Introduction to Database Management Systems

Introduction to Database Management Systems

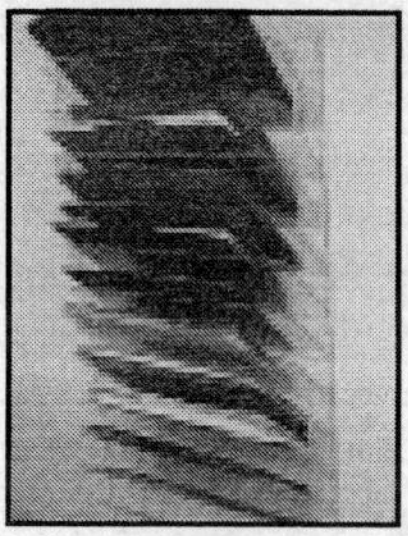

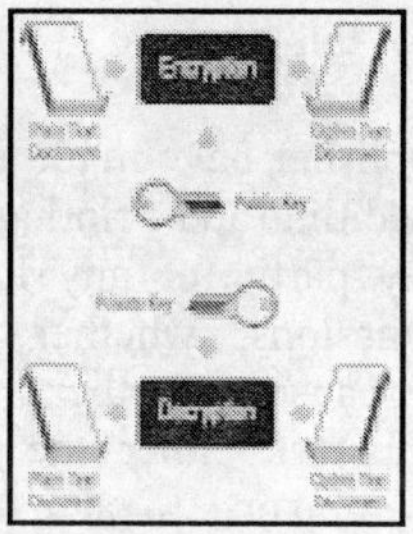

Atul Kahate
PROJECT MANAGER
i-flex Solutions Limited
Pune

Pearson

ISBN 978-81-317-0078-5

First Impression, 2006

Published by Pearson India Education Services Pvt. Ltd, CIN: U72200TN2005PTC057128

Head Office: 1st Floor, Berger Tower, Plot No. C-001A/2, Sector 16B, Noida – 201 301,Uttar Pradesh, India.

Registered Office: Featherlite, 'The Address' 5th Floor, Survey No 203/10B, 200 Ft MMRD Road, Zamin Pallavaram, Chennai - 600044
Website: in.pearson.com; Email:companysecretary.india@pearson.com

Digitally printed in India by Trinity Academy for Corporate Training Ltd, New Delhi in the year of 2025.

To

My Wife Anita
For being the best life partner one could ever hope to find

Daughter Jui
For being so wonderful, lovely, mischievous and cheerful

Son Harsh
For adding some spice to our small but brilliant family

Foreword

Like many technologies in the computer industry, the evolution of databases can be tracked back to research into automating office functions in the 1960s and 1970s. Firms discovered it was becoming far too expensive to hire people to do certain jobs such as storing and indexing files. They began investing in research into cheaper and more efficient mechanical solutions.

In 1970, an IBM researcher named Ted Codd published the first article on relational databases. It outlined an approach that used relational calculus and algebra to allow non-technical users to store and retrieve large amounts of information. Codd envisaged a system where the user would be able to access information stored in tables with "natural language" commands.

The article's significance was not recognised because it was far too technical and relied heavily on mathematics. However, it did lead to IBM starting a research group known as "System R".

Eventually, System R evolved into SQL/DS which later became DB2. The language created by the System R group, SQL (Structured Query Language) has become the industry standard for relational databases and is now an ISO standard.

The first database systems built upon the SQL standard appeared at the beginning of the 1980s from Oracle with Oracle Version 2, and later SQL/DS from IBM, as well as a host of other systems from other companies.

Relational database technology was continually refined during the 1980s. This was due to feedback from customers, the development of systems for new industries and the increased use of personal computers and distributed systems.

By the middle of the 1980s, it had become obvious that there were several fields where relational databases were not practical due to the types of data they used. These areas included medicine, multimedia and high energy physics and they needed more flexibility in how their data was represented and accessed.

This led to research into object oriented databases where users could define their own methods of access to data and how it was represented and manipulated. This coincided with the introduction of Object Oriented Programming languages such as C++ which started to appear in industry at the same time. Since then, in the late 1990s and the early years of this decade, we have seen huge advances in the technology behind running databases and securing them.

Since their arrival, databases have expanded in size from the 8MB of data that System R had been tested with to terabytes of data used for mailing lists, credit card information for banks and so on. With each increase in the amount of storage available, we have seen a corresponding increase in the size and complexity of database systems in operation.

In today's scenario, databases are ubiquitous in all modern corporations, so much so, that professionals carry smaller databases on palmtops or mobile phones. It will be hard to find any successful organisation that does not deploy databases for their key operations. This subject is now being taught and discussed in primary schools in urban areas. This area of technology has spun off a huge cottage industry around it, spanning from the technical support novice to highly specialised very large database management gurus.

It is in light of this background that Atul's book is very significant. Effective database management has become a critical success factor in corporate IT strategy. Although, there are a number of books on this subject available in the market today, ***Introduction to Database Management Systems*** stands out because of the wide range of topics that it covers and the simple and lucid manner in which it explains them. It will be of tremendous value to students of this subject, who can also use it as a reference tool.

While working with Atul over the years, I have always been impressed with his thorough understanding of database management and other related topics. He also has outstanding ability to present his thoughts in the most palatable fashion. I am delighted that he has come out with this book that explains the theory behind database systems, their architectures and issues in a way that even a layman can understand. Atul has put to good use his practical experience while working with us at i-flex, mixed with his very good grasp of theory of databases.

I wish him all the best in his future endeavours.

Deepak Ghaisas
CEO (India Operations)
i-flex Solutions Limited
Pune

Preface

The traditional mechanism for storing computer data was data files. Data files have been immensely popular since the 1960s. The earlier commercially successful programming languages such as COBOL had extensive features related to file processing. In fact, even today, many major computer applications run on file-based computer systems.

However, all this has also changed in the last few decades. Database Management Systems (DBMS) has become a subject of great significance in the Information Technology industry. Most serious business applications need the presence of DBMS in some form or the other. DBMS is replacing files as the de facto standard for storing data that is medium/long term in nature. This is especially true in the case of most newly developed applications.

DBMS is a fascinating subject. Many people confuse it with Structured Query Language (SQL). However, SQL is just one aspect of DBMS technology. Understanding how DBMS technology really works involves the study of many theoretical concepts, such as database design, modelling, transaction management, security, concurrency, and so on.

I have read a number of books on DBMS. Most of them explain DBMS technology quite well, but there is one aspect that I find quite intimidating, and that is the complexity of these books. I have a strong and sincere belief that without using almost any jargon and mathematics, we can study most aspects of the DBMS technology. It is intimidating to see complex mathematics and cryptic symbols one page after the other when learning DBMS. That is the sole reason why I have attempted to keep the material as simple as it can get. The idea is that even a person with very little background in computers will be able to grasp the main concepts in DBMS, and if he/she is interested, can go ahead and study the more complex features.

Here are the main features of the book.

- ***Orientation***: An attempt has been made to cover the topics in an appropriate sequence, so that it is sufficient for the managers/professionals/teachers/students to refer to this book alone for learning about DBMS.
- ***Contents***: The book covers all the major concepts in the DBMS technology that a reader at any level needs to understand.
- ***Style***: An attempt has been made to keep the language very simple and to make the explanations extremely lucid.
- ***Visual approach***: The book features a number of illustrations and diagrams (close to 400) to enable an easier grasp of the subject.
- ***Pedagogical features***: Every chapter contains a list of Key Terms and Concepts, Chapter Summary and self-study questions in the form of True/False questions, Multiple-choice questions and Detailed questions. In addition, Exercises are also provided at the end of every chapter.

The chapter-wise organisation of the book is as follows.

Chapter 1 provides a lot of background material to the subject of DBMS. This chapter covers the basics of storing data. We study the meaning and purpose of file systems with simple examples. We also discuss the various types of data structures used in file systems. The chapter also covers various kinds of file systems/organisations.

Chapter 2 introduces the concept of DBMS. It examines why we need DBMS in the first place. We also study the advantages of DBMS over file-based systems. We then study the basics of SQL. The key concepts in SQL, in the form of Data Definition Language (DDL), Data Manipulation Language (DML), and Data Control Language (DCL) are explained here. We also study dynamic and embedded SQL. The chapter also covers the various DBMS models, namely Hierarchical, Network, and Relational.

Chapter 3 focuses on the most popular of the three DBMS models: the Relational Database Management Systems (RDBMS). After a primer of RDBMS theory, we study relational algebra, and relational calculus. We also take a look at the concepts of database integrity, constraints, keys, and views.

Chapter 4 covers the topic of database design. We take a look at the concepts of functional and transitive dependencies to start with. We then move on to the topic of Normalisation. All the five important Normal Forms are covered in great detail with lots of examples and theory. Then we move on to Entity/Relationship (E/R) modelling.

Chapter 5 explains the beauty of transactions. Transaction management is a very important concept in DBMS. Without transactions, most serious business applications would simply not work. The chapter details what we mean by Transactions, the concept of Recovery, Transaction models, Two phase commit protocol, Concurrency problems, and how Locking can solve them. We also study the idea of Deadlocks and Two phase locking.

Chapter 6 deals with the aspects of Database security. We cover the classification of data and then move on to the kinds of risks we face in computer systems. The chapter moves on to the technical details of Cryptography and Digital signatures. It also covers User and Object privileges. The discussion concludes with an overview of Statistical databases.

Chapter 7 focuses on Query execution and optimisation. We study the impact of using indexes on query performance. There are various ways in which the SELECT queries in SQL can be implemented. We study all the background material related to this. Certain optimisation recommendations are also provided. The chapter also covers the topic of Database statistics.

Chapter 8 explains the idea of Distributed databases. We study the Advantages, Architecture, Issues, Techniques, Query processing, Concurrency control, Recovery, and Deadlocks related to distributed databases. The chapter also covers the idea of Client/Server computing. We end with a small note on C.J. Date's 12 rules related to distributed databases.

Chapter 9 begins with the basic concepts such as data, information, its quality, and value. It then covers the relatively new topics of Decision support systems, Data warehousing, and Data mining. We also discuss the concept of Online Analytical Processing (OLAP).

Chapter 10 deals with the marriage between Object technology and DBMS. We cover the key Object oriented (OO) concepts such as abstraction, encapsulation, and inheritance. We then study their relevance to RDBMS and later on provide a detailed coverage of Object Oriented Database Management Systems (OODBMS).

Chapter 11 covers some modern concepts in DBMS, such as Deductive databases, Internet and DBMS, Multimedia databases, Digital libraries, and Mobile databases.

A number of appendices provide a solid base of Data structures, Case studies, Programming examples, Searching and Sorting techniques, etc.

The following symbols have been used in the book.

1.  Fundamental Concepts

2.  Significant Points

I hope that the book has a significant use for the professionals, teachers and students of DBMS. All the same, I am aware that there may be areas where we can improve. You are most welcome to write to me at *akahate@indiatimes.com* for any comments or suggestions.

ATUL KAHATE

Acknowledgements

Many people have done so much for me over the years that it is just not possible to mention all of them here.

My wife Anita has been the best friend and critic of the manuscript, as ever. She has helped me in so many ways that I cannot simply put it all in words. All I can say is that I am extremely lucky to have such a loving, caring, supporting and understanding partner. I cannot describe the joy that my two small kids Jui and Harsh have brought to my life. Life was so incomplete without them! My parents Dr. Meena and Dr. Shashikant Kahate and all relatives have been standing behind me like a wall, which is very reassuring.

I respect Mr Achyut Godbole more than anyone else for so many reasons. He has always provided encouragement and constructive criticism.

There are so many friends, both at the workplace and outside that I would like to mention, especially the *Tea group* at i-flex, which make the day at the workplace great. All my colleagues have been very understanding, supportive, and encouraging.

I would also like to thank Mr Nandu Kulkarni and Mr Madhusudhan Magadi for allowing me to use my spare time and facilities at the workplace for the development of this book. Colleagues like Ravi Jadhav, Subhabrata Sanyal, Atul Edlabedkar, Ruchi Bhargava, Sandeep Jagnade, Dhananjay Barve, Abhijit Agashe, Sachin Limkar, Mithoo Chakraborty, Javed Attar, Dayakar Vummadi, Amar Gokhale, Richard Saldanha, Subramanian Krishnan, Sunil Gokhale, Bhupendra Porwal, and many others make my day at work wonderful!

Last, but not the least, it is the expertise, enthusiasm and persistence of my Editor K Srinivas of Pearson Education, which has kept me on my toes to try and complete this book in record time. I cannot thank him enough. I would also like to express my gratitude to Shadan Perween of Pearson Education, the Copy Editor of this book. And finally, thanks Deepak for your lively foreword.

ATUL KAHATE

Contents in Brief

Contents

Chapter 1

File Systems

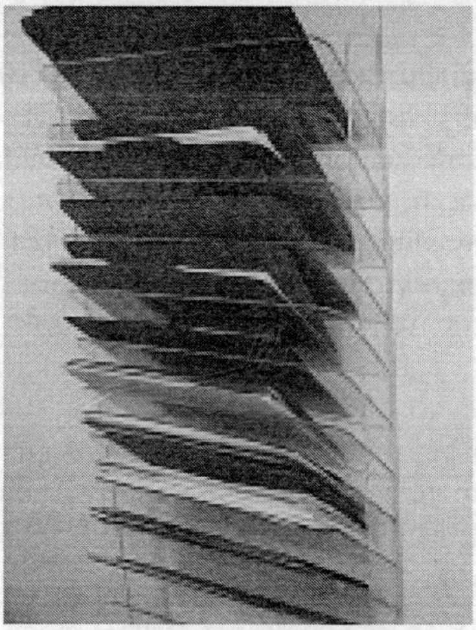

Computer files and file systems have great similarities with traditional files and file systems. Both allow records to be inserted, updated, deleted, searched for, sorted, and so on.

Chapter Highlights

- The Concept of File Systems
- Files and Records
- Various Data Structures Used in File Systems, such as Chains, Pointers and Lists
- Different Types of File Organisations
- Concept of Record Keys and Indexes

1.1 NEED FOR A FILE

We use a lot of **files** in carrying out our day-to-day activities. For example, a college student uses notebooks and journals while a workplace contains many files and registers. Why do we need files at all? The simple explanation is that we cannot remember each and every word and number that is important to us. Hence, we store information in the form of files, notebooks and so on as shown in Fig. 1.1.

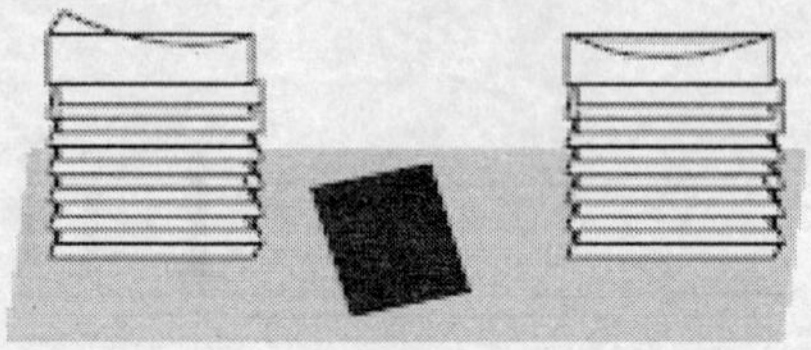

Fig. 1.1 File

In simple terms, a file is a collection of logical information.

Imagine a clerk working in the payroll department of a company that has 10 employees. Since 10 is a small number, the clerk might remember all the details such as basic pay, various allowances and deductions applicable for each one of them. Hence the clerk may not need a file at all! At the end of a month, the clerk would simply take 10 blank pay-slips and write various details in the appropriate columns directly from his memory. However, even this situation does not guarantee perfect payroll processing. What if the clerk leaves the job or is on leave during the end of the month? The person replacing the clerk would take at least some time to remember all the different names and numbers. Furthermore, if the number of employees increases (say to 100 employees), even the old clerk may not be able to remember all the information correctly.

In view of all these problems, it is essential that all such information is recorded somewhere; the easiest option being files or notebooks. If that is done, the clerk can simply use the recorded information at the end of the month to calculate the pay and prepare the pay-slips.

1.2 FILES

Let us assume that the clerk has decided to store the information in the form of files. For understanding the process of filing better, let us discuss it in detail.

1.2.1 Sample File

Let us imagine that the clerk is about to start preparing the pay-slips for this month. As we had seen, the clerk now uses a file to store information such as name, basic pay, days-worked etc. Suppose the company has 1000 employees.

There will be one page of information for each of the 1000 employees, as shown in Fig. 1.2. Thus, there will be 1000 **records** for the clerk to consult while preparing the pay-slips.

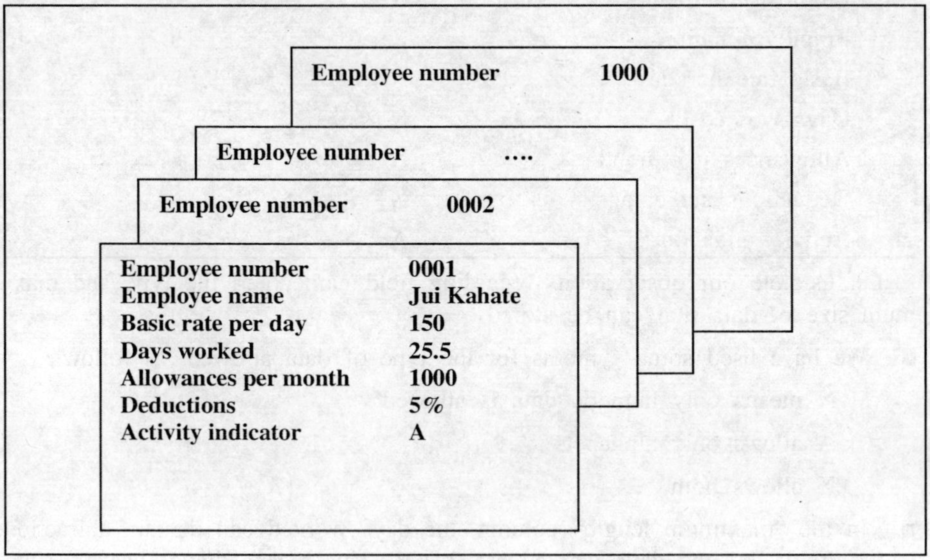

Fig. 1.2 Employee records in a file

A file can contain one or more records.

As the figure shows, the clerk stores the information related to various employees and their pay details (i.e. employee records) in this file prior to the calculation of final pay. Hence, the clerk calls this file *employee file.* In other words, this is the **file name** of this particular file. We need to write an algorithm to prepare the pay-slips in the manual system. The creation of a file would not only simplify the clerk's task, but would also help the person who takes over in his absence. The next few sections build up towards that goal.

Files were used in 1960s, and are used widely in all serious business applications even today. Database systems are slowly replacing most files systems.

1.2.2 Records and Fields

We have seen that in the file there is one page or record per employee. Each of these records contains details such as employee number, name etc. Such a detail is called a **field** or **data item** of the record. A sample record for Jui lists all the available fields. Table 1.1 shows the skeleton of a record, and outlines the information that can be stored in it. This skeleton is also called a **record layout**. Generally, it contains sections such as *field name, type of data* that can be stored (alphabets, numbers or both) and *maximum allowable length* of each field.

Table 1.1 Record layout for the Employee file

Field name	*Type of data*	*Maximum length*
Employee number	N	4
Employee name	X	30
Basic rate per day	N	4
Days worked	N	2 + 1
Allowances per month	N	4
Deductions percentage	N	3
Activity indicator	A	1

Let us note our observations regarding field name, and the type and maximum size of data that can be stored.

- We have used some symbols for the type of data allowed, as follows:

  N means only numeric data is allowed

  A allows only alphabets

  X allows both
- In the "maximum length" column, the days worked can contain a fraction. In Table 1.1 the days worked are 2 + 1. This means that it has two integer positions and one decimal, for example, 23.5 or 12.2. The maximum value in this field can be 99.9. However, in real life, can an employee work for 99.9 days in a month? The specification should, therefore, validate that the entry for this field should not exceed a maximum value of, say 31.0 days, depending on the month for which the record is being created. However, as of now we will not check for this condition so that we keep our observations simple.
- It is always a good idea to make provisions for the future. So, the basic per day section has been designed to allows up to 4 digits. Let us suppose that the basic pays are currently in the range 100 to 500. But sooner or later, an employee might have a basic pay of 1000. Unless we provide for an extra digit, the bigger figure cannot be stored.

1.2.3 Master and Transaction Data

Data can be classified into two types – **master** and **transaction**.

Master data does not change with time. Some examples are employee number and employee name. Days worked and allowances are transaction data, which can change from time to time.

Master and transaction data are kept as separate files with reference to Table 1.1, if some changes have occurred during the month (e.g. recruitment of new employees resignations or increments) we go through a **master maintenance** process to keep the master data up-to-date. All the transactions that take place during the month are collected separately in a *transaction file*.

Finally, both files are read and the payroll is processed. In Table 1.1, we have shown an employee record in which some data is master data and some is transaction data. This kind of mixed data is usually available after both the master and transaction files have been read. The data is extracted after matching the records from both the files for the same employee number, and is further used for the payroll. The process is illustrated in Fig 1.3.

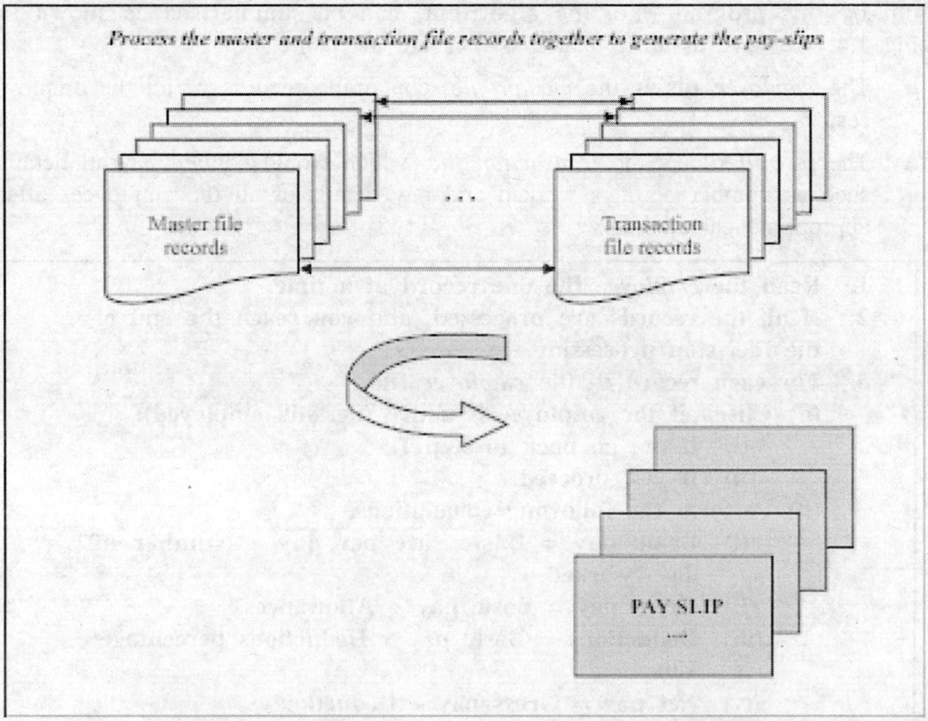

Fig. 1.3 Processing master and transaction files to generate pay-slips

1.3 COMPUTER FILES

Maintaining records and files in the paper format is convenient. It allows easy access to information and does not require any formal training. However, it is far easier and much more convenient to create and maintain files by using computers.

> A computer file contains information arranged in an electronic format.

In concept, computer files are not significantly different from paper files. Computer files also facilitate easy storage, retrieval, and manipulation of data. The major difference between paper files and computer files, however, is that while the former is stored on paper the latter is stored in the form of bits and bytes. Computer files also contain information similar to paper files. A computer file has a name. Thus, if we store employee information in a computer file, we may call it the *employee* file. The computer would recognise the file based on this name. A programmer working with this file can give instructions to the computer to open the file, read from it, write to it, modify its contents, close it, and so on.

For example, if we write a program for payroll processing, the steps carried out by this program (i.e. the algorithm) can be summarised as shown in Fig. 1.4. We have assumed that two files are available:

- The *employee* file is the *master file*, containing records of all the employees.
- The *payroll* file is the *transaction file*, which would contain payroll details such as number of days worked and pay details of all the employees after appropriate calculations.

1. Read the *employee* file one record at a time.
2. If all the records are processed, and you reach the end of the file, stop processing.
3. For each record in the *employee* file:
  (a) Check if the employee is active (i.e. still employed):
    (i) If no, go back to step 1.
    (ii) If yes, proceed.
  (b) Perform the following calculations.
    (i) Basic pay = Basic rate per day x Number of days worked.
    (ii) Gross pay = Basic pay + Allowances.
    (iii) Deductions = Basic pay x Deductions percentage/ 100.
    (iv) Net pay = Gross pay – Deductions.
  (c) Write the employee number, name and above pay details to the *payroll* file with appropriate formatting and go back to step 1.

Fig. 1.4 Payroll processing algorithm

We present the flow chart for this algorithm in Fig. 1.5.

If we look at the payroll-processing program carefully, we will notice that once it starts executing, the program needs very little interaction on the part of the clerk. Suppose there is some sort of mechanism by which the following can be achieved:

1. The input records are put (read) into the input area one by one as desired from the external medium (in this case, the *employee* file stored on the disk).
2. Calculations are done for the record read.
3. The output pay-slips are put (written) into the output area (that is the *payroll* file).

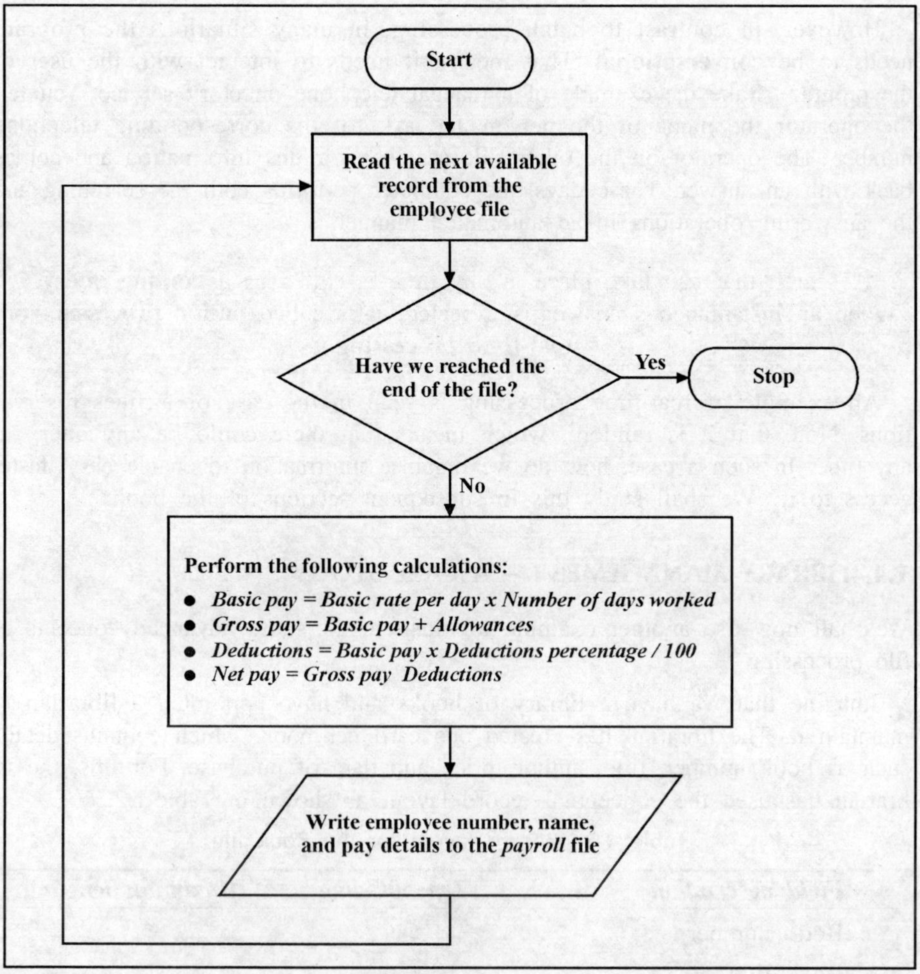

Fig. 1.5 Payroll-processing flowchart

Then the clerk would virtually do nothing until all the pay-slips were printed and filed for distribution. This is similar to a factory where things keep on moving over a belt. The entire cycle starts with the input of spare parts and ends with the production of the end product. Everything moves over a belt, with processes involved at many intermediate stages. This type of processing is called **batch processing**. Batch processing involves a batch of goods manufactured and passed along the conveyer belt. Here, the entire batch of input employee records *moves over* the payroll program. Calculations are performed in each case. The output of the process is the set of pay-slips. This, in fact, was the motivation behind the earlier *batch* computer systems, which aimed at reducing the human drudgery of performing repetitive tasks!

> In batch processing, no or minimum human interaction is required. One program passes control to another in a sequence.

However, in contrast to batch processing, in many situations the program needs to be **conversational**. That means, it needs to interact with the user of the program. Take the example of a manual telephone directory service. You tell the operator the name of the person and ask for the corresponding telephone number. The operator on the other side searches for this information and comes back with an answer. These days, the computer performs both the searching and the answering operations in an automated manner.

A search that can take place at any time is called as an **online query**. When an instantaneous answer is expected, it is called **online processing** or **real-time processing.**

An example of real-time processing is seen in the case of airlines reservations. Note that it is random, which means that there could be any query at any time. In such a case, how do we organise information to enable easy, faster access to it? We shall study this in subsequent sections of the book.

1.4 LIBRARY MANAGEMENT – A CASE STUDY

We shall now use another example to illustrate the more advanced concepts of file processing.

Imagine that we have a library of books and have appointed a librarian to maintain it. The librarian has created one card per book, which contains details such as book number, title, author, price and date of purchase. For this, the librarian has used the conceptual record layout as shown in Table 1.2.

Table 1.2 Record layout for the Book file

Field description	*Type of data*	*Maximum length*
Book number	N	4
Book title	X	100
Author	X	50
Price	N	4
Date of purchase	X	10
Category	X	20
Publisher	X	50

For simplicity, we have not shown the part of the card containing details on borrowing and returning of books. We shall ignore these details throughout the discussion. As soon as a new book comes in to the library, the librarian creates a new card for it. Note that a card is similar to a record and, in technical terms, the entire pile of cards is similar to a file. We shall use the terms interchangeably. The cards arranged by the librarian are shown in Fig. 1.6.

1.4.1 Record Keys

One pertinent question is: why do we need additional data elements such as an employee number in the case of an employee record and a book number in a book record? The reason is quite simple. By using an employee number, we can quickly identify an employee; and similarly, by using a book number, we can uniquely identify a book.

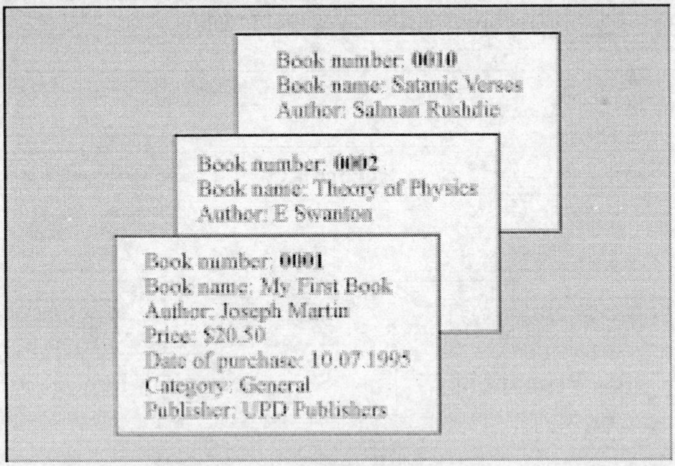

Fig. 1.6 Cards for the books

> A field used to identify a record is called as a **record key**, or just a **key.**

As and when a new book arrives in the library, the librarian creates a new card for the book and gives it the next number in sequence. Since there can be many books with the same title, author or publisher, none of these can be used to uniquely identify a book. Hence, something additional is needed for this purpose. This is achieved by having book number as an extra field in the record.

> A field that can identify a record uniquely is called as **primary key** of the record.

Hence, here the book number is the primary key. Given a book number, we are sure that to get only one record.

> A field that identifies one or more records, not necessarily uniquely, is called a **secondary key.**

For instance, given an author name, we may or may not be able to identify a book uniquely: the library may have two or more books written by the same author. Hence, the author field identifies a group of records. Hence, it is a secondary key. Other secondary keys in this case can be the book title, publisher and so on.

Thus, as shown in Fig. 1.7 a record key can be of two types:

- **Primary key**: Identifies a record uniquely based on a field value.
- **Secondary key**: May or may not identify a record uniquely, but can identify one or more records based on a field value.

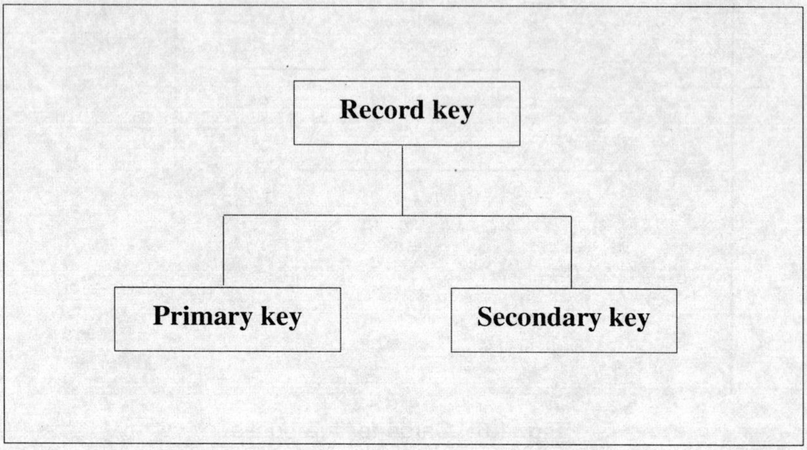

Fig. 1.7 Types of record keys

1.4.2 Searching Records

For simplicity, let us assume that there are only 10 books in the library. Suppose a member wants a list of all the books written by Mahatma Gandhi. The librarian can perform a quick search. He would simply look at one card after another and check if the author's name on the card is Gandhi. If they match, the librarian would inform the member about the book. The algorithm for this process is shown in Fig. 1.8.

Many file systems have become popular, but the two most notable ones are Indexed Sequential Access Mechanism (ISAM) and Virtual Storage Access Mechanism (VSAM). VSAM files dominate the IBM mainframe world even today.

1. **Picks up the next available card.**
2. **Stop if all the cards are exhausted.**
3. **Is the name of the author on the card = *Gandhi*?**
   a. **If yes, show the card to the member.**
   b. **If no, do not show the card to the member.**
4. **Go to step 1.**

Fig. 1.8 Algorithm for retrieving books written by Gandhi

Figure 1.9 shows the corresponding flow chart.

A similar search can be carried out to find the books published by a particular publisher. As we already know, any such inquiry is called as *online query*. The process of looking up the cards is called a **search**. Thus, the records in a file need to be searched in order to respond to an online query.

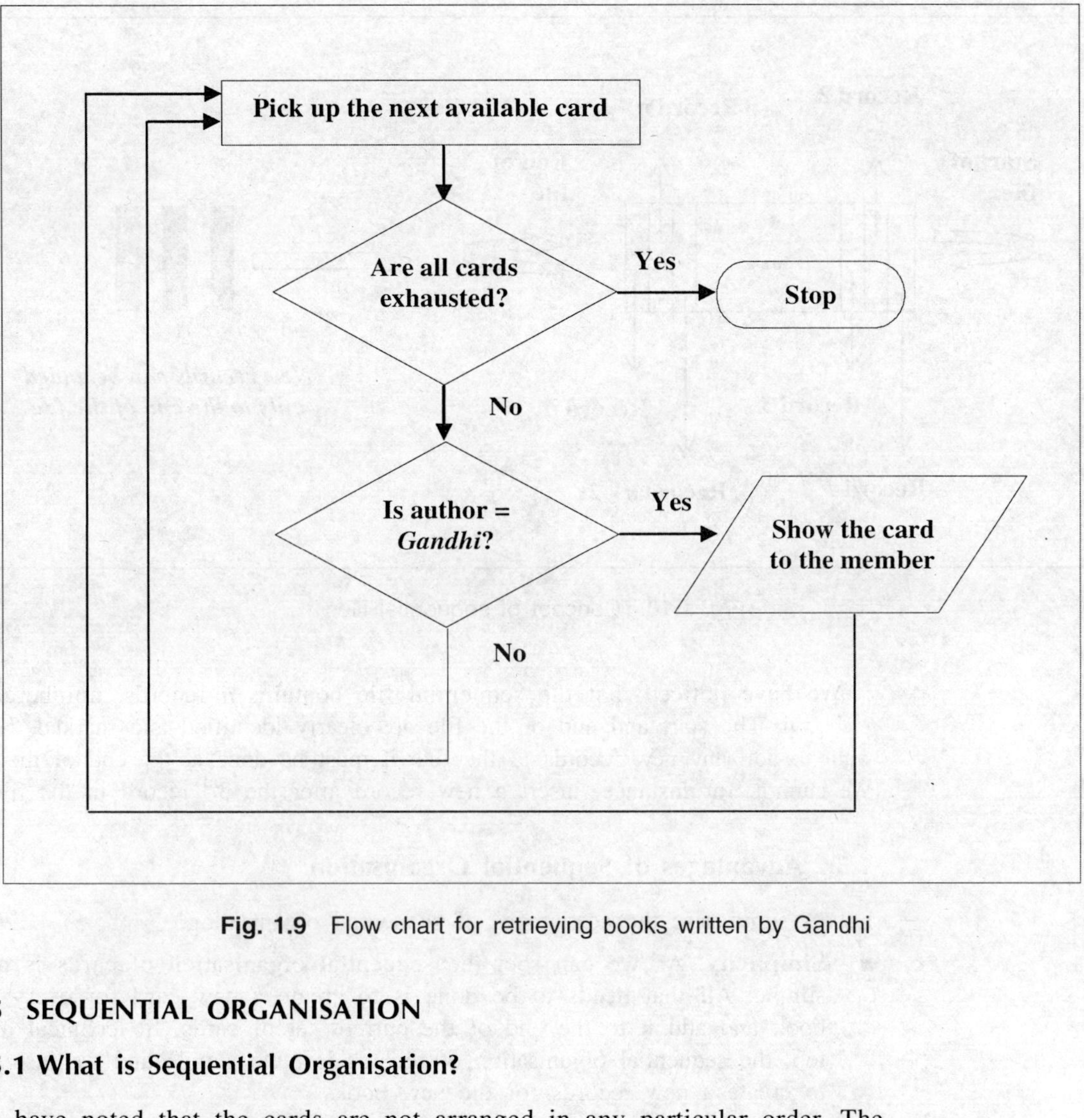

Fig. 1.9 Flow chart for retrieving books written by Gandhi

1.5 SEQUENTIAL ORGANISATION

1.5.1 What is Sequential Organisation?

We have noted that the cards are not arranged in any particular order. The natural order of cards is based on the arrival of books: as and when a new book arrives, a new card is made for it. Hence, the cards are arranged sequentially. In computer terms, the main characteristic of this **sequential organisation** of records is that the records are added as and when they are available. The idea is that a new record is always added to the end of the current file, as depicted in Fig. 1.10.

Note the following:

A file is called as a **sequential file** when it contains records arranged in sequential fashion.

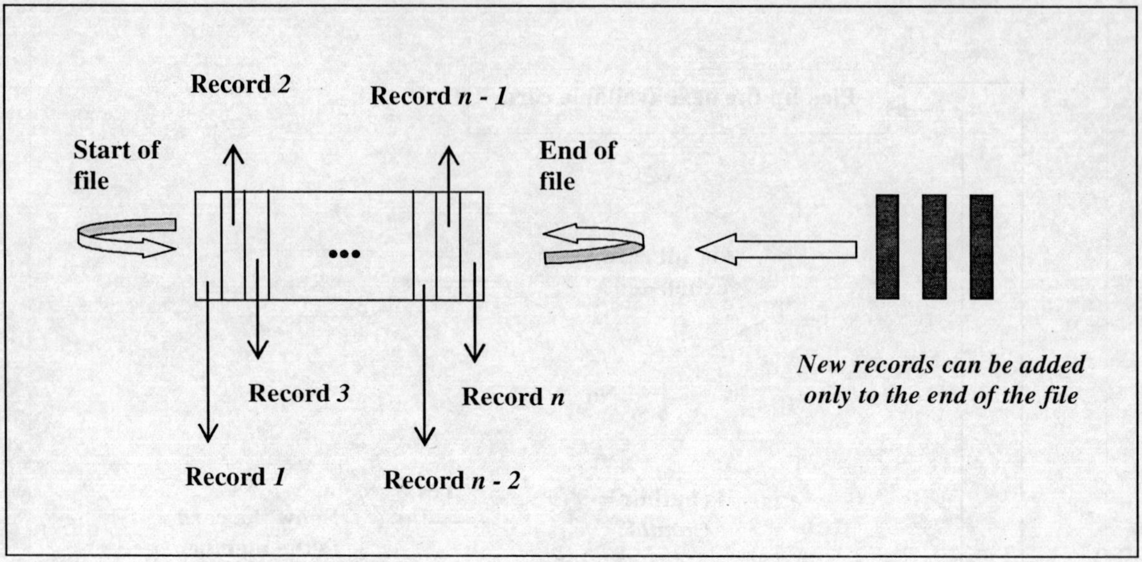

Fig. 1.10 Concept of sequential files

We have noticed that the sequential file contains *n* records, numbered 1, 2, …, n. The start and end of the file are clearly identified and marked. If we want to add any new records to the file, it must be done at the end of the file. We cannot, for instance, insert a new record after the 3rd record in the file.

1.5.2 Advantages of Sequential Organisation

Let us summarise the advantages of sequential organisation.

- **Simplicity**: As we can see, the sequential organisation of cards is quite simple. All that needs to be done is to create a new card for every new book and add it to the end of the current set of cards. In technical terms too, the sequential organisation of records is quite simple and we just need to create a new records for the new books.
- **Less overheads**: We have noticed that in this form of organisation the librarian does not need to maintain any additional information about the books. Maintenance of the cards is good enough. In technical terms, we do not need to keep any *key* or any other extra information on the books file. The file is enough.

1.5.3 Problems with Sequential Organisation

In spite of its simplicity, sequential organisation does have a number of problems. These are mainly associated with the (lack of) searching capability. Let us summarise them.

- **Difficulties in searching**: Since the number of books is quite small in our imaginary library, the current scheme works fine. However, if the number of books goes on increasing, this form of organisation will be clearly inefficient. Suppose our library contains 1000 books instead of 10. If a member now inquires about the books written by *Gandhi*, the librarian would have to start from the first card (that is, card number 1). As in the previous case, he would then check one card after another to see if the author mentioned on it is Gandhi so that he can come up with a list of books written by Gandhi. Note that, now he would have to look at 1000 cards. Clearly, it would take a long time. If there were many such queries, the librarian would be busy in merely answering queries and would not be able to do anything else! Obviously, the main drawback of this scheme is that the librarian has to physically examine every card.

In technical terms, searching information in a sequential file can be a very slow process. For any search operation, we need to start reading a sequential file from the beginning and continue till the end, or until the desired record is found, whichever is earlier. This is both time-consuming and cumbersome.

- **Lack of support for queries**: Sequential organisation is not suitable for answering some queries such as: *Do you have any book written by Gandhi at all?* If the library has one such book, but unfortunately it is the last entry in the file, all cards need to be scanned! In technical terms, it means that to even find out whether something is available in the file or not, the entire file has to be read!

- **Problem with record deletion**: This problem is perhaps not so clear in our example. In an ordinary situation, if the card associated with a book needs to be removed, the librarian can simply remove it from the deck of cards and tear it off. However, in the technical world, we simply cannot delete records in a sequential file. To understand this problem, let us consider a contrived situation wherein the librarian must maintain a number of cards equivalent to the number of books, regardless of whether the book is available or is lost. Thus, if there are 1000 books in the library, there must be 1000 corresponding cards. Thus the card must be maintained even if a book is lost. Perhaps, the librarian can put a special marker (say ***) on the card to indicate the card is void—meaning that the book is lost. The idea is illustrated in Fig. 1.11 for card number 971 (indicating that book number 971 is lost).

Earlier file systems used to be dependent on the physical locations of their records. Modern file systems are quite independent of the actual storage locations.

In any case, the librarian must not remove the card. This is exactly what happens with sequential files on computer disks. When we want to remove a record from a sequential file, the file cannot *crunch* itself automatically. For example suppose that there are 1000 records in a file, each occupying 100 bytes. The file would occupy a total of 1,00,000 bytes on the disk. Now, suppose that we want to delete record number 971 for some reason. We cannot reduce the file size by the size of one record (i.e. 100 bytes) to 99,900 bytes. All we can do is to mark record number 971 in some special fashion to indicate that it should be considered as deleted. The idea is explained in Fig. 1.12.

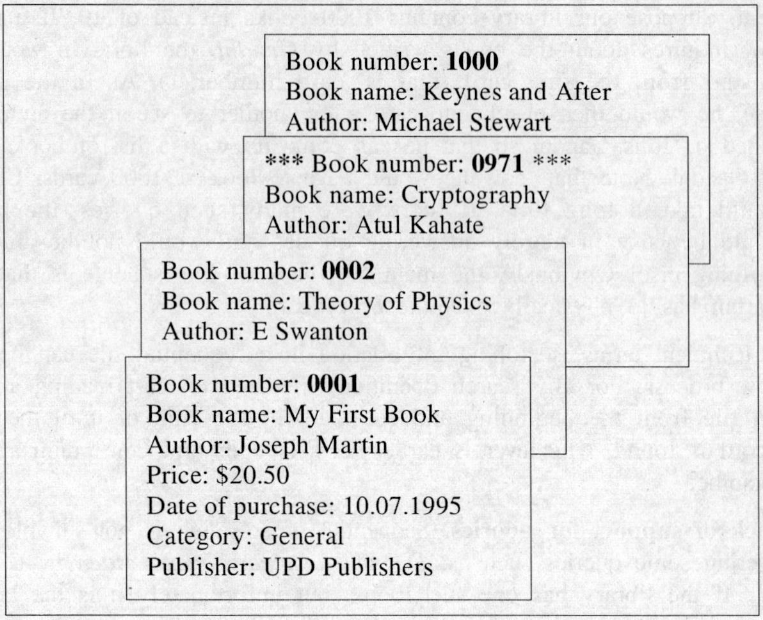

Fig. 1.11 Marking a book as deleted/lost

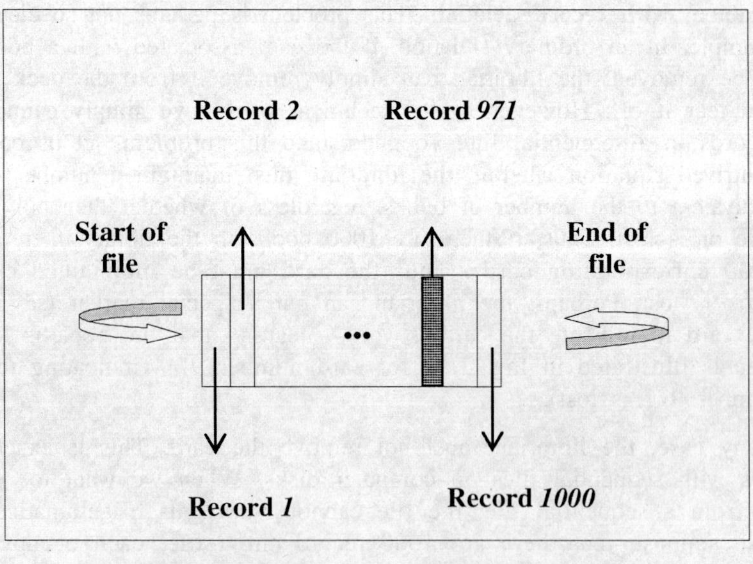

Fig. 1.12 Marking a record as deleted in a file

Also, we cannot reclaim the space freed by the deletion of this record. For this we would need to have a separate program which reads every record from the file and, if it is not deleted, writes to another file. Thus, record number 971 (and any such records, which have been **logically deleted**), would not be written to the second file. In other words, they would get physically deleted. Thus, this second file would contain only the records for the available books. This process is used in many cases where sequential files are used, and is called **file reorganisation**.

In general, sequential search works fine if the number of records is small. However, if the number of records as well as the number of queries is large, it becomes inefficient.

1.6 POINTERS AND CHAINS

In order to overcome the drawbacks of sequential organisation, let us add one more field to the original record layout. Let us call this field *Next by same author*. This field is a **pointer**.

In general, a pointer in a record is a special field, whose value is the address/reference of another record in the same file.

The pointer points to the next book written by the same author as shown in Fig. 1.13. We can see that there is a pointer in Record Number 1, pointing to Record Number 3. This means that the same author has written the books numbered 1 and 3.

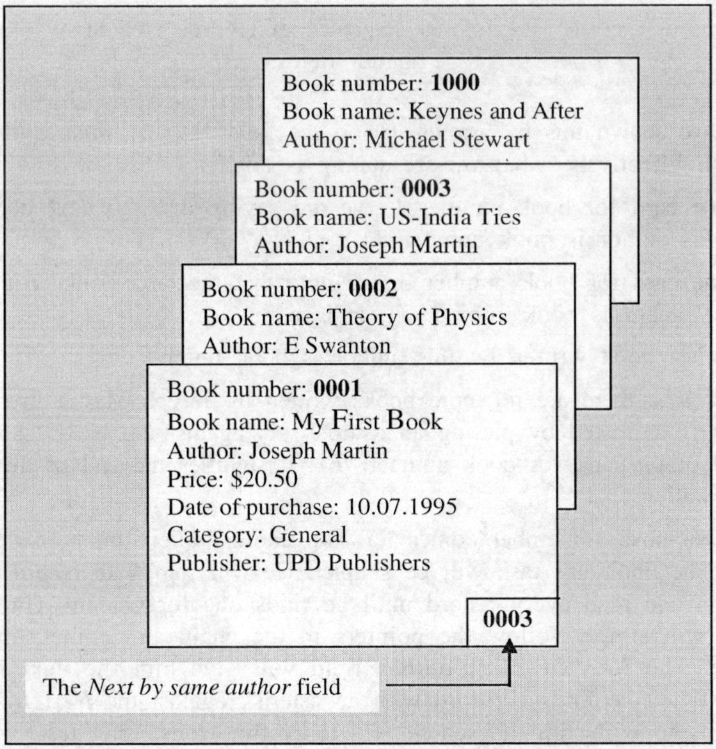

Fig. 1.13 A pointer to the next record

Note the new field added to the record layout. This field gives the book number for the next book written by the same author. Every card will have this additional field. So, when it comes to looking for the next book written by the same author, every card will actually *point to* another card. So, conceptually, we will have the following situation, assuming that book numbers 1, 3, 21 and 761 are written by the same author—Joseph Martin. Figure 1.14 ignores the other details and concentrates on only the pointer field of these four cards.

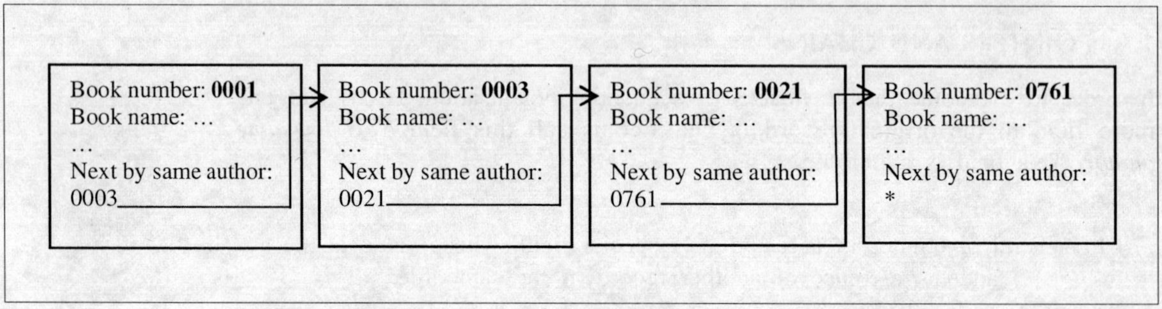

Fig. 1.14 Logical chain of records formed by using pointers

What the additional field does is simple? It forms a **chain** of records. Pointers maintain the chain.

A chain of records is a logical sequence of records created by the use of pointer fields.

We have shown this by arrows. Using the field *Next by same author* creates the chain. Effectively, what we are stating is this:

- In the card for book number 1, we are saying that the next book written by this author is book number 3.
- In the card for book number 3, we note that the next book written by the same author is book number 21, and so on.
- The last book written by this author is book number 761.
- After this, there are no more books written by Joseph Martin in our library. This is indicated by putting an asterisk (*) against the Next (same author) field of the card for book number 761. It signifies the end of the chain for this author.

Now, suppose a member comes up with another query on books written by Gandhi. The librarian's task will be simpler. He will start with record number 1, as before, and read every record until he finds one for Gandhi. Having found that, he will simply follow the pointers in the chain and comes up with the response. The *Next by same author* field will give him the next record for Gandhi. When he finds a record with an asterisk against the *Next by same author* field, he will stop the search. The only time-consuming task will be obtaining the first record for Gandhi. Once that is done, the rest of the search will be a lot quicker. The algorithm for this search is shown in Fig. 1.15.

1. Pick up the first card in the library.
2. If the name of the author = *Gandhi*
   - (*a*) Show the card to the member
   - (*b*) Check the value of the field *Next by same author*
   - (*c*) If this value is a number
     - (*i*) Go to the card specified by this number
     - (*ii*) Go to step 2 (*a*)
   - (*d*) Else (*i.e., the value is* *)
     - (*i*) Go to step 4
3. Else
   - (*a*) Pick up the next card
   - (*b*) Go to step 2
4. Stop

Fig. 1.15 Algorithm for searching books by using pointers

Figure 1.16 shows the corresponding flow chart.

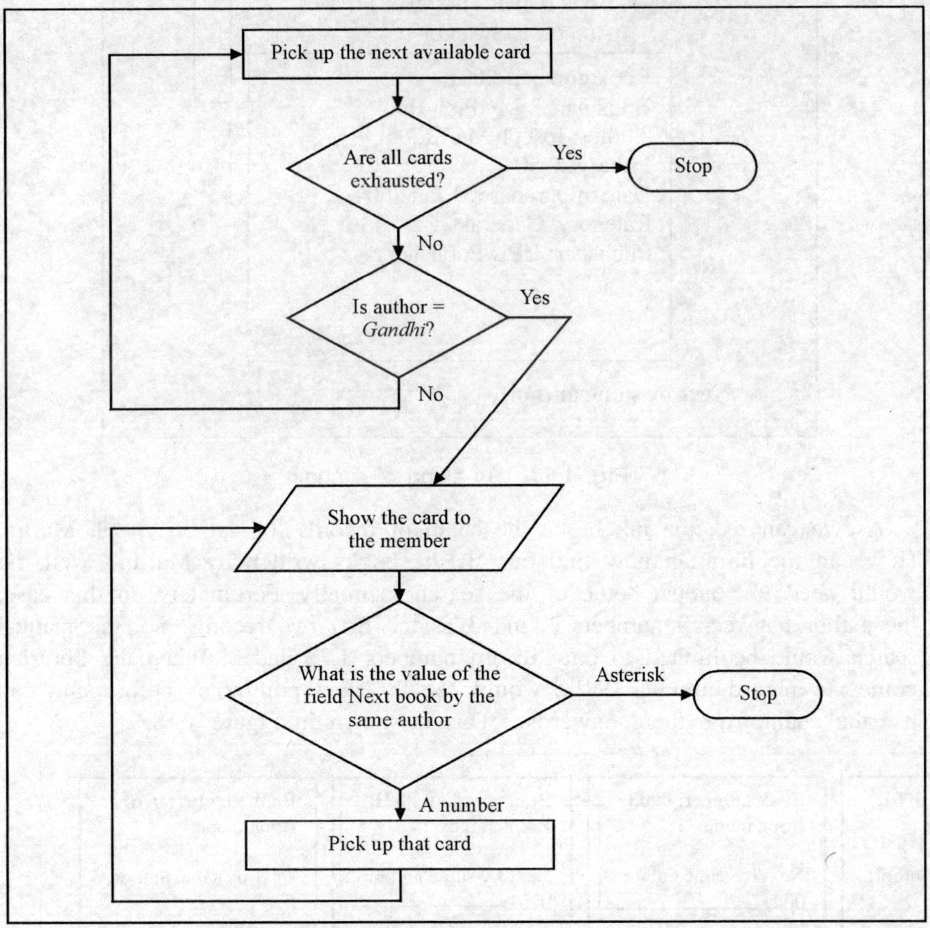

Fig. 1.16 Flow chart for searching books by using pointers

1.6.1 Problems with One-way Chains

What we just saw were **one-way chains**. The *Next by same author* field gives us the next record for the same author in the forward direction only. However, imagine that our librarian goofs up one day. While he is adding some new cards for books that have arrived recently as shown in Fig. 1.17, he spills ink on the first card.

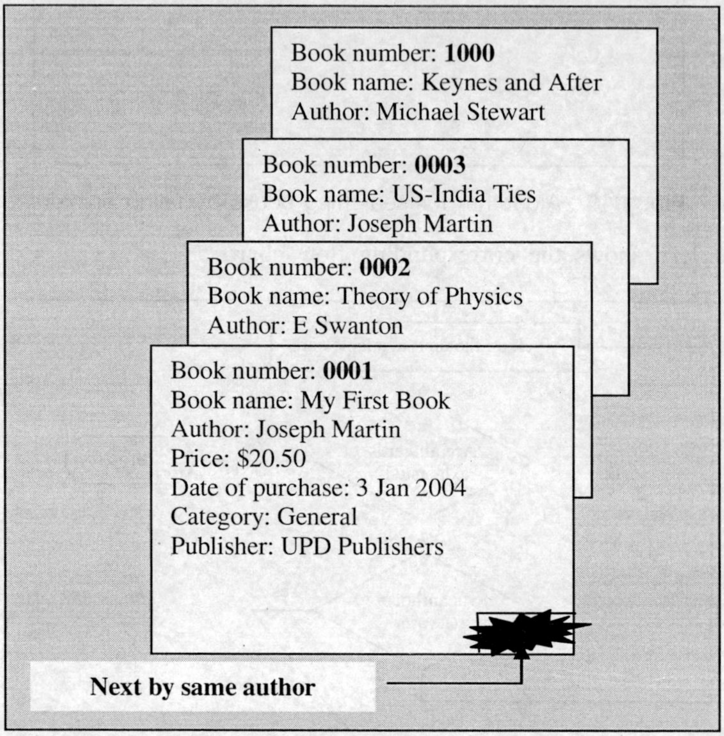

Fig. 1.17 Breaking of a chain

As we can see, the ink broke the chain of records for author Joseph Martin. How can the librarian now find out all the books written by Martin? Well, he would need to conduct some of the search manually. Fortunately, in this case, the author has record numbers 1 and 3 as the first two records. So, the manual search would be limited to only record numbers 1, 2 and 3. When the librarian comes to record number 3, he would see the next pointer as before and can use the chain from there onwards. This is shown in Figure 1.18.

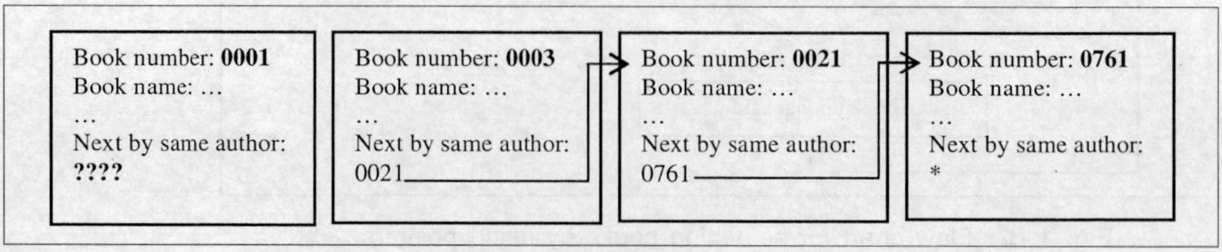

Fig. 1.18 A broken chain

However, imagine that the concerned author's first book was book number 1 and the second was 990! That would mean a sequential search of the first 990 records! From 990, the chain would be available.

> One-way chains can suffer from the drawback of lost/damaged references.

Another problem with one-way chains is that they are unidirectional by nature. Therefore, if anyone wants the third book from the end written by Joseph Martin, there is no direct way of finding it except traversing the whole list from the end to the beginning of the chain, in a reverse manner. As a result, some of the library members may start complaining that their queries are not getting a quick response. What is the solution?

1.6.2 Two-way Chains

The librarian can improve things by creating another logical chain. Until now, the chain of records for an author was unidirectional. Now, the librarian adds another chain—in the reverse direction—such that we now have two pointer fields: one for the *Next by same author* and another for the *Previous by same author*. The former, as before, gives the book number for the next book written by the same author. The *Previous by same author* field gives the previous book written by the same author. We shall call it as the **back-pointer.** Now the cards look as shown in Fig. 1.19.

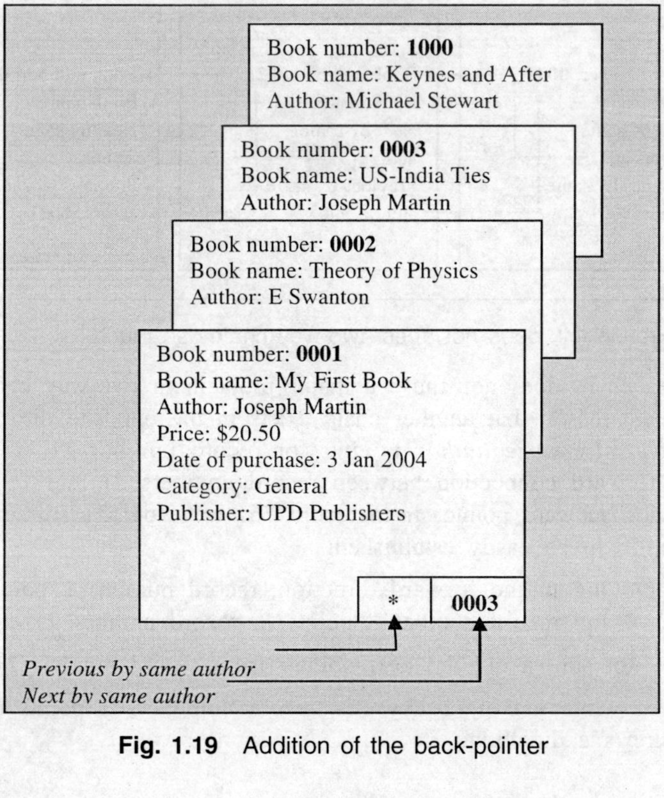

Fig. 1.19 Addition of the back-pointer

Since book number 1 is the first book in our library, there is no book (for this author) prior to it. Therefore, the *Previous by same author* is marked with an asterisk (*). This is a special value, which indicates that there is no previous book in the library for this author. However, the remaining records would have a back-pointer, corresponding to the *Next by same author* field as shown in Fig. 1.20.

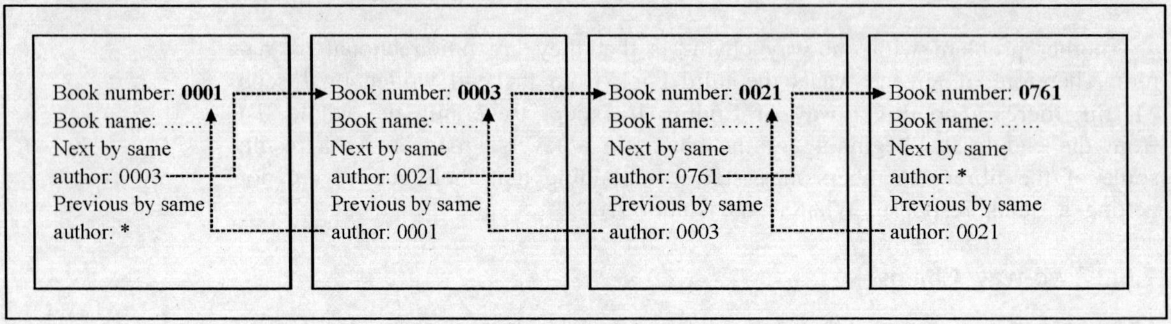

Fig. 1.20 Two-way chains

As the figure shows, we now have two-way chains. The back-pointer points to the previous record for the same author in the chain. Therefore, any query related to the previous as well as the next records for the same author can be easily answered. Now let us see what happens if ink falls on the *Next by same author* pointer of record number 21, as shown in Fig. 1.21.

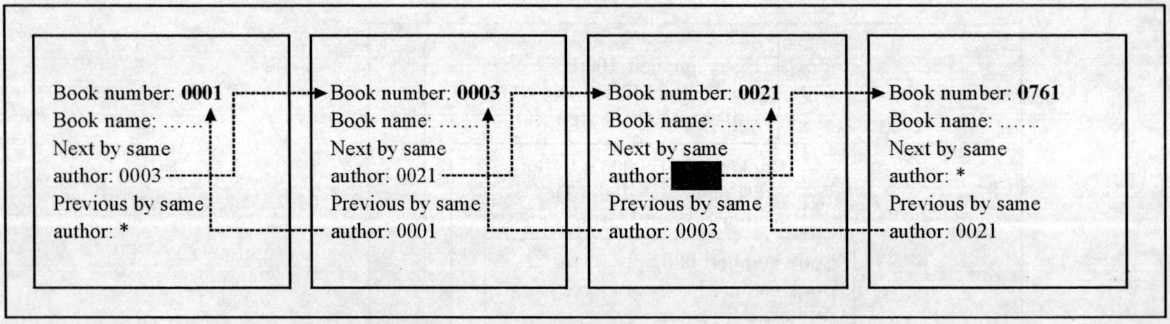

Fig. 1.21 Broken link does not affect two-way chains so much

A broken chain does not cause a major problem in two-way chains. This is for the simple reason that another chain exists in the opposite direction. In this case, the *Next by same author* pointer for record number 21 is lost, due to which the forward connection between record numbers 21 and 761 is broken. However, the backward pointer from record 761 to record 21 still exists. Hence, the following can be easily established:

1. When moving in the forward direction, record number 1 points to record number 3 and record number 3 points to record number 21.
2. We are not sure about the *next* pointer from record number 21.
3. However, while moving backwards, record number 761 points to record 21 in the reverse direction.

Therefore, record number 21 must point to record number 761 in the forward direction. Thus, a *Next by same author* pointer can be reconstructed for record number 21 to point to record number 761. This is called **recovery** of a lost pointer. Thus, we can state the following:

Two-way chains do not suffer from the drawback of lost/damaged references.

What are the disadvantages of two-way chains? Obviously more effort goes into their maintenance. For every new book that is being added, the clerk has to make a *Previous by same author* entry in addition to the *Next by same author* entry. Also, if a book is lost both the previous and next pointers need to be adjusted so that they point to the correct record.

1.6.3 Queries Based on Other Fields

So far, we have been considering queries based only on authors. However, members might be interested in knowing about all the books published by a particular publisher. How do we answer to such queries? Quite simply, in addition to the author field the librarian needs to maintain two-way chains for the

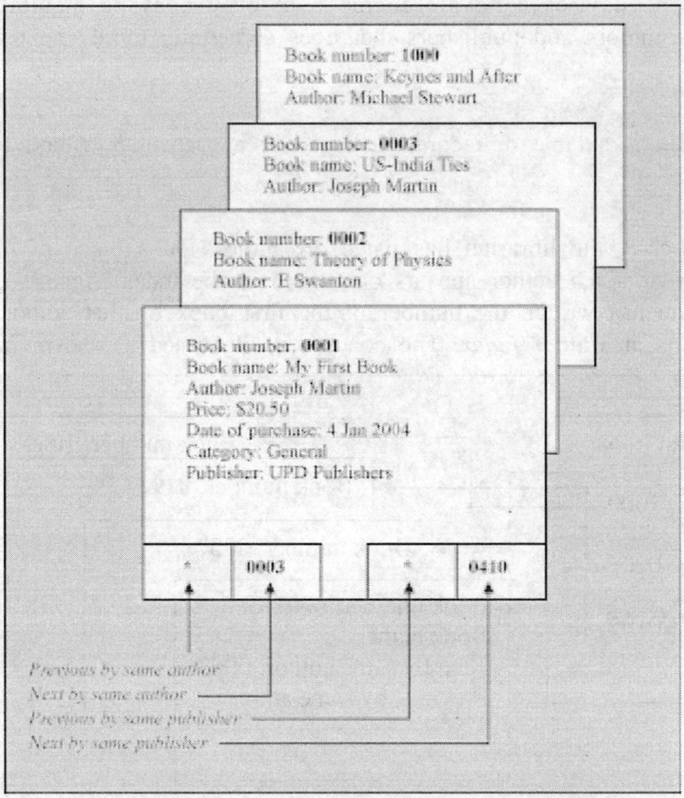

Fig. 1.22 Pointers for publishers in addition to those for authors

publisher field. Thus, we now have four pointers establishing four chains. The first two *next* and *previous* author pointers maintain the author chains. A similar set of *next* and *previous* pointers maintains the publisher chain. The modified record structure now looks like the one shown in Fig. 1.22.

There can be two-way chains for publishers as well. We will not illustrate the chains, as the characteristics of chains must be very clear by now. So, if an inquiry based on the author is made, the librarian would follow the author chains as before. However, if an inquiry is made on the publisher, the new publisher chains would be used. This would facilitate a fast search based on either the author or the publisher. Also, we can have additional chains for other fields such as book title, price and so on, depending on the queries that come up. The downside, as pointed out earlier, is the effort that goes into more maintenance. Every time a book is added to or deleted from the library, the librarian has to adjust upto four or more pointers.

1.7 INDEXED ORGANISATION

1.7.1 Using Indexes

Our librarian is really improving fast. For still faster access to the desired record(s), he devises a novel scheme. Not only does he maintain two-way chains for authors and publishers, but does something more—he maintains **indexes**.

> An index is a table of records arranged in a particular fashion for quick access to data.

In this case, the librarian has listed all authors on a piece of paper in ascending order. Each author appears only once in the index. Against each author, the librarian has written the number of the first book by that author. Therefore, the paper is an *author index*. The concept is illustrated as shown in Fig. 1.23.

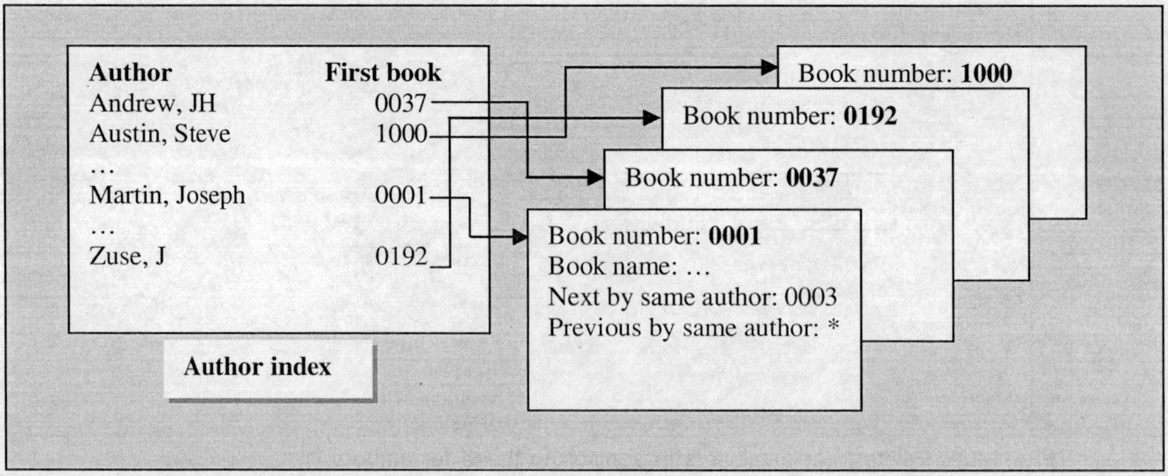

Fig. 1.23 Concept of index and chain

The idea behind this scheme is simple.

1. The author index points to the first record for every author which acts as the entry pointer for that author.
2. As before, the actual records still have two-way chains maintained for each author.

Thus, the search based on a particular author becomes even simpler. The first thing that needs to be done now is to look at the author index. Because it is sorted in alphabetical sequence, an author's name can be found quickly. Thus it provides easy access to the first record number for the selected author. Using this number, we can directly go to the first record for this author by following the logical pointer. From there, the chains assist in the remaining search as before. Thus, a combination of an index and chains makes the search even faster.

Figure 1.24 shows the algorithm for searching all the books written by a particular author quickly by using the index and the chains.

1. Search for the name of the author in the index.
   (a) If the author name is found, go to step 2.
   (b) If the author name is not found, there are no books in the library by this author. Go to step 4.
2. The index provides the first book number for the author. Pick up the card corresponding to that book number.
3. Every card would provide the next book number for that author (with the help of the Next by same author field), if there are more books. Otherwise, it would indicate the end of books for the author with an asterisk. Proceed accordingly for all the cards for this author.
4. Stop processing.

Fig. 1.24 Algorithm for searching all books by one author

For example, suppose someone asks: *Which books written by Zuse are available in the library?* Using the author index, we realise that the first book in our library by this author is number 192. Hence, we can now go directly to record number 192 and then, use the author chain for the remaining records. This saves the time needed for searching the first record for the author. A similar scheme can be arranged for publisher index. We will not go into its details as the same concept is applicable here too.

Can there be further enhancements to our basic scheme of index and chains?

1.7.2 Improvements to Index-chain Method

Just as the chains are two-way, the librarian can make the index two-way too!

That is, rather than keeping an entry for only the first record for an author in the index, he can keep an entry for the first and the last records. If that is done, a two-way chain would be formed. Thus, by using the pointer for the first record in the index, we can traverse the forward chain. For a search from the end, we can use the reverse chain starting with the last record for the author. This would make the search faster in certain situations.

For example, if a member wants to see the latest book by Agatha Christie, we can first look up the new entry in the index (*Last book for this author*). Then, we can simply go to the chain using that book number and identify the record. Clearly, this adds some more overheads to the process of record maintenance, but gives him more flexibility in terms of searching records. However, the more important reason for maintaining two-way chains is to aid recovery. We had previously seen that when a chain based on the *next* pointer is broken, information is lost. Use of two-way chains ensures that vital information is not lost.

The concept is illustrated in Fig. 1.25. Due to space constraints, instead of full book cards only book numbers are shown. Also, not all cards and their pointers are shown. But it should be adequate in making the concept of first and last book entries in the author index clear.

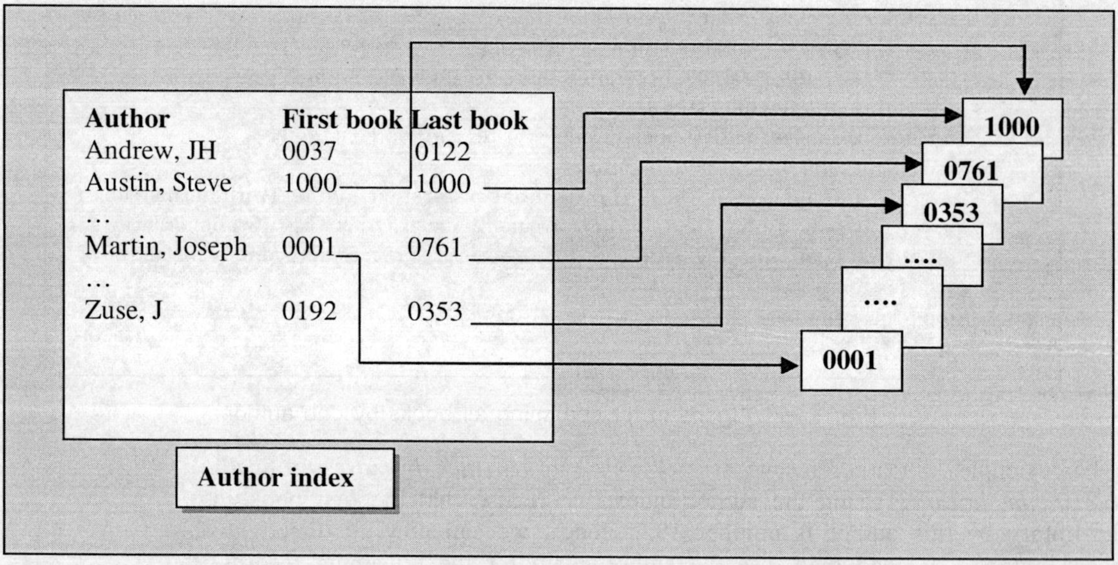

Fig. 1.25 Index with entry for the first and the last records

1.7.3 Maintaining a List of All Items in the Index

The index can be constructed in another manner. We can maintain a list of all the books written by an author in the index. In the index described earlier, only details on the first and the last books were maintained. In the new index, we can list all the book numbers for an author in the second column, as shown in Fig. 1.26. The figure shows only the author index and not the chain.

Author	List of books
Andrew, JH	0037, 0082, 0111, 0147, 0122
Austin, Steve	1000
....	
Martin, Joseph	0001, 0003, 0021, 0761
....	
Zuse, J	0192, 0273, 0353

Fig. 1.26 Author index with list of all books

This system would not only work fine but also give faster results. For example, if someone wants to know about all the books written by Joseph Martin, the above author index would quickly provide the answer. Using the book numbers provided (1, 3, 21, 761) for Joseph Martin, the information can be searched quickly. Note that we need not maintain any chains or next/previous pointers now. The index contains all the information.

The algorithm for this search is shown in Fig. 1.27.

1. **Search for the name of the author in the index.**
   (a) If the author name is found, go to step 2.
   (b) If the author name is not found, there are no books in the library for this author. Go to step 3.
2. **The index provides all the book numbers for the author. Pick up the cards corresponding to these book numbers one-by-one.**
3. **Stop processing.**

Fig. 1.27 Modified algorithm for searching all books by one author

However, the drawback of this scheme is that there is variable number of entries per author. We are not sure how many books per author is allowed in the library: it could be any number. Therefore, maintaining the index could be cumbersome, especially if the number of books written by an author is large. A better scheme is needed for quickly finding such information.

1.7.4 Keeping a Count of Records

Another improvement in the basic scheme could be achieved by keeping **record counts**. For instance, suppose there are four books for Joseph Martin, we can not only keep a record of the first and last pointers for the author in the author index, but additionally, we can also keep a count of the total number of books by the author available in the library, that is 4. This is shown in Fig. 1.28.

Such counts can help in two ways:

(a) Queries such as: *How many books in your library are written by Joseph Martin*? can be answered very quickly without even going to the cards or following the chains.

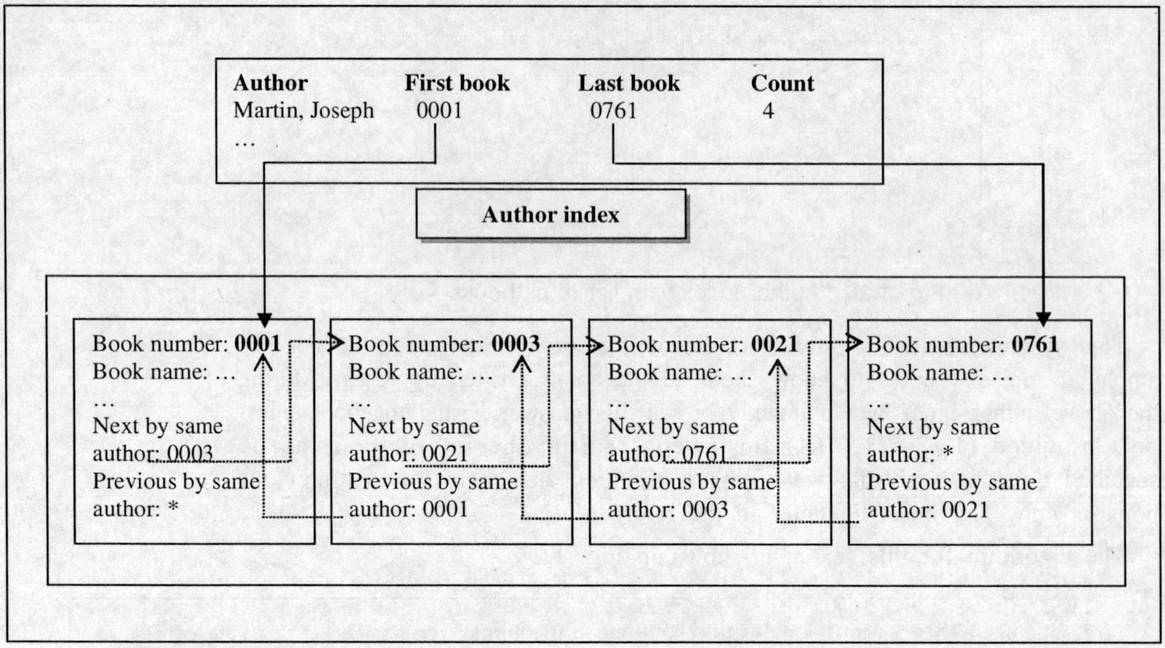

Fig. 1.28 Maintaining the count of records for each author

(b) Errors can be detected early. For instance, since we know that we have four books by Joseph Martin from our index entry, we must obtain the same number when we actually traverse the chains. If we get anything other than four, it means that either the index entry for count is wrong or that the chains are not quite correct. This is called **index corruption**. Either way, a correction is required and walking through the chains help in implementing it.

1.7.5 Complex Queries and Query Optimisation

Maintaining a count of records for a given key can have significant effect on a search. This is especially true in case of a **complex query**. For instance, if someone wants a list of books written by Philip Bailey and published by ACS Publications, we will assume that we have two indexes, one for author and another for publisher. Also, both point to the first and last records in the indexes, respectively for author and publisher. These concepts have already been discussed in detail. However, suppose they do not have a *count* field as yet.

In order to search the books written by an author for a particular publisher, there can be two approaches:

1. First, get a list of all the books written by the concerned author — in this case, Philip Bailey — using the author index and chains. Having found them, look for each of these books in the publisher index and chains.

OR

2. First, get a list of all the books published by the concerned publisher — in this case, ACS Publications — using the publisher index and chains. Having

found them, look for each of these books in the author index and chains.

Both schemes look equally good, but which one should we select? There is no fixed rule. We can either go for the first method, or the second. However, our choice could affect the time required to come up with an answer to the query.

For instance, suppose there are 50 books by Philip Bailey in the library and only three of them are published by ACS Publications. In addition, ACS has published two other books not authored by Philip Bailey. If we use the first method, we would walk through 50 entries in the author chain and then three in the publisher chain. Thus, we would need to go through 53 records altogether.

However, by any luck, if we had selected the second method of searching, we would first go to the publisher index and follow the publisher chain. Thus, we would go through only five records in the publisher chain. Using these five records, we would go through only five records in the author chain. This would mean we go through only ten records altogether. Finally, we would select three records in the author chain out of the five read, for Philip Bailey.

As we can see, depending on the selection, there can be significant **performance improvement** in answering queries. If one opts for the second method, the efforts required for answering the query will be much lesser. This process of resolving queries in a more efficient manner is called **query optimisation**. This can prove to be extremely important as the number of library members increases. Many of them would come up with different sets of queries and the librarian must be able to respond to those as quickly as possible.

Having *count* field in both the indexes would greatly help the process of query optimisation. In the example just discussed, if we would have had such a field in the author as well as publisher indexes, we could have decided about choosing either approach 1 or 2 based on the *count*. From author index count, we get a figure of 50. From the publisher index count, we get five. Clearly, there is enough evidence to start our query evaluation using the second approach. However, in the absence of a *count* field, there is no guarantee that either of the approaches would be better. Maintaining a count of records in the index thus helps to significantly improve results.

Sequential files are worse than audio cassettes in concept. You must not only rewind them to go to a specific location, but you must rewind them completely! Indexed files are like CDs/DVDs; you can go to any specific location of the disk directly.

1.7.6 Indexed Organisation in Computer Files

We have studied the concepts of pointers, chains and indexes with a simple example. Computers organise **indexed files** in a similar manner. That is, one of the fields in the file is the *primary key*, as we have discussed earlier. This field identifies a record uniquely. We should note that the position of this field is the same in all the records. That is, in every record, the primary key field should occupy the same position. The idea is illustrated in Fig. 1.29.

It is interesting to study how computers maintain index files. We have noted that our librarian had to maintain the index separately. Computers do the same. There are various ways of achieving this objective. However, the basic idea is simple and common to most implementation of indexes.

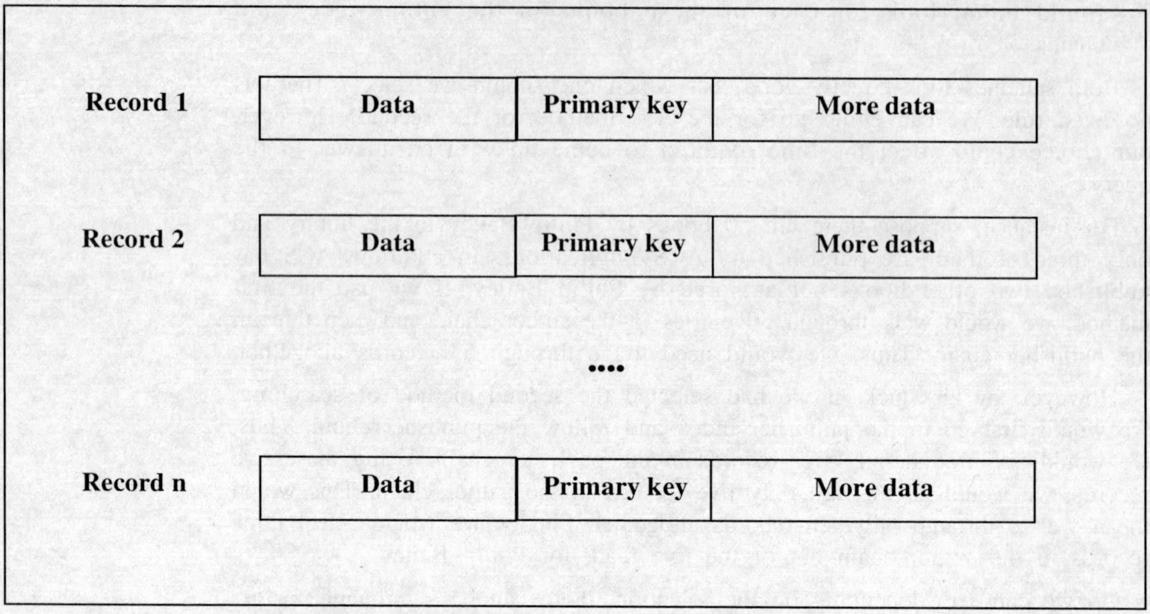

Fig. 1.29 Primary key positions in an indexed file

In order to create and maintain index files, a computer creates a **data file** and an **index file**. The data file contains the actual contents (data) of the record, whereas the index file contains the index entries.

The way files are organised in computers is as follows:

1. The data file is sorted in the order of the primary key field values.
2. The index file contains two fields: the key value and the pointer to the data area. Note the similarity between this organisation and the index mechanism employed by our librarian.
3. One record in the index file thus consists of a key value and a pointer to the corresponding data record. The key value is generally the largest primary key value in a given range of records. The pointer points to the first entry within that range of data records.

This is best illustrated than explained, as shown in Fig. 1.30. Note that there are other ways of organising records in a data file.

Let us understand how this works. We will notice that there are two separate files: an index file and a data file. The index file contains two parts: an index value and a pointer to the data area. Every index value is the highest in a range of data values.

- In the first index entry, the index value is C, which is the highest primary key value in the first data block. Note that the pointer from this index entry points to the start of this range (i.e. A). The address (i.e. memory location) of this on the disk is assumed to be 0, as shown.
- Similarly, the second index entry contains F as the highest primary key value for that range of records, and a pointer to D, which is the start of

the range, and so on. The address (i.e. memory location) of this on the disk is assumed to be 100, as shown.

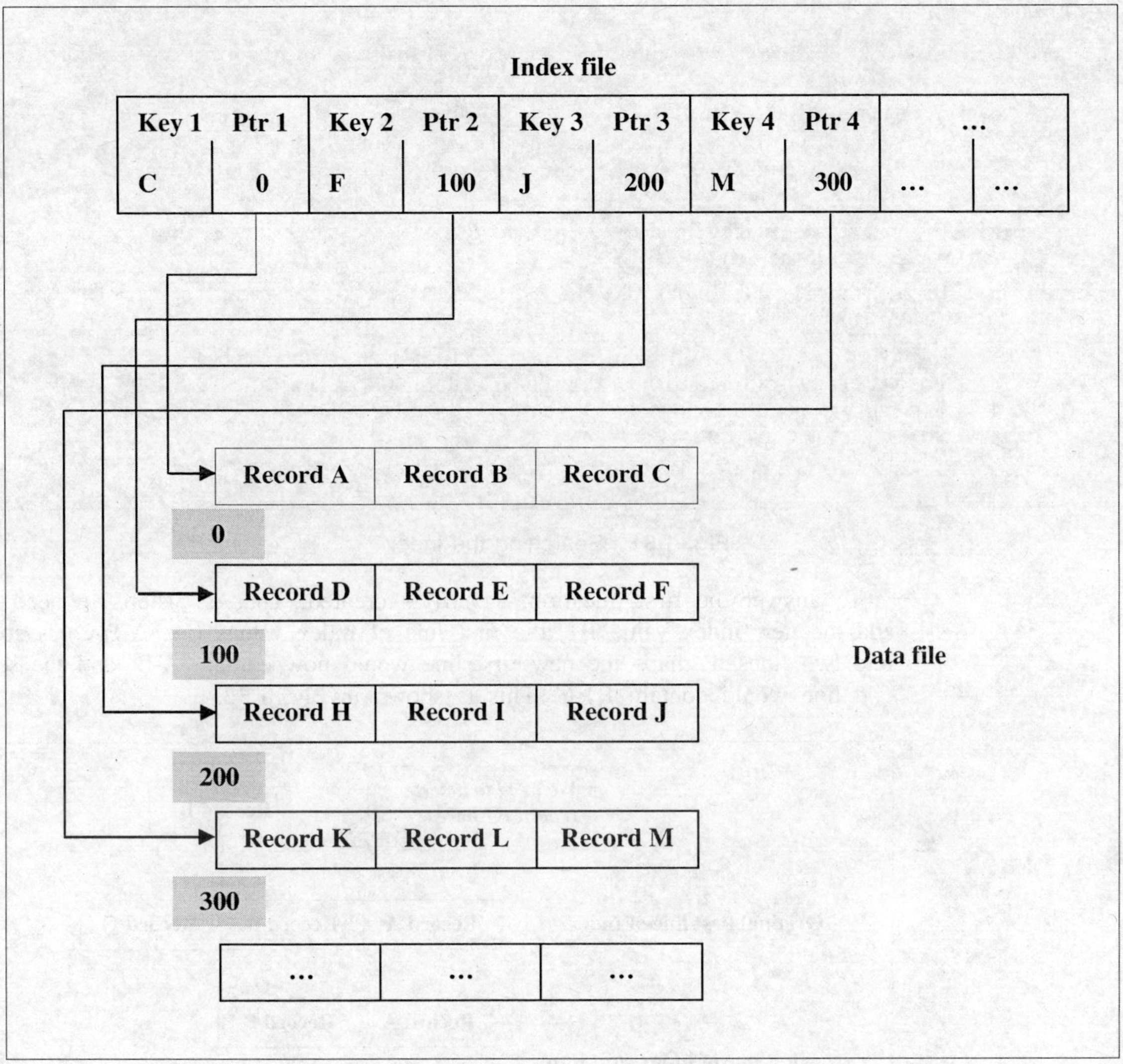

Fig. 1.30 Indexed file organisation

An example of this is shown in Fig. 1.31.

This arrangement works fine. However, we would need to deal with two problems, as follows:

1. How do we insert new index values between any two existing values? For example, suppose we now have an index value called as B1. Where do we store it? Clearly, we do not have any space left in the first range of A-C.
2. What happens if the number of index values becomes too high? Would it not slow down the search?

Example

Suppose we need to search a record with primary key value = L. Then the search would proceed as follows.

(i) A comparison would be made between the highest key value of the first range (i.e. C) and the key value to be searched (L.) Because the value being searched (L) is greater than the highest primary key in the first range (C), the primary key is not present in the first range. So, we must search the next range.

(ii) The highest value in the second range (F) is also lesser than the one being searched (L). So, we move to the next range.

(iii) The highest value in the third range (J) is also lesser than the one being searched (L). So, we move to the next range.

(iv) The highest value in the third range (M) is greater than the one being searched (L). So, the value being searched (L) must be available in this range. So, by using the starting pointer to this range (i.e. pointer to K), we move to the start of this range, and from K, move to L. Thus, our search is complete.

Fig. 1.31 Searching the index

To answer the first question, a *split* is created. That is, when we need to add the new index value B1, the first line of index values (i.e. A-B-C) is split into two lines. Perhaps the new first line would now contain A-B, and the second line would contain B1-C. This is shown in Fig. 1.32.

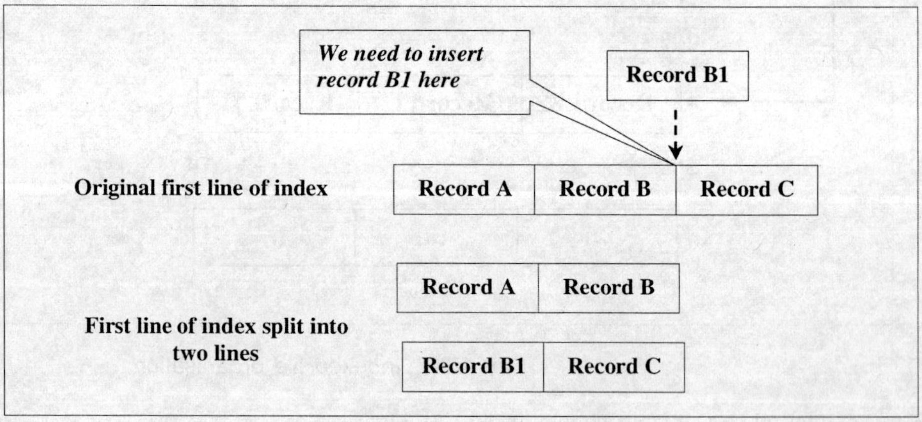

Fig. 1.32 Split in index entries

We can similarly insert any new index entry anywhere. This would necessitate a split in the index, and appropriate adjustments in the address values.

Solving the second problem is equally interesting. We can create an *index of indexes*. In other words, we can create a **multi-level index**. In this type of index, the very first line does not point to the data items as before. Instead, it points to another lower-level index. Depending on the need, this lower-level index may point to yet another lower-level index, and so on. Only the final level of index points to the actual data items.

> A multi-level index contains multiple lines of indexes, the final line pointing to the data items.

The benefit of this scheme is that we can create multiple levels of indexes, accommodating as many index entries as desired. This leaves enough space for future expansions (insertions). Of course, if even this strategy does not suffice, we would create another split in the index, as shown earlier.

A two-level index is shown in Fig. 1.33. To keep things simple, we have shown only two second-level indexes. There would, of course, be four such indexes in the real copy, corresponding to the four entries in the first-level index. We also show only a couple of pointers from the second-level index to the data area.

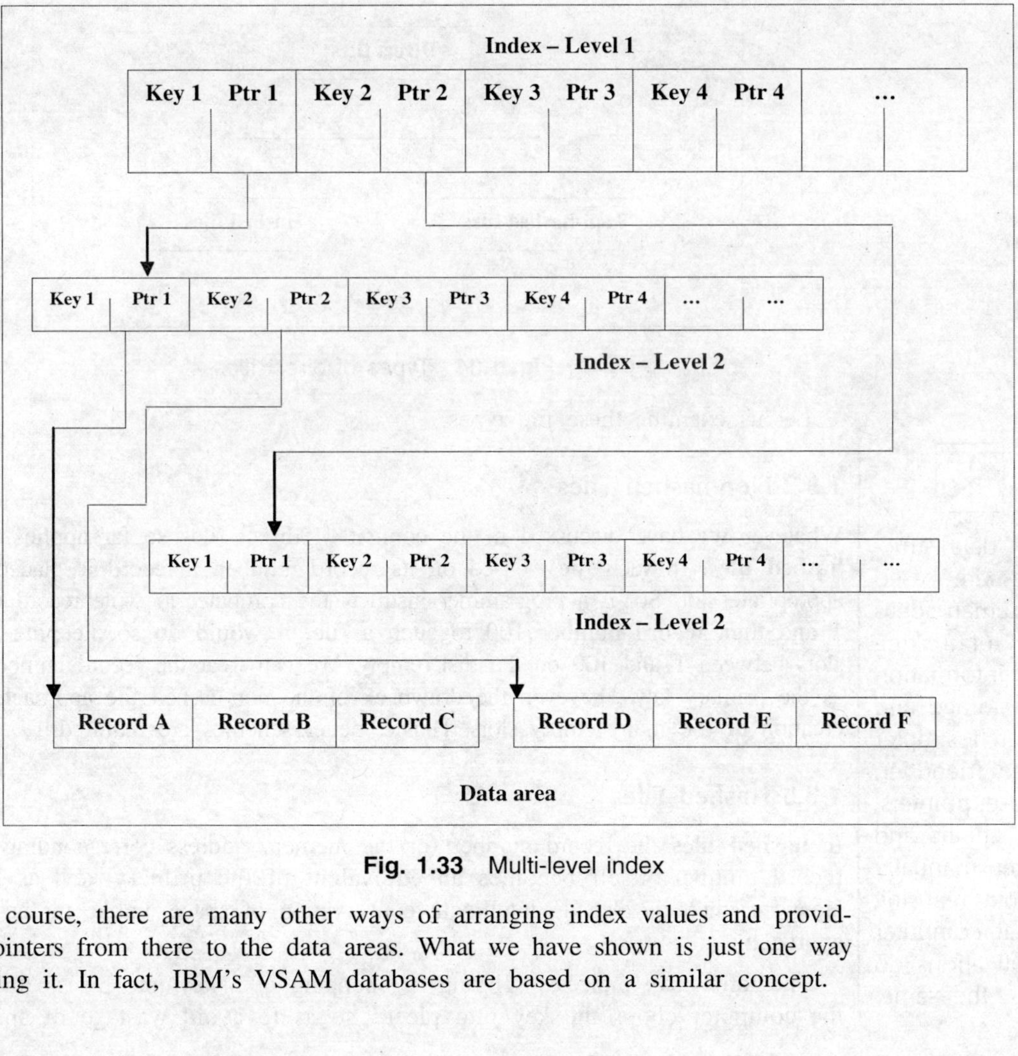

Fig. 1.33 Multi-level index

Of course, there are many other ways of arranging index values and providing pointers from there to the data areas. What we have shown is just one way of doing it. In fact, IBM's VSAM databases are based on a similar concept.

1.8 DIRECT ORGANISATION

1.8.1 Basic Concepts

There is a third popular type of file, called **direct files**. In some technologies, these files are also called **relative files**. There is no concept of an index (and hence that of a primary key) here. The idea is quite simple. All records in a direct file are of the same size. Every record has an associated **record number**. The record number serves the same purpose as a primary key in an index file. Thus, we can ask the computer to provide us with record number 13 (instead of asking for a record whose employee-ID equals A17, for example). In relative files we cannot search records based on a value in a field directly, as can be done in the case of an index file.

Direct files can be classified into two main types as shown in Fig. 1.34.

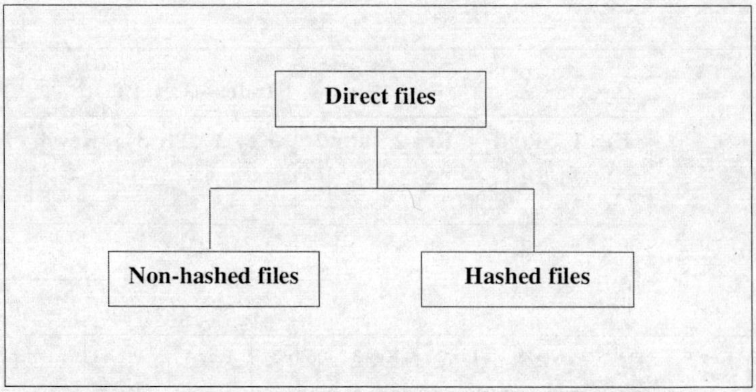

Fig. 1.34 Types of direct files

Let us examine these file types.

All data structures are based on human ideas of making information storage and search simpler and friendlier. We use pointers, chains and indexes manually without realising that computer applications do the same.

1.8.2 Non-hashed Files

Whatever we have discussed in the context of direct files so far applies to **non hashed files**. In such files, based on its record number, a record is placed in its appropriate slot. So, if a programmer instructs the computer to write record number 1 and then record number 100 to such a file, it would do so, keeping the 98 slots between 1 and 100 on the disk empty. We can treat the record number itself as the primary key. However, the drawback of the non-hashed file approach is the creation of too many empty slots. Hence, better schemes are required.

1.8.3 Hashed Files

In **hashed files** the record number (or the memory address corresponding to the record number) itself becomes an equivalent of the primary key, as before. However, there is also an intelligent conservation of space, unlike in the earlier approach.

The term *hash* indicates splitting or chopping of a key into pieces. In effect, the computer chops the key into pieces so as to avoid wastage of space, as illustrated subsequently. There are three primary hashing techniques, as shown in Fig. 1.35.

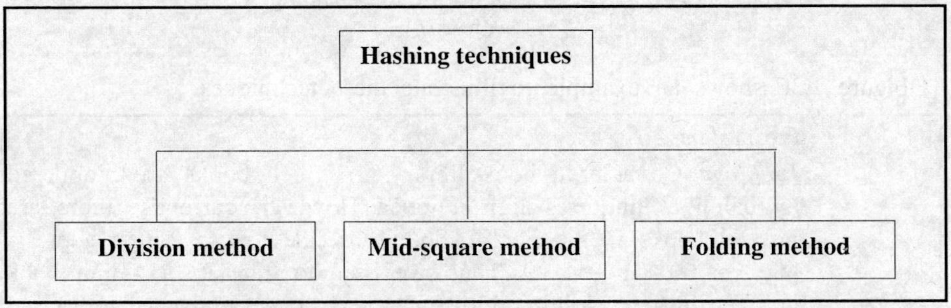

Fig. 1.35 Hashing techniques

The following discussion requires some mathematical concepts and can be safely skipped without any loss of continuity. The reader may instead choose to move to the example that follows the discussion, which explains the concepts in a simpler manner.

To understand these techniques, we need to be familiar with certain terminologies, as follows.

N = Number of records in the file

K = Set of keys that can uniquely identify all the records in the file

- **Division method**: In this method, we choose a number M, such that $M > N$. It is better to choose a prime number as M. Then, the hash function H is defined as follows:

  $H(K) = K \bmod M$

  Just for clarity, K *mod* M means we divide K by M, and take the remainder of the division.

For example, if K is 9875, N is 58 and M is 97, then we have:

$$H(K) = 9875 \bmod 99 = 78.$$

- **Mid-square method**: In this method, we take the square of K (i.e. K^2). We then chop off digits from both the ends of K^2. We will call this final value as L. Therefore, the hash function H is defined as follows:

  $H(K) = L$

For example, if K is 9875, N is 58 and M is 97, then we have:

$$K^2 = 97515625$$

$$H(K) = \text{Middle two digits of } K^2 = 15.$$

- **Folding method**: Here, the key, K, is partitioned into a number of parts, such as K_1, K_2, and so on. The parts are then added together, ignoring the final carry. Thus, the hash function, H, is defined as follows:

  $H(K) = K_1 + K_2 + \ldots + K_n$

For example, if K is 9875, N is 58 and M is 97, then we have:

$H(K) = 98 + 75 = 173$; ignoring the leading 1, we have

$H(K) = 73$.

Figure 1.36 shows an example to illustrate these techniques.

Example

Problem: Consider a book library, in which books are numbered by using a unique 4-digit number. However, currently, there are just 69 books in the library. So, we decide to use 2-digit addressing, i.e. 00, 01, …, 99. Thus, we need to translate a 4-digit book number into a 2-digit address. As examples, translate the actual book numbers 3207, 7147, and 2347 into 2-digit addresses using the three hashing techniques. (Similar techniques would apply for the remaining book numbers).

Solution:

(a) Division method

Select a prime number M close to 99, say 97. Then we calculate $H(K)$ as follows:

(i) $H(3207) = 3207 \bmod 97$ = Remainder of 3207/97 = 6

(ii) $H(7147) = 7147 \bmod 97$ = Remainder of 7147/97 = 66

(iii) $H(2347) = 2347 \bmod 97$ = Remainder of 2347/97 = 19

Thus, the addresses would be 6, 66, and 19 for these three records.

(b) Mid-square method

(i) $K = 3207$ $\quad K^2 = 10284849$ $H(K)$

= Middle two digits of this = 84

(ii) $K = 7147$ $\quad K^2 = 51079609$ $H(K)$

= Middle two digits of this = 79

(iii) $K = 2347$ $\quad K^2 = 5508409$ $H(K)$

= Middle two digits of this = 08

Note that in the third case there are no *middle* digits. So, we choose the fourth and fifth digits from the right, as we had done in the two earlier cases.

Thus, the addresses would be 84, 79, and 08 for these three records.

(c) Folding method

We chop the key K into two parts, and add them, as follows:

(i) $H(K) = 32 + 07 = 39$

(ii) $H(K) = 71 + 47 = 118$; ignoring the leading digit,

$H(K) = 18$

(iii) $H(K) = 23 + 47 = 70$

Thus, the addresses would be 39, 18, and 70 for these three records.

Fig. 1.36 Examples of hashing techniques

KEY TERMS AND CONCEPTS

Batch processing
Chain
Complex query
Data file
Data item
Direct file
Division method
Field
File
File name
File reorganisation
Folding method
Hashed file
Index
Index corruption
Index file
Key
Logical record deletion
Master data
Mid-square method
Multi-level index
Non-hashed file
One-way chain
Online processing
Online query
Performance improvement
Physical record deletion
Pointer
Primary key
Query optimisation
Real time processing
Record
Record key
Record layout
Record number
Recovery of lost pointer
Secondary key
Sequential file
Sequential organisation
Transaction data
Two-way chain

CHAPTER SUMMARY

- A **file** is a collection of logical information. Each file has an associated **file name**.
- A file contains many **records**.
- One record consists of many **fields** or **data items**.
- The skeleton of a file is called its **record layout**.
- **Master data** changes infrequently. **Transaction data** changes quite regularly.
- In **batch processing**, there is no or little human intervention.
- In **online processing**, information needs to be obtained from the computer in real time and provided to the user. **Real time processing** is a special case of online processing.
- A field that identifies a record is called the **record key**, or just the **key**. A **primary key** identifies a record uniquely. A **secondary key** may or may not identify a record uniquely.
- One file can have at the most one primary key, but zero or more secondary keys.

- A **sequential file** contains records arranged in a sequential fashion.
- A sequential file is simple and has lesser overheads. However, it is not easy to search or delete records from such a file.
- A **pointer** is a special field that points to another record in the same or a different file.
- **One-way chains** are created to link related information together in the forward direction.
- **Two-way chains** are created to link related information together in the forward as well as the backward direction.
- An **index** is a table of records arranged in a particular fashion.
- **Query optimisation** means trying to improve the **performance** of the query.
- An **index file** helps faster search of data.
- In a **direct file**, every record is identified based on its record number.
- Direct files can be **non-hashed** or **hashed**.
- Hashing techniques include **division method**, **mid-square method**, and **folding method**.

PRACTICE SET

Mark as true or false

1. In our daily life, we store information in the form of files and registers.
2. A file can contain only one record.
3. The skeleton of a record is called its layout.
4. Master data keeps changing every month.
5. A file that identifies a record is called a record key.
6. In sequential organisation, records are added as and when they are available.
7. A pointer in a record contains the address of another record.
8. Two-way chains suffer from lost/damaged references.
9. The process of resolving queries in a more efficient manner is called performance improvement.
10. Direct files are also called relative files.

Fill in the blanks

1. The details of a record are called ________.

   (a) field (b) record layout

   (c) description (d) file name

2. ________ involves a batch of goods manufactured and passed along the conveyor belt.

   (a) Real time processing (b) Online processing

   (c) Batch process (d) Online query

3. A field that can identify a record uniquely is called ________.
   (a) secondary key (b) primary key
   (c) record key (d) data key
4. A ________ contains the address of another record.
   (a) field (b) data item
   (c) key (d) pointer
5. A chain of records is a ________ created by using pointers.
   (a) physical sequence (b) logical sequence
   (c) connection (d) organisation
6. A ________ is a table of records arranged in a particular fashion.
   (a) file (b) one-way chain
   (c) two-way chain (d) None of the above
7. By using the pointer for the first record in the index, we can traverse the ________.
   (a) forward chain (b) reverse chain
   (c) opposite chain (d) two-way chain
8. In order to create and maintain index files, a computer creates a ________ and a ________.
   (a) data file, key file (b) index file, key file
   (c) data file, chain file (d) data file, index file
9. Inserting a new index entry necessitates a ________ in the index.
   (a) split (b) join
   (c) connection (d) none of the above
10. Another word for *index of indexes* is ________.
   (a) single-level index (b) hashed file
   (c) non-hashed file (d) multi-level index

Provide detailed answers to the following questions

1. Explain the concept of master and transaction files.
2. What is sequential organisation? What are its advantages and disadvantages?
3. What are pointers and chains?
4. Explain the difference between one-way chains and two-way chains.
5. How are indexes used?
6. How are record counts maintained?
7. What are complex queries? What is query optimisation?
8. Explain indexed organisation of computer files.
9. What are the different types of direct files? Explain with examples.
10. What is the difference between non-hashed files and hashed files?

Exercises

1. Write down the layout for a student file containing the following fields:
   - Roll number Number Maximum length 5
   - Student name Character Maximum length 30
   - Rank Number Maximum length 2
   - Total marks Number Maximum length 3
2. Create the above *file* as a *table* in MS-Access.
3. Assume that the student file contains the following data. Show an index for the same.

Roll number	*Student name*	*Rank*	*Total marks*
17	Atul	4	500
90	Anita	3	712
27	Jui	1	910
56	Harsh	2	851

4. Calculate the hash of the roll numbers by using all the three methods.
5. Should the *Total marks* field in the above file be a secondary key? Justify your answer.
6. Learn more about file organisation packages such as ISAM or VSAM.
7. If you know a programming language, study its aspects related to file processing.
8. The C programming language provides for extensive file processing. Learn how to handle files in C.
9. The COBOL programming language facilitates the usage of three types of files. Investigate than and describe how they differ from one another.
10. Study how different operating systems treat files. Contrast between the views of UNIX and Windows about files.

Chapter 2

Introduction to Database Systems

A Database Management System (DBMS) acts as the interface between data stored on the disk and its users. In that sense, it creates a boundary between data and its users.

Chapter Highlights

- Overview of Database Management Systems (DBMS)
- Need for DBMS
- Basics of Structured Query Language (SQL)
- Dynamics and Embedded SQL
- Database Models

2.1 WHAT IS DBMS?

We have studied the concepts of data item (also called field), record and file. We have seen information regarding all the employees being stored in a file called "employee-file". The file contained many records, one per employee. Each employee record consisted of data items such as employee number, name and basic pay. Similar examples of files could be student-file, purchase-order-file, invoice-file and so on.

In typical business environments, it is always essential to be able to produce the right information at the right time with minimum efforts. Assume that a manufacturer of goods uses 10 such different files (one for suppliers, one for customers, one for accounts, etc.). It might not be very easy to answer a query such as:

How many of our customers have credit balance with us for over a month now and whose average purchases from December last year to February this year have been above average?

You can imagine the complexity involved in providing this information. It is not that such a report cannot be generated at all. It certainly can be produced, however, it will require a lot of effort. We shall see the reasons behind this and also study what better systems exist. More specifically, we shall study how a **database** is a better solution than a set of files. Also, a **Database Management System (DBMS)** scores over **File Management System (FMS)** on many counts. We shall explore the reasons behind this. Fig. 2.1 shows this evolution.

The DBMS has evolved over the years from being a simple means of arranging data to a much more sophisticated organisation and retrieval of data as and when required, in real-time. We shall study the different types of databases and understand the differences between them. **Relational Database Management Systems (RDBMS),** about which we shall study too, have become the most popular of them all for many reasons. Our aim is also to see how we can access data from a RDBMS using the **Structured Query Language (SQL).**

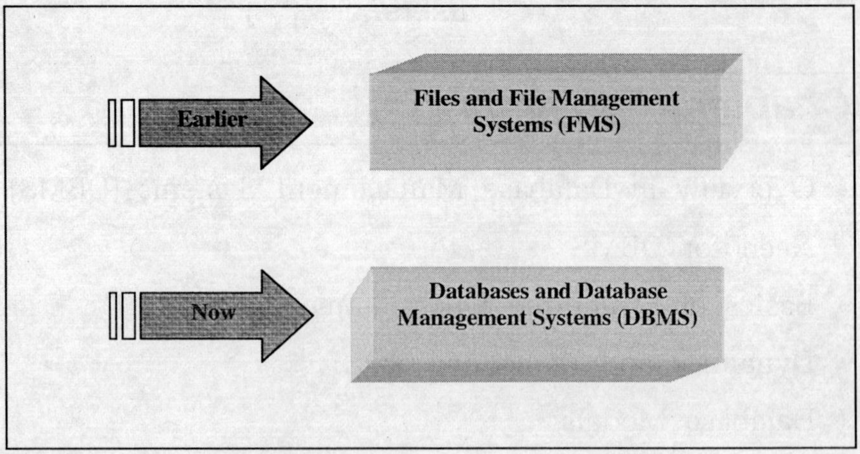

Fig. 2.1 Files, FMS, Databases, DBMS

2.2 FILE MANAGEMENT SYSTEMS (FMS)

We can imagine that a personnel department would use many files in addition to the employee file shown earlier. In fact, the early years of data processing was based on these ideas. Large organisations often had many end-users. Each end-user had a variety of tasks for the computer. For instance, one manager could request for a report of employees who joined after a certain date, another could need information about a specific department, the third could ask about employees in a particular department in a particular grade, and so on. Each such request meant that one or more programs had to be written. Moreover, since there would be many such files in an organisation (for instance, the attendance file, pay-slips file etc), a complex query would mean interaction with more than one file in a single program. Thus, even a simple request could take a few hours of programming effort. This was frustrating, although it was better than a manual system.

The other problem in using files was the tight locking of programs and files. For instance, if someone in the personnel department decided to add a field called *Blood group* to the employee file shown earlier, all programs interacting with the employee file would need a change to accommodate this new field. This was extremely annoying. Since writing new programs is time-consuming and changing existing ones is even more so, changes to a file-based system were approached with a lot of caution.

As the use of computers in an organisation grew, different departments needed to carry out their data processing jobs independent of each other. The obvious consequence of this was a lot of **data duplication** or **data redundancy**.

> Data duplication or data redundancy means multiple (and possibly different) copies of the same data items.

This led to further related problems. For instance, suppose the personnel, payroll and administration departments have different employee files. This meant three problems:

1. Extra efforts to enter the duplicate data.
2. Additional storage requirements.
3. Different values for the same data items, also called as **data inconsistency**.

Database systems became popular in the 1960s when IBM introduced the IMS and IDMS database systems. IMS is a hierarchical database, whereas IDMS is network.

The last problem was the most serious one. For example, each department might follow a different convention for representing information. Thus, one may not know if John Jameson, Jameson J, and J Jameson referred to the same employee or three different people! This problem is shown in Fig. 2.2.

Interestingly enough, the duplication of information was more serious when not done! Imagine that J Jameson left the job. The personnel department would update its employee file. But if one of the other two departments does not, because of a misplaced memo, the consequences could be comical or even damaging. Jameson might continue to receive his salary, or be informed that his chair was being replaced with a modern-cushioned one!

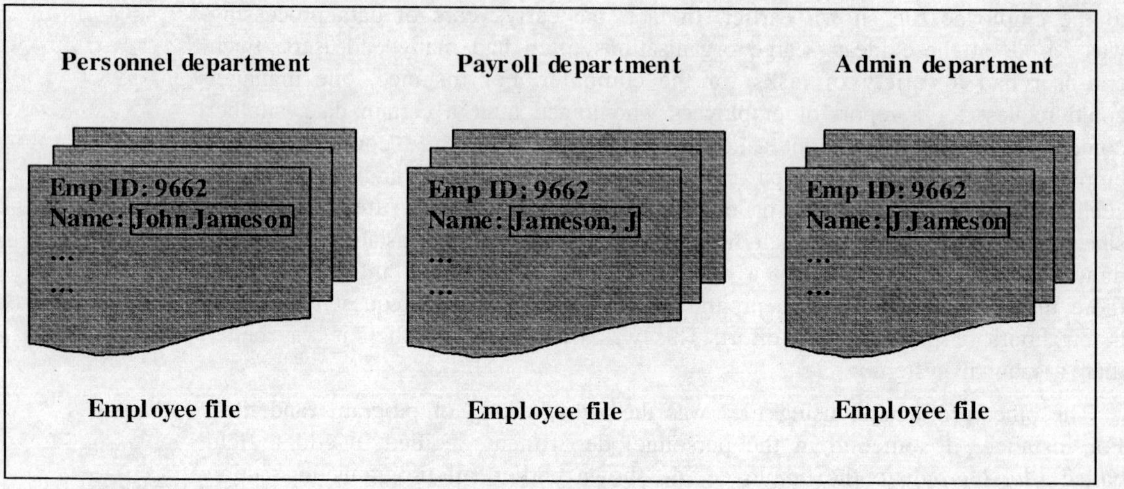

Fig. 2.2 Data inconsistency

The file-based approach is shown in Fig. 2.3. As the figure shows, a variety of application programs interact with a number of files. They are tightly coupled with each other, so that a change in one file could necessitate a change in many programs as explained earlier.

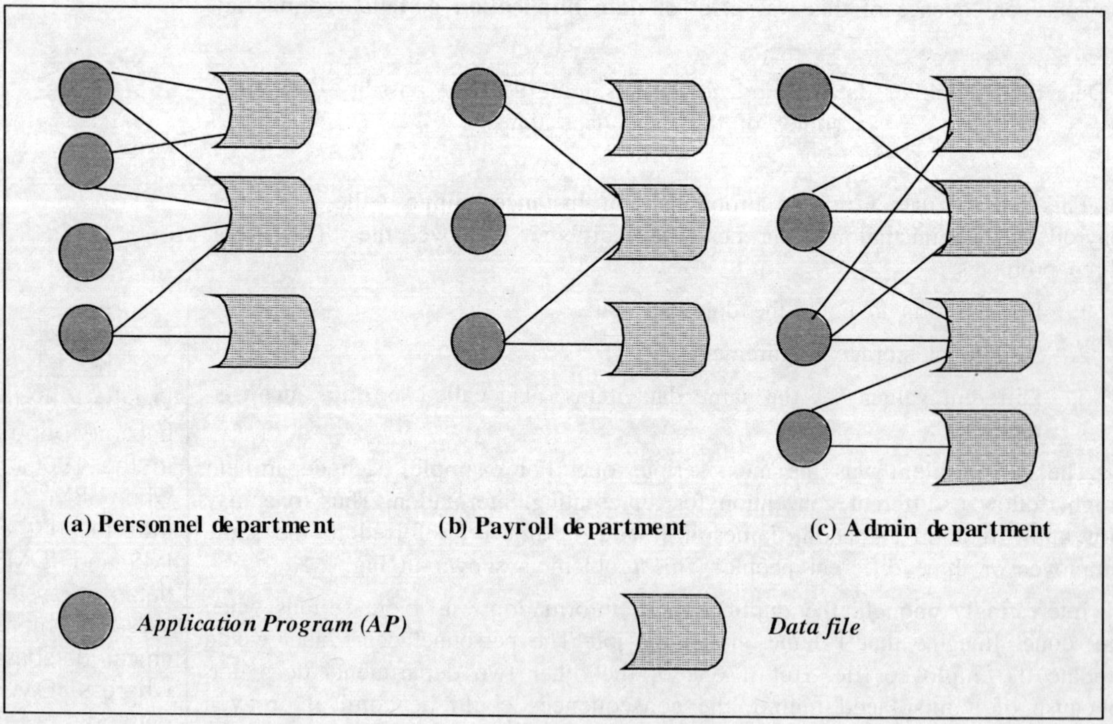

Fig. 2.3 File-based approach

The most important problem was in the area of data consistency. Imagine that a customer invoice is entering the system. It will update customer record for the outstanding amount that the customer owes. It will also add a record to the *invoices register* or *sales daybook* file. It may also add it to the sales statistics file, which maintains product-wise, quarter-wise sales figures. Also imagine that after the system updates the customer record, and before it updates the other two files, the system gets switched off, say due to power cut. What should be done in this case? If the invoice is discarded altogether, the data will be inconsistent (first file updated, but the other two not updated). If, on the other hand, we allow the invoice to be reentered, all the three files will be updated, thus duplicating the updating of the customer record. This is a serious problem and FMS cannot solve it.

FMS suffers from the possibility of lack of data consistency.

DBMS solves such problems by defining a new concept called **transaction** in which all these updates are encapsulated. DBMS has a mechanism to execute the transaction entirely or not execute it at all. This principle of **atomicity** generates consistency, which is absent in FMS.

DBMS solves the problem of the possibility of lack of data consistency by using the concept of transaction.

We shall discuss these concepts later in great detail.

2.3 DATABASE MANAGEMENT SYSTEMS (DBMS)

Although using files was a satisfactory approach for small organisations and businesses, it was not quite easy to work with for larger establishments. Hence, a need for storing information centrally and using it as and when needed was felt. This would take care of the problems with files.

A scheme of grouping a set of **integrated** data files together is called as **database.**

As we shall see, the term *integrated* is extremely important.

A **Database Management System** is a set of prewritten programs that are used to store, update and retrieve a database.

The most important change brought about by DBMS is that the programs no longer interact with the data files directly. Instead, they communicate with the DBMS, which acts as a middle agency. It controls the flow of information from and to the database, as shown in Fig. 2.4.

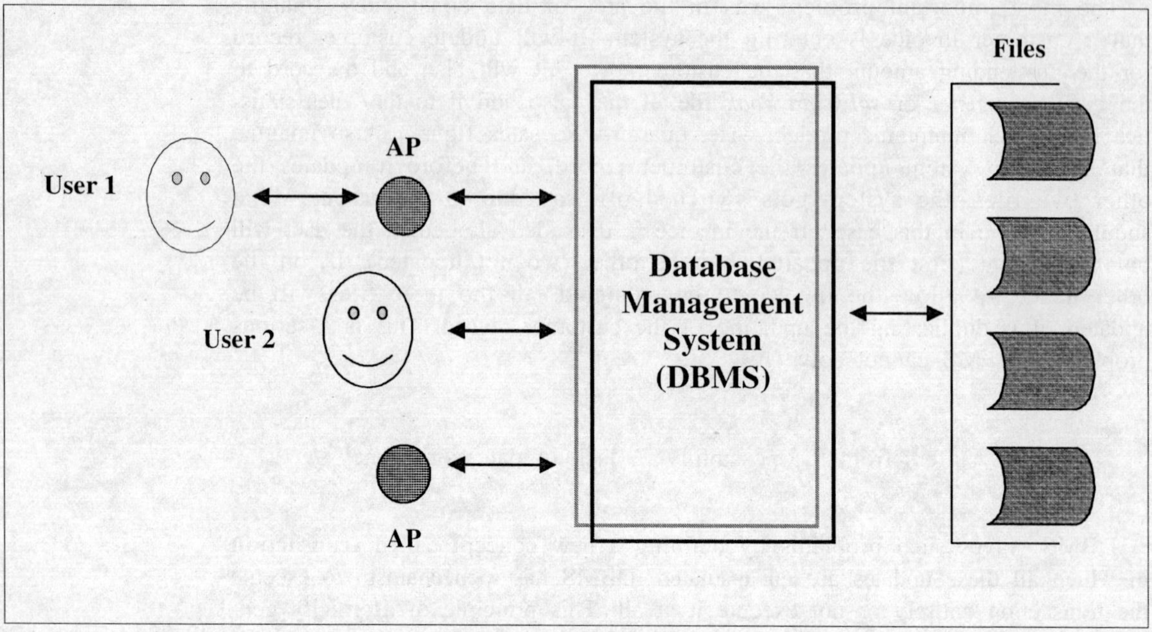

Fig. 2.4 DBMS approach

If we compare this figure with the earlier one, the initial reaction might be that an extra layer of complexity has been added. However, this extra layer is not a cause for worry as it is completely transparent to the end user and, in fact, it helps.

As the figure shows, the files are *integrated*. This means that there is no duplication of data. Instead, all the files are stored together. They are managed by DBMS. In fact, the user or programmer does not even know about the files used by DBMS. DBMS internally uses data structures such as chains, pointers and indexes. However, the user or programmer need not worry about the internal details of how the data is stored such as whether it is on one disk or more, on which sectors, in a continuous pattern or in chunks, in what data structures (e.g. chains/indexes) and so on.

If the user wants to find all the invoices in which the value is > $500, DBMS can produce the result. It may use the indexes on *invoice value* to achieve this, or it may go through the invoices record sequentially. The user need not worry. Only the category of people called **Data Base Administrator (DBA)** need to know the details of data storage. This is because they are concerned with the performance and security aspects of DBMS.

IBM's DB2 rules the world of mainframe databases. Oracle is immensely popular in the non-IBM world.

This is how DBMS hides all the complexities involved in maintaining files and provides a common and simple interface. There is another interesting consequence illustrated in Fig. 2.4. In it, User 2 is interacting directly with the database, without needing to use an application program. This is possible since DBMS provides a set of commands for interacting with and manipulating the database. At the same time, User 1 wants to access/manipulate the database, which is not directly possible by using its set of DBMS commands. Therefore, the user's interaction is through an application program. The third case is a batch program that executes without a user, sitting and interacting with the program/database continuously through a terminal. The batch program executes on its own, once scheduled to run at a specific time. Thus, online (simple and complex) as well as batch data processing is easily handled by DBMS.

2.4 FMS VERSUS DBMS

Let us summarise the advantages offered by DBMS over FMS.

1. **Quicker response** – By using DBMS, in many cases, even end-users can prepare simple reports; extract data directly without the need to write an application program. This facilitates quicker responses to queries and also reduces a lot of unnecessary programming effort. This is not possible in the case of FMS. Extracting data from files requires the writing of programs. The idea is illustrated in Fig. 2.5.

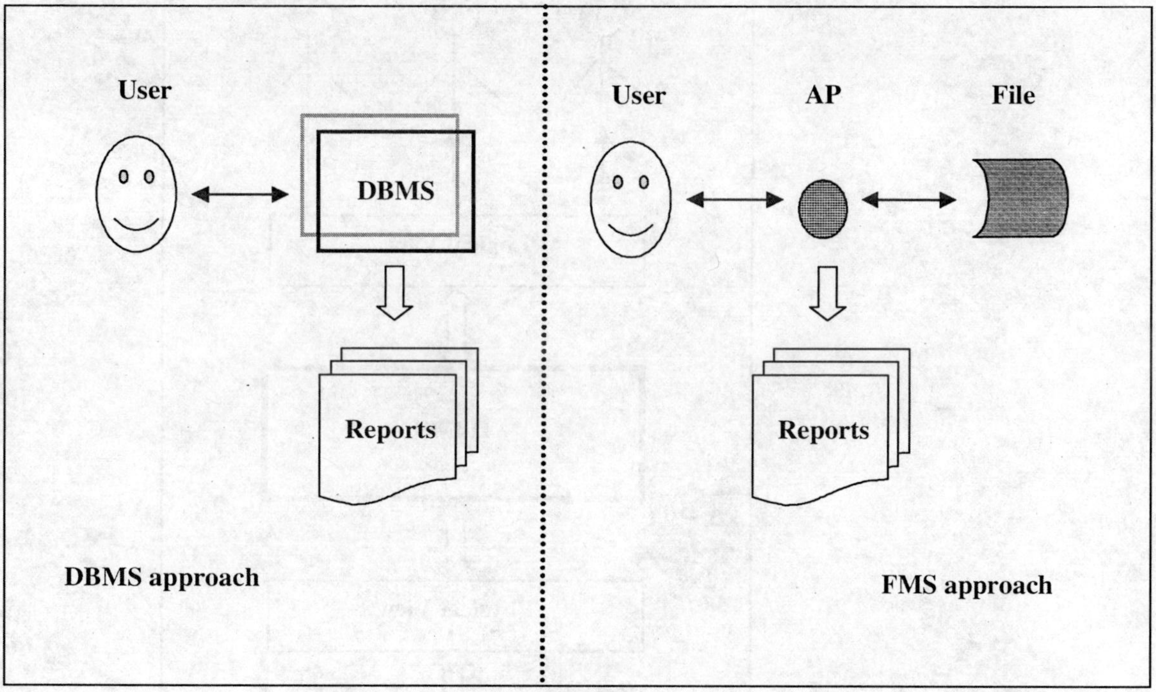

Fig. 2.5 Report generation using DBMS and FMS

2. **Data independence** – One of the most significant features of DBMS that we have already discussed is that it frees the users and/or programmers from the responsibility of knowing the physical details of data. The users need not worry about the size, layout and storage of data. They can concentrate on *what* they want (that is, the **logical view**), rather than *how* to get it (that is, the **physical view**). The DBMS approach handles these internal details on behalf of the users.

> The separation of physical and logical views of data is called as **data independence.**

Another example of data independence is the way the fields or data items are stored physically one after another in a record and the way they are presented to different programs. In fact, once the fields are defined, the program can create their own *logical records* by just stating the names of the data fields in different sequence. The DBMS internally extracts the required fields in the desired sequence and presents them to the application programs. Thus, different programs can have different *views* of the same record. The application programmer has only to bother about the logical record and not to worry about how it is stored. This lends adaptability to DBMS. Fig. 2.6 illustrates the idea.

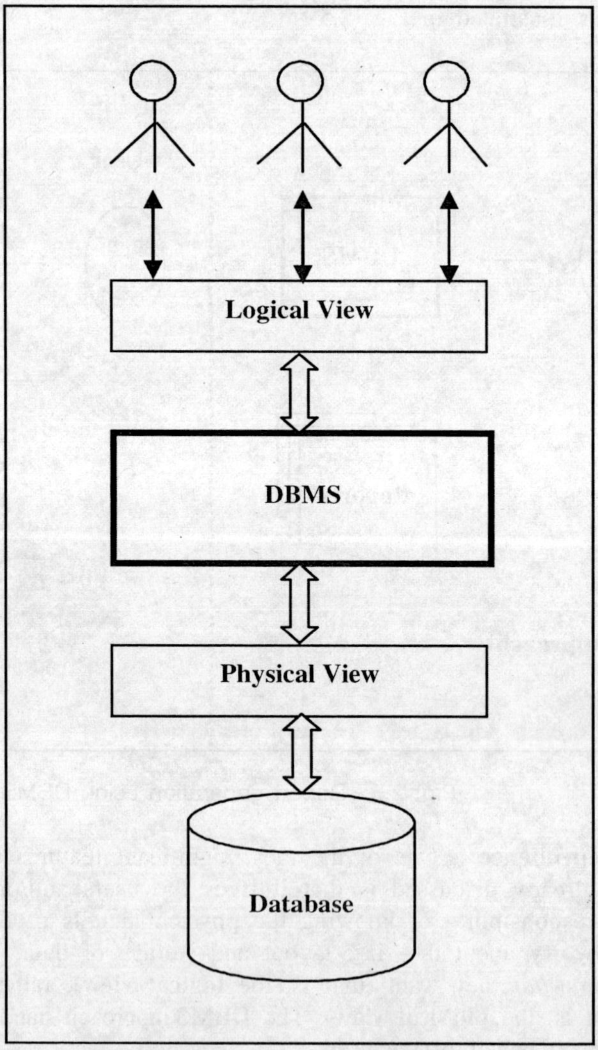

Fig. 2.6 Data independence

Changes to a DBMS are far simpler than those to a file-based system. For instance, in this approach adding the *Blood group* field to the employee record contained in a database is very simple. In contrast to this, a similar change in a file-based system would be much more complicated. The main reason for this is, of course, that the application programs in a DBMS are written with the logical organisation of the database in view.

3. **Security** – The **security** and protection of sensitive information are very important issues. This is handled by a DBMS easily and efficiently. Permissions and access rights can be defined for one user or a group of users so that any unauthorised user cannot update or even read sensitive information. Implementing this needs a lot of effort in a file-based system.
4. **Data sharing –** DBMS offers features that allow easy data sharing. This comes in four aspects/combinations, as shown in Table 2.1.

Table 2.1 Data sharing

Application	*Data*
Old	Old
Old	New
New	Old
New	New

In simple terms, old (i.e. existing) applications can share old or new data. Additionally, new applications can also use old or new data. File systems also allow data sharing. However, it is not as powerful or rich in terms of features as DBMS.

5. **Data redundancy** – We have discussed this earlier. DBMS provides good features so that the redundancy in data can be controlled or minimised, if not completely eliminated. Thus, data duplication is controlled.
6. **Data consistency** – We also discussed this point earlier. DBMS features allow us to make sure that data in a database are consistent. For example, let us assume that an employee E1 is working in department D5 is recorded at two places in a file (or in two separate files) and that the FMS is not aware of this duplication. (In other words, the redundancy is *not controlled*). In such a case, it may easily so happen that one of these entries is updated to say that employee E1 now works in department D8. However, the other entry is not modified. This leads to data inconsistency. This can be taken care of in DBMS.
7. **Transactions** – The concept of transactions is perhaps the most important aspect of DBMS. This simply does not exist in a file-based system, as discussed earlier.

> A transaction is a set of related operations that must be performed completely or not at all.

For example, if 100 dollars are to be transferred from one account to another, debiting one and crediting the other are two activities that must be done to complete this transaction. If only one goes through, it will lead to chaos. The idea is shown in Fig. 2.7.

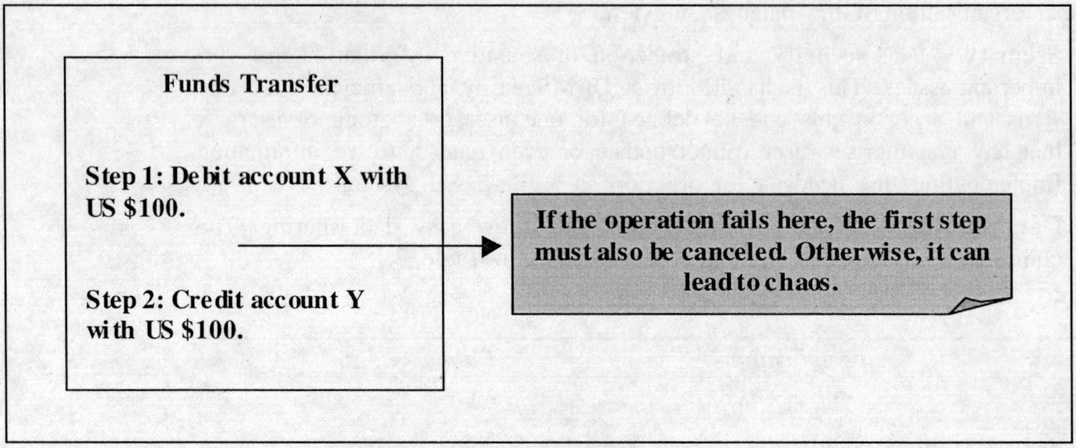

Fig. 2.7 Importance of transactions

For example, the money would disappear from the first account, but would not be credited to the other account. This is shown in Fig. 2.8.

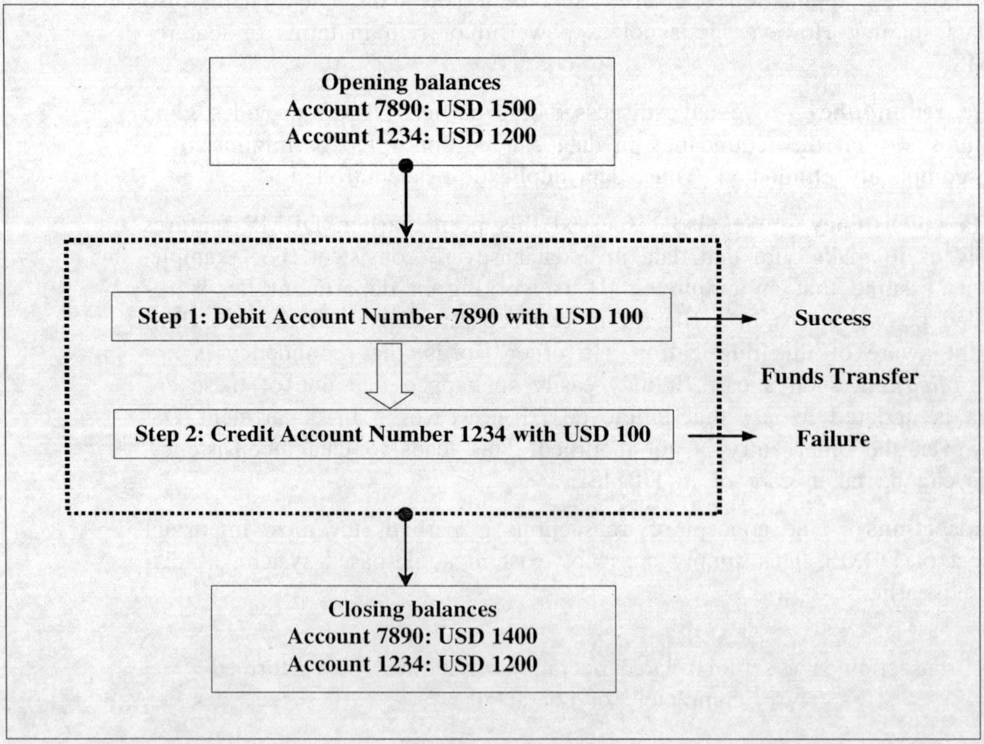

Fig. 2.8 Problems due to lack of transactional capabilities

As a result of this half-successful operation, although account number 7890 would be correctly debited with USD 100, account number 1234 would not be credited with that much amount, leading to chaos.

DBMS supports the concept of transactions and thus allows **data integrity**. This is extremely important for any business application. The way this works is as follows.

Typically DBMS encapsulates all the database updates between two instructions *Start-transaction* and *End-transaction*. *Start-transaction* denotes the beginning of a transaction and *End-transaction* denotes the end of it. All the database updates between these two should be treated as atomic, that is, they are done completely or not done at all.

- If the transaction goes through without any problems, it is **committed** (i.e. all the updates take place).
- However, if it does not go through it, it is **rolled back** (i.e. all the updates done so far have to be undone before we can start again!).

In our earlier example, if step 1 (i.e. debiting an account) is successful, but step 2 (i.e. crediting the corresponding account) is not successful, then the complete transaction would be rolled back. That is, the DBMS would cancel the effect of step 1 as well. The data would thus assume the original state, that is, the one before the debit step happened. This is shown in Fig. 2.9.

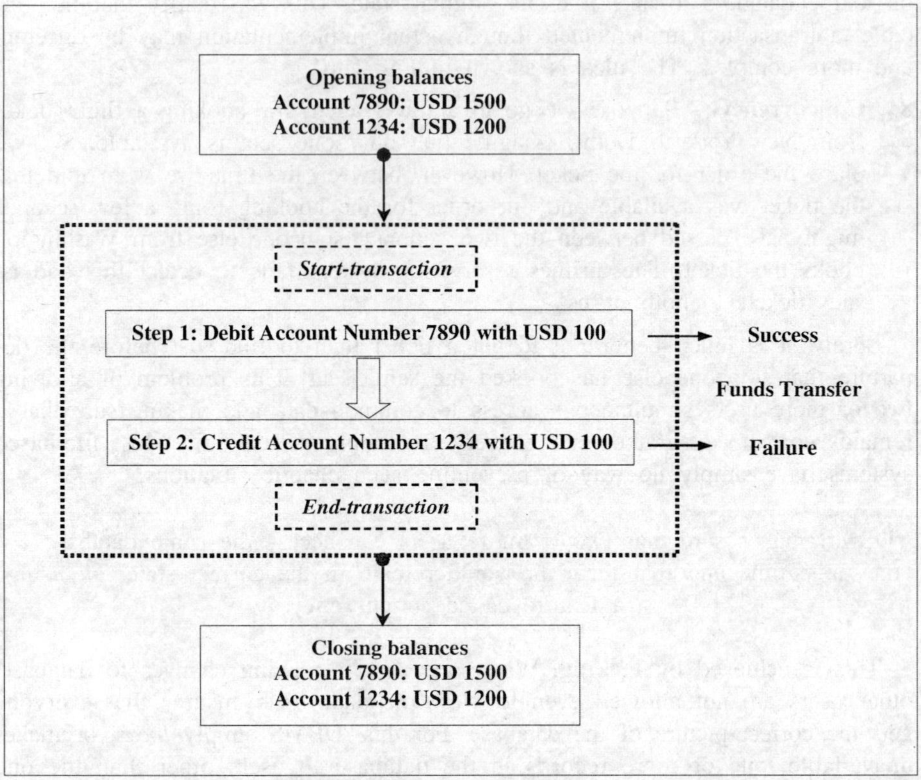

Fig. 2.9 Concept of a transaction

Note that when step 2 fails, both the accounts retain the opening balances as the closing balances. That is, the effect of the debit step is cancelled automatically.

How is this done technically?

To be able to undo database changes, a log of all database changes is kept. The log contains a chronological list of database changes. For undoing a transaction (that is, for rolling it back), the log contains a copy of every database record *before* it was changed. Such records are called *before image records.*

- ***Roll back***: When a transaction needs to be rolled back, the DBMS simply reads all the *before image records* for that transaction from the log and applies them to the database.
- ***Commit***: For committing a transaction, of course, the DBMS might discard all the *before image* records – and also write them in a file for future reference.

For instance, consider our earlier example of transfer of 100 dollars from one account to another. When 100 dollars are taken out from one account, DBMS would write the record as it was - *before subtracting 100 from its balance* – to the log file, and then make changes to it in the database. Now if for some reason, there was some failure and the transaction was aborted, the DBMS has to simply take the *before image* record of the account and write it on to the database to take it to its original state. This will clarify that in principle, a transaction implemented though actual implementation may be different and more complex. The idea is shown in Fig. 2.10.

8. **Concurrency** – Suppose we go to a travel agent for booking a flight ticket from New York to Delhi. Imagine that only one seat is available. So, we place the order for the ticket. However, between the time we were told that the ticket was available and our order for the booking (only a few seconds might have passed between the two actions), someone else from Washington books the ticket. The airlines reservation system fails to detect this and issues tickets to both of us!

Surely, it is much better not to get a ticket than to find just before the departure that someone else has booked the same seat! This problem of allowing two or more users simultaneous access to common data and making sure that it remains correct (integrated) can be very frustrating in real life. Most file-based systems have simply no way of preventing such chaotic situations.

DBMS makes sure that two or more users can access the same database at the same time and that the data would remain in the correct state, by using a feature called **concurrency.**

This is achieved by **locking**. When one user is making changes to database, other users are not allowed even to view the data. This ensures that everyone gets the correct picture of the database. For this, DBMS simply *locks*, or makes unavailable, one or more records in the database to users other than the one who is changing them.

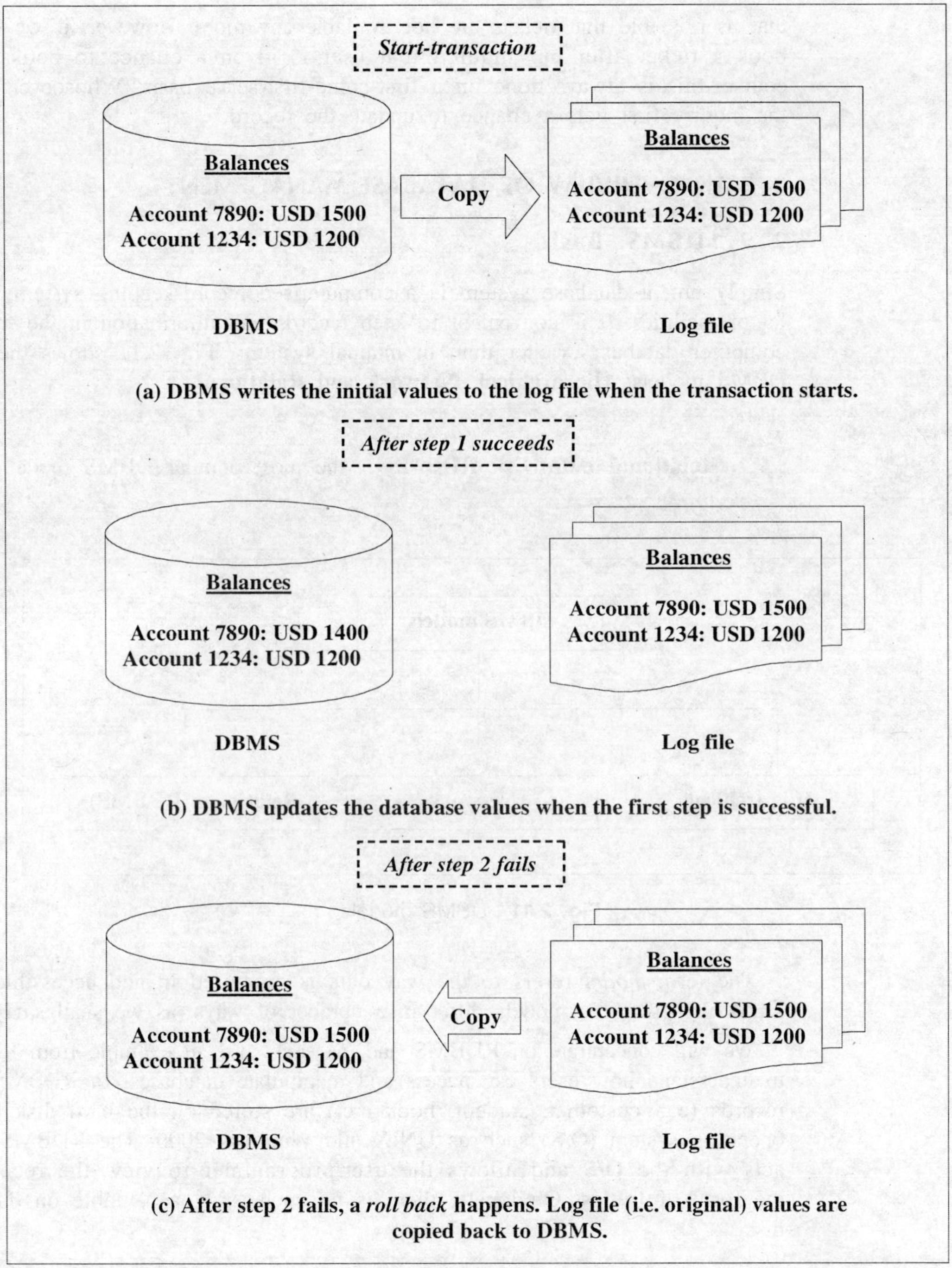

Fig. 2.10 Technicalities behind handling rollbacks

In the above example, when we inquire about the ticket with the intent of booking it, DBMS would internally lock the record. Thus, the other user from Washington is asked to wait until our transaction is over. If we book the ticket, that user is told that tickets are not available any more. However, if we do not book a ticket after our inquiry, that user is given a chance to book it. Of course, this is always done on a first-come-first-serve basis. Whosoever makes the inquiry first gets a chance to update the record.

2.5 AN OVERVIEW OF DATABASE MANAGEMENT

2.5.1 DBMS Basics

Simply put, a database system is a computerised record-keeping system with a lot of facilities. It is convenient to keep records and information in the form of computer databases rather than in manual systems. Fig. 2.11 shows the three DBMS models: **Hierarchical**, **Network** and **Relational**.

Relational DBMS or **RDBMS** is the most popular DBMS model.

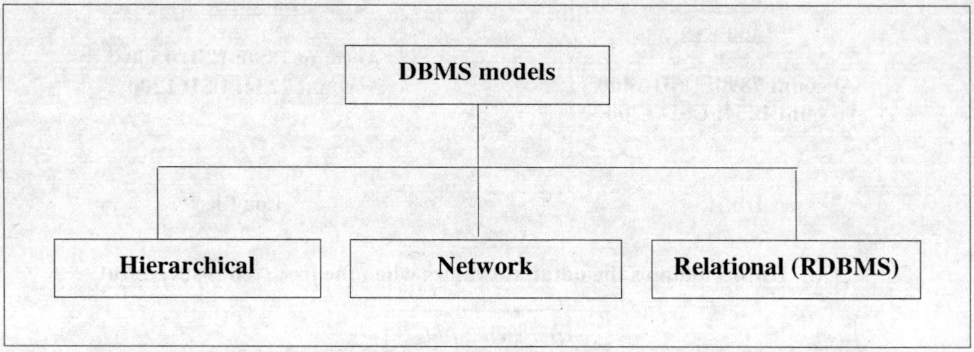

Fig. 2.11 DBMS models

The term *model* refers to the way data is organised in and accessible from DBMS. These three models differ in a number of ways, as we shall study later.

We will concentrate on RDBMS and, as such, use an example from RDBMS to understand how users can access and manipulate databases. In RDBMS, data records (e.g. customer, student, book etc.) are stored on the hard disk by the operating system (O/S) such as UNIX and Windows 2000. The RDBMS interacts with the O/S and allows the user/programmer to view the records in the form of **tables**. Obviously, there is no such thing as a table on the hard disk.

A table is a two-dimensional view of the database.

Suppose I have some books in my collection and I have used a computer database to keep a track of these books in my library, since I intend to purchase many more. (We shall see how to create a database subsequently.) For now, let us assume that the database exists. To see which books exist in my library, I can type a simple command on my computer:

SELECT * FROM Book

We shall look at the details of this command soon. But for now, let us see what happens as a result of this command. The computer comes up with the information I was looking for, on the screen, as shown in Table 2.2.

Table 2.2 Effect of a SELECT command

Id	*Title*	*Author*	*Publication*	*Subject*
1	Computer Fundamentals	AM John	AMC	Computer
2	Operating Systems	Peter Parker	AMC	Computer
3	Computer Networks	AB Simpson	Bernard's	Computer
4	My Autobiography	MK Gandhi	Goyal	Autobiography
5	Chinese Cooking	Rumala Rao	Diwan	Cooking
6	The Freedom Struggle	MK Bose	Bose	General
7	Home PC	PJ Dilbert	AMC	Computer
8	Gardening	SK Das	Das & Das	Home improvement
9	You and Your Dog	ERP Slater	Home and Away	Home improvement
10	Math for Small Children	B Reid	Children Books	Children

As we can see, the information is arranged in the form of a table. So, this table – the Book table – represents a complete listing of all the books I have in my library. Let us dissect the command I had typed:

SELECT – Informs the RDBMS that I want to *select* (or *retrieve*) *something* from *some* table.

* — Indicates that I want to select *all* information from the table.

FROM — Specifies that the table name would follow now.

Book — This is the name of the table from which I want to retrieve data.

Thus, when I want to retrieve any data from any table, I should use a SELECT command. Actually, it is called as **query** in RDBMS terms, and henceforth, we shall also follow that practice.

Now suppose I had decided that tonight, just before going to bed, I would read a book on home improvement. However, I was not sure which book I wanted. So, I enter another simple command:

SELECT * FROM Book WHERE Subject = 'Home improvement'

The computer responds with the result shown in Table 2.3.

C.J. Date has done pioneering work in the area of RDBMS and has demystified the RDBMS principles like no one else. The contribution of E.F. Codd is unmatched in the history of RDBMS.

Table 2.3 Effect of a SELECT ... WHERE query

Id	*Title*	*Author*	*Publication*	*Subject*
8	Gardening	SK Das	Das & Das	Home improvement
9	You and your dog	ERP Slater	Home and Away	Home improvement

Compare this table with the earlier one. You will notice that by adding a WHERE clause, we have filtered our list. The computer does not show the entire table now. Instead, it shows only the records I want. So, it restricts the output and displays books belonging to the *Home improvement* category of subjects. It is not only possible to restrict the number of rows displayed but also the columns. For example, I enter a command:

SELECT Title, Author

FROM Book

WHERE Publication = 'AMC'

The computer displays the result shown in Table 2.4.

Table 2.4 Effect of a SELECT ... WHERE query with column selection

Title	*Author*
Computer Fundamentals	AM John
Operating Systems	Peter Parker
Home PC	PJ Dilbert

We will notice that the computer displays only the book title and author, as requested. Also, it restricts the output to only books published by AMC.

The question now is – who is doing all these filtering of rows and columns based on the conditions I specify? Of course, it is DBMS! DBMS allows me to enter extremely simple commands which I can learn and experiment with quickly. I need not have any formal computer knowledge. I can use simple command in English to see the contents of my database. The DBMS, thus, simplifies the tasks of a common user.

2.5.2 Internal Process

Of course, DBMS has to carry out a number of tasks in order to present a very friendly *face* to the end user. The relationship between the hardware (H/W), the operating system (O/S), the DBMS and the application program (AP) is shown in Fig. 2.12. Of course, the AP is optional, and is not required in the case of simple manipulations like the one illustrated earlier. It is needed when the user wants to perform more complex tasks, which cannot directly be done by typing queries.

Let us imagine that the Results application of a school has an AP to display records of students who have scored marks > 70%, in the alphabetic order. We will assume that a database of student records exists (with an index on percentage of marks maintained by the DBMS internally for faster access). The actual data records and the index records are stored on the hard disk, on various sectors, by the operating system. The O/S keeps track of the sectors allocated to various files of different users and also the sectors that are free. The O/S also provides some access rights denoting who can read or write on which records. Thus, it is only the O/S, which interacts with the H/W to ensure security.

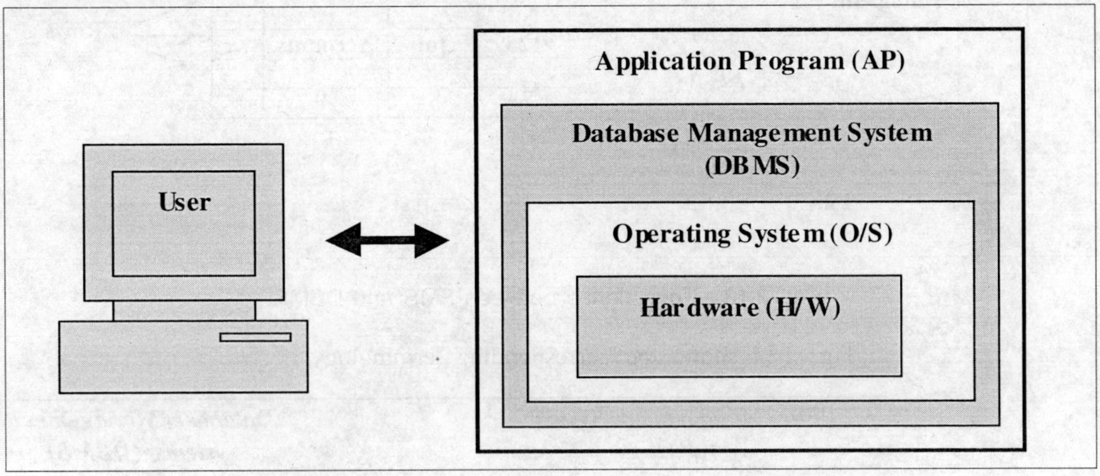

Fig. 2.12 Relationship between H/W, O/S, DBMS and AP

The DBMS builds various data structures like chains/pointers on top of these. Thus, in our example, the user will execute the AP. When the AP needs the specific records (students with marks > 70%), it will make a request to the DBMS. The DBMS will go through the data structures to select the records to be read. After this, the DBMS will make a request to the O/S to read those specific records. The O/S will instruct the H/W (i.e. disk device drivers) to read those records in the memory. The DBMS will present those records to the AP. The AP then can print/display them or perform any calculations or any other action on them as required.

2.5.3 Tables, Rows and Columns

In our example, without stating too much, we used two more terms: **row** and **column**.

A *table* is a set of related pieces of information stored in *rows* and *columns.*

Information, when represented in the form of such rows and columns is called a table in database terminology. Conceptually, a table is similar to what we have been calling a file, so far. Similarly, a column is similar to a field, and a row to a record. These ideas are illustrated in Fig. 2.13.

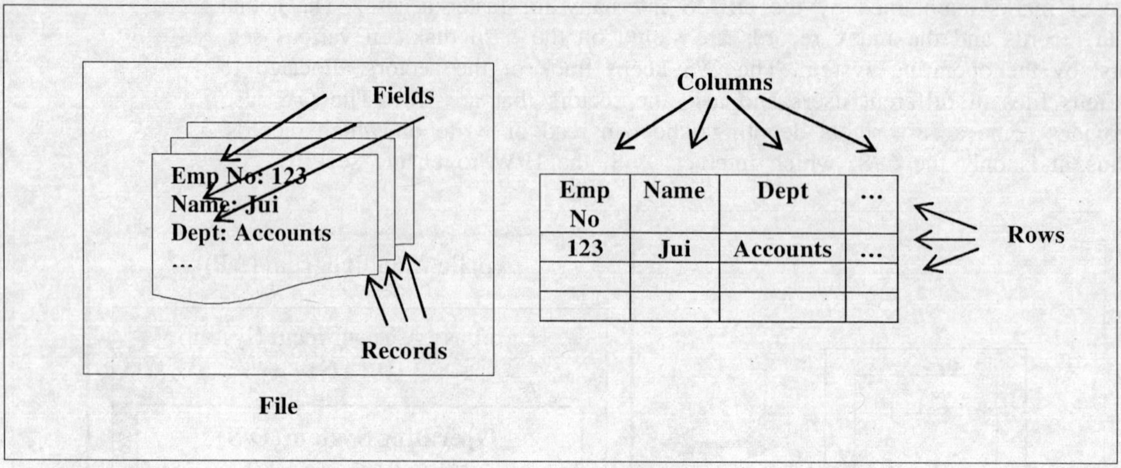

Fig. 2.13 Equivalence between FMS and DBMS

Fig. 2.14 shows the corresponding terminology.

File Management Systems (FMS)	*Database Management Systems (DBMS)*
File	Table
Record	Row
Field	Column

Fig. 2.14 Terminology for FMS and DBMS

Henceforth, we shall use the new terms just introduced. Thus, we can conclude the following:

At the intersection of every row and column, there is one value of interest.

Another important point to note is that many related tables make up a database. This is similar to how many files make up the data portion of a FMS. The concept is illustrated in Fig. 2.15.

When information can be presented in the form of tables in a database, regardless of how it is stored, the arrangement of data is called a **relational database**. The term comes from the fact that data columns are *related* to each other by virtue of their values, and nothing else.

EF Codd first introduced the relational databases in 1970s.

The concept of relational database was based on EF codd's research work on the set theory in relation to computers. Relational databases have gained immense popularity and have captured a large market share mainly due to their simplicity, apart from other standard database features.

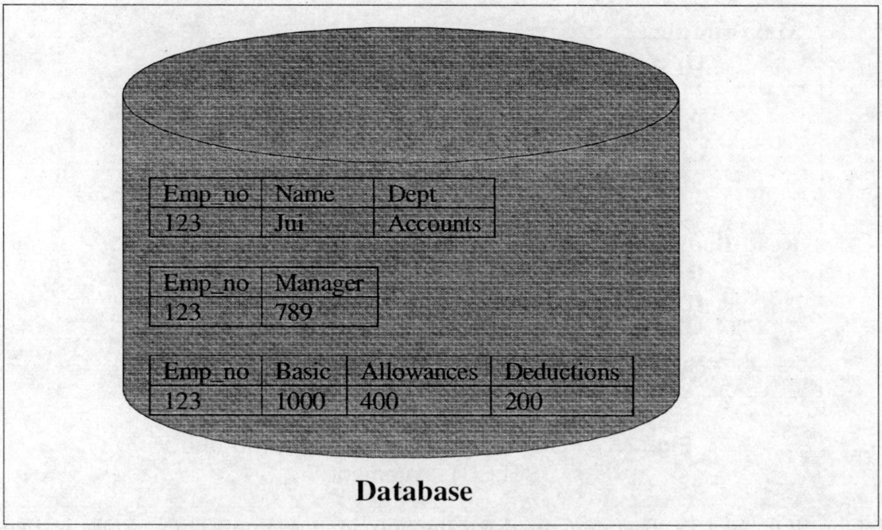

Fig. 2.15 One database contains many tables

2.5.4 SQL and its Power

The language that we use to extract data from a relational database is called **Structured Query Language (SQL)**. Thus, SELECT is a statement in SQL. SQL belongs to the category of **Fourth Generation Languages (4GLs)**. We can produce a list of all the books in a library using a C program, as shown in Fig. 2.16.

```
FILE *fp;
char rec [100];

int main ( )
{
        fp = fopen ("Book.dat", "r"); /* Open file for reading */
        while (!feof (fp))            /* Repeat till end of file is not reached */
                read_book_file ( );   /* Read next record from file */
               fclose (fp);           /* Close file when end of file is reached */
        return 0;
}

read_book_file ( )
{
        fread (&rec, sizeof (rec), 1, fp);
                                      /* C function call for file reading */
        if (feof (fp))                /* If end of file is reached, return back */
                return;
        printf ("%s %s %s %s %s", rec.id, rec.title, rec.author, rec.publication,
        rec.sub);
}
```

Fig. 2.16 C program equivalent to one SELECT statement

The corresponding COBOL program is shown in Fig. 2.17.

```
Main-routine.
        Open Book-file
        Move 'N' to EOF
        Perform Read-Book-file until EOF = 'Y'
        Close Book-file
        Stop run.

Read-Book-file.
        Read Book-file at end move 'Y' to EOF
        If EOF not equal to 'Y'
           Display Id, Title, Author, Publication, Sub
        End-if.
```

Fig. 2.17 COBOL program equivalent to one SELECT statement

Our SQL SELECT statement does the job in one line! Thus, SQL is like a grown-up child who understands an instruction such as *brush teeth* and does not need to be told in detail about how to do it (such as go to wash basin, take the brush, and apply toothpaste). In simple terms, it expects us to tell *what* to do. It will decide *how* to do it! Thus, we are not to bother with opening and closing of files, reading one record at a time, filtering and other such issues.

SQL is, therefore, extremely powerful. It requires only very high-level commands. One SQL command translates into many **Third Generation Language (3GL)** statements, as illustrated above. We can show the equivalence between SQL, 3GLs such as C/COBOL and **Second Generation Languages (2GLs)** such as assembly language, as illustrated in Fig. 2.18. Here, we show a simple instruction provided to some children. If the child is grown up, a simple instruction such as *brush your teeth* would suffice. However, if the child is younger, then we need to provide slightly more detailed instructions — similar to the way we provide instructions in C or COBOL. Finally, if the child is very young, then we must provide very detailed instructions — similar to the way we write assembly language programs.

We should note that SQL is not a product. It is a standard language that many products such as DB2, Oracle, Ingres, Informix, Sybase, SQL Server and MS-Access have adopted. These products are called **Relational Database Management Systems (RDBMS)**. In the following sections, we shall study the basics of SQL in brief.

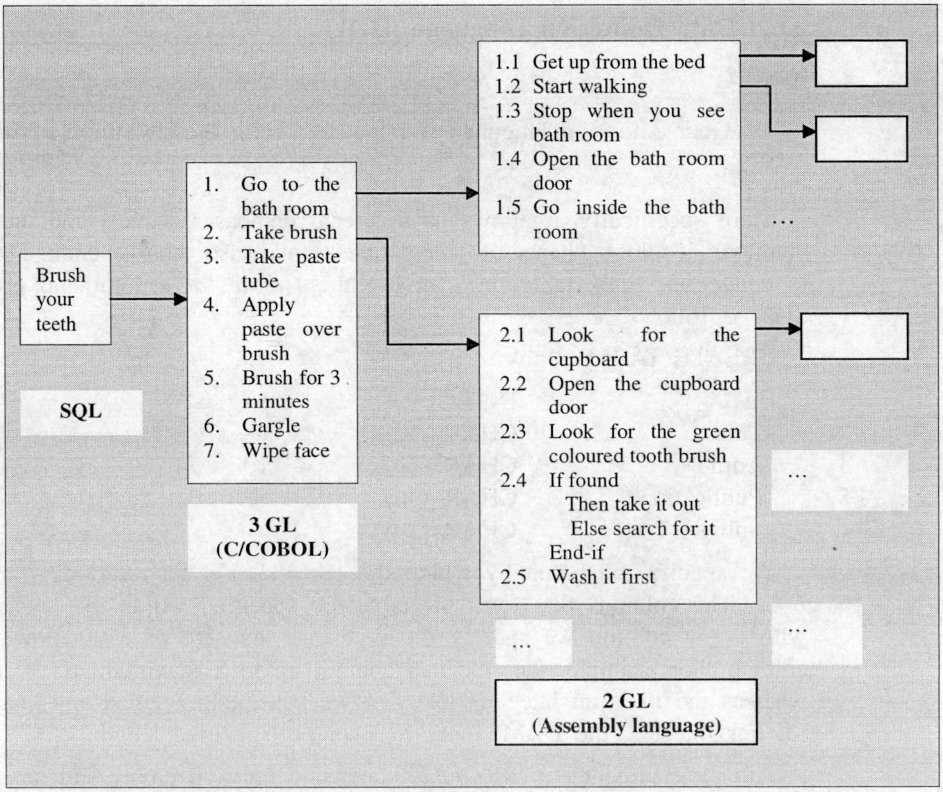

Fig. 2.18 Comparison between SQL and other languages

2.6 BRIEF INTRODUCTION TO SQL

SQL is concerned with three most common tasks needed by any user of a database management system, namely: data definition, data manipulation and data control. SQL allows us to define databases and tables, add/update/view their contents and allows security features. More specifically, SQL commands can be divided into three main categories: **Data Definition Language (DDL)**, **Data Manipulation Language (DML)** and **Data Control Language (DCL)**. These categories are shown in Fig. 2.19.

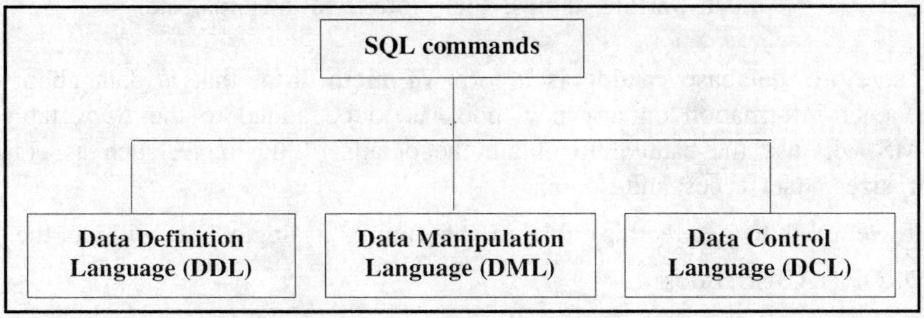

Fig. 2.19 Classification of SQL commands

Let us study each of these.

2.6.1 Data Definition Language (DDL)

Data definition language is concerned with the definition of data.

More specifically, it allows us to create databases, tables, and indexes. Furthermore, it allows changes to these objects and also their deletion. For instance, to create our *Book* table, we can use the *Create table* command provided by SQL as follows:

```
CREATE TABLE Book
(Id             INTEGER,
 Title          CHAR (30),
 Author         CHAR (20),
 Publication    CHAR (30),
 Subject        CHAR (20))
```

We specify the name by which the table should be referred – in this case *Book*. The columns that form the table are specified within the brackets. Along with every column we specify the type and the size of data allowed for that column. For example, the title can contain up to a maximum of 30 characters, whereas the Id is an integer. Note that we have not specified any length for the Id. For integers, the DBMS uses its own pre-specified length.

After executing the *Create table* statement, only an empty structure (called as the template) of the table is created, as shown in Table 2.5.

Table 2.5 Empty Book table structure

Id	*Title*	*Author*	*Publication*	*Subject*

No information about any book exists at this point. All we are telling the DBMS is that there exists a table called *Book* in which there are five columns as specified. The DBMS stores this information in a special area called as **database catalog**.

The catalog is a special area used by the DBMS to maintain information about various tables, their inter-relationships, etc.

Therefore, database catalog is a form of **meta-data**, that is data about data. Whenever information on any new book is to be added to the *Book* table, the DBMS will use the catalog to obtain the details of the table, such as columns, their sizes, data types and so on.

If we need to delete this table in the future, a single line will do the job:

```
DROP TABLE Book
```

The DBMS has to internally update its catalog with the information that no *Book* table exists now. This is hidden from a user. From a user's perspective, the *Book* table no longer exists.

Other simple things such as adding a new column are allowed. For example, if we decide to add a new column — *Price* — to our *Book* table, all we need to do is:

```
ALTER TABLE Book
ADD Price INTEGER
```

As a result, the structure of the *Book* table is modified to the one shown in Table 2.6.

Table 2.6 Modified Book table structure

Id	*Title*	*Author*	*Publication*	*Subject*	*Price*

Indexes allow faster access to data as studied earlier. In SQL, an index can be created as follows:

```
CREATE INDEX BookIndex
ON Book
(Id)
```

What we are asking is to, create an index on the *Book* table and name it as *BookIndex*. Further, the column on which the index is to be created is the book's *Id*. This will enable faster access to books when retrieved using the *Id* (e.g. display all books with *Id* between 20 and 30). We can create an index on any column, or indeed, any combination of more than one column of a table. The index can be in ascending or descending order of column values.

Interestingly, the DBMS might do this by creating chains, pointers, indexes and their combinations. We have already seen how the librarian maintained chains and indexes manually for faster query responses. A similar mechanism is used by DBMS, but it is hidden from the user. The DBMS manipulates the chains and indexes as and when required, internally.

2.6.2 Data Manipulation Language (DML)

2.6.3 Select, Insert, Update and Delete

We have already seen some examples of data manipulation. The SELECT statement allows viewing of the contents of a table in a variety of ways. All or only a few columns, rows or their combinations can be selected, based on the search criteria. SELECT * gives everything: all the rows and all the columns of a table. The WHERE clause does the job of restriction. Only the rows satisfying one or more conditions can be retrieved by using it. SELECT allows selection of one or more columns. For example,

```
SELECT Name, Author
FROM Book
WHERE Author = 'P JONES'
```

This is a very simple data-filtering example. More sophisticated search criteria can be specified. For this, we will use an example for the rest of the discussion.

SQL is a very simple language. It allows manipulation of RDBMS data with great ease and minimum learning curve.

Consider a *Student* table containing details about a student and the marks obtained in various subjects. Let the columns of this table be: *Name*, *Math*, *Science*, *Languages*, *Total*, *Average* and *Result*. Assume that the *Total* and *Average* columns are expected to contain the total marks obtained in the three subject categories and their average, respectively. If the student has obtained less than 35 marks in any of the subjects, the result should be *Fail*; otherwise it should be *Pass*. At the moment, the table looks as shown in Table 2.7.

Table 2.7 Student table – Initial contents

Name	*Math*	*Science*	*Languages*	*Total*	*Average*	*Result*
P Jones	68	90	72			
M Henry	95	92	80			
J Man	29	67	41			
A Bryan	45	60	71			
W Fringe	77	82	64			
A Lawson	55	76	67			
B Marsh	59	52	41			
C Lloyd	81	56	33			
C Adams	32	31	36			

Note that the Total, Average, and Result columns are currently blank. We shall now carry out a variety of operations on this table, to make ourselves familiar with the various aspects of SELECT statement. It will also help us understand the other data manipulation statements.

1. Obtain a list of students who have failed in Math.

   SELECT *

   FROM Student

   WHERE Math < 35

   Output: See Table 2.8.

Table 2.8 Students failing in Math

Name	*Math*	*Science*	*Languages*	*Total*	*Average*	*Result*
J Man	29	67	41			
C Adams	32	31	36			

2. Display names of students who have passed either in Math or Science.

   SELECT Name

   FROM Student

   WHERE Math > 34 OR Science > 34

   Output: See Table 2.9.

Table 2.9 Students passing either in Math or in Science

Name
P Jones
M Henry
J Man
A Bryan
W Fringe
A Lawson
B Marsh
C Lloyd

3. Display names of students who have passed in Languages and also in either Science or Math.

```
SELECT *
FROM Student
WHERE (Languages > 34) AND (Math > 34 OR Science > 34)
```

Output: See Table 2.10.

Table 2.10 Students passing in Languages and in either Science or Math

Name	*Math*	*Science*	*Languages*	*Total*	*Average*	*Result*
P Jones	68	90	72			
M Henry	95	92	80			
J Man	29	67	41			
A Bryan	45	60	71			
W Fringe	77	82	64			
A Lawson	55	76	67			
B Marsh	59	52	41			

Note that C Lloyd's record is not displayed because she has failed in languages.

4. What is the average Math score?

```
SELECT AVG (Math)
FROM Student
```

Output:

60.11

Note that SQL provides many in-built functions such as AVG or MAX, which perform these operations on the specified columns of the table. It should be obvious by now that it is possible to query the *Student* table in a number of ways: almost any requirements can be satisfied with the help of simple SE-

LECT statements. There are many more features of SELECT, which we shall ignore for the moment.

5. What is the maximum score in Languages?

```
SELECT MAX (Languages)
FROM Student
```

Output:

80

The question now is, we have been selecting data from the *Student* table, but who entered it there in the first place? For this, SQL provides an INSERT command. For example:

```
INSERT INTO Student
(Name, Math, Science, Languages)
('P JONES', 68, 90, 72)
```

An INSERT statement will insert one row at a time. We have not manually calculated and entered the values for total marks, average and result. If we were to do that, the purpose of using a computer for database management would be defeated! How can we calculate the totals? For that, another DML statement is required:

```
UPDATE Student
SET Total = Math + Science + Languages
```

Result: See Table 2.11.

Table 2.11 Result of calculating total marks

Name	*Math*	*Science*	*Languages*	*Total*	*Average*	*Result*
P Jones	68	90	72	230		
M Henry	95	92	80	267		
J Man	29	67	41	137		
A Bryan	45	60	71	176		
W Fringe	77	82	64	223		
A Lawson	55	76	67	198		
B Marsh	59	52	41	152		
C Lloyd	81	56	33	170		
C Adams	32	31	36	99		

This would update the Student table with the total marks calculated as a sum of the three subjects. Further, we can find out and store the average marks:

```
UPDATE Student
SET Average = Total / 3
```

Result: See Table 2.12.

Note that *Average* is a column in our table, whereas *AVG* is a build-in SQL function. These two are completely different things.

Table 2.12 Result of calculating averages

Name	*Math*	*Science*	*Languages*	*Total*	*Average*	*Result*
P Jones	68	90	72	230	76.66	
M Henry	95	92	80	267	89.00	
J Man	29	67	41	137	45.66	
A Bryan	45	60	71	176	58.66	
W Fringe	77	82	64	223	74.33	
A Lawson	55	76	67	198	66.00	
B Marsh	59	52	41	152	50.66	
C Lloyd	81	56	33	170	56.66	
C Adams	32	31	36	99	33.00	

Now, the result for the passed students can be determined:

```
UPDATE Student
SET Result = 'Pass'
WHERE Math > 34 AND Science > 34 AND Languages > 34
```

Result: See Table 2.13.

Table 2.13 Determining which students have passed

Name	*Math*	*Science*	*Languages*	*Total*	*Average*	*Result*
P Jones	68	90	72	230	76.66	Pass
M Henry	95	92	80	267	89.00	Pass
J Man	29	67	41	137	45.66	
A Bryan	45	60	71	176	58.66	Pass
W Fringe	77	82	64	223	74.33	Pass
A Lawson	55	76	67	198	66.00	Pass
B Marsh	59	52	41	152	50.66	Pass
C Lloyd	81	56	33	170	56.66	
C Adams	32	31	36	99	33.00	

Finally,

```
UPDATE Student
SET Result = 'Fail'
WHERE Math < 35 OR Science < 35 OR Languages < 35
```

Result: See Table 2.14.

Table 2.14 Determining which students have failed

Name	*Math*	*Science*	*Languages*	*Total*	*Average*	*Result*
P Jones	68	90	72	230	76.66	Pass
M Henry	95	92	80	267	89.00	Pass
J Man	29	67	41	137	45.66	Fail
A Bryan	45	60	71	176	58.66	Pass
W Fringe	77	82	64	223	74.33	Pass
A Lawson	55	76	67	198	66.00	Pass
B Marsh	59	52	41	152	50.66	Pass
C Lloyd	81	56	33	170	56.66	Fail
C Adams	32	31	36	99	44.33	Fail

This would lead to further queries.

1. List the students in the order of merit list.

```
SELECT *
FROM Student
ORDER BY Average DESC
```

Output: See Table 2.15.

Note that ORDER BY is a special clause, which allows us to sort data in the ascending/descending order of a column. In this case, we have specified that the sorting should happen on the basis of the average marks column. Furthermore, a DESC word in the end specifies that the sorting should happen in the descending order of average marks.

Table 2.15 Listing students in order of merit

Name	*Math*	*Science*	*Languages*	*Total*	*Average*	*Result*
M Henry	95	92	80	267	89.00	Pass
P Jones	68	90	72	230	76.66	Pass
W Fringe	77	82	64	223	74.33	Pass
A Lawson	55	76	67	198	66.00	Pass
A Bryan	45	60	71	176	58.66	Pass
C Lloyd	81	56	33	170	56.66	Fail
B Marsh	59	52	41	152	50.66	Pass
J Man	29	67	41	137	45.66	Fail
C Adams	32	31	36	99	33.00	Fail

2. How many students have passed?

```
SELECT COUNT (*)
FROM Student
WHERE Result = 'Pass'
```

Output:

6

3. Which students have failed in more than one subject?

```
SELECT *
FROM Student
WHERE (Math < 35 AND (Science < 35 OR Languages < 35)) OR
      (Science < 35 AND (Languages < 35 OR Math < 35)) OR
      (Languages < 35 AND (Math < 35 OR Science < 35))
```

Output: See Table 2.16.

Table 2.16 Students failing in more than one subject

Name	*Math*	*Science*	*Languages*	*Total*	*Average*	*Result*
C Adams	32	31	36	99	33.00	Fail

Suppose we now want to retain only data for students who have passed the examination. A DELETE statement would do the job:

```
DELETE FROM Student
WHERE Result = 'Fail'
```

Result: See Table 2.17.

Note that we can specify which records are to be deleted. If we do not specify any WHERE clause, that is just say *DELETE FROM Student*, then SQL will delete all *rows* from the *Student* table, making it empty.

Table 2.17 Retaining records of passed students only

Name	*Math*	*Science*	*Languages*	*Total*	*Average*	*Result*
P Jones	68	90	72	230	76.66	Pass
M Henry	95	92	80	267	89.00	Pass
A Bryan	45	60	71	176	58.66	Pass
W Fringe	77	82	64	223	74.33	Pass
A Lawson	55	76	67	198	66.00	Pass
B Marsh	59	52	41	152	50.66	Pass

It should be clear that Data Manipulation Language is extremely powerful. Only four basic statements, namely SELECT, INSERT, UPDATE and DELETE, allows almost any operation on the database.

2.6.4 Multiple Tables and Joins

A database usually comprises of many tables. For example, suppose some other information on the students is available in another table called as *StudentInfo*. It contains the name, address, phone number and date of birth of the students, as shown in Table 2.18.

Table 2.18 StudentInfo table

Name	*Address*	*Phone-Number*	*Date-of-Birth*
P Jones	George Street	1567	12-31-1973
M Henry	Warwick Terrace	2121	02-02-1972
J Man	The Oaks	3131	09-01-1973
A Bryan	Albert Street	5467	11-23-1972
W Fringe	Bush Street	2148	09-06-1972
A Lawson	Woodlands	8514	08-14-1973
B Marsh	The Drive	5806	11-02-1973
C Lloyd	Patrick's Corner	4727	02-04-1973
C Adams	North Street	1584	08-23-1973

Now we wish to call the students up and inform them about the result. For this, we need the student names, averages, results and phone numbers to be displayed together. However, the phone number appears in a separate table, as noted earlier. Thus, we need to combine two tables. This process is called **joining** one table to another. The query would take the form:

SELECT Student.Name, Student.Average, Student.Result, StudentInfo.Phone-Number

FROM Student, StudentInfo

WHERE Student.Name = StudentInfo.Name

Resulting output: See Table 2.19.

Table 2.19 Result of joining two tables

Name	*Average*	*Result*	*Phone-Number*
P Jones	76.66	Pass	1567
M Henry	89.00	Pass	2121
J Man	45.66	Fail	3131
A Bryan	58.66	Pass	5467
W Fringe	74.33	Pass	2148
A Lawson	66.00	Pass	8514
B Marsh	50.66	Pass	5806
C Lloyd	56.66	Fail	4727
C Adams	44.33	Fail	1584

The above statement mentions two table names in the FROM clause. Thus, data is being selected from two tables and compiled in one. As usual, the SELECT statement lists the columns to be selected. Note that the column is prefixed with the table name (as there are two tables now) with a period (.) in-between. For instance, *Student.name* is the *name* from the *Student* table. The main logic is in the WHERE clause. It specifies that the items where the names match are to be displayed. In other words, for a row in the Student table, only one row that has the same name in the Studentinfo table is to be selected. This means that only one row per student is to be displayed. In the absence of this clause, *all* rows of the Student table would be joined to *all* rows of the Studentinfo table! That is, it would result a display of 10 × 10 = 100 rows!

Joins are extremely powerful, but can demand a lot of resources, and thus be slow. Hence, they should be used judiciously.

2.6.5 Nested Queries

> Sometimes, we might need to write one SELECT statement inside another. This is called a **nested query**.

Fig. 2.20 illustrates the concept. The outer SELECT is called as the *outer query*, whereas the inner SELECT is called as the *inner query*, or the **sub-query**.

```
SELECT ....                 ──────> Outer query
     (SELECT ....)          ──────> Inner query (sub-query)
```

Fig. 2.20 Nested query

For instance, suppose we want a list of students whose total marks are greater than the overall average. We would write a nested query like this:

```
SELECT Name, Total ──────────────> Outer query
FROM Student
WHERE Total >
      (SELECT AVG (Total)  ──────> Inner query (sub-query)
      FROM Student)
```

The query works like this:

1. The inner query or the sub-query is executed first, *and exactly once*. Thus, the average of totals for all the students is calculated (which is 187.33).
2. Next, the outer query is executed. For every row of the Student table, the inner query is tested once.

Thus, the query takes the form:

```
SELECT Name, Total
FROM Student
WHERE Total > 187.33
```

Output: See Table 2.20.

Table 2.20 Result of executing nested query

Name	*Total*
P Jones	230
M Henry	267
W Fringe	223
A Lawson	198

Since we have one query within another, this is an example of two-level nested query. In practice, nesting is rarely required beyond three levels.

2.6.6 Data Control Language

Having understood how to create tables and access/manipulate data in them, we must know how to give access to and revoke accesses from various tables to different users. This is extremely important in case of a multi-user database system. We can achieve this with the use of Data Control Language.

Suppose there are two persons working in the personnel department: John and Peter. Only they should have access to the *Employee* table. We can secure access by using the GRANT and REVOKE statements provided by SQL as follows. First, we remove all accesses to the table by everybody.

```
REVOKE ALL ON Employee
FROM PUBLIC
```

Note that ALL means the ability to perform any DML operation such as SELECT, INSERT, UPDATE or DELETE. Thus, we do not allow anyone (because we specify PUBLIC) to perform any operation on the *Employee* table. In other words, PUBLIC means *everybody*.

At this stage, no one can do anything with the *Employee* table. Now, we shall allow only John and Peter the necessary authority to access then *Employee* table.

```
GRANT ALL
ON Employee
TO John, Peter
```

This would allow John and Peter to perform *any* DML operation (namely SELECT, INSERT, UPDATE and DELETE) on the *Employee* table. Suppose at some stage, Peter is on leave and a third employee, David, temporarily takes his place. We need to provide only SELECT access to David on the *Employee* table. This can be done as follows.

```
GRANT SELECT
ON Employee
TO David
```

David cannot update the information in the *Employee* table in any manner. He can just see what it contains.

Thus, SQL enables allowing or taking back accesses to/from sensitive pieces of information very easily. This enforces security and assures the confidentiality of information.

2.7 EMBEDDED SQL

2.7.1 Embedding SQL Statements inside 3GL

We have mentioned that SQL can be used by end users to produce ad-hoc reports and also by application programs. The examples we have seen so far deal with the former.

> When we embed SQL statements in an application program, it is called an **embedded SQL**.

The programming language in which we write SQL statements is usually a 3GL such as COBOL or C. The 3GL is called the **host language**. The reasons we need embedded SQL are:

- Online transaction processing involves formatting of screens for easier data entry and validations. This ensures database integrity. Interactive SQL does not support these features.
- Many applications need batch processing. In this, data are collected together and processed in groups called as batches. Such applications are normally developed by using a host language.

The most interesting aspect of this is that as we know, SQL deals with an entire table at a time. For example, when we issue a SELECT statement, it goes through the entire set of rows in one go and comes back with a result. On the other hand, a 3GL deals with one record at a time. Embedded SQL programming also deals with this issue. Therefore, we need a mechanism by which the entire data returned by a SQL query is examined one row at a time, validations, if any are performed and the row is processed. Then, the second row is examined, validated and processed, and so on. The concept is illustrated in Fig. 2.21. Note that we have a C program, which includes SQL statements embedded inside it.

A question that arises is, how would we know whether a statement belongs to the C portion of the code or the SQL portion? Of course, we would know by looking at the statement itself. For instance, the moment we see a *SELECT* statement, we know that it is an SQL statement. Similarly, we know that *if* is a C statement. However, to remove the scope for any ambiguity, an SQL statement in an embedded SQL program needs to be delimited inside special boundaries. These take the form EXEC SQL and END-EXEC verbs (of course, these differ from one language such as C to another such as COBOL. In C, it is just a semicolon).

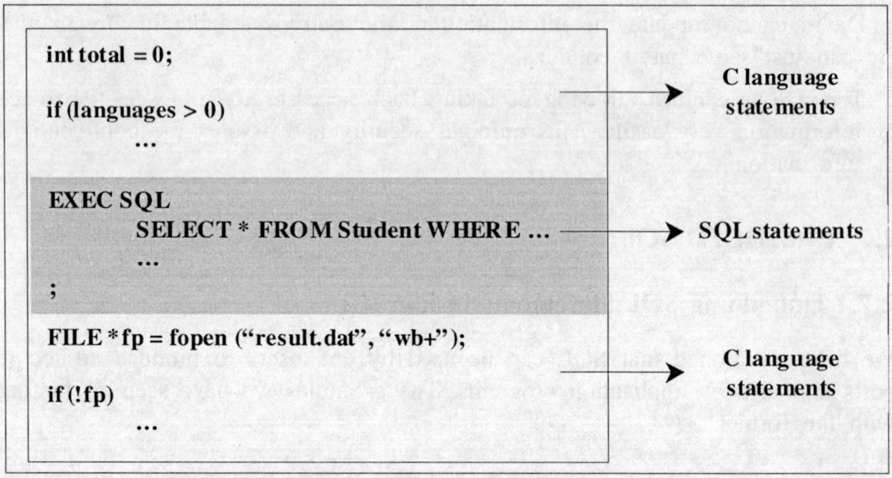

Fig. 2.21 Embedded SQL

2.7.2 Embedded SQL Program Lifecycle

The lifecycle of an embedded SQL program is pretty interesting. We know that a normal C program is compiled and linked before it can be executed. However, an embedded SQL program needs to be pre-compiled before it can be compiled. The difference is shown in Fig. 2.22.

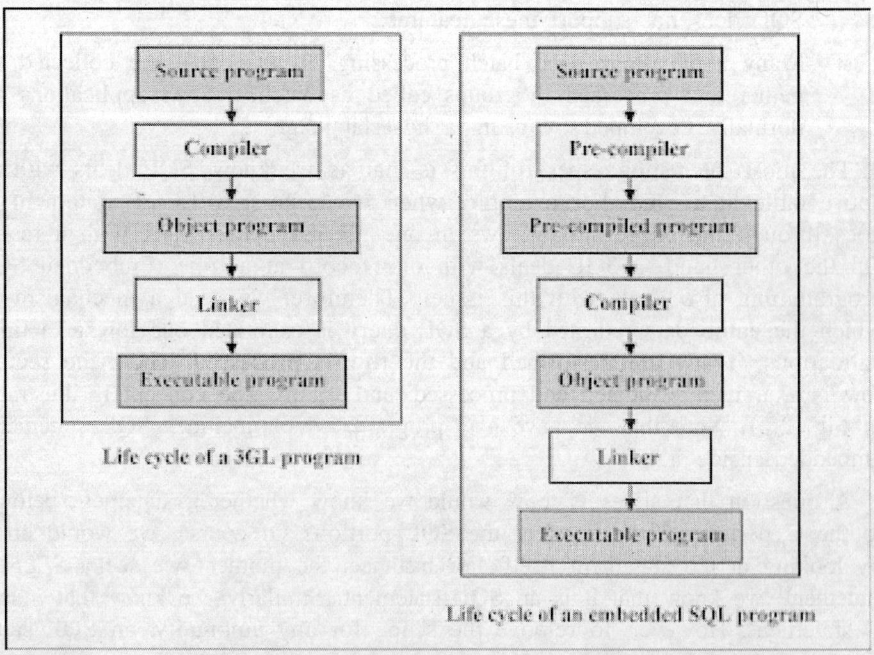

Fig. 2.22 Life cycle of a 3GL program and an embedded SQL program

What is the significance of the pre-compiler and the pre-compilation step? We have noted earlier that any SQL statement inside an embedded SQL program must be inside the boundaries of EXEC SQL and END-EXEC verbs. The pre-compiler precisely looks at these blocks, contained within EXEC SQL and END-EXEC verbs. It ignores everything else. The pre-compiler translates the SQL statements inside these blocks into the appropriate 3GL statements (e.g. C or COBOL, depending on which 3GL is being used). The idea is illustrated in Fig. 2.23.

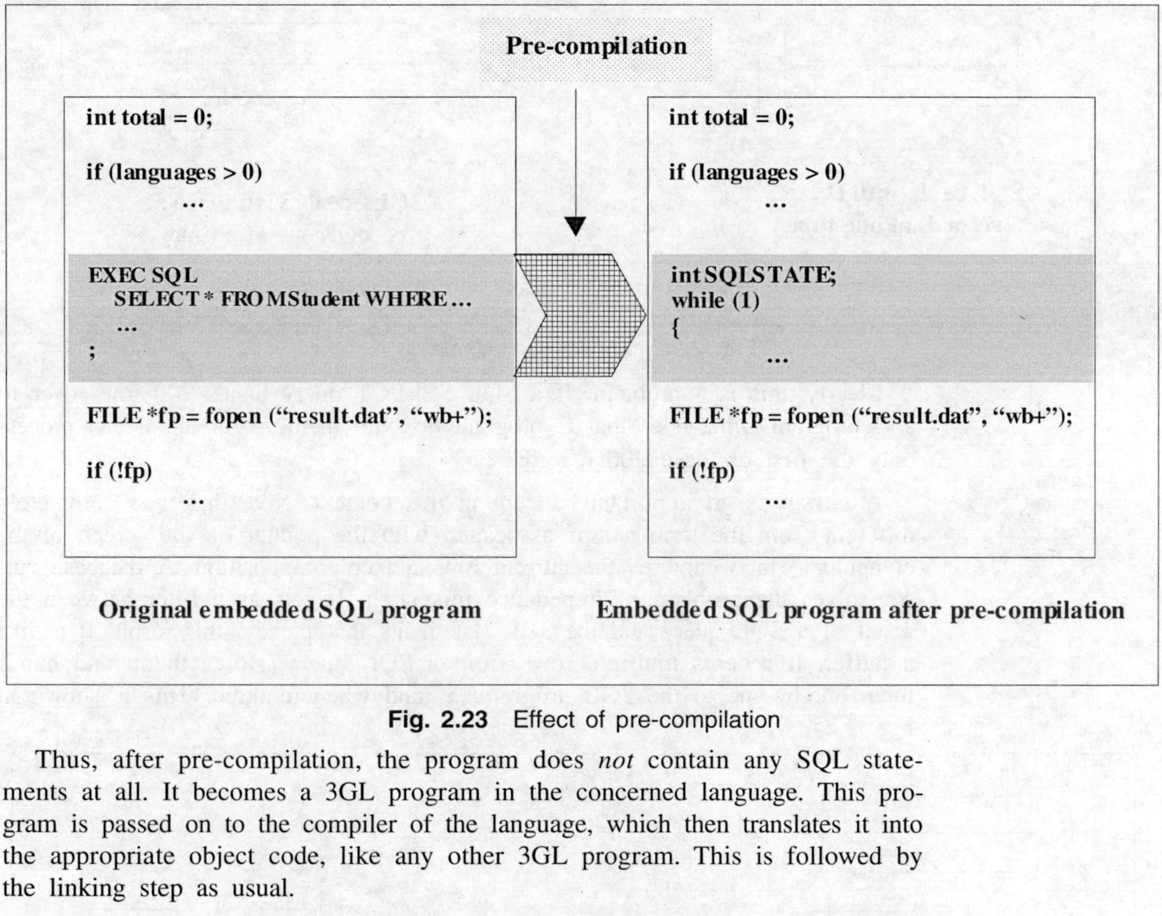

Fig. 2.23 Effect of pre-compilation

Thus, after pre-compilation, the program does *not* contain any SQL statements at all. It becomes a 3GL program in the concerned language. This program is passed on to the compiler of the language, which then translates it into the appropriate object code, like any other 3GL program. This is followed by the linking step as usual.

Because the pre-compiler translates the SQL statements inside an embedded SQL program into the appropriate 3GL statements, the compiler of the language need not change at all. We can summarise this as:

> The pre-compilation stage translates the SQL statements inside an embedded SQL program into appropriate 3GL statements.

2.7.3 Cursors

We have mentioned that SQL deals with multiple rows at a time, whereas 3GLs deal with one record at a time. This means that if we embed SQL statements inside a 3GL program, which return multiple rows from a table, a 3GL program would not be able to handle them. Such a problem is called **impedance mismatch** and is illustrated in Fig. 2.24.

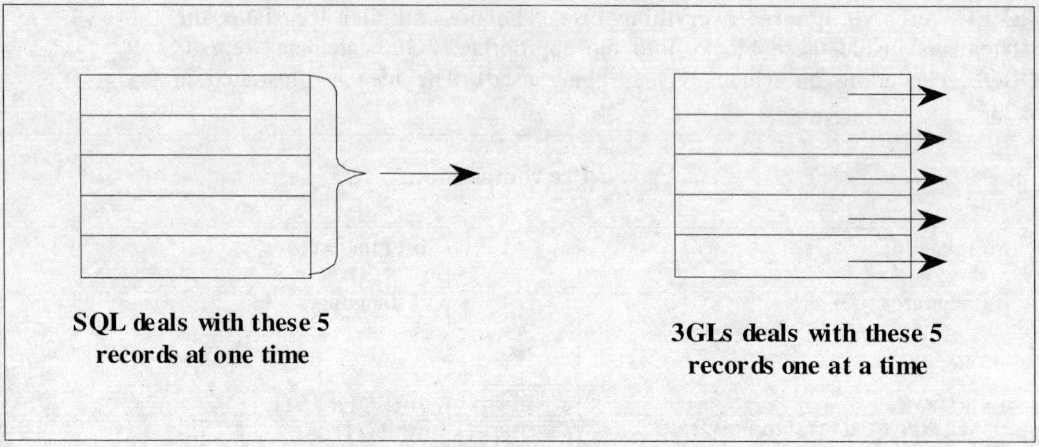

Fig. 2.24 Impedance mismatch

Clearly, this is a problem. If a SQL SELECT query hands 200 rows over to a C program, what does that C program do with them? After all, it can process only the first of these 200 records!

A **cursor** is an important concept in this context. Note that it is completely different from the term *cursor* associated with the pointer on the screen of the computer, which captures the current row and column position. A database cursor solves the problem of impedance mismatch. It acts as a filter between the result of a SQL query and the 3GL statements that process this result. It is like a buffer. It accepts multiple rows from a SQL query, stores them, and hands them one-by-one to the 3GL program, as and when required. This is shown in Fig. 2.25.

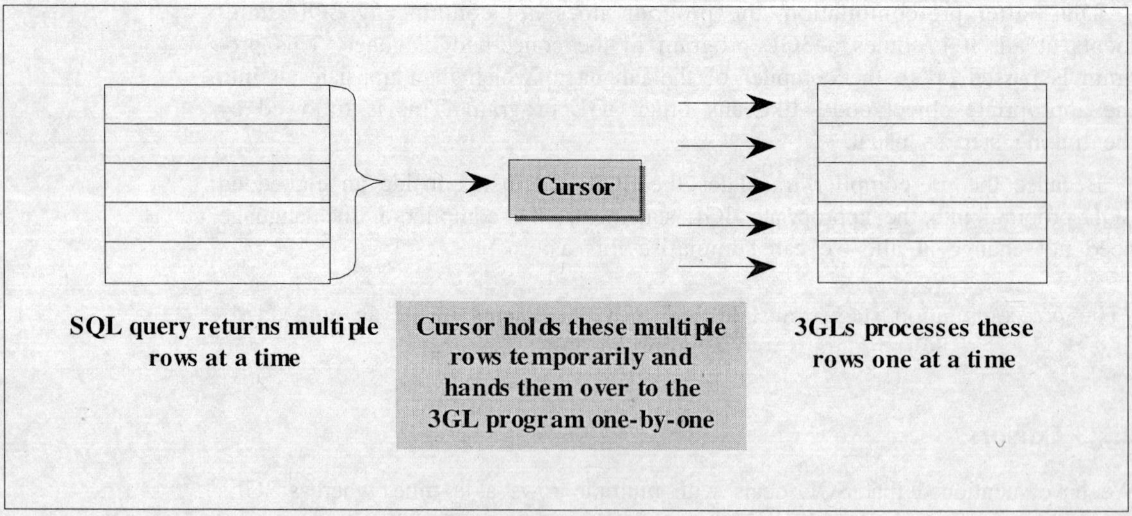

Fig. 2.25 Cursor

In principle, this is similar to the way a spooler works. A spooler allows a user to send a big document for printing and then to continue working on something else. The user need not wait for the printer to print the whole document. It is the spooler which holds the document in its memory while the printer gets ready and accepts the document for printing.

2.8 DYNAMIC SQL

In embedded SQL, the SQL statements to be executed are known at the time of coding the program statements. This is called as **static SQL**. However, in some cases, the SQL statements to be executed are *not* known when the program is written. They might be constructed based on user options or, in fact, be written by the user directly in the form SELECT – FROM – WHERE. Such SQL queries, which are not known prior to their execution, form **dynamic SQL**.

> Dynamic SQL offers the flexibility of writing SQL statements during the program's execution.

However, this comes with two main drawbacks.

1. In case of static SQL, the SQL statements are pre-written. Therefore, if there are any errors in the SQL statements, the pre-compiler points them out. In case of dynamic SQL, the statements are pre-compiled, compiled and executed directly, like an interpreter. So, the errors would also be shown at run time.
2. Static SQL allows the DBMS to do optimisation (discussed later). For example, the DBMS may choose to use a particular index to make the SQL statements execute faster. In the case of dynamic SQL, there is no such provision. Therefore, the SQL statements may not choose the best possible execution path.

Dynamic SQL SELECT statements take the form:

EXECUTE IMMEDIATE <SQL statement>

The EXECUTE IMMEDIATE portion tells the operational environment that the statement belongs to dynamic SQL category.

For example, consider the following dynamic SQL statements. Here, we store the dynamic SQL INSERT statement into a variable called *My_statement*, and pass that variable at the time of execution of dynamic SQL.

My_statament = 'INSERT INTO Student VALUES (10, 'Cryptography', 'Atul', 'THM', 'Security')'

EXECUTE IMMEDIATE:My_statement

Dynamic SQL is useful in the case of online applications. In such cases, it may not be possible every time to anticipate the kind of queries that the user wants to execute. The user may want to construct them at execution time and execute them immediately. For instance, in a shopping cart application on the Internet, the user may choose to buy 0, 1 or 10 items. In such cases, dynamic SQL would facilitate an elegant creation of a query to process these many items. It may not be possible to achieve the same result using embedded SQL.

There is a variation of the dynamic SQL scheme. We can treat an SQL statement as a temporary object and create it repeatedly. The advantages offered by this approach are as follows:

- We can write queries.
- Performance can be far better. This is because the statement is parsed, validated and optimised far ahead of execution time.
- Using parameters, the same statement can be executed in various ways.

In this model, two statements are required: PREPARE and EXECUTE.

The PREPARE statement creates an SQL object that contains the SQL statement to be executed. When this statement is executed, the DBMS examines, interprets, validates and optimises it. It is stored until an EXECUTE (and not EXECUTE IMMEDIATE) statement is encountered. At this stage, the statement is actually executed. This approach is contrasted with the earlier (EXECUTE IMMEDIATE) approach in Fig. 2.26.

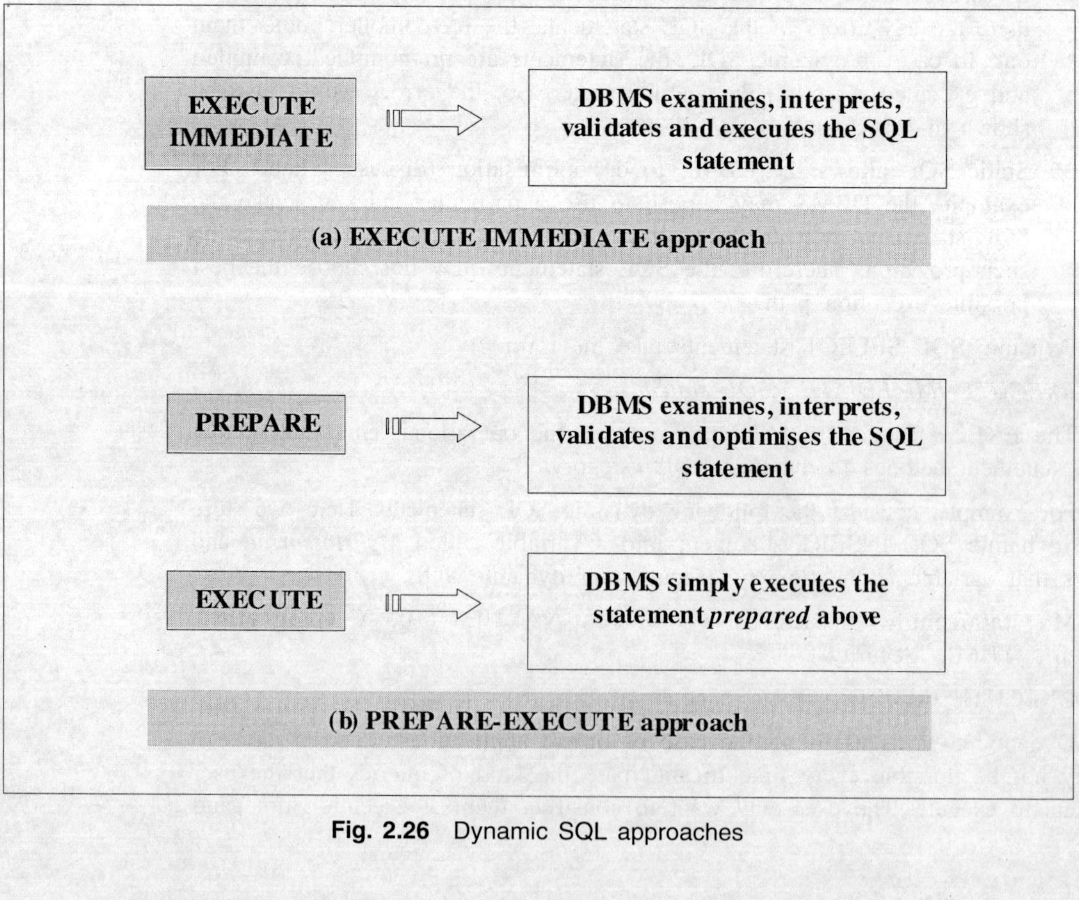

Fig. 2.26 Dynamic SQL approaches

2.9 DBMS MODELS

We have mentioned earlier that there are primarily three DBMS models: hierarchical, network and relational. We have seen relational databases (RDBMS) in operation. We shall not discuss the others in detail as they were developed earlier and they are rarely used today. Only a few legacy *old* systems use them. If we have to maintain them, we have to understand them and that is the only reason that we shall study them.

In these two models (i.e. hierarchical and network), the relationships between records has to be pre-defined. For instance, if one doctor treats many patients, there is said to be a **1:m (1 to many)** relationship between these two record types. The *doctor* record is called a **parent** record and the *patient* record the **child** record. Having established these parent and child records, links are created such as *next patient for the same doctor* as others, which we have studied earlier.

For the pre-decided queries such as *List all patients for doctor XYZ*, this is, in fact, faster. That is why these models were popular. The hardware speeds for RDBMS, which resolves the queries at run time, were not very high. RDBMS really became popular when hardware speeds and response times improved. We will now present a quick overview of all the three models.

2.9.1 The Hierarchical Model

Fig. 2.27 shows a database containing information about students, the courses they have opted for and the marks they have obtained in them. In short, each student can opt for many courses and is given marks in each one of them. Hence, there are three types of record here: students, courses and marks.

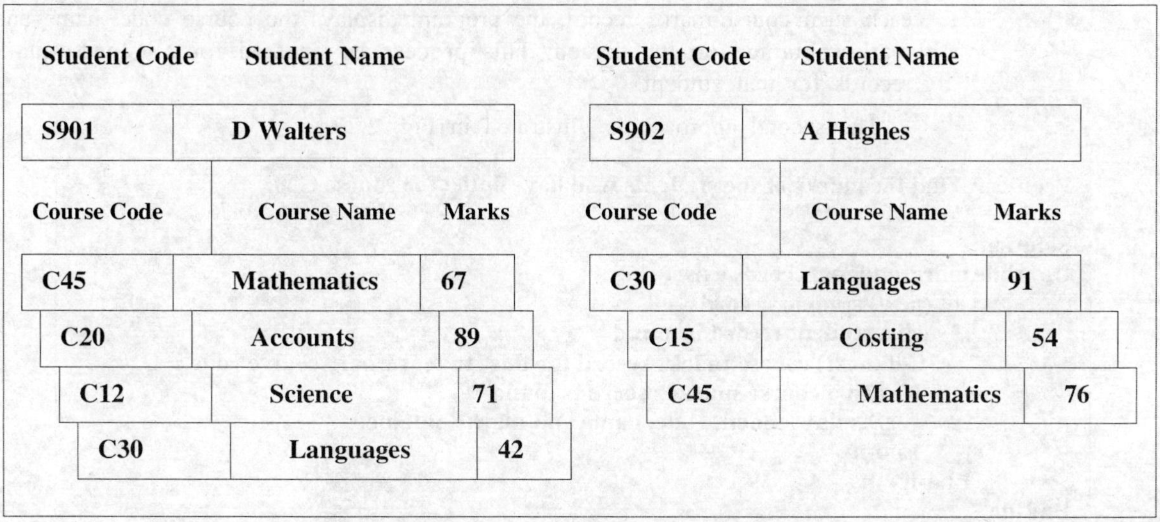

Fig. 2.27 Hierarchical model

The student record, which is at the top of the hierarchy, is called the *parent* or *root*. The course-marks record is a child of the student record type. Hence, we have one parent and one child record. In general, we can have as many child records as needed. Furthermore, each child record can, in turn, have many child records, and so on. However, given a child record type, we can have only one parent. Hence, the hierarchical model is based on the principle of *one-to-many* record types. Let us discuss the operations such as retrieving, inserting, removing and deleting records from such a database.

2.9.1.1 Retrieval There are two main ways to study this. Fig. 2.28 shows the first approach.

Problem: Find the courses opted for and the marks obtained by student S901.

Solution:

```
Get (next) student record where student code = S901
Do while course-marks records exist for this student
        Get (next) course-marks record for this student
        If such a course-marks record is found
            Display course code, name and marks obtained
        End-if
End-do
```

Fig. 2.28 Record retrieval from hierarchical databases – Approach 1

Let us understand how this query would work. The processing would begin with the parent record, that is student. First, a record containing a value of student code = S901 is searched in the database. For this, the database would be read sequentially, starting with the first student record. When a match for S901 is found, the course-marks (children) records for this student are searched. For each such course-marks record, the program displays the course code, name and marks obtained on the screen. This process is repeated for all course-mark records for that student.

The second approach is illustrated in Fig. 2.29.

Problem: Find the marks of the students who have opted for course C20.

Solution:

```
Do while more student records exist
        Get (next) student record
        If such a student record is found
            Get (next) course-marks record for this student where course code = C20
            If such a course-marks record is found
                Display student code, name and marks obtained
            End-if
        End-if
End-do
```

Fig. 2.29 Record retrieval from hierarchical databases – Approach 2

Let us now look at this query. The processing would again begin with the parent record. Actually, the student record is not of importance in terms of search. The search criterion is based on the course code. However, the database would be read sequentially, starting with the first student record. For each student record, the course-marks (children) records for this student are searched. For each such course-marks record, the course code is compared with C20. If such a record is found, the student code, name and marks obtained are displayed on the screen. This process is repeated for all student records in the database.

We will notice that although the two queries are similar, the logic used to resolve them is entirely different. This comes from the fact that the database is arranged in a parent-child fashion. The logic would be reversed if student were the child record type of course-marks record.

2.9.1.2 Insert Since there cannot be a child record without a parent record, we simply cannot have a course-marks record without a student record. So, if a new course is introduced, its details cannot be entered until at least one student opts for it.

2.9.1.3 Delete The only solution for deleting marks is to delete the course-marks record. If we delete all the records of a particular course during deletion of marks, we lose the information that such a course exists. Similarly, if only one student has opted for a course and we delete that student's record, we lose information about the course, too!

2.9.1.4 Update To change the course title for course C30 from Languages to English, the entire database needs to be searched for course C30 and appropriate changes made.

Hierarchical and network database models are almost obsolete. However, many legacy applications rely in them heavily. Threrefore, we need to learn hierarchical and network databases from a practical point of view.

Hence, we can conclude that because of the way the *one-to-many* hierarchy is designed, there are inherent problems associated with such databases. The data manipulation is not easy and might lead to problems. IBM mainframes offer IMS, which is the most popular hierarchical database product.

2.9.2 Network Model

The network model is different from the hierarchical model in one important respect. Unlike the hierarchical model, here we can have *many-to-many* relationships. This means that a parent can have many children, and one child can belong to more than one parent. The network model for the same example is shown in Fig. 2.30.

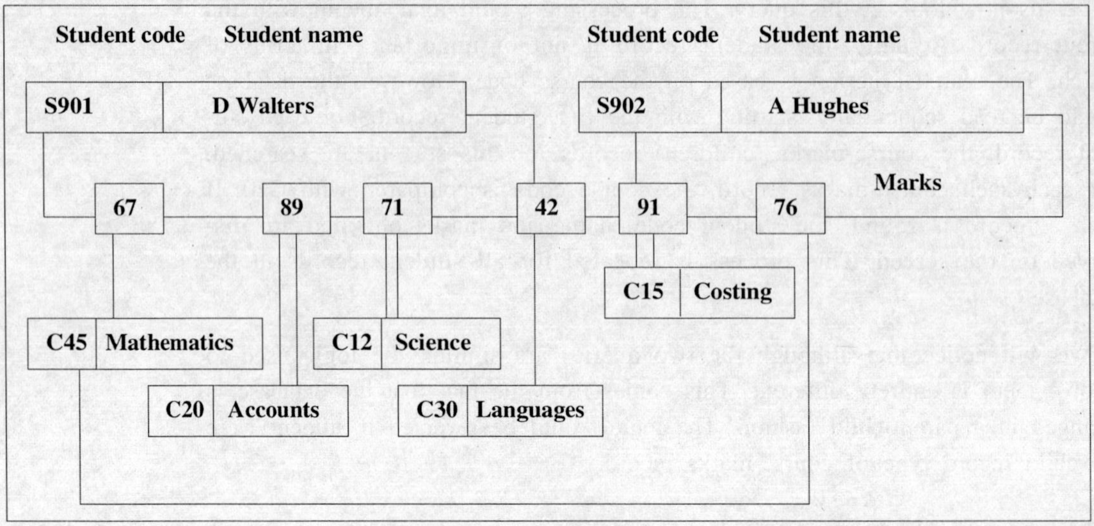

Fig. 2.30 Network model

Here, the database consists of **links** (also called **connectors**). The marks connect the students with the courses they have opted for. Note that the link records are not mere pointers. They are themselves a record – that is, they contain data values. Additionally, they also own the responsibility of connecting parent records with children records. The link records have an interesting property that differentiates network databases from hierarchical databases. The link records allow a child record to exist without any parent record. This is not possible in case of hierarchical databases. The way this is achieved is that a child record has a link record (note that there is no parent record). The other pointer of the link record then points back to the same child record – thus not requiring that it have a parent!

The network model is certainly more complex than the hierarchical model, and it can represent any structure that the hierarchical model represents. Let us look at the various operations to be performed:

2.9.2.1 Retrieval Fig. 2.31 shows the first retrieval operation.

Problem: Find out the courses and marks for student S901.

Solution:

```
Get student record where student code = S901
Do while link records exist for this student
        Find (next) link for this student
        If such a link record is found
                Find course record using this link
                If such a course record is found
                        Display course code, marks
                End-if
        End-if
End-do
```

Fig. 2.31 Record retrieval from network databases – Approach 1

This query works exactly in the same manner as in the case of a hierarchical database. The only difference is the addition of the link records. Rather than looking for a child record directly from a parent record, here we first traverse to the link (marks) record and use that to obtain the child record (course). The rest of the query works in the same fashion and we will not describe it. Fig. 2.32 shows the other query.

Problem: Find the marks of the students who have opted for course C20.

<u>Solution</u>:

```
Get course record where course code = C20
Do while link records exist for this course
        Find (next) link for this course
        If such a link record is found
                Find student record using this link
                If such a student record is found
                        Display student code, marks
                End-if
        End-if
End-do
```

Fig. 2.32 Record retrieval from network databases – Approach 2

Interestingly, this query starts with the child record type (course). Remember that in case of hierarchical databases and even in this kind of query, the execution began with the parent record (student). However, because network databases allow you to start with a child record and then find its parent, the query is more natural. It starts with the course record, rather than the student record. For each course record, it checks the course code. If it matches with the required value (C20), it gets the parent record – that is student record — by using the link record. It then displays the student code and marks. This process is carried out for all course records that belong to course C20.

As we can see, the two queries can be resolved using a very similar logic. This is because the database can be accessed from top to bottom of the hierarchy in the same fashion as from bottom to top.

2.9.2.2 Insert There are no problems in inserting a student record without a course or a course without a student record. They can exist independently until a connector connects them.

2.9.2.3 Delete Deleting any of the record types, that is, student, course or marks, will result in an automatic adjustment of chain.

2.9.2.4 Update Updates also pose no problems and can be done easily.

2.9.3 Relational Model

The main difference between relational and the other two models is the links between different data items. In case of the relational model, the links are entirely due to the values of various data items, and nothing else. There are no internal links, connectors or parent-child relationships. For instance, a student is *connected* to a marks record by virtue of a common student code in both the tables. Table 2.21 shows the earlier example using the relational model.

Table 2.21 Relational model

Student table

Student Code	Student Name
S901	D Walters
S902	A Hughes

Course table

Course Code	Course Name
C12	Science
C15	Costing
C20	Accounts
C30	Languages
C45	Mathematics

Marks table

Student Code	Course Code	Marks
S901	C12	71
S901	C20	89
S901	C30	42
S901	C45	67
S902	C15	54
S902	C30	91
S902	C45	76

Now, let us look at the different operations using the relational databases.

2.9.3.1 Retrieval Fig. 2.33 finds the answer to the first query.

Problem: Find out the courses and marks for student S901.

Solution:

```
Do while marks records exist for student code = S901
        Find next marks record where student code = S901
        If such a marks record is found
            Display course code, marks
        End-if
End-do
```

Fig. 2.33 Record retrieval from relational databases – Approach 1

This query looks pretty simple in comparison to the earlier queries for hierarchical and network databases. It starts with the student record. For each student record, the student code of which is S901, it displays the course code and course name. Note that there is no question of any parent-child hierarchy built into the database itself. A mere *join* would suffice to answer this query. The join internally would use the logic as stated earlier. Fig. 2.34 depicts this.

Problem: Find the marks of the students who have opted for course C20.

Solution:

```
Do while marks records exist for course code = C20
        Find next marks record where course code = C20
        If such a marks record is found
                Display student code, marks
        End-if
End-do
```

Fig. 2.34 Record retrieval from relational databases – Approach 2

This query also looks quite simple. It now starts with the course record. For each course record with a course code of C20, it displays the student code and marks. Again, there is no question of any parent-child hierarchy built-into the database itself. As before, a *join* would be employed, which would internally use the logic stated earlier.

The logic of the queries is not only uniform; it is also simpler to build. As stated earlier, relational databases also make insert, update and delete operations easier. We will not go into the details of the same. Since the three tables exist physically separately, there should not be any adverse effect if operations performed on one table are performed on others.

2.10 DATABASE SYSTEM ARCHITECTURE

We have briefly discussed the concept of levels or views (e.g. logical and physical) that different kinds of users have in relation to a DBMS. We will now discuss it more formally.

Classically, we have three levels of the same DBMS, depending on what type of user we are. Fig. 2.35 shows these three levels.

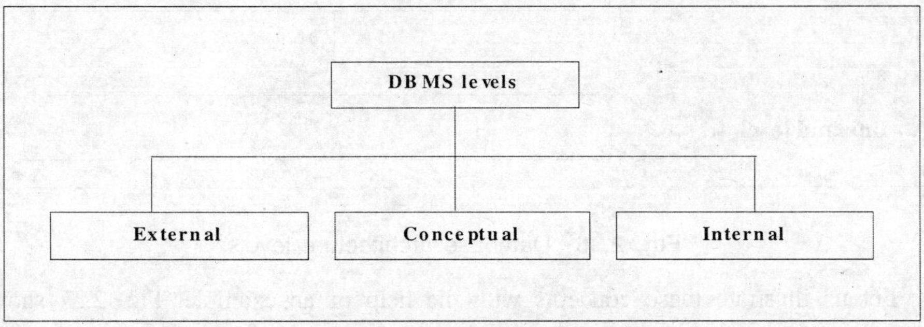

Fig. 2.35 DBMS levels

Let us discuss these three levels now.

- **External level**: This is the view of the database that most end users have. For example, when we talk of *Employee record* or *Student record*, we have the **external view**, also called the **community user view**, in mind. This level represents the end-user view. It is quite abstract in nature and closer to the way a programming language would model a record. For example, an Employee record in C would consist of a *structure* data type, and as a *01 level record* in COBOL. This level sees the data in a database with this view.
- **Conceptual level**: The **conceptual level**, also called the **logical level**, is not tied to a programming language or to a specific technology. It merely describes the data as *any* user would see it, regardless of any technology differences. For instance, this view would inform us that the employee number is a string that can hold 6 characters at the most, and that the employee salary is an integer, and so on. This level offers a layer of indirection between the external and the internal views.
- **Internal level**: The **internal level** provides the **physical view** of the database. More specifically, this view provides information regarding the physical organisation of the data in the database. For example, this view may inform us that the employee record consists of 20 bytes, of which the first 6 are occupied by the employee number, and so on.

It is worth pointing out that there would be as many external views as the number of different types of users of the database. Therefore, there can be many external views for the same database. However, there is always precisely one conceptual and internal view for a database, regardless of the different number or types of users. This is illustrated in Fig. 2.36.

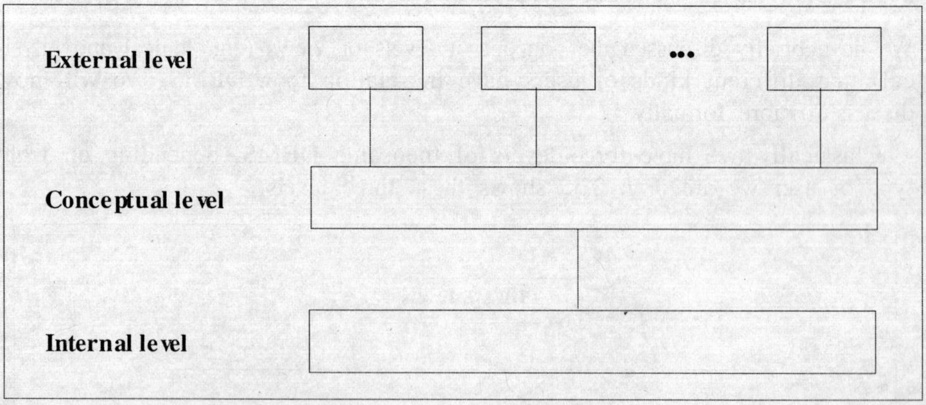

Fig. 2.36 Database architecture levels

Let us illustrate these concepts with the help of an example. Fig. 2.37 shows the different levels of an Employee record.

External (C)

```
struct emp
{
        char emp_no[6];
        char emp_name[30];
        int salary;
};
```

External (COBOL)

```
01 Emp-rec.
        05 Emp-no        pic X(6).
        05 Emp-name      pic X(30).
        05 Salary        pic 9(5).
```

Conceptual

```
Employee
        Employee_number     Character (6)
        Employee_name       Character (30)
        Salary              Number (5)
```

Internal

```
Stored_Emp    Bytes = 20
        Emp#          TYPE=BYTE(6), OFFSET=0
        EmpName       TYPE=BYTE(30), OFFSET=6
        Salary        TYPE=FULLWORD, OFFSET=36
```

Fig. 2.37 Three levels of the DBMS architecture – An example

KEY TERMS AND CONCEPTS

1:m relationship
Atomicity
Child record
Column
Commit
Community user view

- Conceptual level
- Concurrency
- Cursor
- Data consistency
- Data Control Language (DCL)
- Data Definition Language (DDL)
- Data inconsistency
- Data independence
- Data integrity
- Data Manipulation Language (DML)
- Data redundancy
- Data sharing
- Database
- Database Administrator (DBA)
- Database catalog
- Database Management System (DBMS)
- DBMS models
- Dynamic SQL
- Embedded SQL
- External level
- File Management System (FMS)
- Hierarchical DBMS
- Host language
- Impedance mismatch
- Inner query
- Internal level
- Join
- Logical level
- Logical view
- m:n relationship
- Nested query
- Network DBMS
- Outer query
- Parent record
- Physical view
- Physical view
- Relational Database Management System (RDBMS)
- Rollback
- Row
- Security
- Static SQL
- Structured Query Language (SQL)
- Sub-query
- Table
- Transaction

CHAPTER SUMMARY

- A **database** is a well-organised set of data.
- A **Database Management System (DBMS)** is a set of programs that helps us to manage databases.
- **Relational Database Management System (RDBMS)** is the most popular of all DBMS models.
- **Structured Query Language (SQL)** is the language for working with RDBMS.
- **File Management Systems (FMS)** suffers from many drawbacks such as **data redundancy**, **data inconsistency**, lack of **transactions**, and so on.
- Data redundancy refers to duplication of data.
- Data inconsistency refers to different values for the same data items in a database, and is caused by redundancy.
- Transaction is a logical unit of work. It must complete in entirety or not at all, but never only partly.

- DBMS scores over FMS in terms of quicker response, data independence, security, data sharing, data consistency, removing data redundancy and providing for transaction management and **concurrency**.
- In concurrency, one or more users/programs attempt to access the same data at the same time.
- DBMS can be **hierarchical**, **network** or **relational**.
- Hierarchical databases employ parent-child relationships. This poses certain problems in data insertion, updates and deletion.
- Network databases employ parent-child as well as child-parent relationships. They remove some drawbacks of hierarchical databases.
- Relational databases relate data items purely based on their values.
- The equivalent terms for file, record, and field in RDBMS are **table**, **row** and **column** respectively.
- SQL is a very high-level language that provides simple instructions for accessing data from tables.
- SQL consists of three sets of languages: **Data Definition Language (DDL)**, **Data Manipulation Language (DML)** and **Data Control Language (DDL)**.
- DDL is used for creating and destroying tables, indexes, and other forms of structures.
- DML is used to retrieve or manipulate data stored in a database.
- DCL controls the access to various tables, indexes and other structures.
- DML is most widely used and provides four major statements: SELECT, INSERT, UPDATE and DELETE.
- **Joins** can be used to retrieve data from multiple tables.
- **Embedded SQL** programming facilitates the use of SQL with 3GLs such as C and COBOL.
- **Dynamic SQL** provides for entering of SQL queries at execution time, rather than at the development stage.
- A database can be considered as consisting of three layers: **External**, **Conceptual** and **Internal**.
- External view of a database presents the view that the end users have.
- Conceptual view describes the data without stress on any technology or programming language.
- Internal view provides information regarding the organisation of a database.

PRACTICE SET

Mark as true or false

1. Using a set of files is better than using a database.
2. RDBMS is the least popular of the possible DBMS models.
3. Data redundancy means multiple copies of the same data item.
4. Data inconsistency means the same values for different data items.
5. A scheme of grouping a set of integrated data files is called FMS.

6. A transaction is a set of operations that must be performed completely or not at all.
7. Database concurrency is achieved by using the locking mechanisms.
8. A table is a three-dimensional view of data.
9. DML is concerned with data definition.
10. In nested queries, one SELECT statement is written inside another.

Fill in the blanks

1. Data is better organised and is easily accessible by using ________.
   (a) DBMS (b) FMS
   (c) EMS (d) OOAD
2. A ________ is a set of operations that must be performed completely or not at all.
   (a) query (b) command
   (c) data sharing (d) transaction
3. Commit and rollback are related to ________.
   (a) data integrity (b) data consistency
   (c) data security (d) data sharing
4. Data is processed by using ________.
   (a) DDL (b) DML
   (c) DCL (d) DPL
5. When SQL statements are embedded inside 3GL, we call such a program as ________.
   (a) nested query (b) distinct query
   (c) embedded SQL (d) nested programming
6. ________ translates the SQL statements inside a 3GL program into appropriate 3GL statements.
   (a) Compiler (b) Linker
   (c) Loader (d) Pre-compiler
7. If SQL statements are known before the program executes, we call them ________.
   (a) cursor (b) dynamic SQL
   (c) static SQL (d) embedded SQL
8. If SQL statements are not known before the program executes, we call them ________.
   (a) cursor (b) dynamic SQL
   (c) static SQL (d) embedded SQL
9. In ________, we have a strict parent-child relationship only.
   (a) hierarchical databases (b) network databases
   (c) relational databases (d) all of the above

10. In ________, we have a parent-child as well as child-parent relationship.
    (a) hierarchical databases (b) network databases
    (c) relational databases (d) all of the above

Provide detailed answers to the following questions:

1. Explain DBMS and FMS with short explanations.
2. How is DBMS better than FMS?
3. Explain the terms *table*, *row* and *column*.
4. What is SQL? Why is it a powerful language?
5. Explain the terms Data Definition Language, Data Manipulation Language and Data Control Language in SQL.
6. Write a note on embedded SQL.
7. What is a cursor? How is it useful?
8. Explain the difference between static and dynamic SQL.
9. Write a note on hierarchical and network databases.
10. How is relational database technology different from the other two DBMS technologies?

Exercises

1. Write SQL command to create the following table, named *Student*:
   - Roll number Number Maximum length 5
   - Student name Character Maximum length 30
   - Rank Number Maximum length 2
   - Total marks Number Maximum length 3
2. Create the above table in MS-Access.
3. Assume that the *Student* table contains the following data. Write a SELECT statement to print the average marks and the maximum marks.

Roll number	*Student name*	*Rank*	*Total marks*
17	Atul	4	500
90	Anita	3	712
27	Jui	1	910
56	Harsh	2	851

4. Consider the following table (called *Details*) in addition to the above table.

Roll number	*Birth date*
17	7-Apr-1973
90	26-Oct-1972
27	19-Oct-2001
56	22-Dec-2002

Write a SELECT query to print the roll numbers, names, birth dates and ranks of all the students with the help of a join.

5. Produce the same output as above by using a sub-query.
6. Provide read-only access of the *Student* table to all users.
7. How would you ensure that only the user named *User1* can perform insertions in the *Details* table?
8. Study Pro*C or Pro*COBOL to learn more about embedded SQL.
9. Study what is meant by *isolation level* in embedded SQL programming.
10. Learn more about hierarchical and network databases by reading about the products called IMS and IDMS.

Chapter 3

The Relational Model

Ted Codd came up with the relational model which disconnects the logical organisation of a database from its physical storage methods during the early 1970s.

Chapter Highlights

- RDBMS in Depth
- Relational Algebra and Relational Calculus
- Database Integrity and Constraints
- Meaning and Types of Keys
- Views and their Usage

3.1 RELATIONAL DATABASES PRIMER

3.1.1 Tabular Representation of Data

The most natural way of organising data so that even people not familiar with computers can easily understand it is to arrange it in a tabular format. This means that when data is arranged in a two-dimensional table, it can be easily visualised and understood by everyone. These tables have the following characteristics:

1. Each entry in a table occurs exactly once. There are no repeating rows.
2. All data items in the same column are of the same kind.
3. Every column has a distinct name to identify it.

3.1.2 Some Terminology

Readers who do not wish to know about mathematical jargon can skip this section without any loss of continuity. However, for the purists, we shall discuss some of the jargon in relational database technology.

Technologists like to use complex words for simple concepts, which sometimes makes comprehension difficult. Thus, a table is called a **relation** and a database constructed by using such relations is called a relational database. Actually, a relational database is nothing but a *flat* collection of data items.

Relational databases are based on the mathematical theory of relations. As such, the vocabulary used in relational mathematics is used here as well. Also, we can apply the results of relational mathematics to relational databases straightway. This makes predictions of the results of operations on relational databases quite precise.

There are a few more terms that complicate things a bit further. A row or a record is called as a **tuple**. Thus, the following two statements mean the same thing:

- A table is a collection of rows
- A relation is a set of tuples

If there are n columns in the table, then the relation is said to be of **degree n**. Relations of degree 2 are binary, relations of degree 3 are ternary, and so on.

The number of rows in a table is called the **cardinality** of the table. The number of columns in a table is called its **degree**. For example, the table in Fig. 3.1 has a cardinality of 5 and a degree of 4.

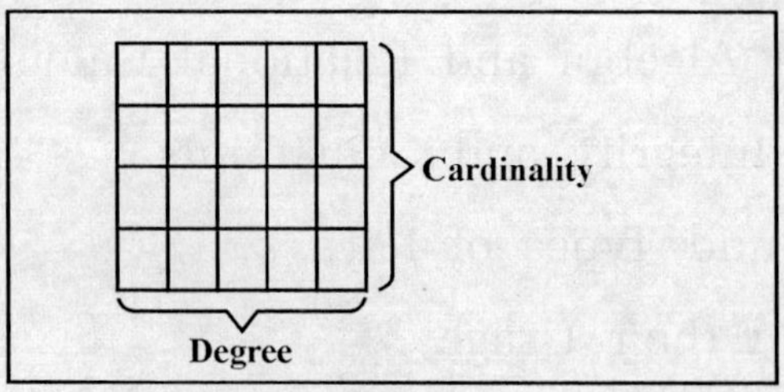

Fig. 3.1 Cardinality and degree

As we shall study soon, a set of values of one column in a table is called a **domain**.

3.1.3 Domains

Domain is an important concept in relational databases.

> A domain is a set of all possible values for a column or a relation.

For example, suppose we have a column called *Student_name* in a *Student* table. Then, the set of all possible student names is the domain. In other words, the domain is similar to a *data type*. We know that integer, string and character are common data types in many programming languages. They define the set of possible values and the rules associated with those values. For instance, when we declare a variable as of type integer in a programming language, we implicitly know the possible range of values that it can accommodate, the arithmetic operations that can be performed on that variable, and so on.

Similarly, *Student_name* is a set of all possible student names. It is as good as a *data type*. However, the idea of a domain has further connotations. Strictly speaking, a domain is a set of values that allows direct comparisons. Thus, there is no point in comparing student numbers with employee numbers, although both are integers. They have *different* domains.

Based on these ideas, we can define a few domains as shown in Table 3.1.

Table 3.1 Examples of domains

Domain	*Significance*
Indian_Phone_Numbers	Set of 8-digit phone numbers valid in India.
Names	Set of names of people.
Department_codes	Set of 3-character department codes valid in an organisation, such as EDP, MKT, ADM, etc.
Player_ages	Set of ages of cricket players; must be between 12 and 75.

We can see that a domain has some or all of the following characteristics:

- Name
- Data type
- Format
- Unit of measurement
- Range or list of allowed values

Relational databases are similar to any tabular organisations of data. In fact, when we create spreadsheets, those are quite similar to the tables in relational databases.

We shall now show the mathematical terms in action, as depicted in Fig. 3.2.

Id	Title	Author	Publication
1	Computer Fundamentals	AM John	AMC
2	Operating Systems	Peter Parker	AMC
3	Computer Networks	AB Simpson	Bernard's
4	My autobiography	MK Gandhi	Goyal
5	Chinese cooking	Rumala Rao	Diwan
6	The freedom struggle	MK Bose	Bose
7	Home PC	PJ Dilbert	AMC
8	Gardening	SK Das	Das & Das
9	You and your dog	ERP Slate	Home and Away
10	Math for small children	B Reid	Children books

Tuple

Relation

Prime key

Domain

Fig. 3.2 Relational database terminology

3.2 RELATIONAL DATABASE CHARACTERISTICS

Relational databases have some peculiar characteristics which distinguish them from file-based structures. We shall now study them.

- **Ordering of rows**: We have seen that a table is a set of rows. A table in relational databases is similar to a *set* of values in mathematics, as shown in Fig. 3.3.

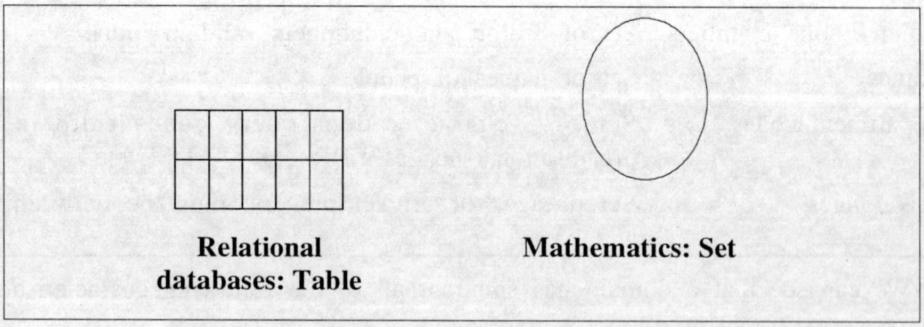

Fig. 3.3 Table is similar to a set

If we think about this concept further, we will note that there is absolutely no importance of the *order* of values in a set in mathematics. Similarly, the order of rows has no significance in a table. This is in stark contrast to files, where the order of records can be quite significant. For example, we talk of the 1st, 2nd and nth record in a file. However, no such terminology is used in the case of rows in a table in relational database.

Of course, physically, a table in a relational database is stored on the disk. Therefore, there is some logical ordering of records. However, this must not be visible, nor should it have any importance from an external or logical perspective.

Ordering of columns: Just as the ordering of rows in a table has no importance, the ordering of columns in a table is also of no significance. As before, we will note that there will be some physical ordering of columns on the disk. However, from an external point of view, this has no meaning.

Atomicity of values: Each value in a row is **atomic** or indivisible. In other words, no value should repeat in the same row. To understand this, consider Table 3.2. Here, we show a *Customer* table containing three columns — *Name*, *Status*, and *Address*. We can see that one customer can have multiple addresses, all stored in the same row. This is non-atomic, and hence, non-relational. We shall later study how to take care of such problems and make such values atomic.

Table 3.2 Non-atomic values in the Address column

Name	*Status*	*Address*
Atul	Inactive	Pune Solapur Mumbai
Anita	Active	Pune Mumbai
Jui	Active	Pune

Table 3.3 shows the atomic view of the same table, which now follows the principle of relational databases.

Table 3.3 Atomic values in the Address column

Name	*Status*	*Address*
Atul	Inactive	Pune
Atul	Inactive	Solapur
Atul	Inactive	Mumbai
Anita	Active	Pune
Anita	Active	Mumbai
Jui	Active	Pune

Uniqueness of rows: In a table, no two rows should be exactly the same. That is, there must be *something* different between any two rows of a table. Some of the values in any two rows may repeat, but not all of them. Table 3.4 shows what is not permitted. We can see that rows 1 and 3 are exactly the same. This is not allowed.

Table 3.4 Repetition of complete rows is not allowed

Name	*Status*	*Address*
Atul	Inactive	Pune
Atul	Inactive	Solapur
Atul	Inactive	Pune
Anita	Active	Pune
Anita	Active	Mumbai
Jui	Active	Pune

Relational database theory consists of two primary concepts, **relational algebra** and **relational calculus,** as shown in Fig. 3.4.

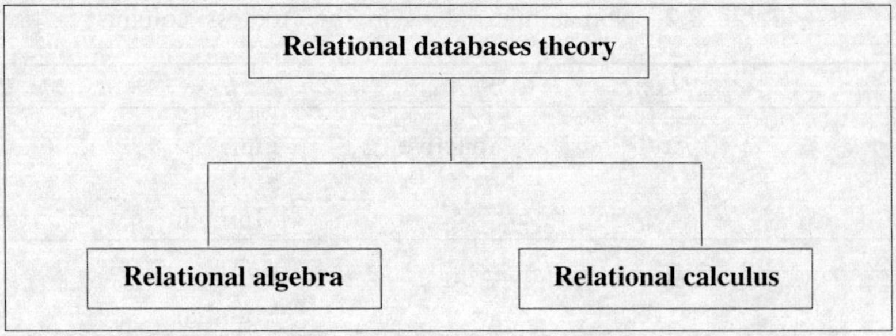

Fig. 3.4 Relational databases theory

Now we shall discuss these concepts.

3.3 RELATIONAL ALGEBRA

3.3.1 Relational Algebra Operators

Relational algebra is a set of operations on relational databases that allow retrieval of data.

There are 8 such operations defined in relational algebra, as listed in Table 3.5.

Table 3.5 Operations specified in relational algebra

Operation	*Meaning*
Restrict	Returns rows that satisfy a specified condition.
Project	Returns rows with specified columns.
Product	Returns rows after combining two tables.
Union	Returns all rows that appear in either or both of two tables.
Intersect	Returns all rows that appear in both of two tables.
Difference	Returns all rows that appear in the first but not in the second of two tables.
Join	Returns rows after combining two tables based on common values.
Divide	Returns all rows that appear after dividing one table by another.

Some of these operations are self-explanatory. However, others are not so easy to understand. Therefore, we shall try to depict them in a diagrammatic form, as shown in Fig. 3.5.

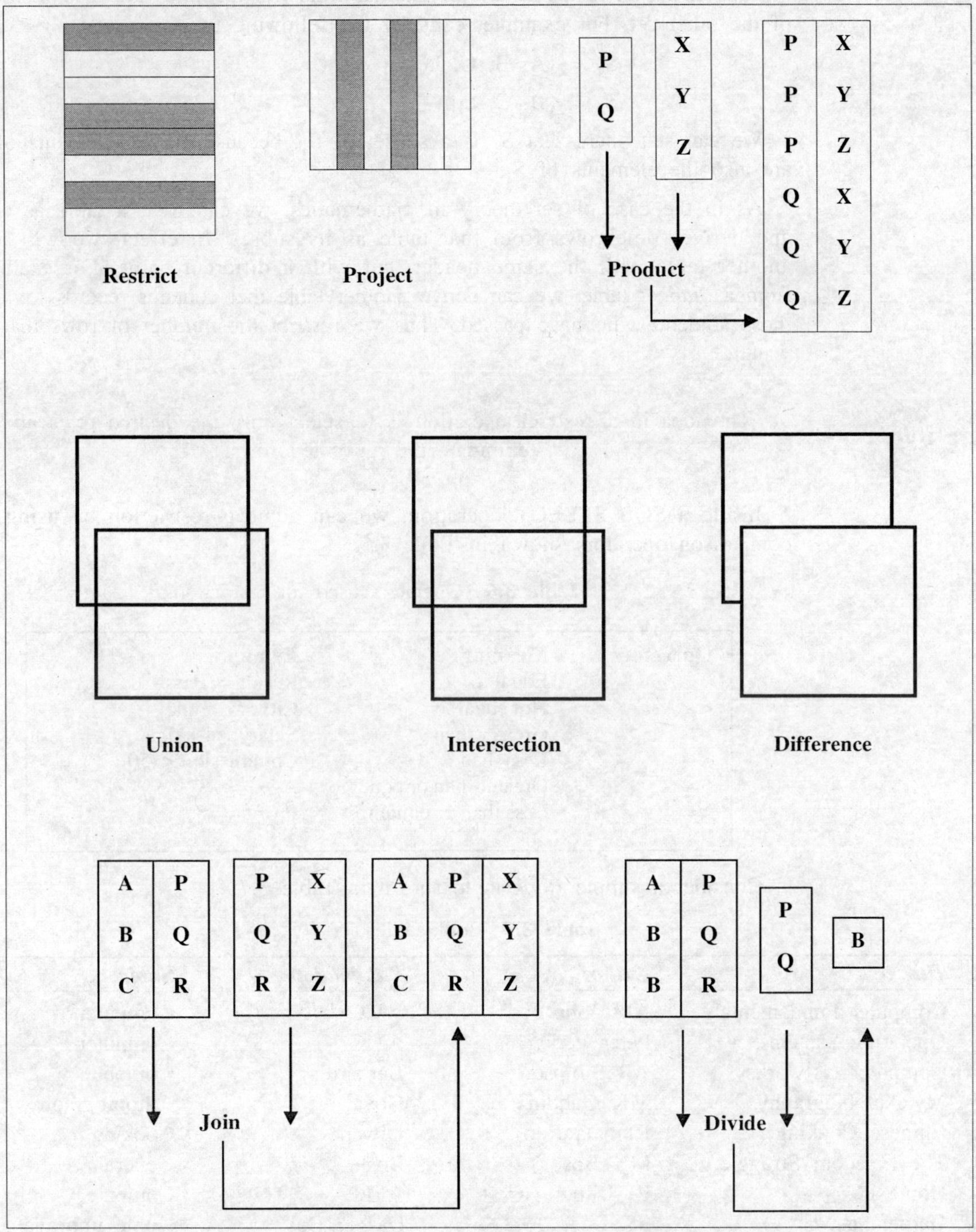

Fig. 3.5 Relational algebra operations illustrated

Let us now discuss these operations one-by-one.

3.3.1.1 Restrict We know that in mathematics, a set can have any number of subsets. A set is the subset of another if all its members are also members of the other set. For example, consider the following two sets:

$$S_1 = \{A, B, C, D, E\}$$

$$S_2 = \{B, C, D\}$$

We can state here that S_2 is a subset of S_1, because all the elements of S_2 are also the elements of S_1.

As in the case of set theory in mathematics, we can treat a table as a set and derive some rows from that table as its subset. In effect, we will have another table with the same header, but with a different name. For example, from a *Student* table, we can derive another table that contains records for only those students who have passed. Thus we *restrict* the number of rows that we want.

> The idea in a **restrict** operation is to select only the desired rows and eliminate the unwanted rows.

Inside a SQL SELECT operation, we can achieve restriction by using the comparison operators shown in Table 3.6.

Table 3.6 Operators used for restriction

Operator	**Meaning**	**Example**
=	Equal to	Result = 'Pass'
<>	Not equal to	City <> 'Pune'
>	Greater than	Salary > 1000
<	Less than	Commission < .50
>=	Greater than or equal to	Age >= 18
<=	Less than or equal to	Profit <= 50

Consider a simple *Book* table shown in Table 3.7.

Table 3.7 Book table

Id	*Title*	*Author*	*Publication*	*Subject*
1	Computer Fundamentals	AM John	AMC	Computer
2	Operating Systems	Peter Parker	AMC	Computer
3	Computer Networks	AB Simpson	Bernard's	Computer
4	My Autobiography	MK Gandhi	Goyal	Autobiography
5	Chinese Cooking	Rumala Rao	Diwan	Cooking
6	The Freedom Struggle	MK Bose	Bose	General
7	Home PC	PJ Dilbert	AMC	Computer
8	Gardening	SK Das	Das & Das	Home improvement
9	You and Your Dog	ERP Slater	Home and Away	Home improvement
10	Math for Small Children	B Reid	Children Books	Children

If we apply the restriction of *Publication* = *'AMC'* to the above table, we will get the result shown in Table 3.8.

Table 3.8 Restrict on Book table

Id	*Title*	*Author*	*Publication*	*Subject*
1	Computer Fundamentals	AM John	AMC	Computer
2	Operating Systems	Peter Parker	AMC	Computer
7	Home PC	PJ Dilbert	AMC	Computer

3.3.1.2 Project We know that the unwanted rows are eliminated in a *restrict* operation. Similarly, we can also eliminate the unwanted columns.

The operation of eliminating columns in a table is called a **project** operation.

Projection operation on a table leads to the formation of another table by copying specified columns of the original table. During the process, if any duplicate rows are found because of this elimination, they are ignored too.

For example, if we consider the same *Book* table defined earlier and perform a projection operation to consider only the *Title*, *Author*, and *Publication* columns, the result is as shown in Table 3.9.

Table 3.9 Project on Book table

Title	*Author*	*Publication*
Computer Fundamentals	AM John	AMC
Operating Systems	Peter Parker	AMC
Computer Networks	AB Simpson	Bernard's
My Autobiography	MK Gandhi	Goyal
Chinese Cooking	Rumala Rao	Diwan
The Freedom Struggle	MK Bose	Bose
Home PC	PJ Dilbert	AMC
Gardening	SK Das	Das & Das
You and Your Dog	ERP Slater	Home and Away
Math for Small Children	B Reid	Children Books

Note that a projection operation does not eliminate any rows, unless there are duplicates. It only eliminates columns.

3.3.1.3 Product We know of Cartesian product in mathematics. Cartesian product of two sets yields a third set. This set contains pairs of elements. Here, the first element in each pair belongs to the first set, and the second element in each pair belongs to the second set.

For example, let us consider two sets as follows.

$S_1 = \{A, B, C\}$

$S_2 = \{D, E, F\}$

Then, the Cartesian product $S_1 \times S_2$ is the following set:

$\{(A, D), (A, E), (A, F), (B, D), (B, E), (B, F), (C, D), (C, E), (C, F)\}$

Similarly, let us consider two tables shown in Table 3.10 and Table 3.11.

Table 3.10 Male table

Person	*Department*
Ram	Accounts
Sham	Sales

Table 3.11 Female table

Person	*Department*
Radha	Accounts
Geeta	Sales

If we decide to obtain a product of these two tables so as to identify the possible marriage pairs, the result would be as shown in Table 3.12. We have slightly modified the column names for ease of understanding, as well as to preserve the uniqueness of the column names.

Table 3.12 Male_Female table

Male_Person	***Male_Department***	***Female_Person***	***Female_Department***
Ram	Accounts	Radha	Accounts
Ram	Accounts	Geeta	Sales
Sham	Sales	Radha	Accounts
Sham	Sales	Geeta	Sales

Thus, we can conclude the following.

Product returns rows after combining two tables.

3.3.1.4 Union In mathematical set theory, the union of two sets is a set that contains elements present in either or both of the sets. In the process, any resulting duplicates are eliminated.

For example, let us consider two sets as follows.

$S_1 = \{A, B, C, D, E\}$

S_2 = {D, E, F, G}

The union of the two sets is the following set:

{A, B, C, D, E, F, G}

The concept of union in relational databases works slightly differently, as follows.

By using **union**, multiple queries can be put together and their output merged.

When we use union, the output of two or more SQL queries is merged into a single set of rows and columns. For example, consider two tables shown in Table 3.13 (*Salespeople* table) and Table 3.14 (*Customers* table).

Table 3.13 Salespeople table

SID	*Sname*	*City*	*Commission*
101	Ram	Pune	10
102	Ana	Pune	12
103	Jyoti	Mumbai	11
104	Raghu	Delhi	14
105	Deepa	Chennai	12

Table 3.14 Customers table

Cnum	*Cname*	*City*	*Orderamt*	*Snum*
201	Amrita	Pune	10000	102
202	Rekha	Pune	12700	101
203	Dheeraj	Delhi	18080	104
204	Prasad	Delhi	12810	104
205	Srinath	Mumbai	15610	103
206	Meena	Chennai	14374	105

Now, let us take a union of sales people and customers based in the city of Pune. Let us assume that we only want to have a look at the sales person/customer numbers and names. That is, the following query in English is constructed:

Select number and name of salespeople working in Pune

UNION

Select number and name of customers residing in Pune

The effect of union is *either or*, or *both*. Thus, we are saying the following:

Give us a list (containing numbers and names) of salespeople and customers based in Pune.

The resulting output is shown in Table 3.15.

Table 3.15 Result of union

Number	*Name*
101	Ram
102	Ana
201	Amrita
202	Rekha

The column headings (that is, Cnum, Cname, Snum, Sname) are changed, because the result is based on two distinct tables. That is, the columns in a union are not extracted from a single table – but from two or more tables. Therefore, the names of the columns from which the output is formed can (and usually does) vary. For instance, here, the number is stored in a column called as Snum in the Salespeople table, and as Cnum in the Customers table.

An important prerequisite for unions is that the output columns should be *union-compatible*. That is, all the SELECT queries that make up the union statement need to select the same number of columns, and their data types should also match. For example, in the above case, we cannot choose Sname from the Salespeople table and Orderamt column from the Customers table. This is because these two columns are incompatible with each other in terms of their data types. In any case, such a union would make little sense.

When we do a union of two or more tables, any duplicates arising out of the operation are automatically eliminated.

3.3.1.5 Intersection In mathematics, the intersection of two sets is the set of elements that are common to both the sets.

For example, let us consider two sets as follows.

S_1 = {A, B, C, D, E}

S_2 = {D, E, F, G}

Then, the intersection of the two sets is the following set:

{D, E}

In the case of relational databases, to perform an intersection operation on two tables, the two tables must be **union-compatible**.

The result of **intersection** is the rows common to the rows produced by the individual queries.

In other words, it is the intersection of the rows produced by two or more queries.

For example, consider two tables as shown in Table 3.16 and Table 3.17.

Table 3.16 Table *A*

Cname	*City*
Ruchi	Pune
Subha	Mumbai

Table 3.17 Table *B*

Cname	*City*
Ravi	Delhi
Ruchi	Pune

If we take an intersection of tables A and B, then the result is as shown in Table 3.18.

Table 3.18 *A* INTERSECT *B*

Cname	*City*
Ruchi	Pune

As we can see, the intersection operator is used in a manner similar to the union operator. However, intersection provides the *and* functionality. If this sounds confusing, let us consider a more useful example of union and intersection.

Let us consider the tables shown in Table 3.19 and Table 3.20. The first table shows the languages that the students are learning, and the second table shows the languages that the teachers teach.

Table 3.19 Student table

Student	*Language*
Ruchi	English
Subha	Hindi
Ruchi	Hindi
Ravi	Marathi

View is a *window* to a database. It allows us to view data in one or more tables and provides for access control. What is more, it allows us to update data in certain cases!

Table 3.20 Teacher table

Teacher	*Language*
Sandeep	English
Sunil	English
Sunil	Marathi
Abhijit	Hindi
Dhananjay	French

Now, let us first do a union as follows:

Select all languages that the students are learning

UNION

Select all languages that the teachers are teaching

The result is shown in Table 3.21. As expected, the languages present in either or both of the tables are shown.

Table 3.21 Result of UNION

Language
English
Hindi
Marathi
French

Now let us do an intersection as follows:

Select all languages that the students are learning

INTERSECT

Select all languages that the teachers are teaching

The result is shown in Table 3.22. As expected, the languages present in *both* the tables are shown. *French*, which is present only in the second table, but not in the first, is not shown.

Table 3.22 Result of INTERSECT

Language
English
Hindi
Marathi

3.3.1.6 Difference In mathematics, the difference between two sets is a set that contains members of the first set that are not in the second set.

For example, let us consider two sets as follows.

S_1 = {A, B, C, D, E}
S_2 = {D, E, F, G}

Then, the difference of the two sets $S_1 - S_2$ is the following set:

{A, B, C}

Similarly, the difference of the two sets $S_2 - S_1$ is the following set:

{F, G}

Like union and intersection, we can perform a difference operation only on those tables that are union-compatible. The difference between tables A and B defined earlier in the chapter (i.e. A – B) is as shown in Table 3.23.

Table 3.23 Difference A – B

Cname	*City*
Subha	Mumbai

Similarly, the difference between tables B and A defined earlier in the chapter (i.e. B – A) is as shown in Table 3.24.

Table 3.24 Difference B – A

Cname	*City*
Ravi	Delhi

The **difference** operator provides a *not* functionality. Thus, we can state:

> When we take the difference between two tables we get rows that are present in the first table but are *not* present in the second one.

3.3.1.7 Join Join joins two or more tables by using operators such as *equal to, not equal to, greater than*, etc.

Joining two (or more) tables has some prerequisites, if it has to be of some practical value:

- The tables should be joined based on a common column.
- The common column should be compatible in terms of domain.

For example, we will consider the *Student* and *Teacher* tables mentioned earlier. Let us join them based on the *Language* column. The condition is that the language in the *Student* table should match that in the *Teacher* table. The result is shown in Table 3.25. Note that we have renamed the *Language* column to preserve uniqueness.

Table 3.25 Joining Student and Teacher tables based on common language

Student	*Student_Language*	*Teacher*	*Teacher_Language*
Ruchi	English	Sandeep	English
Ruchi	English	Sunil	English
Subha	Hindi	Abhijit	Hindi
Ravi	Hindi	Sunil	Marathi
Ravi	Marathi	Abhijit	Hindi

As we have seen, the commonality is based on the *Language* column between the two tables being equal. As we have tested to see if the language is same (or equal), this is called as **equi-join**. This is the most common form of join in relational databases. There are other forms of joins as well. For example, in a **non-equi-join**, we create a join based on an operator such as *not equal to*.

Another important type of join is the **natural join**. In this case, the relationship between tables is already known, and comes out as a result of the natural join operation. For example, let us revisit our *Salespeople* and *Customers* tables. We will recollect that both the tables contain a column called as Snum. This column is a must in the *Salespeople* table, as it is the primary key, and identifies a salesperson uniquely. However, we have also added that column to the *Customers* table to know which salesperson serves which customer. In effect, there is naturally a correspondence between the two tables, based on this common thread of salesperson number. Therefore, we can perform a natural join on these tables based on the salesperson number to see which customer is served by which salesperson. Note that we have given prominence to the customer table here. So, if a salesperson does not serve any customer, her name would not appear in the result. The result is shown in Table 3.26.

Table 3.26 Natural join

Cname	*Sname*
Amrita	Ana
Rekha	Ram
Dheeraj	Raghu
Prasad	Raghu
Srinath	Jyoti
Meena	Deepa

If we observe carefully, we will realise that all the sales people from the *Salespeople* table are present in Table 3.26. This is because every salesperson serves at least one customer. However, let us assume that we have a new salesperson numbered 106 having the record shown in Table 3.27. This salesperson is not assigned to any customer as of now.

Table 3.27 Unassigned salesperson

SID	*Sname*	*City*	*Commission*
107	Deepak	Mumbai	12

If we perform a natural join again, the output will be the same as shown earlier. In effect, this new salesperson would be ignored because he does not have a customer assigned yet. This is fine, as long as what we are looking for is a list of customers and their assigned salespersons. However, if our objective is to see *all* salespeople in the output, regardless of whether they have a customer assigned or not, this objective would not be served.

The form of join we have shown so far is called as **inner join**. On the other hand, when we write a query to bring records of salespeople regardless of whether they have a customer assigned or not, it is called as an **outer join**. An outer join shows both matching as well as non-matching values from the tables being joined.

3.3.1.8 Divide Explaining the **divide** operator is slightly cumbersome. Therefore, we shall straightaway take an example. Let us again consider the *Student* table defined earlier in the chapter. Let us assume that we have another table called as *Language,* as shown in Table 3.28. If we now divide the *Student* table with the *Language* table, we get the result as shown.

Table 3.28 Division example

Student	Language
Ruchi	English
Subha	Hindi
Ruchi	Hindi
Ravi	Marathi

***Student* table**

Divided by

Language
English
Hindi

***Language* table**

Student
Ruchi

Result of the division operation

As we can see, the result is the selection of all the students – in this case just 1 – who know both the English and Hindi languages.

3.3.2 Grouping

Grouping is an additional feature of relational algebra. It facilitates the combination of values based on a common reference. For example, let us consider the *Salespeople* table shown in Table 3.29. The three columns in the table convey the following information:

SID	Salesperson's ID
PID	Product ID
Quantity	Quantity sold

Table 3.29 Salesperson table

SID	*PID*	*Quantity*
S_1	P_1	10
S_1	P_1	12
S_1	P_2	5
S_2	P_2	18
S_2	P_2	7
S_2	P_2	5
S_2	P_3	3
S_2	P_3	12
S_3	P_1	11
S_3	P_2	8
S_3	P_2	1

Let us first group the data based on salesperson ID. This will provide us information regarding the quantity of products sold by each salesperson. The result is shown in Table 3.30.

Table 3.30 Grouping on SID

SID	*Quantity*
S_1	27
S_2	45
S_3	20

Although this information is useful, it would be still better if we had information regarding the quantity of each product sold by each salesperson. That is, the grouping should happen on SID as well as PID. Table 3.31 shows the result.

Table 3.31 Grouping on SID and PID

SID	*PID*	*Quantity*
S_1	P_1	22
S_1	P_2	23
S_2	P_2	12
S_2	P_3	15
S_3	P_1	11
S_3	P_2	9

The SQL language also provides easy-to-use facilities for grouping data based on relational algebra. To achieve the above result, we can specify the following SQL query:

```
SELECT SID, PID, SUM (Quantity)
FROM Salesperson
GROUP BY SID, PID
```

3.4 RELATIONAL CALCULUS

Relational calculus is a formal declarative query language.

At this juncture, it is important to distinguish between relational algebra and relational calculus.

Relational algebra is procedural in nature. In other words, we need to specify what data to be retrieve, and also how to retrieve it. On the other hand, relational calculus is declarative in the sense that we need to only specify *what* data needs to be retrieved. We need not specify *how* to retrieve it. Fig. 3.6 shows the distinction between the two.

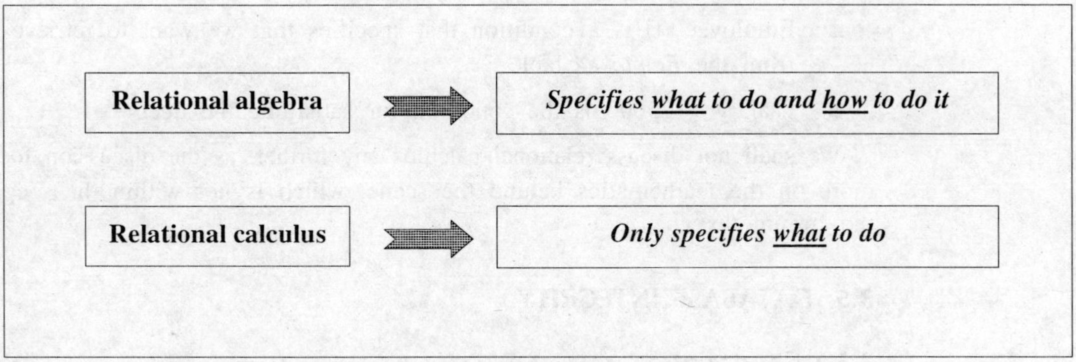

Fig. 3.6 Relational algebra versus relational calculus

Because of this, we can state the following:

- Relational algebra is **procedural**
- Relational calculus is **non-procedural**

In other words, relational algebra is a bit like the 3GLs such as C or COBOL, where we need to specify the algorithms (i.e. sequence of operations) for performing a specific task. On the other hand, relational calculus does not require detailed algorithms to be specified. We need to only mention what needs to be achieved and leave it at that.

Interestingly, any retrieval operation performed by using relational algebra can be performed by using relational calculus, and *vice versa.* In other words, both of them are equal in terms of their capabilities. Their expressive power is identical.

Let us consider an example to understand relational calculus. Suppose we have an *Employee* table and we want to find out the list of employees whose salary is above Rs 25,000. We can write the following SQL query (which is in the form of relational algebra):

```
SELECT Name, Salary
FROM Employee
WHERE Salary > 25000
```

Those not interested in the mathematical theory behind this can skip the next few sentences safely without any loss of continuity.

If we want to write this in the language of relational calculus, then the query takes the following form:

{t.Name | Employee (t) and t.Salary > 25000}

The meaning of this query is as follows:

- t.Name specifies the column to be retrieved (t is called as *tuple variable* in classical terminology)

- Employee (t) is a condition that specifies that we want to retrieve data from the *Employee* table
- t.salary > 25000 is the condition for satisfying the query

We shall not discuss relational calculus any further, as the discussion focuses more on the mathematics behind the scene, which is not within the scope of the current text.

3.5 DATABASE INTEGRITY

3.5.1 Constraints

Database integrity refers to the accuracy or correctness of data in a database.

A database may have a number of integrity constraints. For example, let us revisit the *Salesperson* table. We may have many constraints on this table, such as the following:

- The salesperson ID and product ID must consist of two digits.
- Every salesperson ID and product ID must start with an alphabet.
- Every salesperson ID and product ID must end with a number between 1 and 9.
- Quantity must be a number between 1 and 999.

We can think of any number of additional constraints. For example:

- Salesperson S_2 will be able to sell only product P_2.
- Whenever product P_3 is sold, the quantity must be over 2.

All these constraints would be based on the rules and demands of the business. Therefore, we need to inform the DBMS of such constraints, and make sure that they are not violated.

If the database is empty, there is no problem in specifying constraints. However, if the database already contains some data, then we may have a problem. What if we specify a new constraint, which is already violated in the database? Imagine the same happening in case we have to add the following constraint:

- Salesperson S_2 will be able to sell only product P_2.

What if there is already a record in the *Salesperson* table which shows that salesperson S_2 has sold product P_3? There would be no point in even trying to force this constraint. Therefore, when we specify a constraint on a database, the DBMS has to check if the constraint is currently valid. If it is not, the DBMS will reject the constraint. Otherwise, the DBMS will store it and enforces it with immediate effect. This is shown in Fig. 3.7.

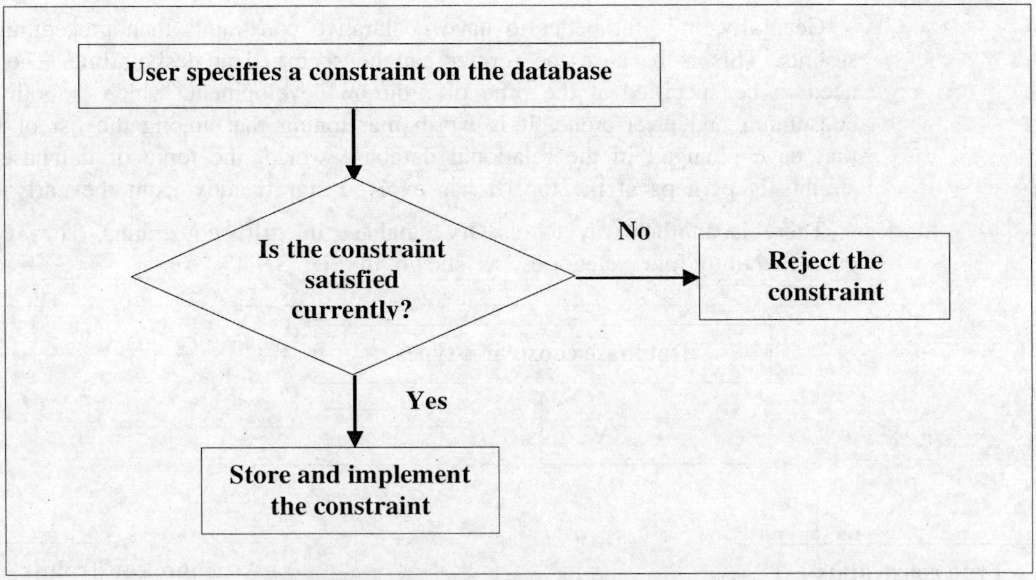

Fig. 3.7 Implementing database constraints

Similarly, there is a need to be able to remove existing constraints.

3.5.2 Declarative and Procedural Constraints

Database constraints can be of two possible types: **declarative** and **procedural**. Fig. 3.8 shows this.

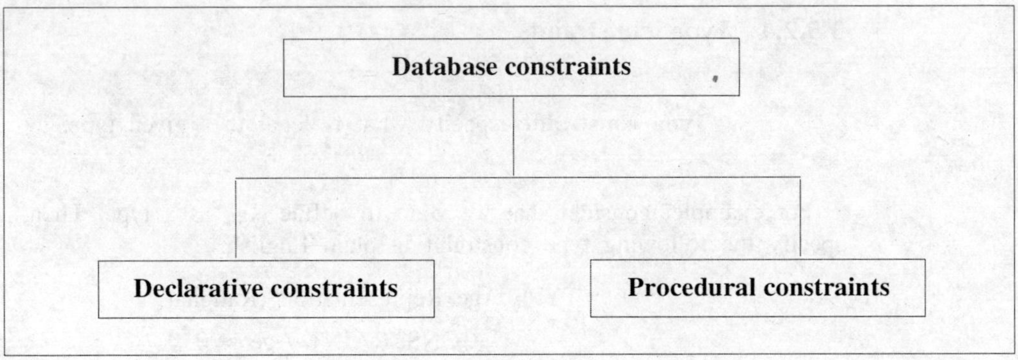

Fig. 3.8 Database constraints

The type of constraints that we have discussed so far falls under the declarative category. In other words, we have considered that these constraints will be specified at the time of table creation or even later. However, they would still be a part of the database design scope.

On the other hand, the procedural constraints come in the form of **triggers** or **stored procedures**. These are precompiled procedures, which can be invoked from an application program.

Generally, it is far better to have declarative constraints than procedural constraints. This is because the former can be specified at design time. The latter need to be specified at the time of program development, which is both time-consuming and error-prone. It is worth mentioning that among the list of things that have changed in the relational database world, the topic of database constraints is perhaps at the top. It has evolved significantly from the early days.

There is another way to classify database integrity constraints. They can be classified into four categories, as shown in Fig. 3.9.

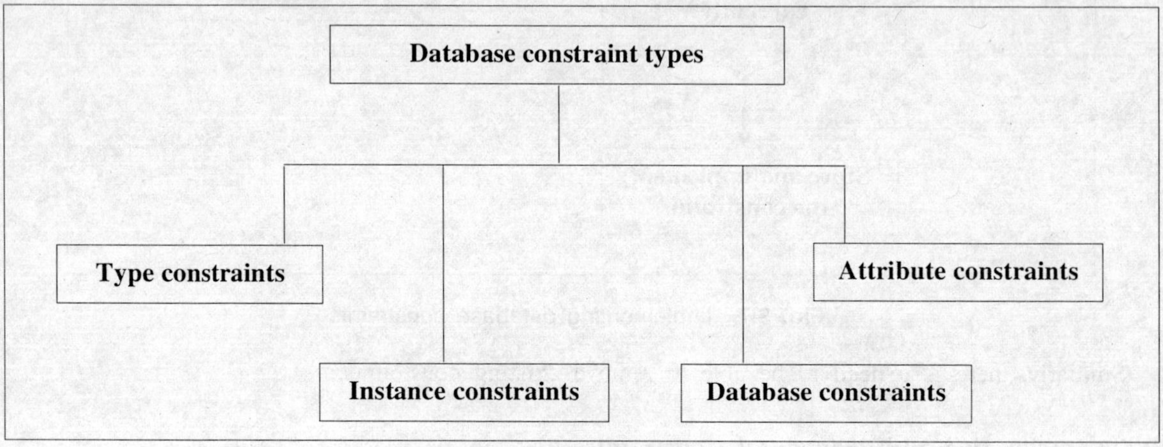

Fig. 3.9 Types of database constraints

Let us discuss these types.

3.5.2.1 Type constraints

> **Type constraints** specify what is legal to a given type.

For example, consider that we want to define *Age* as a type. Then, we can specify the following type constraint in plain English:

TYPE Age Representation (Rational)

CONSTRAINT Age > 0

This constraint specifies that the type *Age* would allow rational numbers with a value greater than 0. In other words, an expression that does not produce a value greater than 0 for *Age* will fail.

3.5.2.2 Attribute constraints

> **Attribute constraints** specify that a specified column is of a specified type.

For example, consider the following declaration:

```
CREATE TABLE Employee
(Emp_No       Integer,
Emp_Name      Char (30),
Department    Char (5),
…
)
```

We can see that the employee number is an integer; the employee name is a string, and so on. These declarations automatically add attribute constraints to column definitions.

In other words, if we attempt to store a string in the employee number column, it will fail.

3.5.2.3 Instance constraints

> **Instance constraints** apply to a specific instance or condition.

SQL provides good features for specifying instance constraints.

For example, consider the following CREATE TABLE statement in SQL:

```
CREATE TABLE Student
(Snum          INTEGER      NOT NULL     PRIMARY KEY,
 Sname         CHAR (30)    NOT NULL,
 Total_Marks   INTEGER      CHECK (Total_Marks <= 100))
```

SQL provides a keyword CHECK for specifying constraints. Here, we have specified a constraint that the total marks of a student cannot exceed 100.

Let us consider another example.

```
CREATE TABLE Salespeople
(Snum          INTEGER      NOT NULL     PRIMARY KEY,
 Sname         CHAR (30)    NOT NULL,
 Region        CHAR (10)    CHECK (Region IN 'West', 'East'),
 Commission    INTEGER      CHECK (Commission < 80))
```

Note how we have specified two different constraints:

1. The region that a salesperson can work in can only be *West* or *East*.
2. The commission paid to a salesperson cannot exceed 79.

A logical question at this stage is: can we combine two or more constraints, so that they work together? Yes, we can, and that is what we will discuss next.

3.5.2.4 Database constraints

> **Database constraints** group two or more instance constraints.

Continuing with the *Salespeople* table, let us assume that only the salespersons in the Northern region are allowed commissions of .20 or above. How can we explain this condition in an IF-ELSE form in plain English?

```
IF Region = 'North'
        Do not bother about the commission value
ELSE
        The commission must be < 20
ENDIF
```

Translating into SQL-like form, this condition becomes as shown below in the table definition. Note that we have got rid of the earlier constraints to keep things simple.

```
CREATE TABLE Salespeople
(Snum          INTEGER      NOT NULL     PRIMARY KEY,
Sname          CHAR (30)    NOT NULL,
Region         CHAR (10),
Commission     INTEGER,
CHECK (Region = 'North' OR Commission < 20))
```

We can also write more complex constraints.

3.5.3 More on Constraints

This discussion raises two questions:

1. Can we specify constraints in SQL only while creating a table? What do we do if a table already exists, and we simply need to add constraints to it?
2. We have still not seen any constraint that applies to multiple rows of a table. The constraints that we have discussed may even reference multiple columns, but still, they apply to the same row in the table. How do we take care of this problem? For example, suppose we want to be sure that all the salespeople in a given region must have the same commission.

RDBMS has two main aspects: Relational algebra and relational calculus. These names come from the fact that RDBMS has its roots in mathematics and set theory.

The answer to the first question is *No*. We can also add constraints to existing tables by using an ALTER TABLE clause.

Using a CHECK constraint cannot solve the problem specified in the second question. There is a work-around when we use *views*. We shall discuss it later.

3.6 KEYS

Keys are fundamental to relational databases. In fact, without keys, relational databases will not be usable at all. The power of relational databases comes from the fact that we can split related data into different tables and logically link them together by using keys. In this context, we need to discuss several terms.

Database keys can be of various types, as follows.

- **Superkey**
- **Key**
- **Composite key**
- **Candidate key**
- **Primary key**
- **Alternate key or Secondary key**
- **Foreign key**

Let us discuss these types of keys.

3.6.1 Superkey and Key

> A **superkey** is a set of columns that uniquely identifies every row in a table, while a **key** is a *minimal* set of such columns.

The word *minimal* comes from the fact that we cannot exclude any column from a key and still identify a row. All the columns that make up the key must be available — otherwise, it is no longer a key. In other words, a key is a minimal set of columns that uniquely identifies or **functionally determines** every column value in a row.

Let us understand this with an example. Consider a simple *Employee* table containing just two columns: *Emp_ID* and *Emp_Name*. Then the concepts of a superkey and a key are illustrated in Fig. 3.10.

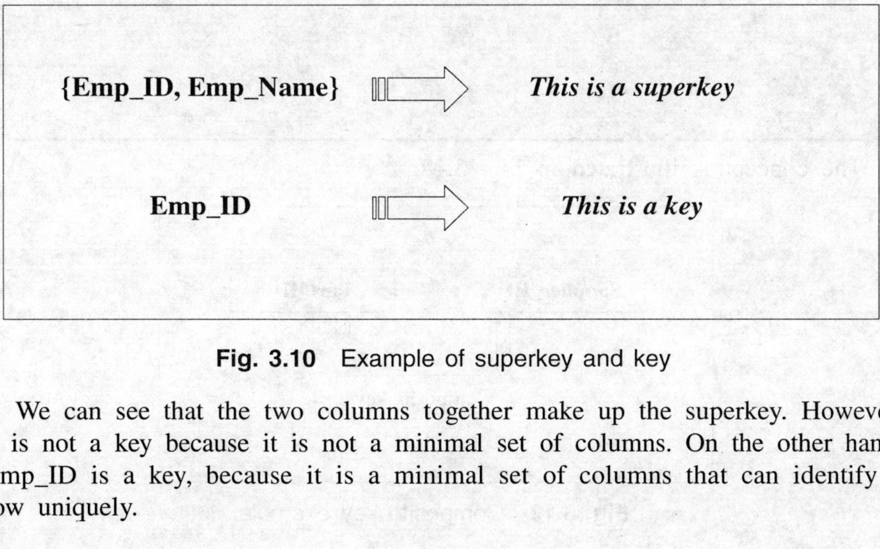

Fig. 3.10 Example of superkey and key

We can see that the two columns together make up the superkey. However, it is not a key because it is not a minimal set of columns. On the other hand, Emp_ID is a key, because it is a minimal set of columns that can identify a row uniquely.

3.6.2 Composite Key

There are situations when a single column cannot constitute a key. This is because a single column cannot uniquely identify every row in the table. Instead, we need to have two or more columns together in order to identify every row in the table uniquely.

A key consisting of two or more columns is called as a **composite key.**

This concept is shown in Fig. 3.11. Here we have a table containing five columns. The first three of them together make up the composite key.

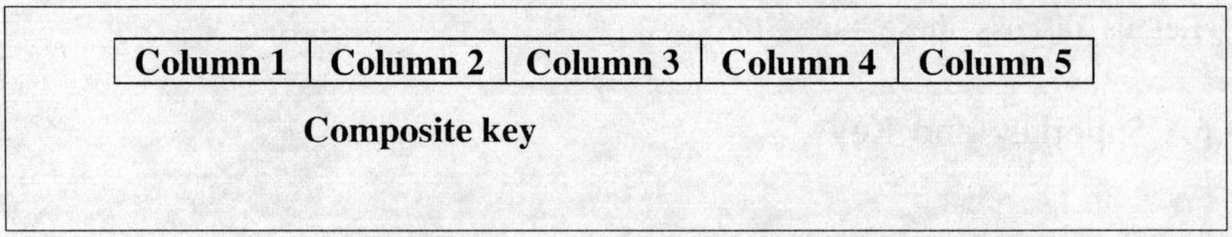

Fig. 3.11 Composite key concept

For example, consider the table structure and data for the *SP* table as shown in Table 3.32. This table tells us which supplier sells which part. As we can see, neither the supplier ID nor the part ID can identify a row in the table uniquely. However, the two of them together can easily identify any row in the table uniquely. Hence, it is a composite key.

Table 3.32 SP table

Supplier_ID	*Part_ID*	*Quantity*
S_1	P_1	10
S_1	P_2	5
S_2	P_2	8
S_2	P_3	6
S_2	P_4	5

The concept is illustrated in Fig. 3.12.

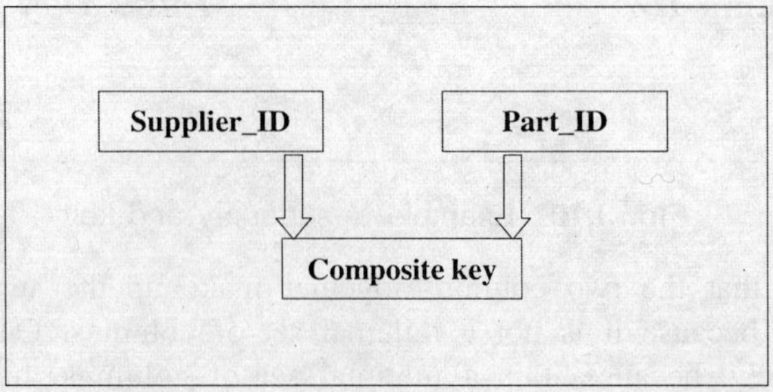

Fig. 3.12 Composite key example

3.6.3 Candidate Key

A table can have more than one set of columns that could be chosen as the key. These are called **candidate keys.**

For example, consider again the *Salespeople* table containing the following columns — Snum, Sname, Region and Commission. From the list of columns, it may appear that apart from Snum, Sname can also be a key. This assumption will prove right as long as we always have unique salesperson names. However, if we cannot make this assumption, Sname cannot be a candidate key. This is shown in Fig. 3.13.

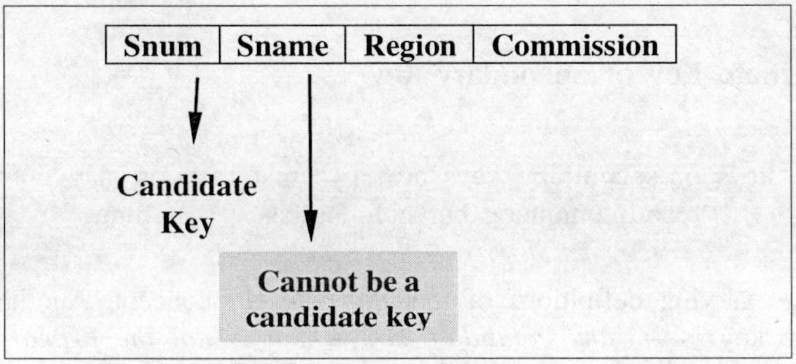

Fig. 3.13 Candidate key possibilities – Example 1

Let us now consider that there is one more column in the Salesperson table, called as PN (short form for Passport Number). Since we can identify a person uniquely based on the passport number, this can certainly be another candidate key. This is shown in Fig. 3.14.

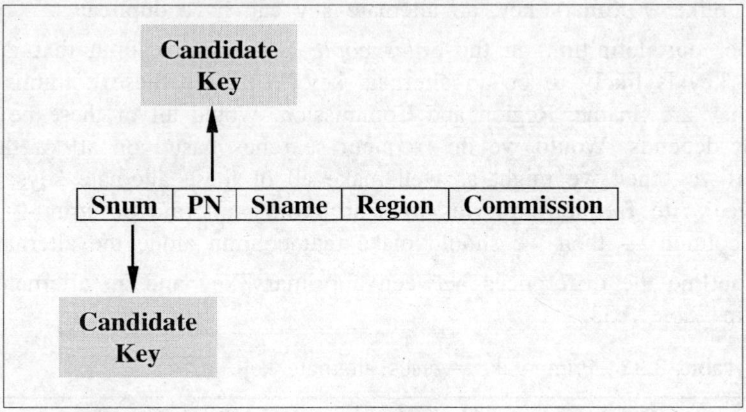

Fig. 3.14 Candidate key possibilities – Example 2

3.6.4 Primary Key

We have discussed the idea of primary keys earlier.

> The **primary key** identifies every record in a table uniquely.

When we have two or more candidate keys, we have to decide which of them becomes the primary key. The criterion for this decision is based on the ease of use in the day-to-day working as well as data entry. Emp_ID, Snum and PN are all examples of primary key.

Sometimes, a table just does not have a primary key. In such cases, we may need to introduce an additional column which contains unique values (such as a running sequence number). That is, we may need to artificially add a primary key.

3.6.5 Alternate Key or Secondary Key

> **Alternate keys** or **secondary keys** are keys that may or may not identify a record uniquely, but help in faster searching.

There are varying definitions of the *alternate key* concept. Another definition of alternate key is — *any candidate key, which is not the primary key is an alternate key*. However, we shall follow the definition mentioned earlier.

The significance of defining an alternate key is as follows:

- The DBMS creates and uses an index based on the alternate key (just as it would, based on a primary key).
- Searching based on an alternate key is quicker than searching based on a non-key column, because of the index.
- Unlike a primary key, an alternate key can have duplicates.

As per our definition, in the *Salespeople* table, any column that is not the primary key is likely to be an alternate key. What are these columns? As we know, they are Sname, Region and Commission. Would all of these be alternate keys? It depends. Would we do frequent searches based on all of these columns? If yes, then we might as well make all of these alternate keys. If, however, we write frequent queries to search only on one column — say the Sname column — then we should make that column alone the alternate key.

We outline the differences between a primary key and an alternate key as shown in Table 3.33.

Table 3.33 Primary key versus alternate key

Primary key	*Alternate key*
Requires the column to have unique values in all the rows.	Uniqueness of values is not required. Duplicates are allowed.
There can be only one primary key per table.	There can be any number of alternate keys per table.
A primary key has to be a candidate key also.	An alternate key may or may not be a candidate key.

3.6.6 Foreign Key

A **foreign key** is a set of columns in one table, which is a key in another table.

Foreign keys are extremely important in the context of table inter-relationships. We have seen the *SP* table, containing the supplier ID, part ID and the quantity. We have not worried too much about finding more details about the supplier and the part, though. For example, what is the name and address of the supplier or what part does the part ID stand for? How do we locate this information?

Relational database works by dividing data into different tables, and then linking them on the basis of common attributes/columns. For example, we would most likely have separate tables for suppliers and for parts. These tables would contain details regarding suppliers and parts respectively. The SP table would be used to establish a relationship between them. The idea is illustrated in Fig. 3.15. We have deliberately not shown the details of the *Supplier* and the *Part* tables, reasons for which will be known soon.

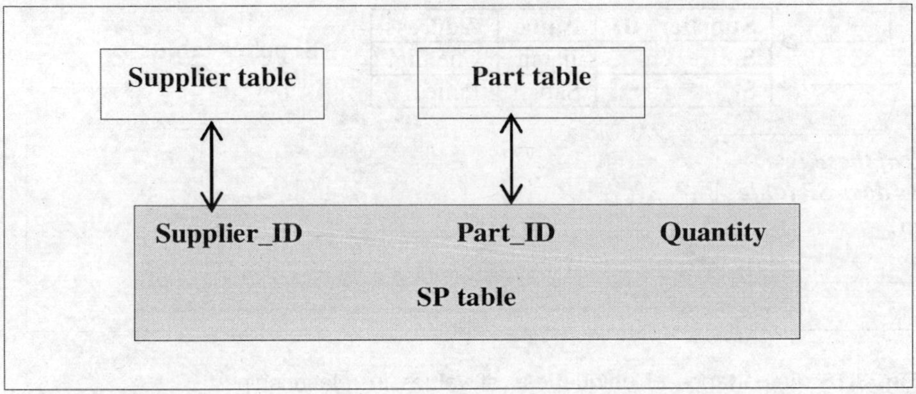

Fig. 3.15 SP table related to the Supplier and Part tables

The next question is, how do we establish the relationships between the *SP* table and the *Supplier* as well as *Part* tables? This is exactly where the vital concept of foreign key comes into the picture.

- Just as we have a Supplier_ID column in the *SP* table, we would also have a similar column in the *Supplier* table. For a given Supplier_ID in the *SP* table, there must be exactly one supplier row in the *Supplier* table.

Similarly,

- Just as we have a Part_ID column in the *SP* table, we would have a similar column in the *Part* table. For a given Part_ID in the *SP* table, there must be exactly one part row in the *Part* table.

Thus, Supplier_ID is the common link between the *Supplier* and *SP* tables, and Part_ID is the common link between the *Part* and the *SP* tables.

More importantly, for a given value of Supplier_ID or Part_ID in the *SP* table, there must be exactly one corresponding row in the *Supplier* and *Part* tables, respectively. Why is it? Let us understand with an example.

Suppose the first row in the *SP* table contains Supplier_ID = S_1. We shall ignore the values in the other columns for this row in the *SP* table. Furthermore, let us assume that the *Supplier* table contains two rows for Supplier_ID = S_1. We shall also ignore the *Part* table for now. The question is: which one of these suppliers does the first row in *SP* table refer to? This problem is shown in Fig. 3.16.

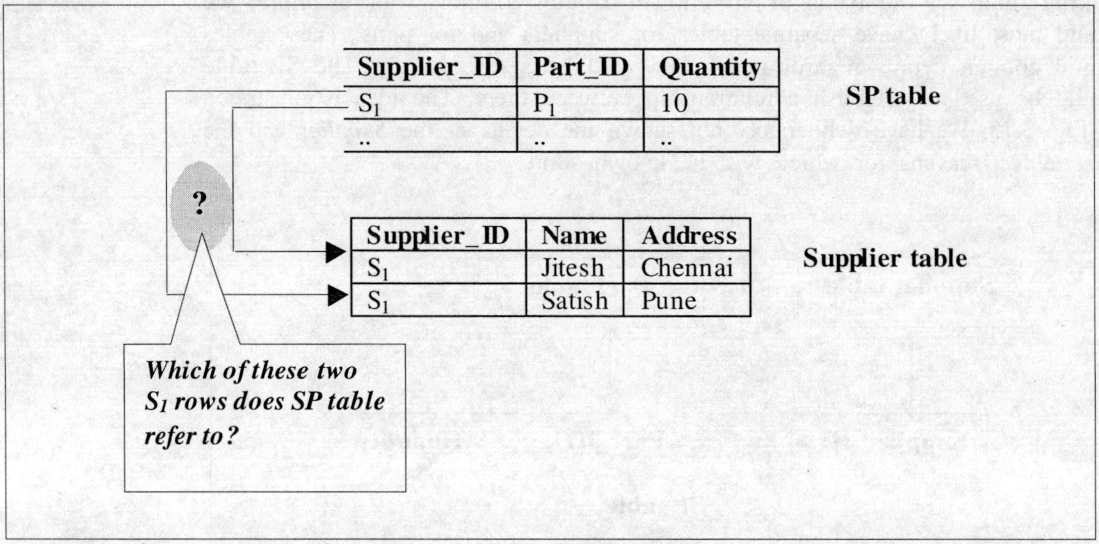

Fig. 3.16 Importance of uniqueness of values in relationships

To ensure that this does not occur, we must allow only one matching entry from the *SP* table to the *Supplier* table for a given Supplier_ID (and also to the *Part* table for a given Part_ID).

Interestingly, the inverse of this is not true. That is, there can be multiple rows in the SP table for the same supplier, that is they can have the same Supplier_ID. After all, Supplier_ID is not the primary key of the *SP* table. So, this makes sense.

We will now expand our earlier diagram to show the internal details of the *Supplier* and *Part* tables to illustrate this. Fig. 3.17 depicts this.

Based on these premises, let us now get our terminology correct. Table 3.34 tabulates the concepts.

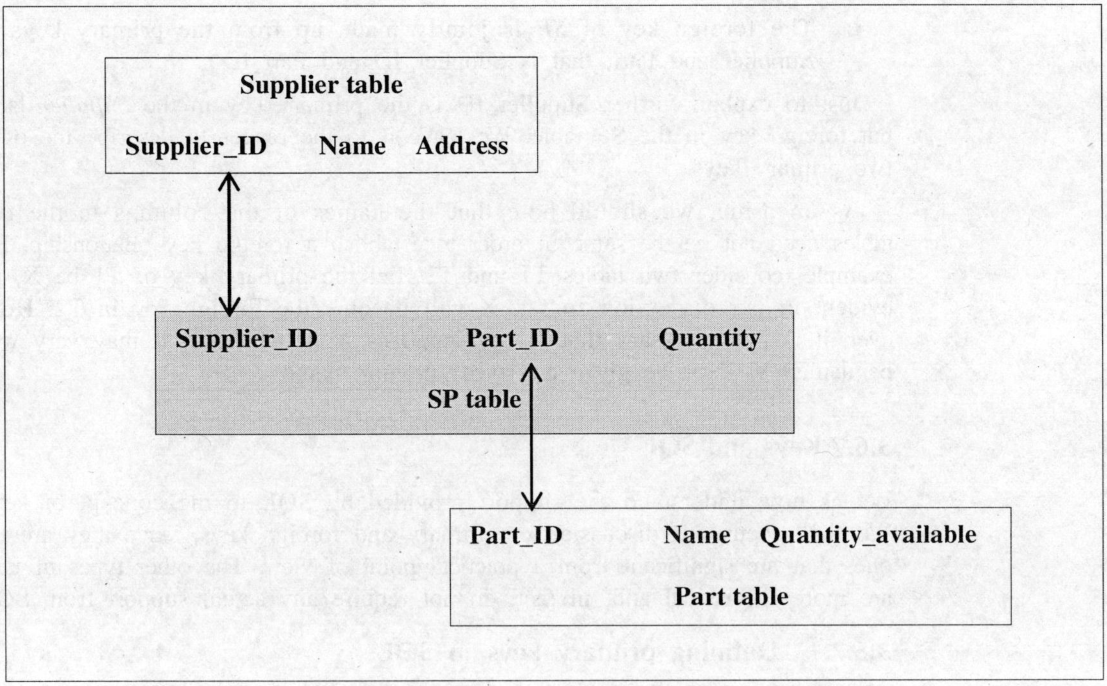

Fig. 3.17 Establishing relationships between tables

Table 3.34 Primary and foreign keys for the example shown earlier

Table	*Primary key*	*Foreign key*
Supplier	Supplier_ID	Supplier_ID of SP table
Part	Part_ID	Part_ID of SP table
SP	Supplier_ID + Part_ID	Supplier_ID of Supplier table
		Part_ID of Part table

Firstly, let us discuss about the primary keys of the three tables. This should be quite easy to understand.

- In the *Supplier* table, Supplier_ID is the primary key.
- In the *Part* table, Part_ID is the primary key.
- In the *SP* table, Supplier_ID + Part_ID is the (composite) primary key.

Now, consider the foreign keys. The primary key of one table generally becomes the foreign key of the other table, if the linking of the two tables is based on that key.

- The foreign key of *Supplier* is (a part of) the primary key of SP, that is Supplier_ID.
- The foreign key of *Part* is (a part of) the primary key of *SP*, that is Part_ID.

- The foreign key of *SP* is jointly made up from the primary keys of Supplier and Part, that is Supplier_ID and Part_ID.

Just to explain further Supplier_ID is the primary key in the *Supplier* table but foreign key in the SP table. We leave it to the reader to describe the other two primary keys.

As an aside, we should note that the names of the columns in the two tables need not be the same in order to establish a foreign key relationship. For example, consider two tables T1 and T2. Let the primary key of T1 be X. As evident in our discussion so far, X will become the foreign key in T2. However, it is not necessary that X be named as X in table T2. It may very well be named Y, Z or be given any other column name.

3.6.7 Keys and SQL

Let us now understand the support provided by SQL to the concept of keys. We shall focus our discussion on primary and foreign keys, since they are the ones that are significant from a practical point of view. The other types of keys are more theoretical and, in fact, do not require any actual support from SQL.

3.6.7.1 Defining primary keys in SQL

> SQL provides a constraint called PRIMARY KEY in order to define a primary key on a table.

As we already know, one table can have only one primary key. The value of a primary key cannot be empty (i.e. NULL).

Let us define the creation statement for the Supplier table, and its associated primary key.

```
CREATE TABLE Supplier
    (Supplier_ID    CHAR (5)     NOT NULL    PRIMARY KEY,
     Name           CHAR (30),
     Address        CHAR (30))
```

As we can see, the PRIMARY KEY constraint defines that the supplier number should be treated as the primary key of this table. Defining primary keys in SQL is that simple!

How do we define a primary key on multiple columns? That is, how can we define a *composite primary key*? For this purpose, we need to apply the PRIMARY KEY clause to all the columns of the composite key together. Let us illustrate this with the example of the *SP* table.

```
CREATE TABLE SP
    (Supplier_ID        CHAR (5)    NOT NULL,
    Part_ID             CHAR (5)    NOT NULL,
    Quantity            INTEGER,
    PRIMARY KEY (Supplier_ID, Part_ID))
```

The primary key is now defined as a composite key on two columns. This definition is not linked to the definition of the individual columns. Instead, it is defined in the end as a separate constraint.

3.6.7.2 Defining foreign keys in SQL

> SQL uses the FOREIGN KEY constraint to define foreign keys.

This constraint restricts the values that we can enter into a table to force a key and its corresponding foreign key to be in sync with each other. For example, consider the following table declaration.

```
CREATE TABLE SP
    (Supplier_ID    CHAR (5)    NOT NULL,
    Part_ID         CHAR (5)    NOT NULL,
    Quantity        INTEGER,
    PRIMARY KEY (Supplier_ID, Part_ID),
    FOREIGN KEY (Supplier_ID) REFERENCES Supplier (Supplier_ID),
    FOREIGN KEY (Part_ID) REFERENCES Part (Part_ID))
```

As before, the table declaration specifies the list of columns, their data types and the primary key. In addition, however, it also specifies two foreign key relationships. Let us dissect this.

```
FOREIGN KEY (Supplier_ID) REFERENCES Supplier (Supplier_ID)
```

This constraint specifies that in the *SP* table, Supplier_ID is a foreign key. Furthermore, it specifies that this foreign key references or corresponds to the Supplier_ID column of the *Supplier* table. We know that Supplier_ID is the primary key of the *Supplier* table.

We leave it to the reader to explain the other foreign key relationship.

Note that even if we omit the word Supplier_ID in reference to the *Supplier* table and write the foreign key as follows, it will be valid.

```
FOREIGN KEY (Supplier_ID) REFERENCES Supplier
```

The reason for this is that the Supplier_ID is named the same in the *SP* as well as *Supplier* tables. However, if the title of this column were, say Supplier_Number in the *Supplier* table, then we must be explicit, as follows:

```
FOREIGN KEY (Supplier_ID) REFERENCES Supplier (Supplier_Number)
```

How else would SQL know what is the equivalent of the Supplier_ID of the *SP* table in the *Supplier* table?

Going one step ahead, we can specify rules or actions regarding the relationships between the two tables based on the foreign keys. For example, suppose we have a supplier S_1 in the *Supplier* table and that there are three rows for

> Database integrity ensures that only valid actions are possible against a database. Database constraints are useful in ensuring this. By using constraints, we can clearly specify what actions are possible against the database and what are not.

this supplier in the *SP* table. What will happen if we delete the row for S_1 from the *Supplier* table? The three rows in the *SP* table would be in a hanging state, as shown in Fig. 3.18.

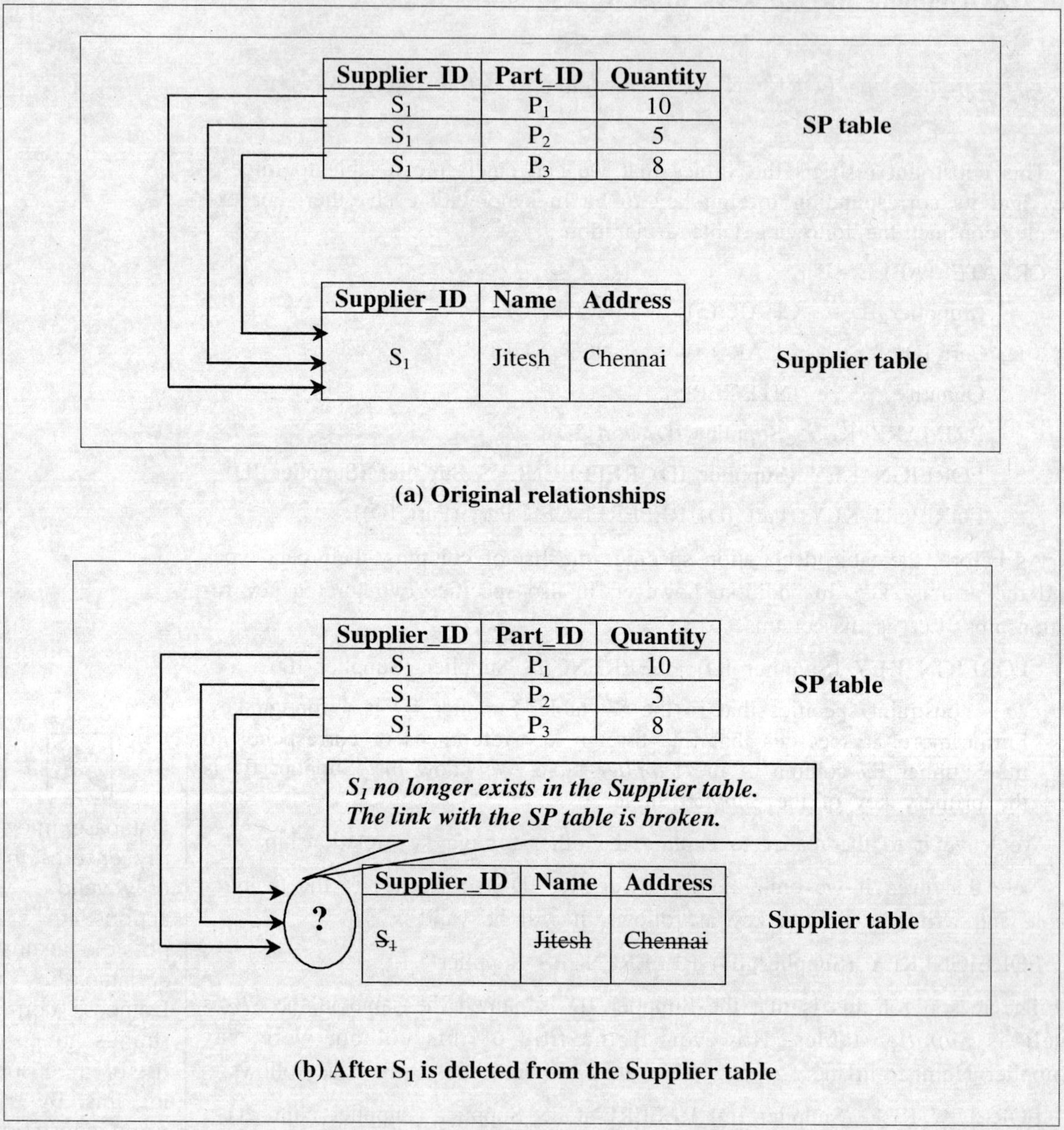

Fig. 3.18 Effect of removing key in one table corresponding to foreign key in another table

To take care of such problems, SQL has some provisions in the form of **referential triggered actions**. We can summarise them as follows.

- *UPDATE rules*: These rules specify what happens to a foreign key value when the primary key in the other table (also called as the **parent key**) is modified. For example, in the above case, a supplier ID, S_1 in the *Supplier* table is changed — say to S_9. We should be able to specify what will happen to the S1 records in the SP table.

DELETE rules: These rules specify what happens to a foreign key value when the row corresponding to the primary key in the other table (i.e. the parent key) is deleted. For example, in the above case, we should be able to specify what should happen to the S_1 records in the *SP* table if we delete the row containing S_1 in the *Supplier* table.

For the above two actions, SQL provides four effects, as summarised in Table 3.35.

Table 3.35 Summary of effects of UPDATE/DELETE on foreign key constraints

Effect	*Description*
CASCADE	The foreign key should change to the new value of the parent key. ■ For UPDATE operations, the foreign key value now becomes the same as the parent key value. For example, in our case, if S_1 in *Supplier* table is changed to S_9, all the S_1 rows in the *SP* table will also be changed to S_9. ■ For DELETE operations, the row in the dependent table containing the foreign key value will be deleted. For example, in our case, if the row containing S_1 as the Supplier_ID in *Supplier* table is deleted, all the S_1 rows in the *SP* table will also be deleted automatically.
SET NULL	The foreign key value is set to NULL. Of course, if the foreign key column has a NOT NULL constraint, then this rule will be violated and an error would be flagged.
SET DEFAULT	The foreign key value is set to the specified DEFAULT value (SQL provides for this feature). If no DEFAULT value is specified, it will be set to NULL. Of course, if the foreign key column has a NOT NULL constraint or has no DEFAULT value specified, then this rule will be violated and an error would be flagged.
NO ACTION	There would be no automatic action taken, and the UPDATE/DELETE statement would be rejected if this leaves the foreign key in an inconsistent state.

Let us add these effects to our table definitions to understand things more clearly. In an example we shall specify that if the parent key in the *Supplier* table is updated, then the same change should be carried out in the SP table. However, if the row containing the parent key in the *Supplier* table is deleted, then the corresponding foreign key in the *SP* table should be set to NULL. This is how the new definition of the *SP* table would look like.

```
CREATE TABLE SP
    (Supplier_ID        CHAR (5)        NOT NULL,
    Part_ID             CHAR (5)        NOT NULL,
    Quantity INTEGER,
    PRIMARY KEY (Supplier_ID, Part_ID),
    FOREIGN KEY (Supplier_ID) REFERENCES Supplier (Supplier_ID)
            ON UPDATE CASCADE
            ON DELETE SET NULL,
    FOREIGN KEY (Part_ID) REFERENCES Part (Part_ID))
```

Let us understand the significance of the FOREIGN KEY clause. We state that the Supplier_ID column in the *SP* table depends on the Supplier_ID in the *Supplier* table. If we update any Supplier_ID in the *Supplier* table, the same change should be propagated to the *SP* table. However, if we delete the row containing a particular Supplier_ID in the *Supplier* table, then we should not delete the row for that supplier from the *SP* table. Instead, we should change the value of the Supplier_ID column for this row to null.

We leave it to the reader to describe other FOREIGN KEY constraints in a similar fashion.

3.7 ENTITY AND REFERENTIAL INTEGRITY

There is (yet) another way of classifying integrity constraints based on the concepts of primary key and foreign key. This classification considers two types: **entity integrity** and **referential integrity**. This is shown in Fig. 3.19.

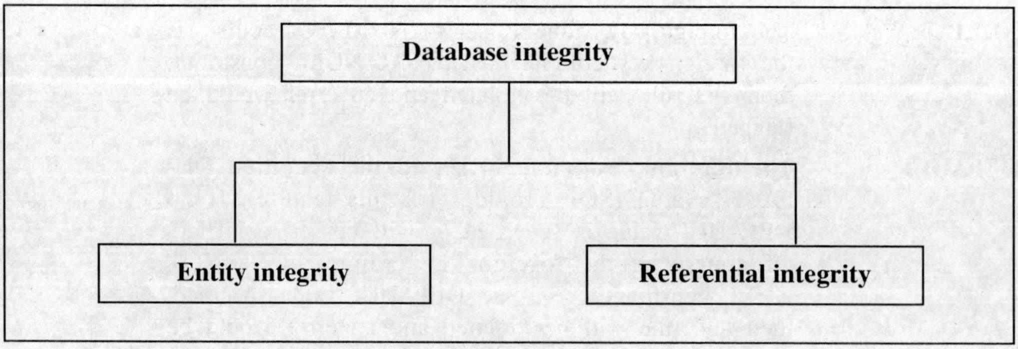

Fig. 3.19 Database integrity types

Let us discuss these in brief.

3.7.1 Entity Integrity

We know that the rows in a table represent real-world entities (such as an employee, a student, a supplier, a part, etc). The key value uniquely identifies every row in the table. Thus, if the users of the database want to retrieve any row from a table or to perform any action on that row, they must know the value of the key for that row. This means that cannot represent any entity in the database unless we can identify it completely, based on the value of a key. Thus, we cannot allow the key (or any part of the key, if it is a composite key) to contain a null value. This is captured in the entity integrity rule, as follows.

> No key column of any row in a table can have a null value.

3.7.2 Referential Integrity

We have discussed foreign keys in great detail. We know that when multiple tables need to be related or linked with each other, we must use foreign keys for doing so. For instance, we had linked the Supplier and *SP* tables based on the Supplier_ID, and the Part and *SP* tables based on the Part_ID. It is, therefore, extremely important that:

- The Supplier_ID in any row of the *SP* table corresponds to a Supplier_ID of the *Supplier* table.
- The Part_ID in any row of the *SP* table corresponds to a Part_ID of the *Part* table.

If such rules are violated, the relation between the tables would be broken. A database in which all the foreign keys either contain null or valid references to other tables is said to observe the *referential integrity* rule. We can summarise the referential integrity rule, as follows.

> Every foreign key must contain a null value or a valid key reference in another table.

3.8 VIEWS

3.8.1 What is a View?

> A **view** is a logical table that derives its data from other tables.

A view does not contain any data of its own. Its contents are taken from other tables through the execution of a query. The *other tables* that provide data to a view are called **base tables**. Base tables usually contain data. As views do not contain any data, when we execute a query on a view, the corresponding base tables are consulted, the appropriate data are fetched, and the view is temporarily populated. When the lifetime of the query is over, the data in the view is discarded.

Thus, a view can be considered as a window to one or more base tables. We can *view* data in these base tables by using a view. Therefore, we can consider a view as very similar to a query.

Let us consider an example. In SQL, we can create a view by using a CREATE VIEW statement. Let us create a view on the *Salespeople* table as follows:

```
CREATE VIEW PuneSalesTeam
        AS SELECT Snum, Sname, City, Commission
        FROM Salespeople
        WHERE City = 'Pune'
```

When we execute this statement, there is no output. Instead, SQL simply informs us that a view named PuneSalesTeam has been created in the database. It is only when we make an attempt to select data from the view that the DBMS looks at the *Salespeople* table, brings out the rows for the salespeople working in Pune, fills the view with this information, and shows it to us.

In mathematical terms, a view is a named expression in relational algebra. When we execute a statement for creating a view, the relational algebra statement is not *executed* by the DBMS. It is simply *remembered*. From a user's point of view, PuneSalesTeam contains data on the sales staff in Pune. However, from the DBMS perspective, the view is empty.

For retrieving data from the view just created, we can use a simple SQL statement as follows.

```
SELECT * FROM PuneSalesTeam
```

In response, we will be provided information/data on the salespeople working in Pune.

Why do we create views when we can retrieve data from the base tables? The main reason is access control. We may wish to show only data pertaining to Pune employees to certain users. In such a case, we can allow them to access the view, but not the base table. Although we shall study this later, the idea should be simple to understand. This has many other interesting implications as well. For example, consider the following view definition.

```
CREATE VIEW SalesView
        AS SELECT Sname, City
        FROM Salespeople
        WHERE City = 'Pune'
```

Think of a key as a column that can *open* a table, just as a key in real life can *open* a lock. Various types of keys can be defined in a database.

Note that we have selected just two columns from the base table. Let us now attempt to execute the following SQL statement:

```
SELECT commission FROM SalesView
```

We have not made the commission column a part of the view. Therefore, the above query will fail. The DBMS will tell us that there is no such column as commission in the SalesView view. This is another facet of the access control feature.

Similarly, the following query would not produce any output:

```
SELECT Sname
FROM SalesView
WHERE City = 'Delhi'
```

Note that only the salespeople from Pune are a part of the view. Hence, there is no question of being able to find any suppliers for any other city in it.

3.8.2 Updating Data through Views

Can data be updated through views? For example, consider the following view definition.

```
CREATE VIEW SalesViewNew
        AS SELECT Snum, Sname, City
        FROM Salespeople
```

Now, let us execute an UPDATE statement on this view, as follows.

```
UPDATE SalesViewNew
        SET City = 'Kanpur'
        WHERE SID = 104
```

This statement will be executed successfully. However, recall that a view itself has no data. It always brings data from a base table. When we update a view, it updates data in the base table. Therefore, in this case, the data corresponding to the salesperson whose ID is 104 would be updated in the *Salespeople* table.

Let us consider another UPDATE statement.

```
UPDATE SalesViewNew
        SET Commission = 50
                WHERE SID = 104
```

This statement would produce any output, because there is no commission column in the view.

We can create views based on summary data. For example, consider the following query.

```
CREATE VIEW SalesSummary
    AS SELECT City, Max (Commission)
    FROM Salespeople
    GROUP BY City
```

The resulting output is shown in Table 3.36.

Table 3.36 Use of GROUP BY clause

City	*Max of Commission*
Pune	12
Mumbai	11
Delhi	14
Chennai	12

We cannot perform any UPDATE operation on this view. In general, an UPDATE statement cannot be executed on any view that is based on a GROUP BY clause.

KEY TERMS AND CONCEPTS

Alternate key
Atomicity
Attribute constraints
Candidate key
Cardinality
Composite key
Database constraints
Database constraints
Database integrity
Declarative constraints
Degree
Difference
Divide
Domain
Entity integrity
Equi-join
Foreign key
Functional dependency
Grouping
Inner join
Instance constraints
Intersection
Join
Join
Key
Natural join
Outer join
Primary key
Procedural constraints
Product
Project
Referential integrity
Referential triggered actions
Relational algebra
Relational calculus
Restrict
Secondary key
Stored procedures
Superkey
Triggers
Tuple
Type constrains
Union
View

CHAPTER SUMMARY

- A table in RDBMS is also called a **relation**.
- A row in RDBMS is also called a **tuple**.
- **Domain** defines a set of all the possible values for a column or a relation.
- RDBMS operations can be classified into **relational algebra** and **relational calculus**.
- Relational algebra is procedural.
- The main relational algebra operations are **restrict**, **project**, **product**, **union**, **intersect**, **difference**, **join**, and **divide**.
- Restrict operation returns rows that satisfy a specified condition.
- Project operation returns rows with specified columns.
- Product operation returns rows after combining two tables.
- Union operation returns all rows that appear in either or both of the tables.
- Intersect operation returns all rows that appear in both of two tables.
- Difference operator returns all rows that appear in the first but not in the second of two tables.
- Join operator returns rows after combining two tables based on common values.
- Divide operator returns all rows that appear after dividing one table by another.
- **Grouping** is a feature of relational algebra that facilitates retrieval of summary values.
- Relational calculus is a formal declarative query language. It is non-procedural.
- **Database constraints** can be used to ensure database integrity.
- Database constraints can be declarative or procedural.
- Examples of database constraints are **type constraints**, **attribute constraints**, **instance constraints** and **database constraints**.
- Type constraints specify the legal values for a type.
- Attribute constraints specify that a column is of a specified type.
- Instance constraints apply to a specific instance or condition.
- Database constraints group two or more instance constraints.
- Database keys allow identification of records.
- Database keys can be classified into **superkey**, **key**, **composite key**, **candidate key**, **primary key**, **alternate/secondary key** and **foreign key**.
- A superkey is a set of columns that identifies every row in a table.
- A key is a minimal set of key columns.
- A composite key is made up of two or more columns.
- If a table has two or more keys, they are the candidate keys.

- A primary key identifies every record in a table uniquely.
- An alternate key (also called as a secondary key) may or may not identify every record in a table uniquely.
- Foreign key relationship allows two or more tables to be related to each other.
- **Entity integrity** mandates that no primary key value can be null.
- **Referential integrity** specifies that every foreign key must contain a null or a valid primary key value.
- A **view** is a logical table derived from other tables.
- View definitions exist physically, but not the data in them.
- Views are used to provide access control and ease of query management.
- We can update data through views, with certain restrictions.

PRACTICE SET

Mark as true or false

1. A table can also be called a relation.
2. A table is a set of tuples.
3. A domain is a set of all possible values in a row.
4. Every value in a row-column combination should be atomic in RDBMS.
5. In the *Restrict* operation, we select only the desired columns.
6. *Product* returns rows after combining two or more tables.
7. Relational calculus is a formal declarative language.
8. Database constraints group two or more instance constraints.
9. A composite key is a set of columns in one table.
10. Entity integrity specifies that a primary key column should not contain null.

Fill in the blanks

1. The number of rows in a table is called as its __________.

   (a) uniqueness (b) dimension

   (c) degree (d) cardinality

2. The number of columns in a table is its ______________.

   (a) degree

   (b) cardinality

   (c) relation

   (d) tuple

3. _________ is a set of operations on RDBMS that allows retrieval of data.
   (a) Relational algebra (b) Cardinality
   (c) Relational database theory (d) Relational calculus
4. The operation of eliminating columns in a table is called ________.
   (a) product (b) project
   (c) union (d) none of the above
5. The result of _________ is the rows common to the rows produced by the individual queries.
   (a) union (b) intersection
   (c) product (d) query
6. ______ is a set of columns that uniquely identifies every row in a table.
   (a) Key (b) Superkey
   (c) Foreign key (d) Candidate key
7. A key consisting of two or more columns is called ________.
   (a) composite key (b) candidate key
   (c) primary key (d) alternate key
8. SQL provides a constraint called __________.
   (a) Secondary key (b) Primary key
   (c) Database key (d) key
9. Every _______ must contain a null or the value of another valid key.
   (a) key (b) foreign key
   (c) primary key (d) alternate key
10. ___________ is a logical table that derives data from other tables.
    (a) Cursor (b) Database
    (c) Table (d) View

Provide detailed answers to the following questions

1. Explain the concept of domains.
2. Explain the term *relational algebra.*
3. Explain the term *relational calculus.*
4. What is database integrity? Explain the term *constraints* with short descriptions.
5. Explain declarative and procedural constraints.
6. Describe a key and a superkey.
7. What are candidate key and composite key?
8. Explain the difference between primary key and foreign key.
9. What is referential integrity?
10. What are views? What is their significance?

Exercises

Account table

Account_Number	Numeric	5
Account_Name	Alphabetic	25
Opening_balance	Numeric	5
Opening_type	Alphabetic	2

Journal table

Account_Number	Numeric	5
Transaction_date	Date	8
Transaction_type	Alphabetic	2
Transaction_Amount	Numeric	5

The Account table specifies the account number, name and the opening balance along with its type (credit/debit). For example, an accountholder can have an opening credit balance of Rs. 10000, which means that the bank owes the accountholder Rs. 10000. Over a period of time, many transactions (debits/credits) happen on the account.

Based on this information, attempt the following.

1. Write SQL code to create the referential integrity constraint between the two tables, based on the Account_number as the common column.
2. Specify a constraint such that if an account number is deleted from the Account table, the corresponding records in the Journal table should also be deleted.
3. Check if the referential integrity condition is violated for any records in the Journal table. (Hint: Use the concept of *outer join*).
4. Find out the meaning of left, right and full outer joins. How would each one of them be relevant to this example?
5. Write an algorithm in plain English that will find out the current balances of all the accountholders. (Hint: Use a combination of 3GL programming and SELECT statements.)
6. Find out the number of transactions for every user on 4 January 2004. (Hint: Use the GROUP BY mechanism.)
7. How can we ensure that the Transaction_type column always contains a value of DR (for debit transactions) or CR (for credit transactions) only? (Hint: Think of constraints).
8. Find a list of accountholders who owe money to the bank (i.e. those having a debit balance). (Hint: Use a combination of 3GL programming and SELECT statements).
9. How would you enforce entity integrity in the Account table?
10. Create a view on the Journal table to allow selection of only the account numbers and amounts for all debit transactions.

Chapter 4

Database Design

Designing databases is a tricky job. Several rules can be applied to make it simpler. If we apply them correctly, data can be stored, updated and retrieved most efficiently.

Chapter Highlights

- Database Design Principles
- Functional and Transitive Dependencies
- Normalisation Principles
- Various Normal Forms
- Entity/Relationship (E/R) Modelling

4.1 DESIGN CONSIDERATIONS

Good database design is critical for ensuring that the data that we want to store is consistent and can be retrieved or updated in the most efficient manner. The problem of database design deals with fitting of a given piece of data into an appropriate logical organisation. Several factors need to be considered during the process, some of which are as follows.

- How many tables should we have?
- How should they be inter-related?
- How many columns should each table have?
- Which columns should be key columns?
- What sort of constraints should we have?

As before, we shall focus our attention to relational databases. Moreover, when we speak of database design here, we are talking about the *logical* aspects of the design and not its *physical* aspects.

4.2 FUNCTIONAL DEPENDENCY

Functional dependency is critical in formulating database design. For two columns, A and B, of a table, we can define the functional dependency between them as follows.

Column B is said to be **functionally dependent** on column A if, given A we can precisely determine B.

For example, consider the following E*mployee* table, shown in Table 4.1.

Table 4.1 Employee table

Emp_ID	*Emp_Name*	*Age*
A101	Anand Joshi	29
A102	Shilpa Kamat	23
A103	Reshama Joshi	34

Do we see any functional dependence between any two columns of the table? Let us consider a combination of the Emp_ID and the Emp_Name columns. Are any of the following statements true?

- Given an Emp_ID, we can certainly determine a precise Emp_Name
- Given an Emp_Name, we can certainly determine a precise Emp_ID

We will observe that the first statement is true, but the second one is not. This is because, Emp_ID is the primary key of the table and, therefore, always unique. However, Emp_Name can repeat and, therefore, can be a duplicate in the table. Thus, we can determine with confidence an employee's name, given her employee ID. However, the reverse is not true.

Thus, Emp_Name is *functionally dependent* on Emp_ID. In symbolic terms, this is written as follows.

Emp_ID $\rightarrow$ Emp_Name

(This should be read as Emp_ID *functionally determines* Emp_Name).

In general, if column A determines the value of column B, then we write it as follows:

A $\rightarrow$ B

(This should be read as A *functionally determines* B).

Of course, there can be several functional dependencies between various columns of a table. For example, in the same table, we can certainly have the following functional dependency:

Emp_ID $\rightarrow$ Age

Let us expand the *Employee* table to add a few more columns and try and deduce some more functional dependencies. The modified *Employee* table is shown in Table 4.2.

Table 4.2 Modified Employee table

Emp_ID	*Emp_Name*	*Age*	*Salary*	*Project_ID*	*Completion_Date*
A101	Anand Joshi	29	10000	BTC	12/12/2005
A102	Shilpa Kamat	23	7000	WAP	11/08/2005
A103	Reshama Joshi	34	25000	WAP	11/08/2005

Now let us list down all the functional dependencies in this table.

- Emp_ID $\rightarrow$ Emp_Name
- Emp_ID $\rightarrow$ Age
- Emp_ID $\rightarrow$ Salary
- Emp_ID $\rightarrow$ Project_ID
- Project_ID $\rightarrow$ Completion_Date

To further clarify, let us also list what cannot be termed as *functional dependencies*.

- Age NOT $\rightarrow$ Emp_ID (because more than one employee can have the same age)
- Salary NOT $\rightarrow$ Emp_ID (because more than one employee can have the same salary)

Moreover, the functional dependency need not always be between two columns. It can be between:

- Two columns
- A column and a set of columns
- Two sets of columns

Physical design of databases refers to the organisation of data on the disk. It is related to aspects such as the cluster size, index creation and cleanup. Logical design refers to the design of the tables, their interrelationships, key definitions, and so on.

4.3 NORMALISATION AND NORMAL FORMS

4.3.1 Decomposition

Decomposition refers to the breaking down of one table into multiple tables.

Any database design process involves decomposition. Interestingly, decomposition is not greatly different from the RDBMS *projection* operation. As we know, during a projection operation, we choose only the needed columns of a table, discarding the rest. We do the same in decomposition. Of course, by *discarding*, we do not mean that the columns are lost forever. It is just that they are placed in another table, where they should logically belong.

To understand the importance of decomposition, we should first revisit the idea of redundancy. We know that redundancy means unwanted and uncontrolled duplication of data. Redundancy not only leads to duplication of data it also has other side effects such as loss of data integrity and data consistency.

Let us consider a simple example.

Suppose we have a table that holds information regarding students and the marks they have obtained in an examination. The table has the following columns:

Roll_number

Student_name

Subject_code

Subject_name

Marks

Let us consider some hypothetical data for this table, as shown in Table 4.3.

Table 4.3 Examination table

Roll_number	*Student_name*	*Subject_code*	*Subject_name*	*Marks*
101	Narendra Limaye	S_1	English	80
101	Narendra Limaye	S_2	Physics	56
101	Narendra Limaye	S_3	Chemistry	63
102	S Gururaj Rao	S_1	English	78
102	S Gururaj Rao	S_3	Chemistry	39
102	S Gururaj Rao	S_4	Biology	91

We can certainly see some redundancy here. For example, the student names appear three times in the table. Similar is the case with the subject. In other words, every time we have more than one row for a student or for a subject, the student name and the subject name would repeat respectively. Thus, is it not a better idea to store the student name and the subject name somewhere else? But where do we store them?

This is precisely the problem of decomposition. What we are essentially trying to do is to minimise data redundancy by way of following a simple rule:

Keep one fact in one place

How we can decompose the *Examination* table. Let us consider that we now break the original table into two tables, as shown in Fig. 4.1.

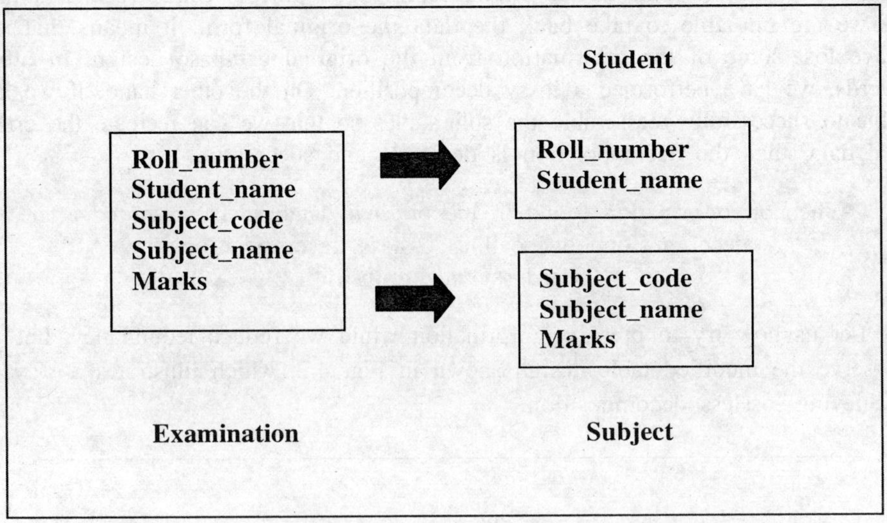

Fig. 4.1 Possible decomposition of the Examination table

Let us now study what we have achieved by performing this decomposition. We now have information on students in the *Student* table, information about various subjects in the *Subject* table. Let us assume that Roll_number and Subject_code are the primary keys of the *Student* table and the *Subject* table respectively. This certainly seems to have taken care of the problem of duplication. Now, for a given student, there will be only one entry (in the *Student* table) and, therefore, student name cannot repeat. Similarly, for a given subject, there will also be exactly one entry (in the *Subject* table), such that, the subject name cannot repeat. This would take care of the problem of redundancy.

However, if we observe the modified table design carefully, we will note that although the problem of redundancy has been solved, we have also introduced another very undesirable problem. Where do we now have the information as to which student has obtained how many marks in which subject? We have lost it! We now simply know that some students exist and some subjects can be chosen. However, we do not know how these two are interlinked.

> Loss of information due to decomposition is called **lossy decomposition.**

Clearly, decomposition cannot be used for redundancy if it leads to loss of information. In other words, lossy decomposition is not acceptable in any case. Therefore, we need to have some form of decomposition in which we do not lose information on either the data in our tables or the interrelationships between the various data items.

How do we figure out if our decomposition is lossy? It is actually quite simple. We need to observe for the possibility (or otherwise) of *reversibility* of the decomposition. In other words, we need to check if, after decomposition, we can reassemble the data in the original form — a process called *recomposition*. If we are not able to take back the data the original form, it means that we have lost some of the information from the original database design. In other words, we have performed a lossy decomposition. On the other hand, if we are able to successfully reassemble the split tables so that we can recreate the original data, then the decomposition is desirable and successful.

> When all information found in the original database is preserved after decomposition, we call it **lossless decomposition** or **non-lossy decomposition**.

Let us now try to preserve information while we reduce redundancy. Let us observe the modified table design shown in Fig. 4.2, which illustrates a way of achieving lossless decomposition.

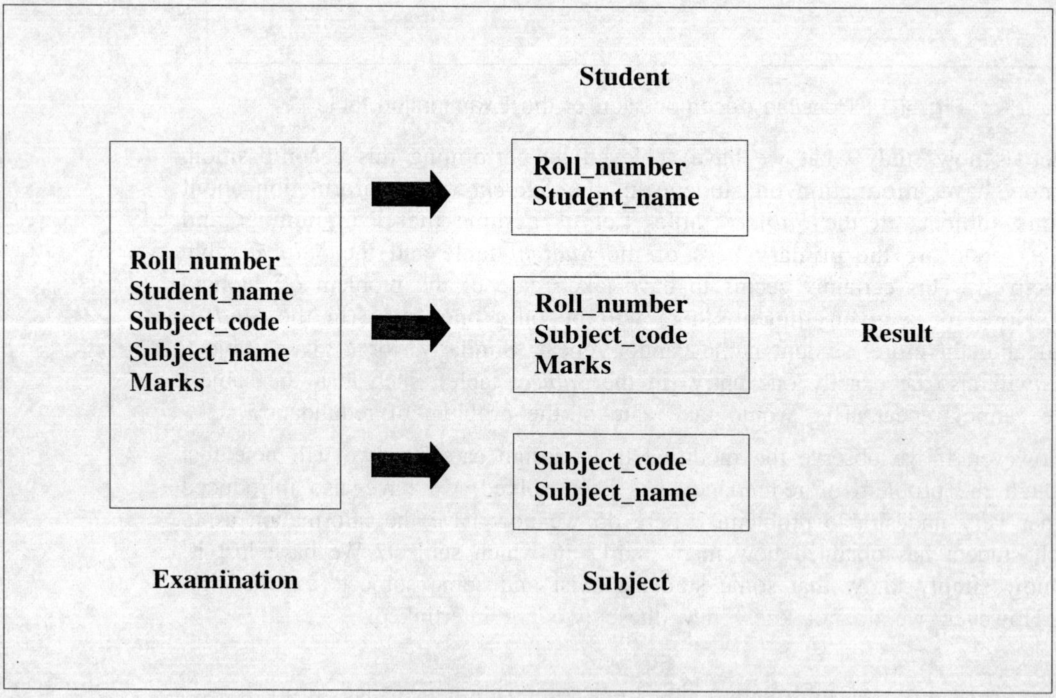

Fig. 4.2 Another possible decomposition of the Examination table

We see that three tables are created as a result of the decomposition process, instead of two. The *Student* and the *Subject* tables continue to exist as before, but the structure of the *Student* table is changed — the *Marks* column no longer exists. The newly created table is the *Result* table. This table shows the marks obtained by a student in a particular subject.

Let us now try to recreate the original information as was available in the *Examination* table. We can obtain a student's roll number, name, subject code and subject opted for, and the marks obtained therein. Can we draw the same information from the three tables? If we observe carefully, we will realise that there are referential integrity relationships as follows:

- Between *Student* and *Result* tables, based on the *Roll_number*
- Between the *Subject* and the *Result* tables, based on the *Subject_code*

Fig. 4.3 shows these relationships diagrammatically.

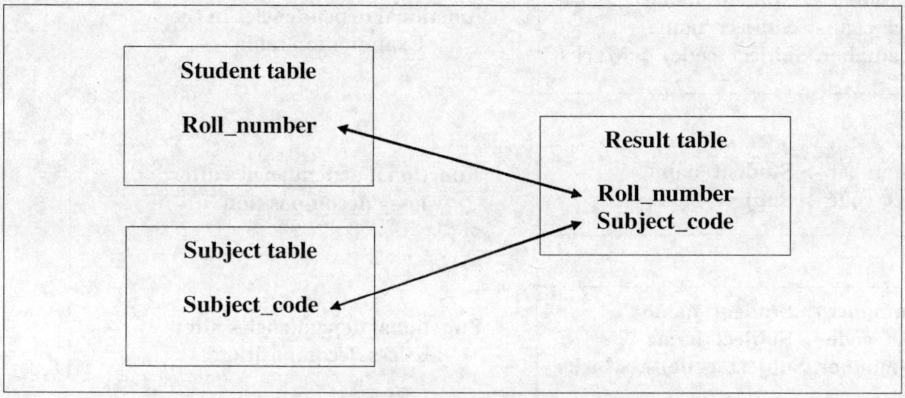

Fig. 4.3 Referential integrity relationships between the three tables

If we join these three tables to perform a recomposition, we would get the following columns (after eliminating duplicate columns):

Roll_number

Student_name

Subject_code

Subject_name

Marks

This is precisely what was contained in the original *Examination* table. Thus, we have been able to preserve the data and the interrelationships between the data elements even after decomposition. Needless to say, this is an example of lossless decomposition.

Another interesting point regarding lossy versus lossless decomposition is its close relation with the concept of functional dependency. Let us list down the functional dependencies in the original table (Examination Table) and after we perform decomposition (both lossy and lossless). This is shown in Fig. 4.4.

We will notice that the original *Examination* table has three functional dependencies. However, when we decompose it into the two-table structure, we lose one of them. Thus, another indicator for identifying whether the decomposition is lossy or lossless is the loss of functional dependencies. Interestingly, when we create the three-table structure (which is a lossless decomposition), we regain the lost functional dependency. Thus, one way to comprehend the nature of decomposition (lossy versus lossless) is to search for any missing functional dependencies, as compared to the original list of functional dependencies. We can summarise this:

> In lossy decomposition, we lose some of the functional dependency relationships while in lossless decomposition, all functional dependency relationships are preserved.

Functional dependencies	
Roll_number -> Student_name **Subject_code -> Subject_name** **(Roll_number, Subject_code) -> Marks**	**Functional dependencies in the Examination table**
Roll_number -> Student_name **Subject_code -> Subject_name**	**Functional dependencies after lossy decomposition**
Roll_number -> Student_name **Subject_code -> Subject_name** **(Roll_number, Subject_code) -> Marks**	**Functional dependencies after lossless decomposition**

Fig. 4.4 List of functional dependencies in the original, lossy and lossless relationships

4.3.2 What is Normalisation?

After the overview of functional dependencies, redundancy and decomposition, it is time to take a look at **normal forms**. Whenever there is talk of *good* database design, the discussion invariably focuses more on the concept of normal forms. Indeed, good database design involves considerable amount of effort in trying to put a table through a series of normal forms. Before we discuss normal forms though, we need to formally define the normalisation process itself.

> **Normalisation** is the process of successive reduction of a given set of relations to a better form.

In other words, normalisation is not very different from decomposition. The only difference between the two is that decomposition does not abide by any formal rules, whereas normalisation does. When we apply a normalisation rule, the database design takes the next logical form – called the **normal form**.

We will consider the example of an *Order* table to illustrate the concept of normal forms. The structure of the table is as follows.

Order_number
Order_date
Customer_number
Item_number
Item_name
Quantity
Unit_price
Bill_amount

These would repeat for as many items as we have for a given order. (applies to Item_number through Bill_amount)

As we can see, the table contains information about the orders received from various customers. The table identifies an order based on the Order_number column. Similarly, Customer_number can identify a customer and Item_number can identify an item uniquely.

Notice that for a given order several items repeat. Therefore, many columns associated with an item, such as the item number, item name, quantity, unit price and the bill amount, also repeat.

4.3.3 First Normal Form (1NF)

> A table is in the **first normal form (1NF)** if it does not contain any repeating columns or repeating groups of columns.

We have noted that in the *Order* table, one order can contain duplicate items. Clearly, this violates the principle of first normal form. Therefore, we can conclude that the *Order* table does not conform to the first normal form in its present state.

As we know, in order to bring the table into the first normal form, we have to take aid of the decomposition technique. More importantly, we need to ensure that the decomposition is lossless.

We shall state a simple process with which a table not initially conforming to the rules of the first normal form can be altered so as to follow the first normal form:

Move all the repeating columns to another table.

What are the repeating columns in the *Order* table? Clearly, they are:

Item_number
Item_name
Quantity
Unit_price
Bill_amount

These columns can repeat many times in the same order. Therefore, we have to move these columns to another table in order to bring the *Order* table in the first normal form. As a result, we now have two tables: (a) the modified *Order* table, and (b) a new table, called *Order_item*, which contains the repeating columns from the original table.

At this stage, let us find out if this decomposition is lossless. As we know, the simplest way to judge this is to check if we are able to produce the original information after joining the new tables. We now have the following two tables:

Order	**Order item**
Order_number	Item_number
Order_date	Item_name
Customer_number	Quantity
	Unit_price
	Bill_amount

Let us join these two tables. But what should the process of joining be based on? There has to be some commonality between the two tables if we have to join them. Quite clearly, there is no such commonality here. Thus, this is a case for *lossy decomposition*.

The way to achieve this commonality is to add another column to the *Order_item* table, so that an item sold is linked to a particular order. Therefore, we need to add the *Order_number* column to the *Order_item* table. This will cause a referential integrity relationship based on this column, to be established between the two tables. *Order_number* will be the primary key in the *Order* table and the foreign key in the *Order_item* table. Therefore, the modified table structures will be as shown in Fig. 4.5, in which the referential integrity relationship is also illustrated.

Order		**Order item**
Order_number	←——→	Order_number
Order_date		Item_number
Customer_number		Item_name
		Quantity
		Unit_price
		Bill_amount

Fig. 4.5 Illustration of first normal form

We can see that it is now possible to join the two tables, based on the *Order_number* such that all information about an order is preserved as well. Thus, this is a lossless decomposition. Incidentally, what should be the primary key of the *Order_item* table? It cannot be *Order_number*, because there can be multiple rows for the same *Order_number* in this table. Therefore, here the primary key should be a combination of the *Order_number* and the *Item_number*. Thus, the primary key is a *composite* or *concatenated* primary key.

Now, are there any repeating values in these two tables? Observing the tables carefully, will show that the redundancy conditions or repeating values have been removed. Therefore, we can say that our tables are in the first normal form.

4.3.4 Second Normal Form (2NF)

A table is in the **second normal form (2NF)** if it is in the first normal form and if all non-key columns in the table depend on the entire primary key.

Based on the rule stated above, let us examine if the tables illustrated in the previous section are in the second normal form. The prerequisites for a database to be in the second normal form are:

All the tables should be in the first normal form and

All the non-key columns in all the tables should depend on the entire primary key

We know that the first condition is already satisfied. Let us study the second condition for both the tables.

(a) Let us start with the *Order* table. This table now contains three columns, namely *Order_number*, *Order_date* and *Customer_number*. The primary key of the table is *Order_number*. From this column (i.e. *Order_number*), we can derive the other non-key columns, namely *Order_date* and *Customer_number*. Similarly, these non-key columns do not depend on each other at all. Therefore, we can state that this table is in the second normal form.

(b) Now, let us study the *Order_item* table. This table contains the columns *Order_number*, *Item_number*, *Item_name*, *Quantity*, *Unit_price* and *Bill_amount*. We know that the primary key here is a composite key, namely *Order_number* + *Item_number*. Can we determine the values of the other (i.e. non-key) columns of the table by using this composite primary key? Not quite! We can determine *Item_name* based on the *Item_number* alone. We do not need the *Order_number* for this purpose. Thus, all non-key columns do *not* depend on the *entire* primary key, but some of them depend only on a *part of* the primary key. In other words, the principle of the second normal form is violated. Same is the case with the *Unit_price* column — this can also be determined with the Item_number alone.

Therefore, we conclude that our database does not follow the second normal form. We need to take some action to rectify this situation. We can follow a simple strategy as follows:

Move columns that do not depend on the entire primary key to another table.

However, before we perform decomposition on the table to bring it into the second normal form, think as to why we need to do so. The technical name for problems associated with such a table structure is **update anomalies**. It refers to the problems that we are likely to face if we maintain the existing table structure. These problems are classified into three SQL operations — INSERT, UPDATE, and DELETE.

- *INSERT* problems: Imagine that we have a new item, which is not yet available in the *Order* table. Can we add information regarding this item in the *Order* table? We cannot. This is because until an order is placed for that item, we cannot insert a row for that item in the *Order* table.
- *UPDATE* problems: Suppose we have a product with *Item_number* = 100 and *Item_name* = Soap. Let us now assume that we wish to assign another product name — Toothbrush — to this Item_number, instead of 'Soap'. We will need to make this change in many rows of this table. This is because this item could be a part of many orders. We will have to locate all of them and make this amendment.
- *DELETE* problems: Let us assume that we currently have just one order for an item with *Item_number* as 105. Further imagine that for some reason, this order gets cancelled and therefore we delete this order record from the *Order* table. As a side effect, we will also end up losing all information about this item itself (such as *Item_code*, *Item_name* and *Unit_price*). This is because there is no other order, which contains information about this item. The only order that we had for this item no longer exists.

The columns that do not depend on the entire primary key are *Item_name* and *Unit_price*. They depend only on the Item_number. Therefore, we need to move these two columns to a new table, say *Item*. By now, you would have realised that we also need Item_number as one column in this table, and it should also act as the primary key of that table. Consequently, the tables would now look as shown in Fig. 4.6.

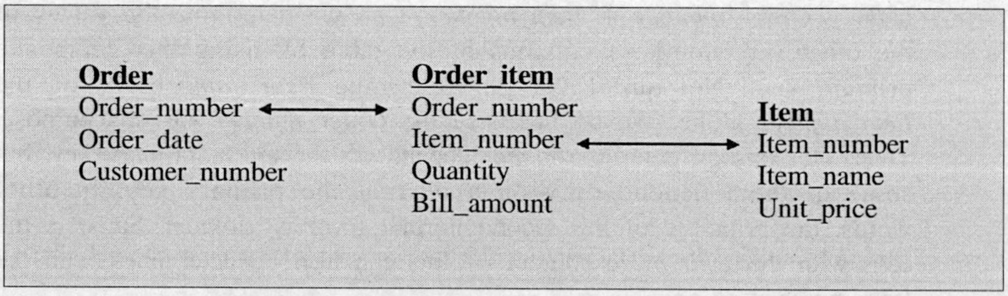

Fig. 4.6 Illustration of second normal form

There is a referential integrity relationship between the *Order_item* and *Item* tables based on the column *Item_number*.

We will not elaborate on the proofs in order to make sure that the table is in the second normal form. It should be easy to check this with the recompositions or joins, as before. However, let us ensure that the *update anomalies* discussed earlier are taken care of with the modified design.

- *INSERT* problems: We can now insert a new item in the *Item* table without needing to have even a single order for this item.
- *UPDATE* problems: We can now easily update the item name and unit price for an item in the *Item* table. We need to make this change only

in this one place (i.e. in exactly one row) and need not touch the *Order* or *Order_item* tables at all.

- *DELETE* problems: Even if we delete an order from the *Order* table, the information about that item is not completely lost. This is because the information on items is now held in a separate table (*Item* table).

4.3.5 Third Normal Form (3NF)

A table is in the **third normal form (3NF)** if it is in the second normal form and if all non-key columns in the table depend non-transitively on the entire primary key.

A simpler way to state the same thing is:

The third normal form requires a table to be in the second normal form. Additionally, every non-key column in the table must be independent of all other non-key columns.

The third normal form definition may sound complex. However, it is very easy to understand. We shall try and demystify it.

So far, we have discussed the concept of functional dependency. To reiterate, a column (B) in a table is said to be functionally dependent on another column (A) if, given A, we can determine precisely one value of B. In other words, there is a direct relationship between A and B.

Another kind of relationship also exists in relational databases. This type of relationship is called **transitive dependency**. It is an indirect relationship between two columns. Let us formally define it.

Given the following conditions:

1. There is a functional dependency between two columns, A and B, such that B is functionally dependent on A.
2. There is a functional dependency between two columns, B and C, such that C is functionally dependent on B.

We say that C **transitively depends** on A.

We can represent this symbolically as:

$A \rightarrow B \rightarrow C$

This should be read as: *C transitively depends on A*. Of course, in the larger picture, B functionally depends on A and C functionally depends on B.

The third normal form states that we should identify all such transitive dependencies and get rid of them.

Let us look for any possible transitive dependencies in our current table structure.

- *Orders* table: There is no such dependency in the *Order* table. The *Order_date* and *Customer_number* columns are functionally dependent on the *Order_number* column.

- *Order_item* table: In this table, the *Item_number* and *Quantity* columns are functionally dependent on the *Order_number* column. However, we cannot say the same thing about the *Bill_amount* column. After all, Bill amount would be calculated as:

Bill amount = Quantity × Unit price

The quantity is available in the *Order_item* table, and the unit price is available in the *Item* table. Thus, the column *Bill_amount* does not depend directly on the primary key of the *Order_item* table. Therefore, this is a case for transitive dependency. Hence, we need to get rid of the *Bill_amount* column.

- *Item* table: Here, the non-key columns *Item_name* and *Unit_price* functionally depend on the primary key of the table, that is *Item_number*. Therefore, there is no transitive dependency in this table.

In summary, we need to get rid of the *Bill_amount* column from the *Order_item* table in order to bring the table into the third normal form. Do we lose any information because of this? Not really. We can always find out the unit price for a given item from the *Item* table. We can multiply that by the *Quantity* column in the *Order_item* table, to find out the bill amount.

Let us be methodical and try to find out the update anomalies for this database design.

- *INSERT* problems: Imagine that we have a new order which contains four items. We would not know the total bill amount beforehand, as it would depend on the items ordered (i.e. the unit price of each) and the quantities supplied. Therefore, we cannot fill the column *Bill_amount*. Thus, we have a problem in insert.
- *UPDATE* problems: Let us assume that after an order is placed, there are some alterations in terms of the quantity or unit price of some of the items. In such a case, we would need to recalculate the total bill amount and update it for all the rows of the order even if one row of the order is changed.
- *DELETE* problems: If we delete one order row for an order consisting of multiple rows (i.e. multiple items), we need to recalculate the total bill amount and update it for all the remaining rows of this order.

Database design is a specialised activity. Here, we determine what data needs to go into which tables, and how tables are related with each other. The idea is to minimise data duplication and also to ensure that there are no problems in updating data in any of the tables.

To avoid such problems, we can bring a table into the third normal form. The rule for this is:

Get rid of any transitive dependencies from the table.

Stated another way:

Remove those non-key columns that depend on other non-key columns.

Thus, our table structure in the third normal form would look as shown in Fig. 4.7.

Let us revisit the update anomalies to see if they are now taken care of.

- *INSERT* problems: Because there is no such column as *Bill_amount* in the *Order_item* table, there is no question of calculating and storing the total bill amount. So, the INSERT anomaly no longer exists.

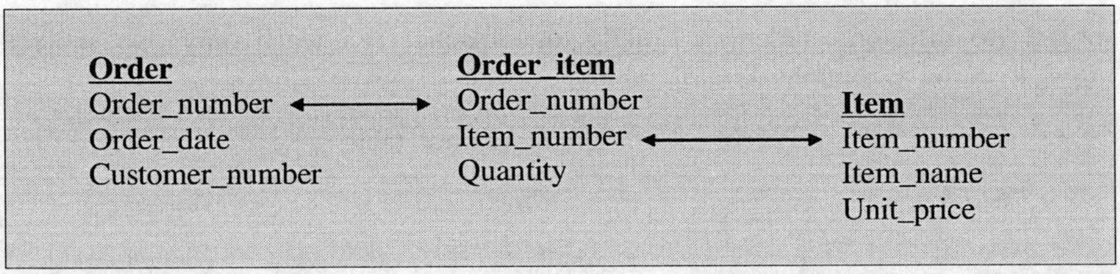

Fig. 4.7 Illustration of third normal form

- *UPDATE* problems: Even if we make changes to any Order row, we need not recalculate or store the total bill amount. Therefore, this UPDATE anomaly is also taken care of.
- *DELETE* problems: Even if we delete one Order row for an order consisting of multiple rows (i.e. multiple items), we need not recalculate the total bill amount or update it. Thus, we have got rid of the DELETE anomaly as well.

4.3.6 Boyce-Codd Normal Form (BCNF)

The first three normal forms provide means to ensure that a table is reasonably normalised. However, all design anomalies are not taken care of yet. The *next* normal form in sequence is not called *fourth normal form,* as we would have expected. Instead, it is called a **Boyce-Codd normal form (BCNF),** named after the creators of this normal form.

Before we study BCNF, we need to familiarise ourselves with a simple term, that is, **determinant**. We have studied the concept of functional dependencies in great detail. We know that if B is functionally dependent on A, that is, A functionally determines B, then the following notation holds good:

$A \rightarrow B$

In such a case, we call A the *determinant.*

Based on this definition, let us define BCNF.

> A table is in Boyce-Codd normal form (BCNF) if the only determinants in the table are the candidate keys.

A more complete but complicated definition is as follows.

> A table is in Boyce-Codd normal form (BCNF) if every column, on which some other column is fully functionally dependent, is also a candidate for the primary key of the table.

Let us now consider an example to understand BCNF. We have a *School* table consisting of three columns: *Student*, *Subject*, and *Teacher*. One student can study zero or more subjects. For a given student-subject pair, there is always exactly one teacher. However, there can be many teachers teaching the same subject (to different students). Finally, one teacher can teach only one subject. Fig. 4.4 shows a sample *School* table.

Table 4.4 Sample School table

Student	*Subject*	*Teacher*
Amol	English	Meena
Amol	Hindi	Shrikant
Mahesh	English	Prasad
Naren	Science	Mona
Naren	English	Meena

What are the functional dependencies in this table?

1. Given a student and a subject, we can find out the teacher who is teaching that subject. Therefore, we have:

   {Student, Subject} → Teacher

2. Given a student and a teacher, we can find out the subject that is being taught by the teacher to the student. Therefore, we have:

   {Student, Teacher} → Subject

3. Given a teacher, we can find out the subject that the teacher teaches. Therefore, we have:

   Teacher → Subject

Now, let us find out the primary key candidates (i.e. candidate keys) for this table.

1. The *Student* and *Subject* columns together can constitute a composite candidate key. This is because, by using these two columns in combination we can determine the remaining column, that is, the *Teacher* column. Thus, one candidate key is {Student, Subject}.
2. The *Student* and *Teacher* columns together can constitute a composite candidate key. This is because by using these two columns in combination, we can determine the remaining column, i.e. the *Subject*. Thus, one candidate key is {Student, Teacher}.
3. Is *Teacher* a candidate key? It is not, because given a teacher name, we can only determine the subject, but not the student name.

We summarise our observations as shown in Table 4.5.

Table 4.5 Functional dependencies and candidate keys for the School table

Functional dependency	*Candidate key*
{Student, Subject} -> Teacher	{Student, Subject}
{Student, Teacher} -> Subject	{Student, Teacher}
Teacher -> Subject	None

It can be seen that we have three functional dependencies but only two of them lead to candidate keys. Thus, we have a situation that can be described as:

There is a functional dependency (i.e. a determinant) without it being a candidate key.

This violates the principle of BCNF. Thus, we conclude that the table is not in BCNF. Let us examine the theoretical and practical aspects (i.e. update anomalies) of this statement.

- *Theory*: Whenever we draw a functional dependency diagram, the determinant (the item on the left side of the arrow) has to be a candidate key. There will be arrows from the candidate keys to the non-key columns. BCNF reaffirms this statement and states that there cannot be arrows from any other column to the non-key columns. If this is not the case, then the table is not in BCNF.
- *Practice (i.e. update anomalies)*:
    - *INSERT* problem: With reference to the *School* table, information about a new teacher cannot be added until we have a student assigned. Similar is the case with subjects.
    - *UPDATE* problem: If the name of a teacher is misspelt, it has to be corrected at many places.
    - *DELETE* problem: With reference to the *School* table, imagine that student Mahesh leaves the school for some reason. Now we need to delete the row for student Mahesh. This can have a very undesirable side effects such that we also lose the information that teacher Prasad teaches English.

Let us now try to convert the data to BCNF. For this purpose, we perform a decomposition operation on the *School* table to create the following two tables: *Student_Subject*, and *Subject_Teacher*. Their definitions are shown in Fig. 4.8.

Table	Columns
Student_Subject	Student, Subject
Subject_Teacher	Subject, Teacher

Fig. 4.8 Database in BCNF

What are the functional dependencies in this new database organisation? As it will be clear soon, there is just one functional dependency now. Given a teacher name, we can identify the subject that she teaches. The other two functional dependencies from the original *School* table no longer exist. What is the impact of the loss of these functional dependencies? Analysing the tables will show that, we can determine the following:

- *Which student is learning which subjects?*

Functional dependency is very high amount of dependency. Given something, we can determine another thing with almost certainty. For instance, given a married man's name, we can determine (i.e. it is functionally dependent on) the wife. Of course, it would not be true if the husband has more than one wife!

- *Which teacher is teaching which subject?*

However, we cannot determine the following:

- *Which teacher is teaching which subject to which student?*

This proves that, the decomposition that we performed is lossy. We should be careful while performing BCNF operations as we may end up losing information in the process. In a nutshell, we may not be able to implement BCNF all the time.

It is worth pointing out that BCNF is actually simpler to understand and implement than 3NF. Unlike 3NF, BCNF does not depend on 2NF. This also means that BCNF does not have the concepts of transitive dependencies.

4.3.7 Fourth Normal Form (4NF)

A table is in the **fourth normal form (4NF)** if it is in BCNF and does not have any independent multi-valued parts of the primary key.

The fourth normal form is related to the concept of a **multi-valued dependency (MVD)**. In simple terms, if there are two columns — A and B — and if for a given A, there can be multiple values of B, then we say that an MVD exists between A and B. If there are two or more such unrelated MVD relationships in a table, then it violates the fourth normal form.

Examples showing MVD (and, therefore, 4NF) tend to be contrived. However, we need to use them in order to illustrate the fourth normal form.

The fourth normal form is theoretical in nature. In practice, normalisation up to and including the third normal form are generally adequate. In certain situations, the designers may also have to look at the BCNF. However, rarely do we see the 4NF being employed for any real-life use.

Let us consider a table in which a student name, the subjects she learns and the languages she knows are stored. One student can learn zero or more subjects and can simultaneously know zero or more languages. Quite clearly, this is a strange relationship but we will overlook this fact in order to understand the theory behind 4NF. We can see that there are two independent MVD facts about this relationship:

(a) A student can study many subjects.

(b) A student can learn many languages.

Table 4.6 shows some sample data from this *Student* table.

Table 4.6 Student table

Student	*Subject*	*Language*
Geeta	Mythology	English
Geeta	Psychology	English
Geeta	Mythology	Hindi
Geeta	Psychology	Hindi
Shekhar	Gardening	English

We can see that Geeta is studying two subjects and knows two languages. Because these two facts about Geeta (namely subjects that she is studying and the languages that she knows) are independent of each other, we need to have four rows in the table to capture this information. If Geeta starts studying a third subject (say gardening), we would need to add two rows in the *Student* table to depict this fact (one for *Language* = *'English'* and another for *Language* = *'Hindi'*) as shown in Table 4.6. This is certainly cumbersome.

The process of bringing this table the fourth normal form is:

Split the independent multi-valued components of the primary key into two tables.

The primary key for the *Student* table is currently a composite key made up of all the three columns in the table — *Student*, *Subject* and *Language*. In other words, the primary key of the table is Student + Subject + Language. Clearly, this primary key contains two independent multi-valued dependencies. Hence, the table violates conditions of 4NF.

Consequently, we need to split these two independent multi-valued dependencies into two separate tables. Let us call them as *Student_Subject* and *Student_Language* tables, respectively. The resulting tables would be as shown in Table 4.7.

Table 4.7 (a) Student_Subject table

Student	*Subject*
Geeta	Mythology
Geeta	Psychology
Shekhar	Gardening

Table 4.7 (b) Student_language table

Student	*Language*
Geeta	English
Geeta	Hindi
Shekhar	English

We can see that this decomposition reduces redundancy with respect to both the independent MVD relationships, that is subjects and languages. Also, if we need to add a new subject for Geeta now, we have to add just one row to the *Student_subject* table. Contrast this with the case, where we had to add two rows for this purpose to the *Student* table. Thus, the update anomaly is taken care of.

4.3.8 Fifth Normal Form (5NF)

A table is in the **fifth normal form (5NF),** also called as **project-join normal form**, if it is in the fourth normal form and every join dependency in the table is implied by the candidate keys.

The fifth normal form is quite theoretical in nature. It is almost never required in practice.

All normal forms up to 5NF perform normalisation with the help of lossless decomposition. This decomposition usually splits one table into two by using a projection operation. However, in 5NF, the decomposition splits the original table into *at least three* tables.

Consider a SPL table shown in Table 4.8. It shows suppliers (S), the parts they supply (P) and the locations to which they supply these parts (L).

Table 4.8 SPL table

S	*P*	*L*
S_1	P_1	L_2
S_1	P_2	L_1
S_2	P_1	L_1
S_1	P_1	L_1

Note that this table does not contain any independent MVD relationships. The parts (P) are supplied to specific locations (L). Hence, they are dependent MVD relationships with the suppliers (S). Therefore, the table is in 4NF. All the same, the table does have some amount of redundancy. For instance, the row S_1-P_1 occurs twice but for two different locations (L_2 and L_1). Therefore, we cannot decompose the table into two tables to remove this redundancy. This would lead to loss of information and, therefore, would be a lossy decomposition. Let us illustrate this with actual decomposition of the SPL table into SP and PL tables, as shown in Table 4.9.

Table 4.9 (a) SP

S	*P*
S_1	P_1
S_1	P_2
S_2	P_1

Table 4.9 (b) PL

P	*L*
P_1	L_2
P_2	L_1
P_1	L_1

Why did we say that this decomposition is lossy? The reason is quite simple. We can still determine:

- *Which suppliers supply which parts?*
- *Which suppliers supply to which locations?*

However, we cannot determine:

- *Which suppliers supply which parts to which locations?*

We can prove this by carrying out a natural join on the two tables (*SP* and *PL*). Quite clearly, this join will be based on the common column P. The result of the join operation is shown in Table 4.10. Let us call it SPL_2.

Table 4.10 SPL_2 table after natural join of the SP and PL tables

S	*P*	*L*
S_1	P_1	L_2
S_1	P_2	L_1
S_2	P_1	L_1
S_2	P_1	L_2
S_1	P_1	L_1

Notice that the fourth row, shown in italics (namely S_2-P_1-L_2), is bogus. Compare the data in this table with the data in the original *SPL* table. The new table contains this additional row, which was not present in the original *SPL* table. Therefore, the natural join operation has produced one unwanted spurious row. This proves that our decomposition is lossy.

Interestingly, if we had decomposed the original *SPL* table into three tables, namely *SP*, *PL*, and *LS*, then the decomposition would have been lossless. Let us prove this. We have already seen the *SP* and *PL* tables. Let us also view the *LS* table, as shown in Table 4.11.

Table 4.11 LS table

L	*S*
L_2	S_1
L_1	S_1
L_2	S_2

Now, let us join together the *SP*, *PL*, and *LS* tables. This process is shown in Fig. 4.9.

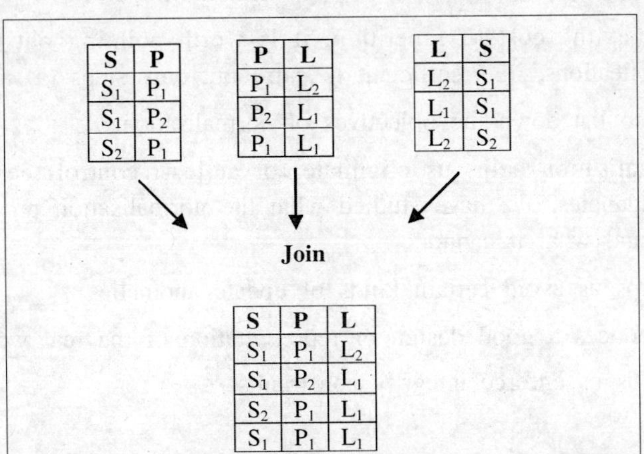

Fig. 4.9 *SPL* table after joining *SP, PL* and *LS* tables

We are able to obtain the original SPL table with the process and the bogus row too disappeares. This proves our earlier theory that in order to bring a table in 5NF, we need to decompose the original table into at least three tables.

In this case, what we are saying is this:

The relation SPL is equivalent to the three projections SP, PL and SL under the following criteria for a given S, given P and given L.

If

S and P appear in SP and

P and L appear in PL and

L and S appear in LS

Then the triplet

S, P and L appears in SPL

4.3.9 Normalisation Summary

Let us summarise what we have studied in normalisation.

(a) Take the projection of the database in the first normal form to eliminate functional dependencies that are not irreducible. This gives us the database in the second normal form.

(b) Eliminate the transitive dependencies from the database in the second normal form. This will give us the database in the third normal form.

(c) Eliminate the functional dependencies where the determinant is not a candidate key. This will give us the database in the Boyce-Codd normal form.

(d) Eliminate any multi-valued dependencies that are not functional dependencies. This will give us the database in the Boyce-Codd normal form.

(e) Eliminate any join dependencies that are not implied by candidate keys. This will give us the database in the fifth normal form.

The first three normal forms are really useful even in practical situations. But when it comes to the Boyce Codd Normal Form and the fourth and fifth normal forms, the situation changes. These are more theoretical in nature and can be ignored in most practical situations.

However, at the cost of repetition, it is worth pointing out that for most practical applications, it is sufficient to carry out only steps (a) and (b) above.

Let us also list down the objectives of normalisation.

(a) Normalisation helps us eliminate (or at least control) certain types of redundancies. We have studied what the normalisation process can control, and what it cannot.

(b) It helps us avoid certain kinds of update anomalies.

(c) It produces a good design or representation of the real world.

(d) It helps us enforce integrity constraints.

4.3.10 Denormalisation

Interestingly, while we have discussed the benefits of normalisation and glorified it endlessly, a completely opposite concept exists. It is called **denormalisation**. We can define denormalisation informally as follows:

> Denormalisation is a process in which we retain or introduce some amount of redundancy for faster data access.

The argument in favour of denormalisation is:

1. Full normalisation is a decomposition process. This causes a relation (i.e. table) to be broken down into many separate or distinct relations.
2. In general, one table at the logical level would internally map to one file in the physical level. Thus, whereas we would have required to access only one physical file for data retrieval/manipulation operations earlier, we would now need to access several files.
3. As a result of the above, the number of I/O operations would also increase by a sizeable proportion.
4. Thus, through normalisation we would get a cleaner database design at the cost of performance.

Let us consider an example of denormalisation. We had considered a database, as shown in Fig. 4.10, as a part of the normalisation process.

Order	**Order_item**	**Item**
Order_number ↔	Order_number	
Order_date	Item_number ↔	Item_number
Customer_number	Quantity	Item_name
		Unit_price

Fig. 4.10 Order database organisation revisited

Let us assume that we have to find the bill amount for each order. For this we would need to:

(a) Read all the records from the *Order_item* table and find out the item number and quantity ordered.

(b) Based on the item number, we find its unit price from the *Item* table.

(c) Multiply the quantity and unit price and arrive at the bill amount for that item.

(d) Add the amount for all items in the order.

Instead, if we add the *Unit_price* column to the *Order_item* table (making it slightly more redundant), we would be able to calculate the bill amount for each item quickly. This would allow us to skip step (b). This would certainly be faster than the above execution, since we would not need to go to the *Item* table, thus saving one I/O operation.

We can think of many such examples, where denormalisation can help speed up the execution but cause redundancy.

However, experts argue against denormalisation in general and this theory in particular. They state that the introduction of redundancy has no theoretical basis. Normalisation is based on strict and proven rules. There is no such concrete basis for denormalisation. Also, the big question is, *how much* denormalisation would we want? When do we decide to stop denormalisation? There are no criteria to decide this. We can go on and on to any level – even to the first normal form.

Consequently, it is not advisable to perform denormalisation unless we have some real-life data to back arguments in favour of denormalisation.

4.4 ENTITY/RELATIONSHIP (E/R) MODELLING

4.4.1 Aspects of E/R Modelling

In the context of database design, there is always reference to the technique of **Entity/Relationship (E/R) modelling.** It is a technique that helps us model real-world systems in the form of software constructs. Several terms need to be discussed in the context of E/R modelling, as follows.

- **Entity**: An *entity* is an object that has its own unique identity. Examples of entity are my car, a book, a road, a window, a dream and so on. The reason we have mentioned so many diverse entities is that an entity can be concrete or abstract. This is the *E* portion of E/R modelling.
- **Entity set**: An *entity set* is a set of entities of the same type. For example, all account holders in a bank can form an entity set called *customer*.
- **Attribute**: An *attribute* is a characteristic of an entity. For example, the colour, size and shape of a car are its attributes. Similarly, the subject, number of pages and author name are the attributes of a book entity.
- **Relationship**: The association between several entities forms a **relationship**. This is the *R* portion of E/R modelling. For example, customer A (an entity) could be associated with account 101 (another entity) to form a relationship between these two entities.
- **Relationship set**: A *relationship set* is a collection or set of relations of similar type.
- **Binary relationship**: The relationship between two entities is called a *binary relationship*.

Let us understand E/R modelling with a simple example. Consider that we want to represent the details of the customers of a bank and it branch. Fig. 4.11 shows the E/R diagram for this relationship.

Note that we have two entities in this relationship, namely *Customer* and *Branch*. Both of these entities have their own set of attributes. For example, a customer has name, address and phone number as its attributes. On the other hand, a branch has name, city and manager as its attributes. The two entities themselves are linked to each other via a relationship set. The relationship set here is the *customer's account*.

Normalisation is breaking down of a table or that of multiple tables into smaller tables to ensure that there is minimum or no anomaly in the design. The idea is to store data in such a manner that there is minimum redundancy of information, and that we are able to find out all the data quickly or update it.

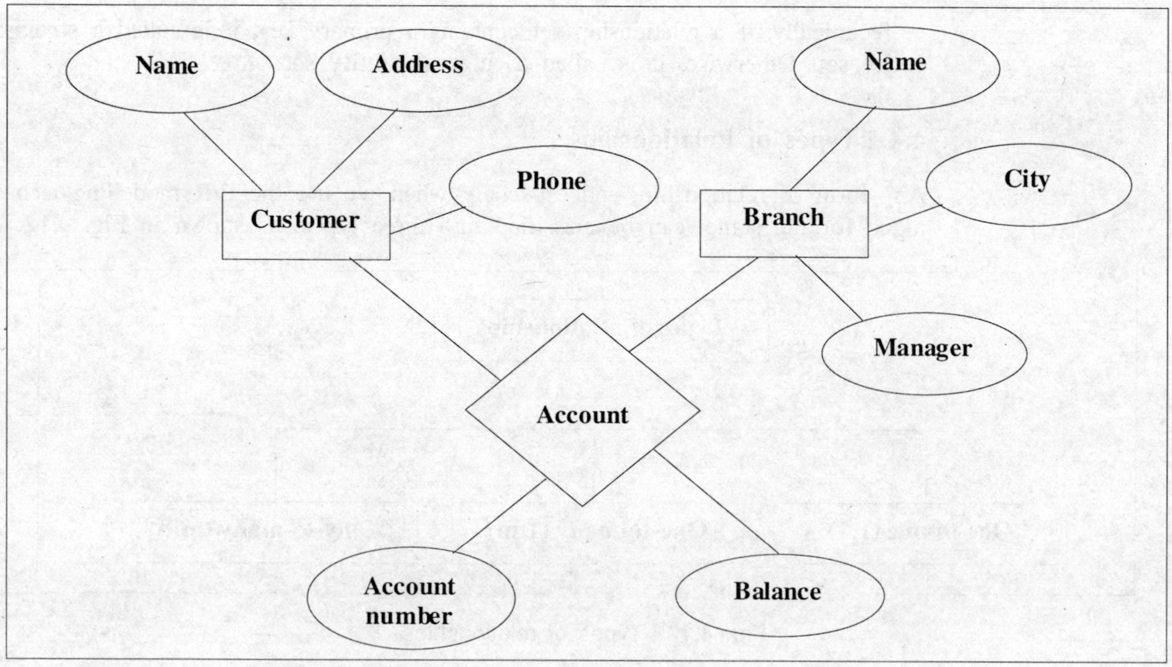

Fig. 4.11 E/R diagram showing the relationship between a bank's branch and its customers

In other words, the branch of a bank has many customers. Each one of them has an account with the branch.

The following points regarding symbols in E/R diagrams should be noted:

- A *rectangle* represents an *entity set*. An entity set roughly maps to a *table* in the RDBMS world.
- An *ellipse* represents an *attribute*. It roughly maps to a *column* of a table in RDBMS.
- A *diamond* represents a *relationship set*. It roughly maps to the *relation* between two tables in RDBMS.
- Finally, a *line* links an attribute to an *entity set* or an *entity set* to a *relationship set*.

This information is tabulated in Table 4.12.

Table 4.12 Symbols in E/R diagrams

Symbol	*Purpose in E/R diagram*	*Equivalent in RDBMS*
Rectangle	Entity set	Table
Ellipse	Attribute	Column
Diamond	Relationship set	Relation
Line	Linking (a) attributes to entity sets or (b) entity sets to relationship sets	Relation

Technically, if a relationship set contains a primary key, it is called a **strong entity set**. Otherwise, it is called as a **weak entity set**.

4.4.2 Types of Relationships

Any form of relationship, and especially when we use the E/R modelling technique for the same, can be classified into three types, as shown in Fig. 4.12.

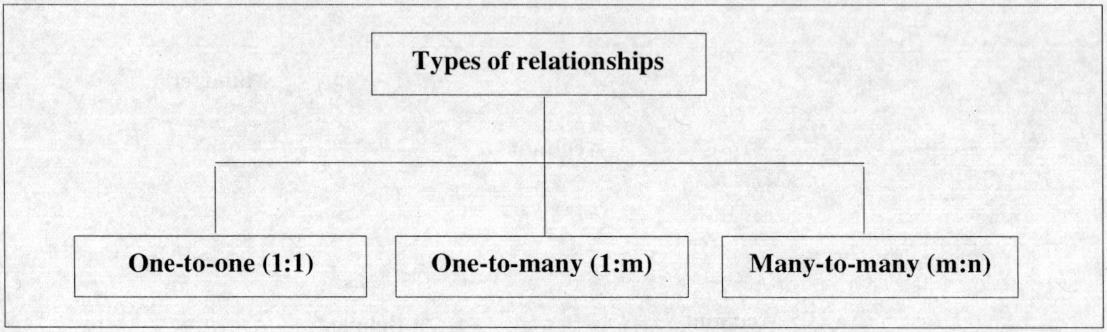

Fig. 4.12 Types of relationships

Let us define these types of relationships.

- **One-to-one (1:1)** – The *one-to-one* relationship, also denoted as **1:1,** is simple. Here, for a given occurrence of an entity (i.e. its value), there is exactly one occurrence of another entity. For example, for a given account number, we can have only one customer. Therefore, there is a 1:1 relationship between an account number and a customer. However, the converse is not true. That is, one customer can hold multiple accounts. Therefore, a 1:1 relationship from a customer to an account.
- **One-to-many (1:m)** – In a *one-to-many* relationship, also denoted as **1:m**, for a given occurrence of an entity (i.e. its value), there can be one or more occurrences of another entity. For example, a branch of a bank can have one or more customers. Therefore, there is a 1:m relationship between a branch and its customers.
- **Many-to-many (m:n)** – In a **many-to-many** relationship, also denoted as **m:n**, there can be one or more values on both sides of a relationship. That is, there can be multiple instances of both the entities that are being related. For example, take another example of a school in which many students learn many subjects. Clearly, there is a m:n relationship here.

The types of relationships can have a great bearing on **database modelling**. In other words, when we create E:R relationships to depict real-world situations, or translate them into database designs, we must know the types of relationships we are trying to model. If we do not do so, we would not be able to decide whether we should create separate tables while transforming the database models into actual table structures or not.

KEY TERMS AND CONCEPTS

Attribute
Boyce-Codd Normal Form (BCNF)
Decomposition
Entity
Entity/Relationship diagram (E/R diagram)
First Normal Form (1NF)
Second Normal Form (2NF)
Third Normal Form (3NF)
Functional dependency
Lossy decomposition
Multi valued Dependency (MVD)
Normal forms
One-to-many relationship (1:m)
Project-join normal form
Weak entity set
Binary relationship
Database modeling
Denormalisation
Entity set
Fifth Normal Form (5NF)
Fourth Normal Form (4NF)
Strong entity set
Transitive dependency
Lossless decomposition
Many-to-many relationship (m:n)
Non-loss decomposition
Normalisation
One-to-one relationship (1:1)
Relationship

CHAPTER SUMMARY

- Database design is related to the logical view of a database.
- **Functional dependency** is an important concept in database design. If column A of a table can determine the value of another column — B, then B is functionally dependent on A.
- **Decomposition** means breaking one table into multiple tables. If we lose information in the process, it is **lossy decomposition**. Otherwise, it is **lossless** or **non-lossy decomposition**.
- **Normalisation** is the process of successive reduction of a given set of relations to a better form. It helps create a very good database design.
- A **normal form** specifies the actions needed to remove the drawbacks in the current design of database. Overall, there are six normal forms, of which the first three are most widely used.
- The **First Normal Form (1NF)** specifies that there must not be any repeating columns or groups of columns in a table.
- The **Second Normal Form (2NF)** specifies that all the non-key columns in table should depend on the primary key.
- A **transitive dependency** is an indirect dependency relationship. If column C functionally depends on column B, and column B functionally depends on column A, then column C transitively depends on column A.
- The **Third Normal Form (3NF)** specifies that all the non-key columns in the table should non-transitively depend on the entire primary key.

- A table is in the **Boyce-Codd Normal Form (BCNF)** if only candidate keys are the determinants.
- If a table has no independent multi-valued parts of the primary key, then it is in the **Fourth Normal Form (4NF).**
- If the candidate keys imply every join dependency in a table, then it is in the **Fifth Normal Form (5NF).**
- Denormalisation is a process of adding some redundancy to a database purposefully so as to improve performance. It has no theoretical basis, and should be discouraged.
- **Entity/Relationship modeling (E/R modeling)** is a technique for modeling real-life systems in the form of software constructs.
- Relationships between two columns can be **one-to-one (1:1), one-to-many (1:m)** or **many-to-many (m:m)**.

PRACTICE SET

Mark as true or false

1. Column B is said to be functionally independent of column A, if given A, we can precisely determine B.
2. Decomposition means breaking one table down into multiple tables.
3. When we lose information due to decomposition, we call it lossless decomposition.
4. In lossy decomposition, all functional dependency relationships are preserved.
5. In lossless decomposition, we lose some of the functional dependency relationships.
6. Normalisation is the process of successive reduction of a given set of relations to a better form.
7. When we apply a normalisation rule, the database design takes the next logical form called the normal form.
8. A table is in the second normal form if it does not contain any repeating columns or repeating groups of columns.
9. A table is in the third normal form if it is in the second normal form and if all non-key columns in the table depend non-transitively on the entire primary key.
10. A table is in the Boyce-Codd normal form if the only determinants in the table are the candidate keys.

Fill in the blanks

1. ________ is critical in formulating database design.

(a) Row-column order (b) Number of tables

(c) Functional dependency (d) None of the choices offered

2. If column A determines the value of column B, then we write it as ________.
   (a) A -> B (b) B ->A
   (c) A <- B (d) B <- A
3. Breaking one table into multiple tables is called ________.
   (a) normalisation (b) composition
   (c) denormalisation (d) decomposition
4. When we preserve information after decomposition, we call it as ________.
   (a) lossy decomposition (b) lossless decomposition
   (c) non-lossy decomposition (d) both b & c
5. ________ is the process of successive reduction of a given set of relations to a better form.
   (a) Normalisation (b) Denormalisation
   (c) Composition (d) Decomposition
6. A table is in the ________ normal form if it is in the ________ normal form and if all non-key columns in the table depend on the entire primary key.
   (a) first, second (b) second, third
   (c) third, fourth (d) second, first
7. The ________ normal form requires a table to be in the second normal form.
   (a) first (b) third
   (c) fourth (d) fifth
8. The ________ normal form is also called as project-join normal form.
   (a) Boyce-Codd normal form (b) first normal form
   (c) second normal form (d) none of the above
9. ________ is a process in which we retain or introduce some amount of redundancy for faster data access.
   (a) Normalisation (b) Composition
   (c) Denormalisation (d) Decomposition
10. ________ technique helps us model real-world systems in the form of software constructs.
    (a) Relationship design (b) Attribute design
    (c) Database design (d) Entity/Relationship modeling.

Provide detailed answers to the following questions

1. Explain the concept of functional dependency.
2. What is decomposition?
3. Define the term *normalisation*.
4. Explain the first normal form.
5. Write a note on the second normal form.

6. Describe the third normal form.
7. Explain the concept of determinant with the help of Boyce-Codd normal form.
8. What is the difference between fourth and fifth normal forms?
9. What is *denormalisation*?
10. Explain the concept of E/R modelling.

Exercises

1. In the following column combinations, identify the functional and transitive dependencies:
   (a) Item ID, Item name, Item price, Quantity sold, Bill amount
   (b) Student ID, Name, Address, Subject, Marks
2. What are the candidate keys in the following relationships?
   (a) Employee code, Employee name, Driving license number, Passport number, Address
   (b) Part ID, Part name, Unit price, Colour, Make
3. What are the primary keys in the following relationships?
   (a) Movie ID, Name, Actor name, Actress name, Director name
   (b) Player name, Runs made, Match number, Ground, Date
4. Consider the following *Student* table. Is it in the second normal form? Provide reasons for your answer. If you think that the database is not in the second normal form, bring it in the second normal form by modifying the design suitably.

■ Roll number	Number	Maximum length 5
■ Student name	Character	Maximum length 30
■ Subject	Character	Maximum length 20
■ Marks	Number	Maximum length 3
■ Total marks	Number	Maximum length 3

5. Is the following modified *Student* table in the third normal form? Why?

■ Roll number	Number	Maximum length 5
■ Subject	Character	Maximum length 20
■ Marks	Number	Maximum length 3
■ Teacher ID	Character	Maximum length 5
■ Teacher Name	Character	Maximum length 20

6. Consider the following table.

■ Player	Character	Maximum length 25
■ Sport	Character	Maximum length 15
■ Coach	Character	Maximum length 25

The primary key is Player + Sport. This table is not in BCNF. Bring it into BCNF. Would it lead to any problems?

7. Consider the following table:

■ Child	Character	Maximum length 25
■ Hobby	Character	Maximum length 25
■ Teacher	Character	Maximum length 25

   One child can have many hobbies. Many teachers can teach the child. There is no dependency between the hobby and the teacher columns. Is this table in 5NF? If not, how would you bring it into 5NF?

8. Draw an E/R diagram for modelling the relationship between students who learn many subjects taught by many teachers. We need to maintain information such as the students' names, addresses and divisions; and the teachers' names and addresses.

9. Would you call a 1:1 relationship a functional dependency or a transitive dependency? Justify your answer.

10. Is a m:1 relationship the same as a 1:m relationship? Why?

Chapter 5

Transaction Processing and Management

Transactions make processing of complex logical operations reliable. Without them, it is hard to imagine serious business applications functioning correctly.

Chapter Highlights

- Transaction
- Recovery Principles
- Transaction Models
- Two-phase Commit Protocol
- Concurrency Issues, Locking and Two-phase Locking

5.1 TRANSACTION

5.1.1 Transactions – Need and Mechanisms

We have discussed the concept of **transaction** earlier. It is now time to take a look at the same in greater detail. We define a transaction as follows.

> A *transaction* is a logical unit of work.

Let us understand the concept of transaction with a simple example. We had earlier taken the case of funds transfer from one account to another to illustrate the concept. Let us now assume that we have a database that tracks the number of items that a firm has sold so far. There are two tables in this database: *Sales* and *Total*. The *Sales* table contains the item code and quantity sold. The *Total* table contains the item code and the total quantity of that item sold so far. Of course, immediate questions arise, such as: (a) Is the *Total* table itself not redundant? (b) Does it not violate the normalisation process? Well, for the time being, we shall ignore such questions and focus on understanding the idea behind transactions.

Imagine that three units of a product, with code P5, have just been sold. Now, we need to update the *Sales* and *Total* tables with this information. The following two simple SQL queries should accomplish this task:

```
INSERT INTO Sales (Item_code, Quantity)
            ('P5', 3)
UPDATE Total
SET Quantity = Quantity + 3
WHERE Item_code = 'P5'
```

At this stage, it is important to clarify that we are considering SQL (and because of that, RDBMS) just as an example. The concept of transactions is not at all restricted to RDBMS. It is a generic concept which covers all kinds of databases. However, because our focus in this book is RDBMS in general, we will discuss transactions with respect to RDBMS.

As already known, there would be an application program which would execute the above two queries. There may be a number of instructions before, in-between, and after these two SQL statements. This idea is shown in Fig. 5.1.

Let us imagine that *after* the execution of the INSERT statement, but *before* the execution of the UPDATE statement a problem such as crashing of the hard disk, power failure or simply an arithmetic overflow occurs. What would be the result? Obviously the *Sales* table would get updated, but the *Total* table would not. This would mean that the total units sold for item P5 would show an incorrect figure as it would not consider the latest sales transaction. (We reiterate that this is bad database design and contrived example. A better mechanism is to get rid of the *Total* table and use an aggregate function such as SUM to find out the total units of an item sold from the *Sales* table itself).

```
// Perform housekeeping tasks.
....
....

// Insert a record in the Sales table.
        INSERT INTO Sales (Item_code, Quantity)
                          ('P5', 3)
....
....

// Update the Total table.
        UPDATE Total
        SET Quantity = Quantity + 3
        WHERE Item_code = 'P5'
....
....

// Program ends here.
```

Fig. 5.1 Program to update Sales and Total tables without a transaction

Transaction is often an over-used and a misunderstood term in computer technology. In daily life, we refer to any kind of operation as a transaction. For example, if we lend money to someone, we call it a transaction. In technical terms, a transaction must be a logical and meaningful unit of work which must be done completely or not at all.

Any program must guard itself against such situations. It is the concept of transaction that helps a program in achieving this objective. We can make a program transaction-enabled, which means that it will execute as a logical unit of work. Thus preventing the database from reaching an inconsistent state. With the use of transactions, a database can always attain a correct state. Let us write the same program such that it now uses the concept of transaction. Fig. 5.2 shows the modified program.

How does a transaction-enabled program differ from the earlier one? The changes are summarised below.

1. The program now starts with a **BEGIN TRANSACTION** statement. This statement informs the database manager that the program involves a transaction, and that the transaction should take effect immediately. We shall soon study the implications of this declaration.
2. Following the INSERT statement, we now have an IF statement. This statement checks to see if the INSERT operation was successful. If it fails for any reason, the program passes control to a paragraph/section named Trans-Error. However, in the case of success, the program passes through and executes the next statement, which is UPDATE.
3. After the UPDATE statement, we have inserted a similar IF statement. In the case of errors, the program jumps to Trans-Error, as before. Otherwise, it jumps to another paragraph/section named Trans-Success.
4. In Trans-Error, we perform a **ROLLBACK** operation and terminate the program. On the other hand, in Trans-Success, we perform a **COMMIT** and end the program.

```
// Perform housekeeping tasks.
....
....

BEGIN TRANSACTION

// Insert a record in the Sales table.
        INSERT INTO Sales (Item_code, Quantity)
                          ('P5', 3)

        IF there is an error
                GO TO Trans-Error
        END-IF

// Update the Total table.
        UPDATE Total
        SET Quantity = Quantity + 3
        WHERE Item_code = 'P5'

        IF there is an error
                GO TO Trans-Error
        ELSE
                GO TO Trans-Success
        END-IF

Trans-Error:
        ROLLBACK Transaction
        End program

Trans-Success:
        COMMIT Transaction
        End program
```

Fig. 5.2 Transaction-enabled program to update Sales and Total tables

Of course, there are better ways to write a program to make it more structured. More specifically, we can get rid of the GO TO statements by using nested IF-ELSE or other constructs. However, we shall ignore these for the sake of simplicity.

The important aspect of the above process is that only when both the SQL statements (i.e. INSERT and UPDATE), that update the database, complete successfully do we perform a COMMIT. If any one of them fails, we immediately perform a ROLLBACK.

In other words, we now treat the INSERT and UPDATE operations as one logical unit of work. This is precisely what we wanted to achieve. Thus, *creating a sales record* is no longer a two-step process for the external world. It is actually an atomic operation. Internally, the DBMS manages this two-step process in a transaction-enabled environment to achieve the state of atomicity (or consistency).

One very interesting fact is often overlooked. Do we realise that the database is actually *not* consistent for a temporary period? Note that if the INSERT statement is successful before the UPDATE statement, the database is *not* consistent. In this case, we have updated just one table and not the other. Therefore, the database is not accurate. However, the transaction hides this temporary inconsistency and provides an abstraction that makes the overall operation atomic and consistent. It is another matter that *within* a transaction, the database could temporarily attain an inconsistent state. The idea is shown in Fig. 5.3.

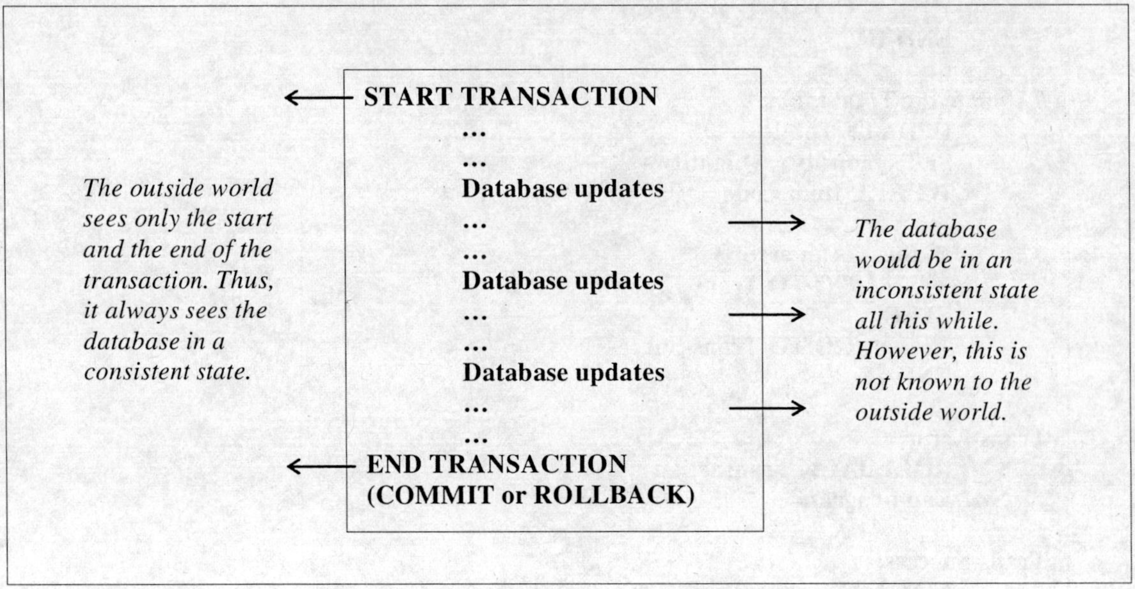

Fig. 5.3 Transaction hides the internal inconsistencies from the external world

A transaction is not a single database operation but a sequence of such operations. What is significant, though, is that it transforms the database from one consistent state to another. The initial consistent state of a database is indicated by the BEGIN TRANSACTION declaration, and the final consistent state by the END TRANSACTION (or COMMIT/ROLLBACK) operation. As we have mentioned earlier, any inconsistent state that the database attains during the execution of the transaction is not known to the outside world. The transaction hides them.

5.1.2 Transaction Processing (TP) Monitor

Various types of errors can occur during the execution of a program, such as power failure, nonnumeric data error, memory error and so on. Therefore, we cannot expect that things would not go wrong and therefore, have to prepare for such situations. In fact, we need to assume that things might go wrong at times, and provide for such problems. A **Transaction Processing (TP) system** (also called **Transaction Processing monitor (TP monitor)**), provides for the next best option. The TP monitor is a special program that oversees transaction processing in a DBMS. It allows the system to avoid or recover from problematic situations. It ensures an *all-or-none* operation. Thus, the TP monitor ensures that while a transaction may consist of many steps, it is a single atomic operation as far as the outside world's perspective is concerned.

When it sees a COMMIT statement, the TP monitor informs the DBMS that the database is in a consistent state In effect, it asks the DBMS to make the updates made during the lifetime of the transaction permanent on the physical database. However, when it encounters a ROLLBACK statement, it realises that there is some error. Hence, it asks the DBMS to rollback or undo all the changes made as a part of the transaction. This concept is shown in Fig. 5.4. Here we must clarify one technical detail. When we say that *the DBMS makes changes permanent to the database*, we do not imply that the actual tables are updated immediately. Instead, what we mean is that the DBMS guarantees that the updates would not be lost. Internally, it may keep the data in its buffers and provide other mechanisms (discussed later) to ensure this.

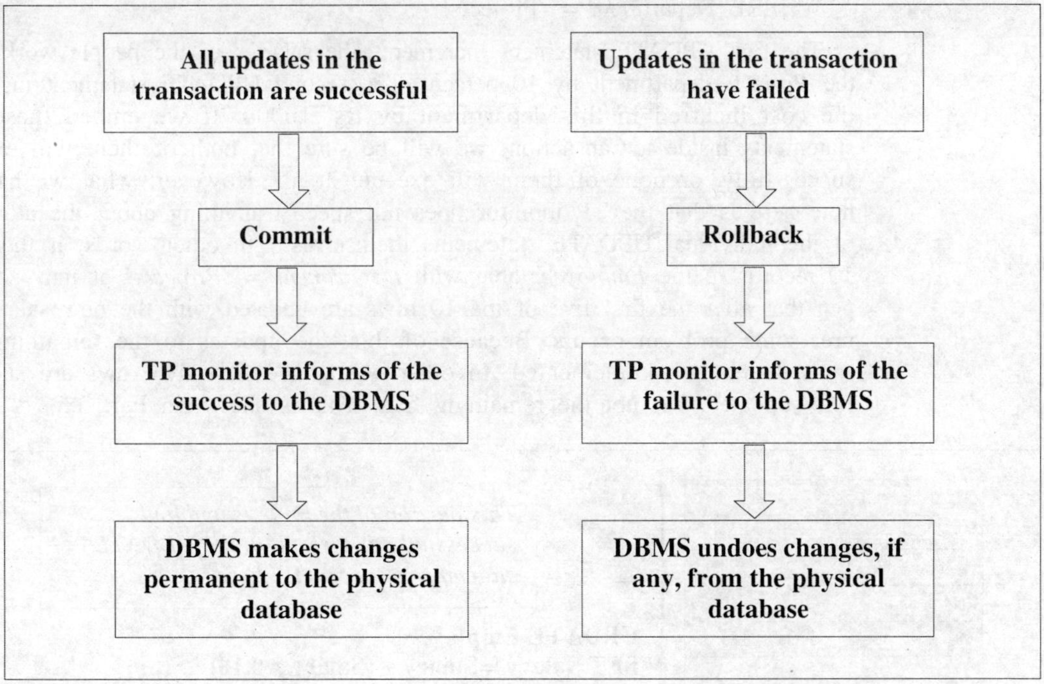

Fig. 5.4 Effect of Commit and Rollback on the database

Although it is fine to know about the COMMIT and ROLLBACK operations conceptually, it is also important to understand how they are achieved in real life. A **system log** or **journal** is used for this purpose. This is a file that contains the details of all modifications to data (i.e. INSERT, UPDATE and DELETE statements), and the before-and-after images of the objects being updated. We shall soon study this in more detail.

For the time being, we should note that whenever there is a ROLLBACK operation, the system restores the corresponding log entry. In other words, it restores an object to its last consistent state.

Another important point that must be stressed is that although a transaction makes a series of database operations atomic, individual statements must be atomic in the first place! Thus if we put two UPDATE statements inside a transaction, the TP monitor guarantees that the result of these two statements is atomic. However, it does not give any assurance regarding the atomicity of these two statements themselves. For example, consider the following two statements.

```
UPDATE Employee
SET Salary = Salary + (Salary * 0.10)
WHERE Department = 'Projects'
UPDATE Projects
SET Cost = Cost + 10000
WHERE Department = 'Projects'
```

The first UPDATE statement increments the salaries of the people working in the *Projects* department by 10 percent. The second UPDATE statement increases the cost incurred in this department by Rs. 10000. If we embed these two statements inside a transaction, we will be sure that both of them will execute successfully, or none of them will execute at all. However, what we have to note here is that the TP monitor does not specify anything about the atomicity of the individual UPDATE statements themselves! In other words, if there are 10 records in the *Employee* table with *Department = 'Projects'*, it may so happen that after the first five of the 10 rows are updated with the new salary figure, some problem occurs. Because of this, the updates to the remaining five rows do not get implemented. In other words, the first five rows are successfully updated, but not the remaining five! This is shown in Fig. 5.5.

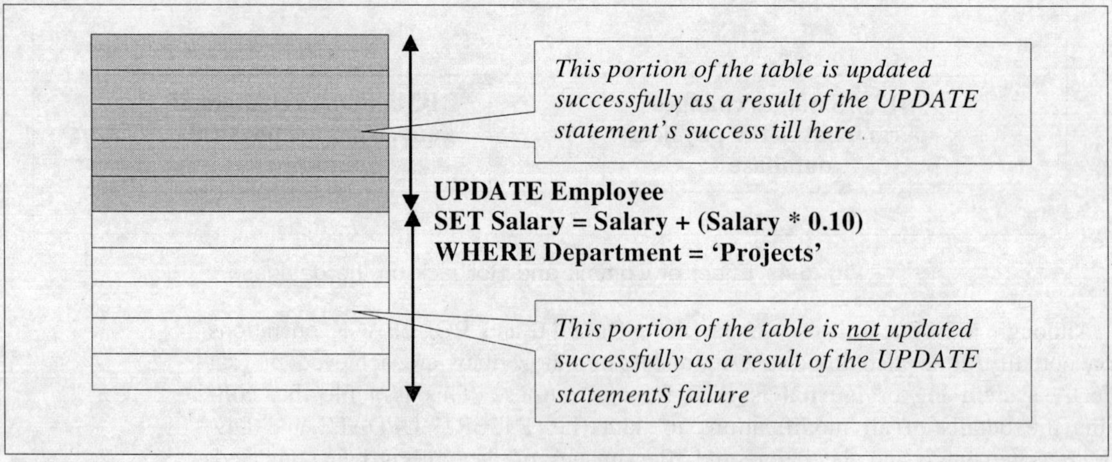

Fig. 5.5 Atomicity of a single update operation

TP monitors do not provide any guarantees regarding such atomicity. Ensuring that the portions of an individual statement are atomic is the responsibility of DBMS. It must ensure that one statement is executed in its entirety or not at all. It cannot allow a statement to make partial updates successful and the remaining ones unsuccessful. Note that we are referring to the INSERT, UPDATE and DELETE statements together as *database updates*.

Another point that should be noted is that one program can contain one or more transactions. Therefore, there may be multiple COMMIT and ROLLBACK statements in the same program. These are not necessarily related to each other. Fig. 5.6 shows an example of a program that contains two transactions. The first transaction is successful and, therefore, committed. The second transaction is unsuccessful and, therefore, rolled back.

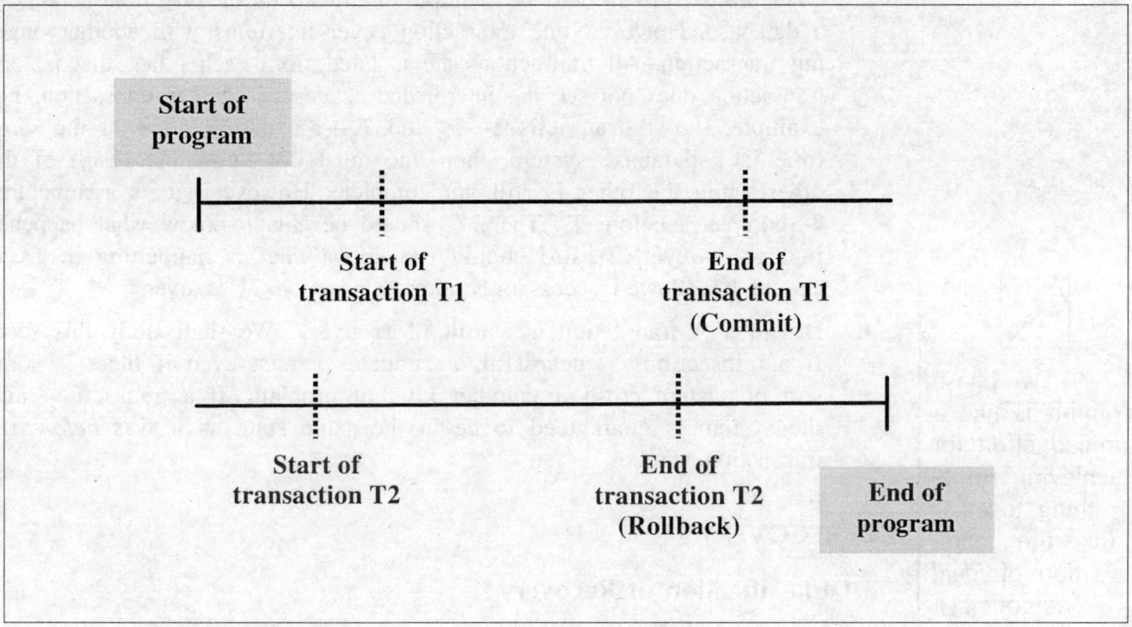

Fig. 5.6 One program can contain multiple transactions

This is quite interesting. Inside one program, not only can there be multiple transactions, but they can have different status, that is success (COMMIT) and failure (ROLL BACK).

5.1.3 Transaction Properties

Transactions are said to depict the ACID properties. Each alphabet in ACID stands for a keyword, as follows:

- *A* stands for Atomic
- *C* stands for Consistent
- *I* stands for Isolation
- *D* stands for Durable

Let us understand the above.

- **Atomic**: A transaction is atomic in nature. This means that it executes exactly once, and ensures that either all the updates to database are completed successfully, or none are implemented at all.
- **Consistent**: We have studied this earlier. A transaction ensures that a database is in a consistent state after it completes (either successfully or in an aborted state). Furthermore, we know that the database consistency is end-to-end (i.e. a database is consistent before a transaction starts and after it ends, but during the lifetime of a transaction, it may not be consistent).
- **Isolation**: A transaction provides isolation from other transactions. In other words, there could be multiple simultaneous ongoing transactions in a database. However, one transaction never interferes with another ongoing transaction. All transactions are isolated from each other, that is, one transaction does not see the intermediate states of another transaction. For example, if two transactions—T_1 and T_2—are taking place at the same time in a database system, then one must not know the result of the other while the other is still not complete. However, let us assume that T_1 completes before T_2. Then, T_2 should be able to know what happened in T_1. However, T_1 still should not know what is happening in T_2. It should be allowed access only after transaction T_2 is over.
- **Durable**: A transaction is a **unit of recovery**. We shall study this soon. If a transaction is successful, its updates persist even if there is some sort of system crash or another kind of problem. If a transaction fails, the system is guaranteed to be in the same state as it was *before* the transaction started.

Two-phase commit is like a unified effort for achieving something together (like the definition of *ideal democracy*). When everybody agrees to do something, the result is much better! In two-phase commit, precisely the same thing happens. All concerned done or even if one participant says *no*, the action is cancelled. It is a collective decision.

5.2 RECOVERY

5.2.1 Classification of Recovery

The concept of **recovery** is closely related to transaction processing. It refers to the recovery of the database itself. Using recovery, we can restore a database to a consistent state. We can perform recovery operations by making copies of the same information elsewhere in the system, so that any missing piece of information can be reconstructed. Note that this is completely different from the ideas related to data redundancy and normalisation.

We can classify recovery as shown in Fig. 5.7.

Let us briefly explain the meaning of these items.

- **Transaction recovery**: This term refers to the recovery of data from transaction failures. Whatever we have discussed so far falls into this category. More specifically, **transaction recovery** talks of recovery of data related to a single transaction. It is not linked with the global system or its state.
- **System recovery**: This category refers to more serious, global failures. **System recovery** is linked with the entire system as a whole. It is not

associated with a single transaction. Clearly, its implications are far more serious as compared to transaction recovery. System recovery is classified further into two sub-categories, as we shall discuss soon.

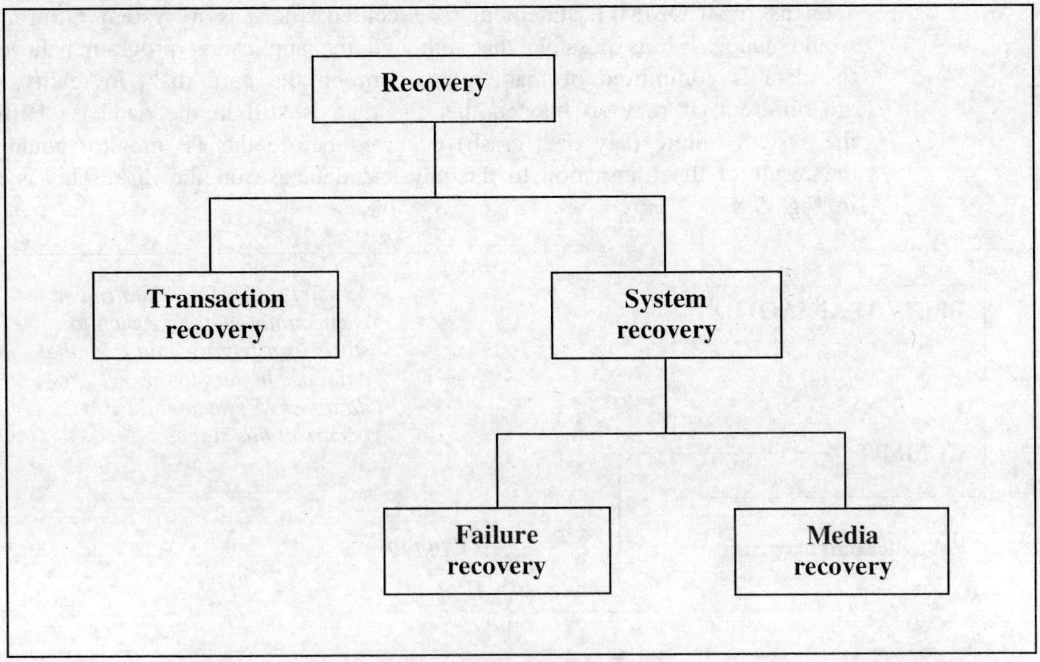

Fig. 5.7 Classification of recovery

We have studied transaction recovery in detail. Hence, we shall not repeat the discussion. We shall now take a look at system recovery.

5.2.2 System Recovery

System recovery can be classified into two categories, as follows.

- **Failure recovery**: This is necessary when a system fails because of reasons such as power failure. However, **failure recovery** is not associated with the media, such as the hard disk. Failure recovery is necessary to recover from *soft* failures so that the associated transactions are not affected.
- **Media recovery**: The failures in this category are caused because the media that hold the data, such as the hard disk, fail. This affects the database, the media, and the transactions that were being processed the time of the media failure. **Media recovery** is, thus, an attempt to recover from such problems.

Let us now discuss the two categories in detail.

5.2.2.1 Failure recovery System failures caused by reasons such as power failure, loss of main memory contents or loss of data in the database buffers need to be examined and dealt with. System recovery is the solution to such problems. When a system failure occurs, invariably the status of all the ongoing transactions is lost. Therefore, a rollback needs to be performed immediately.

Another interesting situation can also occur as a result of system failure. Imagine that a transaction was successful. So, we do a COMMIT on the transaction, and rest assured that the database is in a consistent state. However, as soon as the COMMIT statement is executed, there is a system failure. What would happen? It is possible that although the application program believes that the data is committed or made permanent on the hard disk, in reality, things are different. It may so happen that the data is still in the database buffers as the system failure (say disk crash) occurred before the TP monitor could apply the result of the transaction to the physical database on the disk. This is shown in Fig. 5.8.

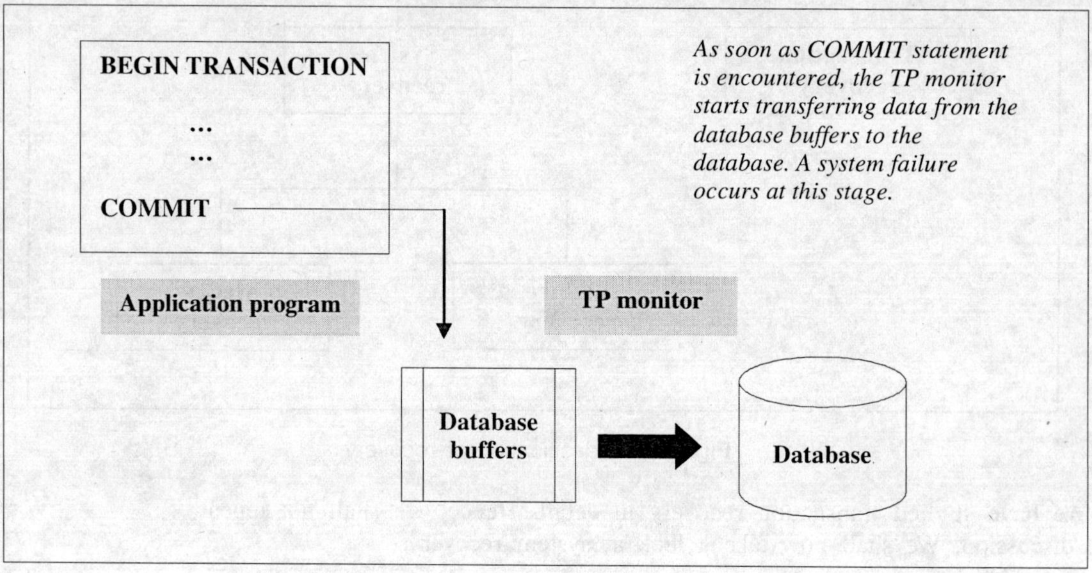

Fig. 5.8 System failure after COMMIT but before physical updates to the database

The result of such a failure is that the database may be in an inconsistent state when the system recovers. How can a system take care of such situations and deal with the emanating problems?

The only way to recover from such failures is to write these values to the log *before* the system failure occurs such that the system restarts, the TP monitor should be able to find these values from the log and write them onto the database. Thus, when a COMMIT statement is encountered, the system should first write the updated values to the log. It should then make attempts to write these updated values to the database. This technique, wherein the log entries precede the database changes, is called a **write-ahead log**.

At this juncture, another question arises—how would the system know which transactions should be redone and which ones should be undone? For this purpose, the system keeps taking periodic **checkpoints** (also called **synch-points**). The taking of check points is a two-step process:

(a) The contents of the database buffers are written (called as **force-written**) to the database.

(b) When this is successful, the system writes special **checkpoint records** to the log. A checkpoint record is a list of transactions that were in progress when the checkpoint was being taken.

We shall illustrate this concept with the help of an example shown in Fig. 5.9. Suppose we have five transactions—A, B, C, D and E. These transactions start and end at different times. Also, two time slots are important, namely:

- TC: This is the time when the last checkpoint was taken.
- TF: This is the time when the system failure occurred.

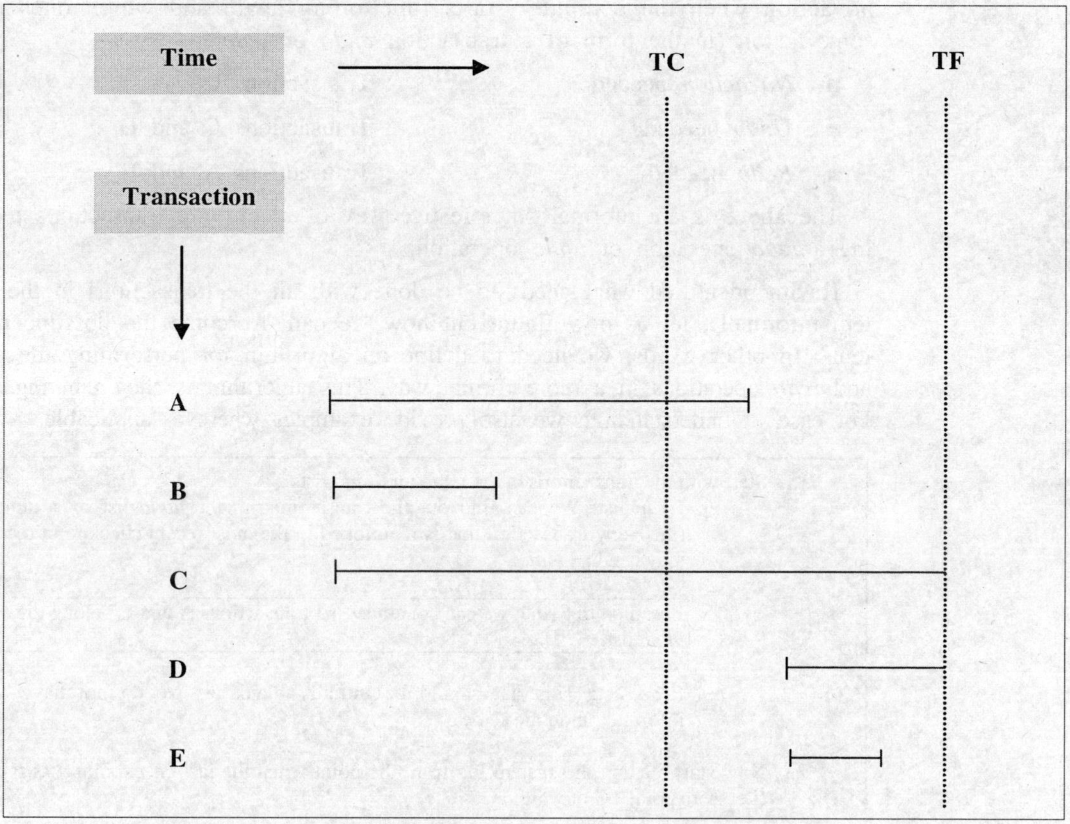

Fig. 5.9 Process of taking checkpoints

Armed with this information, we will draw a hypothetical chart that shows the progress and status of the five transactions A, B, C, D and E.

Let us now examine what is happening with the five transactions.

- *Transaction A*: This transaction started before the checkpoint was taken at time TC. It successfully commited before the system failure occurred. A checkpoint of this transaction was taken at time TC.
- *Transaction B*: This transaction started and also got completed before the checkpoint was taken at time TC.

- *Transaction C*: This transaction started before the checkpoint was taken at point TC and was not completed when the system failure occurred at time TF.
- *Transaction D*: This transaction started after the checkpoint was taken at time TC and was not completed when the system failure occurred at time TF.
- *Transaction E*: This transaction started after the checkpoint was taken at time TC and was completed before the system failure occurred at time TF.

Based on the above descriptions, we need to decide which transactions need no action when the computer starts functioning again and which ones need some action (in the form of a transaction *undo* or *redo*).

- *No action* needed : Transaction B
- *Undo* needed : Transactions C and D
- *Redo* needed : Transactions A and E

The above is an informal but effective way of identifying transactions requiring a *redo* operation or *undo* operation.

Having identified what needs to be done with all the transactions in the system informally, let us now figure out how we can overcome the possible problems. In other words, we need to define an algorithm for performing the *undo* and *redo* operations in a more formal way. This algorithm is shown in Fig. 5.10. For ease of understanding, we also provide examples wherever applicable.

1. Start with the transactions in the *undo* and *redo* lists.
   a. *Undo* list: We can find out the transactions in the *undo* list by a simple rule—any transaction that is mentioned in the most recent checkpoint record may need an *undo*.

      > Based on this rule, we can conclude that transactions A and C belong the *undo* list.

   b. *Redo* list: This list should be initially blank, as we do not have any information on the same.
2. Now start reading the system log from the point when the last checkpoint was taken (i.e. from point TC onwards).
3. Any transaction that has a *BEGIN TRANSACTION* entry in the system log needs to be added to the *undo* list.

   > Based on this rule, transactions D and E need to be added to the *undo* list, which now comprises transactions A, C, D and E.

4. If there is a *COMMIT* entry for a transaction in the system log, move that transaction from the *undo* list to the *redo* list.

   > Based on this rule, transactions A and E would now move from the *undo* list to the *redo* list. So, the *undo* list now is C, D and the *redo* list is now A, E.

Fig. 5.10 Algorithm for identifying transactions that need an *undo* or *redo* operation

We can see that the formal algorithm also yields the same list of *undo* and *redo* transactions as was found by the informal procedure earlier.

Having identified the transactions that need an *undo* operation or a *redo* operation, we do the following:

(a) Work backwards in the system log (i.e. from point TF backwards) and undo the transactions that belong to the *undo* list (i.e. transactions C and D). In simple terms, this means that any data update to any tables that occurred as a part of these two transactions need to be reversed. This is called **backward recovery**.

(b) In the next step redo the transactions that belong to the *redo* list (i.e. transactions A and E). For this, move in the forward direction from the time the last checkpoint was taken (i.e. time TC). To do so, apply the database updates specified in the log since the time the last checkpoint was taken. This is called **forward recovery**.

It is important to state that only when the system recovery is complete can the system accept any new work.

5.2.2.2 Media recovery **Media recovery** is not strictly related to DBMS. However, because media failures can affect a DBMS and its processing severely, we will discuss it in brief.

Media recovery refers to the recovery attempts undertaken when a storage medium, such as a hard disk, that holds a database crashes. Usually, there is a backup procedure that ensures that the database is backed up once a day or so (the frequency can change, depending on requirements). What happens to the transactions that have taken place since the last backup when a media failure occurs? How do we recover any data lost because of such a failure?

For this purpose, a two-step process is used, as follows:

1. Firstly, we need to restore or reload a database from its backup or dump. This would take the database into the state it was in when the last backup was taken.
2. The system log is then used to *redo* all the changes. For this purpose, we need to consider all the activities in the system log since the time the last backup was taken.

This also makes one point clear—the media for transaction processing, system logs and backups must be different. If they are the same, then there is little hope of recovering from *any* sort of failure.

Note that in the case of media failures, there is no place for *undo* activities. This is because such transactions are completely lost. In other words, there is nothing to *undo*. Instead, what we require is a dump/restore or unload/load utility.

- The dump portion of the utility backs up a database as and when needed.
- The restore portion recreates a database from an earlier dump.

Fig. 5.11 illustrates these concepts.

We use recovery principles quite often in our daily life. For example, when we submit original documents for any reason (e.g. insurance claim, getting a visa), we take a photocopy of the same as a precaution. Database recovery operations do the same thing. They take a copy of the data that exists before any update operations are performed in a transaction-enabled environment, so that we can back out in the case of any problems.

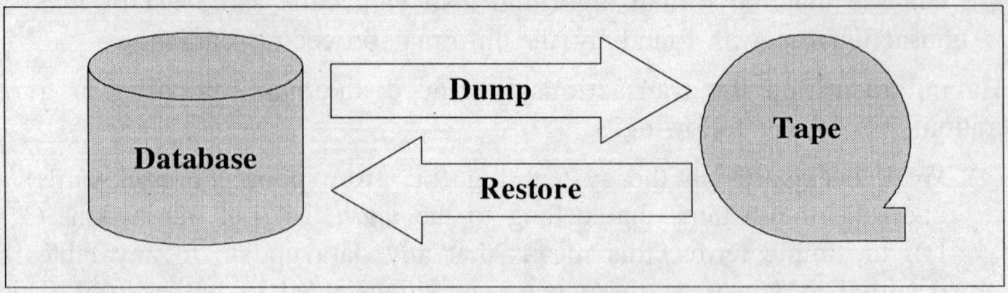

Fig. 5.11 Dump and restore concepts

5.3 TRANSACTION MODELS

Transaction models can be classified into three major types: **flat, chained** and **nested**, as shown in Fig. 5.12.

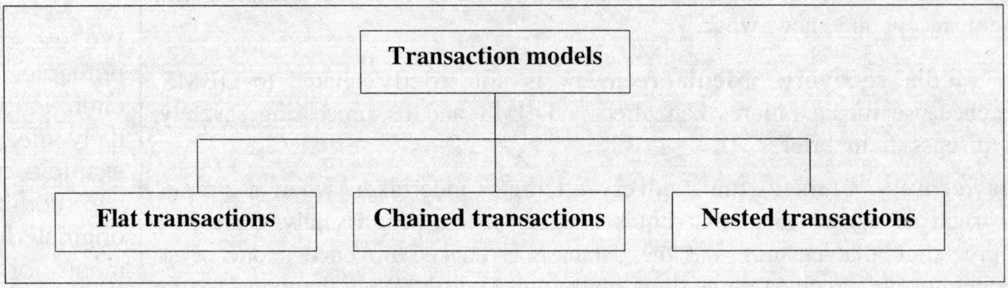

Fig. 5.12 Transaction models

These models are based on questions like:

- When should a transaction start?
- When should a transaction end?
- When should the effects of a transaction be made visible to the outside world?
- What is the right way of recovery in the case of transaction failures?

Depending on the answers to these questions, let us discuss the three transaction models in brief.

5.3.1 Flat Transactions

Flat transactions involve three main steps:

- The transaction begins with an identifier such as *BEGIN TRANSACTION*, which identifies that a transaction has begun.
- In the second step (which is actually the main reason why the transaction is required), the actual operations in the transaction (such as database reads, updates, deletions or insertions) take place.
- If the second step is successfully completed in all respects, the third step finalises the transaction with the help of an identifier such as *COMMIT*.

However, if even a single operation in the second step fails, the third step cancels the *whole* transaction, which is signified by a *ROLLBACK* operation. This is shown in Fig. 5.13.

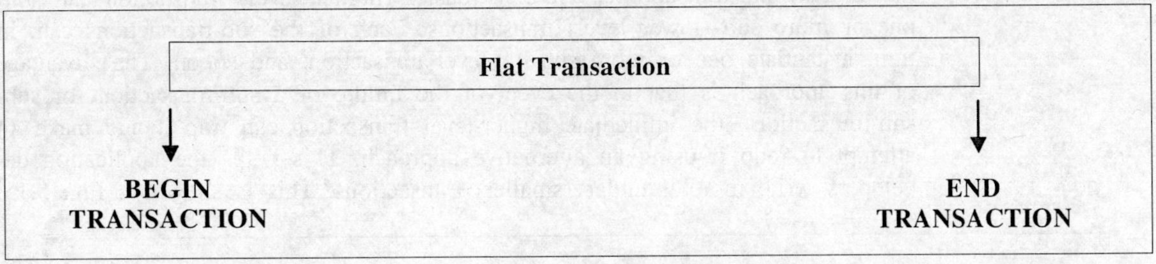

Fig. 5.13 Flat transaction

As evident, the approach taken by flat transaction is quite simple and straightforward. Therefore, it is very widely used in real practice. However, it also has some weaknesses. For example, suppose a transaction needs to update one million records in a single database. Assume that the transaction is almost through and has updated 999900 out of the one million records when an error occures. Obviously, to maintain consistency, the transaction must be aborted (i.e. rolled back) and all the database updates done up to this point will need to be discarded! Such an experience can be quite wasteful and frustrating.

5.3.2 Chained Transactions

In chained transactions, we have many mini-transactions within a main transaction. Therefore, extending our earlier example, we can have one mini-transaction for every 1000 records, and thus commit the database changes after every 1000th *update* call in an update operation involving one million records. With this scheme, in the event of any error, we need not roll back the whole transaction – we need to roll back the last 999 updates at the most. Clearly, this is highly convenient. This is shown in Fig. 5.14.

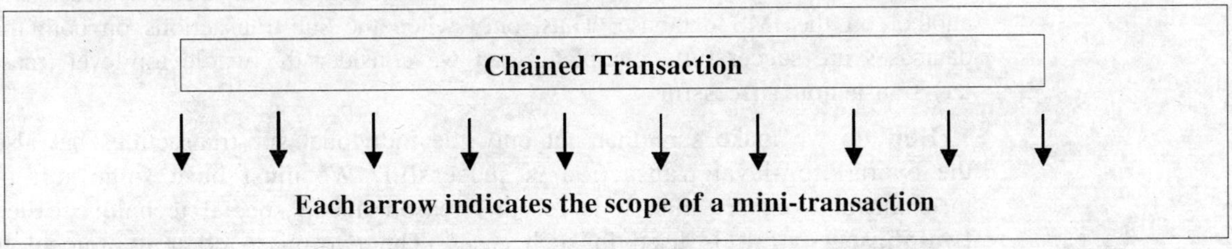

Fig 5.14 Chained transaction

We will realise that this is quite similar to taking periodic checkpoints. The only difference between the checkpoints that we had discussed earlier and these checkpoints is that the former is handled at a system level (i.e. by the DBMS), whereas the latter is an application-level feature in which the application programmer provides for periodic checkpoints.

5.3.3 Nested Transactions

The concept of **nested transactions** introduces a hierarchical relationship of master and sub-transactions. Here, a master (higher level) transaction can start one or more sub (lower level) transactions. Each of the sub-transactions can, in turn, instantiate one or more sub-sub-level transaction, and so on. The advantage of this approach is that in the event of the failure of a sub-transaction (or sub-sub-transaction), the immediate higher-level transaction can trap it and make an attempt to redo it using an alternative approach. This helps the application developers write more granular (smaller) transactions. This is shown in Fig. 5.15.

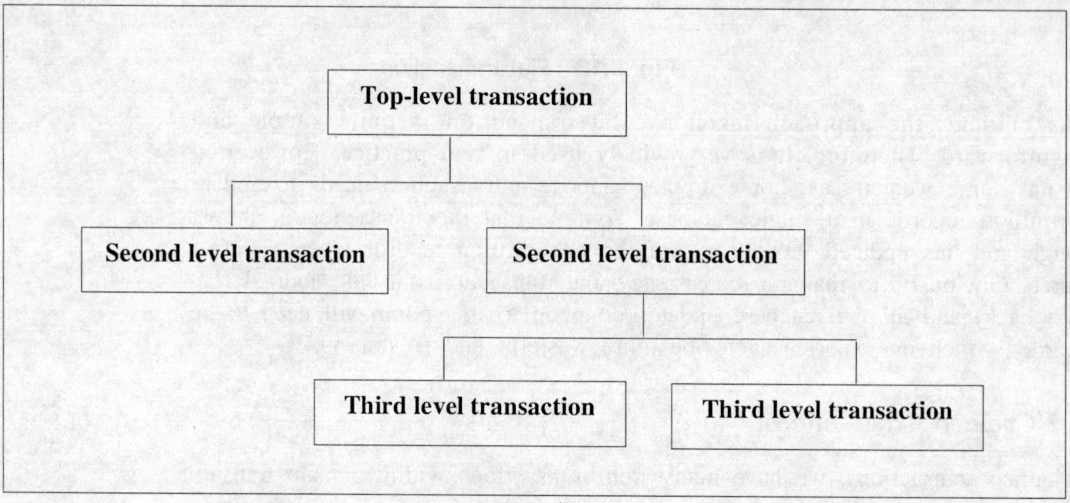

Fig. 5.15 Nested transaction

5.4 TWO-PHASE COMMIT

At times, nested transactions can span across databases. For example, one top-level transaction may consist of one sub-transaction on the DB2 database and another on the IMS database. Thus, only when the sub-transactions on both the databases are successfully completed can we consider the whole top-level (master) transaction successful.

How do we make sure that not only the individual sub-transactions but also the overall top-level transaction is successful? We must have some sort of mechanism to ensure this. It is for this reason that a special technique called **two-phase commit** is used in such cases. The two-phase commit protocol is used to synchronise updates on two or more databases that run on physically different computers. This ensures that either all of them succeed or all of them fail. Thus, it is a *transaction of transactions*.

The database as a whole, therefore, is not left in an inconsistent state. To achieve this, a central **coordinator** (one of the database machines) is designated, which coordinates the synchronisation of the commit/rollback operations. Other **participants** in the two-phase commit protocol have the right to either say *OK, I can COMMIT now* or *No, I cannot COMMIT now*. Accordingly, the central coordinator takes a decision about committing the transaction or rolling it back. For committing, the central coordinator must get an OK from all the participants. Even if one of the participants cannot commit because of reason, all the participants must roll the transaction back. This works as follows:

- **Phase 1 (Prepare phase)**: In this phase, the central coordinator sends a *Prepare to COMMIT* message to all the participants of the transaction. In response, each participant sends either a *Ready to COMMIT* or *Cannot COMMIT* message back to the central coordinator, depending on whether they can go ahead with the committing of the transaction or not. This is shown in Fig. 5.16.

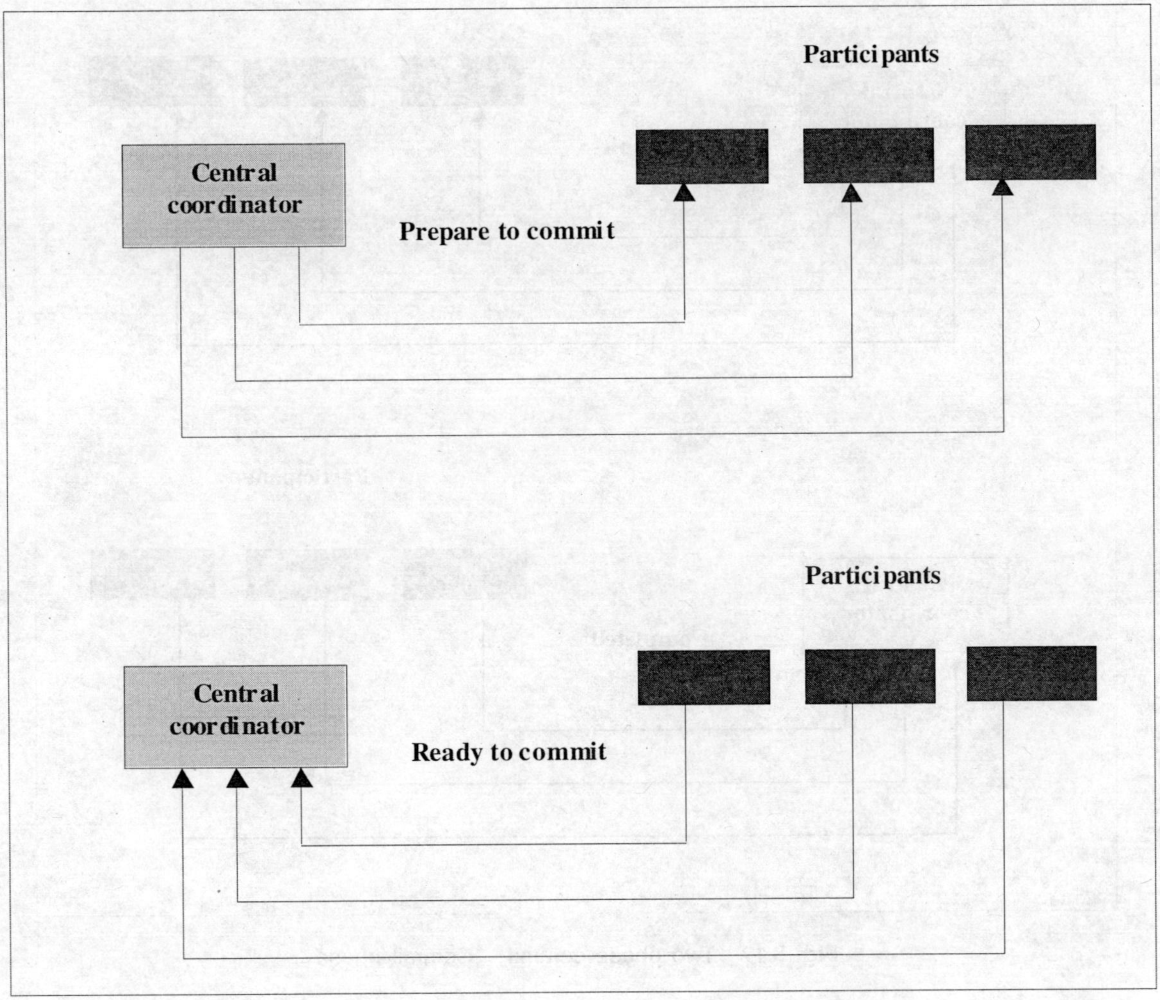

Fig. 5.16 Two phase commit – Prepare phase

- **Phase 2 (Commit phase)**: Only if the central coordinator receives a *Ready to COMMIT* reply from all the participants in Phase 1, can it send a *COMMIT* message to all the participants. Otherwise, it sends a

ROLLBACK message to all the participants. Assuming that the central coordinator has sent a *COMMIT* message, all the participants now commit the transaction and send a *Completed* message back to the coordinator. If any of the participants fails in the commit process, for any reason, that participant sends back a *ROLLBACK* message to the central coordinator. If the central coordinator receives even one *ROLLBACK*, it asks all the participants to roll back. Otherwise, the whole transaction is considered as successful. This is shown in Fig. 5.17.

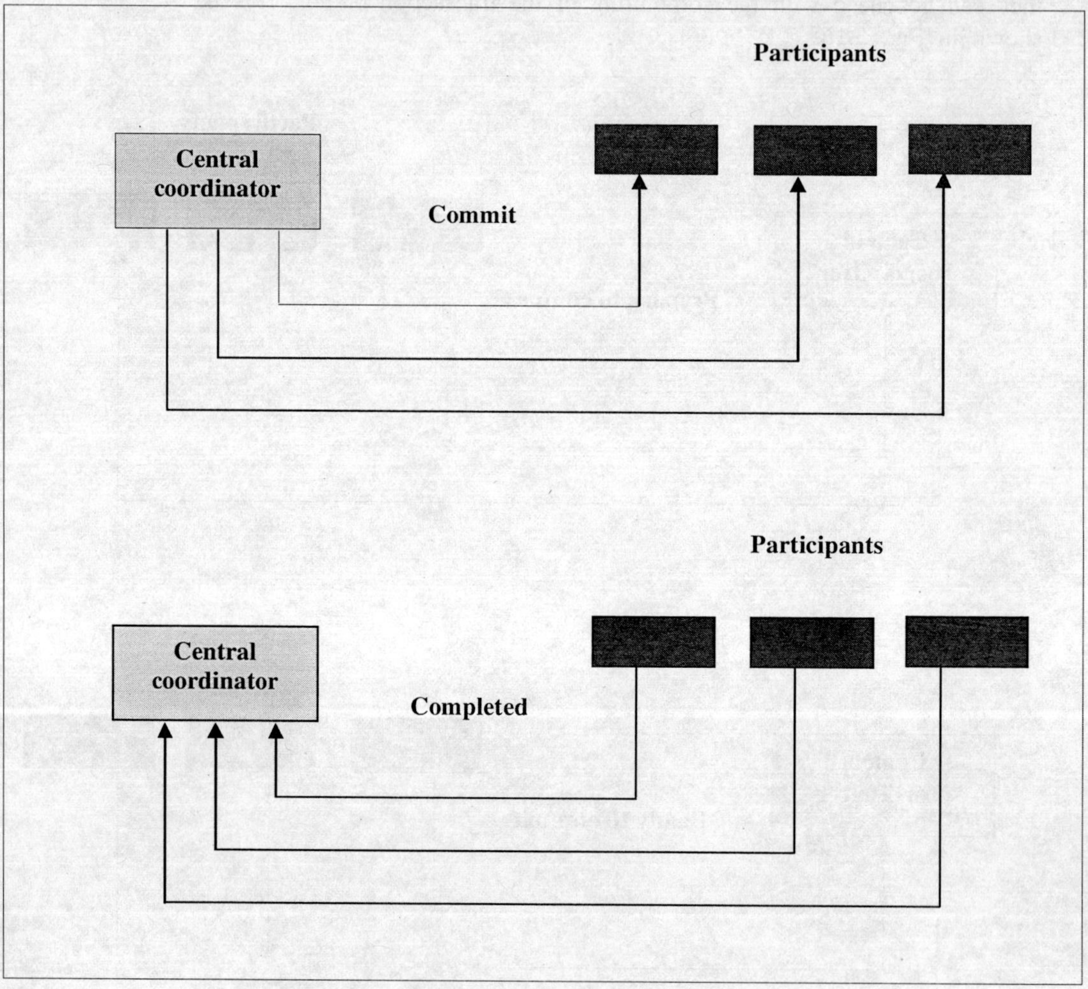

Fig. 5.17 Two phase commit – Commit phase

5.5 CONCURRENCY PROBLEMS

A database can have multiple transactions running at the same time. This is called **concurrency.**

These **concurrent transactions** may perform various database updates simultaneously. Therefore, a mechanism is required to ensure that these transactions do not interfere with each other.

> A mechanism which ensures that simultaneous execution of more than one transaction does not lead to any database inconstancies is called **concurrency control mechanism.**

Suppose transaction A is updating table X. What if another transaction, B, also updates the same table X a bit later, before transaction A is complete? Clearly, this would lead to a lot of problems and as a result. Table X may not retain its integrity. This is precisely the kind of problem that can occur in the absence of concurrency control mechanisms. Any such problem is called **concurrency problem**.

Classically, concurrency problems are classified into four categories, as shown in Fig. 5.18.

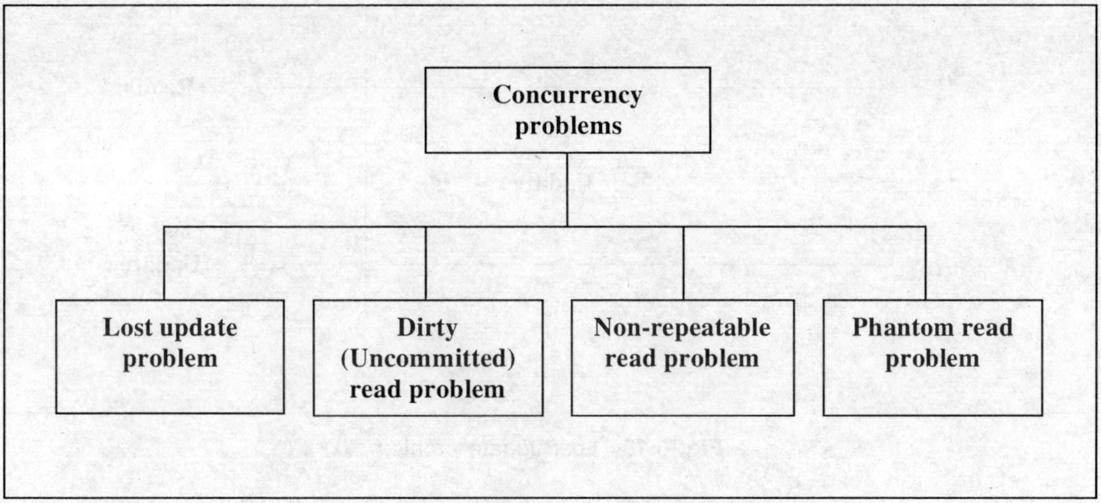

Fig. 5.18 Concurrency problems

Now we shall discuss these problems which are best explained with the help of examples, rather than explanations. So, we shall use examples to illustrate the possible problems in the various categories of concurrency problems.

5.5.1 Lost Update Problem

Consider the situation depicted in Fig. 5.19.

The sequence of events is as follows:

1. At time t_1, transaction A reads a row r of a table.
2. At time t_2, transaction B also reads the same row r.
3. At time t_3, transaction A updates a column value in row r.
4. At time t_4, transaction B updates the same column value in row r.

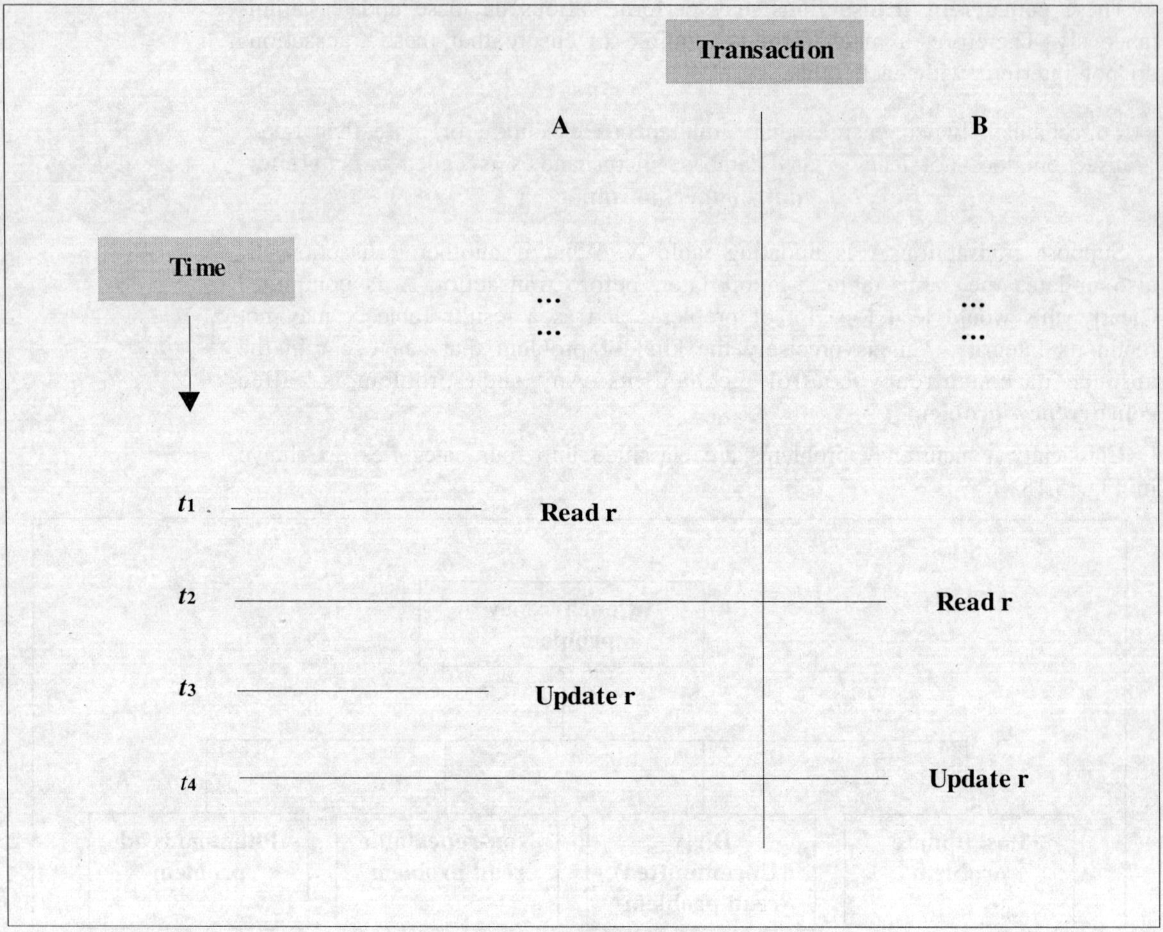

Fig. 5.19 Lost update problem

The result of this sequence of events is that the update made by transaction A in step 3 is overwritten or lost because of the update made by transaction B in step 4. Therefore, such a problem it is termed as the **lost update problem**.

Let us illustrate this with the help of an example in SQL as shown in Fig. 5.20.

We can see that at times t_1 and t_2, transactions A and B respectively read (SELECT) the value of the column *Salary* from table *Employee* for *Emp_number* 101. The value turns out to be 10000. At time t_3, transaction A increments the salary value to 12000, and commits its changes. Next, at time t_4, transaction B sets the salary value to 14000 without even looking at what transaction A has done in step 3.

It can be argued that even if these (i.e. A and B) were not concurrent transactions, (say transaction A happens today and transaction B happens a week later) the result would have been the same. That is, transaction B would have anyway overwritten the updates of transaction A. Then, is this a concurrency problem at all? Well, it is. Ideally, any update operation should know what it is trying to update and also the value before it begins updating. That *is* the problem here. More specifically, transaction B believed that the value of the *Salary* column for this employee was 10000 (whereas it was actually 12000) and then set it to 14000. So, was the intention to add 4000 to the value that it believed to be current? If that was the case, would it have added just 2000 if it knew that the current value is actually 12000 and not 10000 or did it want to add 4000 to whatever was the current value (in which case, the final value should have been 16000)? All this creates confusion.

Time	Transaction A	Transaction B	State of the database
	...	...	
	...	...	
t_1	SELECT salary FROM Employee WHERE Emp_Number = 101;		Salary = 10000
t_2		SELECT salary FROM Employee WHERE Emp_Number = 101;	Salary = 10000
t_3	UPDATE Employee SET Salary = 12000 WHERE Emp_Number = 101; COMMIT;		Salary = 12000
t_4		UPDATE Employee SET Salary = 14000 WHERE Emp_Number = 101; COMMIT;	Salary = 14000

Fig. 5.20 Lost update – SQL example

Of course, such problems could also be avoided by writing the queries in another fashion. For instance, transaction A could have written the following query:

```
UPDATE Employee
SET Salary = Salary * 1.20
WHERE Emp_Number = 101;
COMMIT;
```

Next, transaction B could have written the following query:

```
UPDATE Employee
SET Salary = Salary * 1.40
WHERE Emp_Number = 101;
COMMIT;
```

Now, the intention of both the transactions–A and B–is quite clear. The two transactions wanted to increment the current value of salary by 20% and 40% respectively, whatever the current value may be.

To summarise, the updates made by transaction A are overwritten or lost in this problem.

5.5.2 Dirty (Uncommitted) Read Problem

The **dirty (uncommitted) read problem**, also called **uncommitted dependency problem**, is caused when a transaction (say A) retrieves, or even worse, updates a row updated by another uncommitted transaction (say B). We need to discuss two cases in this context.

Case 1

Fig. 5.21 illustrates the first case. Here, transaction A retrieves a row updated but not yet committed by transaction B.

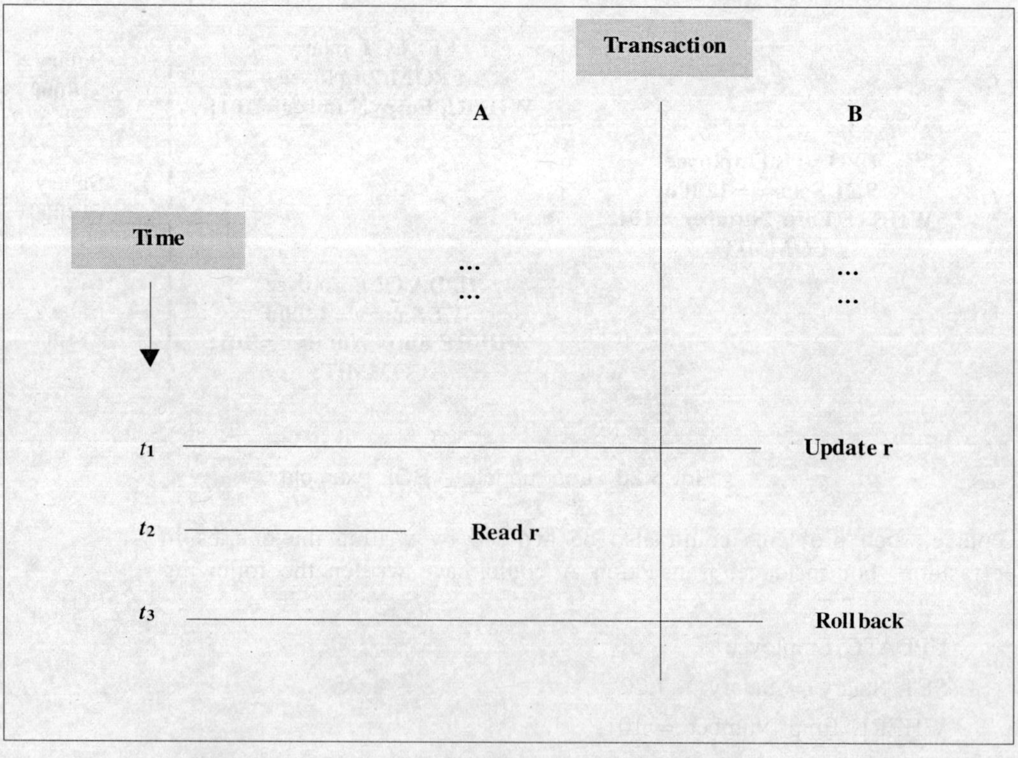

Fig. 5.21 Dirty (Uncommitted) read problem: Case 1

The sequence of events is as follows.

1. At time t_1, transaction B updates a row r of a table.
2. At time t_2, transaction A reads the same row r.
3. At time t_3, transaction B does a *ROLLBACK*.

The problem with this scheme is that at time t_2, transaction A has retrieved a row that has an uncommitted value. After transaction B does a *ROLLBACK* at time t_3, this uncommitted value disappears from the table. Therefore, if transaction A performs any action based on this value, it would be faulty.

In other words, at time t_2, transaction A believes that the value in the row is as *before* time t_1, whereas, in reality, it has seen a non-existent value, which is going to disappear soon.

It is also worth noting that transaction B cannot be blamed for this problem. It has faithfully performed an update, only to realise later that the update operation should not have been executed. Therefore, in its own right, it has done a *ROLLBACK*. It does not even know that transaction A would suffer because of this.

Fig. 5.22 shows an example of this problem.

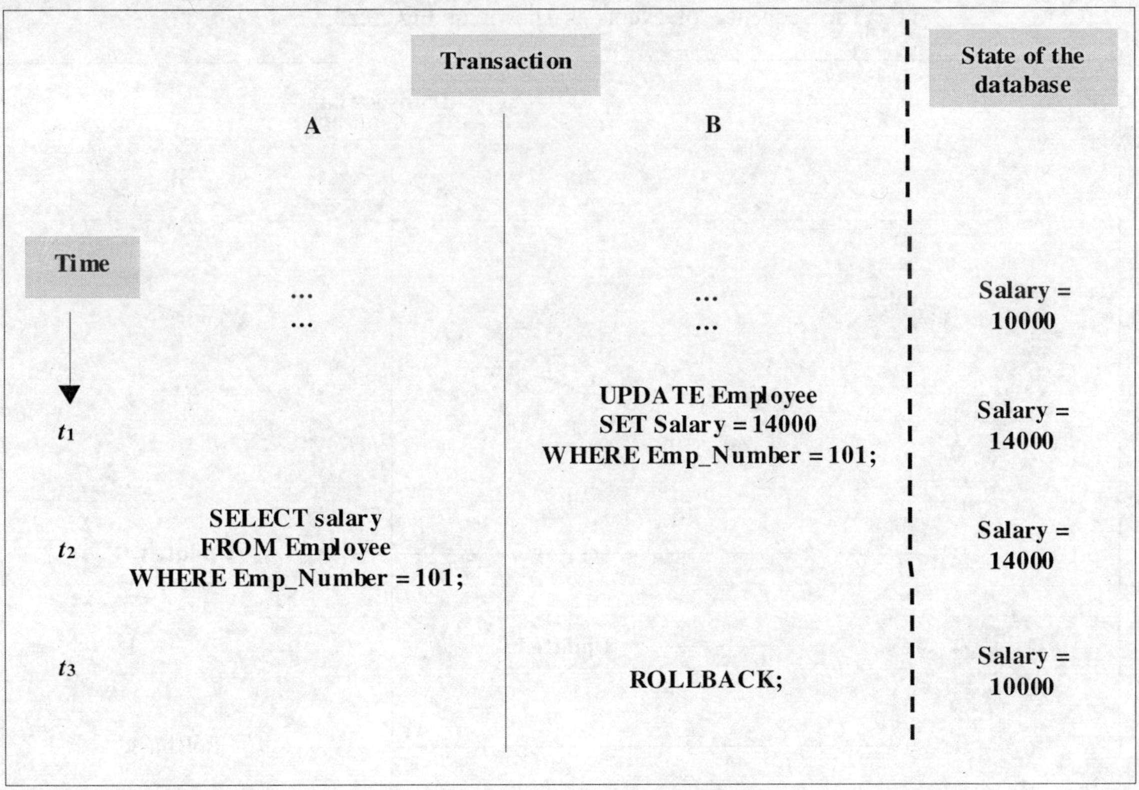

Fig. 5.22 Dirty (Uncommitted) read problem: Case 1 – SQL example

We can see that at time t_1, transaction B updates the salary for employee number 101 to 14000. However, it neither commits the transaction, nor rolls it back. Let us assume further that at time t_2, transaction A selects the same row, thus fetching a value of 14000. For some reason, the update performed by transaction B at time t_1 has problems. Therefore, at time t_3, transaction B performs a *ROLLBACK*. Thus, the value of salary again becomes 10000. Now imagine that transaction A performs a few operations, such as taking a decision based on the value of salary for this employee, at the non-existent time t_4. Note that this decision is based on the assumption that the value of the salary is 14000, whereas it actually is 10000. Thus, we can see that transaction A performs a *dirty read*, also called as an *uncommitted read*, at time t_2. This transaction subsequently gets rolled back and thus transaction A it is misled.

Case 2

This problem is quite similar to the problem in the earlier situation except for one difference. Recall that in the earlier case, at time t_2, transaction A performs a dirty (uncommitted) read. In other words, it retrieves a value that is not committed, and which subsequently gets rolled back. Now, the problem is worse. Transaction A does not retrieve a value that is not committed – it updates it once more after which transaction B overwrites it anyway, by doing a *ROLLBACK*.

The sequence of events is shown in Fig. 5.23.

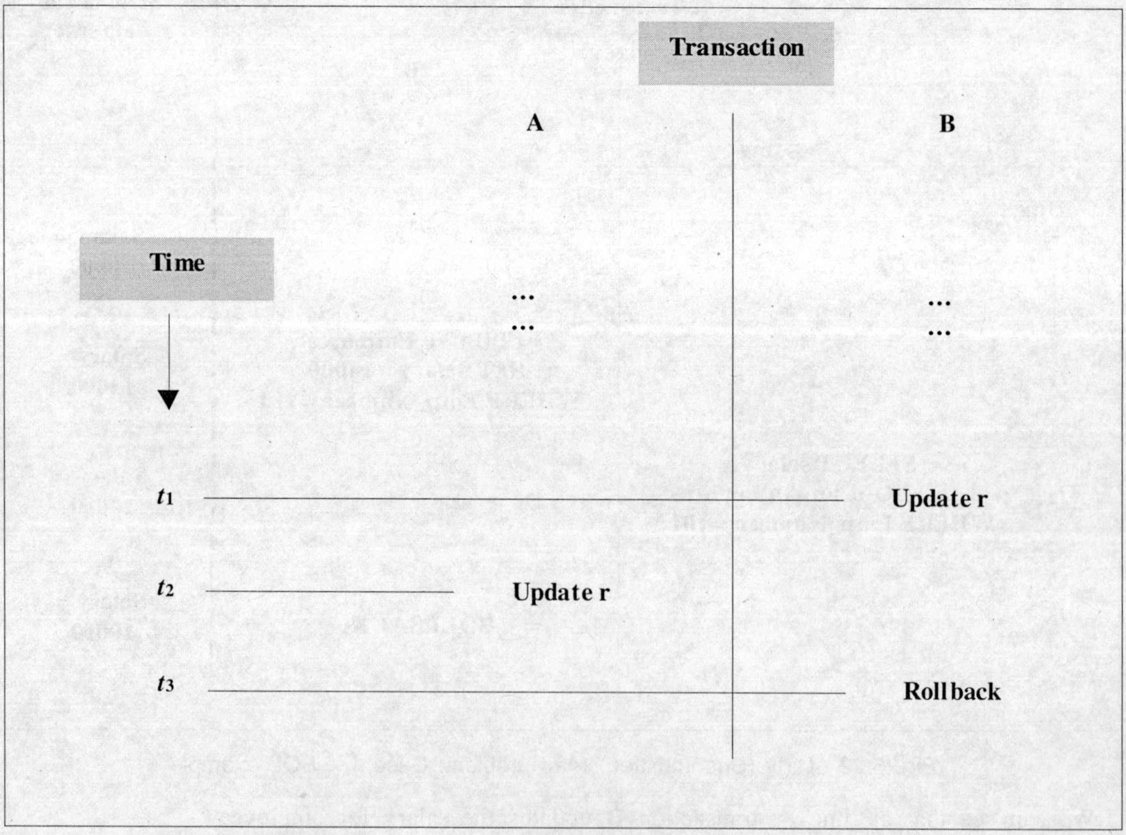

Fig. 5.23 Dirty (Uncommitted) read problem: Case 2

As we can see, there are two updates now, one over the other, in quick succession. After this, the transaction that made the first update (transaction B) does a *ROLLBACK*. As a result, the update done by transaction A at time t_2 is lost. At the end of time t_3, the database would go back to the state that it was in prior to time t_1. Transaction B thinks that it has rolled back its update done at time t_1. Instead, it has unknowingly rolled back the update done by transaction A at time t_2.

Let us illustrate this problem with the help of an example, as depicted in Fig. 5.24.

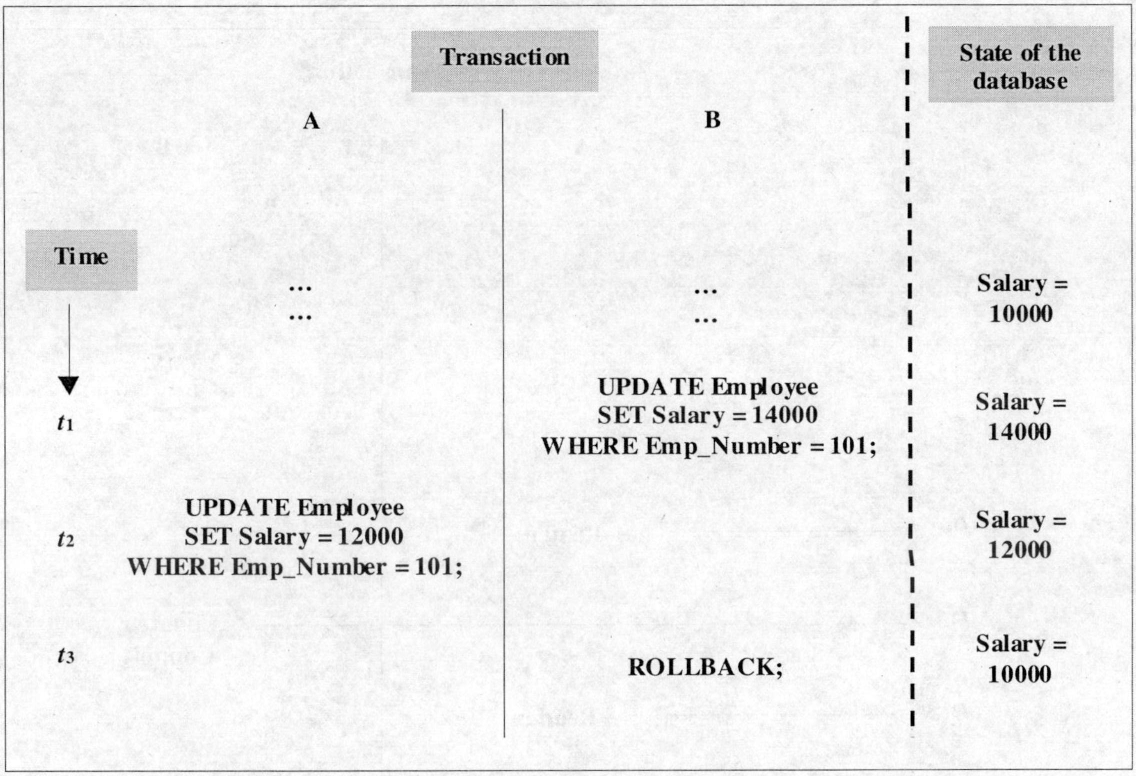

Fig. 5.24 Dirty (Uncommitted) read problem: Case 2 – SQL example

The initial value of salary for employee number 101 is 10000. At time t_1, transaction B updates it to 14000 without committing its changes. At time t_2, transaction A overwrites it with 12000, again without performing a *COMMIT*. At time t_3, transaction B performs a *ROLLBACK*, undoing the changes done by both transactions A and B at times t_1 and t_2. Thus, the database goes back to the state, which it was in prior to time t_1. In other words, salary is again 10000.

5.5.3 Non-Repeatable Read Problem

The **non-repeatable read problem**, also known as the **inconsistent analysis problem**, occurs when a transaction sees two different values for the same row within its lifetime. For example let us assume that transaction A retrieves a row from a table, after which transaction B updates the same row and commits its changes. Immediately afterwards, transaction A once again retrieves the same row from the same table. Because transaction B has updated the row in the meantime, transaction A would now see a value that is *different* from the value it had retrieved earlier. We can see that transaction B cannot repeat its reading operation (actually, the results of its read operation do not repeat). Hence the name *non-repeatable read*.

Fig. 5.25 shows the idea behind a non-repeatable read problem.

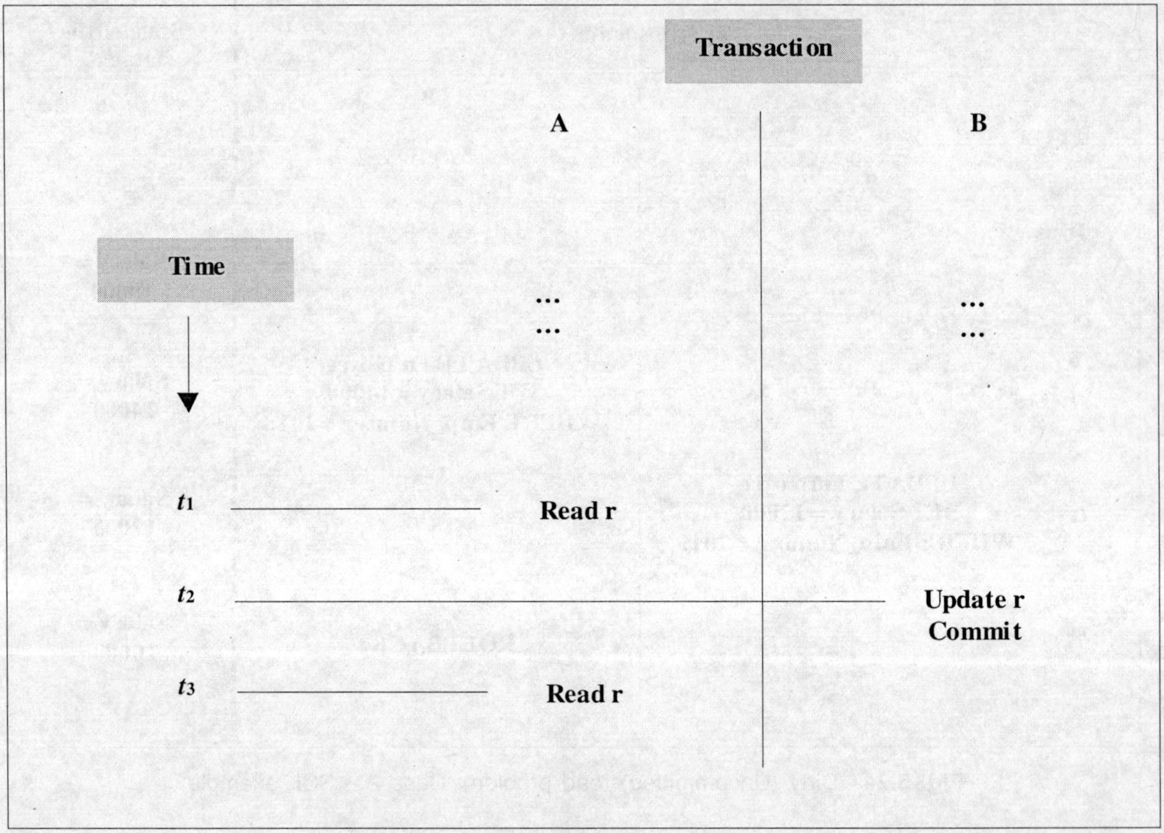

Fig. 5.25 Non-repeatable read problem

The sequence of events is as follows.

1. At time t_1, transaction A reads a row r of a table.
2. At time t_2, transaction B updates the same row r, and performs a *COMMIT* operation.
3. At time t_3, transaction A again attempts to retrieve the same row r. Because transaction B has changed the value of the row r at time t_2, transaction A will now get a value that is different from what it had obtained at time t_1.

Note that this is quite different from the *dirty (uncommitted) read problem*, studied earlier. Here, we are talking about one transaction A being fooled because the other transaction B has committed its changes during the lifetime of A. This can be a problem, if transaction A needs to perform some sort of decision-making operation based on the old value. For example, what if transaction A reads the database, performs some operations, and again reads the database to derive a new value based on the old value. It would get inconsistent results.

We shall consider two examples to illustrate this problem, since it can be quite easily confused with the *dirty (uncommitted) read problem*. Fig. 5.26 shows the first example.

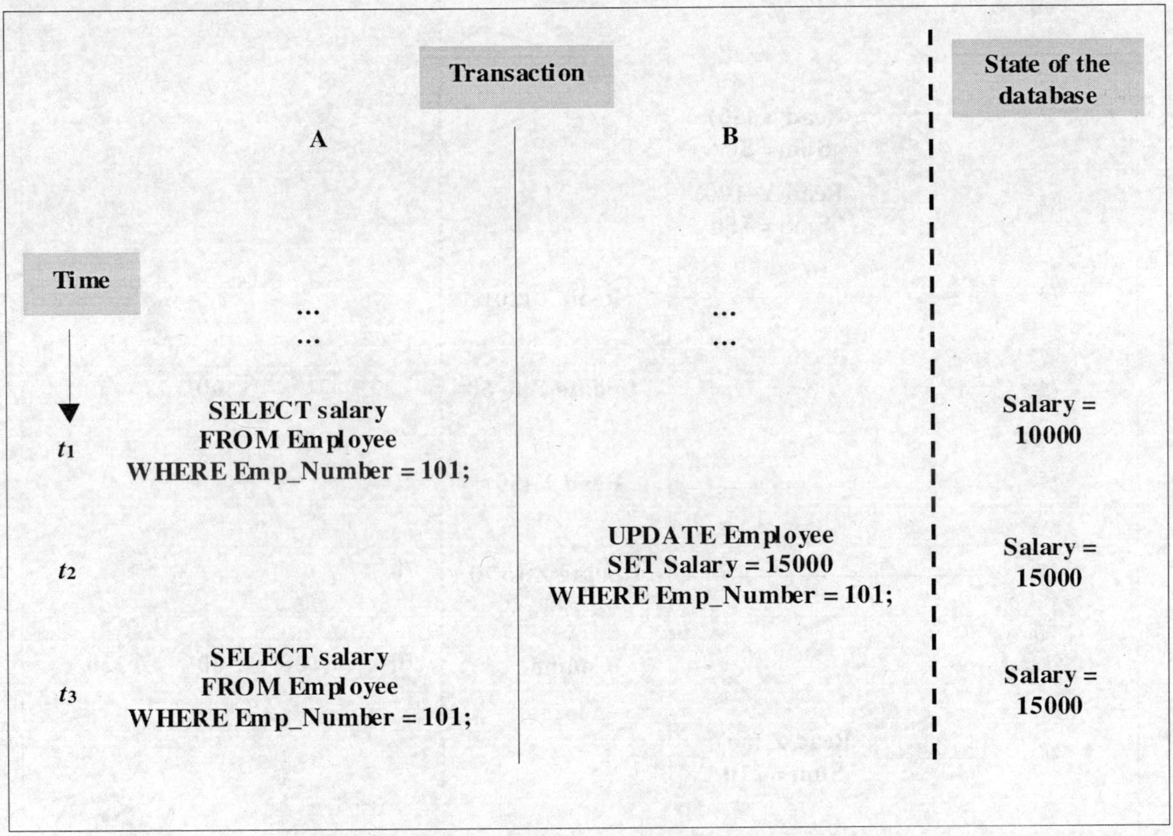

Fig. 5.26 Non-repeatable read problem: SQL example

Transaction A reads the salary value as 10000 and as 15000 at times t_1 and t_3 respectively. These two steps can take place within a few seconds. In the meantime, transaction B has changed the value of the salary from 10000 to 15000 at time t_2. This change fooled transaction A.

Let us consider a more detailed example, which can explain the problem in depth, as illustrated in Fig. 5.27. We shall avoid SQL syntaxes to save space.

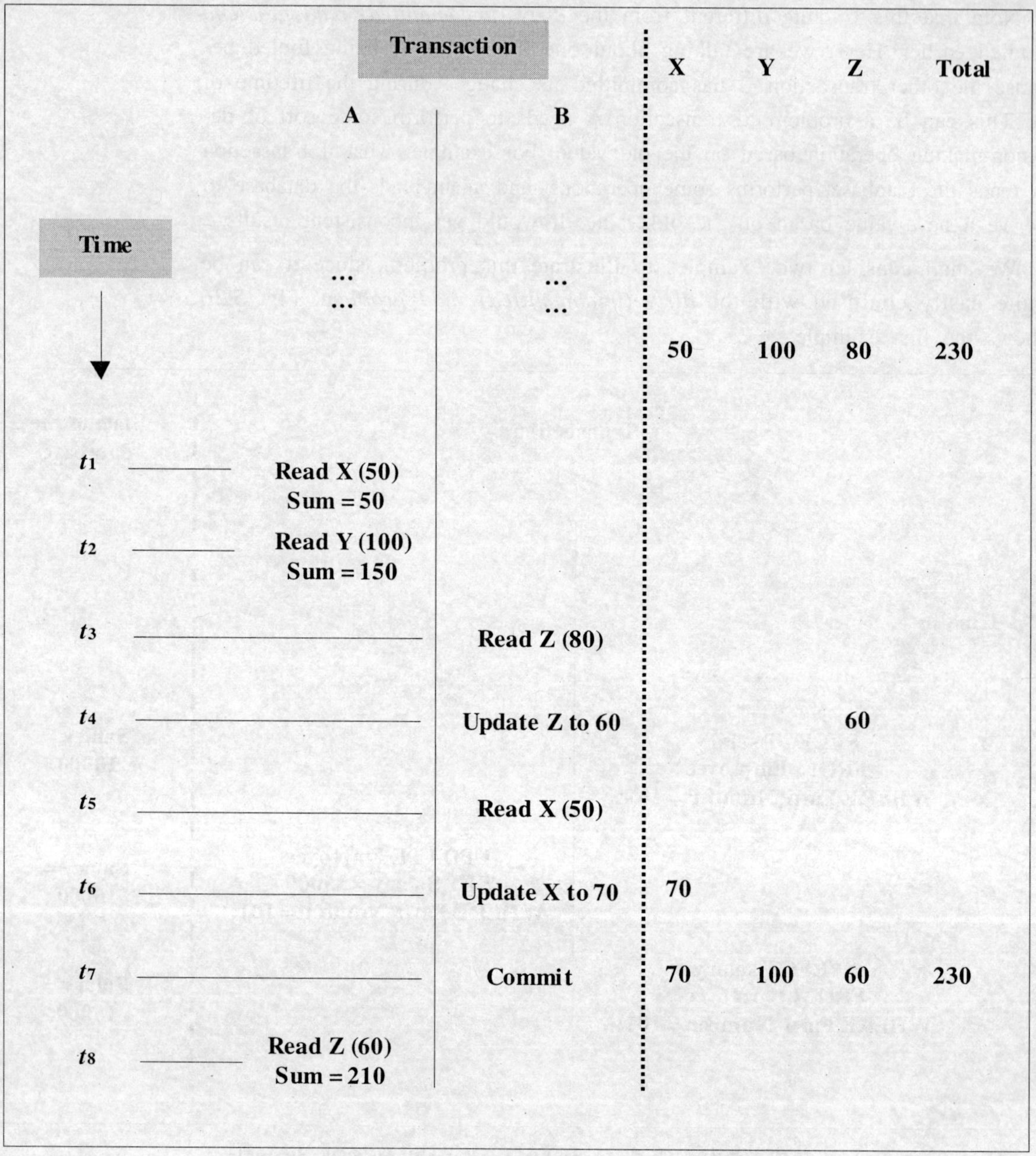

Fig. 5.27 Non-repeatable read problem: second example

We consider three variables—X, Y, and Z. Transaction A wants to add the values of these three variables to calculate the sum. It performs three read and summation operations at time t_1, t_2 and t_8. In the meantime, transaction B reads and updates the value of Z at times t_3 and t_4 and that of X at times t_5 and t_6. It commits its changes at time t_7. Therefore, between times t_2 and t_8, the state of the database changes considerably. Thus, transaction A calculates the sum of X, Y and Z as 210 based on the original values of X (50) and Y (100) and the changed value of Z (60). However, it does not realise that X is also changed to 70 and, therefore, the sum of X, Y and Z should actually be 70 + 100 + 60 = 230, and not 210.

5.5.4 Phantom Read Problem

The **phantom read problem** (also called as **phantom insert problem**) is a special case of the *non-repeatable read problem*. We know that in the example the *non-repeatable read problem* occurs when transaction B does some updates before transaction A completes its reading operations. In the *phantom insert problem*, however, transaction A is fooled because transaction B inserts a row before it completes its reading operation. In principle, it is similar to the *non-repeatable read problem*. This is shown in Fig. 5.28.

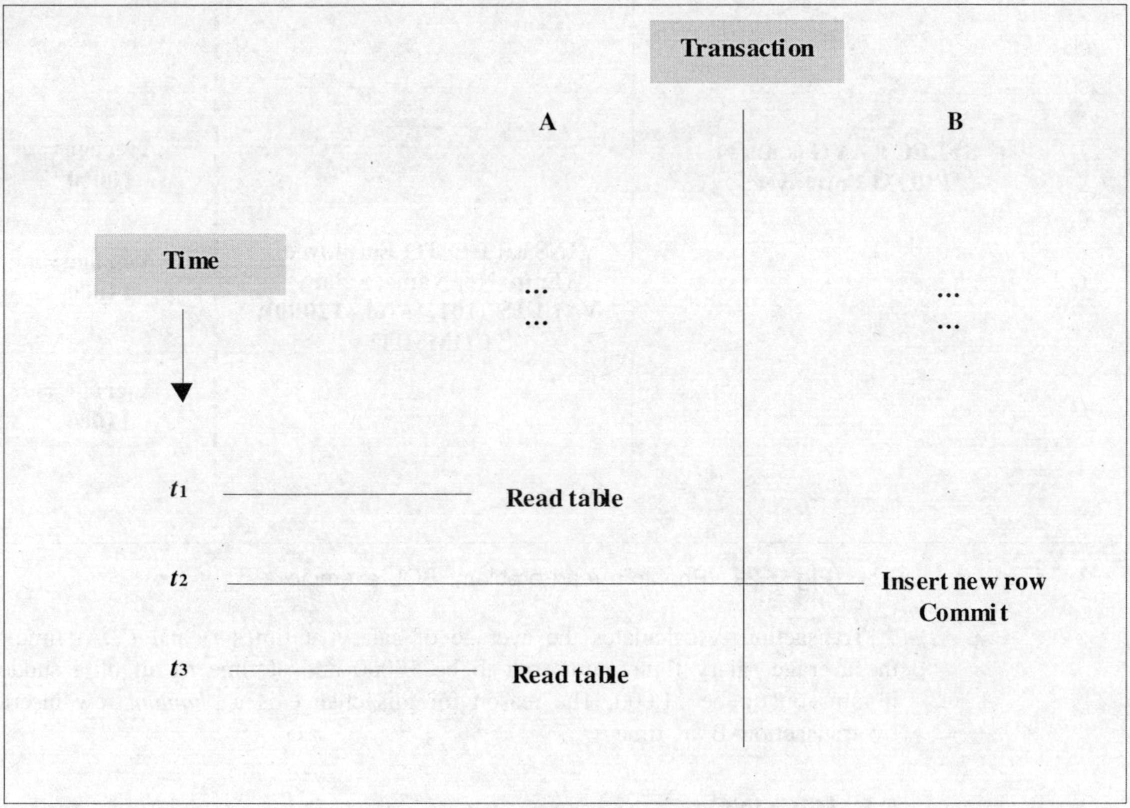

Fig. 5.28 Phantom read problem

In the given case, the sequence of events is as follows.

1. At time t_1, transaction A reads some rows of a table.
2. At time t_2, transaction B inserts a new row in the table, and performs a *COMMIT* operation.
3. At time t_3, transaction A again attempts to retrieve the same rows as it had done at time t_1. Because transaction B has inserted a new row at

time t_2, transaction A will now get a value that is different from what it had obtained at time t_1.

Let us understand this with a simple example, as shown in Fig. 5.29.

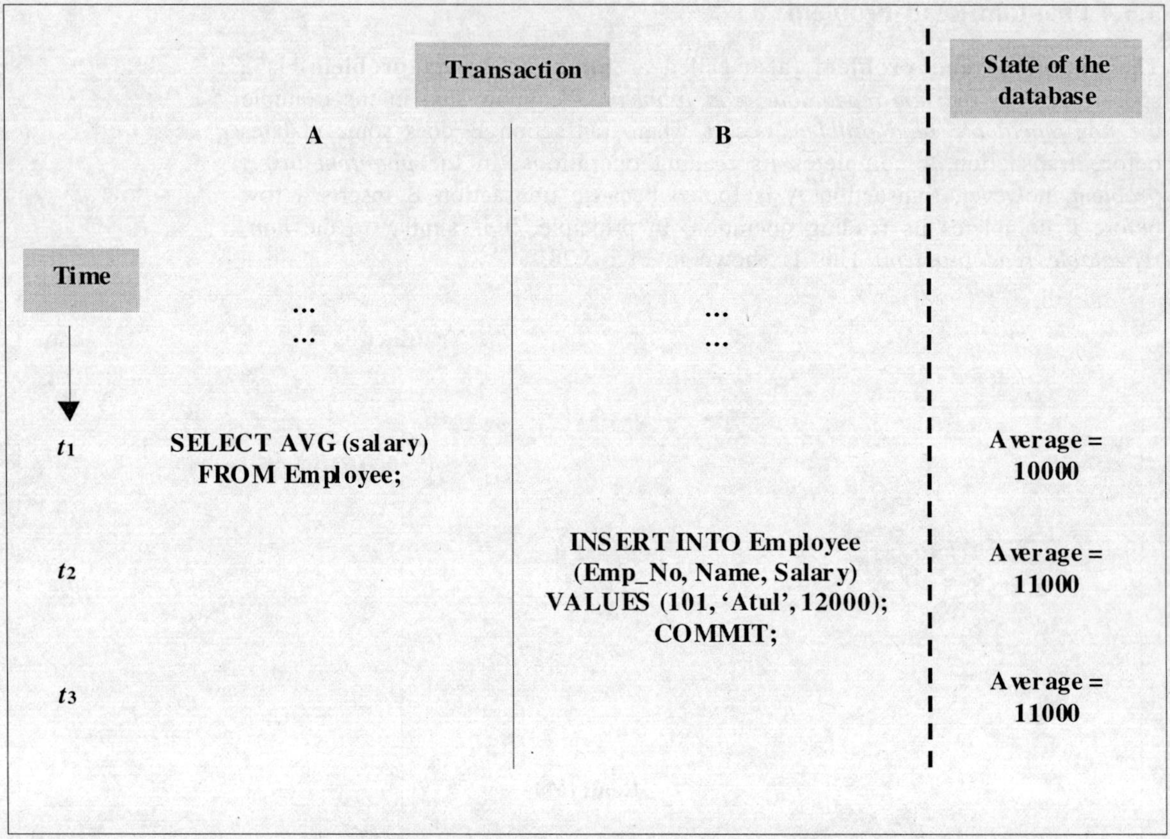

Fig. 5.29 Phantom read problem: SQL example

Transaction A calculates the average of salary at times t_1 and t_3. At time t_1, the average salary figure turns out to be 10000 and at time t_3, all of a sudden, it turns out to be 11,000. The reason for this change is a *phantom* row inserted by transaction B at time t_2.

5.6 LOCKING

The concept of **locking** is used to solve concurrency problems. The idea behind this concepts is that when one transaction needs an object (for example, a row in a database table), it should acquire a **lock** on that object. In other words, it should *lock* the *other transactions* in the system *out of* that object. This would disallow those transactions from making any changes to that object. In effect, it can do any changes that it wants, without encountering any problems. Locks can be classified into two types: **exclusive (X)**, also called **write** and **shared (S)**, also called **read**. This is shown in Fig. 5.30.

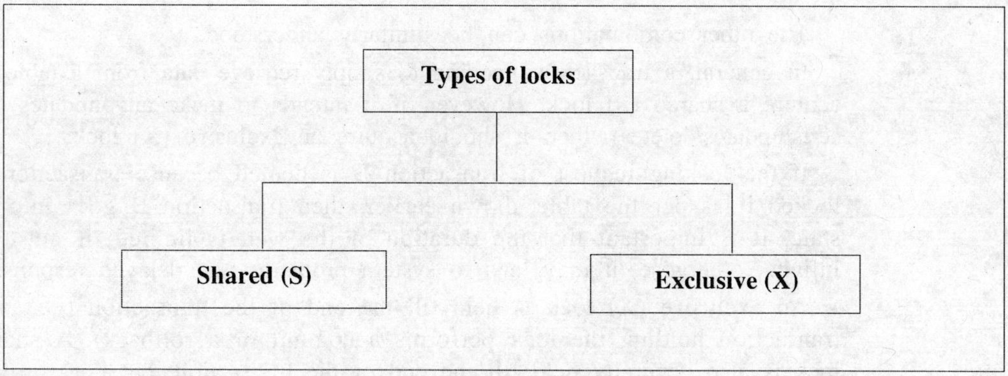

Fig. 5.30 Types of database locks

The properties of these types of locks need to be clarified. Let us assume that we have two transactions, A and B, in our database system.

- If transaction A locks a row r in the table in the exclusive mode (X), then transaction B or any other transaction cannot acquire either an exclusive lock (X) or a shared lock (S) on the same row.
- If transaction A locks a row r in the table in the shared mode (S), then transaction B or any other transaction cannot acquire an exclusive lock (X) on the same row, but it can acquire a shared lock (S) on the same row.

(Note that although we talk of "locking a row", in reality it means either locking a table or locking a page of rows.)

We can prepare a matrix to show these results, as in Table 5.1.

Table 5.1 Locking possibilities

Lock held → *Lock requested* ↓	*X*	*S*	*No lock*
X	No	No	Yes
S	No	Yes	Yes
Any	Yes	Yes	Yes

The way this table should be read is as follows:

A column indicates a lock that is already acquired. A row indicates a lock that is being requested.

For example, we shall consider two samples.

(a) If transaction A holds an exclusive lock (X) on a row r (See column titled X) and transaction B requests for a shared lock (S) on the same row r (See column titled S) then it is *not* allowed.

(b) If transaction A holds a shared lock (S) on a row r (See column titled S) and transaction B requests for a shared lock (S) on the same row r (See column titled S), then it *is* allowed.

Database recovery can be implemented in various ways. Some database technologies make updates to the back up of the tables, and not the tables themselves until a transaction is committed. Upon commit, they apply these changes from the backup to the actual tables. Some other databases apply changes directly to the database tables, and in the case of failures, read the backups for restoration of old values. How this is implemented is not so important as long as we are able to recover data in some manner.

The other combinations can be similarly understood.

In general, a transaction needing to simply retrieve data from a table should acquire a shared (S) lock. However, if it intends to make any updates (i.e. inserts/updates/deletes), then it should acquire an exclusive (X) lock.

If the locking request of transaction B is denied because transaction A has locked it as per the table shown earlier, then transaction B goes into a wait state. It is important that the duration of the wait is limited; it must not be infinite, otherwise, it may lead to system problems and delayed responses.

An exclusive (X) lock is held till the end of the transaction (i.e. until the transaction holding the lock performs a commit or a rollback). A shared (S) lock is also generally held till the end of the transaction, but not always.

5.7 CONCURRENCY PROBLEMS REVISITED

Armed with the facility of locking, let us revisit our concurrency problems to see if they can be solved now. We shall not discuss these problems in detail, as they have been covered earlier. We shall simply focus on the possible solutions to these problems.

5.7.1 Lost Update Problem Revisited

Armed with locking, consider the problem depicted in Fig. 5.31.

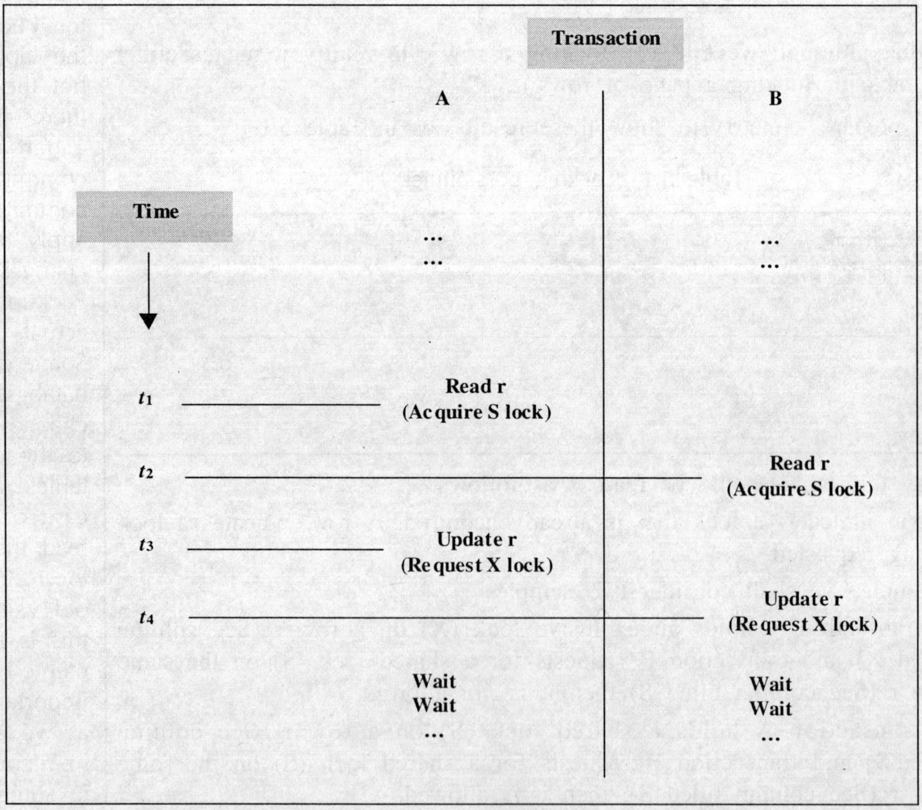

Fig. 5.31 Lost update problem revisited

There is no change in events between times t_1 and t_2. Note that transactions A and B implicitly acquire a shared (S) lock on row r at times t_1 and t_2 respectively, as they want to perform a read operation. At time t_3, transaction A makes an attempt to update row r. This causes transaction A to automatically request for an exclusive (X) lock. However, because transaction B already has a shared (S) lock on the row, this request of transaction A is not fulfilled. At time t_4, transaction B wants to perform an update, and therefore, requests for an exclusive (X) lock. This request is also not granted, because transaction A possesses a shared (S) lock since time t_1.

As a result, both transactions A and B wait from time t_3 and t_4 respectively. More specifically:

- Transaction A is waiting for transaction B to release something (i.e. a lock on row r).
- Transaction B is waiting for transaction A to release something (i.e. a lock on row r).

This situation is peculiar, and is defined as follows.

> A **deadlock** occurs when two or more transactions wait at the same time for others to release their locks, so that they can proceed.

In other words, this situation is called as deadlock and is also known as **deadly embrace**.

We shall discuss deadlocks in detail soon. For now, we realise that although locking seems to have solved the problem of concurrency in the case of *lost update*, it has also introduced a new one – that of the deadlock.

Locking of tables can provide significant benefits in terms of ensuring that we are not causing any accidental problems due to concurrency issues. When a user locks a table, another user cannot update it, thus preventing any actions that would cause the database to reach an inconsistent or invalid state.

5.7.2 Dirty (Uncommitted) Read Problem Revisited

We know that the dirty (uncommitted) read problem is caused when a transaction (say A) retrieves, or even worse, updates a row updated by another uncommitted transaction (say B). Let us revisit this with the introduction of locking as shown in Fig. 5.32.

The sequence of events is as follows.

1. At time t_1, transaction B performs an update on row r, thereby acquiring an exclusive (X) lock.
2. At time t_2, transaction A needs to perform a read operation on row r. Therefore, it requests for a shared (S) lock on the row. This request is not be granted, as transaction B still holds an exclusive (X) lock.
3. At time t_3, transaction A is waiting for transaction B to release its lock, and free row r. Transaction B obliges, by performing a *ROLLBACK* operation, which causes the lock to be released.
4. At time t_4, transaction A obtains the shared (S) lock that it was looking for. It can now proceed with its data retrieval operation.

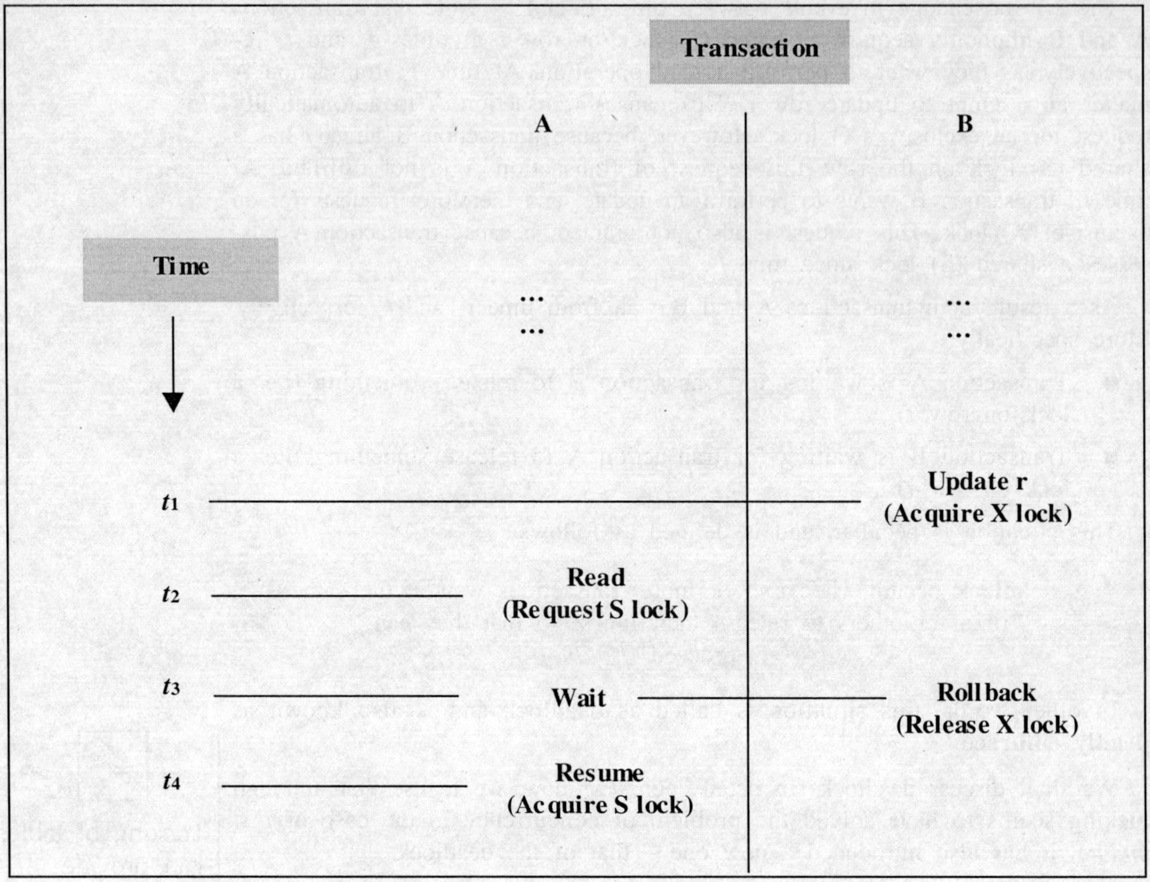

Fig. 5.32 Dirty (Uncommitted) read problem revisited

We can see that locking solves the problem of *dirty (uncommitted) read*.

If transaction A needs to perform an update, rather than a read, at time t_2, things do not change much. The only thing that would change is that transaction A would now request for an exclusive (X) lock, instead of a shared (S) lock. This request would be granted only after transaction B releases its lock at time t_3. As we can see, this is quite similar to the steps discussed above.

5.7.3 Non-repeatable Read Problem Revisited

We know that the *non-repeatable read problem*, also known as the *inconsistent analysis problem*, occurs when a transaction sees two different values for the same row within its lifetime. Fig. 5.33. shows the *non-repeatable read problem* after incorporating the locking mechanisms.

The sequence of events is as follows.

1. At time t_1, transaction A reads row r of a table. Therefore, it implicitly acquires a shared (S) lock on the row.

2. At time t_2, transaction B wants to update the same row r. Therefore, it requests for an exclusive (X) lock on the row. However, because transaction A has already acquired a shared (S) lock, transaction B must wait.
3. At time t_3, transaction A again retrieves the same row r. Because it already holds a shared (S) lock on the row, this is not a problem at all. Note that transaction B is waiting.
4. At time t_4, transaction A releases its shared (S) lock. Transaction B is still waiting.
5. At time t_5, transaction A does not hold a lock on the row. Therefore, transaction B would be granted an exclusive (X) lock on the row, as desired. Transaction B can now perform an update operation, as required.

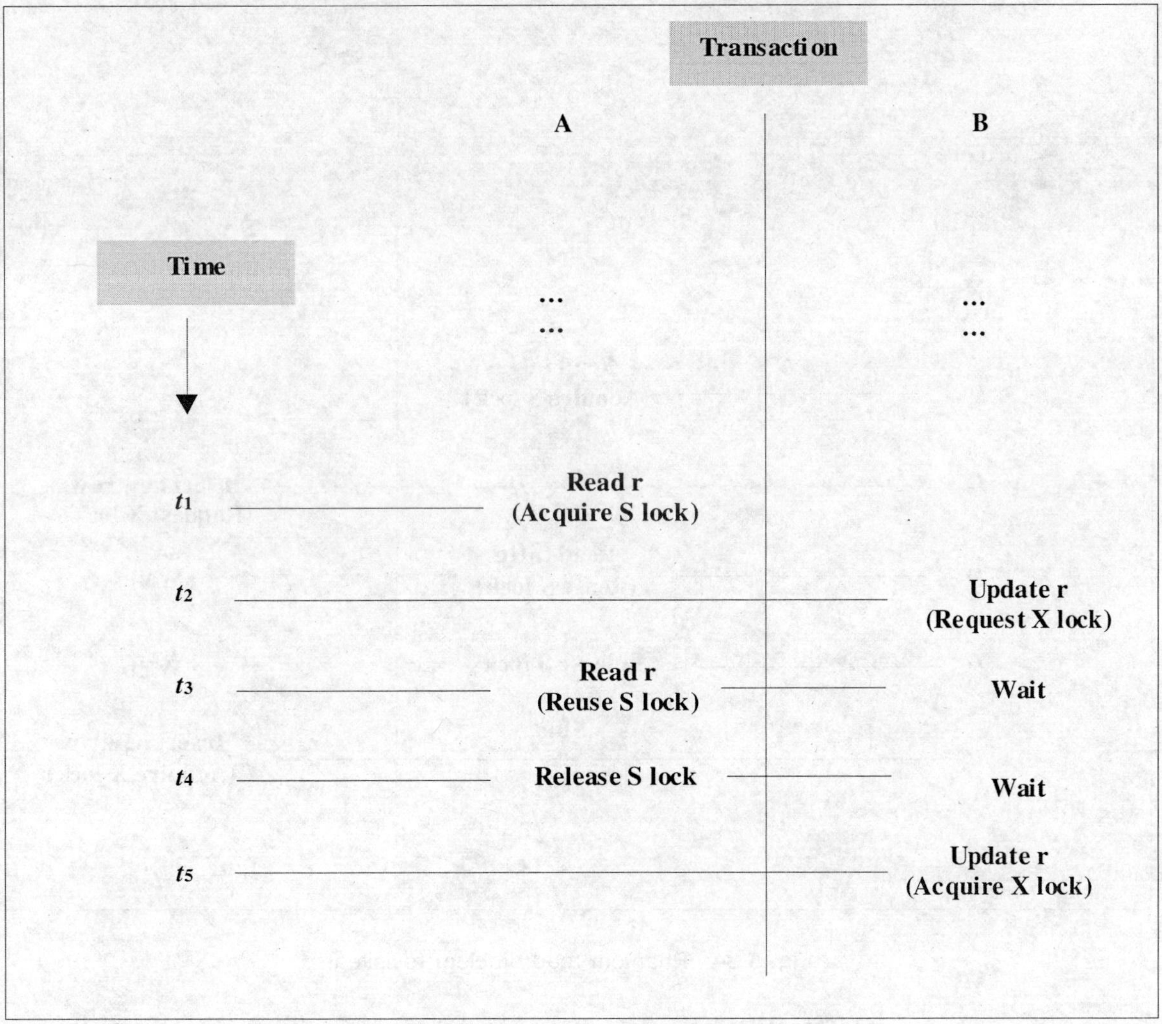

Fig. 5.33 Non-repeatable read problem revisited

We can see that locking has solved the problem of *non-repeatable read* as well.

5.7.4 Phantom Read Problem Revisited

We know that the *phantom read problem* (also called as *phantom insert problem*) is a special case of the *non-repeatable read problem.* In the *phantom insert problem,* transaction A is fooled because transaction B inserts a row before it completes its reading operation. Otherwise, it is similar to the *non-repeatable read problem.* We show the effect of locking on this problem in Fig. 5.34.

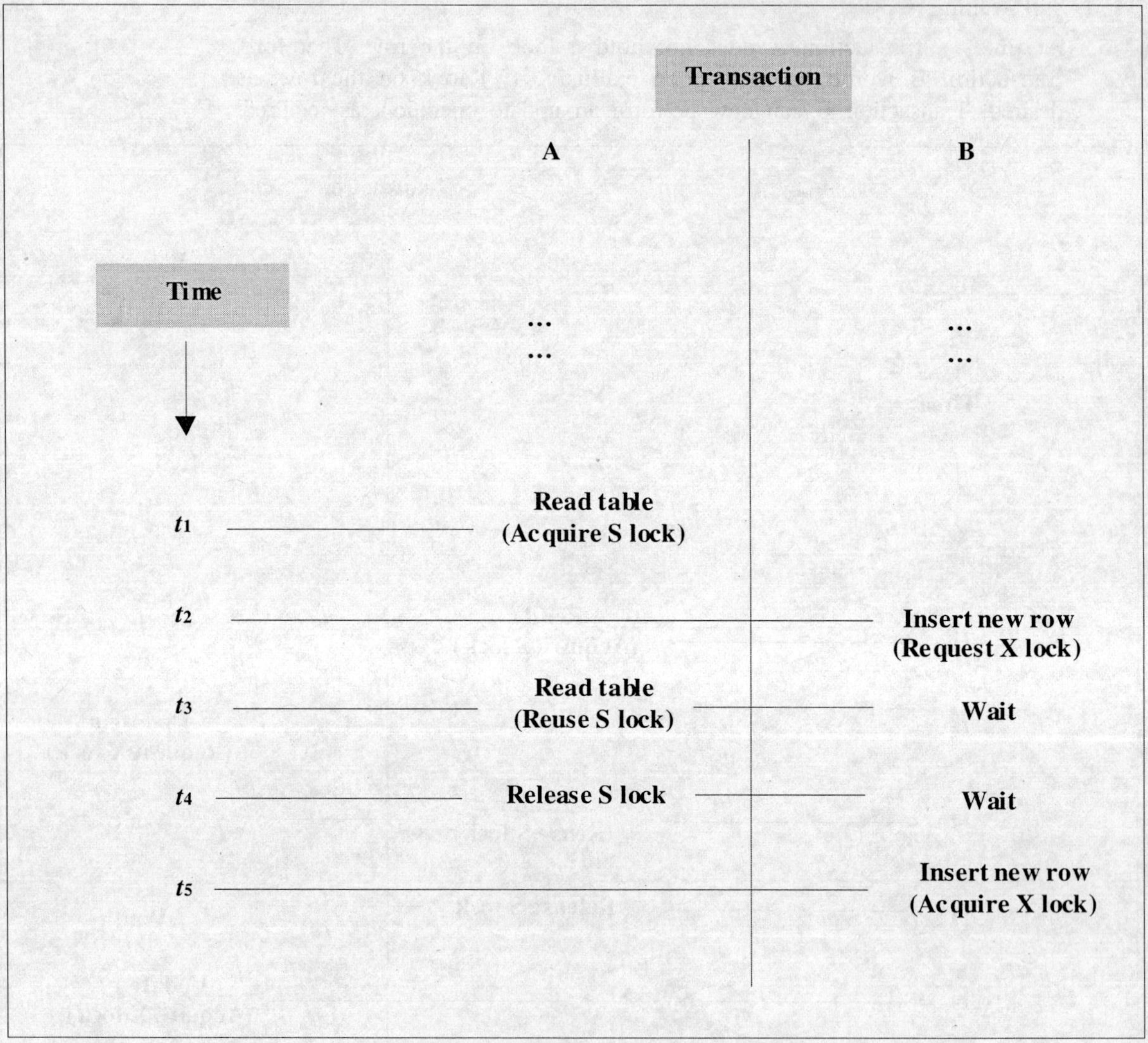

Fig. 5.34 Phantom read problem revisited

The sequence of events is exactly the same as was in the case of the *non-repeatable read problem.* Hence, we will not describe it, except pointing out that the only change is that transaction B intends to insert a row, rather than updating one. Other things remain the same.

5.8 DEADLOCKS

We have touched upon the concept of deadlocks earlier. Deadlock is a specific case of concurrency problem. A concurrency problem can be resolved and yet it can lead to a deadlock. There are several ways in which we can illustrate a deadlock. For the present, we shall depict a very simple case.

- Transaction A holds a lock on Table T_1. Another transaction B also wants to acquire a lock on the same table.
- Transaction B holds a lock on Table T_2. Transaction A also wants to acquire a lock on the same table.

This situation is depicted in Fig. 5.35.

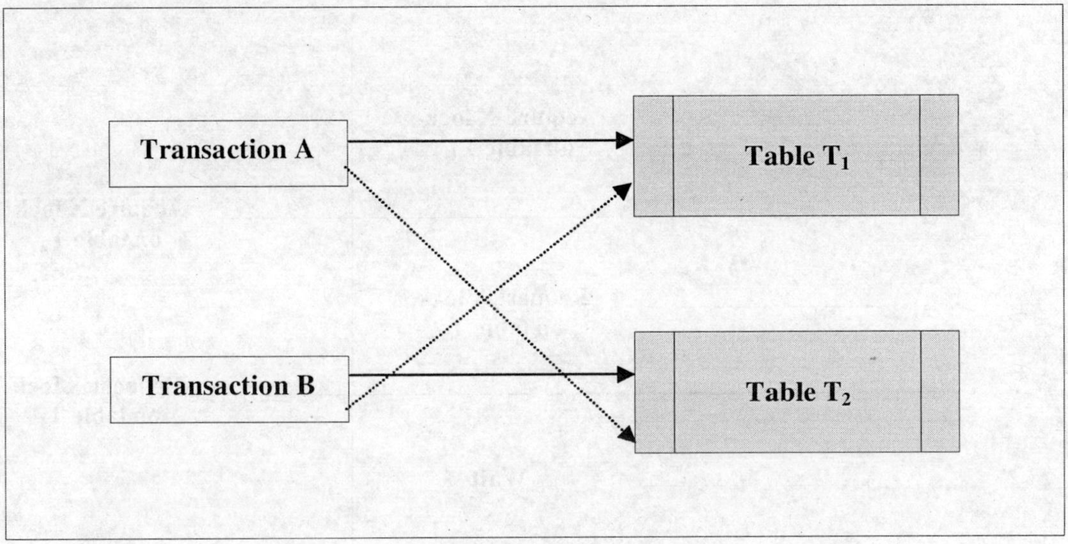

Fig. 5.35 Concept of Deadlock

The thick lines show a lock that is already acquired (e.g. transaction A on Table T_1 and transaction B on Table T_2). The dotted lines show a lock that is desired (e.g. transaction A on Table T_2 and transaction B on Table T_1).

We will realise that unless transaction B gives up its lock on Table T_2, transaction A cannot proceed. On the other hand, unless transaction A gives up its lock on Table T_1, transaction B cannot proceed.

Thus, both the transactions A and B depend on each other to release their respective locks. This can never happen automatically. Hence, it is a condition in which a transaction waits endlessly for resources held by another. This is precisely what is called a *deadlock*. We can illustrate this with the help of a time graph, as shown in Fig. 5.36.

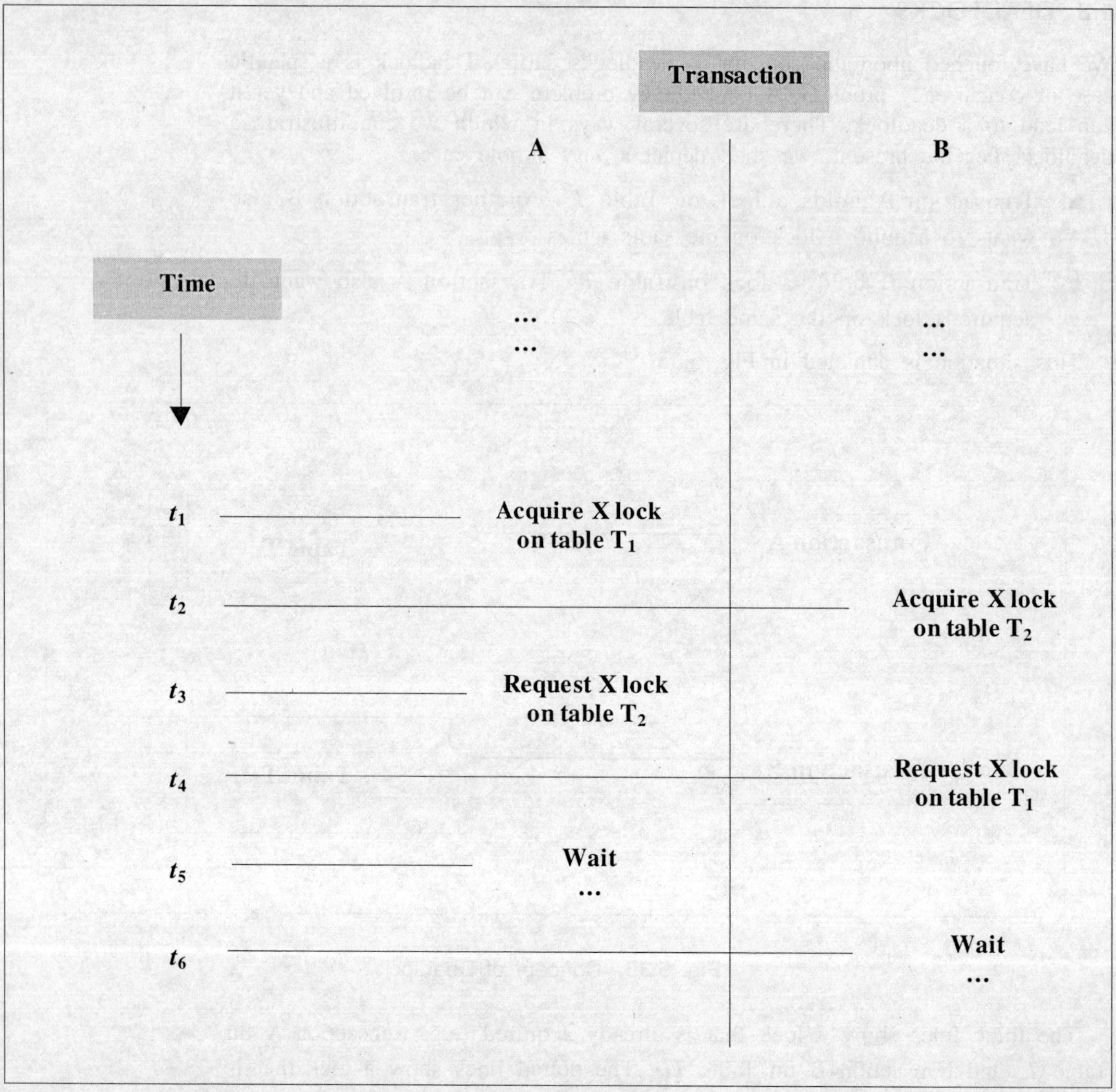

Fig. 5.36 Deadlock

The sequence of events is as follows.

1. At time t_1, transaction A acquires an exclusive (X) lock on Table T_1.
2. At time t_2, transaction B acquires an exclusive (X) lock on Table T_2.
3. At time t_3, transaction A requests for an exclusive (X) lock on Table T_2.
4. At time t_4, transaction B requests for an exclusive (X) lock on Table T_1.
5. At time t_5, transaction A enters into a wait state, as it cannot get a lock on Table T_2.
6. At time t_6, transaction B enters into a wait state, as it cannot get a lock on Table T_1.

Thus, we enter into a deadlock.

How do we resolve a deadlock? For this purpose, one of the transactions (called the **victim**) needs to be identified/detected. This transaction is then rolled back. This causes all the locks that it has acquired to be released. After this, the other transactions that have been waiting because of the deadlock can proceed.

Thus, in our example, we must roll back either transaction A or transaction B. This would free the system resources for the other transaction and allow it to complete. After the completion, we can restart the rolled back transaction from scratch. Of course, when such an action is taken, it is always advisable that the users of the transaction being rolled back be quickly informed about this.

5.9 TRANSACTION SERIALISABILITY

> If the result of the execution of a set of transactions is the same as executing them serially, one-by-one, then these transactions are **serialisable**.

In other words, a given set of transactions executes perfectly if it is serialisable.

The following theory is proposed in the context of serialisable transactions.

(a) Individually, these transactions are supposed to be all right. This is because they transform the database from one consistent state to another.

(b) Therefore, it should be all right to execute them one after the other in *any* order. This is because all these transactions are independent of each other.

(c) Therefore, an interleaved (or combined) execution is also acceptable if the result is the same as the serial execution of these transactions. That is, a set of these transactions is then serialisable.

If we revisit the set of transactions that we have been discussing so far, we would note that none of them was serialisable. That is, transactions A and B were being executed in an interleaved manner. By using the concept of locking, we actually *forced* these sets of transactions to become serialisable. That is, we enforced executions such as *First A then B* or *First B then A*. No longer did we allow *Some A some B* or *Some B some A*.

> Any execution of a set of transactions (either interleaved or serialised) is called as its **schedule**.

If we execute the transactions strictly in a sequence, one at a time, then the schedule is called a **serial schedule**. On the other hand, if there is an overlap of transactions, then the schedule is called **interleaved schedule** or **non-serial schedule**. Two transactions are equivalent if they produce the same results, regardless of the order in which they execute, i.e. they move the database from one consistent state to another.

It is extremely important to note that two different transaction schedules (either serial or interleaved) involving the same transactions may yield *different* results, and yet they are correct! For example, consider two transactions, A and B, as shown in Fig. 5.37.

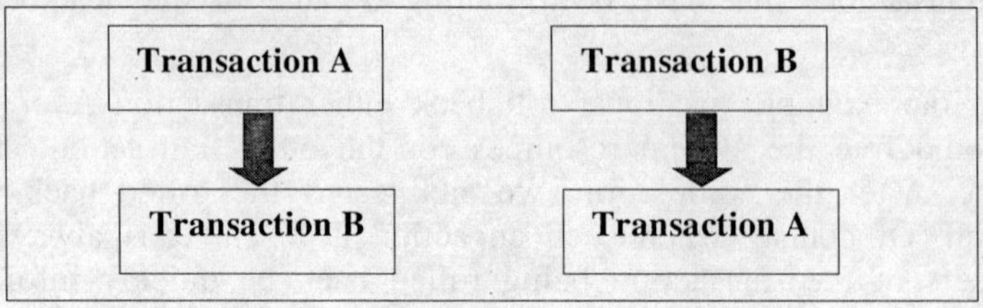

Fig. 5.37 Different transaction schedules

Let us assume that these transactions are operating on a value T whose initial value is 50. Note Fig. 5.38 to see how dramatically different the results are, if the execution is *First A then B* versus *First B then A*.

	Value of T
Initial	**50**
Transaction A	
T = T + 100	**150**
Transaction B	
T = T / 2	**75**

Schedule: Transaction A followed by Transaction B

	Value of T
Initial	**50**
Transaction B	
T = T / 2	**25**
Transaction A	
T = T + 100	**125**

Schedule: Transaction B followed by Transaction A

Fig. 5.38 Different transaction schedules may produce different results

The reason we state that either sequence of transactions (i.e. either of the schedules) is acceptable, is because both leave the database in a consistent state. Transaction management does not have a say about which transaction should start first, that is which transaction should get precedence. This is a decision left best to the software application.

5.10 TWO-PHASE LOCKING

Two-phase locking is a protocol that guarantees that if all the transactions obey it, all the possible interleaved schedules become serialisable.

Before we proceed, the most important thing to remember is that this protocol is completely different from the *two-phase commit* protocol. Except for the similarities in naming, these two protocols are unrelated in theory as well as practice.

In other words, this protocol ensures serialisability of any schedule, provided it adheres to the conditions specified by the protocol. This protocol mandates the following.

(i) A transaction must acquire a lock on any object that it intends to open (i.e. work with).

(ii) After releasing a lock, a transaction must never attempt to acquire any more locks.

Thus, a transaction consists of two phases:

(a) In the **acquire phase**, a transaction goes on acquiring locks as and when it needs to open new objects.

(b) The **release phase** is indicated by a single *COMMIT* or *ROLLBACK* operation.

This protocol is shown in Fig. 5.39.

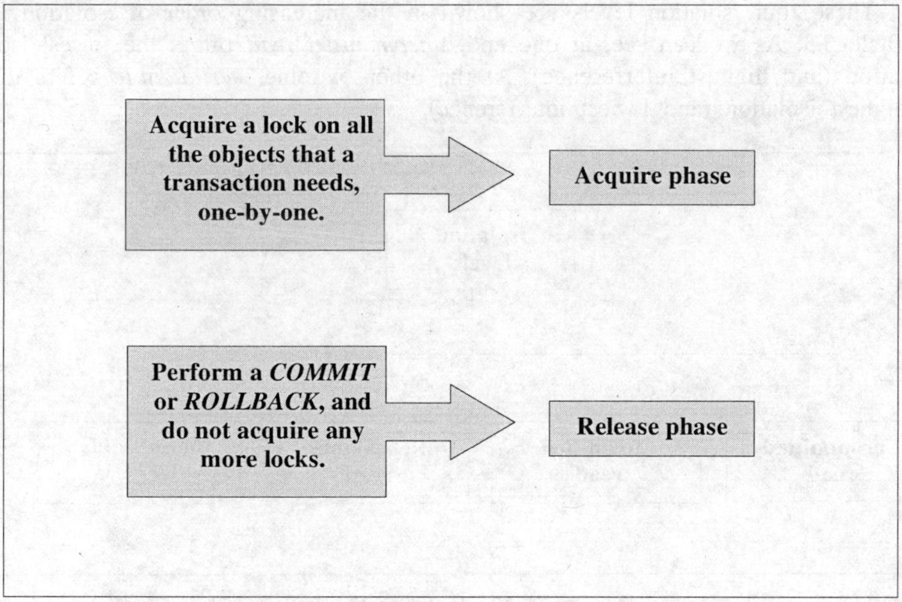

Fig. 5.39 Two-phase locking protocol

5.11 ISOLATION LEVELS

Isolation level is defined as the degree of interference that a transaction can tolerate in a concurrent operation.

The higher the isolation, the lesser is the interference and, therefore, lesser is the concurrency. But higher isolation also awaits lesser overall system throughput. This is shown in Table 5.2.

Table 5.2 Effect of isolation levels

Isolation level	*Interference*	*Throughput*
Low	High	High
High	Low	Low

If a transaction has to be serialisable, then it must not be interrupted at all. In other words, it must not be interfered with and the degree of interference must be 0. Thus, the isolation level must be a maximum. This is fine in theory, but almost impossible to achieve in practice.

SQL provides four possible isolation levels. A transaction could be assigned one of these four possible isolation levels before it starts. The business requirements and priority of a transaction together determine the isolation level that must be chosen for that transaction. The four isolation levels are **read uncommitted**, **read committed, repeatable read** and **serialisable**. They are shown in Fig. 5.40.

These four isolation levels are shown in the increasing order of isolation in Table 5.3. As we can see, at one end, *uncommitted read* offers the lowest isolation (and highest interference). At the other extreme, *serialisable* offers the highest isolation (and lowest interference).

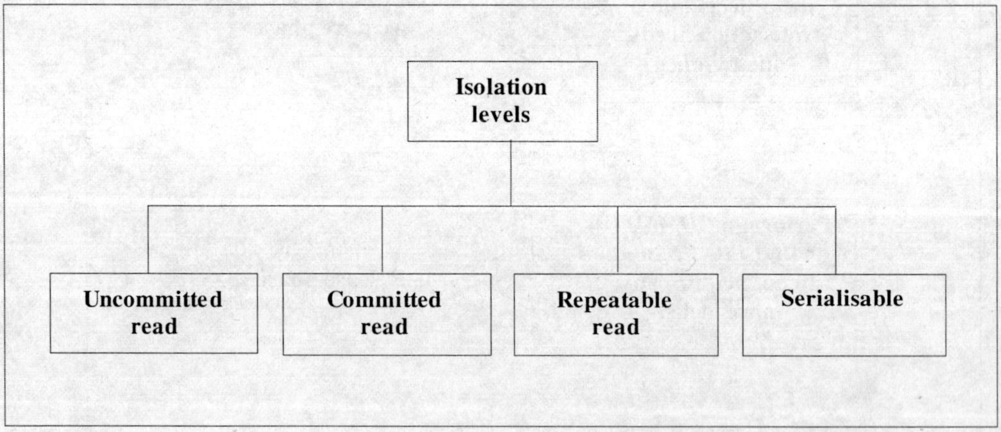

Fig. 5.40 Isolation levels

Table 5.3 Effect of isolation levels

Isolation level	*Isolation*	*Interference*
Uncommitted read	Lowest	Highest
Committed read	Medium	High
Repeatable read	High	Medium
Serialisable	Highest	Lowest

Let us now describe the effects of these isolation levels.

- **Uncommitted read**: This isolation level offers the lowest isolation. As a result, the same query can return different results if executed multiple times, regardless of whether the changes are committed or not.
- **Committed read**: This isolation level allows the same query to return different rows, but only if the transaction that made the updates to the database committed its changes.
- **Repeatable read**: This isolation level allows phantom inserts, but prevents everything else (including the *repeatable read problem*).
- **Serialisable**: This isolation level offers the highest isolation. It treats every transaction as a separate entity and does not provide any space for the occurance of concurrency problems. In other words, it makes a scheme of transactions completely serialisable.

We tabulate the effects of various isolation levels on concurrency problems in Table 5.4.

Table 5.4 Effect of isolation levels on concurrency problems

Isolation level	*Lost update*	*Dirty (Uncommitted) read*	*Non-repeatable read*	*Phantom read*
Uncommitted read	**No**	**Yes**	**Yes**	**Yes**
Committed read	**No**	**No**	**Yes**	**Yes**
Repeatable read	**No**	**No**	**No**	**Yes**
Serialisable	**No**	**No**	**No**	**No**

We shall provide one example that shows how to interpret this table.

If the isolation level is *uncommitted read*, then the *lost update* concurrency problem cannot occur. However, the other three problems can occur. Similarly, the other three isolation levels can be understood.

KEY TERMS AND CONCEPTS

ACID properties
Atomicity
Chained transaction
Commit
Concurrency problems
Consistency
Deadlock
Dirty (Uncommitted) read problem
Exclusive (X) lock
Flat transaction
Forward recovery
Acquire phase
Backward recovery
Checkpoint record
Commit phase
Concurrent transaction
Coordinator
Deadly embrace
Durability
Failure recovery
Force-writing
Inconsistent analysis problem

Interleaved schedule
Isolation
Isolation level
Journal
Lock
Lost update problem
Media recovery
Nested transaction
Non-repeatable read problem
Non-serial schedule
Participant
Phantom insert problem
Phantom read problem
Prepare phase
Read committed
Read lock
Read uncommitted
Release phase
Repeatable read
Rollback
Schedule
Serial schedule
Serialisable
Serialisable transaction
Shared (S) lock
Synch-point
System log
System recovery
Transaction
Transaction Processing (TP) monitor
Transaction recovery
Two-phase commit
Two-phase locking
Write lock
Write-ahead log

CHAPTER SUMMARY

- A **transaction** is a logical unit of work. It signifies that all the operations must be executed in entirety or not at all. A transaction must not execute partially.
- A transaction consists of distinct steps, namely Begin transaction, ***Commit/Rollback***, and End transaction
- If a transaction is committed, all the database changes made inside the transaction are made permanent.
- If a transaction is rolled back, all the database changes made inside the transaction are undone.
- A **Transaction Processing (TP) monitor** ensures that transactions are performed as expected.
- A **system log** or **journal** is used internally to record database operations. It is used while committing or rolling back a transaction.
- A transaction has four properties, together called as *ACID*.
- The letter A in *ACID* stands for **atomicity**. It means that a transaction must execute exactly once completely or not at all.
- The letter C in *ACID* stands for **consistency**. It means that when it ends a transaction must leave the database in a consistent state.
- The letter I in *ACID* stands for **isolation**. It means that transactions must not interfere with each other – they must be completely isolated from each other.

- The letter D in *ACID* stands for **durability**. It means that a transaction must make its changes permanent to the database when it ends.
- Database recovery consists of **transaction recovery** and **system recovery**.
- **Transaction recovery** deals with individual transactions.
- **System recovery** deals with all the transactions in a system as a whole.
- System recovery is sub-classified into **failure recovery** and **media recovery**.
- Failure recovery deals with soft errors, such as power failure.
- Media recovery deals with disk errors.
- DBMS takes frequent **checkpoints**, which are used in the recovery process.
- Transactions can be **flat, chained** or **nested**.
- **Two-phase commit** protocol is used to perform multiple transactions that execute on different databases/computers.
- **Concurrency** means multiple transactions running at the same time.
- Concurrent execution of transactions can lead to four possible problems, called as concurrency problems. These are: **lost update, dirty (uncommitted) read, non-repeatable read** and **phantom read**.
- In the lost update problem, one transaction overwrites the changes of another transaction.
- In the dirty (uncommitted) read problem, one transaction reads an uncommitted value of another transaction.
- In the non-repeatable read problem, one transaction sees two different values for the same row in two successive executions.
- In the phantom read problem, one transaction inserts a row in the table while the other transaction is half-way through its browsing of the table.
- **Locking** helps solve concurrency problems.
- Locks can be **shared (S)** or **exclusive (X).**
- If a transaction obtains a shared lock on a row, it means that the transaction wants to read that row.
- If a transaction obtains an exclusive lock on a row, it means that the transaction wants to update that row.
- **Deadlock** is a specific concurrency problem wherein two transactions depend on each other for something.
- Transaction **serialisability** ensures that the transactions are being executed successfully.
- **Two-phase locking** protocol guarantees that a set of transactions becomes serialisable.
- **Isolation level** is the degree of interference that a transaction can tolerate in a concurrent operation.
- SQL defines four isolation levels: **read uncommitted, read committed, repeatable read,** and **serialisable.**

PRACTICE SET

Mark as true or false

1. A transaction is a logical unit of work.
2. A COMMIT statement indicates the end of a transaction.
3. Transactions are said to depict the ACID properties.
4. If a transaction executes only halfway, the system becomes unstable.
5. In nested transaction we have many mini-transactions within a main transaction.
6. A database can have multiple transactions running at the same time. This is called concurrency.
7. The non-repeatable read problem is also known as the inconsistent analysis problem.
8. A deadlock occurs when two or more transactions wait at the same time for others to release their locks, so that they can proceed.
9. Locking solves the problem of phantom read.
10. If there is an overlap of transactions, then the schedule is called as serial schedule.

Fill in the blanks

1. A transaction processing system is also called as ________.

   (a) TP monitor (b) transaction monitor
   (c) processing monitor (d) monitor

2. ________ is/are used for COMMIT and ROLLBACK operations.

   (a) System log (b) Journal
   (c) Both a and b (d) None of a, b or c

3. Failure recovery and media recovery fall under ________.

   (a) transaction recovery (b) system recovery
   (c) database recovery (d) none of a, b and c

4. Check-points are sometimes also called as ________.

   (a) crash-points (b) sync-points
   (c) function-points (d) none of a, b or c

5. Flat, chained, nested are the types of ________.

   (a) locks (b) transaction models
   (c) database models (d) system models

6. In ________ transactions, we have hierarchical relationship between master and child transactions.

   (a) chained (b) flat
   (c) overlapped (d) nested

7. The phantom read problem is a special case of ________.
   (a) non-repeatable read problem
   (b) uncommitted read problem
   (c) lost update problem
   (d) nested read problem
8. If we execute the transaction strictly in sequence, one at a time, then the schedule is called a ________.
   (a) serial schedule
   (b) interleaved schedule
   (c) non-serial schedule
   (d) simple schedule
9. ________ is a protocol that guarantees that if all the transactions obey it, all the possible interleaved schedules become serialisable.
   (a) Single-phase locking
   (b) Two-phase locking
   (c) Isolation levels
   (d) Scheduling
10. ________ is defined as the degree of interference that a transaction can tolerate in a concurrent environment.
   (a) Key
   (b) Locking
   (c) Transaction
   (d) Isolations level

Provide detailed answers to the following questions.

1. Explain the concept of transaction processing monitor.
2. Explain ACID properties of transactions.
3. Explain recovery types with short description.
4. What are the various transaction models?
5. Explain the concept of concurrency problems.
6. Describe the lost update problem.
7. Explain the dirty read problem.
8. What is the non-repeatable read problem?
9. Explain locking mechanism with short descriptions.
10. Describe the concept of deadlock.

Exercises

1. Is the concept of a transaction needed in a single-user, single-database environment?
2. Does the concept of transaction apply only to computer-based operations? Is the idea of a transaction important even in our daily life?
3. Investigate whether your bank ensures transaction management.
4. Would concurrency problems occur if there are only two transactions in the system, and both are performing read-only operation? Why?
5. Which concurrency problems can happen if one transaction is reading and another is updating data?
6. Can we do logging by using a database? What are the pros and cons of this approach?

7. Find out the various isolation levels defined in the different DBMS products such as Oracle, SQL Server and DB2.
8. How can one code nested transactions programmatically? Write a short algorithm for it.
9. What are the various TP monitors available in the market?
10. Think of a practical situation where two-phase commit would be needed.

Chapter 6

Database Security

Security of information has become perhaps the most significant issue of modern computing. Modern security mechanisms also take care of message integrity, confidentiality, and non-repudiation. The essense is to take a message and transform it to make it non-understandable.

Chapter Highlights

- Classification of Data
- Meaning of *Information Security*
- Principles of Security
- Introduction to Cryptography and Encryption Technologies
- Database Security and Statistical Databases

6.1 DATA CLASSIFICATION

6.1.1 Importance of Data

It is important to know which data is more important and which is not. As we know, all data is not equally important to an organisation. Thus, some data might be critical, some *nice to have*, and finally, some completely irrelevant. Therefore, we must be able to classify data and based on such classification attach importance and priorities to it. We can then take the toughest measures to protect the most critical data and reasonable steps to protect the data that is useful to some extent.

Data classification also helps in ensuring that data is protected in the most cost-effective manner. Any security mechanism involves basic costs, overhead and maintenance costs. The importance of data must be ascertained in order to ensure that the right data is being protected and to determine if the data being protected actually needs that sort of protection. Data classification is a very important tool to this effect.

Protecting digital information is not significantly different from protecting information in paper form. For example, we sign cheques to ensure that any alterations can be detected and dealt with. This can also ensure that we are authorising a payment. Similarly, we can digitally sign a document on a computer to protect it against unauthorised alterations and to ensure that nobody can tamper with them.

Each class of data has separate requirements and processes related to how the data is accessed, made use of, and destroyed when no longer necessary. For example, in an organisation, confidential information might be accessible only to the senior management. Therefore, some broad-level requirements for making this data accessible can be specified as follows:

- At least two persons must enter their access codes
- The data cannot be printed on paper
- Each and every action taken by the user while accessing the data must be recorded in detail into an audit log

Such data may require degaussing and destruction of media when it is no longer useful.

Some other information may be classified as slightly sensitive, but not that confidential. Such data might be accessible to a large group of people. Only a user ID and password may be used to access such data. The audit log may not be very detailed and the actual auditing process may happen infrequently. The data may be printed and while destroying it normal processes, such as formatting the disk, may be good enough.

The remaining information can actually be public property. All employees may be able to access it. No specific auditing or destroying mechanisms may be required.

6.1.2 Private Organisations versus Military Classifications

Organisations choose different security models and employ varying security practices, based on the classification of data. The type of organisation and its aims and objectives mainly determine the level of security models and practices. One organisation that is keen on high-level security measures is the military. Military organisations are highly concerned about disclosing their data to any outsider.

On the other hand, private organisations are more worried about the integrity and availability of data. This is shown in Fig. 6.1.

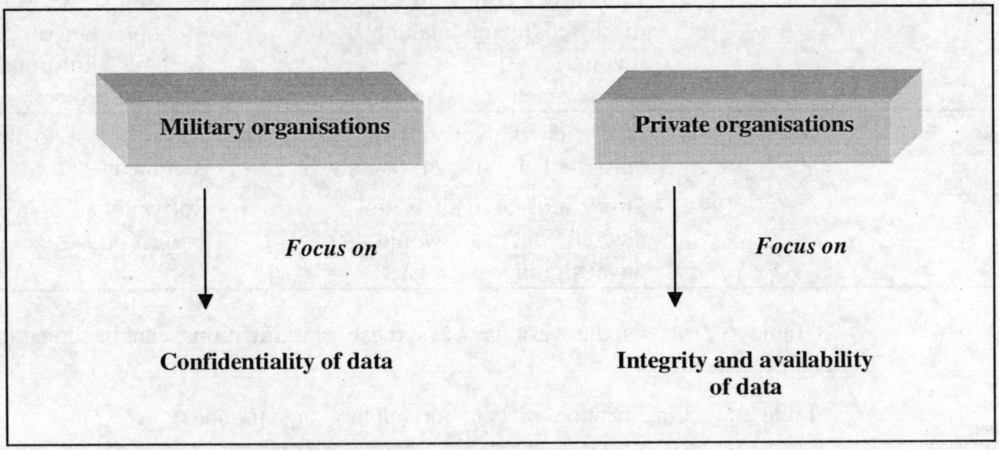

Fig. 6.1 Varying focus on data security

These factors greatly influence the way different types of organisations classify data. Before it implements data classification mechanisms, an organisation, be it military or private, must take decisions regarding the sensitivity mechanisms that they would employ. For instance, one organisation may choose to use only two classifications: confidential and public. On the other hand, another organisation may choose top secret, confidential, sensitive and public as its classifications. Table 6.1 shows the various ways these classifications can be done for private business organisations.

Table 6.1 Classification of data for private organisations

Classification	*Description*	*Example*
Sensitive	■ Needs special measures to ensure the integrity of data ■ Protects from unauthorised changes and deletion ■ Demands a very high assurance of accuracy and completeness	■ Profits, earnings, forecasts ■ Financial information ■ Details of operations
Confidential	■ Must be accessible within the organisation only ■ Can seriously affect the organisation if compromised	■ Program code ■ Plans to beat competition ■ Trade secrets
Private	■ Personal information ■ Should be used within the organisation ■ Unauthorized disclosure outside can affect people in the organisation	■ Human resource details ■ History of personnel ■ Medical records

Classification	*Description*	*Example*
Proprietary	■ Can affect competitiveness if disclosed in an unauthorised manner	■ Functional specifications of a product or service ■ Technical information about a project
Public	■ Any data that cannot be classified as any of the above ■ Disclosure of data is not desired, but also would not have significant impact	■ Next project to be executed ■ Software used in a project

Table 6.2 shows the various ways these classifications can be done for military organisations.

Table 6.2 Classification of data for military organisations

Classification	*Description*	*Example*
Secret	■ Very important data ■ Can cause harm to the nation's interests if disclosed in an unauthorised manner	■ Details of nuclear operations ■ Plans for the troops in a state
Confidential	■ Must be accessible within the organisation only ■ Can seriously affect the organisation if compromised	■ Details of the plans for the next quarter ■ Evaluation regarding arms and ammunition
Top secret	■ Very serious implications to the nation (and to the world) if disclosed	■ Details of weapons to be used in a war ■ Spy satellite information
Sensitive but unclassified	■ Secret but not so important as compared to the above classifications ■ Still can cause serious damage, if disclosed	■ Personnel records ■ Medical records
Unclassified	■ Any data that cannot be classified as any of the above ■ Disclosure of data is not desired, but would not have significant impact	■ Recruitment plans

We will note that the only category that is common to private businesses and military organisations is the *confidential data*. Let us now have a pictorial view the levels of sensitivity for these two types of organisations, as is shown in Fig. 6.2. As we can see, the topmost category specifies the most sensitive information, whereas the category at the bottom represents the least sensitive information.

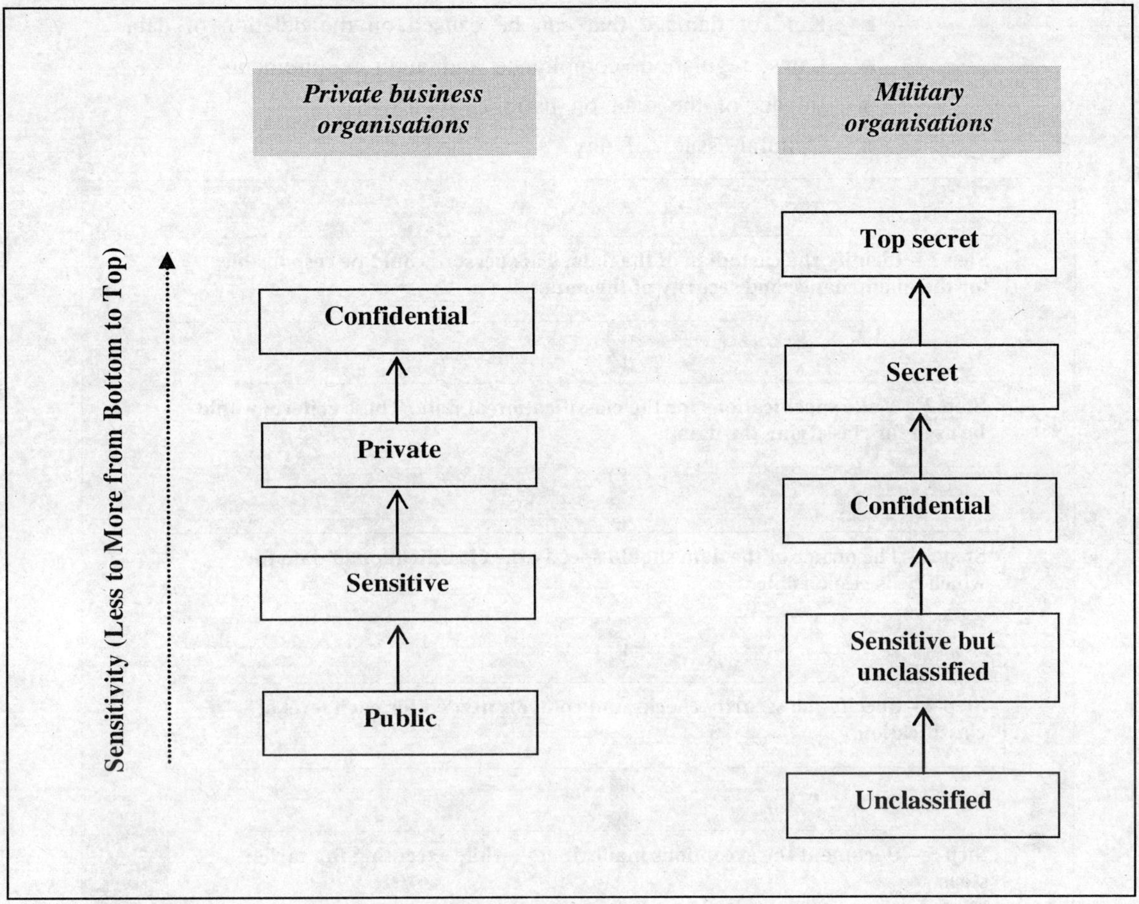

Fig. 6.2 Sensitivity levels of data for private and military organisations

Once they decide on the mechanism to be employed, organisations (private or military) need to come up with the criteria that they would like to adopt to for each category of information. Some of them are listed below. An organisation can use them for ascertaining the sensitivity of data.

- Who should access this data?
- Who should maintain this data?
- Where should the data be kept/stored?
- Who should be allowed to reproduce the data?
- Which data need special identification tags and labels?
- Usefulness of data
- Age of data
- Criticality of data

- Kind of damage that can be caused on the disclosure of data
- Kind of damage that can be caused on the modification of data
- Kind of damage that can be caused on the deletion of data
- Laws, regulation, compliance and audit requirements
- Impact of the data on national security
- Cultural issues, if any

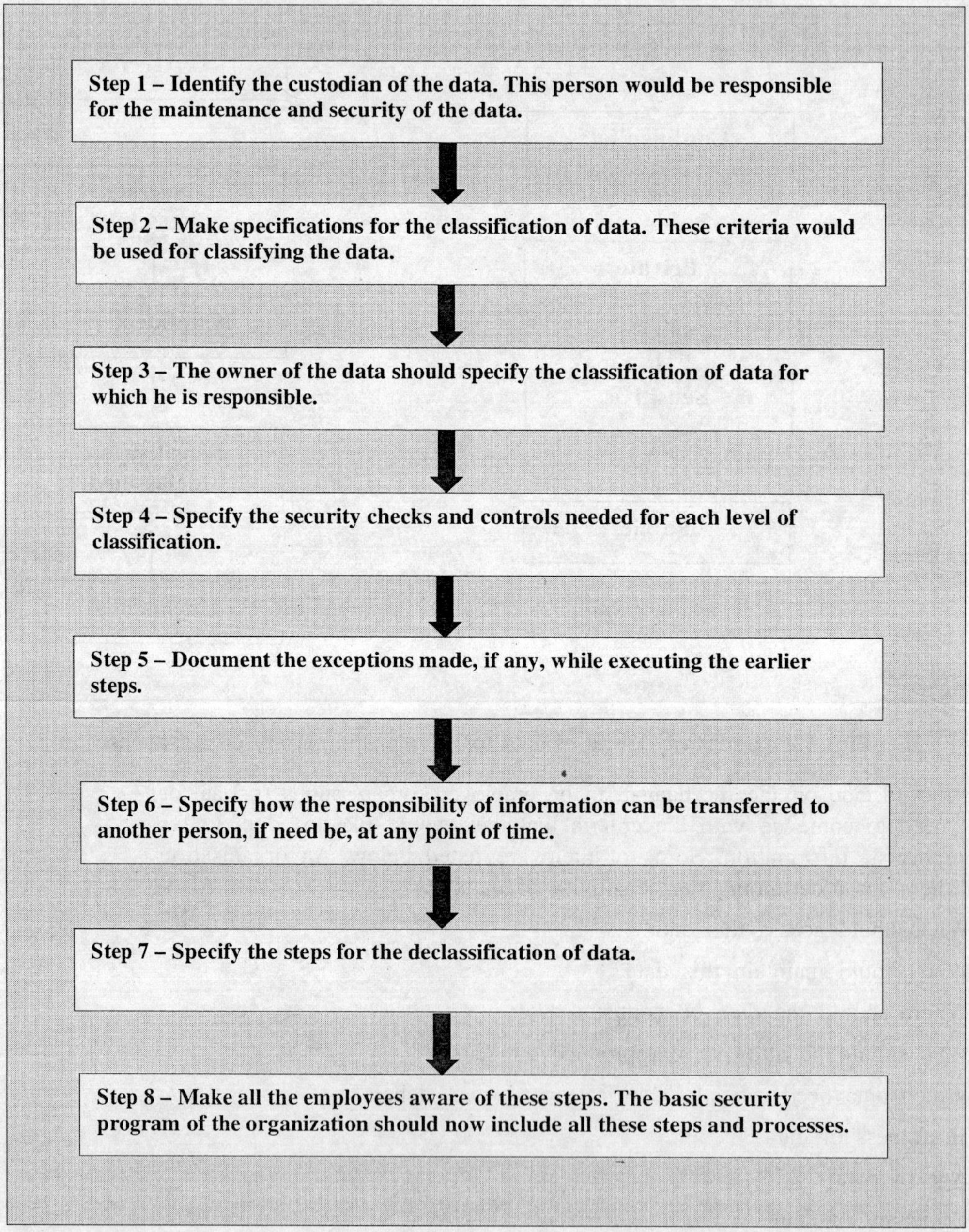

Fig. 6.3 Procedure for classification of data

Having classified data and selected the most appropriate sensitivity mechanism, the next logical step is to specify how each classification needs to be dealt with. It is necessary to now define the provisions for access control, identification and tagging needs. It is also necessary to specify how data should be entered, stored, maintained, transmitted and destroyed. Any pending issues pertaining to audits, monitoring and compliance need to be tackled. Different classifications come with different degrees of security and so, have different requirements.

We can now outline the procedure for classification of data, as shown in Fig. 6.3.

6.2 THREATS AND RISKS

There are certain principles of security. If these principles are broken, then the security of the information is under threat. It then poses significant risks to the information. Let us assume that person A wants to send a paper check worth $100 to person B. What are the factors that A and B will think of in such a case? Person A will write the check for $100, put it inside an envelope, and send it to B.

- Person A would like to make sure that no one except B gets the envelope, and even if someone does they do not get to know about the details of the check. This is the principle of **confidentiality**.
- Persons A and B would like to ensure that no one can tamper with the contents of the check (such as the date, amount, signature and payee details). This is the principle of **integrity**.
- Person B would like to be confident that the check has indeed come from A, and not from someone else posing as A (in which case it could be a fake check). This is the principle of **authentication**.
- What will happen if B deposits the check in the bank, the money is transferred from A's account to B's, and then A denies having written or sent the check? The court will use A's signature to disallow A to refute this claim and settle the dispute. This is the principle of **non-repudiation**.

These are the four chief principles of security related to data. We shall discuss all these security principles in the next few sections.

6.2.1 Confidentiality

> The principle of *confidentiality* specifies that only the sender and the intended recipient(s) should be able to access the contents of a message.

Confidentiality gets lost if an unauthorised person is able to access the contents of a message. An example of compromising the confidentiality of a message is illustrated in Fig. 6.4. As we can see, user A has sent a message to user B. Another user, C (an *attacker*), somehow accesses this message, which is not desired and therefore defeats the purpose of confidentiality. This type of attack is called **interception**.

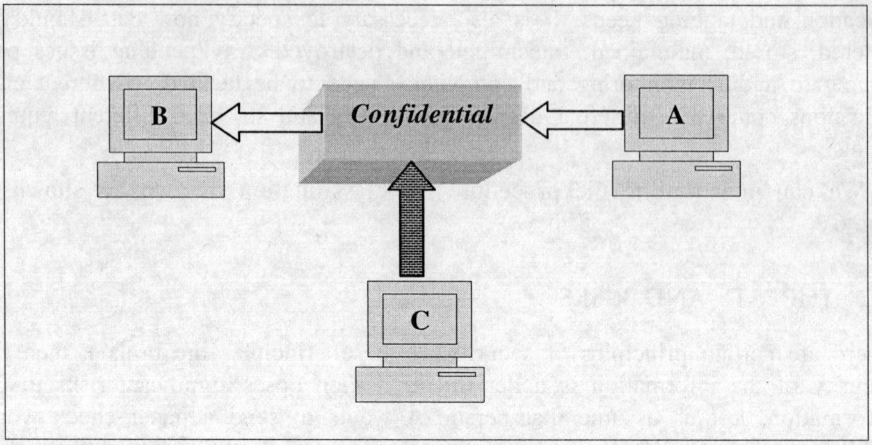

Fig. 6.4 Loss of confidentiality

6.2.2 Authentication

> *Authentication* helps establish proof of identity.

The authentication mechanism ensures that the origin of a message or document is correctly identified. For instance, suppose user C sends an electronic document over a computer network to user B by posing as user A. How would user B know that the message has come from user C, who is posing as user A? A real-life example of this could be a case of user C, posing as user A, sending a purchase request to merchant B. The merchant might willingly send the goods to C thinking that user A has requested for the goods! This concept is shown in Fig. 6.5. This type of attack is called **fabrication**.

Fig. 6.5 Absence of authentication

6.2.3 Integrity

> When the contents of a message are altered after the sender sends it, but before it reaches the intended recipient, we say that the *integrity* of the message is lost.

For example, suppose a check for $100 is issued to pay for books bought from the US. However, when the issuer sees his next account statement, he is amazed to see that the check has resulted in a payment of $1000! This is a case of loss of message integrity and is illustrated in Fig. 6.6. Here, user C alters the contents of a message originally sent by user A, which was actually meant for user B. User C somehow manages to access it, alter its contents, and send the changed message to user B. User B has no way of knowing that the contents of the message have been altered after user A had sent it. User A also does not know about this change. This type of attack is called **modification**.

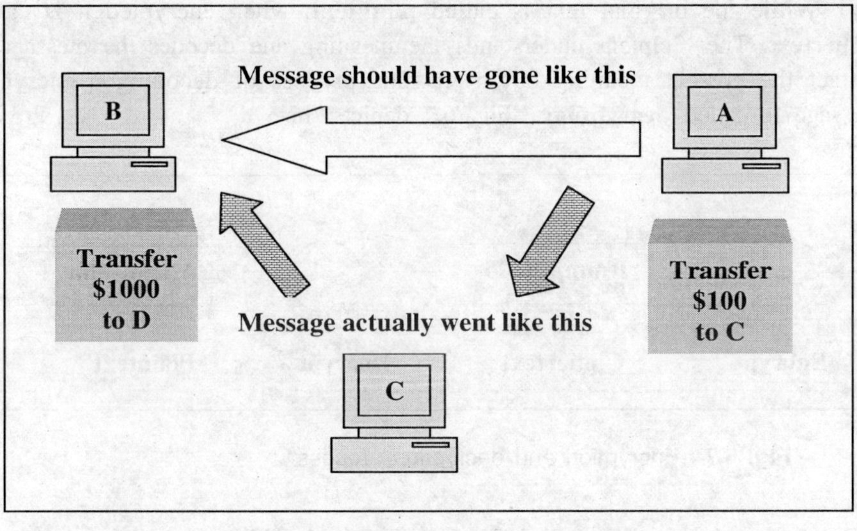

Fig. 6.6 Loss of message integrity

6.2.4 Non-repudiation

There are situations where a user sends a message and later denies having sent it. For example, suppose user A sends a funds transfer request to bank B. After the bank executes the funds transfer as per the instructions A says that the funds transfer instruction to the bank was never sent! Thus, A repudiates, or denies, the funds transfer instruction.

> The principle of *non-repudiation* defeats possibilities of denying something after having done it.

6.3 CRYPTOGRAPHY

In simple terms, **cryptography** is a technique of encoding and decoding messages so that they are not understood by anybody except the sender and the intended recipient. We employ cryptography in our daily life when we do not want a third party to understand what we are saying. For instance, you can have a convention wherein *Ifmmp Kpio* actually means that you are saying hello to your boyfriend John (that is, *Hello John*!). Here each alphabet of the original message (i.e. H, e, l, etc.) is changed to its next immediate alphabet (i.e. I, f, m, etc.). Thus, *Hello* becomes *Ifmmp*, and *John* becomes *Kpio*. Thus, when John makes a phone call to you and your husband is around, you say *Ifmmp Kpio*! Only you and John know its meaning!

Cryptography uses the same basic principle. The sender and recipient of the message decide on an encoding and decoding scheme and use it for communication. In technical terms, the process of encoding messages is called **encryption**. While the original text is called **plaintext**, when encrypted it is called **ciphertext**. The recipient understands the meaning and decodes the message to extract the correct meaning out of it. The process of decoding a encrypted message is called **decryption**. Fig. 6.7 depicts this.

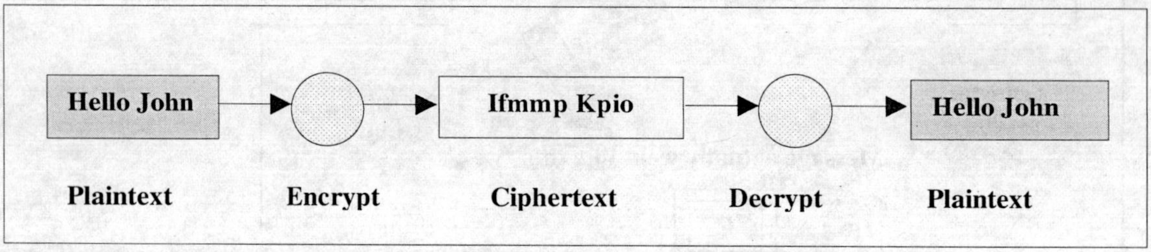

Fig. 6.7 Encryption and decryption process

Note that the sender applies the encryption algorithm and the recipient applies the decryption algorithm. The sender and the receiver must agree on this algorithm for any meaningful communication. The algorithm basically takes one text as input and produces another as the output. Therefore, the algorithm contains the intelligence for transforming messages. This intelligence is called the **key**. Only the persons having intelligence about the message transformation, that is access to the key, can encrypt and decrypt the messages.

6.3.1 Types of Cryptography

Based on the number of keys used for encryption and decryption, cryptography can be classified into two categories: **symmetric key cryptography** and **asymmetric key cryptography**, as shown in Fig. 6.8.

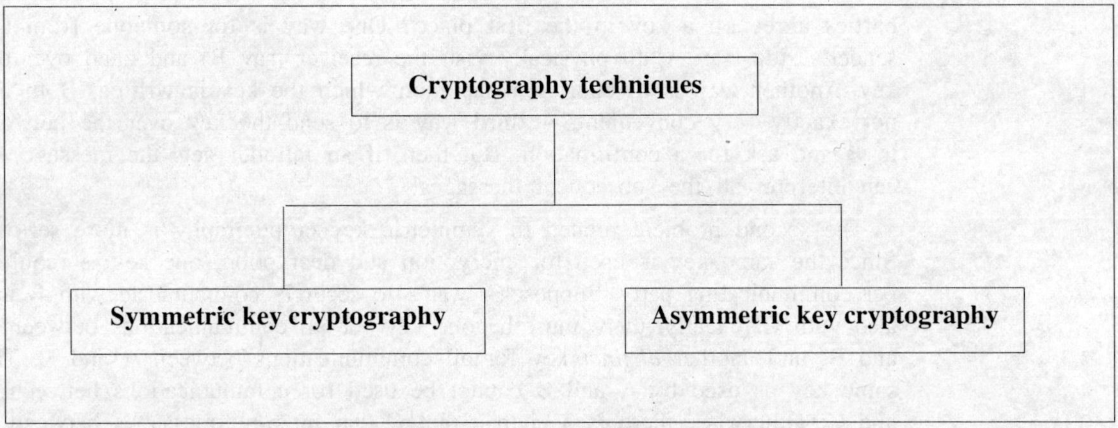

Fig. 6.8 Types of cryptography

6.3.1.1 Symmetric key cryptography Also called **secret key cryptography**, in this scheme only one key is used and the same key is used for encryption and decryption of messages. Obviously, both the parties must agree upon the key before any transmission begins and nobody else should know about it if it is to remain effective. The example in Fig. 6.9 shows how symmetric key cryptography works. Basically the key changes the original message to an encoded form at the sender's end, while at the receiver's end, the same key is used to decrypt the encoded message, thus deriving the original message out of it. IBM's **Data Encryption Standard (DES)** uses this approach. It uses 56-bit keys for encryption.

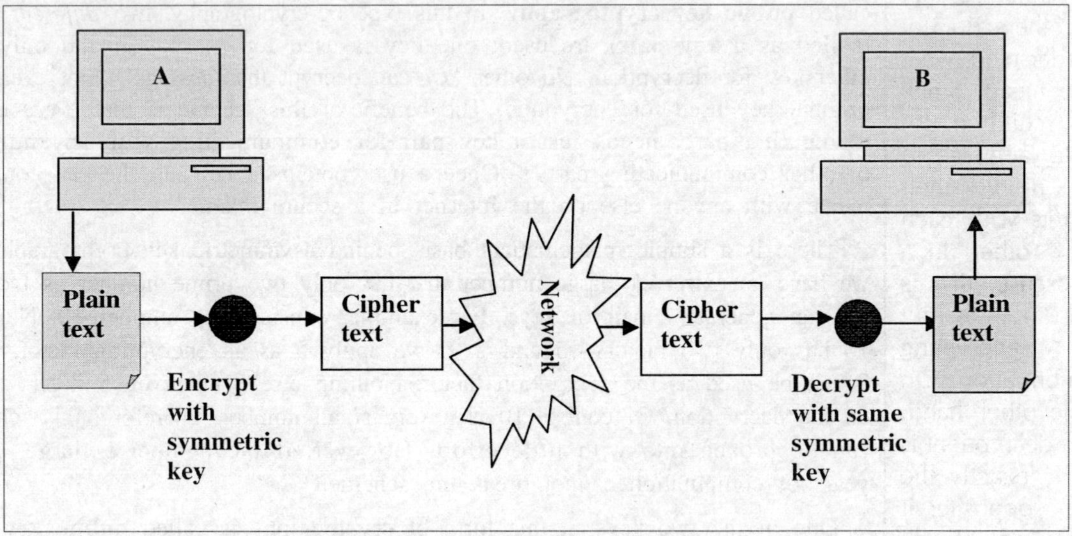

Fig. 6.9 Symmetric key cryptography

In practical situations, symmetric key cryptography has a number of problems; one problem being that of key agreement and distribution. How do two parties agree on a key in the first place? One way is for someone from the sender's side (say A) to physically visit the receiver (say B) and hand over the key. Another way is to courier a paper on which the key is written. Both are not exactly very convenient. A third way is to send the key over the network to B and ask for a confirmation. But then, if an intruder gets the message, he can interpret all the subsequent messages!

The second problem related to symmetric key cryptography is more serious. Since the same key is used for encryption and decryption, one key is required per communicating party. Suppose A wants to securely communicate with B and also with C. Clearly, there must be one key for all communications between A and B; and another *distinct* key for all communications between A and C. The same key as used by A and B cannot be used for communications between A and C. Otherwise, there is a chance that C can interpret messages between A and B, or B can do the same for messages between A and C! Since the Internet has thousands of merchants selling products to hundreds of thousands of buyers, using this scheme would be impractical because every buyer-seller combination would need a separate key!

Thus IBM's DES has been found to be vulnerable. Therefore, better symmetric key algorithms have been proposed and are in active use. One way is to simply use DES twice with two different keys (called as DES-2). A stronger mechanism is DES-3, wherein key-1 is used to encrypt first, key-2 (a different key) is used to re-encrypt the encrypted block, and key-1 is used once again to re-encrypt the doubly encrypted block. DES-3 is quite popular and is in wide use. Other popular algorithms are IDEA, RC5 and RC2.

Encryption is like codifying something so that others do not understand what we mean. Small children use code language to discuss their secrets with each other. In a sense, that is nothing but encrypting information. On the other hand, decryption is exactly the opposite; it transforms codified information back into normal, readable form.

6.3.1.2 Asymmetric key cryptography This is a better scheme and is also called **public key cryptography**. In this type of cryptography, two *different* keys (called as a **key pair**) are used; one key is used for encryption and only the other key for decryption. No other key can decrypt the message – not even the original key used for encryption. The benefit of this scheme is that every communicating party needs just a key pair for communicating with any number of other communicating parties. Once a user obtains a key-pair, he can communicate with anyone else on the Internet in a secure manner.

There is a simple mathematical basis behind asymmetric key cryptography. If we have an extremely large number that has only two prime number as factors, we can generate a pair of keys. For example, consider the number 10. Number 10 has only two factors—5 and 2. If we apply 5 as an encryption factor, only 2 can be used as the decryption factor. Nothing else – not even 5 itself – can do the decryption. Of course, 10 is a very small number. Therefore, this scheme can be broken into with little effort. However, if the number is large, even years of computation cannot break the scheme.

One of the two keys in this form of cryptography is called **public key** and the other **private key**. If we want to communicate over a computer network such as the Internet in a secure manner we would need to obtain a public key and a private key. We can generate these keys by using standard algorithms. The private key remains with the user as a secret and must not be disclosed to anybody. However, the public key is for the general public. It is disclosed to all parties that one wants to communicate with. In this scheme, in fact, each party or node publishes his public key. Using this, a directory can be constructed where the various parties or nodes (i.e. their IDs) and their corresponding public keys are maintained. One can consult this and get the public key for any party that one wishes to communicate with by a simple table search. Suppose A wants to send a message to B without having to worry about its security. Then, A and B should each have a private key and a public key.

- A's private key should be known only to A. However, A's public key should be known to B.
- Only B should know B's private key. However, A should know B's public key.

The working of such a system of simple:

1. When A wants to send a message to B, A encrypts the message using B's public key. This is possible because A knows B's public key.
2. User A sends this message (encrypted with B's public key) to B.
3. User B decrypts A's message using his private key. Note that only B knows about his private key. Thus, no one else can make any sense out of the message even if one manages to intercept it. This is because the intruder does not know about B's private key and only B's private key can decrypt the message.
4. When B wants to send a message to A, exactly the reverse of the above takes place. B encrypts the message using A's public key. Therefore, only A can decrypt the message with the use of his private key.

This is illustrated in Fig. 6.10.

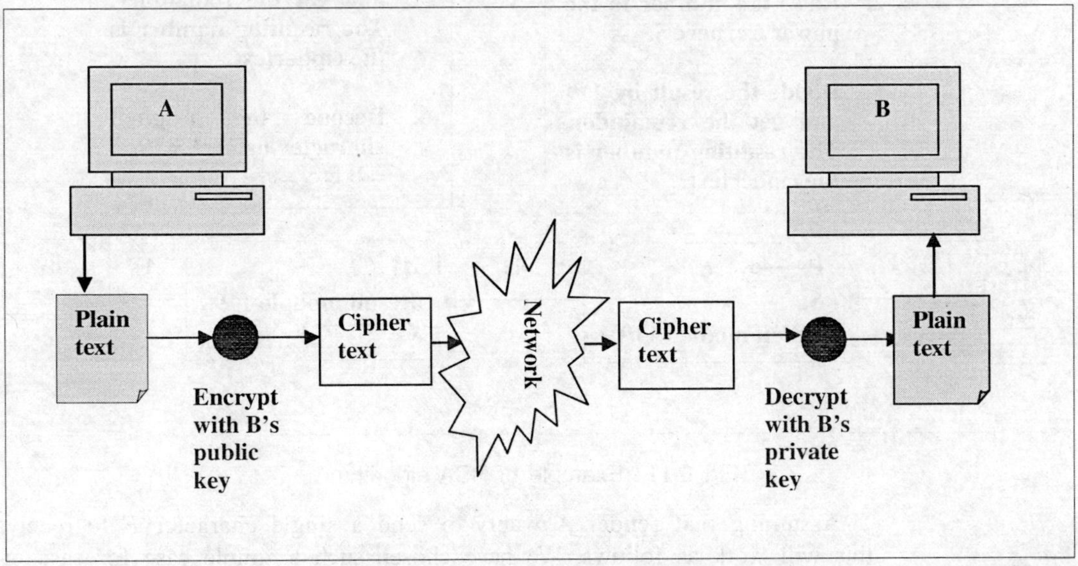

Fig. 6.10 Asymmetric key cryptography

The RSA algorithm

Let us examine a practical example of public key encryption. In 1977, Ron Rivest, Adi Shamir and Len Adleman at MIT developed the first major public key cryptography system. This method is called as Rivest-Shamir-Adleman (**RSA**) scheme. Even today, it is the most widely accepted public key solution. It solves the problem of key agreement and distribution so that there is no need to send thousands of keys across the network just to arrive at an agreement. All one needs to publish is one's public key. All public keys can then be stored in a database which can be consulted by anyone. However, the private key only remains with the original user. Thus, it requires a very basic amount of information sharing among users.

The RSA algorithm is based on the fact that it is easy to find and multiply large prime numbers, but extremely difficult to factor their product. The following discussion about RSA is a bit mathematical in nature, and can be safely skipped in case you are not interested in knowing the internals of RSA. However, if you are keen to know the mathematical details, you can continue reading. Let us now understand how RSA works. Fig. 6.11 shows an example of the RSA algorithm being employed for exchanging encrypted messages.

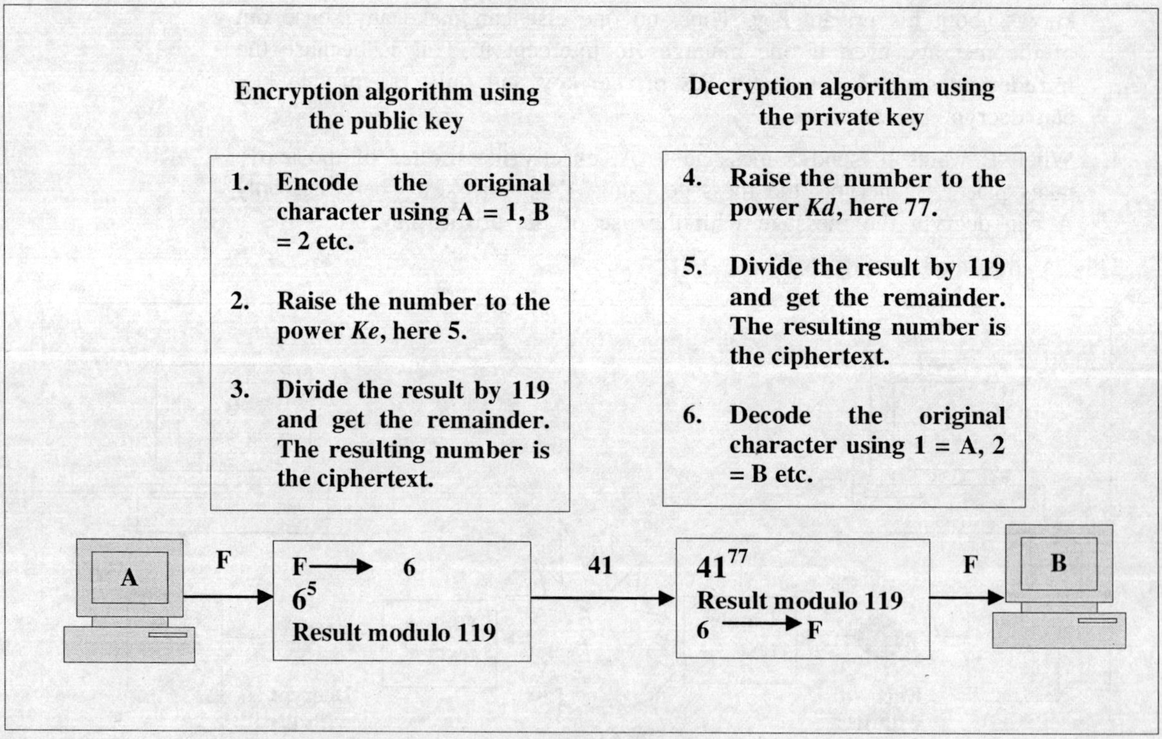

Fig 6.11 Example of RSA algorithm

Assuming that sender A wants to send a single character *F* to receiver B this will work as follows. We have chosen such a simple case for ease of understanding. Using the RSA algorithm, the character *F* would be encoded as follows.

1. Use the alphabet-numbering scheme (i.e. 1 for A, 2 for B, 3 for C and so on). As per this rule, 6 would represent F. Therefore, at first F would be encoded to 6.
2. Choose any two prime numbers, say 7 and 17.
3. Subtract 1 from each prime number and multiply the two results. Thus, we have (7 – 1) × (17 – 1) = 96.
4. Choose another prime number, say 5. This number, which is the public key, is called *Ke* in the RSA terminology. Therefore, Ke = 5.
5. Multiply the two original prime numbers of step 2. We have 17 × 7 = 119.
6. Calculate the following:

   (Original encoded number of step 1)^{Ke} modulo (Number of step 5) that is 6^5 modulo 119, which is 41.
7. The number thus obtained (41) is the encrypted information to be sent across the network.

At the receiver's end, the number 41 is decrypted to get back the original letter *F* as follows.

1. Subtract 1 from each prime number and multiply the two results— (7 – 1) × (17 – 1) = 96.
2. Multiply the two original numbers, that is, 17 × 7 = 119.
3. Find a number *Kd* such that when we divide (*Kd* × *Ke*) by 96, the remainder is 1. After a few calculations, we can come up with 77 as *Kd*.
4. Calculate 41^{Kd} modulo 119. That is, 41^{77} modulo 119. This gives 6.
5. Decode 6 back to F from the alphabet numbering scheme.

It might appear that anyone who knows about the public key *Ke* (5) and the number 119 could find the secret key *Kd* (77) by trial and error. However, if the private key is a large number, and another large number is chosen instead of 119, it will be extremely difficult to crack the secret key. This is what is done in practice.

6.4 DIGITAL SIGNATURE

Using the techniques described earlier, we can *sign* a computer-generated document or message just as we sign a check. A message thus signed contains our **digital signature**. This also involves the same principles of encryption and decryption.

Statistical database are like summary reports. You can make out the overall happenings in a database, but it is not so easy to identify individual pieces of information.

Signing a document digitally involves the following steps:

1. The sender calculates a unique value called **message digest** or **hash** of the message (say MD_1).
2. The sender encrypts the message digest with its private key. This is the digital signature of the message (say DS).

3. At the receiver's end, the original message and the corresponding digital signature are received.
4. The receiver also calculates its own message digest of the message (say MD_2).
5. The receiver decrypts the digital signature (DS) of step 2 with the public key of the sender. This gives the receiver the message digest as was calculated by the sender in step 1 (MD1).
6. The receiver now compares MD_1 with MD_2. If the two match, the receiver is sure that the message sent by the sender in step 2 authentic and not tampered with.

The process is shown in Fig. 6.12.

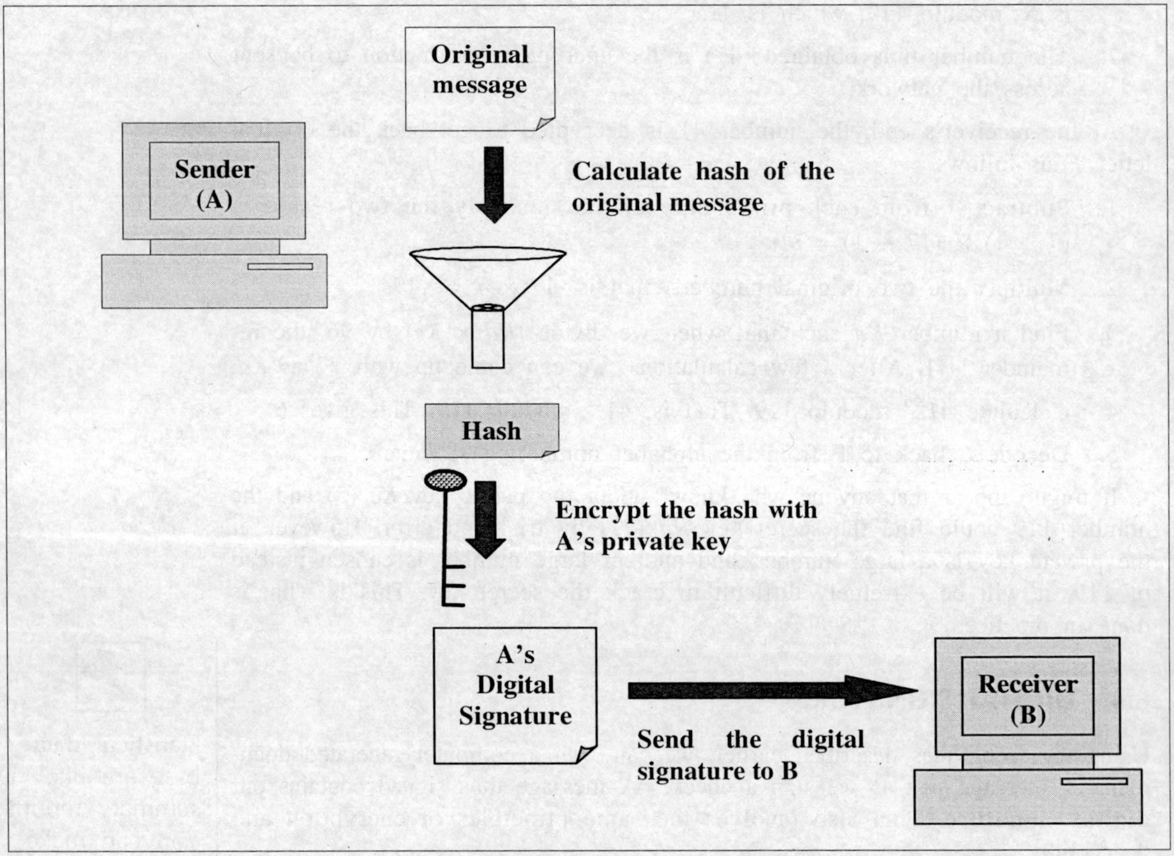

Fig. 6.12 Digital signature process

The other important feature supported by digital signatures is **non-repudiation,** that is, a sender cannot deny having sent a message. With IT laws in place in various countries, this has legal implications as well. Since a digital signature requires the use of the private key of the sender (which is supposed to be known only to the sender), once a message is digitally signed, it can be legally proven that the sender had indeed sent the message.

This can be very useful in tricky situations. For instance, suppose a user authorises a bank payment transaction over the Internet. After the payment is made, the user claims that the transaction was never performed. In such situations, which can be very common as the use of the Internet for conducting business transactions becomes widespread, digital signatures can play a crucial role. They can help settle legal disputes.

6.5 DATABASE CONTROL

Using the concept of **database control**, we can specify who can access a database. Database access can be granted in two ways. In other words, there are two types of database control: **discretionary control** and **mandatory control**. This is shown in Fig. 6.13.

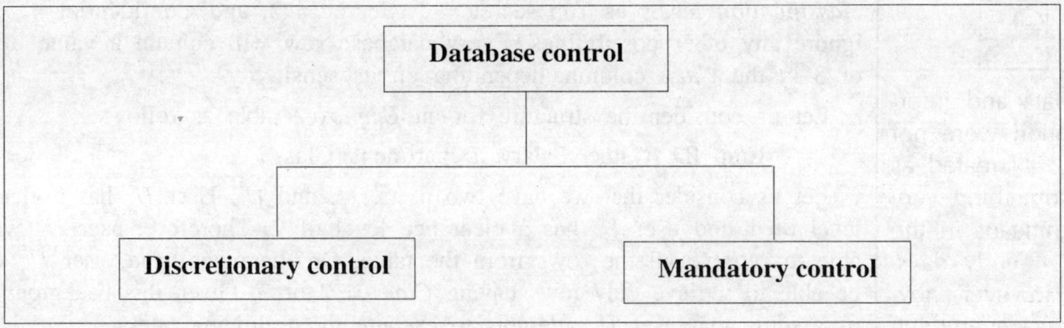

Fig. 6.13 Types of database control

Let us discuss what these types of control mean.

6.5.1 Discretionary Control

> In this type of database control, the users of the database system have **access rights**, also called **privileges**.

For example, we can define conditions such as:

(a) User U_1 can access table T_1 but not table T_2.

(b) User U_2 can access table T_2 but not table T_1.

This type of database control is very common and very flexible. We can define database authorisations, which tell us what the users of the database can do. In other words, database authorisations are exactly the opposite of database constraints.

We shall discuss this type of control in greater detail with SQL syntaxes and examples.

6.5.2 Mandatory Control

Here, each database object (e.g. table) has a **classification level** (e.g. top secret, secret, confidential, sensitive, unclassified) and each database user has a **clearance level** (e.g. top secret, secret, confidential, sensitive, unclassified).

This is a very rigid scheme. A user can access a database object only if she has an appropriate clearance level. Military or government organisations generally opt for this form of database control. After the US Department of Defense (DoD) published their guidelines regarding this type of control, database vendors have started implementing them.

The implementation of classification and clearance levels is quite interesting. In it each user ID has an associated *clearance level*. Suppose we want to implement the authorisation levels at the row level, every row of every table in the database would have an additional column, called as *Class*. This column indicates the *classification level*. Let us suppose that we codify the *clearance/classification levels* as Top secret = 1, Secret = 2, and Confidential = 3; and ignore any other possibilities. Every database row will contain a value of 1, 2 or 3 in the *Class* column, depending on its sensitivity.

Data and information were not treated as something very significant in the early days. However, now almost everything is computerised and automated. With the advent of electronic commerce and the proliferation of the Internet, data has become even more significant, and is now treated as a very precious commodity. Loss of data or damage to data is as bad as, or at times worse than, damage to or loss of paper money.

Let us consider the structure for an *Employee* table as follows:

Emp_ID, Name, Salary, Department, Class

Let us consider that we have two users, U_1 and U_2. User U_1 has a clearance level of 1 and user U_2 has a clearance level of 2. Therefore, user U_1 will be able to retrieve all the rows from the table. On the other hand, user U_2 would be able to retrieve only rows having *Class* = 2 or 3. Given this background. let us assume that user U_2 attempts to execute the following query:

```
SELECT Name, Salary
FROM Employee
WHERE Salary > 1000
```

In this case, the DBMS would automatically modify this query as follows:

```
SELECT Name, Salary
FROM Employee
WHERE Salary > 1000 AND Class >= 2
```

Note that the DBMS figures out that the clearance level of user U_2 is 2 and, therefore, prevents the user from retrieving rows whose class level is 1. Similarly, other attempts of the user to work with class level 1 would be defeated. For example, if user U_2 attempts to insert a row in the *Employee* table, then the DBMS would set the *Class* value to 2 or 3 for that row, and only then perform the insertion operation.

6.6 USERS AND DATABASE PRIVILEGES

Before we discuss the various security mechanisms of controling database access, let us discuss a few points which will help us understand the basics of RDBMS security.

- Database users are theoretically similar to the users of an operating system. However, there are many differences between the two types of users.
- Database users are typically authenticated with the use of user name and password. However, in most cases, this may not be visible to the end user.
- All objects under the control of a specific user are considered as belonging to the same schema.
- In technical terms, a database user is sometimes called as Authorisation Identifier (Authorisation ID).
- All the operations performed by a user on a database during one set of events is said to make up one *database session.* Another name for this is *database connection.* In it a user opens a connection to a database, performs the intended tasks and then breaks the connection. However, to establish the connection, the user must have the appropriate authentication credentials.
- A user is allocated a set of privileges. These privileges decide what the user can and cannot do.

6.7 TYPES OF PRIVILEGES

At a broad level, database privileges can be classified into two types: **system privileges** and **object privileges**, as shown in Fig. 6.14.

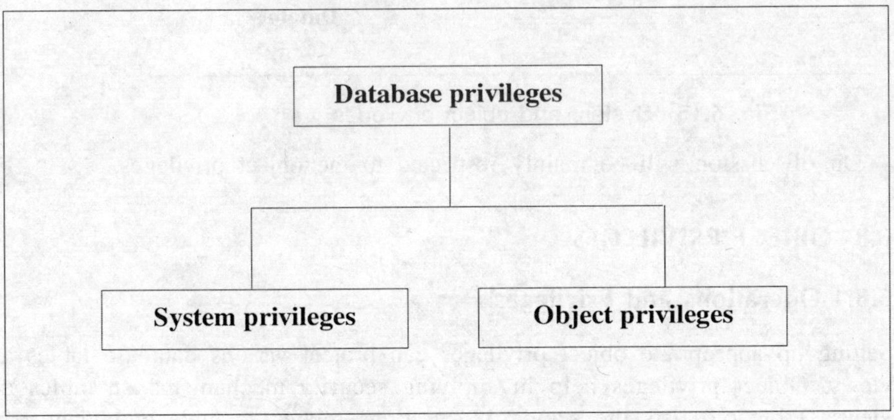

Fig. 6.14 Types of database privileges

Let us discuss the two types of privileges in brief.

- **System privileges**: These privileges are related to the access of the database. They govern things such as permission to connect to the database, the right to create tables and other objects and database administration permissions. These types of privileges are not standardised across various RDBMS products.
- **Object privileges**: These privileges are focused on a particular database object in question, for example, a table or view. Object privileges are standardised and do not depend on a particular RDBMS product. They

have been a part of the RDBMS technology right from its inception and, i.e. such, have become far more standardised across various RDBMS products. However, various RDBMS products also provide specific object privileges in addition to the basic set of object privileges that is standard and uniform for all the RDBMS products.

The idea of system and object privileges is shown in Fig. 6.15.

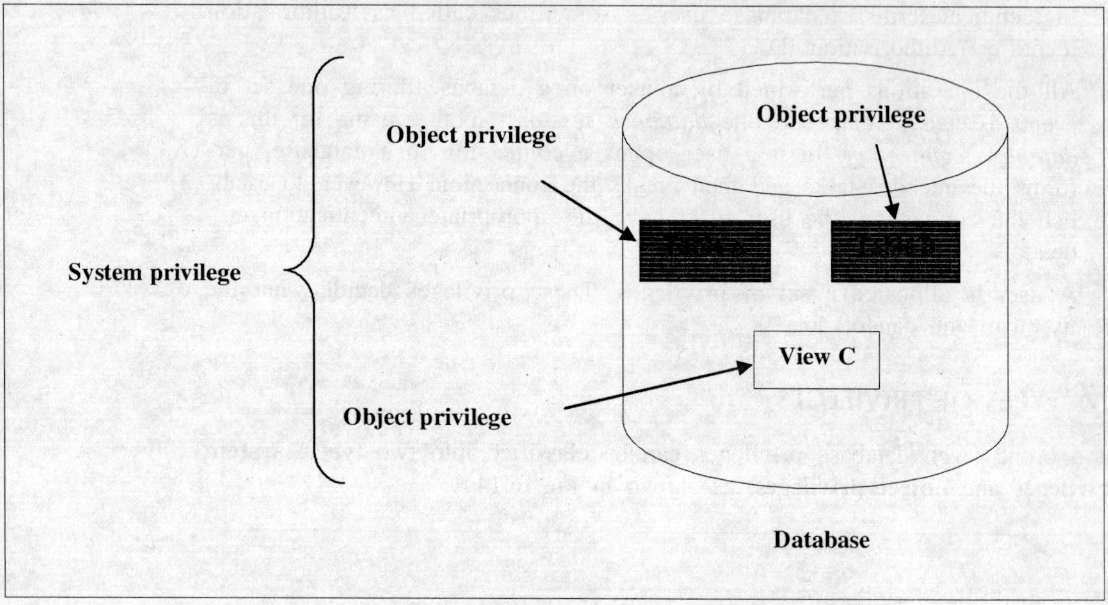

Fig. 6.15 System and object privileges

Our discussion will be mainly restricted to the object privileges.

6.8 OBJECT PRIVILEGES

6.8.1 Operations and Privileges

Setting up appropriate object privileges can protect various database tables and views. Object privileges help in applying security mechanisms on tables and views. Table 6.3 lists the standard operations related to table and view privileges.

Table 6.3 Object privileges

Operation	*Privilege specifications*
ALTER	If a user has this privilege on a table, that user can change the structure of the table by using an ALTER TABLE statement. Note that this privilege is related to tables only. This is not applicable to views.
SELECT	The user having this privilege on a table can query that table. It means that the user is allowed to access data from that table.

Operation	*Privilege specifications*
INSERT	A user with this privilege can create new data. That is, the user can add new rows to a table.
UPDATE	This privilege allows the user to change the data in a table. This privilege can be restricted to specific columns in a table. For example, if a table contains five columns named A through E, we can restrict the update privilege of the user to columns B and E only.
DELETE	A user with this privilege can delete one, more, or all rows in the specific table.
REFERENCES	A user with this privilege can declare a foreign key relationship that is based on one or more columns of the table as the parent key. The access can be limited to a few columns of the table. This privilege is specific to tables. It cannot be applied to views.
DROP	A user with this privilege can drop (i.e. delete) the table itself. Note that this is *different* from the DELETE operation privilege. In the case of DELETE, the user can delete one, more, or all rows of a table – that is the data in the table. However, the user cannot touch the structure or the existence of the table. In the case of DROP, however, the user can delete the table itself. This means that not only all the data in the table will vanish, but the table definition/structure (and therefore, all the depending definitions/structures such as indexes and views) will also vanish.
INDEX	If this privilege is allowed, the user can create an index on a table.

Note that the table or view owner has all these privileges by default. The owner can, in turn, give these privileges to the other users. This is described in the next section.

6.8.2 Granting Object Privileges

The **GRANT** statement is used to give database privileges to other users.

The general syntax of the GRANT statement is shown in Fig. 6.16.

GRANT <privilege/operation> ON <object name> TO <user name>;

Fig. 6.16 Granting privileges to other users

For example, suppose Prashant is the DBA. Obviously, Prashant would have all the privileges on the database and its objects, such as tables and views. Now suppose Prashant wants to give Ana (another user), a privilege to perform SELECT operation on a table called Sales. In such a scenario, Prashant can execute the following statement:

GRANT SELECT ON Sales TO Ana;

After Prashant executes the statement, Ana can execute a SELECT statement on the Sales table. Prior to this, she would not have been able to do this. Of course, even after the granting of privileges, Ana would only be able to execute the SELECT statement on the Sales table (unless Prashant has already given her other privileges).

When a user issues a GRANT statement to the RDBMS, the RDBMS cannot execute it blindly. The most important check it must perform is to ensure that the user who is issuing the command has the necessary privileges to grant the specified privileges to other user(s). The RDBMS has to be satisfied that the user issuing the GRANT command is the owner of the object (i.e. table or view) or has the necessary privileges to do so. If the user does not have sufficient privileges to grant privilege to other users, the RDBMS refuses to execute the GRANT command. A simple flow chart for this check is shown in Fig. 6.17.

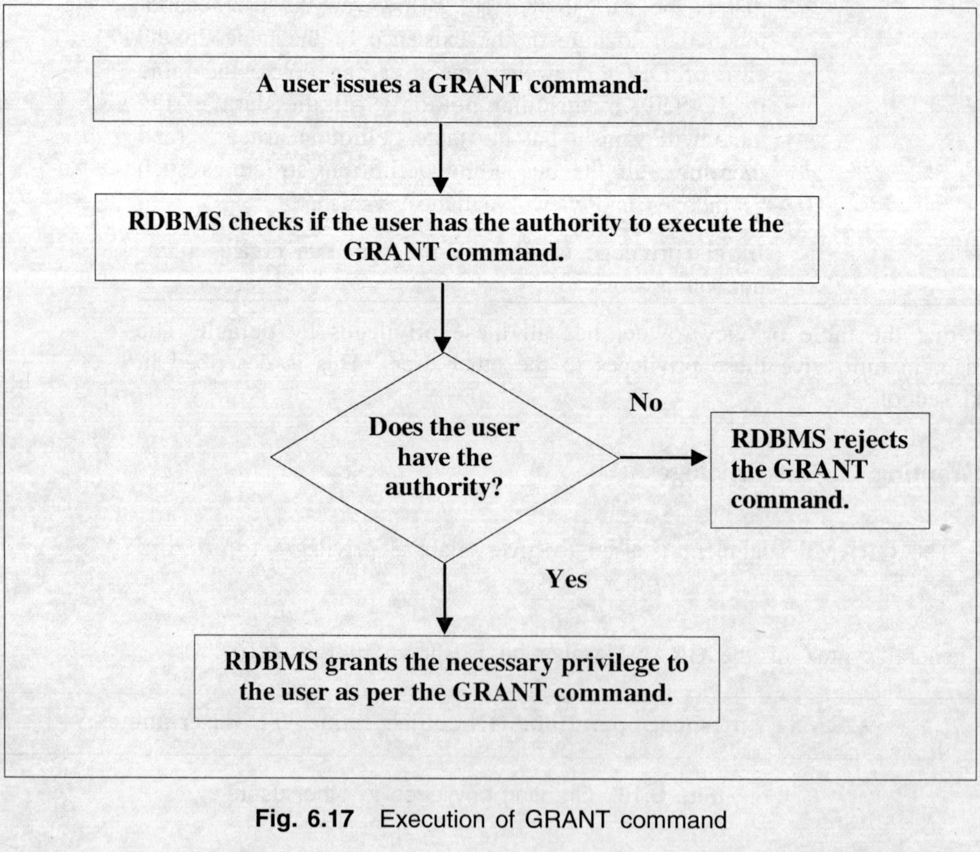

Fig. 6.17 Execution of GRANT command

Another important point is that even if the GRANT operation is successful, the user who has received the necessary privileges cannot grant them to other users. That is, when GRANT is successful, it only allows the user receiving the privileges to perform the specified operations. However, it prevents that user from handing over privileges to other users.

For example, let us assume that Prashant has successfully granted the SELECT privilege to Ana on the Sales table. Let us further assume that there is a third user by the name Radhika, who also does not have the SELECT privilege on the Sales table. Just because Ana has now obtained the SELECT privilege on the Sales table, she cannot simply give Radhika the same privilege. Only Prashant or another user who has the rights to give grants to other users can give the SELECT privilege on the Sales table to Radhika, or any other user. This idea is shown in Fig. 6.18.

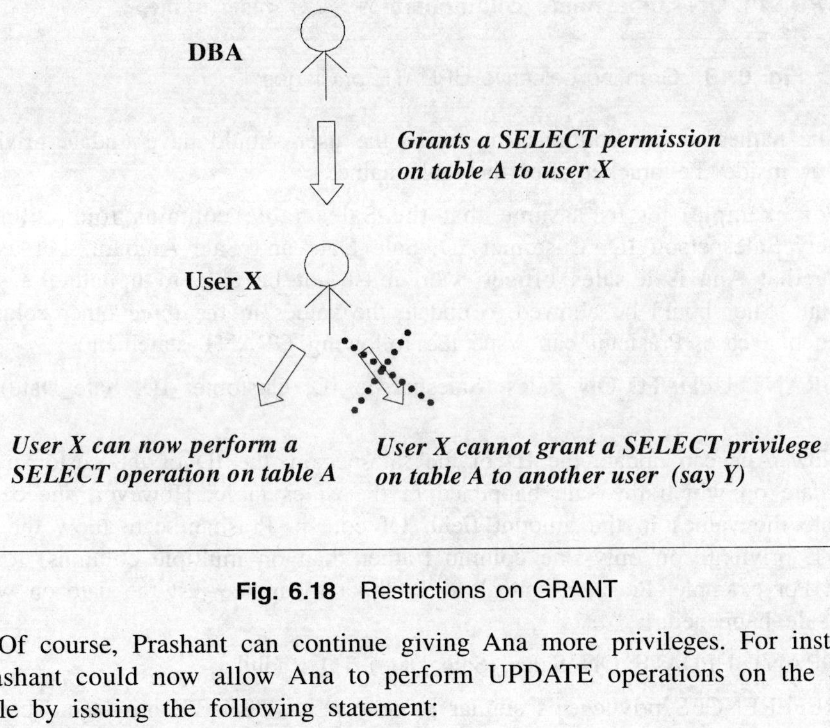

Fig. 6.18 Restrictions on GRANT

Of course, Prashant can continue giving Ana more privileges. For instance, Prashant could now allow Ana to perform UPDATE operations on the Sales table by issuing the following statement:

GRANT UPDATE ON Sales TO Ana;

Various other combinations of the basic technique are possible. For instance, Prashant can allow the SELECT and INSERT privileges to Ana by using just one statement:

GRANT SELECT, UPDATE ON Sales TO Ana;

Similarly, Prashant can give one privilege to multiple users at the same time. For example, Prashant can allow both Ana and Radhika the SELECT privilege by using a single statement:

GRANT SELECT ON Sales TO Ana, Radhika;

Finally, Prashant can hand out multiple privileges to multiple users at the same time. For example, Prashant can allow both Ana and Radhika the SELECT and UPDATE privileges by using a single statement:

GRANT SELECT, UPDATE ON Sales TO Ana, Radhika;

6.8.3 Restricting Object Privileges to Certain Columns

After Prashant issues the UPDATE privilege to Ana on the Sales table, Ana can update values in any column of that table. This sort of situation is not desired by many who meant users to be able to update only specific columns of a table. If privileges are to be restricted to certain sections only, the syntax of the GRANT command changes slightly. With reference to the UPDATE command, the syntax for restricting a privilege to certain columns is shown in Fig. 6.19.

GRANT UPDATE ON <table name (column names)> TO <user name>;

Fig. 6.19 Granting selective UPDATE privileges

The names of the columns for which the user should have update privilege appear inside the bracket after the table name.

For example, let us assume that the Sales table contains four columns, namely Salesperson_ID, Customer_ID, Sale_Date and Sale_Amount. Let us assume that Ana is a sales officer, who must not be able to update the sales amount. She should be allowed to update the values in the three other columns. In such a case, Prashant can issue the following GRANT statement:

GRANT UPDATE ON Sales (Salesperson_ID, Customer_ID, Sale_Date) TO Ana;

Now, Ana can update the ID of the salesperson, the ID of the customer and the date on which the sale happened in the Sales table. However, she cannot update the values in the amount field. Of course, Prashant can allow the UPDATE privilege on only one column (rather than on multiple columns) to any user. For example, Prashant can allow Radhika to update just the date on which the sale happened:

GRANT UPDATE ON Sales (Sale_Date) TO Radhika;

REFERENCES privilege is similar in concept to UPDATE privilege. The idea behind REFERENCES privilege can be summarised thus:

When user A grants the REFERENCES privilege to user B, user B can create a foreign key reference on a table owned by A.

For example, Prashant can allow Kapil the privilege of using the salesperson ID and customer ID columns of the Sales table as parent keys to any of the foreign keys in his table. For this, Prashant needs to execute the following statement:

GRANT REFERENCES (Salesperson_ID, Customer_ID) ON Sales TO Kapil;

Assuming that Kapil has another table called SalesDetails, for which he needs to set up this foreign key relationship with the Sales table, the conceptual will look as shown in Fig. 6.20.

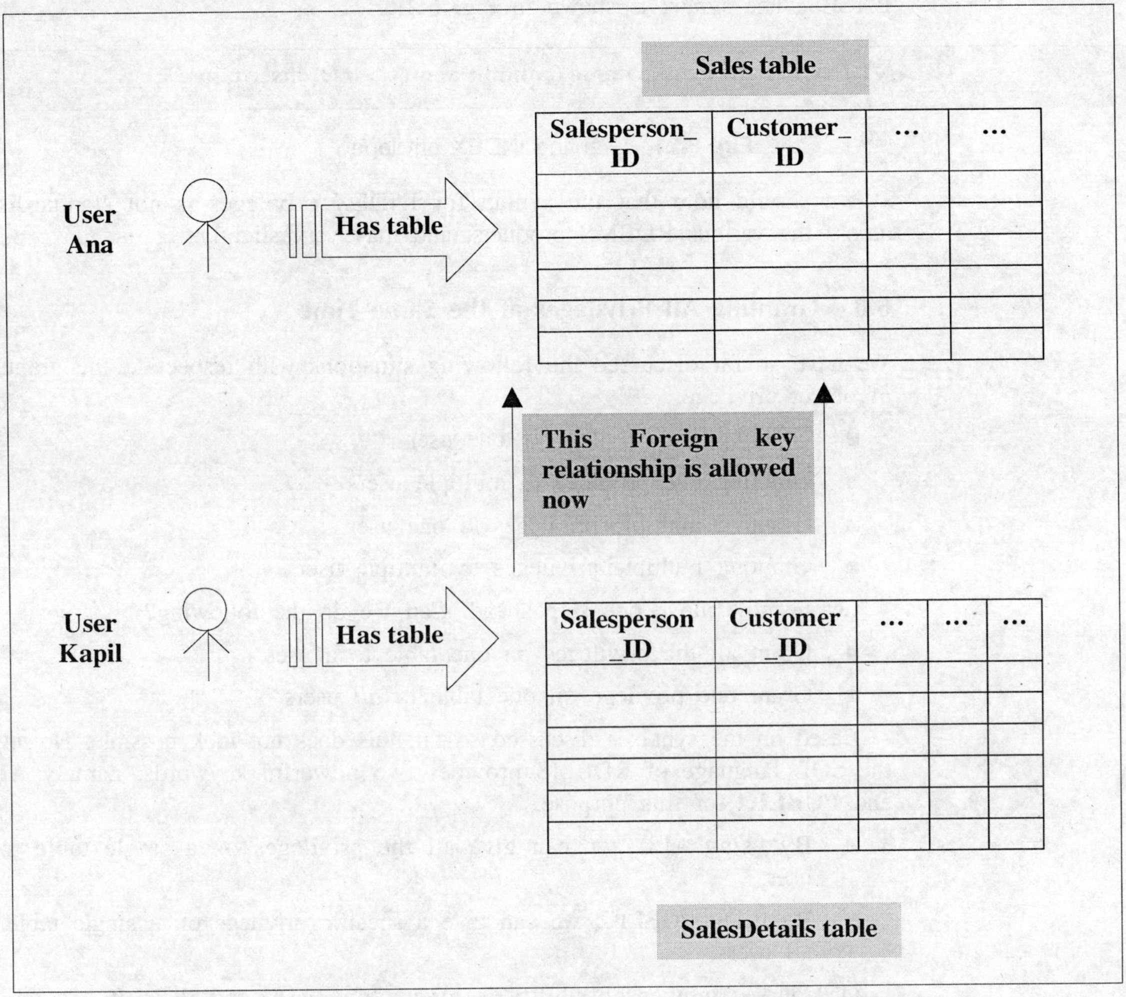

Fig. 6.20 Effect of allowing the REFERENCES privilege

Like in UPDATE privilege, we can omit the column names in the REFERENCES privilege as well. That is, we can allow the foreign key constraint to be put on all or any of the columns in a table. For instance, Prashant could execute the following statement:

GRANT REFERENCES ON Sales TO Kapil;

As a result of executing this statement, Kapil can base the foreign key of his table on any or all columns of the Sales table.

The INDEX privilege is used to create an index on a tablc.

As we know, an index is used to speed up access to the rows of a table. It is a set of lookup entries against the actual rows in the database table. The syntax for granting INDEX privileges is the same as the one for REFERENCES. The syntax is shown in Fig. 6.21.

GRANT INDEX ON <table name (column names)> TO <user name>;

Fig. 6.21 Granting INDEX privilege

We should note that the syntax for INDEX privileges is not standardised across the various RDBMS products, and may vary slightly.

6.8.4 Granting All Privileges at the Same Time

We have so far discussed the following situations with respect to the granting of object privileges:

- Granting one privilege to one user
- Granting one privilege to multiple users
- Granting multiple privileges to one user
- Granting multiple privileges to multiple users

Let us now move one step ahead. Can we do the following?

- Grant all the privileges on one table to a user
- Grant one privilege on one table to *all* users

Based on the syntaxes discussed so far, this does not look possible. However, the SQL language of RDBMS provides two powerful keywords, namely **ALL** and **PUBLIC** for this purpose.

- By using ALL, we can give all the privileges on a single table to a user.
- By using PUBLIC, we can give a specific privilege on a single table to all users.

Of course, another possibility is to combine ALL and PUBLIC, in which case, the following happens:

By using ALL and PUBLIC together, we can give all the privileges on a single table to all the users.

Let us discuss these concepts with a few examples.

Suppose Prashant wants to give all the privileges on the Sales table to Kapil. Then, Prashant can execute the following command:

GRANT ALL PRIVILEGES ON Sales TO Kapil;

The keyword PRIVILEGES is optional. So, the above statement is equivalent to the following statement:

GRANT ALL ON Sales TO Kapil;

Similarly, Prashant can give SELECT privilege on the Sales table to all the users with the help of the following command:

GRANT SELECT ON Sales TO PUBLIC;

As a result, all the users in the system would now be able to execute the SELECT statement on the Sales table. This has been made possible by using just one powerful statement.

What would happen if Prashant executes the following statement?

GRANT ALL ON Sales TO PUBLIC;

Quite clearly, all users would be able to perform all the operations on the Sales table. That is, all users would now have all the privileges on the Sales table. Quite clearly, this is a very dangerous command from a security perspective. It must be used with great caution and only after understanding its implications. Otherwise, it can lead to disaster.

We can now summarise the syntaxes of the ALL and PUBLIC keywords, as shown in Fig. 6.22 and Fig. 6.23. Fig. 6.24 shows the syntax for combining them.

GRANT ALL ON <table name> TO <user name>;

Fig. 6.22 Using the ALL keyword

GRANT <privilege>ON <table name> TO PUBLIC;

Fig. 6.23 Using the PUBLIC keyword

GRANT ALL ON <table name> TO PUBLIC;

Fig. 6.24 Combining the ALL and PUBLIC keywords

6.8.5 Allowing Others to Grant Privileges

So far, we have discussed cases in which only one person, who is either the DBA or owns rights on the objects can give privileges on those objects to other users. Does it mean that only one user is responsible for giving privileges to other users all the time? This seems to be a limiting factor in a big database implementation, where there could be thousands of tables and hundreds of users. If only one person has to deal with all the responsibilities of access rights, she can quickly get overloaded.

Precisely to deal with this problem, SQL provides a feature by which a person at the DBA level can not only grant privileges to other users but can also allow those users to grant privileges to more users. The idea is shown in Fig. 6.25.

Here, the DBA has granted certain privileges to users A, B and C. What is notable, however, is that the DBA has granted the special privilege of *granting privileges* to others to user B only. This means that user B not only has certain privileges on certain objects, but can, in turn, grant certain privileges to any user.

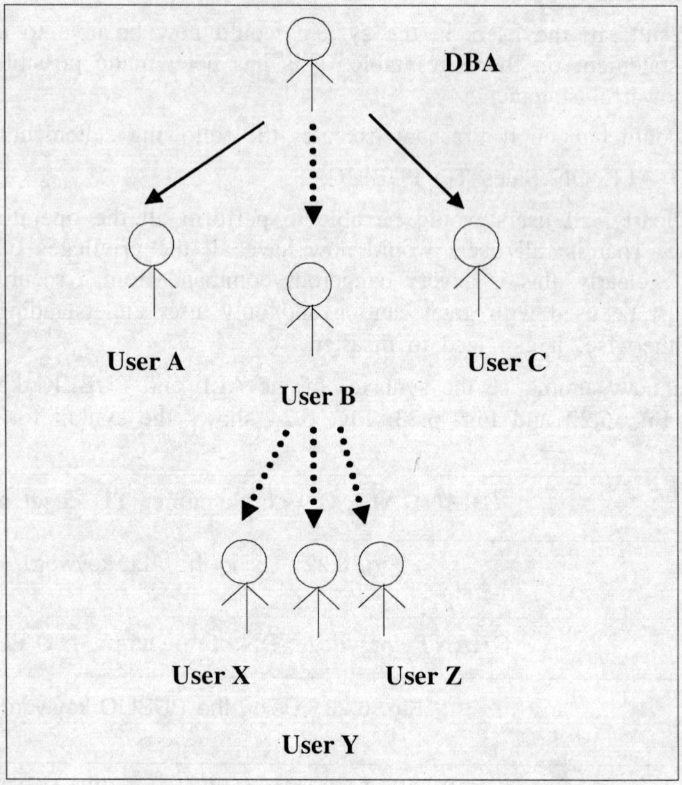

Fig. 6.25 Granting the privilege to grant privileges to others

What would be the syntax for doing this? The DBA (say Prashant) would need to use the keywords WITH GRANT OPTION while granting object privileges to user B (say Radhika). The command would be as follows:

GRANT SELECT ON Sales TO Radhika WITH GRANT OPTION;

This statement means that Prashant wants to give the SELECT privilege on the Sales table to Radhika. In addition, Prashant also wants Radhika to be able to grant privileges to other users in a similar fashion. As we have noted earlier, this is achieved by using the keywords WITH GRANT OPTION.

Of course, because Prashant has given just SELECT privilege to Radhika on the Sales table, Radhika would also be able to give only SELECT privilege to other users. Radhika cannot, for instance, give an UPDATE privilege on the Sales table to other users, simply because she herself does not have it in the first place!

Now, Radhika can grant SELECT privilege to Kapil as follows:

GRANT SELECT ON Sales TO Kapil;

As a result, Kapil can now access the Sales table with the SELECT privilege. Better yet, Radhika could have allowed Kapil to grant privileges further to other users with the help of the following command:

GRANT SELECT ON Sales TO Kapil WITH GRANT OPTION;

In general, the syntax for giving the rights to grant privileges to others is specified as shown in Fig. 6.26.

GRANT <privilege> ON <table name> TO <User name> WITH GRANT OPTION;

Fig. 6.26 Using the WITH GRANT OPTION keywords

6.9 TAKING AWAY PRIVILEGES

What if Prashant is told that Radhika is leaving the organisation and she must not be able to access the Sales table (for that matter, any table, but we shall ignore this here)? How can Prashant take back the privileges that he had given to Radhika earlier? For this purpose, the **REVOKE** command can be used.

By using a REVOKE command, a privilege granted earlier can be taken back.

For example, Prashant can execute the following command:

REVOKE SELECT ON Sales FROM Radhika;

Prashant can take back multiple privileges with the help of the following command:

REVOKE SELECT, INSERT ON Sales FROM Radhika;

Better yet, Prashant can revoke all the privileges of Radhika at one shot as follows:

REVOKE ALL ON Sales FROM Radhika;

Similarly, Prashant can revoke the UPDATE and INSERT privilege from Ana and Radhika using a single command as follows:

REVOKE UPDATE, INSERT ON Sales FROM Ana, Radhika;

An interesting question arises here. Suppose Prashant had granted certain privileges to Ana WITH GRANT OPTION. Further, Ana had granted certain privileges on the same table (Sales) to Kapil, again WITH GRANT OPTION. If Prashant now withdraws the privileges of Ana on the Sales table, what happens to Kapil's privileges? Going one step ahead, what happens to the privileges that Kapil may have granted to other users, and so on? For this, we should remember the following rule:

When we revoke a privilege that was granted WITH GRANT OPTION, all the users who had received the privilege because of that grant option also lose it.

Thus, Kapil and anyone else who got the privileges on the Sales table directly or indirectly from Ana would lose them.

Similarly, a user can revoke a privilege only if she had originally granted it. A user cannot take away the privilege given by another user.

6.10 FILTERING TABLE PRIVILEGES

So far, we have not mentioned anything about restricting the privileges to specific areas of a table. That is, when Prashant gives the Sales table SELECT privilege to Ana, she can access all rows and all columns of that table. There are situations when this is not desirable. Instead, it may be necessary to provide access to a user only to certain columns, certain rows or a combination of the two. For example, let us mention a few cases of this situation.

- Ana must have access only to the Salesperson ID and Customer ID columns of the Sales table.
- Radhika should be allowed to access sales that happened on 7 June 2003 only.
- Kapil should be able to see only the Sales date and Sales amount for sales below $100.

Cryptography is a very old technique for protecting information. Over the years, it has become richer and more and more sophisticated, especially with the usage of computers. Modern cryptography techniques are quite comprehensive in nature and are hard to break into. But attackers find newer ways of breaking in, and the security experts need to keep working on still better techniques to deal with them.

Clearly, in order to deal with such requirements, the normal mechanism of providing privileges is not good enough. We must have some means of providing access only to the information as the business case demands. To deal with such cases, database views should be created, and then privileges should be given on those views.

For example, to deal with the case of Ana gaining access only to the Salesperson ID and Customer ID columns of the Sales table, two steps are needed: (a) Create a view containing only these two columns, and (b) Give Ana a privilege on this view, and not on the Sales table (also called the *base table*). The commands for this two-step process are as follows:

```
CREATE VIEW Anasview AS
    SELECT Salesperson_ID, Customer_ID  ------>  Creation of the view
    FROM Sales;
GRANT SELECT ON Anasview TO Ana;  ------>  Giving privileges on the view
```

Note that Ana does not have an access to the Sales table. However, she is given SELECT privilege on the view called Anasview. Since this view contains only two columns in which she is interested, the purpose of restricting Ana's access only to these columns is achieved.

Let us now examine our second requirement:

Radhika should be allowed to access sales that happened on 7 June 2003 only.

It should not be difficult to imagine that the following statements would do the trick:

```
CREATE VIEW Radhikasview AS
    SELECT *                          ——→ Creation of the view
    FROM Sales
WHERE Sale_date = '7 June 2003';      ——→ Giving privileges on
                                          the view
GRANT SELECT ON Radhikasview TO Radhika;
```

Note that in the case of Radhika, we have filtered rows, rather than columns. In the case of Anasview, we had filtered the columns and not the rows. Note that the filter can be applied to rows as well as columns. For instance, let us examine the last case:

Kapil should be able to see only the Sales date and Sales amount for sales below $100.

In this case, the creation of the view should be based on the filtering of rows as well as columns, as shown below.

```
CREATE VIEW Kapilsview AS
    SELECT Sale_date, Sale_amount     ——→ Creation of the view
    FROM Sales
WHERE Sale_amount < 100;              ——→ Giving privileges on
                                          the view
GRANT SELECT ON Kapilsview TO Kapil;
```

Let us now consider another situation in which we change the SELECT privilege of Kapil to UPDATE. We also allow him access to all the columns in the table. Thus the two commands in the above operation would now look as follows.

```
CREATE VIEW Kapilsview AS
    SELECT *                          ——→ Creation of the view
    FROM Sales
WHERE Sale_amount < 100;              ——→ Giving privileges on
                                          the view
GRANT UPDATE ON Kapilsview TO Kapil;
```

What would be the result of this change? Kapil would now be able to update any columns pertaining to the Sales table via the Kapilsview view. This is a very useful feature. However, unless used carefully, it can prove very dangerous, at times. If we examine carefully, we would realise that Kapil can, if he desires, change the amount of a transaction record to a value greater than 100, whereas he is supposed to access only records that are valued at less than 100.

Another powerful feature which is used to prevent such situations, is the CHECK OPTION. When this option is specified, the user can perform updates to the base table through the view, but only within the boundaries of the view definition. Thus if the CHECK OPTION is specified, Kapil can update the sales amount of a record only to a value less than 100. This makes good sense because Kapil is allowed to access and update only those records whose sales amount is less than 100. If Kapil sets the amount of a record to a value greater than or equal to 100, the whole purpose of restricting Kapil's privileges in the first place would be lost! The modified definition of the view would look as follows:

```
CREATE VIEW Kapilsview AS
    SELECT *                    ———→ Creation of the view
    FROM Sales
WHERE Sale_amount < 100
WITH CHECK OPTION;
```

The GRANT statement would remain unchanged. Because we have inserted the WITH CHECK OPTION clause, Kapil can update the value of the sales amount for any record. However, he can only change it to a value less than 100.

6.11 STATISTICAL DATABASES

One attempt to thwart attacks on databases is the possible use of **statistical databases**.

> A statistical database allows queries based on aggregate information, but not based on the information of individual rows.

For example, if we are using a statistical database of employee and payroll information, the following question is quite legal:

What is the average pay of the male employees in this organisation?

However, the following question is quite illegal:

What is the salary of Deepa?

Note that the first question is based on cumulative data, whereas the latter is based on an individual row.

This property of statistical databases is shown in Fig. 6.27.

The benefit of this approach is quite obvious. Individual data can be protected quite easily, as it is not accessible even to the authorised users of the database system. At the most, an attacker can retrieve aggregate information, which is useful in some ways, but not to a very large extent.

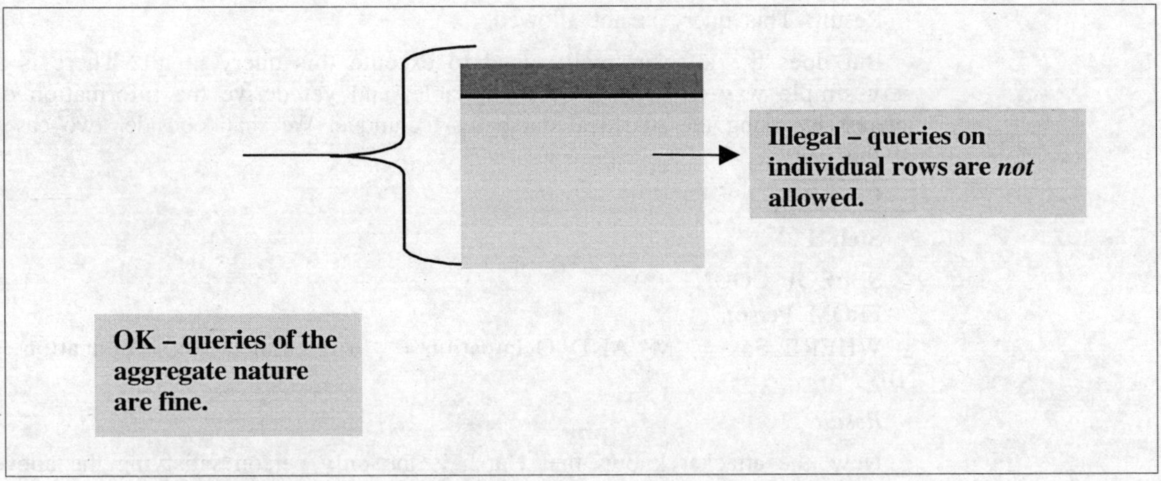

Fig. 6.27 Statistical databases – What can and cannot be done?

Having made this statement, it is extremely important to understand that statistical databases do not solve all security problems. For example, if an attacker obtains a lot of information by executing a number of aggregate queries, then it might happen that the person will be able to actually obtain information even about individuals! This process is called *deduction of confidential information by inference*. We shall illustrate this with an example. Consider a Person table as shown in Fig. 6.4.

Table 6.4 Person table

Name	*Sex*	*Occupation*	*Salary*	*Education*
Atul	M	Programmer	8000	MBA
Ana	F	Manager	12000	LLB
Jui	F	Journalist	7000	MA
Harsh	M	Programmer	8500	BE
Shashikant	M	Doctor	15000	MD
Meena	F	Doctor	17000	MBBS
Kedar	M	Doctor	16000	MD
Gauri	F	Doctor	14000	MBBS

Let us assume that an attacker wants to know Harsh's salary. The attacker knows that Harsh is a male, is educated up to BE (Bachelor of Engineering) and works as a programmer. However the attacker does not have an access to this table. Instead, he can access it in the form of a statistical table and execute queries of aggregate nature on this table. Thus, if the attacker executes the following query, it would fail – the DBMS would refuse the execution.

```
SELECT Salary
FROM Person
WHERE Name = 'Harsh'
```

Result: This query is not allowed.

But does the attacker really need to execute this query at all? There is a very simple way to bypass the main table, and yet derive the information of interest by using the statistical databases technique. We shall consider two cases of this.

Case 1

Step 1

```
SELECT COUNT (*)
FROM Person
WHERE Sex = 'M' AND Occupation = 'Programmer' AND Education = 'BE'
```

Result: 1

Now, the attacker knows that Harsh is the only person satisfying the above criteria in the *Person* table. Next, the attacker performs a simple trick.

Step 2

```
SELECT SUM (Salary)
FROM Person
WHERE Sex = 'M' AND Occupation = 'Programmer' AND Education = 'BE'
```

Result: 8500

Note that the attacker is able to compromise the database security without any problems. In the process, only legitimate queries have been run against the statistical database.

Case 2

Of course, things may not be so simple every time. But the attacker can find more interesting ways of beating the complexity. Consider the following.

Step 1

```
SELECT COUNT (*)
FROM Person
WHERE Sex = 'M'
```

Result: 4

The attacker knows that there are four males in the *Person* table.

Step 2

```
SELECT COUNT (*)
FROM Person
WHERE Sex = 'M' AND (NOT (Occupation = 'Programmer'))
```

Result: 2

The attacker knows that there are two male programmers and two male non-programmers in the *Person* table.

Step 3

```
SELECT MAX (Salary)
```

```
FROM Person
WHERE Sex = 'M' AND (NOT (Occupation = 'Programmer'))
```

Result: 8500

The attacker knows that the Harsh's salary could be 8500.

Step 4

```
SELECT MIN (Salary)
FROM Person
WHERE Sex = 'M' AND (NOT (Occupation = 'Programmer'))
```

Result: 8000

The attacker knows that the Harsh's salary could be 8000.

Thus, although unable to find out Harsh's exact salary, the attacker is able to find out the range of Harsh's salary!

KEY TERMS AND CONCEPTS

Access rights
Authentication
Classification level
Confidentiality
Data Encryption Standard (DES)
Decryption
Discretionary control
Fabrication
Integrity
Key pair
Message digest
Non-repudiation
Plaintext
Privileges
Public key cryptography
Secret key cryptography
Symmetric key cryptography
Asymmetric key cryptography
Ciphertext
Clearance level
Cryptography
Database privileges
Digital signature
Encryption
Hash
Interception
Mandatory control
Modification
Object privileges
Private key
Public key
RSA algorithm
Statistical database
System privileges

CHAPTER SUMMARY

- The importance of data varies from one organisation to another.
- Data can be classified as sensitive, confidential, private, proprietary and public.
- There are four major concepts related to the security of data: **confidentiality**, **integrity**, **authentication** and **non-repudiation**.
- **Confidentiality** means keeping a secret.
- **Integrity** means preserving the contents of a message between the sender and he receiver.

- **Authentication** means identifying a user or a system before they can access any data.
- **Non-repudiation** means preventing the denial of an action.
- Security can be achieved by using **cryptography**, an art of codifying data/messages.
- Cryptography involves **encryption** and **decryption**.
- In encryption, a readable message is transformed into an unreadable format.
- In decryption, an unreadable message is transformed back into its original readable format.
- Encryption and decryption are based on two aspects: **algorithm** and **key**.
- If the communicating parties use the same (single) key, the encryption is called **symmetric key encryption**.
- If the communicating parties use two different keys, the encryption is called **asymmetric key encryption**.
- **Digital signature** prevents repudiation.
- Database control can be classified into two types: **discretionary control** and **mandatory control**.
- Database privileges can be divided into **system privileges** and **object privileges**.
- SQL provides rich features for database control and privilege enforcement.
- Privileges can be granted to or revoked from a database user.
- Privileges can apply to tables, columns, indexes, references and so on.
- **Statistical databases** can protect database information to a certain extent. They contain only summary information.

PRACTICE SET

Mark as true or false

1. All organisations have the same sensitivity to data.
2. Private organisations treat secret data as the most sensitive.
3. Cryptography is the same as compression.
4. Encryption means encoding of data.
5. Decryption means decoding of data.
6. In asymmetric key cryptography, two keys are used per party.
7. RSA is a symmetric key encryption algorithm.
8. In SQL, GIVE command is used to give privileges to users.
9. In SQL, no user can give privileges to other users.
10. Statistical databases contain only aggregate information.

Fill in the blanks

1. The highest sensitive data in the case of private organisations is the ________ data.

   (a) confidential (b) private

   (c) sensitive (d) public

2. The lowest sensitive data in the case of private organisations is the ________ data.
   (a) confidential (b) private
   (c) sensitive (d) public
3. The highest sensitive data in the case of military organisations is the ________ data.
   (a) top secret (b) secret
   (c) confidential (d) unclassified
4. The lowest sensitive data in the case of military organisations is the ________ data.
   (a) top secret (b) secret
   (c) confidential (d) unclassified
5. The principle of ________ ensures that only the sender and the intended recipients have access to the contents of a message.
   (a) confidentiality (b) authentication
   (c) integrity (d) access control
6. If the recipient of a message has to be satisfied with the identify of the sender, the principle of ______ comes into picture.
   (a) confidentiality (b) authentication
   (c) integrity (d) access control
7. If we want to ensure the principle of ________, the contents of a message must not be modified while in transit.
   (a) confidentiality (b) authentication
   (c) integrity (d) access control
8. Allowing certain users specific accesses comes in the purview of ________.
   (a) confidentiality (b) authentication
   (c) integrity (d) access control
9. SQL uses the ______ command to provide users the necessary privileges.
   (a) provide (b) handover
   (c) grant (d) allow
10. ________ privileges apply to individual users.
    (a) Object (b) Table
    (c) Index (d) System

? Provide detailed answers to the following questions

1. Write a note on classification of data.
2. Discuss the principles of security.
3. What is the difference between integrity and confidentiality?
4. Why are authentication and non-repudiation critical?
5. What is cryptography?

6. Explain the difference between symmetric and asymmetric key cryptography.
7. Explain the GRANT and REVOKE commands.
8. What is the grant option?
9. What are statistical databases?
10. Do statistical databases guarantee a very secure environment? Why?

Exercises

1. During World War II, a German spy used a technique known as *Null Cipher*. With the use of this technique, the actual message is created from the first alphabet of each word in the message that is actually transmitted. Find out the hidden secret message if the transmitted message is *President's embargo ruling should have immediate notice. Grave situation affecting international law, statement foreshadows ruin of many neutrals. Yellow journals unifying national excitement immensely.*
2. Consider a scheme involving the replacement of alphabets as follows:

Original	A	B	C	...	X	Y	Z
Changed to	Z	Y	X	...	C	B	A

   If Atul sends a message *HSLDNVGSVNLMVB*, what should Ana infer from this?
3. Study the role of XOR operation in cryptography.
4. Encrypt the following plain text bit pattern with the supplied key, using the XOR operation, and state the resulting cipher text bit pattern.

Plain text	10011110100101010
Key	01000101111101101

5. Transform the cipher text generated in the above exercise back to the original plain text.
6. Consider a plain text message I AM A HACKER. Encrypt it with the help of the following algorithm:
   (a) Replace each alphabet with its equivalent 7-bit ASCII code.
   (b) Add a 0 bit as the leftmost bit to make each of the above bit patterns 8 positions long.
   (c) Swap the first four bits with the last four bits for each alphabet.
   (d) Write the hexadecimal equivalent of every four bits.
7. Write a C program to perform the above exercise.
8. Investigate what a digital certificate is and how it is useful.
9. Learn about an algorithm called Advanced Encryption Standard (AES).
10. Find out the various built-in cryptographic capabilities in different RDBMS products.

Chapter 7

Query Execution and Optimisation

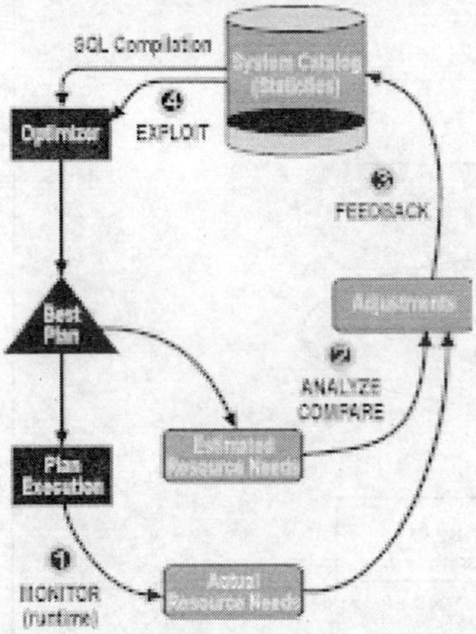

Database operations are quite expensive in terms of the CPU time usage and the wait time for the user. Optimising them helps tremendously in terms of boosting the overall throughput.

Chapter Highlights

- Internals of Query Execution
- Fundamentals of Query Optimisation
- Examples of Optimisation
- Recommendations for Query Optimisation
- Database Statistics

7.1 QUERY PROCESSING

The DBMS performs a number of steps while executing a query. The conceptual view of this process is shown in Fig. 7.1.

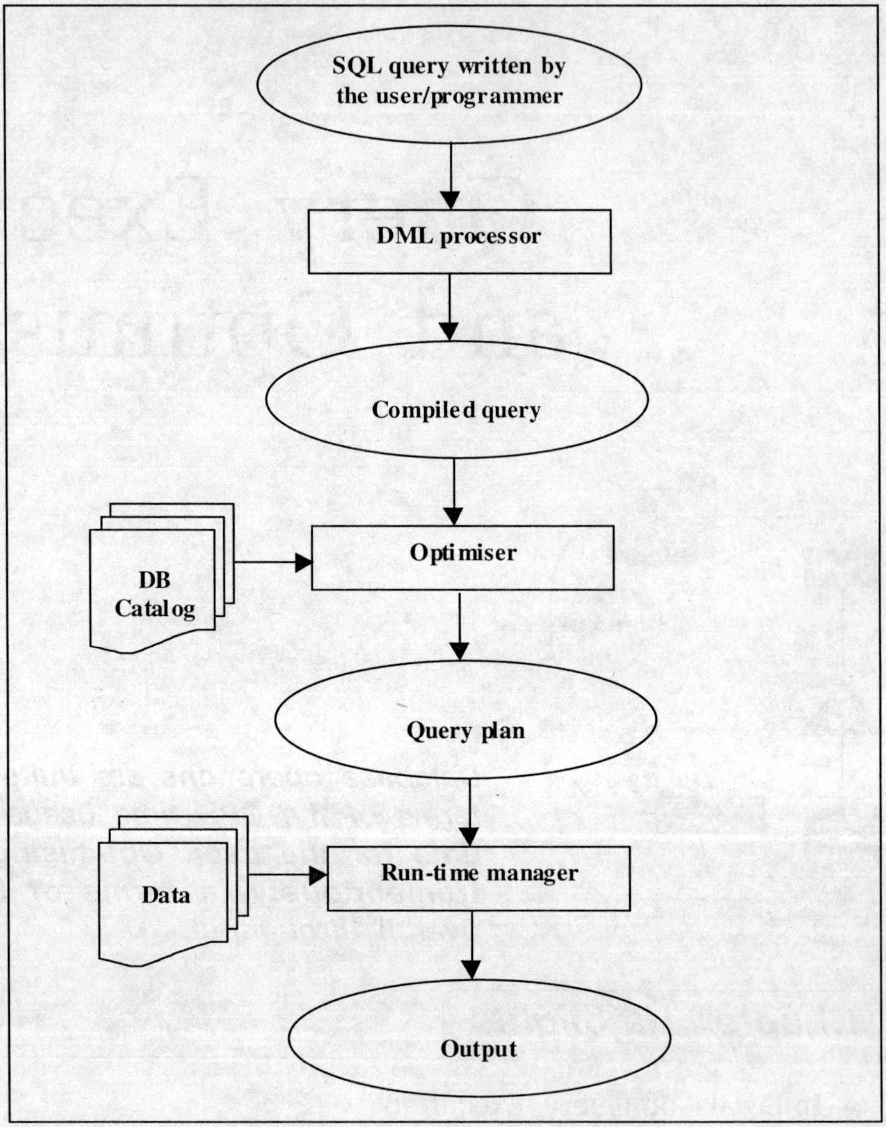

Fig. 7.1 Query execution process

There are several ways to do the same thing. Optimisation means choosing the best approach of all the available ones. It is a bit like time management. Depending on how best we manage our time, we can complete no, just one, a few, or many tasks in the best possible manner.

Another way of depicting this is captured in Fig. 7.2.

Now, let us discuss these steps.

1. **Decomposition**

   In this step, the SQL query written by the user/application programmer is transformed into an internal form. The SQL syntax is changed into a machine-understandable form (called **internal representation**). Other nomenclatures for this form are abstract **syntax tree** and **query tree**.

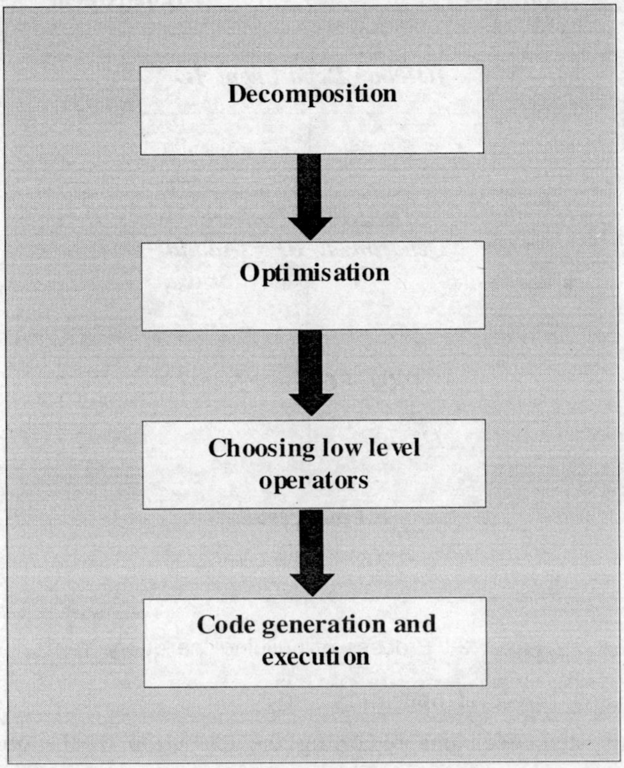

Fig. 7.2 Query execution – Another view

Consider the following SQL query, which finds out the names of employees who work in the *Admin* department:

```
SELECT Name
FROM Employee A, Department B
WHERE A.Department_ID = B.Department_ID
    AND B.Department_name = 'Admin'
```

The step-by-step process of building a query tree for this query is shown in Fig. 7.3.

2. **Optimisation**

   This is the step in which the optimiser performs a number of optimisation processes. In this step, the optimiser also transforms the query into an internal form, called **canonical form**. This involves improving the original query, so that it can be executed better. The optimiser also calculates the possible **cost of the query**. The resulting code is an optimised version of the original code.

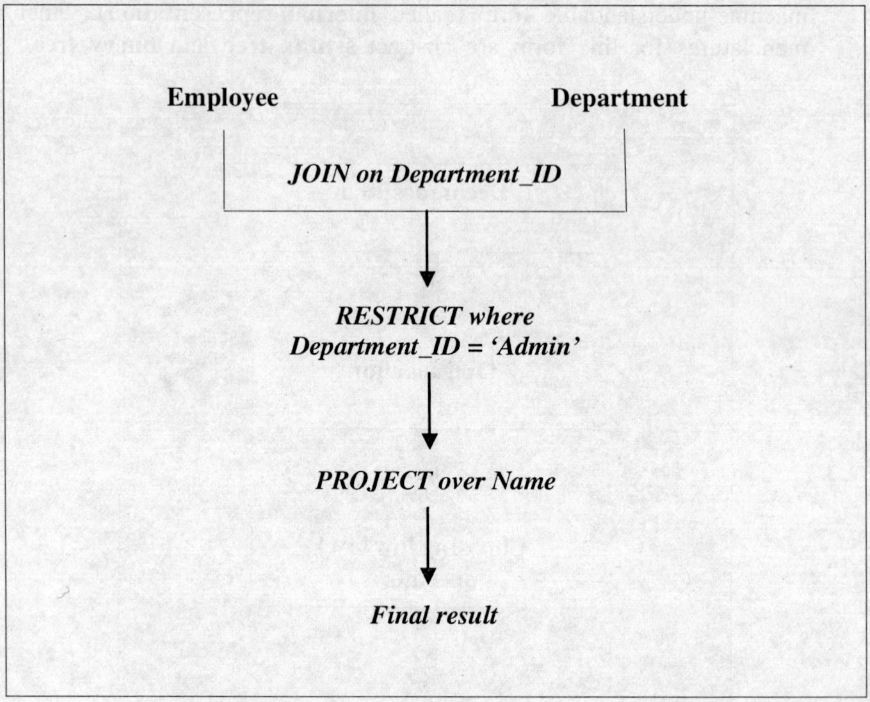

Fig. 7.3 Process of building the query tree

3. **Choosing low-level operators**

   In this step, decisions regarding the execution of the query are taken. They may include the possible use of indexes, physical paths of the database, and so on. Examples of low-level operations are join, projection and restriction. There are usually interdependencies among them. For instance, a selection operation may require sorting, duplication elimination and filtering. For every low-level operation, the optimiser can perform a pre-defined set of implementation procedures. Every such procedure has a cost associated with it. The cost is a function of many factors, such as CPU utilisation, disk I/O, memory requirements and communication needs. Based on current database information from the database catalog (e.g. indexes, page sizes etc), the interdependency information and the cost, the optimiser chooses one or more possible procedures. This is called **access path selection**.

4. **Code generation and execution**

   In this step, the optimiser generates the **query plans** and chooses the cheapest among them. A query plan is a group of possible implementation procedures in which each procedure is a low-level operation. There can be multiple plans for a query and one of them is chosen depending on the cost. The final cost of a query is the sum of the costs of the individual implementation procedures. This may not always be accurate, since it is based on results that are temporary/intermediate in nature.

7.2 USING INDEXES

We know that an index provides quicker access to data. Conceptually, database index is similar to the index provided at the end of a book. We know that an index in a book contains a list of important words, arranged in ascending order, along with the page numbers on which the word found. This is shown in Fig. 7.4.

A			
	...		
	...		
	Aim	...	2, 8, 10
	Air	...	89, 151, 189, 192
	Alter	...	27, 161
	...		
	...		
B			
	...		
	...		
	Boat	...	90, 153, 209
	Brand	...	6, 34
	...		
	...		

Fig. 7.4 Index concept

A database index is not very different. It contains the following:

- A list of values in the specified column (on which the index is created) – This is similar to the words in the book index shown here.
- The row identifiers in which these values occur – This is similar to the page numbers of a book on which the word is located.

Surprisingly, indexes are not really considered while relational databases are designed. In contrast, indexes are very much a part of the logical design stage in most other file or database systems. However, in the case of relational databases, indexes can be created, modified and deleted without changing the inherent database design or application logic. The only difference that this sort of operation leads to in is the change in performance (which becomes either better or worse, depending on what is done). The idea is illustrated in Fig. 7.5.

Non-relational systems

Data design = File/Table design + Index considerations

Relational databases

Data design = File/Table design

Indexes come later

Fig. 7.5 Index considerations

In most cases, the optimiser chooses the most effective index. Thus, the focus of the people who participate in database design and maintenance activities should be to provide a good set of indexes, and then rely on the optimiser to make use of them. This leads to the most effective use of analysis time and also provides for the best possible performance.

7.3 OPTIMISER FUNCTIONALITY

Throughout the rest of the chapter, we shall consider an *Employee* table and a *Department* table with the structures shown in Fig. 7.6.

Employee_number	Name	Department_number	Salary

Employee table

Department_number	Name	Office	Floor

Department table

Fig. 7.6 Sample table structures

The optimiser can use one of the two techniques shown in Fig. 7.7 to execute any given query that involves two or more columns.

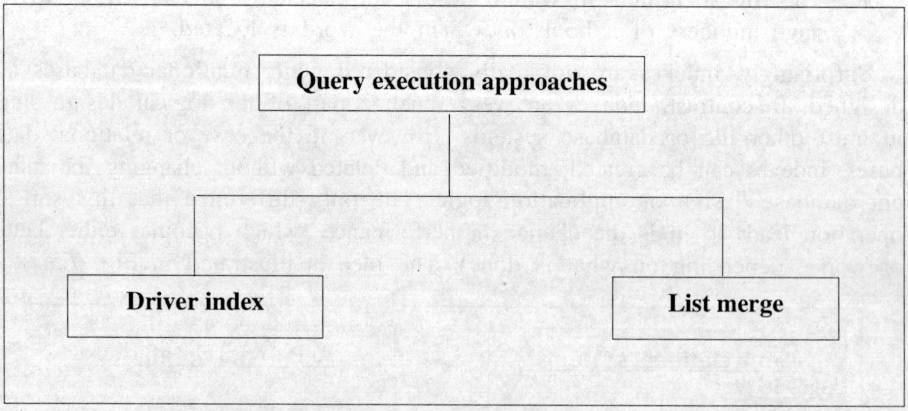

Fig. 7.7 Query execution approaches

Let us discuss these approaches. To understand these approaches, we shall take the example of the following query:

```
SELECT *
FROM Employee
```

WHERE Department_number = 10

AND Salary >= 5000

7.3.1 Driver Index

In the **driver index** approach, the optimiser avoids reading the database table twice, for the two conditions joined by AND. That is, it performs the reading only for one of the conditions, and once a list of rows matching this condition is prepared, it applies a filtering based on the second condition. This is illustrated in Fig. 7.8.

```
Read the first row based on the Department_number index

While End-of-Index on Department_number is not reached

        If Department_number = 10
                If Salary >= 5000
                        Add the employee details to the list of records found
                End-if
        End-if
        Read next row from the Department_number index
End-while
```

Fig. 7.8 Driver index approach

Note that the database is read based on the index on the Department_number column. This means that the optimiser would start reading from the first instance where Department_number = 10 is found. It would read all the rows where this condition is met. Whenever it finds salary of 5000 or above in any row, it would add this row to a temporary list. After all the rows for Department_number 10 are read, the list would contain the rows that match the WHERE condition specified in the query earlier (i.e. it would contain a list of employees who work in department 10, and earn a salary of 5000 or more).

7.3.2 List Merge

This approach is much costlier than the *driver index* approach. Therefore, as far as possible, it should be avoided. In this approach of **list merge**, the optimiser does the table scan twice, that is reads the table twice. The first table scan is for the expression *before* the AND clause, and the second scan is for the expression *after* the AND clause. The algorithm used by this approach is shown in Fig. 7.9. The list of employees in department 10, and those who earn a salary of 5000 or above, are a part of List-B.

We can clearly see that the *list merge* approach is quite cumbersome and time-consuming. As far as possible, we should force the optimiser to disallow this approach.

```
Read the first row based on the Department_number index

While End-of-Index on Department_number is not reached

        If Department_number = 10
                Add the employee details to the list of records found (say List-A)
        End-if
        Read next row based on the Department_number index

End-while

        If the above list (i.e. List-A) is not empty

                Read the first row based on the Salary index

                While End-of-Index on Salary is not reached

                        If Salary >= 5000
                                Add the employee details to the list of records found (say List-B)
                        End-if

                        Read next row based on the Salary index
                End-while

        End-if
```

Fig. 7.9 List merge approach

We can clearly see that the list merge approach is quite cumbersome and time-consuming. As far as possible, we should force the optimiser to disallow this approach.

The DBMS has a special piece of concept built-in, called as the optimiser. The optimiser decides how to deal with database operations so as to make them effective and fast.

7.4 IMPLEMENTING SELECT

Let us take a look at how some of the SELECT SQL queries are implemented and executed by the optimiser.

7.4.1 Simple SELECT

A simple SELECT statement means that the FROM clause contains just one table, and the WHERE clause also contains straightforward conditions. The options for implementing such a SELECT statement are as follows.

1. **Sequential search**

   Sequential search, also called linear search, is the simplest approach to any computer-based search operation. Here, every row of the table is retrieved. If the column values match the selection criteria, then the row is selected in the output. No intelligent processing is involved.

Sequential search is the traditional mechanism of searching for information. It is very simple to understand, but can be very poor in performance at times. As the name says, the process of searching for information in a sequential search is sequential (or one after the other). Given a list of items, the algorithm shown in Fig. 7.10 can be used to find if a particular item exists (or does not exist) in the list.

1. Start with a number K = 1.

2. If there are still more items in the list
Compare the Kth element in the list with the item to be searched.
Else
Item is not found in the list. Stop.

3. If a match is found
The item is found in the list. Stop.
Else
Add 1 to K, and go back to step 1.

Fig. 7.10 Sequential search

The important point in this algorithm is that we start with the first item in the list and go up to the end of the list, or until the item to be searched is found, whichever is earlier.

Table 7.1 shows the number of times this algorithm is likely to be executed, depending on the best, average and worst possible cases. We assume that the list contains *N* items.

Table 7.1 Sequential search: Likely number of iterations

Case	*Meaning*	*Number of iterations*
Best	The item to be searched is the first item in the list	1
Average	The item to be searched is found *somewhere* close to the middle of the list	N/2
Worst	The item to be searched is the last item in the list, or it does not exist at all	N

Note that the average number of iterations (N/2) is most likely over a period of time. Thus, if we have 10,000 items in a list, on an average, it would require (10,000/2), that is, 5,000 iterations.

2. **Binary search**

Binary search is a vast improvement over sequential search. However, unlike sequential search binary search cannot always be used, because for it to work, the items in the list must be sorted (in ascending or descending order). In RDBMS terms, this means that there must be an index on the column on which binary search is being performed—this is a prerequisite for binary search. Note that this condition is not at all essential in the case of a sequential search (although sequential search works equally fine with a sorted/unsorted list). If the list to be searched for a specific item is not sorted, binary search fails.

The approach employed by binary search is called *divide-and-conquer*. Assume that a list contains 1000 elements, which are sorted in ascending order of their values. An item x is to be searched in that list. The approach used by binary search algorithm is as shown in Fig. 7.11.

1. Divide the original list into two equal-sized logical halves. Let us call them *Half-1* and *Half-2*. In this case, the original 1000-element list will be split into two halves, each containing 500 elements.

2. Compare x with the last (i.e. 500th) element of *Half-1*. There are three possibilities:

a. The value of x matches with that of the 500th element of *Half-1*. If this is the case, the search is successful. Therefore, display an appropriate message and stop processing.

b. The value of x is greater than that of the 500th element of *Half-1*. Note that our list was originally sorted in the ascending order. Thus, if the value of x is greater than the last element of *Half-1*, it means that x is definitely not one of the first 500 elements in the 1,000-element array.

c. The value of x is less than that of the 500th element of *Half-1*. Note that our list was originally sorted in the ascending order. Thus, if the value of x is less than the last element of *Half-1*, it means that if x is in the list, it must definitely be one of the first 500 elements in the 1,000-element array.

Fig. 7.11 Binary search

This is summarised in Table 7.2.

Table 7.2 Next action depending on the outcome of binary search

Outcome	*Next action*
(a) x = Last element of Half-1	Stop processing.
(b) x > Last element of Half-1	Search for x within *Half-2*.
(c) x < Last element of Half-1	Search for x within *Half-1*.

- Clearly, case (a) is quite simple and there is nothing to discuss. So, we shall now concentrate on case (b) and case (c).
- In case (b), we need to look for x in *Half-2*. So, we can safely discard *Half-1* altogether and worry only about *Half-2*. We shall use the same

approach as before. We will now divide *Half-2*, made up of 500 elements, into two halves, each consisting of 250 elements. Let us call these two halves of *Half-2* as *Half-2-1* and *Half-2-2*. We now compare x with the last element of *Half-2-1*. This will also have three possibilities—(a), (b) or (c)—as discussed earlier. Depending on that, we can stop processing, or divide *Half-2-1* or *Half-2-2* into two halves, and so on. We stop when either a match for x is found, or when we split the list so much that it cannot be split any further.

- Case (c) is similar to case (b). However, we shall describe it completely, for the sake of completeness. In case (b), we need to look for x in *Half-1*. So, we can safely discard *Half-2* altogether and worry only about *Half-1*. We shall use the same approach as before and divide *Half-1*, made up of 500 elements, into two halves, each consisting of 250 elements. Let us call these two halves of *Half-1* as *Half-1-1* and *Half-1-2*. We now compare x with the last element of *Half-1-1*. This will also have three possibilities—(a), (b) or (c)—as discussed earlier. Depending on that we can stop processing, or divide *Half-1-1* or *Half-1-2* into two halves, and so on. We stop when either a match for x is found, or when we split the list so much that it cannot be split any further.

An example would help make this discussion clearer. Suppose we have a list of numbers arranged in the ascending order—from 1 to 10—as follows.

1 2 3 4 5 6 7 8 9 10

Assume that we are searching for number 8 (x) in the list. The search would proceed as follows.

1. Firstly, divide the original list into two halves, the first half containing numbers 1-5, and the second half containing numbers 6-10.
2. Compare x (i.e. 8) with the last number of the first half (i.e. 5). Since 8 > 5, from our earlier logic, case (b) is true. This means that we should discard the first half (i.e. 1-5) and look for x in the second half (i.e. 6-10). Thus, our new list looks as follows.

   6 7 8 9 10

3. Now, we divide the current list (i.e. 6-10) into two halves, one containing the numbers 6-7 and the other containing the numbers 8-10. We now compare x (i.e. 8) with the last element of the first half (i.e. 7). Since x (i.e. 8) is greater than this, case (b) again stands to be proved. Therefore, we again discard the first half (i.e. 6-7) and use only the second one. Accordingly, our new list now looks as follows.

   8 9 10

4. We now divide the current list into two halves. The first half would contain 8, and the second half would contain 9 and 10. We now compare x (i.e. 8) with the last element of the first half (i.e. 8). Since a match is found, case (a) is true. So, we display an appropriate message, indicating that the element to be searched has been found, and stop processing.

The more the optimised a query, the faster it executes, and the better is the overall throughout. Query optimisation can be done at two levels: (a) Leaving it to the DBMS to decide about optimisation, and (b) Taking steps to do the optimisation ourselves. It is better to use a combination of the two techniques.

Note that the binary search required just two *compare* operations. In contrast, a sequential search would have required 8 *compare* operations. Thus, binary search can be really fast. Of course, more the number of elements in the list to be searched, more effective is binary search, as compared to sequential search. For smaller lists, the overhead involved in sorting the list so as to allow binary search can be more than performing a sequential search. Thus some judicious decision-making is required in such cases to compare the advantages of sequential search versus binary search.

3. **Using primary index for searching one row/record**

   By using a primary index, the record being searched can be directly located, without scanning through the table. This is a very simple option and we have discussed it at length on many occasions. It is shown in Fig. 7.12.

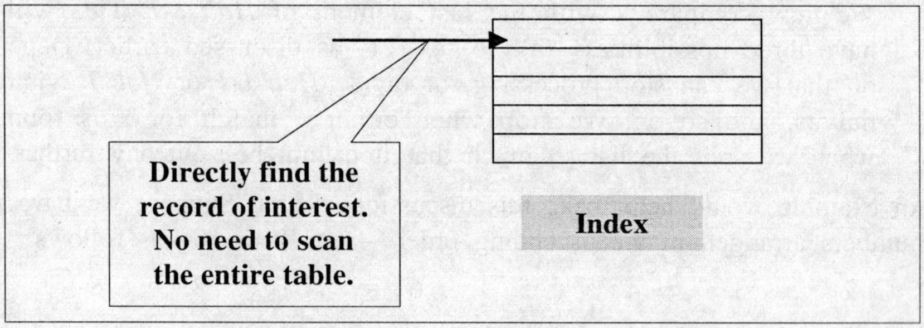

Fig. 7.12 Use of primary index to search one record

4. **Using primary index to search for multiple records**

   This option is a variation of the earlier method. Here, relational operators such as <, >, <=, >= are used. The idea is to use the index to look up the start of a set of matching records, and then to retrieve all the preceding or following matching records, as per the comparison condition. The concept is illustrated in Fig. 7.13.

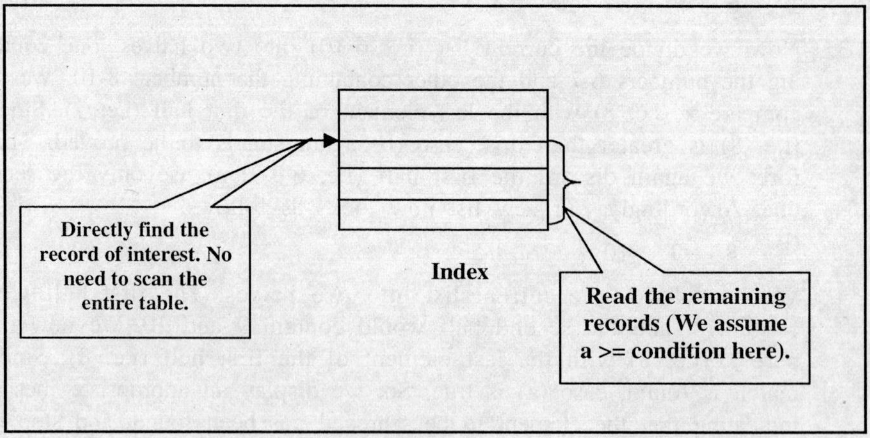

Fig. 7.13 Use of primary index to search multiple records

7.4.2 Complex SELECT Implementation

A complex SELECT statement is a **conjunctive condition**. This means that it contains many conditions joined with an operator such as AND or OR. The following techniques can be used to search for information in a complex SELECT statement.

1. **Conjunctive index using individual index**

   In this approach, we assume that an index is available on an individual column. It is used, just like the approaches described earlier in the case of simple SELECT.

2. **Conjunctive index using combination index**

   If two or more columns are involved in a query, then we may use a combined index on these columns.

7.4.3 JOIN Implementation

The JOIN condition in an SQL query can be implemented in various ways. Some of the possible techniques are described below.

1. **Nested-join**

   The **nested loop join**, also called **brute force**, joins every row of the *outer* table with every row of the *inner* table. It then checks if the two rows satisfy the join condition. This is quite expensive, as we can imagine.

2. **Single-join**

   In **single loop join**, we assume that an index exists for one of the two (or more) columns being joined together. Let us consider that the join is based on two columns, C_1 and C_2. We assume that an index exists on C_1. Given this background, the way this retrieval works is shown in Fig. 7.14.

(i)	Retrieve every row from the table corresponding to column C_2.
(ii)	For every row corresponding to column C_2, use the index on C_1 to find a match directly.

Fig. 7.14 Single loop join concept

The conceptual view of this is shown in Fig. 7.15.

3. **Sort join**

   In the **sort join** approach, it is assumed that both the columns that are being joined have an index on them. So the idea is to read both the tables using the index sequentially – thereby reading them in ascending/descending order. We then match (i.e. join) rows that have the same value in both columns. Because the tables would be read in a sorted order, this approach would also work quite fast.

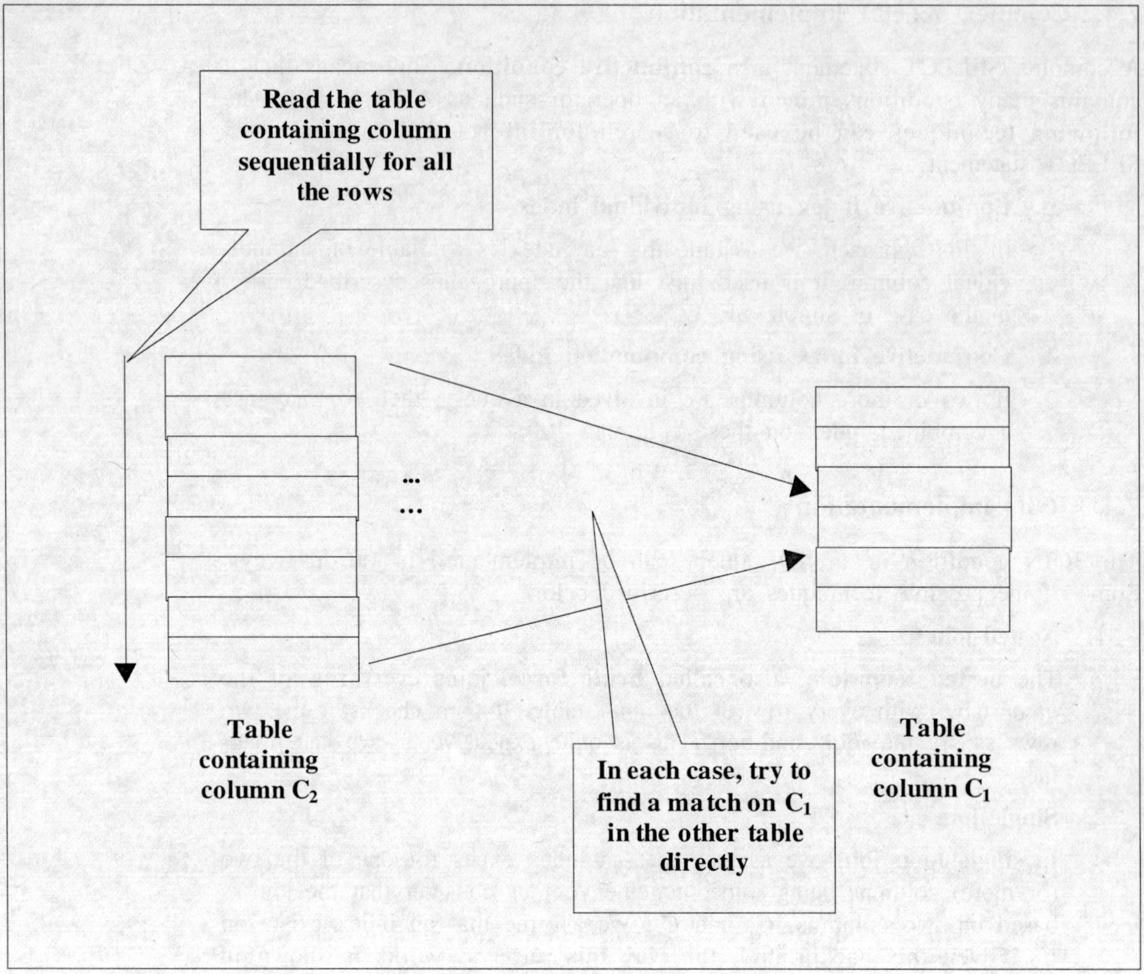

Fig. 7.15 Single loop gain concept

7.4.4 PROJECT Implementation

The implementation of the projection operation is quite simple. We simply need to think of and limit the retrieval to the few columns that the query mentions. The only variation is that we may need to think of duplicate elimination if the DISTINCT SQL clause is used.

7.4.5 SET Operator Implementation

Implementation of the set operators, such as Cartesian product, union, intersection and difference can be quite expensive. They are briefly described below.

1. **Cartesian product**

   This is the most expensive of all query operations. Assuming that we want to take the Cartesian product of two tables—A and B—the result is the combination of every row of A with every row of B, with all the attributes of A and B. Clearly, this puts lots of demands on the CPU, memory and disk space. In fact, whenever possible, one should avoid Cartesian products.

2. **UNION, INTERSECT and DIFFERENCE**

   These operations can work on union-compatible tables. Variations of the basic list-merge technique are used here.

   (a) **UNION**: One needs to scan and merge the tables in question concurrently. After this, whenever a row is found in the merged result, it is retained. If it is found multiple times, duplicates are rejected and just one of them is retained in the result.

   (b) **INTERSECT**: The only difference between this and UNION is that here, a row is retained only if it is found twice in the merged list.

   (c) **DIFFERENCE**: It is retained in the result only if there is a row from the first table and no corresponding row from the second table.

7.4.6 Aggregate Functions Implementation

Examples of aggregate functions are MIN, MAX, AVG, SUM and COUNT. Indexes are quite useful for the implementation of these functions. For instance, consider the following query:

```
SELECT MAX (Salary)
FROM Emp
```

Clearly, the last (right) entry in the index can be used here. Similarly, for the MIN function, the first (left) entry in the index can be used.

7.5 OPTIMISATION RECOMMENDATIONS

Let us now list down some of the most notable recommendations in the field of database performance optimisation.

Recommendation 1: Focus on the WHERE clause in the query.

The WHERE clause is the prime focus of the query optimiser. In fact, every column listed in the WHERE clause is a possible candidate for an index. We need to find out if we should:

1. Create indexes on some of them, or
2. Leave the database in its current state (without a defined index), or
3. Delete an index that is present

We can see that Emp_number is the primary key of the table. Therefore, an index is almost inevitable on this column. However, we should also examine to see if there are frequent queries based on the other columns (e.g. *WHERE Salary BETWEEN 10000 and 20000*). If so, we should create an index for the same.

Recommendation 2: Use narrow indexes.

We can create an index either on one column or on multiple columns. The recommendation is to use as many single-column indexes as possible. The reason for this recommendation is that single-column indexes provides the optimiser with a number of options to choose from. The optimiser can have a number of permutations and combinations because of this. Instead, if the indexes are based on multiple columns, then the optimiser does have too many choices, but to use the indexes as they are (or to discard them altogether).

At the same time, it is worth emphasising that there should not be unnecessary indexes. We should remember that although indexes speed up query processing considerably, they could also slow down the overall processing; because they need to be updated every time there is any database change (i.e. when we execute an INSERT, UPDATE or DELETE statement). Therefore, there is a definite cost associated with maintaining indexes.

Recommendation 3: If there are two or more AND constructs in a query, put the most limiting expression first (most limiting refers to the one that returns the minimum number of rows).

We know that A AND B is true if both A and B are true. Keeping this in mind, the most effective way of evaluating the expression A AND B is to have A < B. This is because, the smaller the A, the more is the number of rows eliminated even without requiring to evaluate B. We need to evaluate B only if A is true. By choosing A as the minimum between A and B, this process can be optimised to the best possible level.

Several simple tricks can help in optimisation. For example, in an OR operation, it is better to have the condition that is most likely to be satisfied on the left of the OR operator. On the other hand, in the case of AND, it is better to keep this condition on the right side of the AND operator.

Let us consider an example. Study the queries, shown in Fig. 7.16. We are interested in finding a list of employees who are working in department number 10 and are earning a salary of Rs 5000 and above. We assume that there is an index based on both the columns referred to in the WHERE clause (i.e. Department_number and Salary).

```
SELECT *
FROM Employee
WHERE Department_number = 10
AND Salary >= 5000
```

(a)

```
SELECT *
FROM Employee
WHERE Salary >= 5000 AND
Department_number = 10
```

(b)

Fig. 7.16 Coding the most limiting expression first in a query containing AND

The first query [i.e. Query (a)] would be more effective if the number of employees belonging to department number 10 is lesser than the employees earning a salary of 5000 or above. However, the second query [i.e. Query (b)] would be more effective if only a few employees earn a salary of 5000 or above, but a far greater number of employees belong to department 10.

Recommendation 4: If there are two or more OR constructs in a query, put the expression that returns the maximum number of rows, first.

We know that A OR B is true if either or both of A and B are true. Keeping this in mind, the most effective way of evaluating the expression A OR B is to have A > B. This is because, the bigger the A, the more is the number of rows eliminated even without requiring to evaluate B. We need to evaluate B only if A is false. By choosing A as the maximum between A and B, this process can be optmised to the best possible level.

We can see that this description is exactly the opposite of the description for the previous case. The major difference, of course, is that the positions of A and B are reversed when we move from AND to OR.

We will go further into this recommendation. Interested readers can relate the earlier example to this one.

Recommendation 5: In the case of a join; put the table with the minimum number of qualified rows last in the FROM clause, and the first in the join expression of the WHERE clause. Then AND the join expression with a column >= ' ' (blank) to force the optimiser to choose this expression as the driver during query evaluation.

Suppose we want to join the Employee and Department tables based on the Department_number field. The simple and commonly-used approach is shown in section (b) of Fig. 7.17. However, section (a) shows an unusual approach, which is quite interesting.

The DBMS maintains various kinds of information and statistics to help in optimisation. The DBMS decides whether to use indexes, whether to do complete table scans or not, and so on, based on a number of parameters, and figures out the best way to accomplish this.

SELECT * FROM Employee A, Department B WHERE B.Department_number > 0 AND A.Department_number = B.Department_number	SELECT * FROM Employee A, Department B WHERE A.Department_number = B.Department_number
(a)	**(b)**

Fig. 7.17 Join recommendation

Let us assume that the Employee table contains 5000 rows and the Department table contains 20 rows. What we have done in case (a) is to force the optimiser to go for a *driver index* strategy, instead of a *list merge* strategy as we want the optimiser to mandate Department.Department_number as the driver. The expression *WHERE B.Department_Number > 0* ensures this. In other words, because we are driving the query based on this expression, only 20 rows would be returned first, corresponding to the 20 rows in the Department table. Then, the optimiser would try and find matching values only for these 20 rows in the Employee table. In contrast to this, approach (b) is a simple join. Therefore, the optimiser would join the 5000 rows of the Employee table with the 20 rows of the Department table, and then perform a filtering operation based on the WHERE clause. Clearly, approach (a) is far better.

Recommendation 6: User ORDER BY, even if it is redundant, causes the performance to improve.

Suppose we want to find a list of employees who earn a salary of 5000 or above, in the order of the employee numbers. Consider the two equivalent queries shown in Fig. 7.18.

```
SELECT *
FROM Employee
WHERE Employee_number > 0
AND Salary >= 5000
ORDER BY Employee_number
```

(a)

```
SELECT *
FROM Employee
WHERE Salary >= 5000
ORDER BY Employee_number
```

(b)

Fig. 7.18 Using redundant ORDER BY clause

We assume the following:

1. The Employee table is indexed on the Employee_number column.
2. The value of Employee_number is greater than zero.
3. There is no index on the Salary column.

In order to evaluate the query to find the list of employees earning a salary of 5000 or more, the optimiser has two options:

(a) Retrieve all rows based on Employee_number. Remove rows with Salary < 5000. Note that no sorting operation is required here as the index based on the Employee_number would be in use.

(b) Retrieve rows containing a salary value of 5000 or above. This means that the full table needs to be scanned, and the result sorted.

Option (a) is better as there is no index on the Salary column, and there would be few rows matching the criteria of Salary >= 5000. As against this, in approach (b), we must read all the rows in the Employee table, accepting only those rows where Salary >= 5000. Note that the index on the Employee_number column would not be used in this case.

Approaches (a) and (b) mentioned here correspond to approaches (a) and (b) in the figure shown earlier. Clearly, approach (a) is better.

Recommendation 7: Be aware of the fact that LIKE may not be optimised.

Let us assume that we want to find a list of employees whose name consists of four characters, starts with character A and ends with L. The standard approach to find this information is shown in section (b) of Fig. 7.19. However, an unusual but interesting approach is shown in section (a) of the figure.

(a)	(b)
SELECT * FROM Employee WHERE Name BETWEEN 'AAAL' AND 'AZZL' AND Name LIKE 'A__L'	SELECT * FROM Employee WHERE Name LIKE 'A__L'

Fig. 7.19 Optimising in the case of LIKE

Note that we have limited the searching operation in case (a) by adding an extra clause in the WHERE condition. This clause filters the rows for names and then hands over control to the LIKE clause. This ensures that a lot of filtering has already been done. This does not happen in case (b) and, therefore, can cause the query to take longer time to run.

Recommendation 8: If the table is small, force the optimiser not to use an index.

Suppose there are only 1000 rows in the Employee table. We want to find a list of employees who earn a salary of more than 5000. Let us assume that we do have an index on the Salary column. Then, we can write the query to find the required list of employees in two ways, as shown in Fig. 7.20.

(a)	(b)
SELECT * FROM Employee WHERE Salary > 5000 + 0	SELECT * FROM Employee WHERE Salary > 5000

Fig. 7.20 Forcing the optimiser for not using an index

In case (a), because of the change in the WHERE clause, the optimiser is fooled and believes that it cannot use the index on the Salary column. This expression forces a full table scan. This is recommended, because the size of the table is small. The whole table can be read in one disk access. However, if it were not the case, then query (b) would be recommended. Query (b) would always cause at least two disk accesses to be made, one for the index portion and one for the data portion.

Recommendation 9: Use OR instead of UNION if the predicate columns are not indexed.

Consider the two queries shown in Fig. 7.21.

```
SELECT *
FROM Employee
WHERE Employee_number = 10
OR Department_number = 10
```

(a)

```
SELECT *
FROM Employee
WHERE Employee_number = 10
UNION
SELECT *
FROM Employee
WHERE Department_Number = 10
```

(b)

Fig. 7.21 OR versus UNION

We assume that for some reason, the Employee_number and Department_number columns are not indexed. Many optimisers perform optimisation only if a query contains a single WHERE clause in a single SELECT statement. In query (b), two SELECT statements are executed. Thus, two separate passes are required. In the first pass, the optimiser looks for rows matching employee number 10, and in the second pass, the optimiser looks for rows matching department number 10. It then joins these lists and performs a filtering operation. This is not the case with approach (a), which is better.

7.6 DATABASE STATISTICS

A DBMS maintains information on the various tables and other database objects, such as indexes. This information is called as database statistics. Some examples of **database statistics** are shown in Table 7.3.

Table 7.3 Database statistics examples

Database object	*Statistics maintained*
Table	Number of rows, Number of pages occupied on the disk
Column	Number of distinct values in the column, Maximum and minimum values, If the column has an index – 10 most frequently occurring values in the column with their frequencies
Index	Levels of the index, Pages in the index

Whenever the DBMS takes decisions about optimising a query, it refers to these database statistics. Of course, this is internal to the DBMS. Neither the programmer nor the end user needs to know anything about it. However, the Database Administrator (DBA) needs to monitor database statistics quite closely and take corrective actions as and when needed.

KEY TERMS AND CONCEPTS

Abstract syntax tree
Brute force
Conjunctive condition
Driver index
Linear search
Nested loop join
Query plan
Sequential search
Sort join
Binary search
Canonical form
Database statistics
Internal representation
List merge
Query optimisation
Query tree
Single loop join

CHAPTER SUMMARY

- The DBMS performs a number of steps while executing a query.
- A query goes via the DML processor, optimiser, and run-time manager.
- The four main steps in query execution are decomposition, optimisation, choosing low-level operations and execution.
- Usage of indexes can greatly speed up query execution.
- **Database optimiser** enhances the speed of query execution.
- There are two approaches for query execution: **driver index** and **list merge**.
- In driver index approach, the optimiser avoids reading a table more than once.
- In list merge, the optimiser scans a table twice.
- The DBMS may use **sequential search** or **binary search** for implementing the SELECT operation.
- Sequential search is a process of scanning all the rows in a table. It is quite costly.
- Binary search is a process of scanning very few rows in a table. It is quite efficient, but it needs data to be sorted in an ascending or descending order.
- Apart from what the optimiser does internally, the programmer/DBA can think about a number of recommendations to speed up query processing.
- **Database statistics** can help determine the parameters in query execution and why it is executing slowly.

PRACTICE SET

Mark as true or false

1. Query optimisation is not important at all.
2. Query optimisation is a complicated process.
3. The DBMS does not have an inbuilt query optimiser.
4. In addition to what a DBMS can do, the DBA can also perform query optimisation.
5. Sequential search is faster than binary search.
6. Binary search requires that the data be sorted in an ascending or descending order.
7. There are no standard query optimisation recommendations.
8. Driver index is faster than list merge.
9. Indexes can greatly enhance query performance.
10. Database statistics contain information regarding the database objects.

Fill in the blanks

1. The first step in query processing is ________.
   (a) decomposition (b) optimisation
   (c) choosing low level operations (d) execution
2. The last step in query processing is ________.
   (a) decomposition (b) optimisation
   (c) choosing low level operations (d) execution
3. In _______, the query is transformed into an abstract syntax tree.
   (a) decomposition (b) optimisation
   (c) choosing low level operations (d) execution
4. The output of the _______ is that the query is transformed into a canonical form.
   (a) decomposition (b) optimisation
   (c) choosing low level operations (d) execution
5. In the ________ approach, the table is scanned only once.
   (a) list and join (b) list merge
   (c) driver index (d) list driver
6. In the ________ approach, the table is scanned twice.
   (a) list and join (b) list merge
   (c) driver index (d) list driver
7. In ______, the entire table is scanned.
   (a) sequential search (b) index search
   (c) direct search (d) binary search

8. In ______, the entire table is not scanned.
   (a) sequential search (b) index search
   (c) direct search (d) binary search
9. A complex SELECT statement is called as a ______.
   (a) sub-query (b) join
   (c) filter (d) conjunctive condition

Provide detailed answers to the following questions

1. What is query optimisation?
2. What are the steps in query processing?
3. What is an optimiser?
4. How can indexes help in query optimisation?
5. What is the driver index approach?
6. Discuss the list merge approach.
7. Describe the sequential search process.
8. How does binary search work?
9. Detail any two query optimisation recommendations.
10. What are database statistics?

Exercises

1. Study the differences in the way a query executes in the various RDBMS products.
2. Is it always better to leave query optimisation decisions to the DBMS? Why?
3. If we have an AND condition in the query, what should be our strategy?
4. If we have an OR condition in the query, what would be our strategy?
5. Read about correlated sub-queries and think about their optimisation.
6. Is join faster than a sub-query in general? Why?
7. Read about a concept called *hit rate*. What significance does it have over query optimisation? (Hint: It is related to the number of records being processed against the number of records in a file/table).
8. When would you *not* use an index?
9. Can we specify that an index *not* be used in file processing? Can we do so in the case of database processing?
10. Why are update operations costly on tables that have indexes?

Chapter 8

Distributed Databases

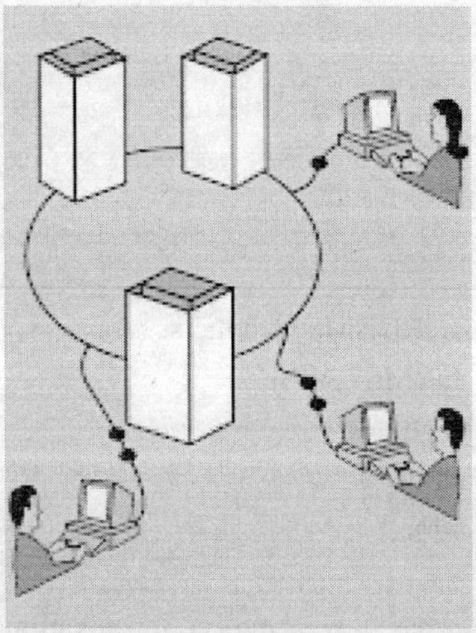

Distributed databases allow sharing of data across cities, states, countries, and continents. It is truly a magnificient technology, which was unthinkable even a few years ago.

Chapter Highlights

- Data Distribution
- Principles of Distributed Databases
- Issues in Distributed Databases
- Client/Server Computing
- Date's 12 Rules for Distributed Databases

8.1 DISTRIBUTED DATABASE CONCEPTS

The technology behind computer networks and data communications has had profound implications on the way computers work. Computer networks make it possible to connect multiple computers to each other. These computers can be located in the same/different buildings, cities, states, countries and even continents. This provides great flexibility to applications that make use of the computers and the networks that connect them. This flexibility is in terms of the distribution of processing logic and data across these networks, unlike earlier, when everything was **centralised**. Many modern applications and databases are **distributed**. In simple terms, this means that the processing logic and the data used by it need not be physically located on a single computer. Instead, it can be spread across multiple computers, which are connected to each other in some form.

> The great idea of **distributed databases** was born when the technology of databases was married to the concept of networking.

The idea is illustrated in Fig. 8.1.

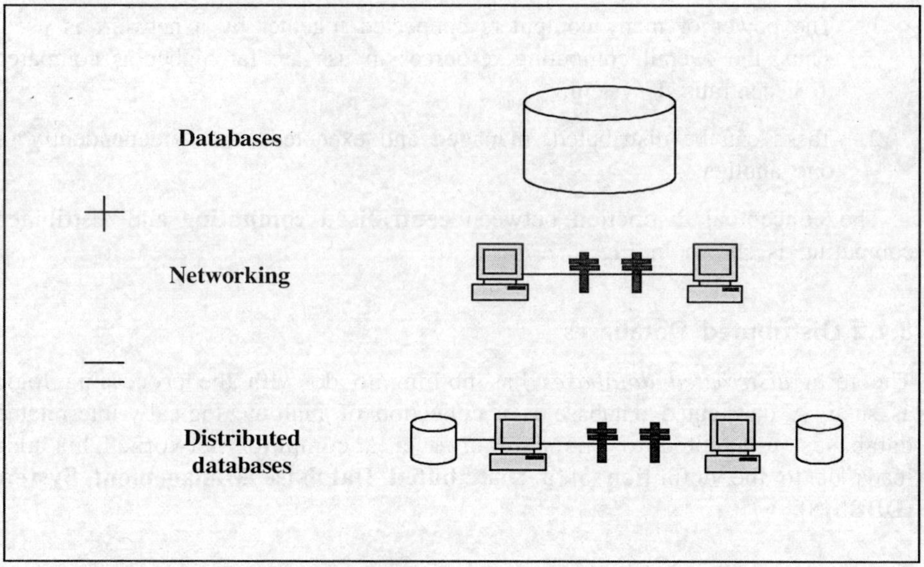

Fig. 8.1 Distributed databases = Databases + Networking

As we can see, the computers connected by a network have their own databases. At this point, however, we will not describe the intricacies, and instead, focus on the broad level concepts. We shall examine the internal details of such schemes and all the issues therein later in this chapter.

Data distribution is no longer a feature that is *good to have*. It is almost mandatory now, with the globalisation of data, widening of boundaries, and the tremendous impact of the Internet on our life.

The concept of distributed databases took off with the advent of wired and wireless data communication facilities. It assumed greater significance when the Internet was born. Now that the Internet has become an extremely important medium for conducting business worldwide, distributed databases have become the most effective technology for sharing data across distances.

At this stage, it is important to distinguish between two terms: *distributed computing* and *distributed databases*. Although related, these terms mean different things.

8.1.1 Distributed Computing

In the case of **distributed computing**, also called **distributed processing**, there are a number of processing elements connected by a computer network. These processing elements cooperate with each other in order to perform a task (i.e. the overall application logic). The idea is to divide a big problem into small chunks, and execute these chunks on different computers, thus solving it in an efficient manner.

The main benefits of this scheme are as follows:

1. The power of many computers connected together by a network is used. Thus, the overall computing resources in use are far higher as compared to a centralised system.
2. Tasks can be distributed, managed and executed fairly independently of one another.

The conceptual distinction between **centralised computing** and distributed computing is shown in Fig. 8.2.

8.1.2 Distributed Databases

The term *distributed databases* has nothing to do with the processing logic as such. A distributed database is a collection of multiple logically-interrelated databases, connected to one another over a computer network. This also leads us to the definition of a **Distributed Database Management System (DDBMS).**

> A DDBMS is a set of programs that manages a distributed database.

The fundamental concept behind a distributed database is: the fact that a database is physically distributed across many computers should be hidden from the users. The users perceive a distributed database as a single database which is physically located on a single computer. The users have no idea – in fact, they should *not* have an idea – that the database is scattered across many computers. This concept is shown in Fig. 8.3.

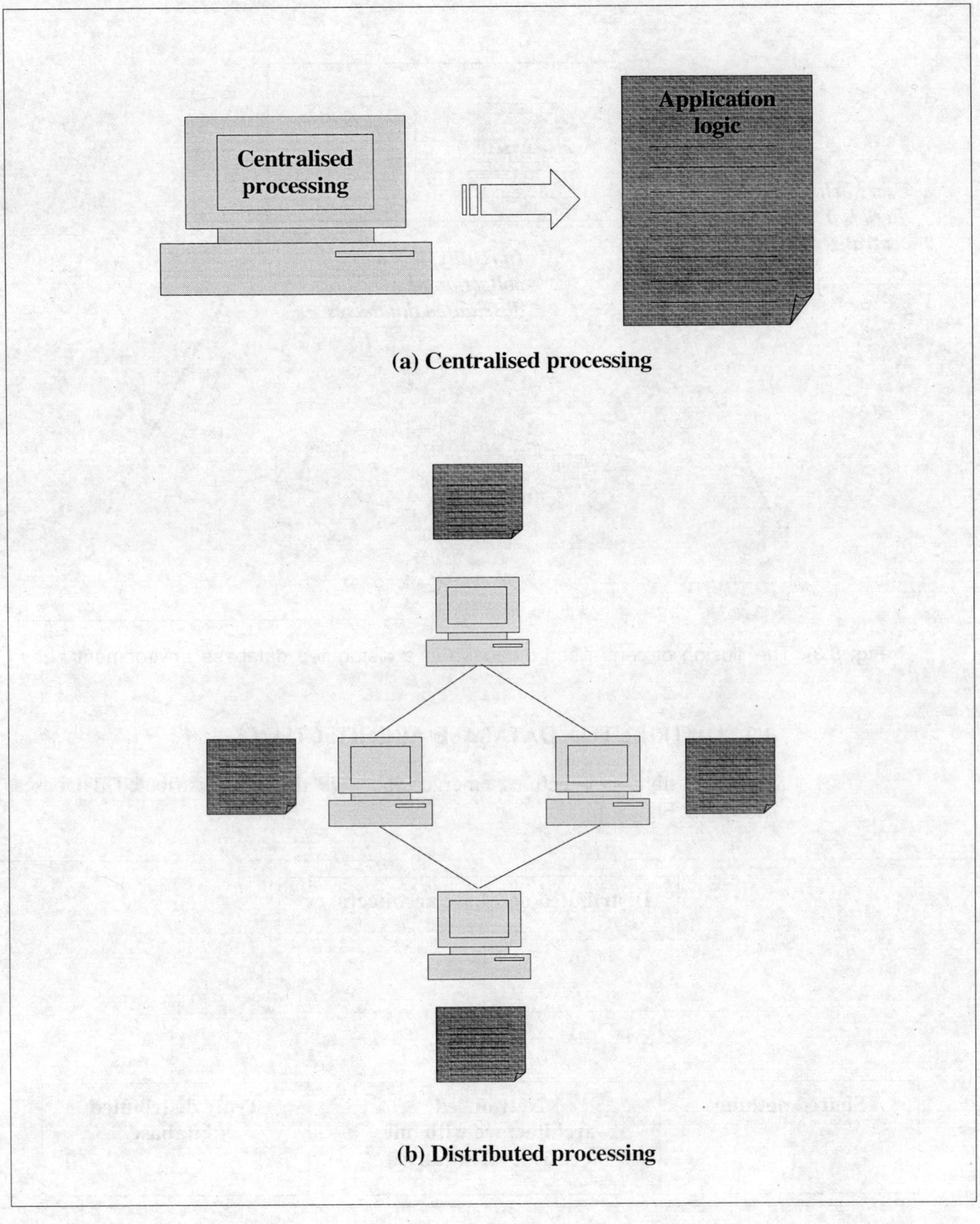

Fig. 8.2 Centralised versus distributed processing

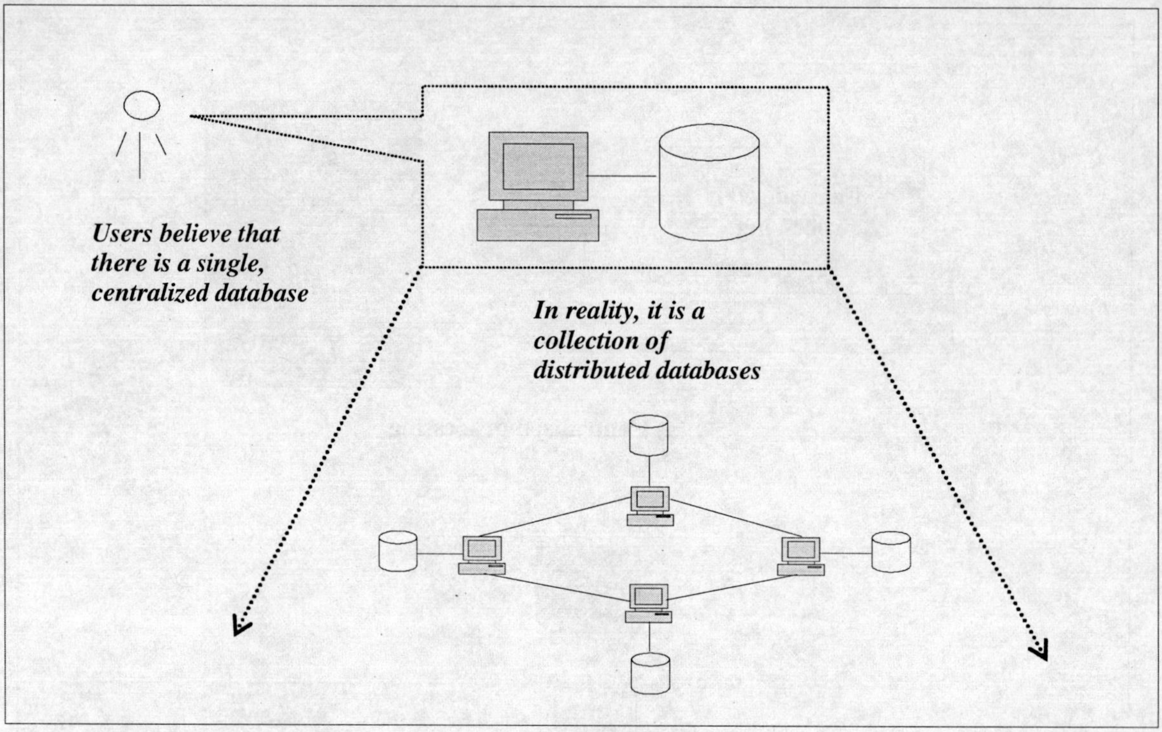

Fig. 8.3 The illusion of centralised database in a distributed database environment

8.2 DISTRIBUTED DATABASE ARCHITECTURES

Three possible architectures emerge when we think of distributed databases, as shown in Fig. 8.4.

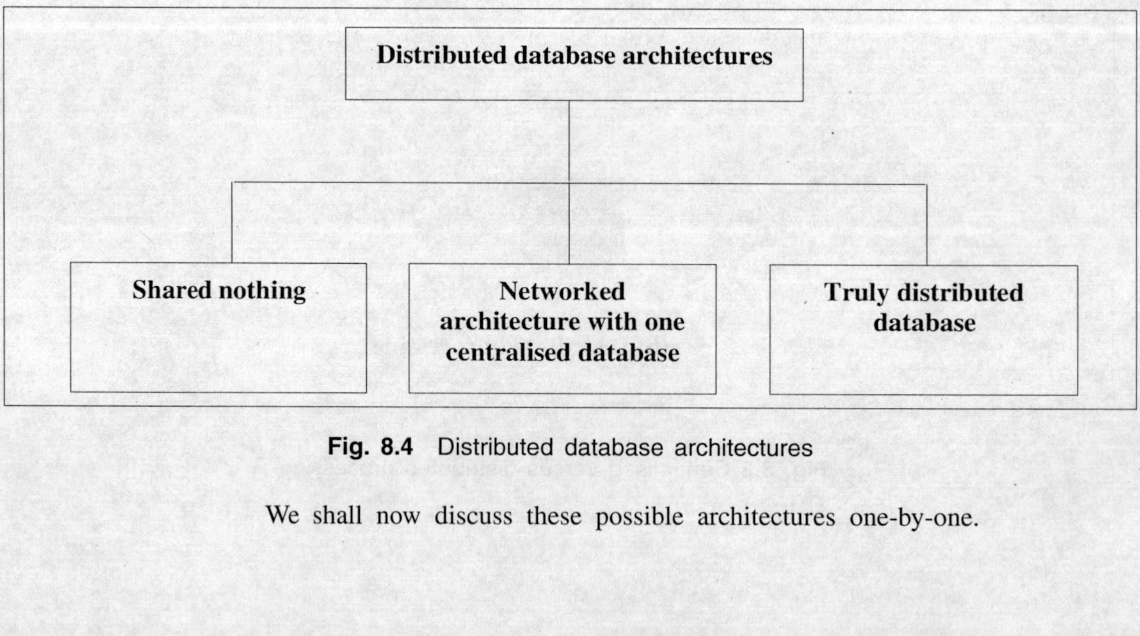

Fig. 8.4 Distributed database architectures

We shall now discuss these possible architectures one-by-one.

- **Shared nothing**

  In this type of architecture, different computers are connected to one another to form a distributed environment. However, as the name (**shared nothing**) suggests, every computer has its own database. No computer shares its database with any other computer. Thus, although this is a distributed environment containing computers connected together by a network, the data itself is not shared at all. This idea is shown in Fig. 8.5.

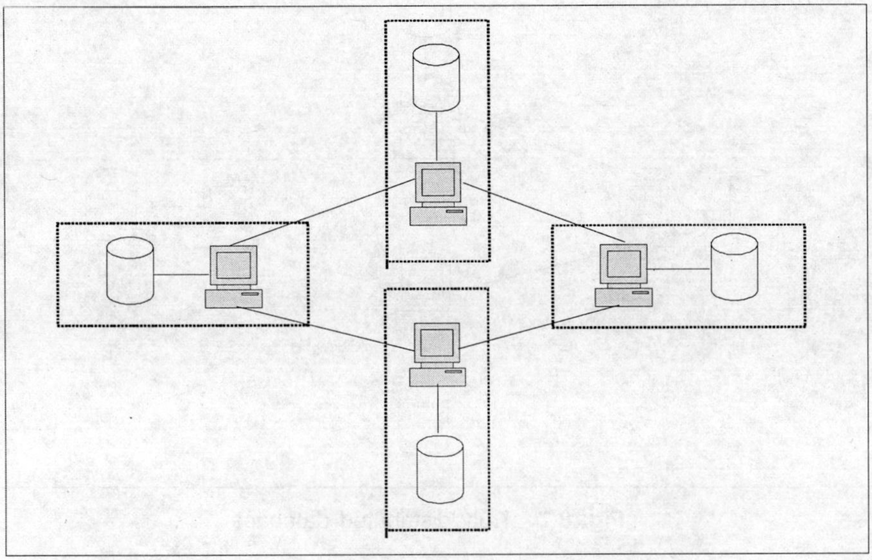

Fig. 8.5 Shared nothing architecture

- **Networked architecture with one centralised database**

  In the **networked architecture with one centralised database**, there is one common database which is shared by all the computers in the distributed environment. Thus, all the applications on the distributed computers share a single database. This architecture is shown in Fig. 8.6.

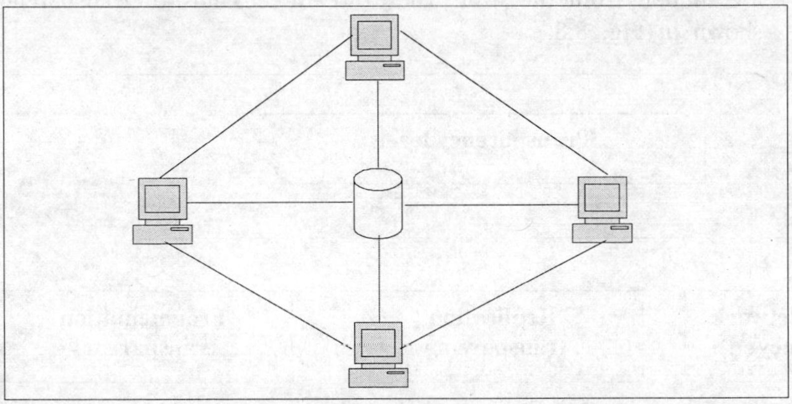

Fig. 8.6 Networked architecture with one centralised database

- **Truly distributed database**

  The **truly distributed database** architecture is shown in Fig. 8.7. Here, every computer in the distributed environment has its own database. However, all these databases are shared, unlike in shared nothing architecture.

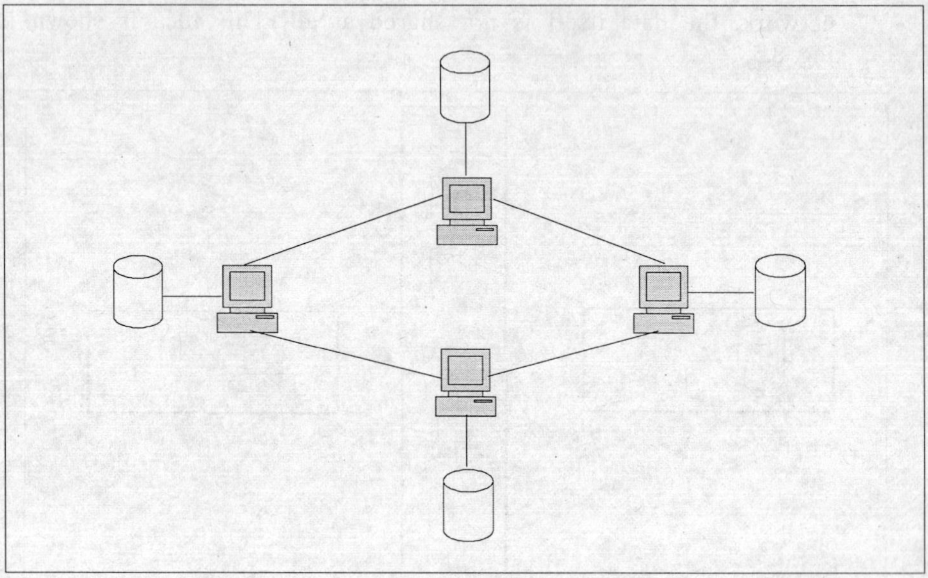

Fig. 8.7 Truly distributed database

8.3 ADVANTAGES OF DISTRIBUTED DATABASES

Let us now take a look at the major advantages of distributed databases.

1. **Management of distributed data with different transparency levels**

   A distributed database provides various kinds of transparencies, or abstraction levels. In other words, the internal complexities of certain things are hidden from the user. There are three kinds of transparencies, as shown in Fig. 8.8.

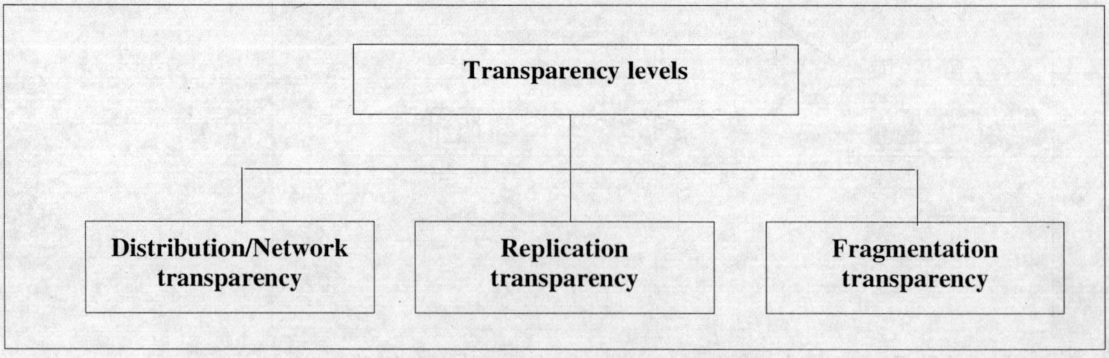

Fig. 8.8 Types of transparencies

(a) **Distribution/Network transparency**: The principle of **distribution transparency**, also called **network transparency**, hides the details of where the actual tables are physically stored. The users need not be aware of these physical locations of the databases. From the user's point of view, there is a single, unified database to work with. This kind of transparency can be sub-divided into two categories, as shown in Fig. 8.9.

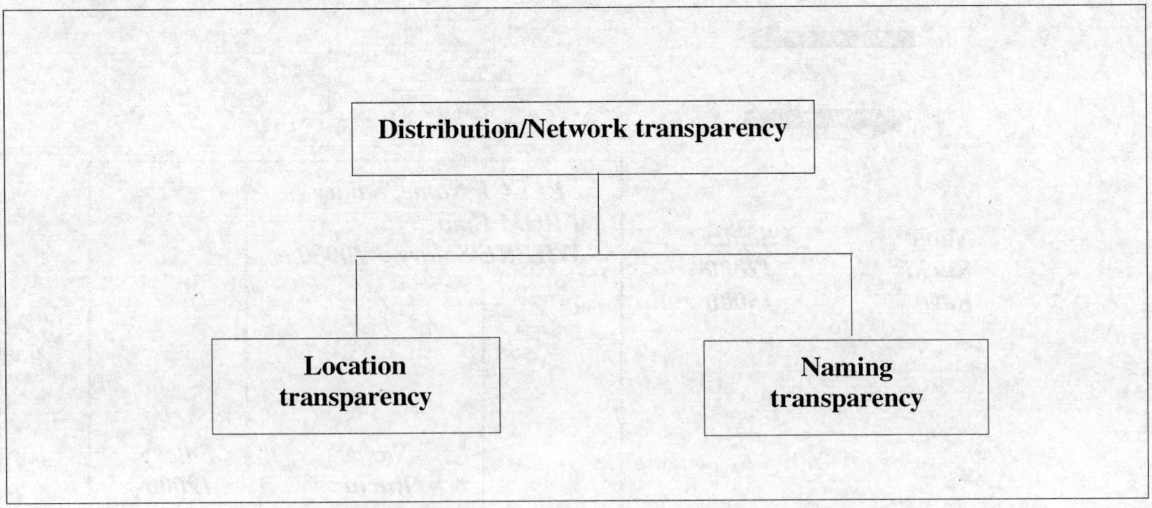

Fig. 8.9 Distribution/Network transparency types

- **Location transparency**: Here, the user is not aware that the command entry and execution happen on different computers. In other words, the user may enter a command (such as an SQL SELECT query) on computer A. Internally, because of the distributed nature, the query may actually be routed to another computer, B where it would be executed. The result of the query would be returned back to computer A, and presented to the user. However, the user would not be aware of this at all and may think that the query was actually executed on computer A. Thus, the location of the execution is transparent to the user. Hence it is called **location transparency**. The idea is shown in Fig. 8.10.

The portion shown inside the box (where computer A forwards the query of the user to computer B, and the result returned by computer B to computer A) is hidden from the user. All that the user feels she is doing is to enter a query and get an answer.

- **Naming transparency**: Apart from the fact that the user is not aware of the location of the actual database, there is one more point of substance. The user must not need to add any extra information to help the DDBMS identify that the *Employee* table is located on computer B, and not on computer A. For example, the user need not specify by putting in like Employee@B. The DDBMS should take care of this fact, thus providing a **naming transparency** to the user.

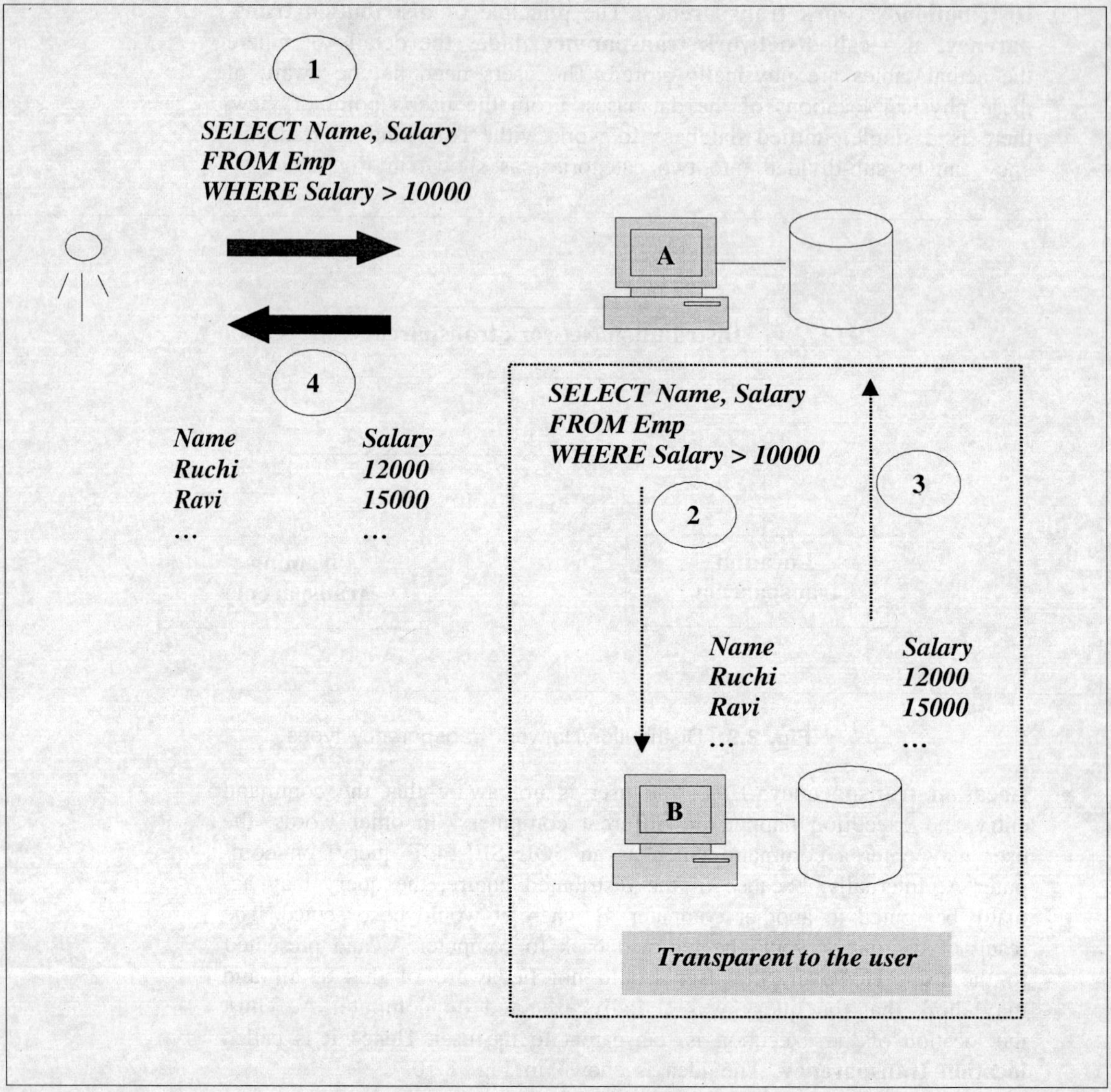

Fig. 8.10 Location transparency

(b) **Replication transparency**: In a distributed database environment, it is quite possible that the same set of data elements exist at multiple locations/sites. This is to provide better availability, performance and reliability. As before, the user need not be aware of this **replication transparency**. We shall later study the significance of *replication transparency*.

(c) **Fragmentation transparency**: In **replication**, the same sets of data elements are present on multiple computers. In **fragmentation**, a table is divided either horizontally (i.e. *sliced* into rows) or vertically (certain columns are selected) to create fragments of the original database. These fragments are then distributed across the DDBMS. These two methods are respectively called as **horizontal fragmentation** (as shown in Fig. 8.11) and **vertical fragmentation** (as shown in Fig. 8.12). Regardless of the type of fragmentation, the user should not be aware of its presence.

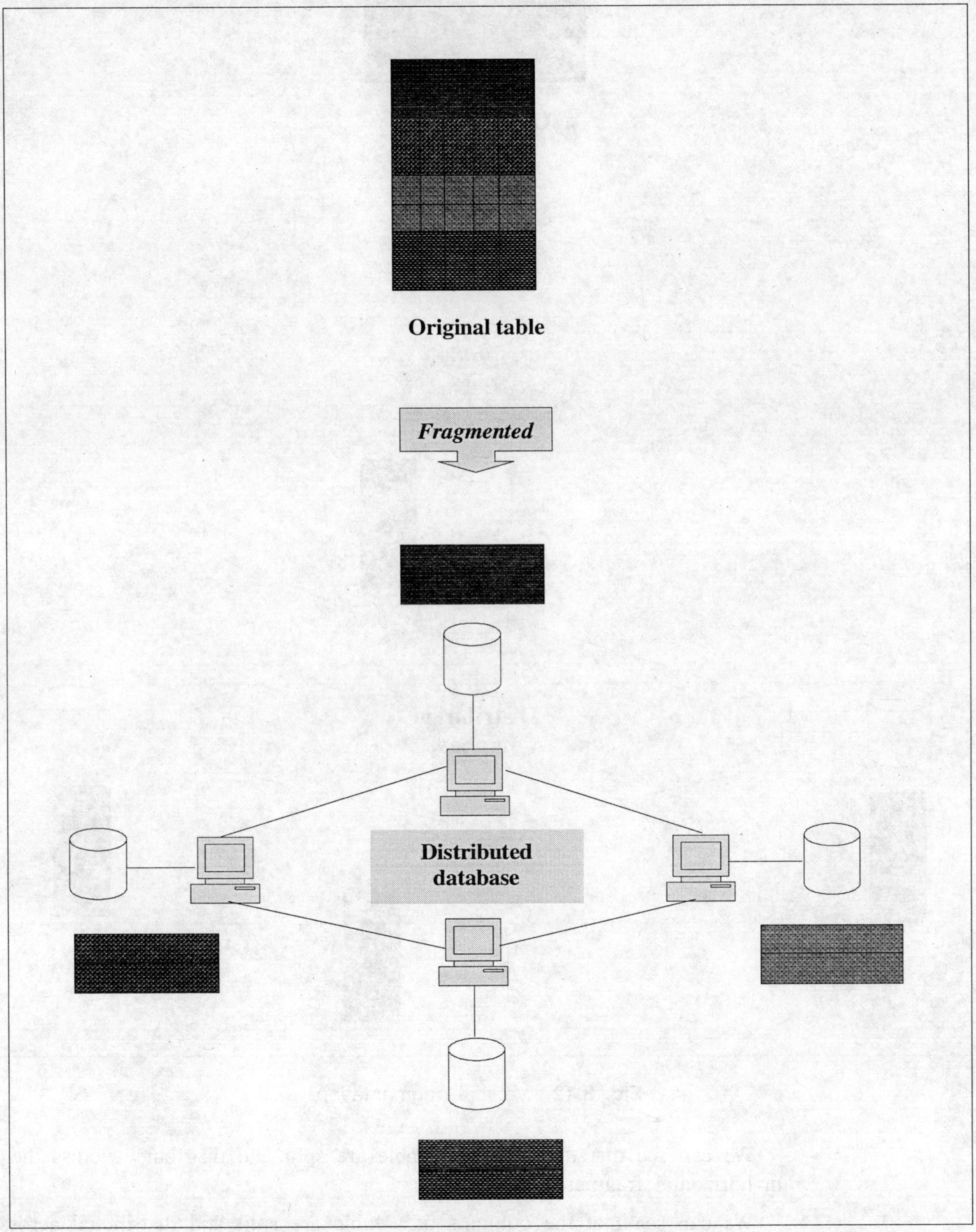

Fig. 8.11 Horizontal fragmentation

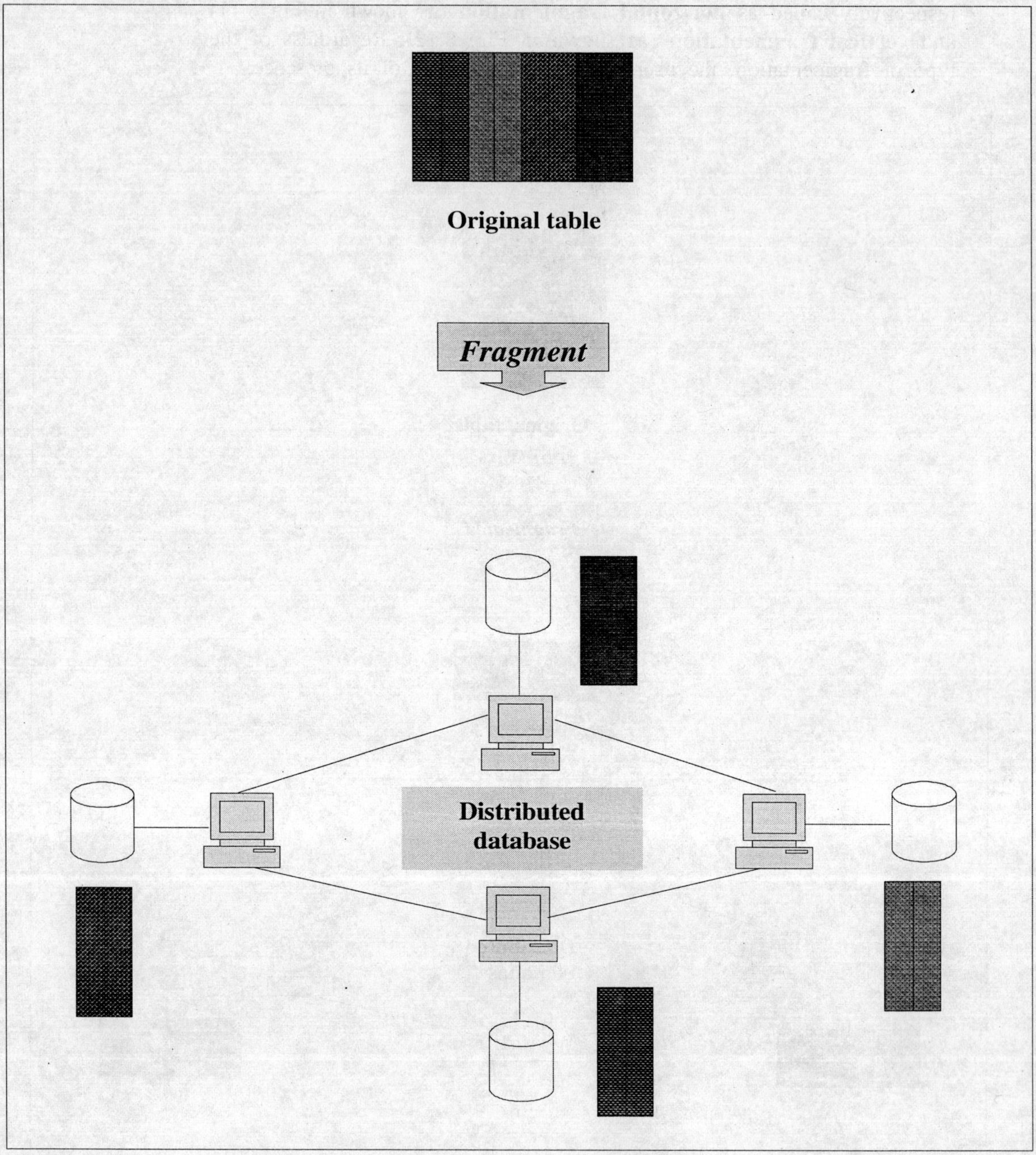

Fig. 8.12 Vertical fragmentation

We can see that the rows of a table are split and distributed across the sites in horizontal fragmentation.

We can see that the columns of a table are split and distributed across the sites in vertical fragmentation.

2. **Better reliability and availability**

> **Reliability** ensures that a system is always running. **Availability** means the continuous availability of a system in a finite time interval.

Because multiple computers share the responsibility and burden of database processing, even if one of them fails, the others can continue working. This is in stark contrast to a centralised system, where if the main computer that holds the database fails, the whole system comes to its knees. Apart from reliability and availability, distributed database systems have one more advantageous feature. Because data can be replicated, even some data of the failed site may be available with other sites that are still functioning.

3. **High performance**

A trick to ensure high performance can be employed in distributed database systems. The idea is simple: Keep data closest to the place where it is most often required. This is referred to as **data localisation**. Because of this, the requirements in terms of the CPU access, I/O transfer, and communication delays are minimised. Moreover, because of fragmentation every site has a smaller database rather than the complete database. This also helps in performance and throughput.

4. **Easy to expand/change**

Because of its localised nature, distributed databases are easier to expand/change. The scope of expansion and changes is local, and does not impact other portions of the system too much. This is quite unlike a centralised database system, where changes can be very complex and time-consuming.

8.4 DISTRIBUTED DATABASE REQUIREMENTS

> Data distribution is in the form of either maintaining copies of the same data at various locations (replication) or splitting it in such a manner that we can always join these broken portions to reconstruct the data in the original form (fragmentation).

Listed below are the requirements of distributed database systems.

1. **Tracking data** – As compared to a non-distributed (i.e. simple) DDBMS, a DDBMS has to perform several additional tasks. These tasks come up because of the nature of distributed databases. As we know, distributed databases can contain data elements that are distributed, fragmented and/or replicated. As such, the DBMS must keep track of exactly where the fragments or replicated pieces of data elements exist. Accordingly, it needs to maintain additional information about these aspects. This is useful when one needs to retrieve data from the database.
2. **Distributed query processing** – Apart from managing the distribution, fragmentation and replication of data, the DBMS also needs to perform the distributed query processing carefully. Data is distributed and, therefore, so should be the query. This is because the query needs to go to the various sites or locations of the database and perform the query operations on the

data stored there. In addition, it must merge the results of these operations in order to create the final output. As we can imagine, this would involve not only the query parsing and execution logic, but also other aspects such as optimisation. The idea of distributed query execution is shown in Fig. 8.13.

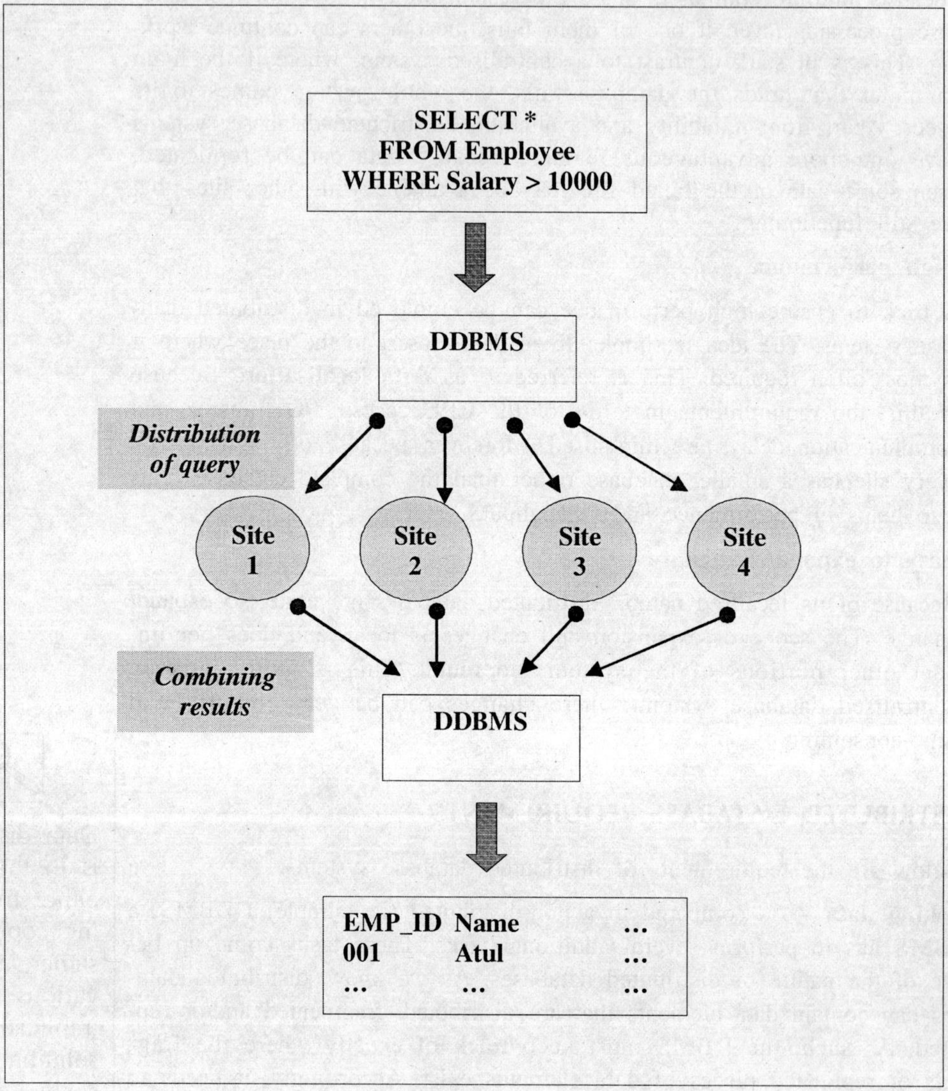

Fig. 8.13 Distributed query processing

3. **Distributed transaction management** – Distributed query processing is the first challenge for DDBMS in terms of coordinating the activities of the various sites participating in a distributed environment. The tougher challenge is to coordinate all of them in order to perform **distributed transactions**.

A *distributed transaction* is one in which multiple sites participate to perform a logical unit of work.

We have studied the **two-phase commit** protocol earlier. This protocol enables the sites participating in a distributed database environment to carry out transaction processing. We shall not discuss it here again.

4. **Management of replicated data** – One of the options for implementing distributed databases is to replicate data. This poses its own challenges. For example, suppose we have three sites, A, B and C containing replicated data. What should be done if a user modifies some of this data at site A? Should we perform the same modifications to sites B and C? If not, the synchronisation of data would be lost. If we do perform the same modifications to sites B and C though, it may lead to poor performance because every such update and its replication means overheads in terms of database locking, communication overheads and transaction processing. Clearly, a DDBMS needs to evaluate all the possible options, their pros and cons and take a decision accordingly.
5. **Distributed data recovery** – Data recovery in non-distributed databases is challenging enough and when data is distributed, it becomes even worse! We now need to know what happens to the various data elements that are replicated or distributed across multiple sites for each transaction may span across many sites. For example, in a distributed Funds Transfer transaction, the debit may happen on site A, but the credit may need to be effected on a different site, say B. This means that the database logging mechanisms are more complex and have to gear up for data recovery as well. The *undo* and *redo* processing discussed earlier now applies to the databases stored on different sites. Therefore, there must be coordination between these sites. Perhaps one *master log* can be made responsible for the overall recovery operation and can drive the logs on the other sites. This is shown in Fig. 8.14.

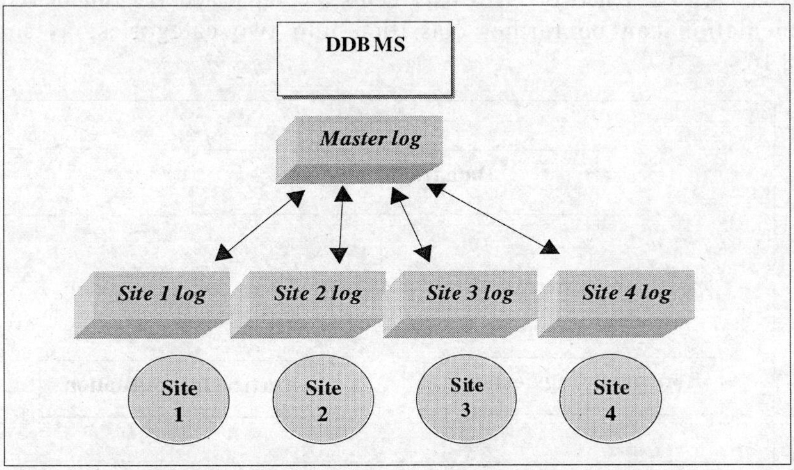

Fig. 8.14 Distributed data recovery through logging

6. **Security** – Maintaining security of data in a distributed environment is not easy. Now users are not located at a single place and therefore, uniform procedures, practices and access control mechanisms are not simple to implement. Determining who can access which data and perform which actions needs to be carefully thought out and implemented. Even worse, due to replication and fragmentation of data, sites can have data that does not *belong* to them. Therefore, it becomes even more important to safeguard data and other database objects from possible attacks.

8.5 DISTRIBUTED DATABASE TECHNIQUES

We have studied that there are two primary ways in which a database can be distributed. Fig. 8.15 shows these approaches.

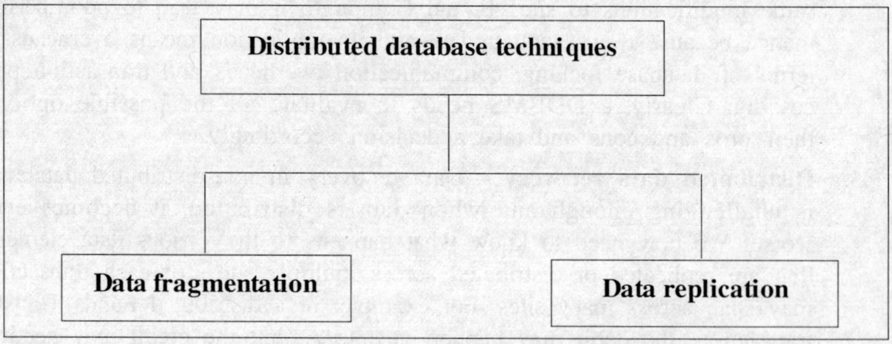

Fig. 8.15 Distributed database techniques

We shall recap these concepts in brief.

8.5.1 Data Fragmentation

In **data fragmentation**, the tables of a database are physically fragmented and distributed across a network. No data items are replicated (i.e. duplicated). Data fragmentation can be further classified into two categories, as shown in Fig. 8.16.

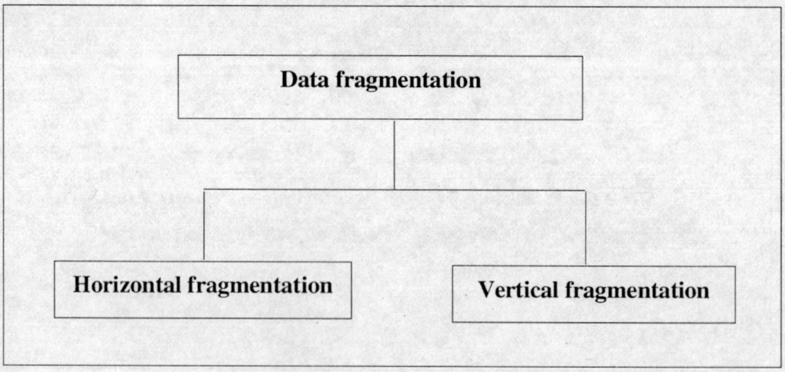

Fig. 8.16 Data fragmentation classification

Let us discuss these.

- **Horizontal fragmentation**: In the **horizontal fragmentation** approach, we take a subset of the rows in a table. A simple WHERE condition can do this job. In addition, a projection operation by using the SELECT clause can also retrieve either the required or all columns. In many practical situations, it is common to see only one column being retrieved. For example, a horizontal fragmentation on the *Employee* table can retrieve employee names working in departments named *Admin*, *Projects* or *Finance*. Note that when we retrieve only the employee name from all the columns in the *Employee* table, it is a projection operation. On the other hand, the retrieval of only the employees working in the three named departments is a selection operation (i.e. horizontal fragmentation).

  A special case of horizontal fragmentation is **derived horizontal fragmentation**. In this case, the fragmentation of a table also causes the other related tables to be fragmented. For example, when we perform horizontal fragmentation on the *Employee* table as discussed above, we may also bring in the locations for the relevant rows (i.e. the rows for the three departments) from the *Department* table to the same site. That way, all the information regarding those departments and their employees will be available at one place. The idea is shown in Fig. 8.17.

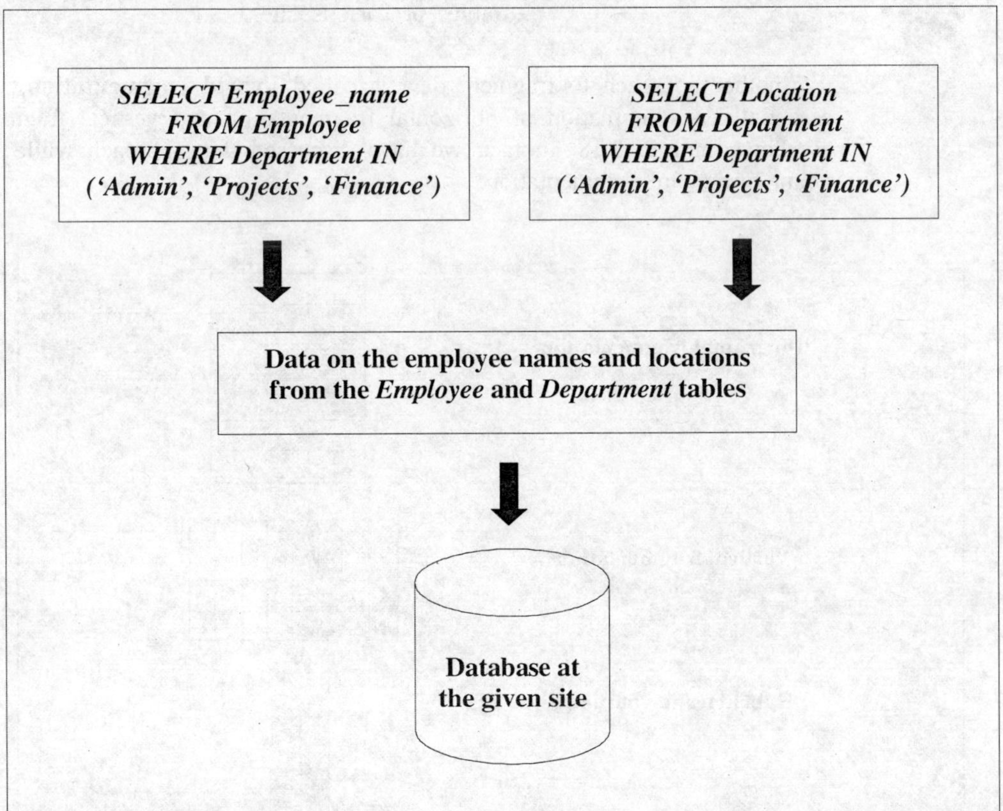

Fig. 8.17 Derived horizontal fragmentation

- **Vertical fragmentation**: In the **vertical fragmentation** approach, we take a subset of the columns in a table. This is a projection operation. For example, we could select only the employee name and salary from the *Employee* table and maintain this information at a site. Importantly, vertical fragmentation should be done in such a way that it should be possible to join or merge back the fragments to construct the original table. For example, suppose the *Employee* table contains the following columns:

  Employee_number, Name, Salary, Age, Sex, Department

  We may then fragment this table at two sites, containing the following columns respectively:

Site 1 – Employee_number, Name, Salary

Site 2 – Employee_number, Age, Sex, Department

Note that we have maintained the primary key column (i.e. Employee_number) at both the sites. This is done in order to be able to recreate the original *Employee* table (by joining the above two tables based on the Employee_number column) as and when needed.

Thus, we can state the following:

> In vertical fragmentation, the primary key is a part of all the fragmented tables at various sites.

Another approach to fragment data is called **hybrid fragmentation**, which is essentially a combination of horizontal fragmentation and vertical fragmentation, as shown in Fig. 8.18. In fact, we have discussed this approach while studying about horizontal fragmentation.

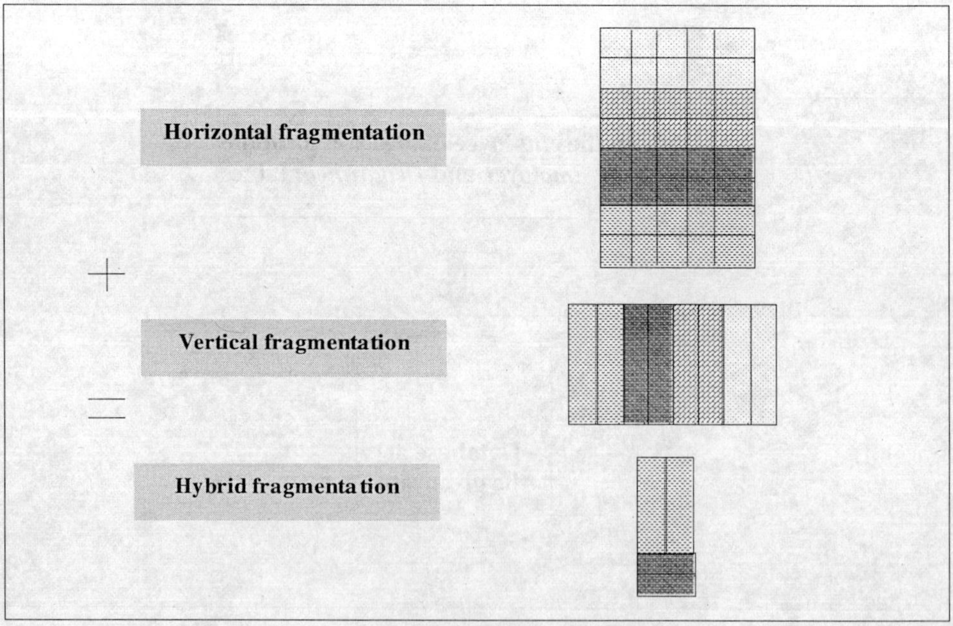

Fig. 8.18 Hybrid fragmentation

8.5.2 Data Replication

In **data replication**, the same copy of data is available at more than one site.

In other words, we create some amount of redundancy. Two most important reasons for employing this strategy are as follows:

(a) The data can be made available at the site where the information is requested for, or at least at a site close to it. This minimises the data transmission requirements.

(b) Overall data availability is increased. If one site is down, we can retrieve data from another site (i.e. a copy of the same data).

Data replication (or no replication at all) can be performed in three ways, as shown in Fig. 8.19.

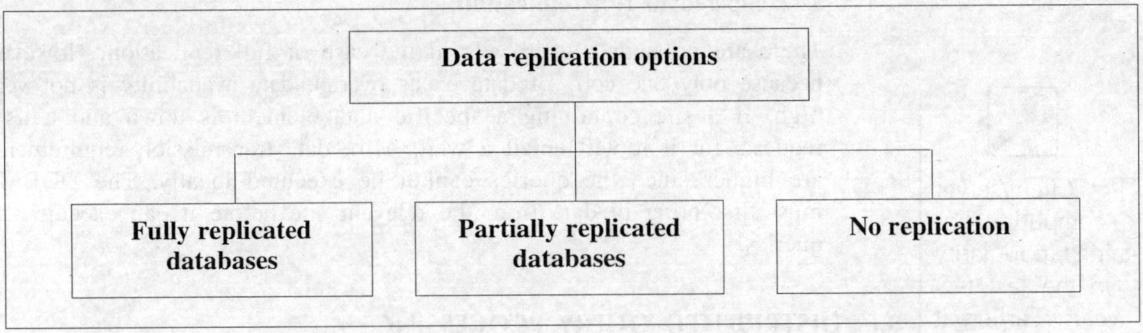

Fig. 8.19 Data replication options

Let us examine the different types of replication now.

In a **fully replicated database** environment, all the sites contain the full database.

- **Fully replicated databases**: Every data element is available at every site in this type of database. This increases data availability and fault tolerance by many folds. In other words, almost all queries can be executed locally, without needing to retrieve any data from another site. Also, the performance of query execution is quite high, because of its nature (i.e. local execution).

  However, there are certain drawbacks of this scheme as well. Most notably, the overall performance, including that of the update operations, is bad. This is because when a user updates the database at one site, the changes made must be replicated to all the other sites in order to maintain data integrity and consistency. Moreover, concurrency and data recovery are not easy to achieve.

In a **partially replicated database** environment, some of the databases/tables are replicated at some of the sites.

- **Partially replicated databases**: In this form of replication environment, not every database element is present at every site. Which databases to replicate, how, and where is a decision specific to an environment. In general, databases that are viewed more than they are updated should be replicated. This provides better performance without too many overheads.

An environment that has **no replication**, a data element is stored at exactly one place.

- **No replication**: In the replication environment, no other copy of the database exists at any other site. This is the other extreme of replication, as compared to **full replication**.

  There are no update overheads in the case of full replication. However, because only one copy of data exists overall, data availability is not very high. If a site containing a specific data element is down and a user requests for it it will entail a wait. Also, data transmission requirements are higher since the queries cannot be executed locally. The DDBMS must first bring in data from the relevant site before it can execute any queries.

Client/server computing has gained popularity in the last few years. Earlier, it was expected that the powerful server computer (e.g. a mainframe) would do almost everything related to the application, and that the user's computer would be quite *dumb* in nature. No longer is it the case now. The users want to be able to use their computer also as a participant in the application execution in true sense.

8.6 DISTRIBUTED QUERY PROCESSING

A DDBMS has to take care of execution of queries that are distributed. In other words, one query has to refer to tables at multiple sites. This involves certain critical decisions, which we shall now discuss.

8.6.1 Costs

The most important cost in a DDBMS environment is related to data transmission. This it is quite logical as even, in a centralised (non-distributed) environment, there are many types of costs, such as the CPU time, memory requirements, hard disk space and so on. However, because the query is entered and executed on a single site, there is no question of data transmission costs.

This is not true in the case of distributed queries. Here, we incur all the costs that are associated with a centralised environment and, in addition, we also acquire data transmission costs. The idea is illustrated in Fig. 8.20.

Because the data is not available at a centralised location, we must first transmit it from one site to another. We may also need to transmit intermediate results. The strategy should always be to try and minimise these data transmission requirements.

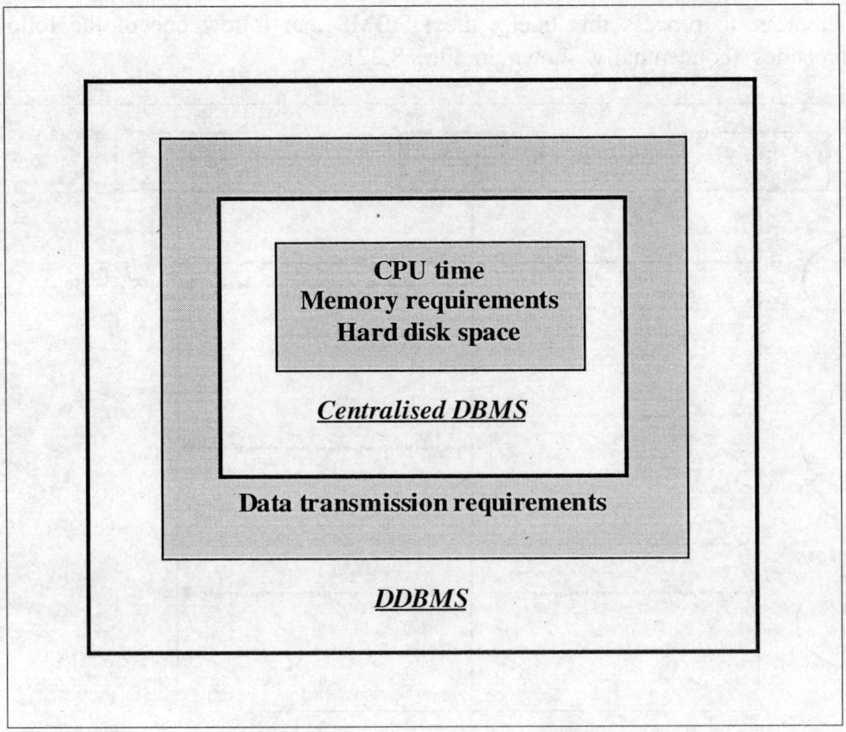

Fig. 8.20 Centralised and DDBMS query processing requirements

Let us consider an example to illustrate this. Suppose we have just three sites numbered 1, 2 and 3. Of these sites, sites 1 and 2 contain one table each, as shown in Fig. 8.21.

Site 1	Site 2
Employee table (Contains 200 bytes per record, and 15,000 such records)	*Department* table (Contains 50 bytes per record, and 150 such records)

Fig. 8.21 Data distribution example

A user at site 3 (called the **result site**) executes the following query:

SELECT Emp_Name, Salary, Department_Name

FROM Employee, Department

WHERE Employee.Department_Number = Department.Department_Number

Let us assume that every employee definitely has a department number assigned. Therefore, this query would produce 15,000 rows. Also, let us assume that the output of the query is 50 bytes. In other words, every output line contains 50 bytes.

In order to process this query, the DDBMS can follow one of the following approaches (conceptually shown in Fig. 8.22).

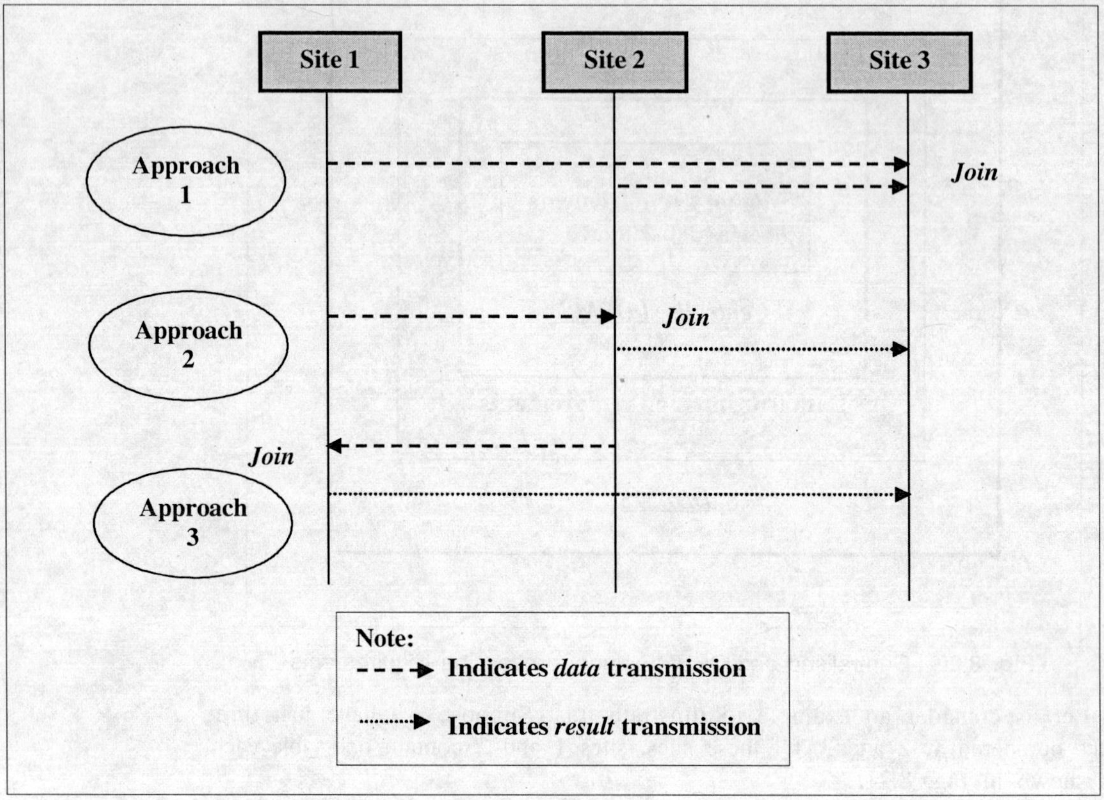

Fig. 8.22 Distributed query processing – Possible approaches

Let us now discuss these approaches.

(a) Transfer the *Employee* and *Department* tables to site 3 and do a join. This will lead to the following steps:

(i) Transfer *Employee* table from site 1 to site 3. This means transfer of 200 × 15,000 bytes, or 30,00,000 bytes.

(ii) Transfer *Department* table from site 2 to site 3. This means transfer of 50 × 150 bytes, or 7,500 bytes.

(iii) At site 3, perform the join and show the result to the user.

Thus, the total data transmission requirement would be worth 30,07,500 (30,00,000 + 7,500) bytes.

(b) Transfer the *Employee* table to site 2 and do a join. Transfer the result of this operation to site 3. This will lead to the following steps.

(i) Transfer *Employee* table from site 1 to site 2. This means transfer of 200 × 15,000 bytes, or 30,00,000 bytes.

(ii) Perform the join operation at site 2 and send the results to site 3. This will cause 50 × 15,000, or 7,50,000 bytes of data to be transferred from site 2 to site 3.

(iii) At site 3, show the result to the user.

Thus, the total data transmission requirement would be worth 37,50,000 (30,00,000 + 7,50,000) bytes.

(c) Transfer the *Department* table to site 1 and do a join. Transfer the result of this operation to site 3. This will lead to the following steps:

(i) Transfer *Department* table from site 2 to site 1. This means transfer of 50 × 150 bytes, or 7,500 bytes.

(ii) Perform the join operation at site 1 and send the results to site 3. This will cause 50 × 15,000, or 7,50,000 bytes of data to be transferred from site 2 to site 3.

(iii) At site 3, show the result to the user.

Thus, the total data transmission requirement would be worth 7,57,500 (7,500 + 7,50,000) bytes.

Clearly, approach 3 is the most desirable as it requires the minimum amount of data transfer.

8.6.2 Semi-join

We will note that although several approaches exist for distributed query processing, all of them involve the transfer a great amount of data from one site to another. Better techniques, which minimise the amount of data transmission between sites, exist.

> **Semi-join** is a technique that attempts to minimise the amount of data that needs to be transferred between sites during distributed query execution.

Semi-join reduces unwanted data transmission, thus reducing the load on the communication links. As a result, the overall performance of distributed query processing is a lot better than otherwise. The technique is simple—minimise the number of rows and columns before sending the data to another site. How can this be done? Let us understand with a simple example.

The Internet is also a special case of client/server computing. The Web browser is the client, and the Web server is the server here.

Suppose we need to join two tables—A and B—located at different sites. Table A is located at site 1, and table 2 is located at site 2. So far, we have studied that we need to:

1. Send table A from site 1 to site 2 and do a join at site 2, or
2. Send table B from site to 2 site 1 and do a join at site 1.

The approach to be chosen depends on the size of the two tables (whichever is smaller should be selected). Semi-join improves upon this. Rather than sending the entire table, it sends just the column(s) on which the join is to be achieved. This dramatically reduces the amount of data that needs to be transmitted from one site to another. Conceptually, this is shown in Fig. 8.23.

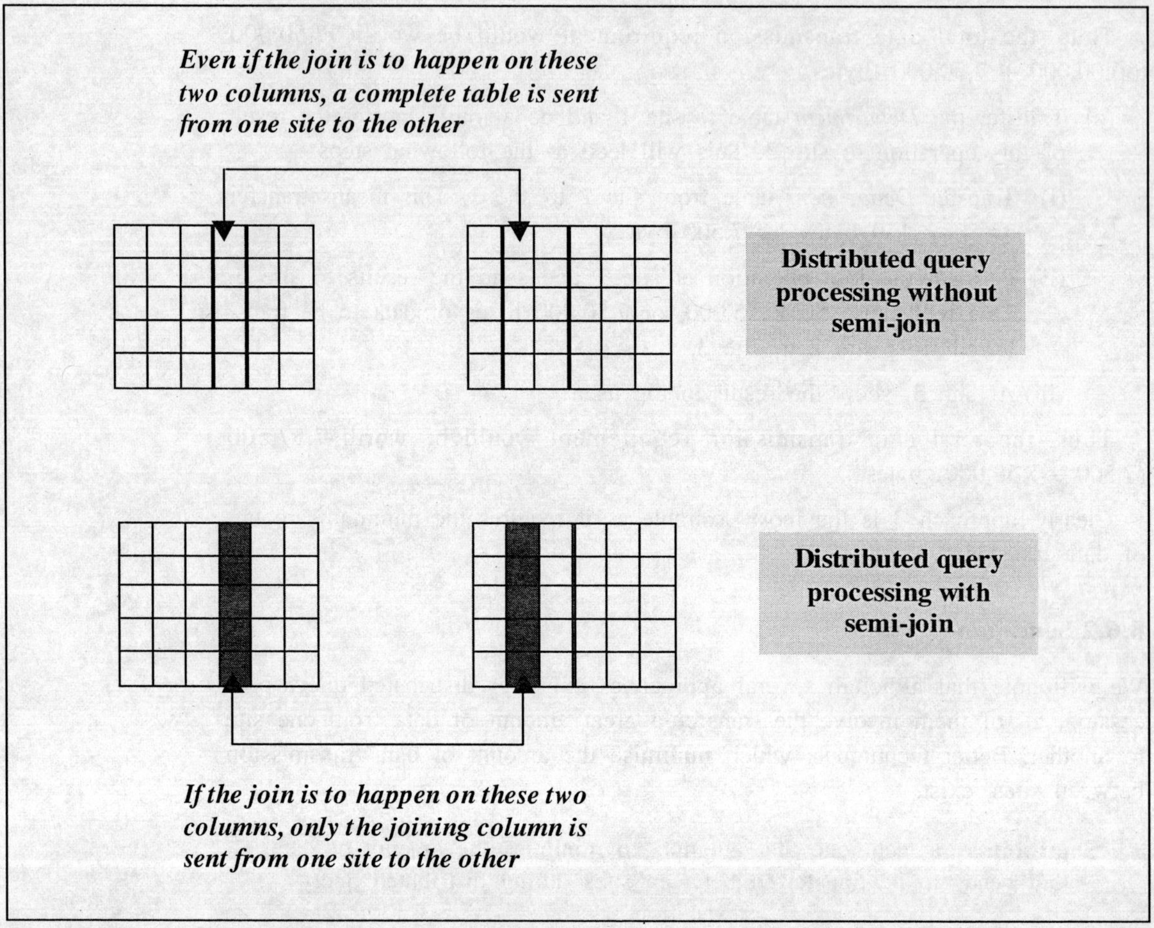

Fig. 8.23 Distributed query processing with and without semi-join

Let us understand this better with an extension of the same example discussed earlier, in which we had concluded that approach 3 was the best, as it involved minimum amount of data transfer.

Let us assume that the join was to happen on the Department_ID columns of the *Employee* and *Department* tables. We shall assume that the size of this column is 5 bytes. Therefore, the transfer of only this column from site 2 to site 1 would now involve $5 \times 150 = 750$ bytes, instead of 7,500 bytes as in the earlier case (refer to the previous section for more details). The saving achieved by semi-join is small here, but it can be quite significant in some other cases.

8.6.3 Distributed Query Decomposition

When working with distributed databases, two main options are available for the processing of queries, as shown in Fig. 8.24.

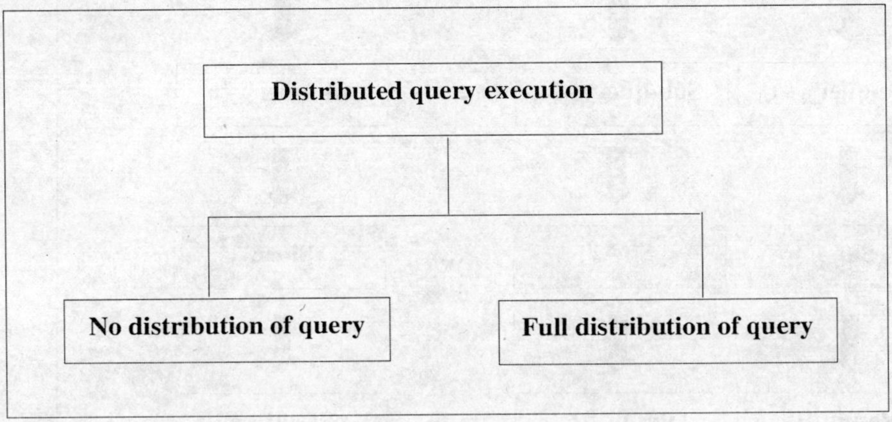

Fig. 8.24 Distributed query execution

Let us now discuss these approaches.

- **No distribution of query**: This approach is quite simple. The user is responsible for working with data fragments and/or replicated data. For instance, if the user is interested in finding out the names and salaries of employees working in department 5, he is completely responsible for locating this information. The user must specify which copy of the replicated database should be chosen (i.e. from which site the table should be taken). Moreover, the user is responsible for ensuring data integrity and consistency among all the participating sites.
- **Full distribution of query**: In this approach, the query is issued as though the user is working on a centralised database. There is no notion of distribution of data from the user's point of view. It is the DDBMS which takes all decisions regarding the retrieval of appropriate tables from various sites. The DDBMS performs a task called **query decomposition** for this purpose. The technique is simple–the DBMS breaks the user's query into smaller queries. Each smaller query is called a **sub-query** and it executes at the respective sites chosen by the DDBMS. The results of all the sub-queries are finally combined to produce the output. The DDBMS maintains and user information regarding the fragmentation, replication and distribution of data for this purpose. This is shown in Fig. 8.25.

Also, the user does not handle tasks such as maintaining data integrity and consistency between the various sites. The DDBMS performs these tasks for the user.

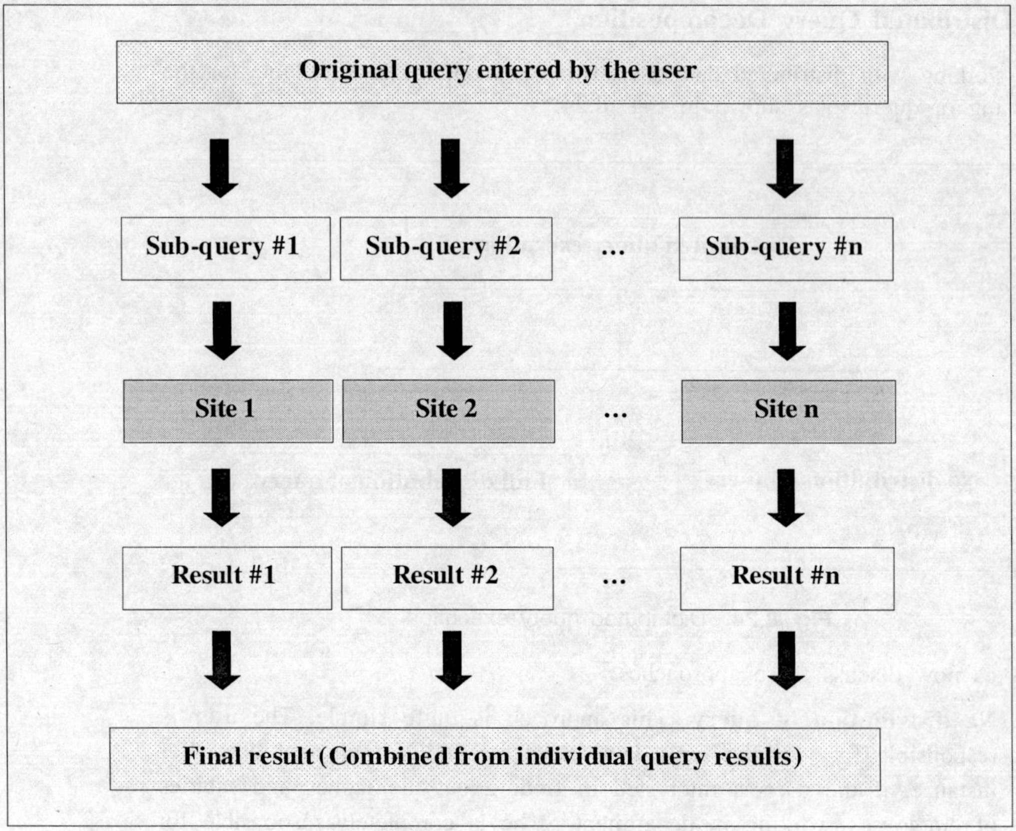

Fig. 8.25 Query decomposition

8.7 DISTRIBUTED CONCURRENCY CONTROL AND RECOVERY

8.7.1 Concurrency and Recovery Problems

Several problems arise while dealing with concurrency control and recovery issues in distributed database systems. These problems are specific to distributed databases, and are not observed in centralised database systems. Some of the main problems are listed below.

- **Site failure**: There are situations when one or more sites in a DDBMS fail. In such situations, it is important that the DDBMS continues functioning. When the sites resume functioning, they must be brought back to the state of the other sites. In other words, the consistency and integrity of the database must be restored.
- **Network problems**: Many times, the communication network fails, causing one or more sites to be cut off from the rest of the sites in a DDBMS environment. An extreme case is when the sites in a DDBMS environment are cut into two portions. This is called **network portioning**. In this case, a site can communicate with other sites that belong to

the same side of the partition, but not with any site that belongs to the other side of the partition.

- **Data duplication**: Because of data replication, the same multiple copies of data may exist. Hence, the DDBMS needs to monitor these copies and make sure that the database is consistent and is in a recoverable state, if and when problems arise.
- **Distributed transactions**: There may be problems when a transaction spans across multiple sites in terms of some sites being successful in committing/rolling back their changes, but others not being able to do so. We know that the two-phase commit protocol is used in such situations.
- **Distributed deadlocks**: In a centralised DBMS, a deadlock occurs at a single site. It is quite easy to detect and deal with such a deadlock. However, in a DDBMS, a deadlock may occur in any one or many of the multiple sites. This situation is called as **distributed deadlock**. The DDBMS must be able to handle such situations.

Here we shall discuss some of the steps taken in order to deal with such problems in a DDBMS environment.

8.7.2 Distinguished Copy

Data replication helps achieve better performance in a DDBMS environment. However, it also poses a major challenge due to the possibility of data inconsistency. In order to deal with such situations, the concept of **distinguished copy** may be used. The idea is simple–if a data item (say a table) exists at three sites, one of the copies is designated as the distinguished copy (or the main copy) and the other two copies depend on it. Any locking and unlocking that needs to be done because of transactions is applied to the distinguished copy. The idea is illustrated in Fig. 8.26. Here, the same table–A–occurs at sites 1, 2 and 3. The table at site 2 is the distinguished copy. The other two tables (at sites 1 and 3) depend on the table at site 2.

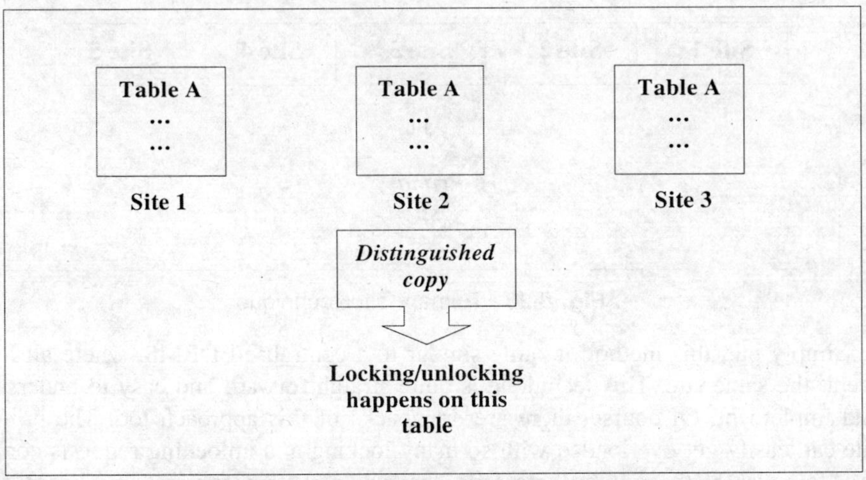

Fig. 8.26 Distinguished copy concept

The concept of distinguished copy can be used to deal with concurrency and recovery issues to a great extent. Based on how we choose to model it, there are three possible techniques, as shown in Fig. 8.27.

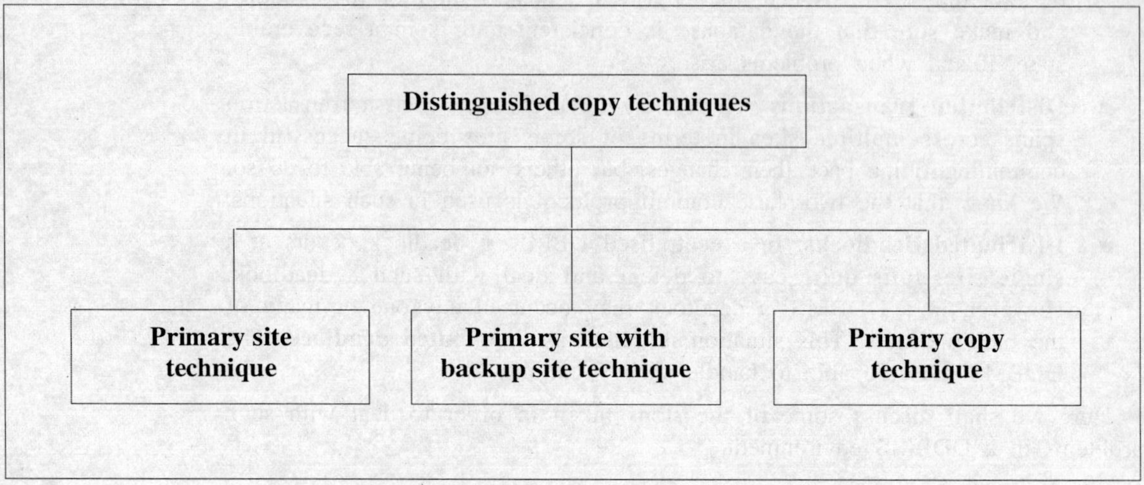

Fig. 8.27 Distinguished copy techniques

The term **coordinator site** needs to be discussed before we study these three techniques. A coordinator site is the one that contains the distinguished copy of the data item under consideration. In other words, the coordinator site is the main site for that data item.

8.7.2.1 Primary site technique In this technique, one **primary site** becomes the coordinator site for *all* data items, as shown in Fig. 8.28. Thus, all locking and unlocking happens at the primary site.

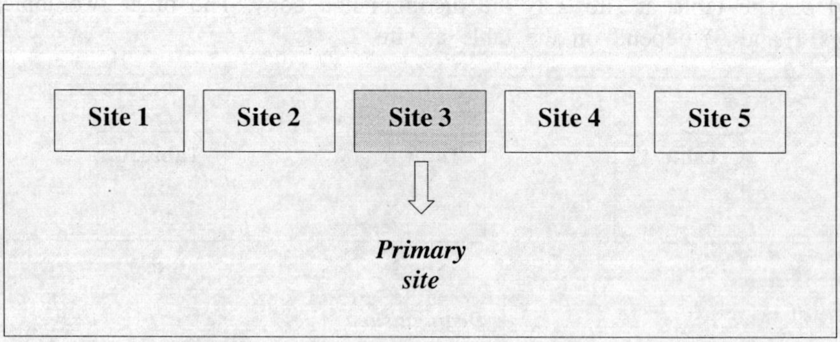

Fig. 8.28 Primary site technique

Simply put, this method is quite similar to a centralised DBMS, where all locks are at the same site. This technique is quite straightforward and easy to understand and implement. Of course, there are drawbacks of this approach too. The primary site can easily get overloaded with so many locking and unlocking requests coming in. Moreover, if the primary site fails, the whole system comes to its knees quite quickly. This is because the primary site is the only one that controls the transaction management aspects of the DDBMS. In other words, system availability and reliability can be at stake.

8.7.2.2 Primary site with backup site technique This approach deals with the problem of primary site failure. A site designated as **backup site** takes over from the primary site if and when the latter fails. The idea is illustrated in Fig. 8.29.

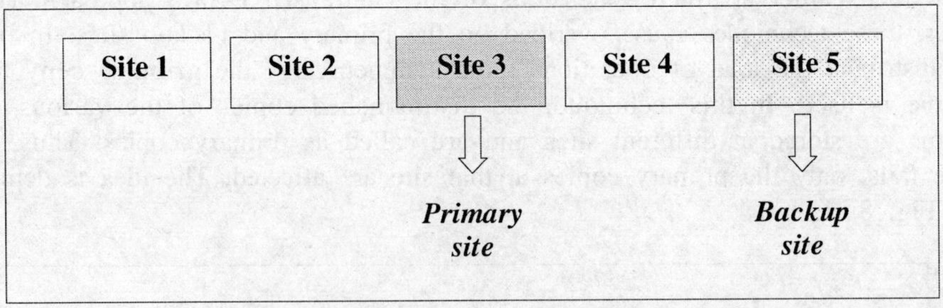

Fig. 8.29 Primary site with backup site technique

Locking and unlocking happens at both the sites – that is the primary site and the backup site. If the primary site fails, the backup site becomes the primary site and a new site is chosen as the new backup site, as shown in Fig. 8.30. The only problem that occurs in case of primary site failure is a small delay for these changes to take peace, after which the DDBMS can resume its operation.

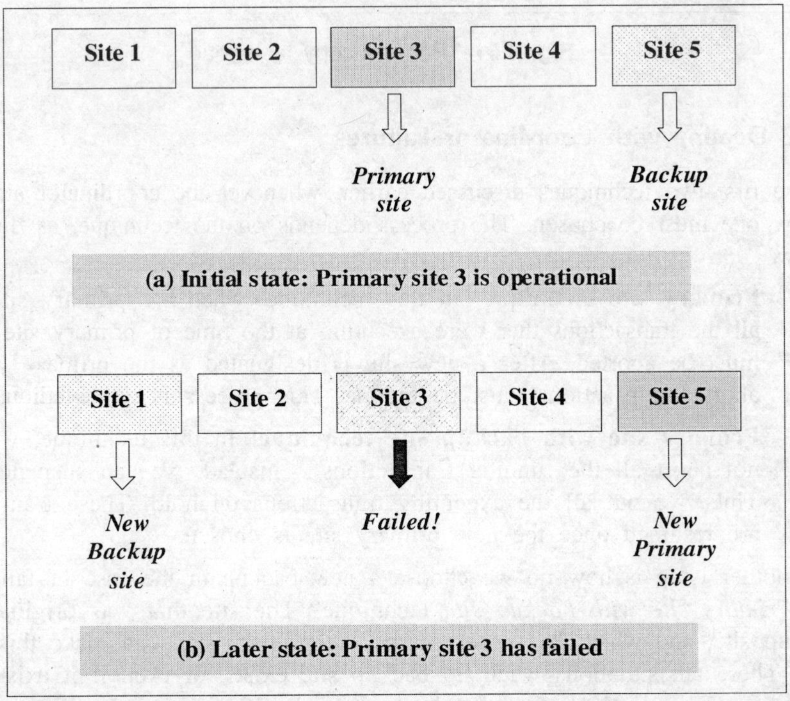

Fig. 8.30 Primary site failure in Primary site with backup site technique

The main disadvantage of this scheme is that all locking and unlocking operations must happen at two sites–the primary site and the backup site. Consequently, the overall system performance is not very high. Moreover, the primary site and the backup site can be overloaded with too many locking/unlocking requests.

8.7.2.3 Primary copy technique We have noticed that the two techniques described earlier are mere extensions of the centralised DBMS approach. However, these techniques cause overload on the primary and backup sites. In order to distribute the load of operations more symmetrically, the **primary copy** technique is used. In this technique, the distinguished copies of the various data items are stored at different sites and are called as primary copies. Thus, if a site fails, only the primary copies at that site are affected. The idea is depicted in Fig. 8.31.

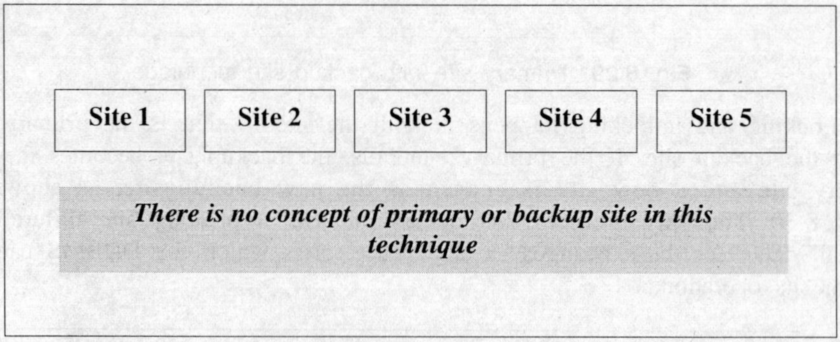

Fig. 8.31 Primary copy technique

8.7.3 Dealing with Coordinator Failures

In the first two techniques discussed earlier, whenever the coordinator site fails, a new one must be chosen. The process depends on the technique, as discussed below.

- **Primary site technique**: In this technique, when the primary site fails, all the transactions that were executing at the time of primary site failure must be aborted. After a new site is designated as the primary site, the aborted transactions must be redone. This process is quite tedious.
- **Primary site with backup site technique**: In this technique, we need not abort all the running transactions – instead, we can suspend them. Thus, we put all the executing transactions on hold. These transactions are resumed once the new primary site is chosen.

Another issue is how do we choose a new backup in the case of failures in the *Primary site with backup site* technique? The site that was originally the backup site, and which has now become the primary site, can make this selection. There are situations when no backup site exists, or even if it exists, it is down. In such situations, a mechanism called **election** is used. In this process, a site that needs to deal with the coordinator site realises that the coordinator site is down based on its repeated unsuccessful attempts at eliciting some sort of information from the (failed) coordinator site. This site now sends a message to all the other sites in the DDBMS, proposing to take over the role of the coordinator. These other sites either choose to select it, or disallow it. In the process, a few more sites may also declare their election. The site that gets the highest number of votes can then become the new coordinator site.

Fig. 8.32 shows an example of election.

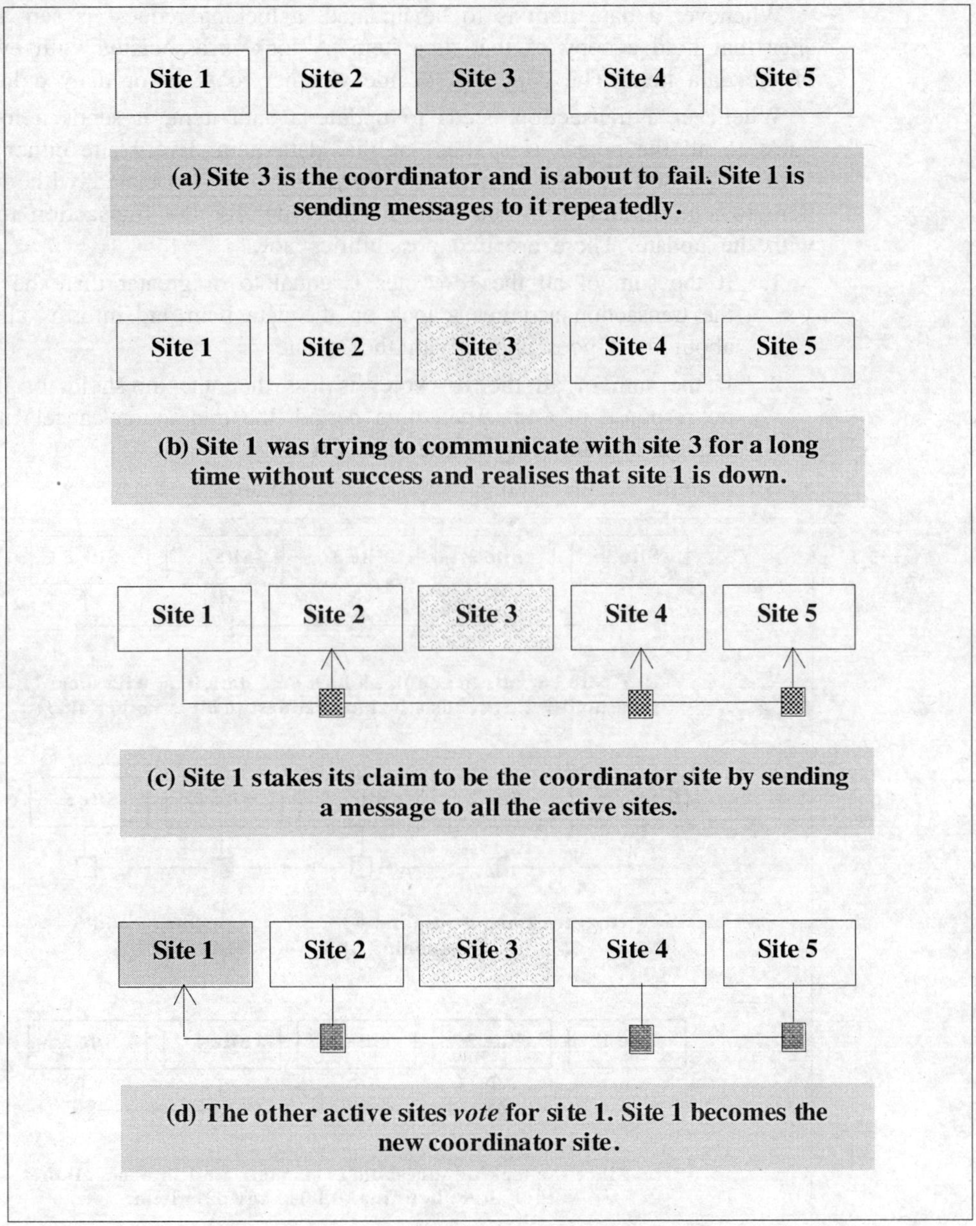

Fig. 8.32 Example of election

8.7.4 Voting Method

Another approach of achieving concurrency control in a DDBMS environment is to use the **voting method**. So far, we have discussed methods of achieving concurrency control based on the concept of distinguished copy. That is, we designate one of the sites as the holder of the distinguished copy of the replicated data item. There is no such concept as a distinguished copy in the voting method.

Whenever a data item is to be updated, a locking request is sent to all the sites that hold a copy of that data item. A lock is associated with every copy of the data item. The copy can decide whether to grant or deny a lock.

Whenever a transaction needs to update a data item, it sends a locking request to all the copies (i.e. sites) of that data item. Every site either responds with a *Yes* or *No*. This response is called a *vote*. Associated with every data item is a minimum threshold that must be met for the transaction to proceed with the update. There are two possibilities now.

1. If the sum of all the *Yes* votes is equal to or greater than the threshold, the transaction acquires a lock on the data item and informs all the sites about it. It goes ahead with the update.
2. If the sum of all the *Yes* votes is less than the threshold, or if there is no response in a specified time period, the transaction cancels its locking request and informs all the sites about it.

An example of the voting method is shown in Fig. 8.33.

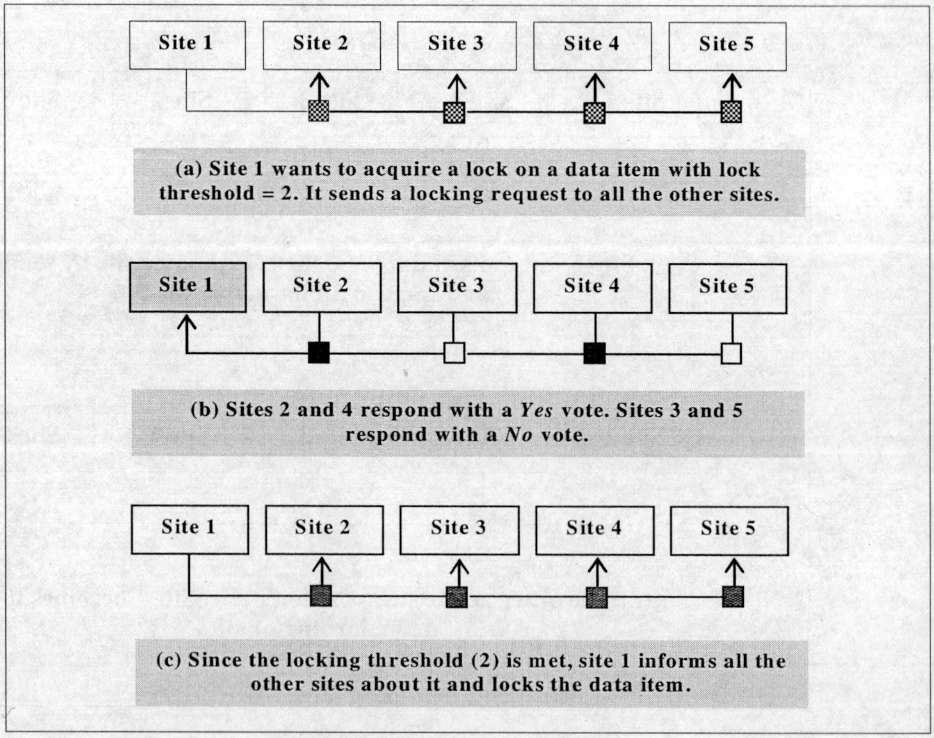

Fig. 8.33 Example of voting

Voting is more distributed in nature, as there is no dependence on a single distinguished copy. However, because of the number of locking requests/responses and voting messages that need to travel between sites, it is slower.

8.7.5 Distributed Recovery

Logging in centralised DBMS systems ensures a swift recovery from failures. In distributed systems, however, things are not so simple. Imagine that site A has sent a message to site B. If B does not respond, what should A do? There are three possible reasons for B not responding, as follows:

1. The message from A to B did not reach B at all, due to communication problems.
2. B was down when A sent the message. So although the message was delivered to B, B could not respond.
3. B did receive the message from A and sent a response. This response was lost due to communication problems.

These possibilities are shown in Fig. 8.34.

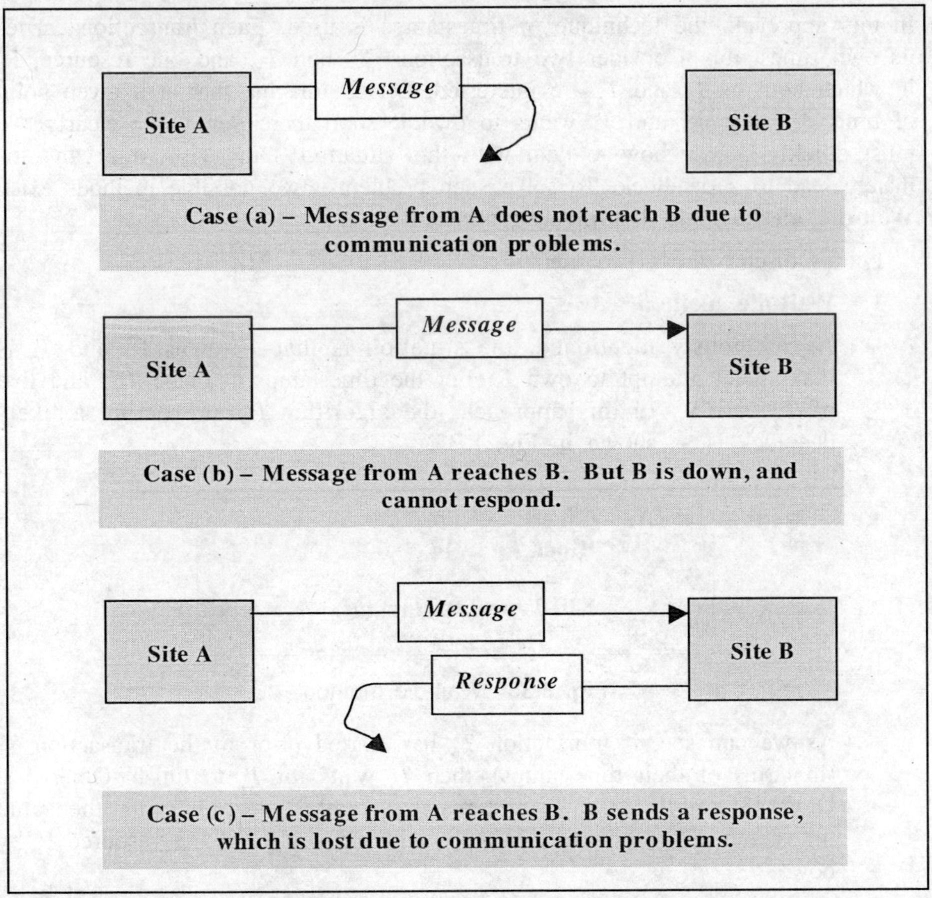

Fig. 8.34 Possible problems in communication between two sites

Clearly, if such problems occur during communication between sites in a DDBMS environment, carrying out transactions or performing recovery operations would be extremely tricky. When a distributed transaction needs to take place, the COMMIT operation cannot happen unless all the participating sites are ready to commit their changes. The two-phase commit protocol is used to ensure this.

8.8 DISTRIBUTED DEADLOCKS

Like almost everything else in distributed systems, deadlocks offer a great design challenge. Dealing with deadlocks even in a non-distributed environment is not easy; coupled with the challenge of multiple sites, the task becomes even tougher.

We shall discuss three strategies related to deadlocks in a distributed environment: *Prevent a deadlock*, *Avoid a deadlock*, *Detect a deadlock*.

8.8.1 Prevent a Deadlock

In this approach, the technique of timestamps is used. Each transaction carries its own timestamp. Consider two transactions, T_1 and T_2, and one resource, R, in which both of T_1 and T_2 are interested. Let us imagine that at a given point of time, T_1 owns R, and T_2 wants to own R soon thereafter. Quite clearly, we must quickly decide how to deal with this situation. Otherwise, this can ultimately lead to a deadlock. To solve such problems, two possible methods exist: **Wait-die method** and **Wound-wait method**.

Let us discuss these two methods.

1. **Wait-die method**

   As previously mentioned, the situation is that T_1 owns R, and T_2 is making an attempt to own R. Let the timestamp of T_1 be TS_1 and that of T_2 be TS_2. In this approach, the algorithm for preventing a likely deadlock is as shown in Fig. 8.35.

```
If TS2 < TS1
        Block T2
Else
        Kill T2 and Restart it
```

Fig. 8.35 Wait-die method

As we can see, if transaction T_2 has started prior to the transaction T_1 (in terms of their timestamps), then T_2 waits for T_1 to finish. Otherwise, DDBMS simply kills T_2 and restarts it after a while (with the same timestamp, TS_2), hoping that T_1 would have released the resource R by now.

To summarise, an older transaction gets a higher priority. Also, we can see that a killed transaction is restarted with its original timestamp value.

That allows it to retain its older priority (which would be higher than most other transactions, when it restarts).

2. **Wound-wait method**

This technique takes a different approach, as compared to the earlier method. Here, we start off with a similar comparison. We compare the timestamps of T_1 and T_2 (i.e. TS_1 and TS_2, respectively). If TS_2 is less than TS_1 (which means that T_2 had started prior to T_1), we kill T_1. (Note that in the earlier case, we had blocked T_2). If, however, T_1 has started earlier, we halt T_2. This process is shown in Fig. 8.36.

```
If TS2 < TS1
        Kill T1
Else
        Halt T2
```

Fig. 8.36 Wait-die method

To summarise, in this approach, we grant immediate access to the request of an older transaction by killing a newer transaction. This means that an older transaction never has to wait for a younger transaction (unlike the earlier approach).

8.8.2 Avoid a Deadlock

After a lot of research, DDBMS designers have concluded that they cannot avoid a deadlock in a distributed environment. There are two main reasons for this:

1. In order to avoid deadlocks completely, every site in the distributed system needs to be aware of the **global state** (i.e. information about all the other sites). This is clearly impossible, because the states of the sites would keep on changing constantly, and even if they communicate these changes to each other, there would be inevitable delays, making the information obsolete. As such, this requirement of global state will never be met.
2. Maintaining global state, if at all, would entail tremendous amount of overheads in terms of network transmission/communication, processing and storage overheads.

8.8.3 Detect a Deadlock

In the process of detecting deadlocks, transactions are allowed to obtain access to shared resources. If a deadlock occurs because of this, it is detected. In such a situation, one of the transactions must release its share of resources.

The trouble in implementing this scheme in the case of a DDBMS is that every site has knowledge of the local transactions only. It cannot know about other sites and their transactions (i.e. global state). Therefore, it cannot help in deadlock detection. Consequently, some sort of arbitration is needed to detect deadlocks in DDBMS. Three solutions are proposed to handle this situation, as follows:

- **Centralised control**: In this approach, one site is designated as the control site, and it decides how to detect and come out of deadlocks. All other sites provide information to this site, and abide by its rules. This approach has the advantage of simplicity, but also has the drawbacks of big overheads in terms of communications, storage and the danger of control site failure. The last point is most relevant as in such a case the entire system could come to a halt.

- **Hierarchical control**: This creates a tree-like structure. Here, the site designated as parent detects deadlocks of its subordinate sites and takes an appropriate decision.

- **Distributed control**: This is a democratic approach, wherein all the sites are treated as equal. All the sites need to cooperate with each other. There is a big amount of information exchange, resulting in substantial overheads.

As we can see, all the approaches have their advantages and disadvantages. Accordingly, the decision of choosing one of them is left to actual problem specification, which differs from one situation to another.

8.9 CLIENT/SERVER COMPUTING AND DDBMS

8.9.1 Client/server Computing

The term **client/server architecture** (also called **client/server computing** or **client/server model**) is very common in computer literature. It is also very important from the context of DDBMS.

Although it sounds complex, it is actually very simple to understand. In fact, it is used in our daily lives as well. For instance, when I use the tea vending machine to get some tea, the machine is serving me. Thus, the tea vending machine is the server, which serves tea to me – the client. When I go to a dentist for operation on my teeth, the dentist serves me – the customer, as shown in Fig. 8.37. Therefore, the dentist is the server in this case and I am the client. Note that in both the examples, the servers (tea vending machine and the dentist) wait for clients (me) to start the action or a dialog.

C.J. Date has provided rules for distributed databases. The more rules that a DBMS complies with; the better it is likely to be.

In computer terms, client and server are both computer programs. These two programs reside on different computers. The idea behind this is quite simple. If two or more programs have to interact with each other for performing a task, one must wait for requests from the other. In this context, the server program is a **passive program** that waits for requests from clients. Therefore, a server program endlessly waits for requests from one or more clients. A client, on the other hand, is an **active program** that initiates a request for the services of that server.

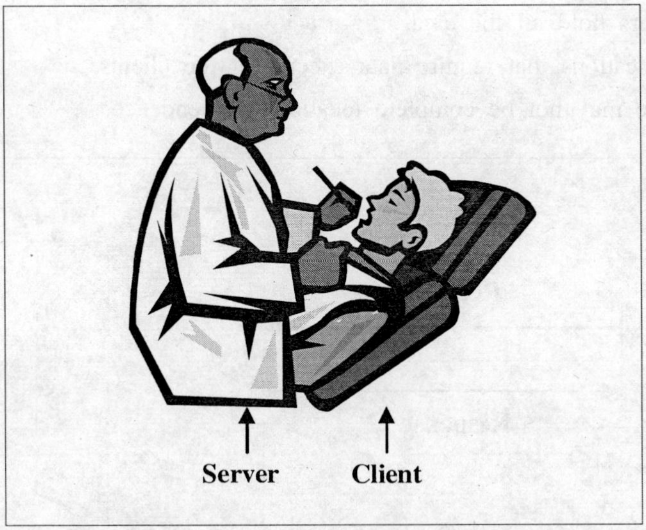

Fig. 8.37 Client and server

Note that a client and a server are both programs, although the 'computers' that run these programs are commonly and erroneously termed as *client* and *server*, respectively. But the terminology has become quite common these days, more so because hardware vendors add to the confusion by advertising their powerful computers as *servers*, whereas what they actually mean are computers that are capable of running server programs due to their high memory, hard disk and processor capabilities. We will, therefore, use these terms in either fashion.

Thus, when one computer requests for the services of another computer, it is called as client/server computing. The services could be anything. For example, a server computer could store files in which a client computer may be interested. Or, in a LAN environment with multiple clients and a server sharing an expensive printer, the server could have the printing hardware and software installed, which all client computers might use for printing. Thus, the term client/server can apply to a variety of applications. Normally, for a computer to act as a server, relatively larger disk and processing capacity are needed. Also, the server must have an operating system that supports multitasking (e.g. UNIX, Windows 2000). The reason for this is simple. There could be multiple requests from different clients at the same time to the same server. For each such request, the server operating system creates a task. The operating system queues these tasks and executes them according to the scheduling algorithm in the operating system.

The common way to depict client/server computing is shown in Fig. 8.38.

8.9.2 Client/server Computing and DDBMS

In the context of DDBMS, client/server computing can be called as a special case of distributed computing, which has the following properties:

(i) There may be one or more clients and servers.

(ii) Servers hold all the data.

(iii) Applications that require data execute at the clients.

(iv) There may not be complete location independence.

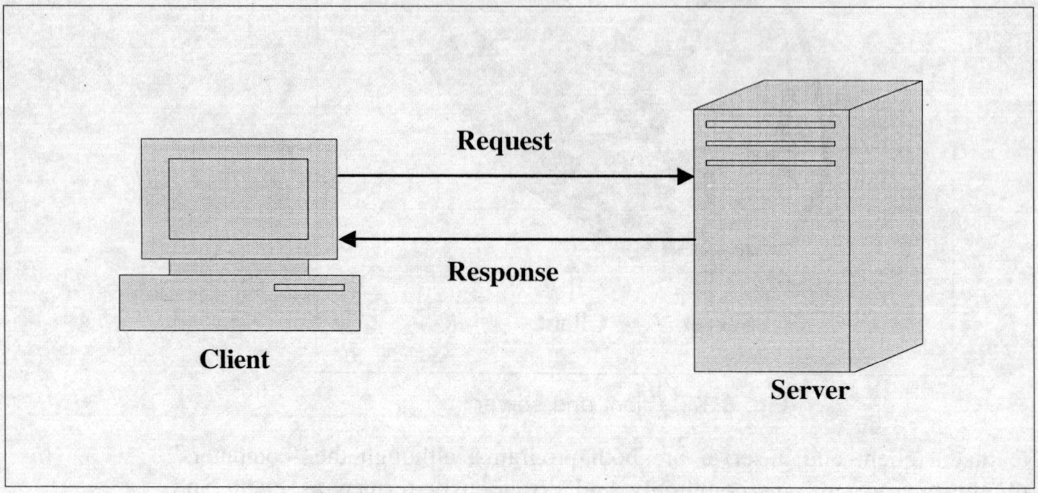

Fig. 8.38 Client/server concept

Effectively, we are saying that servers hold the databases and clients use them. Based on this understanding, we can think of two possible scenarios.

1. Multiple clients access a single server, as shown in Fig. 8.39.
2. One client accesses multiple servers, as shown in Fig. 8.40.

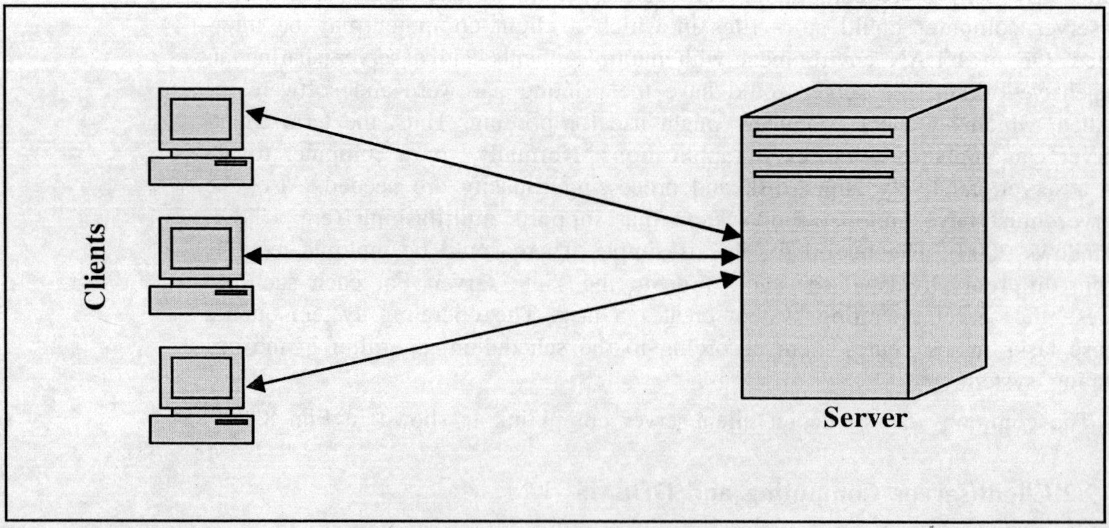

Fig. 8.39 Many clients, one server

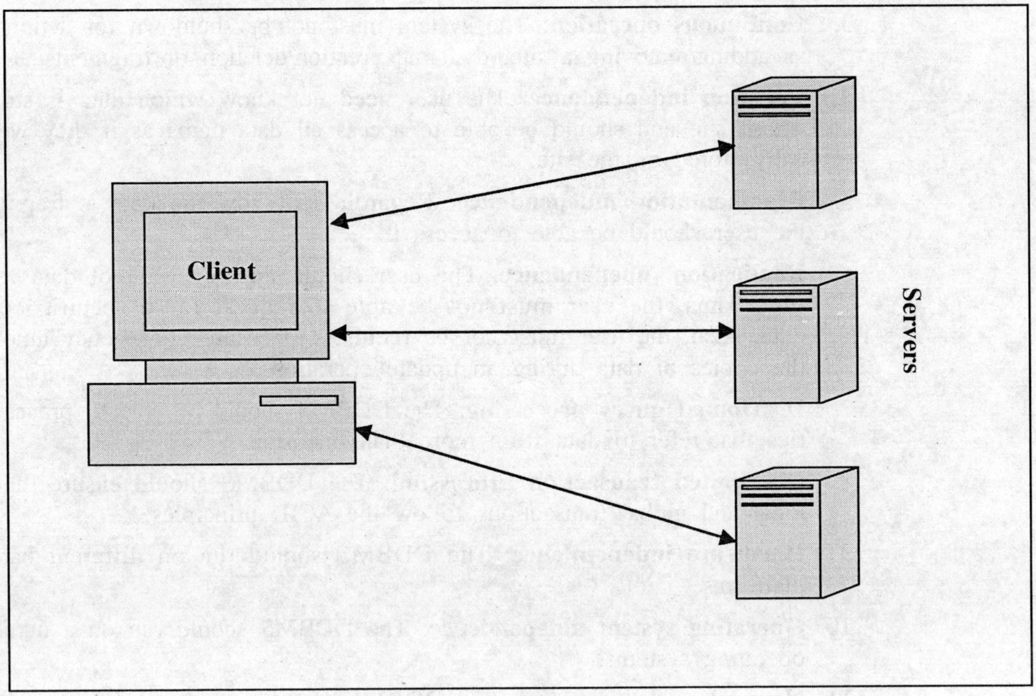

Fig. 8.40 One client, many servers

The second architecture (one client, many servers) can be classified further into two categories, as follows.

(a) The client accesses multiple servers. However, at any given point in time, the client accesses only one server. That is, the client's individual database request is directed to exactly one server, not to multiple servers. Thus, a single request cannot fetch data from two or more servers.

(b) The client can access multiple servers at the same time. A single database request may fetch data form multiple servers.

We will realise that in case (a), the user must know which server holds which data elements. This information would be used to request data from a specific server. In case (b), the user need not possess this information. The user would send request for data as if the set of servers is actually one server.

8.10 DATE'S 12 RULES

C.J. Date has specified 12 rules for or expectations from a DDBMS. We list them below.

1. **Local autonomy**: Every site in a DDBMS should be autonomous. That is, it should own and manage local data and operations.
2. **No dependence on a single site**: The DDBMS should not depend on one site without which it cannot function. Thus, operations such as transaction management, query optimisation and execution, deadlock handling and so on should not depend on a single server.

3. **Continuous operation**: The system must not be shutdown for actions such as adding/removing a site, dynamic creation/deletion of fragments at sites.
4. **Location independence**: The user need not know which data is stored at which site and should be able to access all data items as if they were locally stored on the site.
5. **Fragmentation independence**: Regardless of how the data is fragmented, the user should be able to access it.
6. **Replication independence**: The user should not be aware of data replication. Thus, the user must not be able to request for a specific copy of data. Also, the user must not be required to ensure consistency among all the copies of data during an update operation.
7. **Distributed query processing**: The DDBMS should be able to process queries that refer to data from more than one site.
8. **Distributed transaction processing**: The DDBMS should ensure that both local and global transactions follow the ACID principles.
9. **Hardware independence**: The DDBMS should run on different hardware platforms.
10. **Operating system independence**: The DDBMS should run on a number of operating systems.
11. **Network independence**: The DDBMS should run by using a variety of network types and networking protocols.
12. **Database independence**: It should be possible to construct a DDBMS out of many DBMS, which are different in nature, architecture and data models.

KEY TERMS AND CONCEPTS

Active program
Availability
Avoid a deadlock
Backup site
Centralised applications
Centralised computing
Centralised control
Client
Client/server computing
Coordinator site
Data replication
Derived horizontal fragmentation
Detect a deadlock
Distinguished copy
Distributed applications
Distributed computing
Distributed control
Distributed Database Management System (DDBMS)
Distributed databases
Distributed deadlock
Distributed processing
Distributed recovery
Distributed transaction
Distribution transparency
Election
Fragmentation
Fragmentation transparency
Full replication
Fully replicated database
Global state

Hierarchical control
Horizontal fragmentation
Hybrid fragmentation
Localisation
Location transparency
Naming transparency
Network partitioning
Network transparency
Networked architecture with one centralised database
No replication
Partially replicated database
Passive program
Prevent a deadlock
Primary copy
Primary site
Query decomposition
Reliability
Replication transparency
Semi-join
Server
Shared nothing
Sub-query
Truly distributed database
Two-phase commit
Vertical fragmentation
Voting method
Wait-die method
Wound-wait method

CHAPTER SUMMARY

- Databases can be **centralised** or **distributed**.
- **Distributed DBMS (DDBMS)** manages distributed databases.
- Three possible DDBMS architectures exist: **Shared nothing, Networked architecture with one centralised database**, and **Truly distributed database**.
- In the shared nothing architecture, each computer has its own database.
- In the networked architecture with one centralised database, there is one common database that is shared by all the computers.
- In a truly distributed database, every computer in the distributed environment has its own database. However, all these databases are shared.
- **Location transparency** is a concept in which a user need not be aware of the physical location of a database in a distributed environment.
- In **naming transparency**, the user need not provide any additional information regarding the name of a database.
- A database can be divided horizontally or vertically. This is called as **fragmentation**.
- In **horizontal fragmentation**, a database is divided on the basis of rows.
- In **vertical fragmentation**, a database is divided on the basis of columns.
- Distributed databases offer better reliability and availability as compared to centralised databases. They offer higher performance, and are easy to expand/change.
- Many issues exist in managing distributed databases, such as tracking data, distributed query processing, distributed transaction management, managing replicated data, distributed data recovery, and security.
- Data distribution can happen in the form of replication or fragmentation.

- Data replication can be in the form of **Full replication, Partial replication**, or **No replication.**
- Distributed query processing involves determining the cost of the query. The cost depends on the way it is executed internally.
- Because distributed query processing can be quite expensive, **semi-join** is used to minimise this traffic. Here, an attempt is made to pass minimum data between sites during a distributed query execution.
- A query in the distributed environment can be distributed completely or not at all.
- A number of problems can occur in the area of distributed concurrency control and recovery. Problems such as site failure, network failure, data duplication, distributed transactions and distributed deadlocks can make this quite a challenge to deal with.
- One of the solutions to deal with replicated distributed database problems is to identify a **distinguished copy**. This is treated as the main copy among the replicated ones.
- Three techniques are used in conjunction with distinguished copy concept: **Primary site technique, Primary site with backup site technique,** and **Primary copy technique.**
- The concepts of **election** and **voting method** are used to deal with the failure of the coordinator site.
- Two methods are available to deal with distributed deadlocks: **Wait-die method** and **Wound-wait method**.
- **Client/server computing** is closely related to DDBMS.
- Two client/server architectures are mainly possible; such as **one server multiple clients, one client multiple servers**.
- CJ Date has specified 12 rules for a DDBMS to qualify as really trustworthy.

PRACTICE SET

Mark as true or false

1. A centralised database is the same as a distributed database.
2. The task of a DDBMS is quite complex.
3. In the shared nothing architecture, each computer has its own database.
4. Naming transparency is related only to the location of a database.
5. If a database is divided on the basis of rows, it is called as vertical fragmentation.
6. Data replication can never happen.
7. Semi-join is the same as outer join.
8. A query can be distributed across multiple sites.
9. We can attempt to avoid a distributed deadlock.
10. Election method is used if a participant site fails.

Fill in the blanks

1. In the network architecture with one centralised database architecture, there is/are ______ databases overall.
   (a) 0 (b) 1
   (c) 2 (d) more than 2
2. In ___________, the user need not be aware of the physical place of the database.
   (a) location transparency (b) name transparency
   (c) site transparency (d) area transparency
3. In _______, all the sites contain all the data elements.
   (a) full replication (b) partial replication
   (c) no replication (d) All of the above
4. The ________ protocol is used to govern distributed transactions.
   (a) granular locking (b) normalisation
   (c) concurrency (d) two phase commit
5. We need to determine the _______ of a distributed query in order to judge its performance.
   (a) value (b) amount
   (c) time (d) cost
6. One approach to deal with distributed concurrency is the use of _________.
   (a) unique records (b) locking
   (c) distinguished copy (d) unique copy
7. The idea behind semi-join is to ___________.
   (a) maximize traffic between sites (b) minimize traffic between sites
   (c) put more load on the coordinator site (d) put more load on the participating sites
8. The voting method is used in case the ________ fails.
   (a) main site (b) coordinator site
   (c) participant site (d) follower site
9. A client is _________.
   (a) active program (b) passive program
   (c) active and passive program (d) None of the above
10. A server is _________.
    (a) active program (b) passive program
    (c) active and passive program (d) None of the above

Provide detailed answers to the following questions

1. Distinguish between centralised and distributed systems.
2. Discuss the approaches to distributing data.
3. What are the advantages of distributed databases?
4. List the challenges faced by distributed databases.
5. What are fragmentation and replication?
6. What are the issues in distributed transaction management?
7. What is semi-join?
8. Discuss the concepts of election and voting.
9. What is client/server computing?
10. List down at least five of the twelve rules specified by CJ Date regarding DDBMS.

Exercises

1. What would one look for while designing the architecture of a DDBMS?
2. Why do you think is the two-phase COMMIT protocol required?
3. Are DDBMS closely related to distributed operating systems? If yes, in what sense?
4. Read about the following terms: Distributed query, Distributed transaction, Distributed request.
5. Many Websites use the mirroring technique. Is it related to DDBMS?
6. Is parallel computing related to DDBMS in any ways?
7. Why is there a need for TP monitors such as EJB and MTS when DBMS products themselves support transaction management features?
8. Investigate the problems in distributed file systems.
9. Study more about remote computing protocols such as Remote Procedure Call (RPC), COM/CORBA, and IIOP. How are they related to DDBMS?
10. Why do you think is there a need for location transparency and name transparency?

Chapter 9

Decision Support Systems, Data Warehousing and Data Mining

Modern computing is largely about decision-making. The success of organisations depends on how correct and timely the decisions are. Data warehousing and data mining are powerful tools to this effect.

Chapter Highlights

- Data and Information
- Discussion of Decision Support Systems (DSS)
- Detailed Coverage of Data Warehousing
- Introduction to Data Mining
- Concepts in Online Analytical Processing (OLAP)

9.1 INFORMATION AND DECISION MAKING

9.1.1 Data and Information

Data means raw facts.

Data can be of numerous types, such as:

- Mark sheets of students
- Pay-slips of employees
- File of purchase and sales receipts

When we process data to achieve meaningful results, it becomes **information**.

For example, the data items listed above can become information of some sort, as follows:

- Result summary of an examination
- Payroll report of a month
- Purchase and sales register

Thus, information can be defined as data acquired by informing or by being informed. It is knowledge derived from data, study, experience, and research. Information is not raw facts whereas data is.

The relation between data and information is shown in Fig. 9.1.

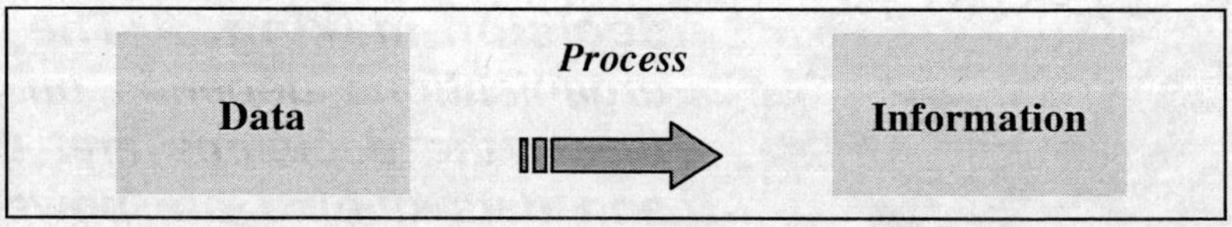

Fig. 9.1 Data and information

9.1.2 Need for Information

The secret of any successful organisation lies in how much information it has, and how it uses that information to achieve its objectives. Any organisation aims at delivering a product, or providing a service. Of course, some organisations may be non-profit making, in which case their focus is on providing free aid, medical help, or education to deprived people. For any organisation to be successful, profit making or otherwise, the flow of information is vital. This flow of information may or may not be connected directly to the usage of computers. However, it is important that all the concerned people in an organisation have access to the right information that they seek.

Organisations are usually made up of groups, such as Administration, Finance, Payroll, Projects, Human Resources, as so on. Within each group there is usually a hierarchy of people, such as the managers, the middle management the clerical cadre and so on. An organisation chart depicts these levels and their functions. It also tells us about the reporting hierarchy and, thus indicates who holds the power of taking decisions. Usually, the decision-making process consists of aspects shown in Fig. 9.2.

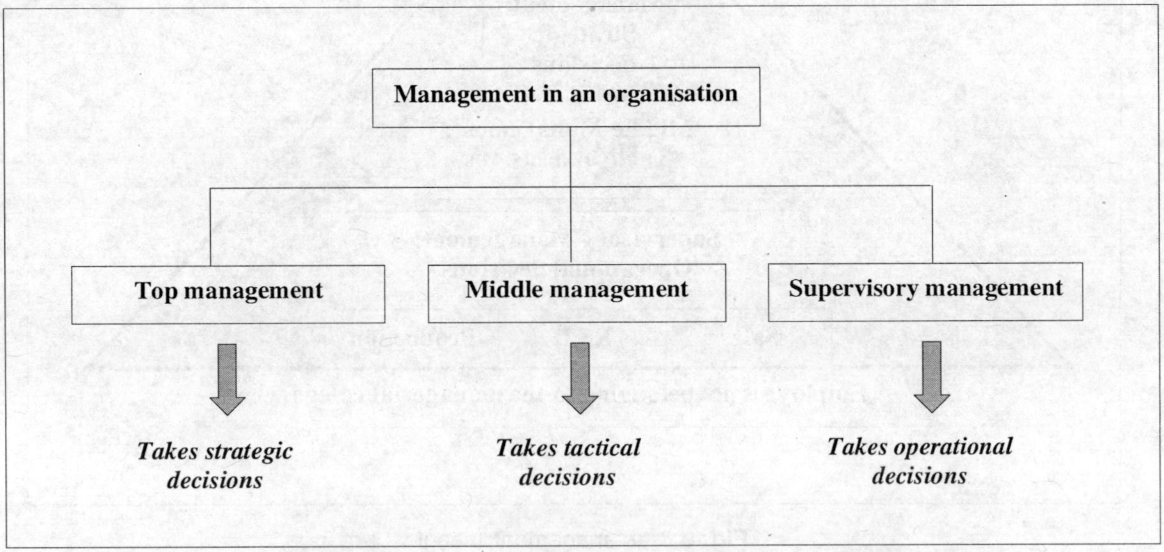

Fig. 9.2 Levels of management and the decision-making process

Let us discuss this in brief.

- **Top management**: The top management is concerned with **strategic decisions**. For instance, the Chief Executive Officer (CEO) or the President of a company deals with the long-term strategic decisions, which are likely to affect the organisation in the medium to long term. For example, the CEO may decide that the organisation needs to tap the US market in the next three years, or that the sales in the next five years should double.
- **Middle management**: The middle management takes **tactical decisions**. Division managers, Section managers, Sales managers, HR managers, are all middle managers. They take decisions for the implementation of the strategic decisions taken by the top management.
- **Supervisory management**: The supervisory managers take **operational decisions**. The focus of these managers is mainly the supervision of staff, monitoring of day-to-day progress of events and taking of corrective actions as and when needed.

Another way of representing the management structure is with the help of the management triangle, which shows the hierarchy of people in an organisation. This is shown in Fig. 9.3.

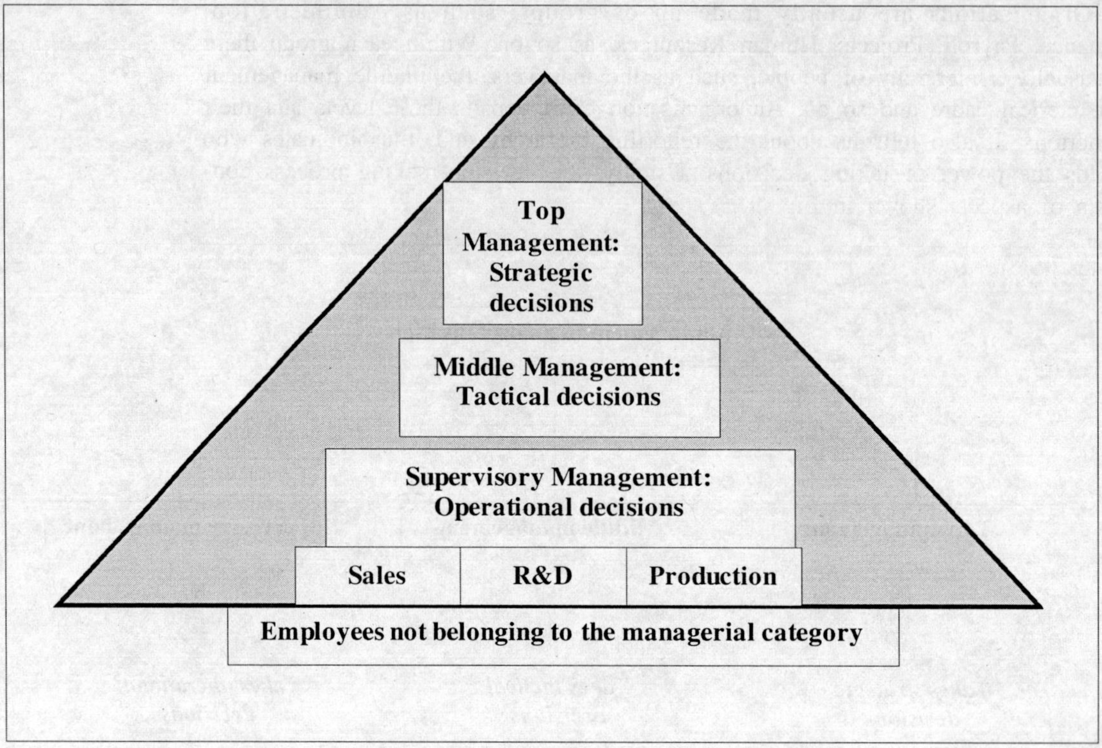

Fig. 9.3 Management triangle

9.1.3 Quality of Information

In order to take decisions at various levels, the managers in an organisation need different kinds of information. The different types of information can be classified as shown in Fig. 9.4.

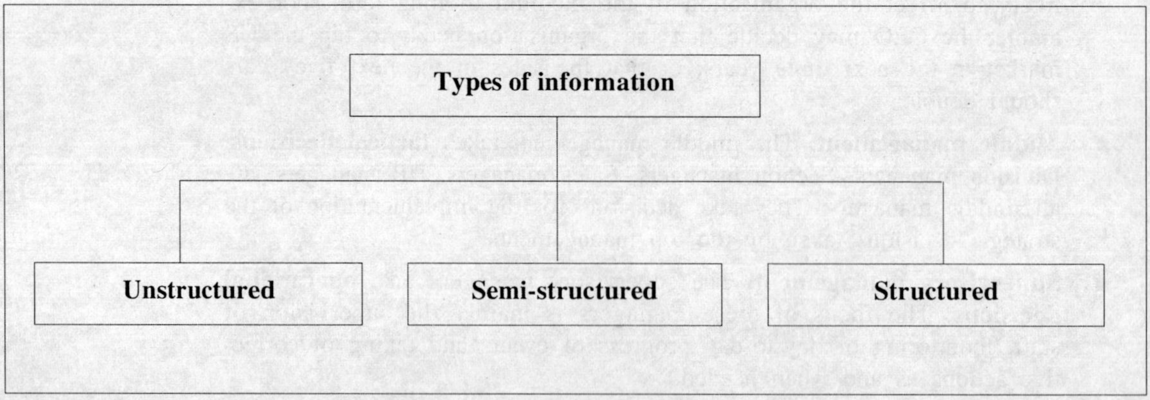

Fig. 9.4 Types of information

The types of information are discussed in brief on next page.

- **Unstructured information**: This type of information is summarised, may be outdated, subjective in nature and related to future events. It deals with a number of areas and covers activities inside and outside of an organisation.
- **Semi-structured information**: This type of information is a combination of the other two types of information.
- **Structured information**: This type of information is up-to-date, detailed, not subjective and concerned with past events. It deals with a small range of facts and deals with the internal details of an organisation.

9.1.4 Value of Timely Information

Information is used to take decisions, convey and evaluate actions, find results and exchange ideas. For information to be effective, data must be processed as soon as it is available and the information must be communicated to those who need it immediately.

Information is always in great demand. However, the main problems related to quality of information are accuracy and timely availability. In today's global marketplace, this need is even more acute. Corporations require information for taking decisions and extending relationships with customers, suppliers and partners.

The information used by organisations comes in from various different systems and sources. It is stored and organised in different databases. In this regard, **data warehousing** has rapidly become a novel and popular business application. Builders of data warehouses consider their systems to be key components of their IT strategy and architecture. There has been tremendous progress in terms of the hardware and software for developing products and services that specifically target the data warehousing market.

A **data warehouse** is the organised data that is situated after and outside the normal operational systems.

In simple terms data warehousing refers to the systematic manner of storing historical data, so that it can be retrieved and used effectively and speedily. The term *data warehouse* itself suggests that here data is stored just as physical warehouses store goods and materials. This is significant because it indicates that data is as important as the physical goods and services that it helps to produce, and produce better.

Decision Support Systems (DSS) are used to create knowledge bases, which are useful in taking decisions about organisational needs.

9.1.5 Historical Data

As we know, the primary focus of a computer-based system is the currently operational systems based on transactions and the data that they process. Normally, in any operational system, there are **master databases** such as customer database, supplier database, product database, and so on. Transactions such as orders, receipts, invoices, payments and returns update these databases continuously. The idea is illustrated in Fig. 9.5.

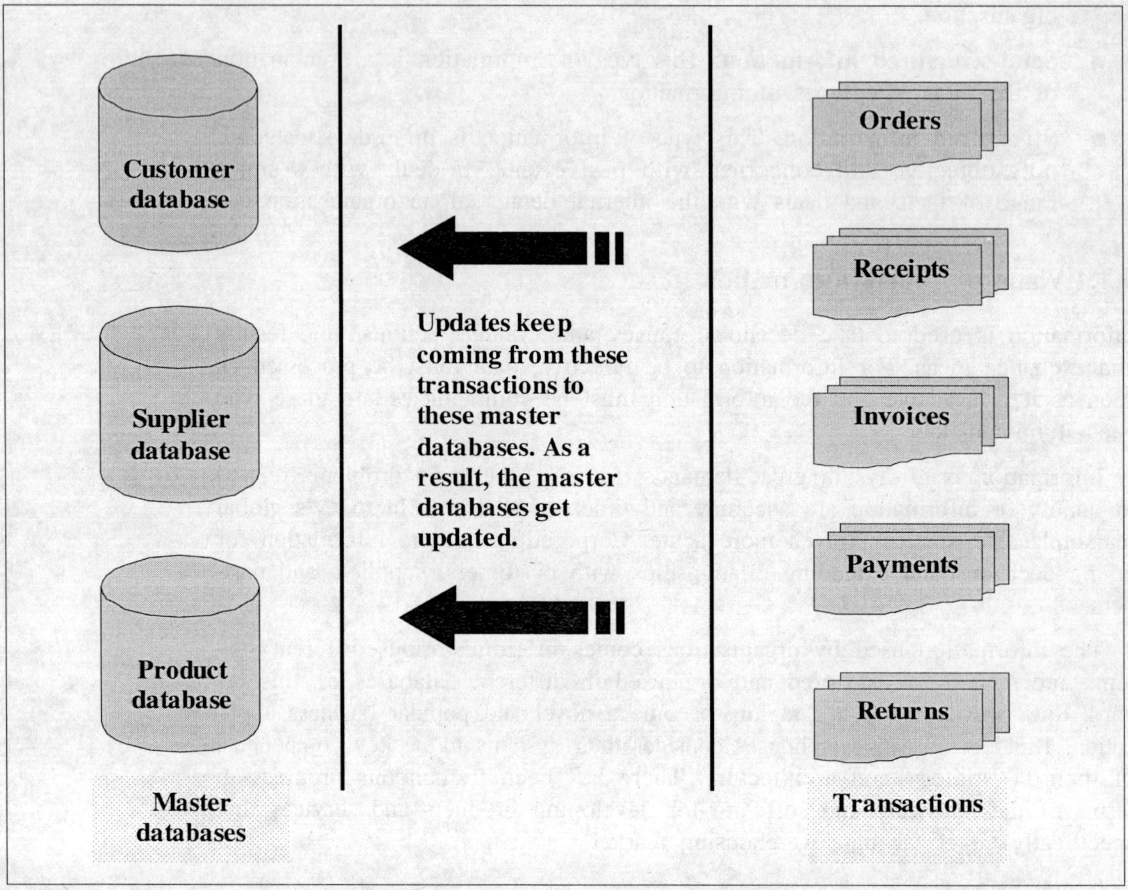

Fig. 9.5 Transactions update master databases

The DBMS ensures the integrity of these databases through rollbacks and other processes. In operational databases, not only are updated master databases maintained but also transactions, at least for some time for reporting and analysis. This is exactly where the problems related to data storage begin. How much data should be kept current and how much data should be archived, and when? It is not practical to keep data in the operational systems for long periods of time when not needed. For achieving this, a structure was designed for archiving data that the operational system has processed. The basic requirements of the running and archive systems are totally different. The running systems need performance, whereas the archive systems need flexibility and also bigger scope. It is not advisable to hamper the currently running systems with loads of archive data.

All early business data processing was done using mainframe computers. Although this has changed over the years, more than 70 per cent of business data processing is still done by mainframe systems. The most important reason behind this is that these systems are robust and fast and can store large amounts of data even if they are bulky and not so user-friendly. Therefore, the programs running on them for decades (embodying vast business knowledge and rules) are incredibly difficult to carry or **port** to a new platform or application. Such systems are called **legacy systems**. The data in such systems, when archived, goes on large tapes to remote data centers. An organisation needs many reports from the archive data. Thus, the programming effort for producing these reports is huge.

Of late, the increasing popularity of the personal computer has introduced many new tools/programs for business data analysis. With this, the gap between a computer programmer and the end user has reduced to some extent. Business analysts have many of the tools required (e.g. spreadsheets, advanced word processors) for data analysis and their graphic representation. In fact, due to this, many managers developed their own **Decision Support Systems (DSS)** based on these tools.

However, such data was usually created independently without any reference to the huge number of transactions residing on the main system; or if it was derived from it, the reports were not timely as it took a long time to process the large amount of archived and current data to produce the result of the query. Due to this, many chose the former approach. As a consequence, hundreds of different unconnected, and sometimes, inconsistent, systems arose on the desktops of business managers. A problem with this scheme is that it makes data fragmented and oriented towards very specific needs. Each user obtains only the information that he needs. Due to the lack of standardisation, the data fragments tend to be incapable of addressing the requirements of multiple users. Data warehousing addresses this issue in an effective manner, so that the individual pieces of knowledge and intelligence no longer remain isolated and scattered.

Data processing was a very common term since the 1960s. Electronic Data Processing (EDP) departments were set up to take care of data processing needs of businesses, military and other institutions. Over the years, this definition was changed to Information Technology (IT). Now, the term EDP is near-obsolete, although a few organisations still like to use it for their computing operational needs.

9.2 WHAT IS A DATA WAREHOUSE?

There are many definitions of a data warehouse, for example the one we saw in the introduction. Going one step further, we can say that a data warehouse is a systematic organisation of data that originates either inside an organisation or outside of it; and which is needed for historical purposes. Examples of data that can go into a data warehouse are: details of orders of a particular product for the last two years and a public database that contains the sales information of all competitors.

The idea is to organise the data in such a way that the summaries of historical data are kept along with the detailed transactions; such that a majority of the high-level management queries can be resolved quickly. Thus, a data warehouse forms the backbone of decision support systems. An important point is that the data stored in data warehouses is not for changes, but for drawing long-term conclusions. This is the main difference between an ordinary operational DBMS and a data warehouse. Any operational transaction (order, invoice, cash recipient etc.) updates a regular operational DBMS. However, data warehouse is updated only at certain intervals and only summaries of transactions may be produced.

For faster response time and flexibility, the data warehouse may be organised around the concept of Multidimensional DBMS or MDBMS instead of Relational DBMS or RDBMS. This is another way in which it differs from ordinary DBMS. In data warehousing, normalisation of data is not important even if it enhances speed or responsiveness in answering a query; whereas in DBMS, normalisation is done.

Let us illustrate the difference between operational data and a data warehouse with the help of a diagram as shown in Fig. 9.6.

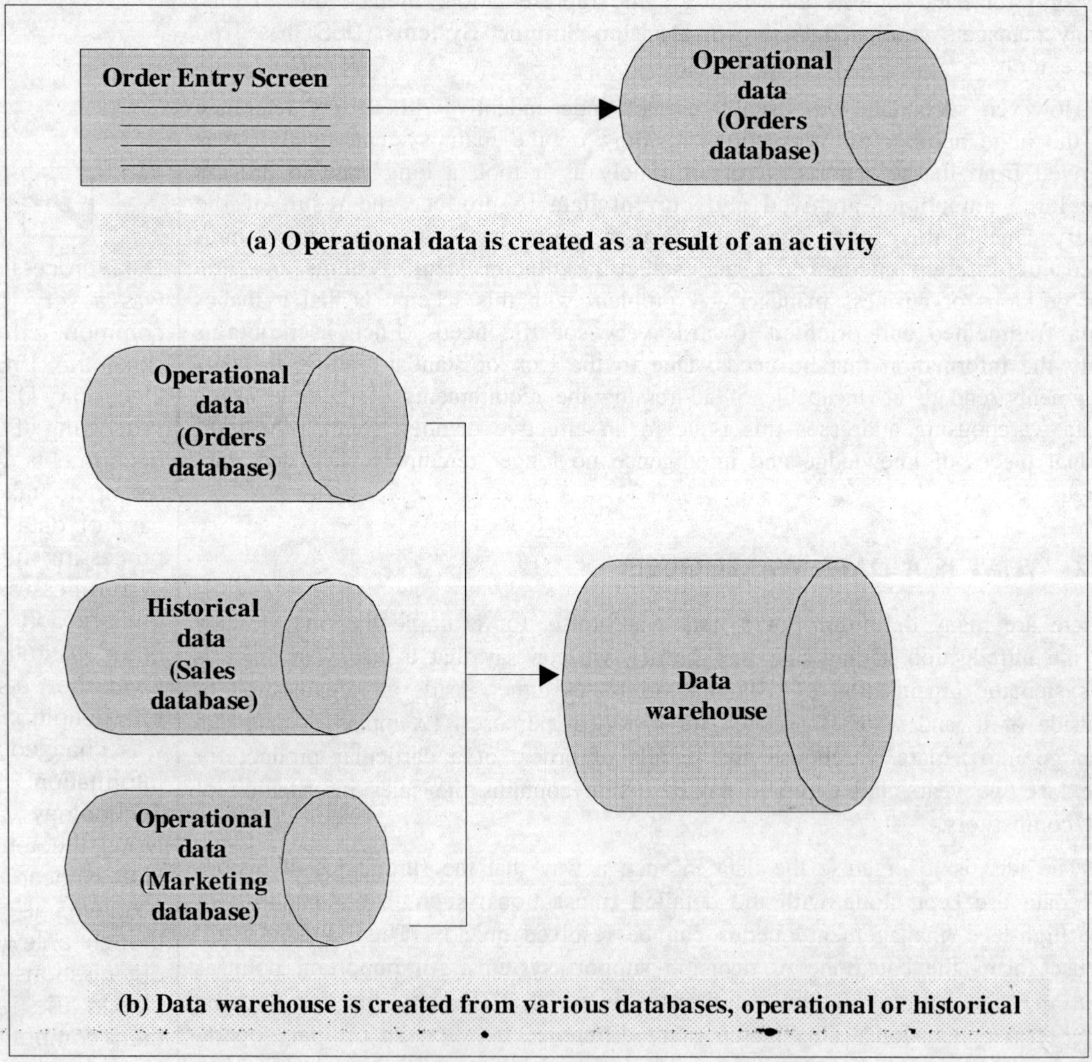

Fig. 9.6 Operational data and a data warehouse

As the figure shows, data warehousing involve a coordinated, planned and periodic copying of data, from various sources both inside and outside an organisation, into an environment that is optimised for analysis and processing of that data. Clearly, the main reason for data warehousing is the inability of the traditional computer systems to provide an organised and systematic access to data. If traditional systems could take care of the problem, data warehousing would not exist in the first place! If you could keep all the data in high-performance disks in the form of databases and retrieve it as and when needed across groups and locations, there would be no need to duplicate it! But as we saw earlier, this is not the case and therefore, data warehousing has emerged as a necessary step in managing historical data.

With the use of data warehousing, companies can identify sales trends, patterns of customer or vendor behaviour or product failure far more quickly than it was possible earlier. Today, data warehousing products that use the Internet as a means of sourcing and delivering data are also available.

9.3 DATA WAREHOUSING CONCEPTS

Having looked at the traditional use of archive data and explored some of the factors paving the way for the evolution of data warehouses, we will now turn our attention to studying the key characteristics of a data warehouse.

- **Warehousing data outside the operational systems**

  The whole idea behind data warehousing is that the data stored for business analysis can be accessed most efficiently if it is separated from the data in the running systems. The reasons for separating the current data from analysis data have not changed significantly with the evolution of data warehousing systems. These reasons are related to performance issues and ease of maintenance. It is desired that the current data be accessible faster and with lesser efforts as compared to historical data. Therefore, the two should be kept separate.

- **Integrating data from more than one operational systems**

  As discussed, for data warehousing systems to be successful, data from different operational systems can be combined. When the data needs to be brought together from more than one application, it is expected that this integration be done at a place independent of the source applications. Before the evolution of structured data warehouses, analysts would perhaps combine data extracted from more than one operational system into a single spreadsheet or a database. The data warehouse may very effectively combine data from multiple source applications such as sales, marketing, finance and production. Many large data warehouse architectures allow for the source applications to be integrated into the data warehouse on an incremental basis. The main reason for combining data from multiple source applications is the ability to cross-reference data from these applications. For example, the sales and orders data might be combined with the forecasts and the targets to do a variety of analyses.

Imagine a company with seasonal sales. The management may want to know the orders backlog, actual sales and sales forecast for the next month (current/operational data) along with the sales data of the same month for the last 10 years (historical data). In this case, if we summarise the historical/archive data that the management is likely to require in the future for analysis, admit it in the data warehouse and integrate it along with the operational data (i.e. link it to records based on keys such as product code, customer etc.), it will help. But, for this, the data warehouse analysts have to analyse the management's current and future requirements for decision support reports/queries in order to be able to structure and design the data in the data warehouse.

- **Differences between transaction and analysis processes**

  The primary reason for separating data for business analysis from operational data is performance degradation on the operational system. This degradation can happen due to the analysis processes. Operational systems always require high performance and quick response time. Operational systems are designed for acceptable performance for pre-defined transactions. For instance, an order processing system might specify the number of active order taken and the average number of orders in each hour. Even though many of the queries and reports that are run against a data warehouse are predefined, it is nearly impossible to accurately predict the activity against a data warehouse.

  This is why, at the cost of data redundancy/duplication, data warehouse is built with some operational data and some historical summarised data for fast reports/queries.

- **Data is mostly non-volatile**

  Another important attribute of the data in a data warehouse system is: it is brought to the warehouse after it has become permanent. This indicates there are no modifications to be made in the data after it is in the data warehouse. This saves data warehousing systems the burden of maintaining transaction and database integrity (rollback etc.) and enhances speed.

> Data warehousing means maintaining older data, and making it available as and when needed in the best possible format and access mechanism. It has gained immense popularity with the advent of Customer Relationship Management (CRM) systems.

- **Data saved for longer periods than in transaction systems**

  Data from most operational systems is archived after it becomes inactive. For example, an order may become inactive after a set period from the fulfillment of the order; or a bank account may become inactive after it has been closed for a period of time. Large amounts of inactive data mixed with operational data can significantly degrade the performance of any transaction. Since the data warehouses are designed to be archives for the operational data, they are saved for a very long period.

Thus, in comparison to operational systems, data warehousing systems contain data that is non-volatile, historical and can tolerate with slower responses. These distinctions are very important and are summarised in Fig. 9.7.

In short, the separation of operational data from analysis data is the most fundamental data warehousing concept. Not only is the data stored in a structured manner outside the operational system, but businesses today are also allocating considerable resources to build data warehouses.

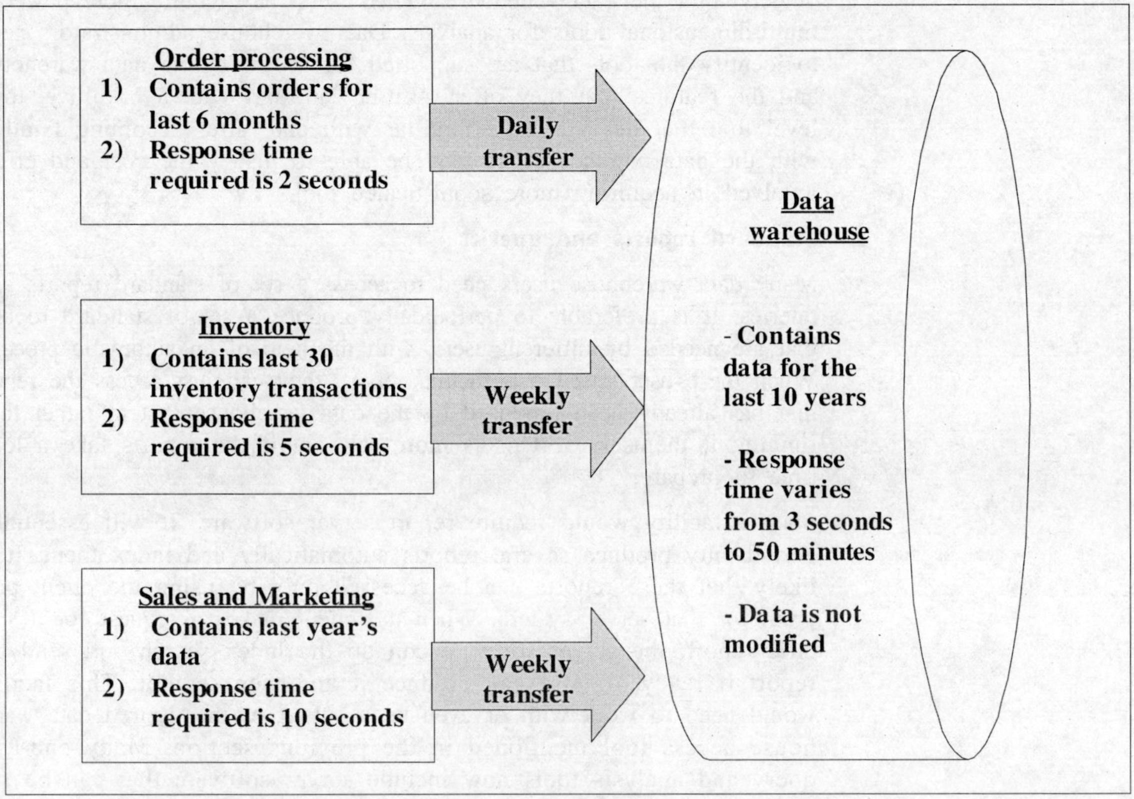

Fig. 9.7 Transfer of data from operational systems to a data warehouse

- **Using a data warehouse for better business processes**

  Having understood what a data warehouse is and its construction at a broad level, let us review the processes supported by a data warehouse. Some of the processes involved in a data warehouse are predefined and not much different from traditional data analysis activity. However, other activities such as multi-dimensional data analysis and information visualisation were simply not available in traditional analysis tools and methods. They have been developed recently and form a very important part of a data warehouse system. This has been shown with the help of a figure later in the chapter.

- **Tools to be used against the data warehouse**

  One of the objectives in the creation of a data warehouse is to make it as flexible and as open as possible. It is not desirable to spend too much in terms of software and training for using a data warehouse. The data warehouse should be accessible by most end-user tools and platforms. However, it is not possible to make every feature of the data warehouse available from every end-user tool.

Primitive tools such as simple querying facilities built into common spreadsheet programs may be sufficient for a user who only needs to quickly refer the data warehouse. Other users may require more powerful multi-dimensional tools for analysis. Data warehouse administrators need to identify the tools that are supported for access to the data warehouse and the features that they offer. A user can start with a primitive, low-level tool that he is already familiar with and, after becoming familiar with the data warehouse, he may be able to justify the cost and effort involved in acquiring more sophisticated tool.

- **Standard reports and queries**

  Many data warehouse users need to access a set of standard reports and queries. It is preferable to periodically produce a set of standard reports that are needed by different users, with the help of an automatic process. When these users need a particular report, they can just access the report that has already been produced by the data warehouse system rather than running it themselves. This is more relevant if the reports take a long time to prepare.

  Such a facility would require report server software. It will essentially periodically produce several reports automatically and index them. It is likely that these reports can be accessed only by using the client program for that server system. When the client makes a request for a specific report, the server software can do the index search and send the report if ready, or else can produce it and then send it. This facility would need to work with or even be a subset of the desired data warehouse access tool mentioned in the previous section. Many end-user query and analysis tools now include server software that can be run with the data warehouse to produce reports and query results. Keeping up with technology developments, these tools are now providing a web interface for accessing reports. The data warehouse users and administrators need to consider any reports that are likely to become standard reports for the data warehouse on a continual basis.

- **Queries against summary tables**

  The summary reports in a data warehouse can form the basis of analysis. Simple filtering and summation against the summary views can be a major analysis activity against a data warehouse. These summary views contain predefined standard business analysis, based on certain rules. For instance, the product summary view may be the basis for a very large number of queries. Different users could choose different products and the time periods for product sales queries. These queries provide quick response and they very easy to build.

- **Data mining**

  Often, the reports and queries run on the summary data are sufficient to answer quite a few *what* business questions. A drilling down into the real data provides answers to *why* and *how* queries. This process is called **data mining**.

A data-mining user starts with summary data and drills down into the detailed data looking for arguments to prove or disprove a hypothesis. Data mining tools are evolving rapidly to satisfy the need to understand the behaviour of business units such as customers and products. These tools will go through the heaps of detailed data to find some correlations – again multidimensional – such as if a customer is from New York, then he is likely to place orders worth $500 or above for three successive months starting August (probability = 80%). It is up to the management to validate them or take them seriously. Data mining can use a lot of modern techniques such as **neural networks**. to find these correlations and find some *method to madness* in huge archive data.

- **Interface with other data warehouses**

  Chances are that a data warehouse system is interfaced with other applications that use it as the source of operational system data. Also, a data warehouse may provide data to other data warehouses or smaller data warehouses called **data marts**.

  The operational system that interfaces with the data warehouse often become increasingly stable and powerful over a period of rime. As the data warehouse evolves into a reliable source of data that has been consistently moved from the current operational systems, many applications find that a single interface with the data warehouse is much easier and more functional than multiple interfaces with the operational applications. However, much of the operational state information is not carried over to the data warehouse. Thus, data warehouse is obviously not a replacement option for the operational systems. This is shown in Fig. 9.8.

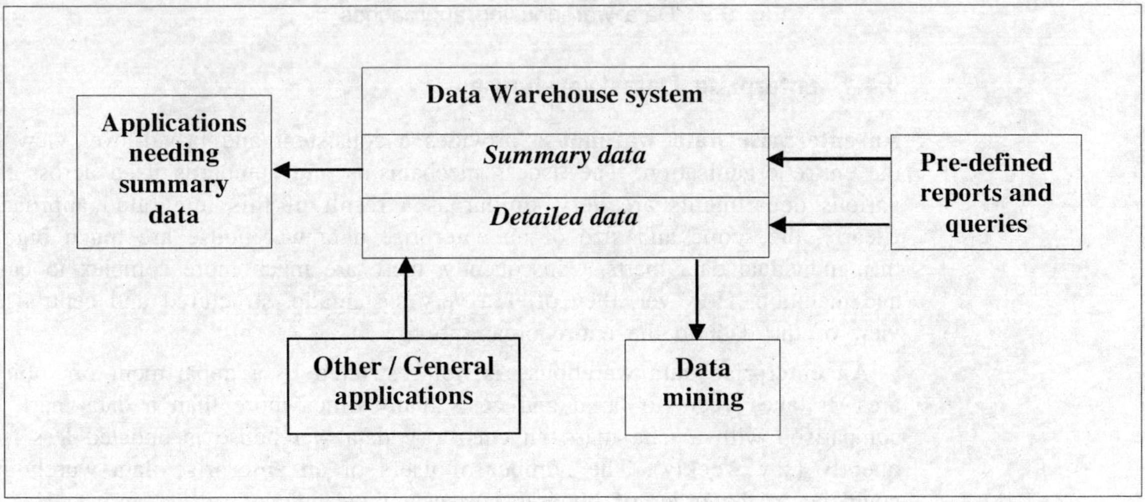

Fig. 9.8 Systems interacting with a data warehouse

The figure shows the analysis processes that run against a data warehouse. Although, to a large extent, the activity against data warehouses is primitive querying, reporting and analysis, sophistication of analysis at the high end is fast evolving. More importantly, all analysis done at a data warehouse is easier and cost-effective as compared to the earlier methods. This simplicity is still the main attraction of data warehousing systems.

9.4 DATA WAREHOUSING APPROACHES

A data warehouse can be simple or it can be complex and the approach to creating a warehouse is determined accordingly. Three major categories of approaches are: **enterprise data warehouse, data mart** and **operational data store**. This is shown in Fig. 9.9. These approaches differ in size and complexity. Let us discuss them one by one.

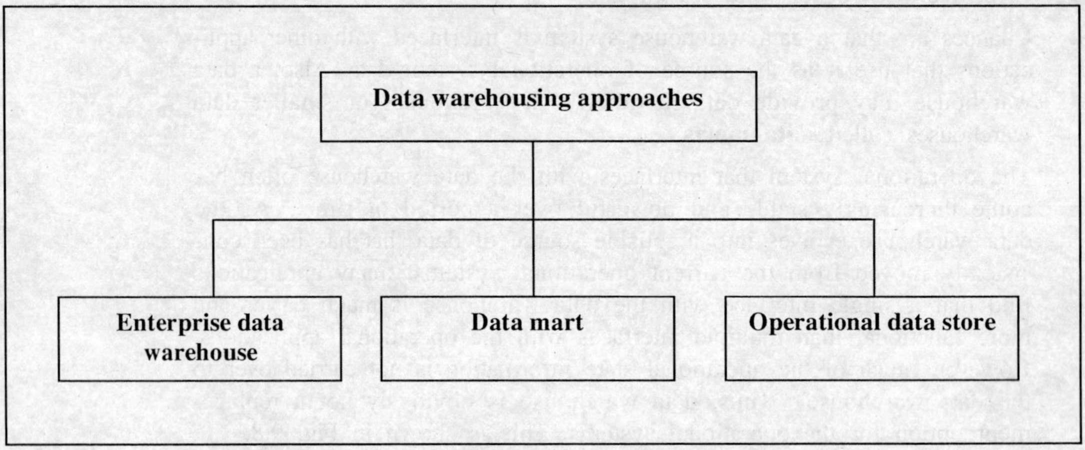

Fig. 9.9 Data warehousing approaches

9.4.1 Enterprise Data Warehouse

An **enterprise data warehouse** provides a consistent and broad-level view of the entire organisation. The access mechanisms and standards used across the various departments are very similar as a result of this integrated approach. Clearly, the scope and size of an enterprise data warehouse are much bigger than individual data marts. Consequently, these are much more complex to build and maintain. However, they offer a very systematic, structured and centralised view of the data to the entire organisation.

An enterprise data warehouse is not restricted to a department or subject area. It takes years to build and costs many times more than a data mart. In comparison with a data mart, an enterprise data warehouse is updated less frequently (say weekly). The number of users of an enterprise data warehouse could be in the order of hundreds or even thousands.

9.4.2 Data Marts

A data mart is a subset of a data warehouse. Rather than looking at the global picture, a data mart is restricted to a particular subject area. A data mart is usually created specifically for a department or a business process to enable better decision-making. Therefore, there can be a number of data marts, each focusing on a subset of the overall business. People often need quick solutions to improve their departments or focus areas. An enterprise data warehouse for the whole enterprise usually takes a long time to build. Rather than waiting for it to be created, data marts are preferred by these departments. The challenge in this approach is the consistency and the interaction in the future.

Data marts are of two types as shown in Fig. 9.10.

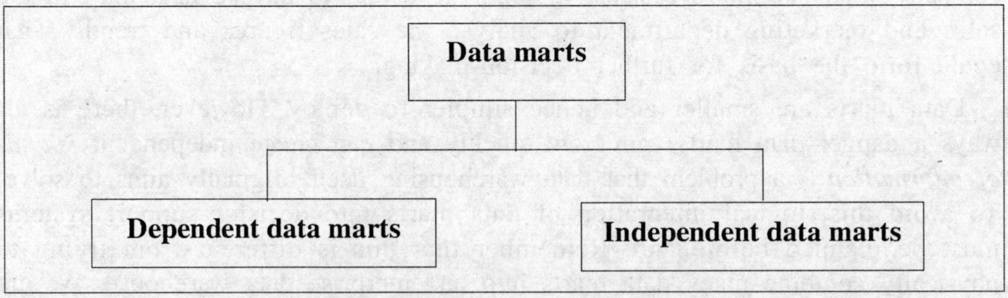

Fig. 9.10 Types of data marts

9.4.2.1 Dependent data mart In this case, the data mart does not have an existence of its own in terms of extracting the data. The data in a **dependent data mart** is actually brought from the enterprise data warehouse. Hence, it is a subset of the latter. The enterprise data warehouse *feeds* data to the smaller, focused data marts. This is shown in Fig. 9.11 (a). You need to build the enterprise data warehouse first and then extract data marts for better performance, access and management.

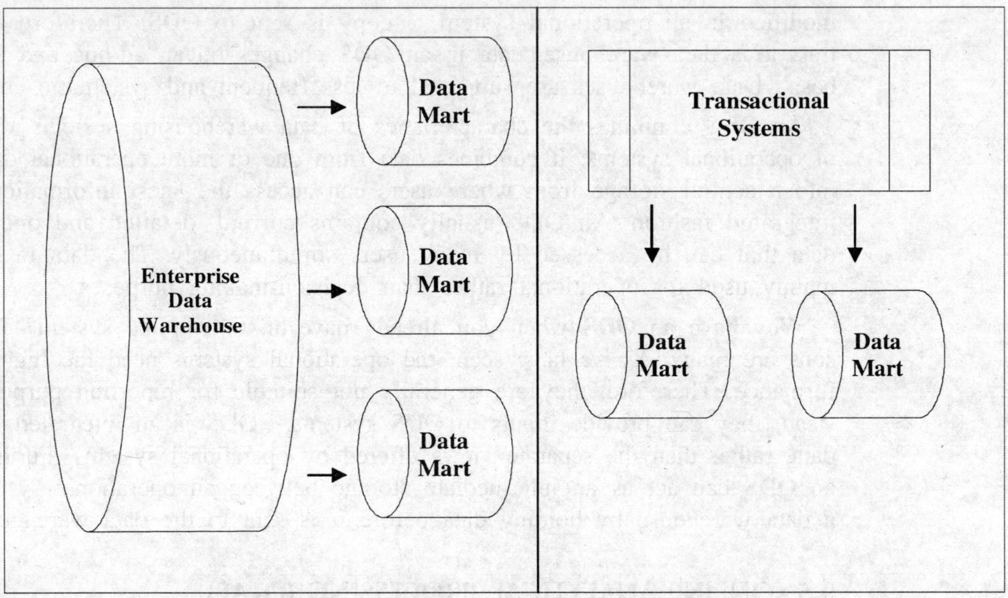

(a) Dependent data mart (b) Independent Data mart

Fig. 9.11 Types of data mart

9.4.2.2 Independent data mart An **independent data mart** does not depend on an enterprise data warehouse. Instead, it derives the data from transactional systems directly and operates independently of the enterprise data warehouse. This is shown in Fig. 9.11 (b). It must be pointed out that integrating many such independent data warehouses to form a single enterprise data warehouse is not easy, unless it is planned accordingly right at the beginning.

Data marts are useful for focusing on specific areas. For example, when a company wants to improve sales, it might be useful to have a data mart in the sales and marketing department to analyse the sales figures and trends. That could form the basis for further decision-making.

Data marts are smaller and hence simpler to deploy. However, there is always a danger–data marts can grow quickly and can create independent *islands of information* – a problem that data warehousing itself originally aims to solve! To avoid this, logical integration of data marts into decision-support systems must be planned beforehand. Remember that this is different from trying to physically combine many data marts into an enterprise data warehouse. We are not talking about physical integration here. It is the overall application integration that is being referred to.

9.4.3 Operational Data Stores

The concept of **operational data store (ODS)** is relatively new. It is used to provide time-sensitive decision-support and operational reporting. Usually, an ODS is built from an operational system and is restricted in the form of subject area. An ODS contains integrated and subject-related integrated data from transactional systems. The data itself may be in a summary or detailed form. As data is modified in an operational system, a copy is sent to ODS. Therefore, in contrast to a data warehouse, data in an ODS changes on an ad-hoc and frequent basis. Data warehouses are subjected to less frequent and systematic changes.

An ODS combines the characteristics of data warehousing systems with that of operational systems. It combines data from one or more operational databases into a central storage from where users can access the latest information in an integrated fashion. An ODS usually contains current, detailed and operational data that can be accessed by many users simultaneously. The data in ODS is mainly used for operational rather than decision-making purposes.

Why have an ODS when you already have an operational system? The reasons are many. As we have seen, the operational systems need the highest performance. Therefore, they are generally not suitable for reporting purposes. Instead, they can provide inputs to ODS systems. ODS is an integrated view of data, rather than the separate views offered by operational systems. Furthermore, an ODS can act as an intermediate storage between an operational system and a data warehouse by holding data before it is sent to the data warehouse.

9.5 ONLINE ANALYTICAL PROCESSING (OLAP)

Data warehousing can be understood better by comparing the normal **On-Line Transaction Processing (OLTP)** data management activities to the **On-Line**

Analytical Processing (OLAP) activities. Whereas OLTP systems are used for supporting day-to-day business operations, OLAP systems are decision-support systems. OLTP applications capture primitive data about business and are mostly transaction-oriented. On the other hand, OLAP systems need access to operational as well as historical data. Thus, OLAP applications tell an organisation what needs to be done, by analysing data and producing decision-support reports used by business managers. Also, OLTP applications help the organisation to actually act on these decisions! In many ways, OLTP applications are the basic ingredients of the Information Technology (IT) department of an organisation. On top are OLAP applications which provide various add-ons for quick decision-making on customer-care and services, increasing revenues, and so on. Clearly, OLAP applications need a data warehouse for these purposes.

Traditionally, creating, using and managing decision-support systems required a number of specialised tools and databases. However, there were several limitations, such as:

- Lack of analytical sophistication
- Database layout limitations
- Inability to handle or process large amounts of data

For overcoming these limitations, organisations made use of many technology solutions, such as data warehousing/data mining and OLAP tools.

OLAP applications provide ways and means to analyse complex data, based on natural and intuitive set of business rules and dimensions, such as the profit figures per market, territory and product. Additionally, OLAP insulates a common user from the technical details of data storage and organisation. Thus, even non-technical users can use OLAP to perform analysis based on the available data. OLAP applications provide for complicated computations, which include sophisticated time-series analysis and also random ad-hoc interactive analysis. Example of the latter is a sales manager starting with a low-performing market and tracing the cause of the problem all the way down to a small feature in one product.

Decision support systems usually have limitations in performing detailed analysis due to one or more of the following reasons:

OLAP is a generic term for a group of decision support applications. Data is usually entered into a relational database through an online system that supports the notion of transactions. Once it is in the database, data is offloaded, reformatted and accessed in special ways to improve the execution and answer complex queries, which is not possible otherwise.

OLAP is categorised into four categories as shown in Fig. 9.12.

9.5.1 Desktop OLAP

Desktop OLAP is also called as **client-side OLAP**. Examples of this category are products that send data from a server to a client desktop computer. The data processing is mainly client-centric. It is used for end-user reporting and analysis. Small data warehouses are the best bet for desktop OLAP.

Online Analytical Processing (OLAP) is different from Online Transaction Processing (OLTP). OLAP is more closely related with decision-making, whereas OLTP is associated with day-to-day operations of computer systems which may or may not be related to decision-making.

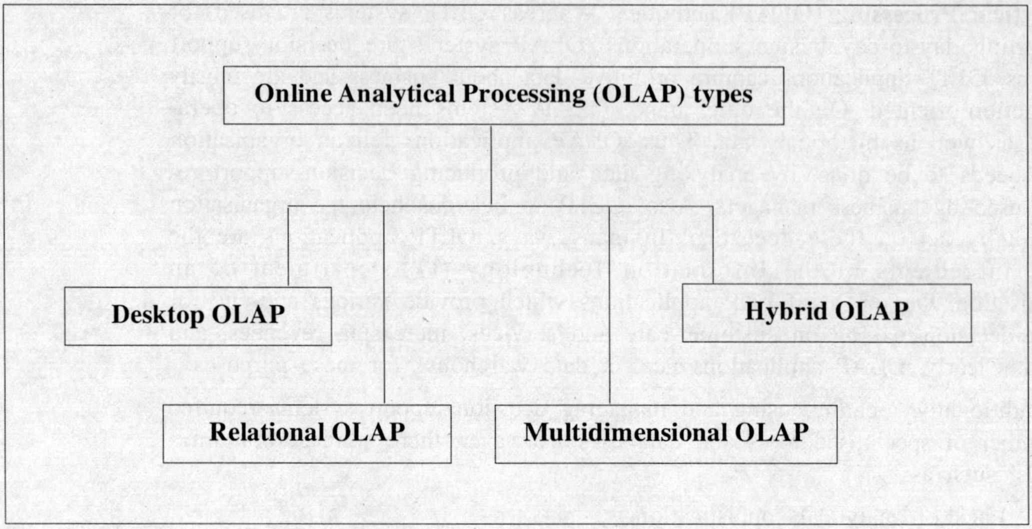

Fig. 9.12 Types of OLAP

9.5.2 Relational OLAP (ROLAP)

The **Relational OLAP** stresses on query execution and processing inside the source database from where data was picked up. In ROLAP, records are stored as rows and columns. This gives a flat view of the data as shown in Fig. 9.13. The figure shows the number of tourists in a season at different places, preferring different lodging types. This might be useful in certain cases. However, for a more detailed analysis, this may not be sufficient.

Season	Place	Lodging type	Tourists (in thousands)
1994	Hawaii	Motel	50
1994	Miami	Hotel	100
1995	Goa	Camping	70
1996	Alps	Private	23

Fig. 9.13 A Relational data visualisation using ROLAP

9.5.3 Multidimensional OLAP (MOLAP)

Multidimensional OLAP is a specialised server-side database. It takes data from relational databases of transactional environments and stores it in a unique format. This allows faster query execution. Data at summary level is usually stored, and thus offers multiple views or dimensions of the original data. Especially useful in forecasting, financial planning and budgeting, the main characteristics of MOLAP are fast access to summary data and data analysis combined with data updates.

Let us contrast MOLAP from ROLAP diagrammatically. Contrast Fig. 9.14 with the earlier one to get a multidimensional view of the same data (the data are different, the main aim is to show the differences between ROLAP and MOLAP).

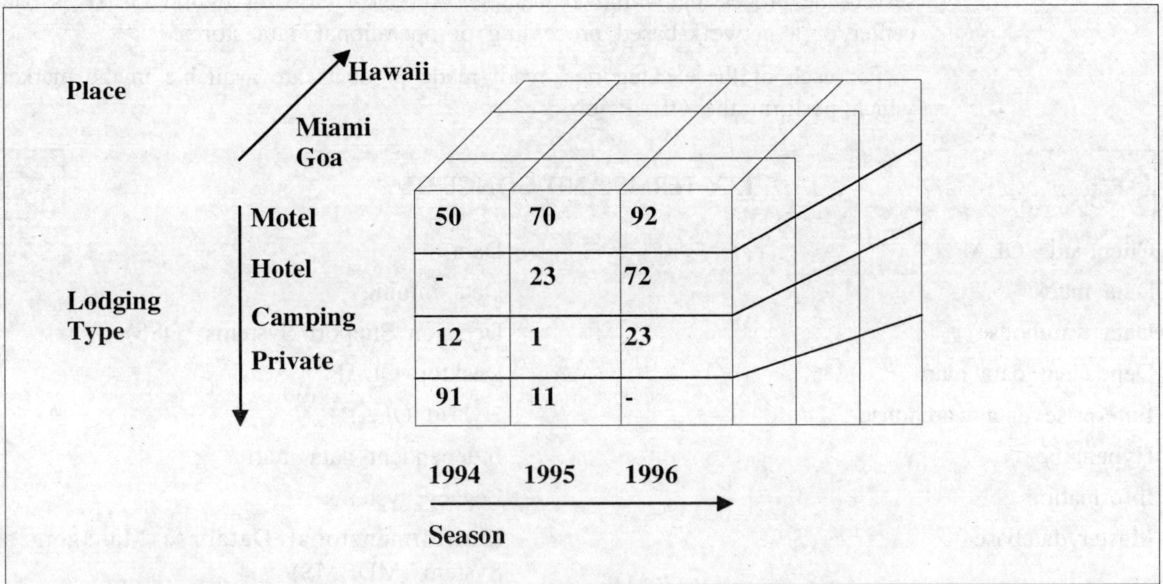

Fig. 9.14 Example of MOLAP

The name *multidimensional* comes from the fact that the data view is not just two-dimensional, but in the form of **hypercubes**. For example, the product data can be analysed against time and different locations–clearly a case for multi-dimensional analysis. This can be done even with relational databases, but not without compromising on access speed and complexity, as explained below.

A specialised **Multidimensional Database Management System (MDBMS)** is used in MOLAP. The internal design of an MDBMS differs from that of a conventional Relational Database Management System (RDBMS). MDBMS is more suitable for data warehousing applications and offers better access performance. While an RDBMS is optimised for data updates, an MDBMS is optimised for data access. A standard RDBMS joins two tables at a time. However, if you want to join three tables, two separate steps are required: first join A and B to form an intermediate table, say T; and then join table T with C. As a generalised convention, joining *n* tables needs *(n-1)* joins. However, using what is called as a **star join**, an MDBMS can join up to eight tables at one go. This improves performance tremendously.

Other reasons that make MDBMS perform much better in comparison to RDBMS are attributed to the fact that an MDBMS is read-only. Therefore, no transaction support, locking and log maintenance are required.

9.5.4 Hybrid OLAP

Hybrid OLAP is a combination of MOLAP and ROLAP. Such requirements are felt with relation to products that need to support both the client-side and server-side processing within a database. A typical case for hybrid OLAP is data center or a network-based processing of operational data stores.

For each of these categories, ready-made products are available in the market, which perform the OLAP job.

KEY TERMS AND CONCEPTS

Client-side OLAP	Data
Data mart	Data mining
Data warehouse	Decision Support Systems (DSS)
Dependent data mart	Desktop OLAP
Enterprise data warehouse	Hybrid OLAP
Hypercube	Independent data mart
Information	Legacy systems
Master database	Multidimensional Database Management System (MDBMS)
Multidimensional OLAP (MOLAP)	Neural networks
Online Analytical Transaction Processing (OLAP)	Online Transaction Processing (OLTP)
Operational Data Store (ODS)	Operational decisions
Port	Relational OLAP
Semistructured information	Star join
Strategic decisions	Structured information
Tactical decisions	Unstructured information

CHAPTER SUMMARY

- Information is necessary for the successful running of any organisation.
- People at various levels, including the managerial staff, need information to carry out their day-to-day activities.
- Raw facts are **data**, which, when processed, become **information**.
- Information can be **structured, semistructured,** or **unstructured**.
- A **data warehouse** is the organised data that is situated after and outside the normal operational systems.

- A data warehouse is a systematic organisation of data that originates either inside an organisation or outside of it, and which is needed for historical purposes.
- The main characteristics of a data warehouse system are: it is outside the operational systems, it integrates data from more than one operational system, it is different from transaction-based systems and has longer life.
- A **data-mining** system starts with summary data and drills down into the detailed data looking for arguments to prove or disprove a hypothesis.
- Three major categories of approaches are generally made in the context of data warehouses: **enterprise data warehouse, data mart** and **operational data store**.
- An enterprise data warehouse provides a consistent and broad-level view of the entire organisation.
- A data mart is a subset of a data warehouse. Rather than looking at the global picture, a data mart is restricted to a particular subject area.
- The **operational data store (ODS)** is used to provide time-sensitive decision-support and operational reporting.
- The data in a **dependent data mart** is actually brought from the enterprise data warehouse.
- An **independent data mart** does not depend on an enterprise data warehouse. Instead, it derives the data from transactional systems directly and operates independently of the enterprise data warehouse.
- **Online Analytical Processing (OLAP)** applications tell an organisation what needs to be done by analysing data and producing decision-support reports used by business managers.
- OLAP can be classified into **Desktop OLAP, Relational OLAP, Multidimensional OLAP** and **Hybrid OLAP**.

PRACTICE SET

Mark as true or false

1. Data is the same as information.
2. Data is raw facts.
3. Information is unprocessed data.
4. Senior management needs data.
5. Data warehouse deals with live data.
6. Data mining and data marts mean the same thing.
7. An independent data mart does not depend on an enterprise data warehouse.
8. ODS stands for Online Decisions and Support.
9. OLTP and OLAP mean different things.
10. MOLAP is the same as hybrid OLAP.

Fill in the blanks

1. Raw facts are called as ________.
   (a) data (b) information
   (c) entropy (d) none of the above
2. Unprocessed information is ________.
   (a) data (b) detail
   (c) entropy (d) none of the above
3. Senior management takes _______.
   (a) strategic decisions (b) tactical decisions
   (c) operational decisions (d) all decisions
4. Middle management takes _______.
   (a) strategic decisions (b) tactical decisions
   (c) operational decisions (d) all decisions
5. Supervisory management takes _______.
   (a) strategic decisions (b) tactical decisions
   (c) operational decisions (d) all decisions
6. Data warehouse deals with _______.
   (a) past data (b) live data
   (c) data of the future (d) None of them
7. _______ deals with the entire organisation.
   (a) Data mine (b) Data mart
   (c) Data mart (d) Enterprise data warehouse
8. _______ is a subset of a data warehouse.
   (a) File (b) Table
   (c) Data mart (d) Data mine
9. In a _______ we start with summary data and then move into detailed data.
   (a) data mine (b) data mart
   (c) data mine (d) enterprise data warehouse
10. _______ is a combination of _________ and _________.
    (a) Hybrid OLAP, ROLAP, MOLAP (b) MOLAP, ROLAP, desktop OLAP
    (c) ROLAP, desktop OLAP, hybrid OLAP (d) ROLAP, MOLAP, hybrid OLAP

Provide detailed answers to the following questions

1. Discuss the terms data and information.

2. Why is information useful to organisations?
3. Discuss the levels of management and the information that they need.
4. What is a data warehouse? What are its types?
5. Describe the term *data mart.*
6. What are dependent and independent data marts?
7. What is data mining?
8. What is OLAP?
9. What is a MOLAP?
10. Discuss the term ODS.

Exercises

1. What is Management Information System (MIS)?
2. How are forecasts related to information?
3. Why has past data gained so much of prominence in the last few years?
4. Study any one data-warehousing project.
5. Which RDBMS products support data warehouse concepts?
6. Is it easier to perform data mining by using a file system as compared to a DBMS? Why?
7. In which fields is MOLAP more useful?
8. Find information about data warehousing tools.
9. Is data warehousing related to Enterprise Application Integration (EAI)? Investigate.
10. Study the concept of information overload.

Chapter 10

Object Technology and DBMS

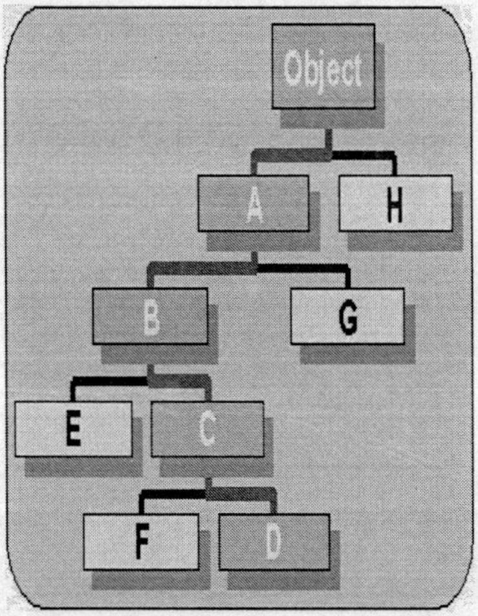

Most modern computer software development is based on object-oriented principles. Objects can be organized, classified, created, detstroyed and so on.

Chapter Highlights

- Object Technology
- Object Oriented (OO) Fundamentals
- Relevance of OO Technology to RDBMS Technology
- Design of OO Systems in Relation to RDMS
- Object Oriented Database Management Systems (OODBMS)

10.1 AN INTRODUCTION TO OBJECT TECHNOLOGY

As the name suggests, the basis of *object technology* is an **object**. The revolution brought about by **object technology** can be largely attributed to the idea of objects. What is an object afterall?

> At the simplest level, anything that we see, touch, smell or feel is an object.

Thus, the book that you are reading now is an object, each page itself is an object, and you are also an object! Well, this is a fairly loose definition of the term object. Let us be a bit more technical, and understand what the term object means.

The basics of object technology can be traced back to the 1960s. A language called as Simula (abbreviation for *Simula*tion language) first used the ideas of object technology. It was designed to build precise models of complex and large physical systems (e.g. big buildings, aircrafts, machines, etc.), which could consist of thousands of components. In Simula, models were defined as objects. For instance, the wing of an aircraft is an object, which is turned by another object called shaft, and so on.

In the world of computer technology, an object is a self-contained unit which contains both operations as well as data. Note that this is dramatically different from what we had discussed so far. In the procedural approach, we had mainly talked about the operations, and introduced data only at the very end. Even then, we had clearly mentioned that operations and data are separate entities in a program. Now, we are talking about operations and data as two portions of a single entity, which we call an object. Data is no longer considered in isolation – it is tightly coupled with an object. This idea is shown in Fig. 10.1.

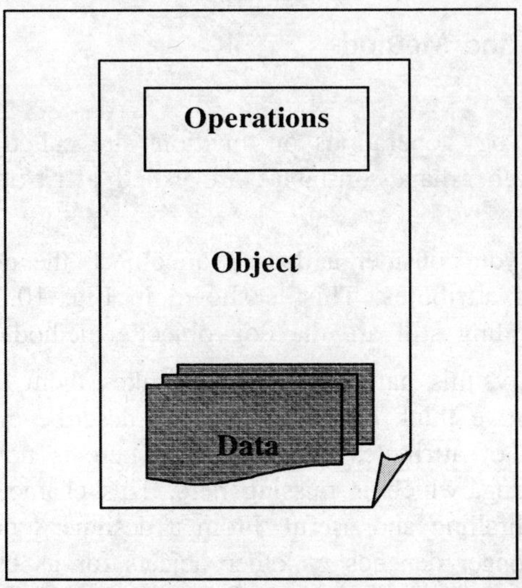

Fig. 10.1 Object = Operations + Data

Object technology has evolved since the days of traditional Structured Systems Analysis and Design (SSAD). Object-oriented systems are supposed to provide significant benefits in terms of reuse and maintainability of software. Relational databases and object technology are quite opposite of each other in their view of applications and data. Therefore, they must be brought to a common platform to make their interaction smoother.

Also note that we have not mentioned the term *program* here. We are talking about *objects*. How do objects relate to a program, then? Well, in the world of object technology, a program actually becomes a collection of well-defined objects. We no longer talk about a program as a collection of operations and data; instead, we call it as a group of objects, as shown in Fig. 10.2.

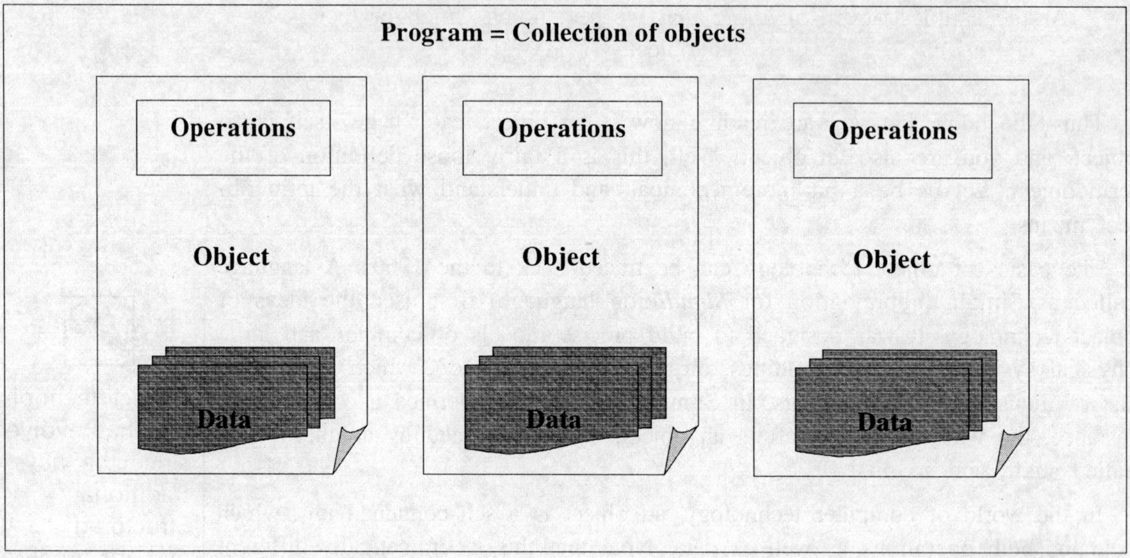

Fig. 10.2 Program in object technology

For example, in a billing application, the objects could be customer, invoice, payment, inventory, and so on. All these objects would interact with each other as and when needed to constitute an application program. Similarly, in a geometric application, the various objects could be circle, triangle, line, and so on.

10.1.1 Attributes and Methods

In object technology, operations or functions are called **methods**. On the other hand, variables are called **attributes.**

For instance, if you consider a dog as an object, the dog's eyes, ears, nose, legs tail are all its attributes. This is shown in Fig. 10.3. Similarly, barking, eating, running standing still are the dog object's methods.

Quite interestingly, this nature of objects makes them self-sufficient. For instance, the moment we think of a dog, we can describe everything about a dog (either in the form of attributes or methods). There is nothing more about the object, that is the dog, which is missing here. This characteristic of object technology is quite enthralling and useful. From a designer's perspective, this means that an object no longer depends on other objects for its own features and characteristics. Similarly, from a programmer's point of view, an object can be constructed as a black box which is completely self-contained and can be safely guarded from the outside world.

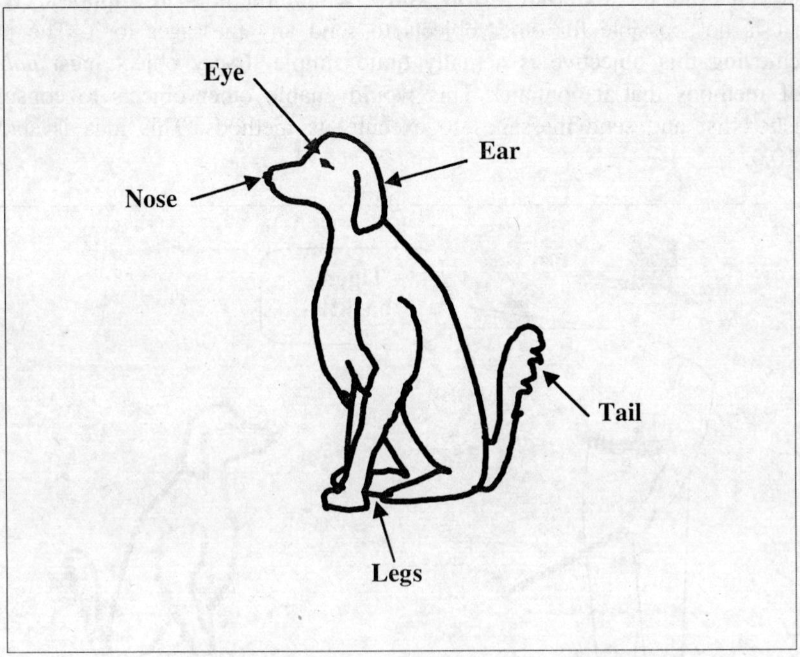

Fig. 10.3 Dog object and its attributes

10.1.2 Messages

However, the self-sufficient nature of objects raises a question. We know that a dog can bark. But how can we instruct a dog to bark? Unless we are able to do so, the dog object, although complete in its own respect, would be quite useless to the external world. This means that we must be able to have a mechanism by which we can instruct the dog to perform the desired action. Object technology provides this facility in the form of **messages**.

> We can pass a *message* to an object, requesting it to perform a specific action.

In the real world, objects can interact with each other in a number of ways, and for a variety of purposes. To achieve this, one object can send a message to another object. This message requests the called object to perform one of its methods. This idea is shown in Fig. 10.4, in which a message is being passed on to the dog, which causes it to invoke its *bark* method.

This leads us to another question. How do we know that a dog can bark? Well, that might be easy, consider an object called as *student* and assume that we are interested in finding out the student's birth date. How would we know what message we should send to the student object, so that it can send us the student's birth date? We cannot simply assume or hope that the student object would contain a method for this purpose. Consequently, as it turns out, each object must let the external world know which methods it supports. Without this, it is not possible for other objects to send any messages to it. The process of achieving this objective is actually quite simple. Every object must *publish* a list of methods that it contains. This would enable other objects to consult this published list and send messages to execute its methods. This idea is shown in Fig. 10.5.

Fig. 10.4 Sending a message to the *dog* object to invoke its *bark* method

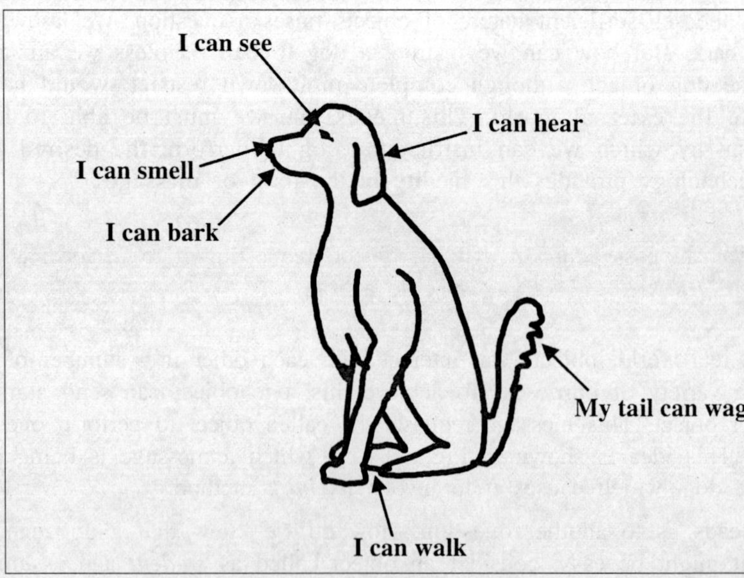

Fig. 10.5 List of methods published by the *dog* object

Thus, an object A can send a message to object B, requesting it to execute one of its methods. Similarly, object B can invoke any method of object A by sending a message, and so on, as shown in Fig. 10.6.

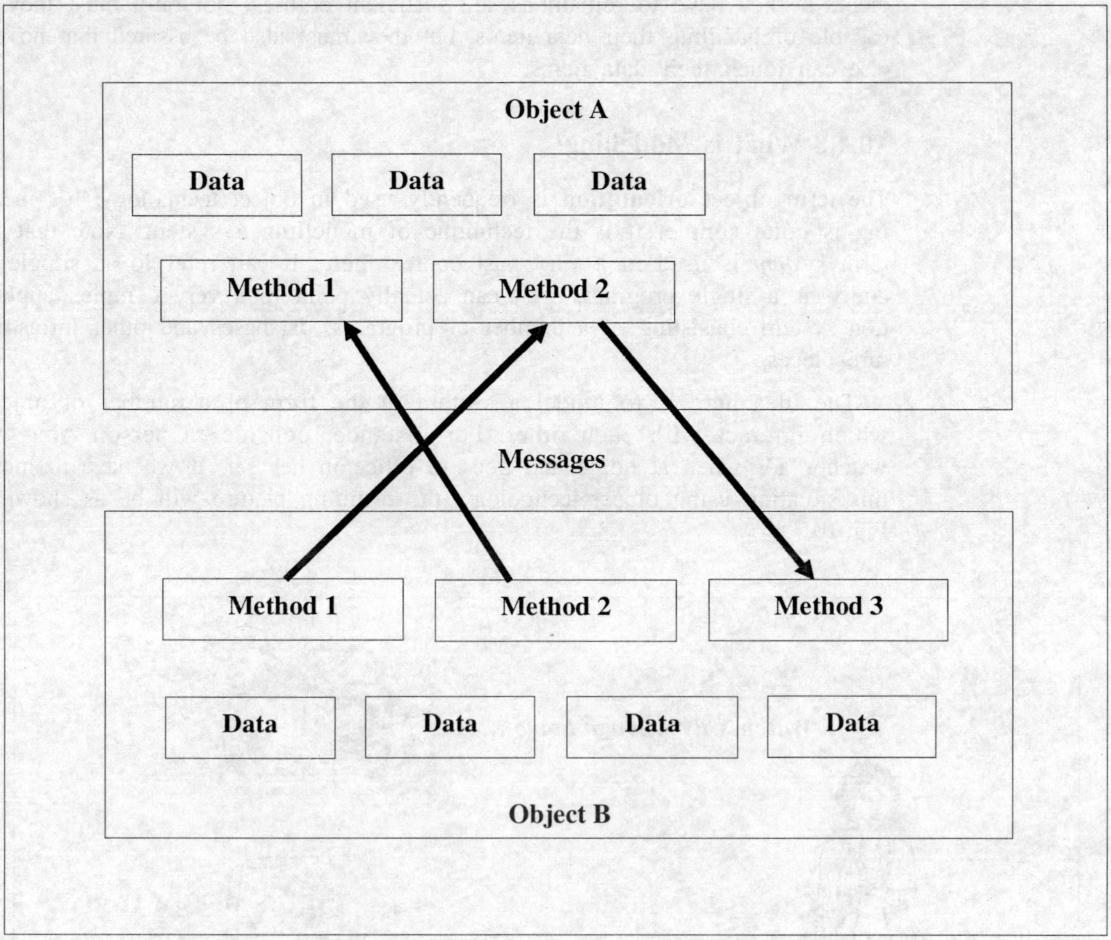

Fig. 10.6 Objects send messages to each other to call each other's methods

The diagram also brings a very crucial point to the fore. Note that an object can send a message to another object, requesting it to execute its method. However, an object does not seem to have an access to another object's data. This is indeed true. In general, an object cannot access another object's data. An object *hides* its data from the outside world, which is exactly the opposite of what it does with its methods (which it *publishes* to the entire world). Of course, in the real world of softwares, there are slight variations to this concept. However, at this juncture, it is safe to assume that an object guards its data safely, and does not allow an outsider to access it. However, it exposes its methods to everyone else.

If you think of it, this is quite sensible. Allowing data access to more than one entity almost always leads to some sort of problems. Object technology recognises this pitfall early, and makes the boundaries between objects quite explicit when it comes to handling data items. This is even more significant in the case of object technology, since we have been calling objects as self-sufficient. If they have to remain as self-sufficient entities, not only must they be capable of handling their data items, but they must also be assured that no one else can touch their data items.

10.1.3 What is Modelling?

The term **object orientation** is frequently used in object technology. It's meaning is quite simple. It is the technique of modelling a system. Note that the term *system* is used in a very vast context here. It can refer to as simple an entity as a single program, or it can actually point to a very complex application system consisting of a number of programs, databases and other infrastructure pieces.

The idea here is to model a system in the form of a number of objects which interact with each other. For instance, consider a person Ana who watches TV when at home and goes to office in her car. If we have to model this situation using object technology, the resulting picture will be as shown in Fig. 10.7.

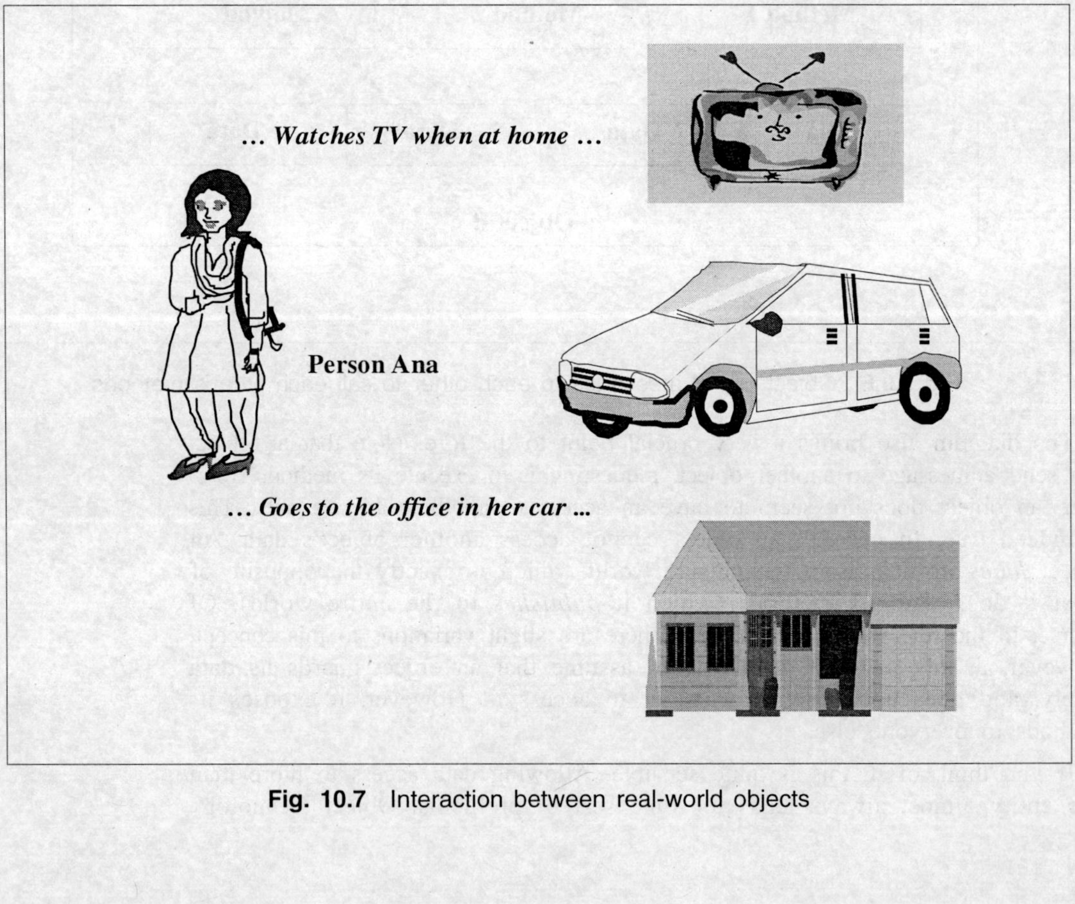

Fig. 10.7 Interaction between real-world objects

As we can see, the beauty of this scheme is the minimum differences in the way we perceive the various objects (e.g. Ana, TV, office, car) and the way they can actually be modelled in a computer-based system. We think of computer objects in the same breath as real-world objects. This is a revolutionary concept in the computer world, where analysts and designers are generally forced to think in terms of computer-based entities such as databases, programs, and so on, right from the beginning. Now, they can think of real-world objects as, well, *objects*! This principle, which reduces the gap between what we perceive and how we model, is called 'reduction in the semantic gap'. As we can guess, the semantic gap is the gap between the outside view of an object, and its implementation/model. This is shown in Fig. 10.8.

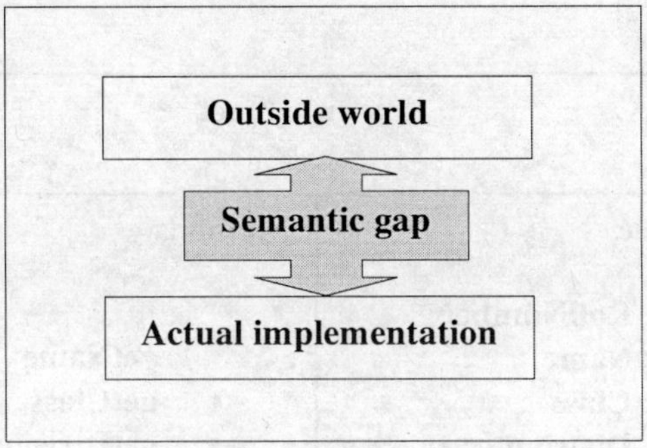

Fig. 10.8 Semantic gap

The smaller the semantic gap, the better, simply because it means that objects can be modelled as closely as possible to their real-world form.

The two main benefits of a small semantic gap are: (a) It makes the process of understanding the requirements of modelling easy, and (b) It makes the process of modifications to software simpler. The second point is important because a smaller semantic gap means that objects are as highly self-contained as possible and, therefore changes to one object do not greatly affect other objects in the system.

10.1.4 Practical Example of an Object

We have discussed the concept of object at great length, and have considered examples that are usually not relevant to real-world computer programming. Therefore, let us now try to model an object that represents student information – an example that is very close to real-world computing.

Typically which information about a student would we like to store? The basic minimum set of information could consist of roll number, name, class, division, gender and date of birth. Of course, there could be many such categories, but for simplicity, we shall ignore them. It should be clear from our discussion so far that each of these information pieces can be modelled as an attribute. As we know, the second aspect of any object is methods. What should be the methods for this object? From our earlier discussion, an object must tightly hold all its attributes to its chest, and reveal whatever it wants only in the form of methods. Therefore, in this case, if another object wants to know the date of birth of a student, the student object must provide a method which provides this information (i.e. date of birth). Similarly, the student object should also provide methods that obtain or get information on the name, class, division and gender, given a roll number. Since these methods *get* information about a student, we can name them as getName, getClass, getDivision, and so on. Thus, our student object would look as shown in Fig. 10.9.

This should give us a fairly good idea as to how objects look in real-life. In fact, the code written to declare a student object in an object-oriented language, such as Java or C++, is actually not dramatically different from the way we have written it here!

Student object

Attributes	**Methods**
• **RollNumber** • **Name** • **Class** • **Division** • **Gender** • **DateOfBirth**	• **getName** • **getClass** • **getDivision** • **getGender** • **getDateOfBirth**

Fig. 10.9 Student object

10.1.5 Classes

Another key concept related to object technology is that of **class**. A class is a generic form of objects. For example, Tom, Ram, John and Ana are all persons. We can treat each one of them as an object. However, at a broader level, we can group them as belonging to a generic class called *person*. Similarly, truck, train, airplane and car are all vehicles. Therefore, we can treat all of them as objects, and make vehicle a generic entity; which means that *vehicle* would be a class. Numerous such examples can be given. However, the point is that a class is a generic template, whereas an object is a specific instance of that template. This idea is shown in Fig. 10.10.

Understanding the concept of a class from a programming perspective is actually quite easy. Recall how we declare an integer or a floating point number in a programming language such as Java or C#. It is done using the following syntaxes:

```
int i;
float f;
```

(Note: We shall ignore minor syntactical errors in order to keep the discussion simple rather than make it technically correct and complicated).

Vehicle class

Objects of the Vehicle class: Truck, Train, Airplane, and Car

Fig. 10.10 Class and objects

What do these declarations convey? They tell us that i is going to be a number, which is an integer, whereas f is a floating point number. In comparison to our earlier discussion, are there certain equivalences? Well, we can consider *int* and *float* as similar to classes, and *i* and *f* as similar to objects of these two classes, respectively. Taking this idea a step further, can we declare an object (say car) for the vehicle class? The following statement in Java or C# should achieve it.

vehicle car;

Thus, we have a very important idea, as illustrated in Fig. 10.11.

Class	**Object**
int	**i**
float	**f**
vehicle	**car**

Fig. 10.11 Classes and objects

This should help us understand the relationship between classes and objects very clearly. Just as integers, floating-point numbers are generic templates (i.e. classes); and so can be other types such as vehicle, student and person. For every such class, we can declare one or more specific instances (i.e. objects).

This is shown in Fig. 10.12, in which we have a class and three objects corresponding to that class, with their unique identifiers.

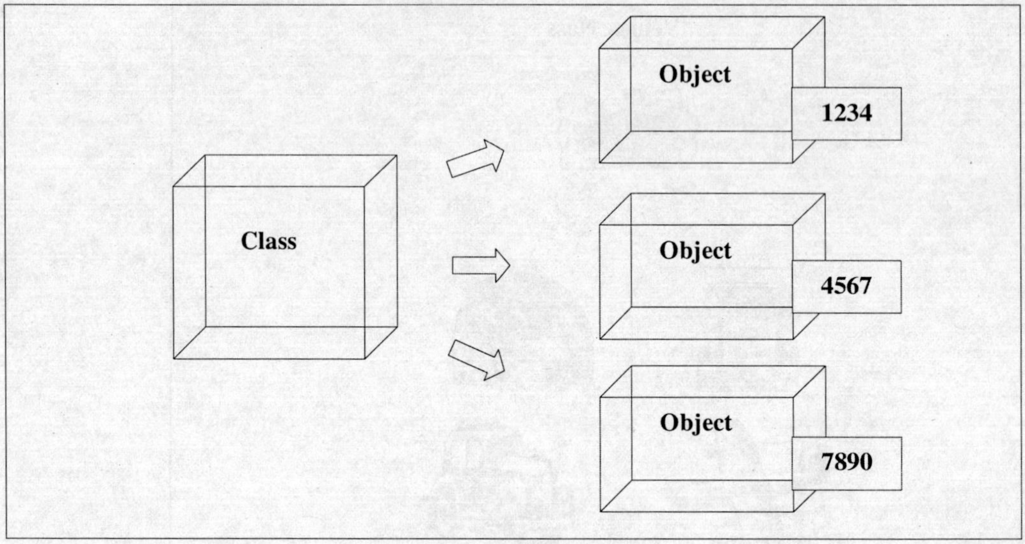

Fig. 10.12 Class and objects

This description also tells us something more about classes and objects. A class has general characteristics, which all its objects automatically inherit. For instance, when we think about an *int*, we immediately perceive a number that cannot have fractional part or a value exceeding a maximum. Therefore, when we declare any number (say *i*) as an integer, it automatically obeys all these restrictions. Extending this concept, when we declare a *student* class, and *ana* as an object of this student class, *ana* automatically picks up all the default characteristics of the student class, such as roll number, name, date of birth, and others.

10.1.6 The Essence of Classes and Objects

Let us now revisit the question on how to declare classes and objects in a programming language, such Java or C#. For that, let us consider the same example of declaring an integer. We know that declaring an integer i takes the following simple form.

```
int i;
```

We know that *int* is the class here, and *i* is its object. An interesting observation is, we simply declare i as belonging to the category of integers. It automatically *knows* that it cannot store fractions, values beyond a certain range, and so on. Similarly, we should be able to simply declare *ana* as a *student*, and *ana* should automatically pick up all the characteristics of a student from the perspective of our current discussion (i.e. roll number, name, date of birth, etc). The following statement should do the trick:

```
student ana;
```

Unfortunately, things do not work this way. The reason for this is quite simple. Programming languages define certain classes as standard or default, which means that the compiler of the programming language *knows* how to deal with these classes. Examples of these are the basic data types, such as integers and floating point numbers. Thus, the moment we declare *i* as type *int*, the compiler enforces all the characteristics of integers with reference to i. However, when we declare *ana* to be of type *student*, the compiler has absolutely no clue as to what a *student*, and therefore, *ana*, means. Therefore, the declaration of *ana* as a *student* would fail. This means that we must first inform the compiler what a *student* means. Only when we tell the compiler what characteristics a student has, can we create instances or objects of it.

A data type, such as student is thus made up of many basic data types like integers, strings, floating point numbers, and so on, as shown in Fig. 10.13.

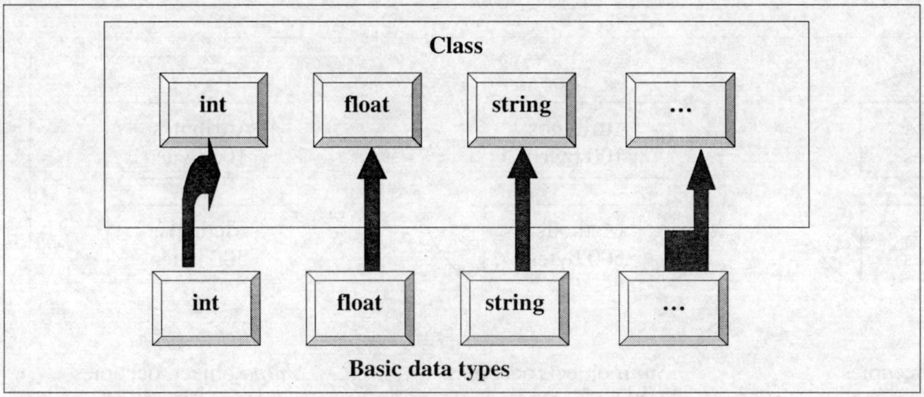

Fig. 10.13 Class is made up of a combination of many basic data types

The declaration of a student class in Java is shown in Fig. 10.14. Do not worry about the syntactical details. Concentrate only on the concept.

```
public class student {
    private int RollNumber;
    private String Name;
    private int Class;                  Attributes
    private char Division;
    private String DateOfBirth;

    public int getName ( );
    public int getClass ( );
    public int getDivision ( );         Methods
    public int getDateOfBirth ( );
}
```

Fig. 10.14 Declaration of student class

Now, the compiler knows what the meaning of a *student* class is. It treats an object of this *student* class in a manner that is not completely different from an integer variable. Thus, it simply considers *student* as a higher-level data type. Now, the following statement makes sense to the compiler:

student ana;

It now knows that *ana* can have a roll number, name, class, and other attributes and that another object can send a message to her to obtain her name, class, division, and so on.

One clarification is necessary at this juncture. Consider the above *student* class. Let us assume that the attributes of the *student* class require 100 bytes of memory in the computer's RAM, and that the methods of the *student* class occupy 500 bytes of memory. Then, the memory representation of the *student* objects Ajay, Sunil and Shilpa would look as shown in Fig. 10.15.

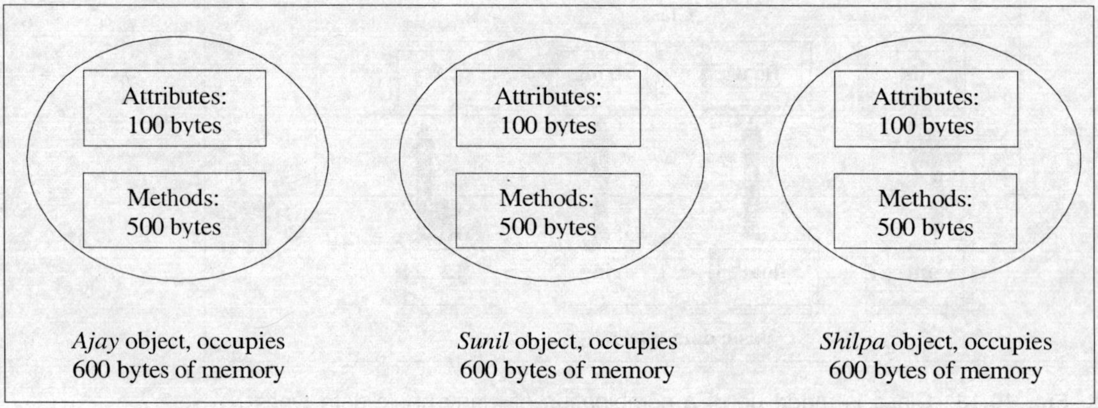

Fig. 10.15 Memory consumption of objects (as it first appears)

Can we think of an improvement here? What would the attributes and methods of the *student* objects contain?

- The attributes for these different objects would certainly have different values. For instance, the names of the students are different (note that the name is one of the attributes of the student). Similarly, their role numbers, classes, divisions, and other attributes are likely to be different.
- What about the methods? We can see that every object would access the same method (i.e. the same code) of the class. There is nothing unique for every object, here.

Does this mean that we cannot share the attributes of different objects, but can share methods? Certainly, this is possible, and in fact this is how object technology implements attributes and methods. All the objects of a class have their own set of attributes, which is not shared with any other object. However, all the objects of a class share its methods. This saves on the memory of the computer and makes implementation of object methods easier. Thus, in the case of the *student* class, where we had 600 bytes of memory requirement per object, we would now need just 100 bytes per object. In addition, we would also need a common pool of 500 bytes of memory shared by all the objects for the methods portion.

Thus, the 1800 bytes that we would have needed for three student objects (3 objects, each of size 600 bytes) can be replaced with just 800 bytes (3 objects, each of size 100 bytes, plus a common area of 500 bytes for memory). This is shown in Fig. 10.16.

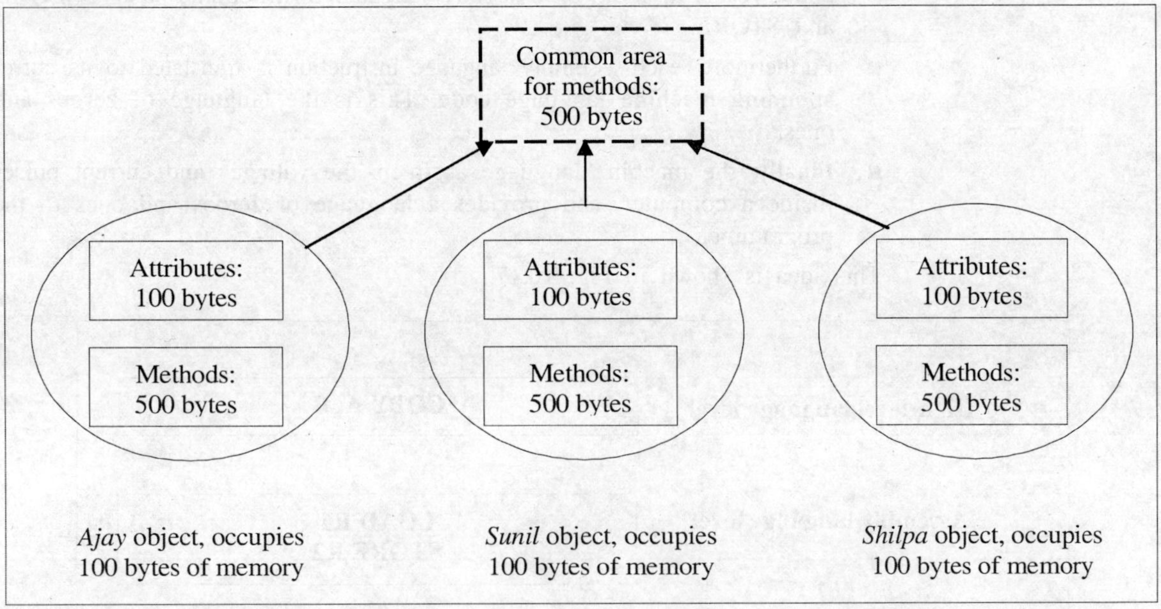

Fig. 10.16 Memory consumption of objects (as it actually is)

10.2 ABSTRACTION

The concept of **abstraction** is very important in object technology. It is one of the most fundamental concepts in this area. Interestingly, abstraction is an extremely useful concept in our daily lives too. For example, we normally do not consider a book to be made up of many pages and diagrams, or a car to be made up of 100 different parts. If we do that, it would be difficult to cultivate the thinking process. Instead, we think of all these things as sub-parts of a book or a car object, respectively. Internally, these objects have a specific set of attributes (pages, spare parts) and behaviours (can be read, can be turned right). This allows us to think about these objects in an abstract fashion. Thus, we can read a book and drive a car easily. We are not bothered about their technical details. We think about objects as a whole.

Even in technical terms, abstraction is actually not restricted only to object technology. All programming languages support abstraction at various levels. Let us understand this.

- A high-level language provides the programmer with keywords, variables, functions, and so on. For example, a high-level language would contain instructions such as ADD, COPY, MOVE, and others (or their equivalents). For instance, an instruction *COPY A, B* could mean copy the contents of variable B to variable A.

- An assembly language is at a *lower* level in the sense that one instruction in a high level language maps to one or more assembly language instructions. For instance, a COPY instruction in a high-level language could result in multiple assembly language instructions, such as LOAD and STORE.
- Furthermore, each assembly language instruction is translated to its corresponding machine language code. This is the language of zeroes and ones.
- Finally, the machine language abstracts the voltages and current pulses inside a computer, and provides a language of zeroes and ones to the programmer.

This idea is shown in Fig. 10.17.

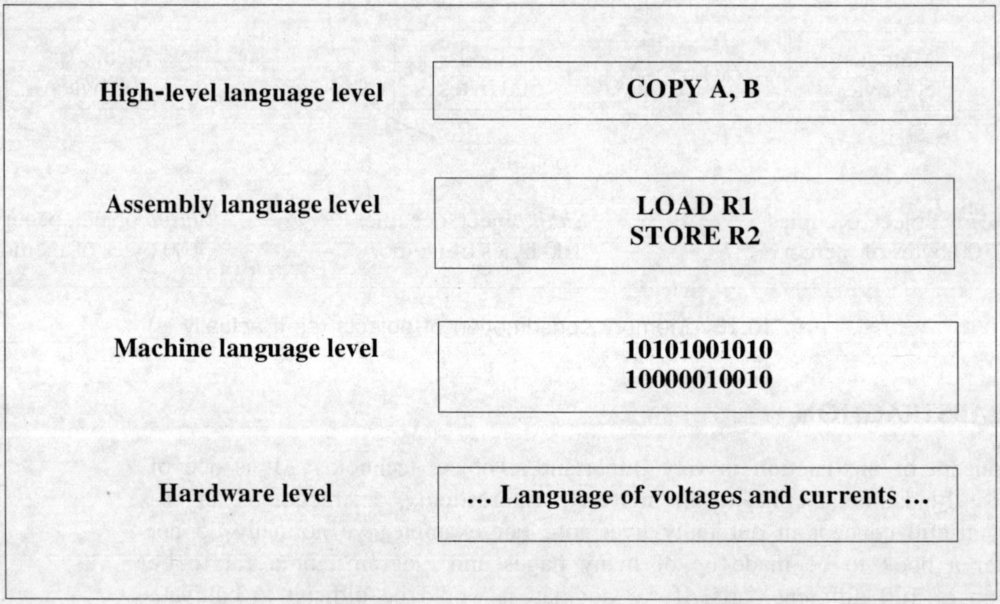

Fig. 10.17 Abstraction in programming languages

We must clarify that the idea of abstraction in object technology has more to do with the abstraction of objects themselves.

One observation must be stated. The object-oriented concepts are not limited to programming alone. The computer software's life has different steps such as analysis (understanding the problem), design (mapping the solution to the problem in terms of data structures), programming (actually writing the program code for the created designs) and storing data (traditionally in the form of files or databases). The object technology experts recommend that the true benefits of object technology can be realised only by applying it through the whole process.

An analyst has to identify different objects, their properties (attributes and methods), how they are going to interact with each other (messages) to achieve various functionalities, produce reports and create queries of the system. Then the analyst has to write specifications for the methods of the different objects. The programmer can then write programs. It is at this stage that object-oriented languages such as Java or C# can be used for coding. These languages allow you to define and manipulate objects. Ordinary languages such as C or COBOL do not allow definition of objects (although enterprise COBOL is evolving). Thus, they cannot be used for object-oriented systems. Similarly, we can perform the analysis in a traditional, structured way, which is process-oriented (where no objects are identified) and still use object-oriented languages such as C++ or Java. We will not get the real benefit of object technology in this case. For real benefit, the whole approach, from the beginning to the end, has to be object-oriented.

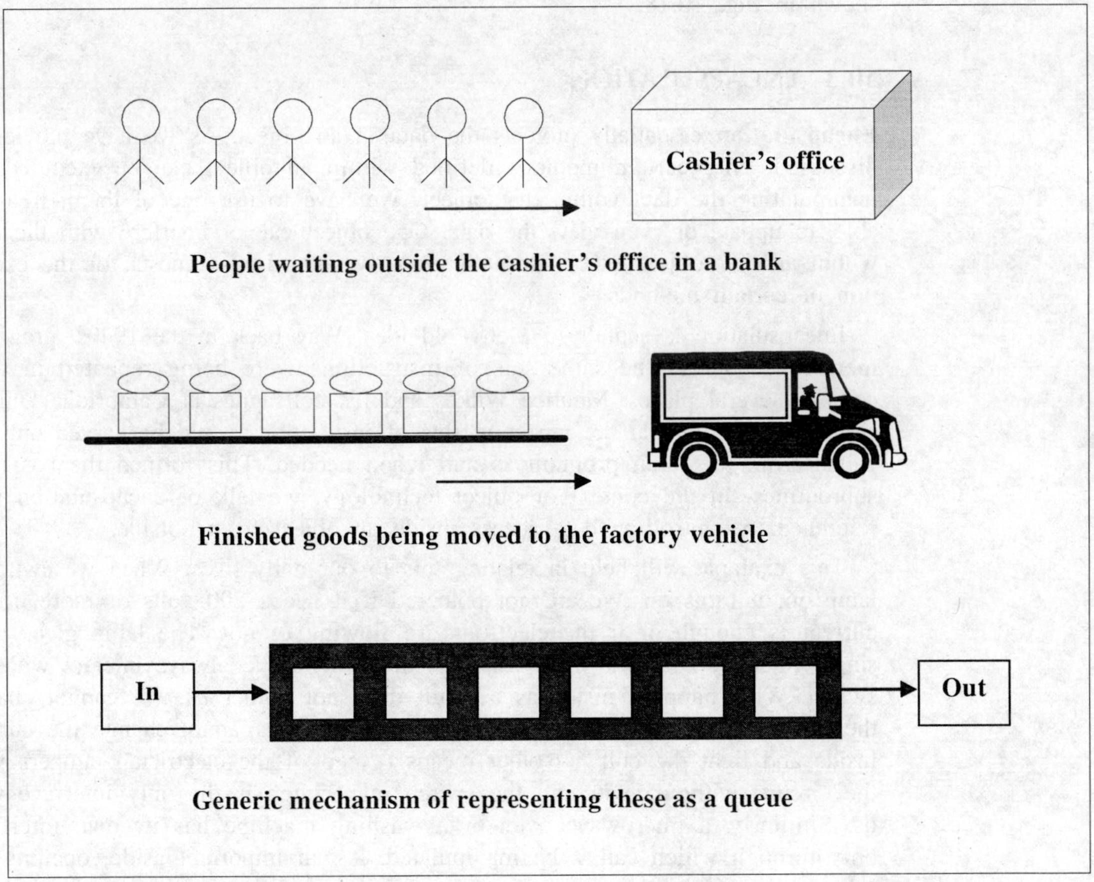

Fig. 10.18 Abstraction can be used to generalise similar ideas

Abstraction allows an analyst to concentrate only on the essential aspects of objects and to ignore their non-key aspects. It facilitates postponing of many decisions to as late a date as possible. This also means that the analyst does not make commitments regarding the design or implementation. Thus, the analyst can focus only on the actual problem at hand (i.e. analysing a system and its requirements), rather than worrying about the implementation details. In other words, abstraction allows an analyst to think about *what* needs to be done, rather than *how* to achieve it. Because this analysis model is at a high level of conceptualisation, it can be reused in the later stages of a software project, such as design coding, testing and implementation.

Let us consider another example of abstraction. We normally stand in a queue when we visit a bank, a pizza shop, post office, and so on. In a similar way, the finished goods in a factory also move in sequence to form a queue. Let us assume that we need to represent these ideas in a computer program. We can apply the principles of abstraction here. That is, we can abstract the two ideas, and think only about the concept of a (generic) *queue*. We can apply the same principle in both the examples, using a single abstraction. The idea is shown in Fig. 10.18.

10.3 ENCAPSULATION

Encapsulation essentially protects the data in an object. As we have previously discussed, only certain methods defined within an object can be executed for manipulating the data within that object. We have to use one of them, if available, to update or even view the data. One object cannot interfere with the data within another object except through properly authorised requests for the execution of certain methods.

Encapsulation is actually a pretty old idea. Way back in the 1940s, programmers realised that the same sets of instructions were being repeated in their code at several places. Maurice Wilkes and his colleagues at Cambridge University soon realised that the repeating sets of instructions could be carved out and called from the main program as and when needed. This formed the basis for subroutines. In the context of object technology, we talk of encapsulation with reference to controlling data access inside an object from outside.

This example will help in relating this to our daily lives. When we switch a lamp on, it turns on. We are not bothered if it needs 200 volts or more, if the current is enough or if the electrons are flowing or not. The lamp gives us a single interface to work with, which is the switch. We always interact with the switch. What happens inside as a result does not bother us. We cannot change the lamp's state without the switch. For instance, we cannot change the current inside and light the bulb by other means (except if the electrician tampers with the circuit) without switching the switch on. Switch is the only interface with us. Similarly, a microwave oven or a washing machine has its own interface, only through which can it be manipulated. As an important aside, opening the microwave oven door or turning the washing machine on does not switch on our lamp. Thus, an action on one object does not cause any change to another object, except through structured messaging, as we will learn later. Every object responds only to its own interface and nothing else.

Encapsulation is a very powerful tool in object-oriented technology. Once an object is ready, all one needs to know is its methods or interfaces. How they are implemented internally (i.e. the program code of the methods) is not of any interest. An object is expected to perform a specific, pre-defined task without worrying about any side effects. To ask an object to do a specific pre-defined task, its methods are called. Suppose there are two methods in an employee object for creating a new employee record and updating some of the fields. This can be as shown in Fig. 10.19.

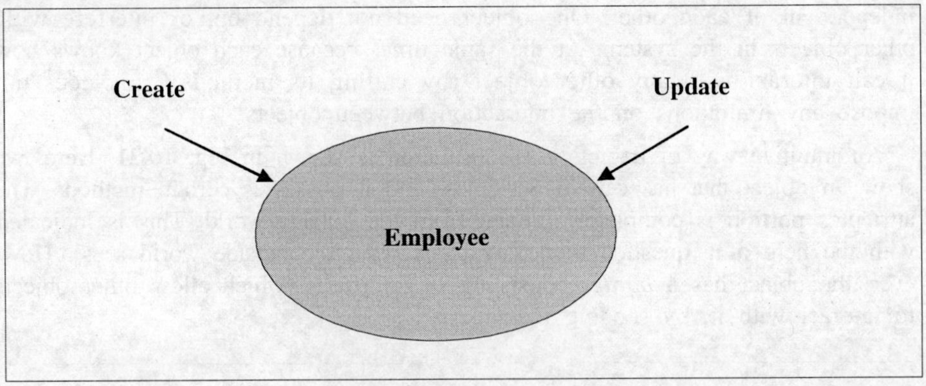

Fig. 10.19 Encapsulation

As the figure shows, an employee object gives the view of a black box. It tells the outside world that its interface is made up of two methods: create and update. How they work internally is not known. In fact, hardly anything else is known about the employee object apart from these two method names. To update the address of an employee, for example, the update method must be called and the new address should be passed to that method. That is the whole idea. Other objects need not know anything about the internal structure of the employee object such that the internal structure of the employee object can be changed without affecting other objects.

This concept is shown in Fig. 10.20 with another example. Here, an account-holder object sends a message *transfer* to an ATM object to transfer funds from itself to another account. The account-holder object does not know the ATM object works internally. However, the ATM object performs the funds transfer successfully and returns an acknowledgement in the form of a receipt to the account-holder object. This is precisely what the account-holder object expects, anyway!

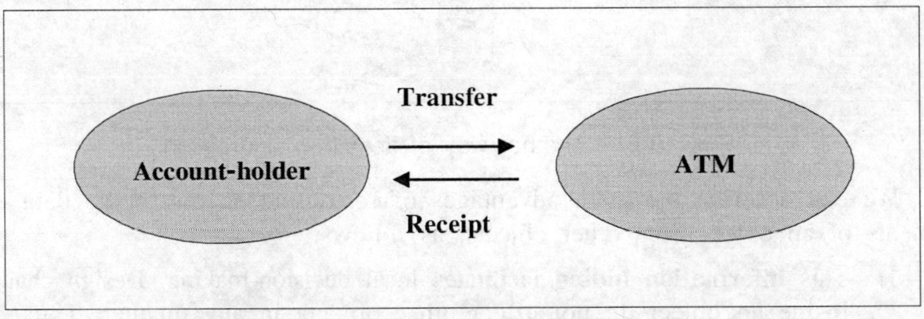

Fig. 10.20 Encapsulation enables simple message passing between objects

Thus, the main idea of encapsulation is *hiding of internal details* of an object. This means that the changes to the internal details of one object do not cause many rippling changes to other objects in the system. These changes to an object could be due to different reasons, such as change in requirements, bug fixing, performance improvement, as on.

By using the idea of encapsulation, objects become self-sufficient and fairly independent of each other. One object need not depend on, or interfere with, other objects in the system. At the same time, because each object knows how it can interact with any other object (by calling its methods), this does not impose any limitations on the interaction between objects.

An intuitive way of depicting encapsulation is shown in Fig. 10.21. Here, we show an object that has certain attributes, and it possesses certain methods. The attributes portion is completely hidden from the outside world. This is indicated with the help of a question mark (which is what the outside world sees). However, the object has a *border* consisting of interfaces, which allow other objects to interact with it, by sending messages.

Object technology specifies many features that are expected to make software engineering and development better. Examples of these features are abstraction (focus on what needs to be done, not how to do it), inheritance (create hierarchies of objects so as to make data and code sharing effective), polymorphism (allow the same method to perform different tasks, depending on the context), and so on.

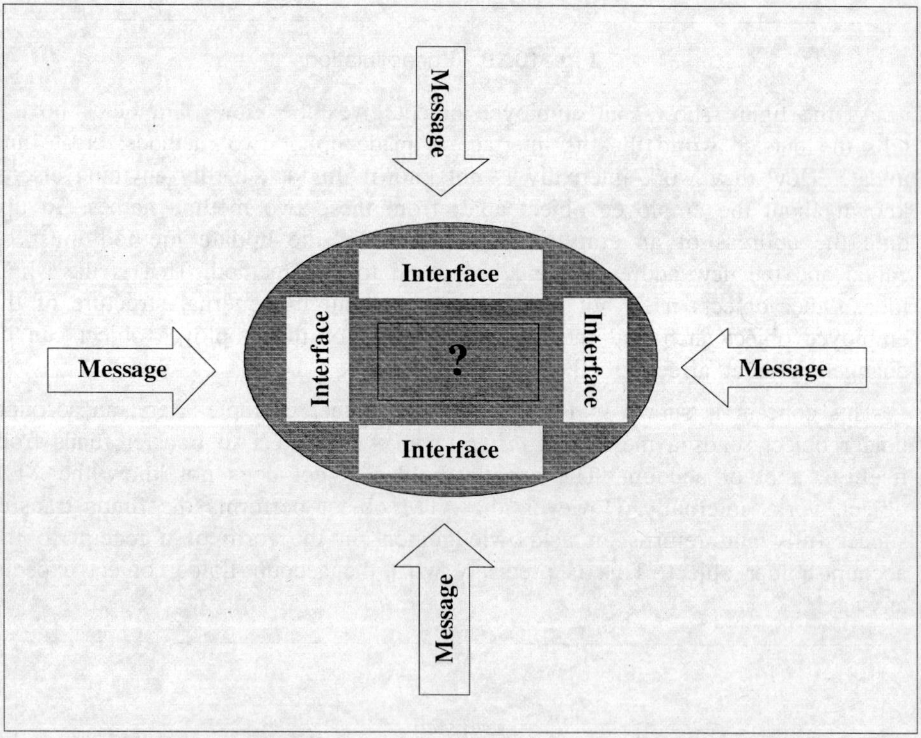

Fig. 10.21 Another way of depicting abstraction

We can describe the main advantages of restricting access to the data elements of an object from other objects, as follows:

1. This **information hiding** facilitates local decision-making. Design changes inside an object do not affect other objects in any manner. Thus, the designers of an object are free to make changes to the object in any

manner, as long as they do not change the external interface of the object to the outside world.

2. This facilitates decoupling of the internal representation details of an object from the way others see it. This also means that others cannot make any alterations to an object.

10.4 INHERITANCE

> **Inheritance** is the process by which one object acquires the properties of one or more other objects.

It involves sharing of attributes and operations or methods among classes based on a hierarchical relationship. Note that this is different from association or aggregation.

A class can be created at a broad level and then refined progressively into finer **subclasses**. Each subclass incorporates, or *inherits* all the properties of its **super class** to which it can add its own properties. It is interesting to notice that deriving the common attributes of more than one object creates a class. Inheritance extends this basic concept so that the classes themselves can be **generalised**. This means, a super class now shares common attributes among different classes. This is a very interesting and important idea.

To take a simple example, *vehicle* can be defined as a class at a broad level—it would be the super class. Cars, scooters and mopeds are all different kinds of vehicle. Suppose the super class *vehicle* has an attribute called *tires;* the attribute value indicates the number of tires for a vehicle. Thus, while the attribute would be common to all vehicles, the *value* of the attribute would differ. For example for a car the value would be 4; for a scooter, it would be 2, and so on. Therefore, rather than defining the attributes in each type of vehicle, it can be defined at the top of the hierarchy, that is in the *vehicle* class.

The *vehicle* class is the super class. The different vehicle types are the subclasses. Each vehicle type (subclass) automatically inherits all the properties – such as *tires* – of the *vehicle* class (super class). Wherever they differ, the differences would be added in the subclass. For instance, tires of a car would be different from the tires of a scooter. However, from the viewpoint of the super class *vehicle*, all tires are the same. It is then up to the subclass to point out the differences (by defining additional attributes). The super class would provide only the basic minimum features. Take another example of the attribute *horn.* The horn of a scooter would produce a different sound from that of a car. However, the super class *vehicle* would provide only a basic *sound* attribute. It is then up to the subclass to add more attributes such as *beep* and *blow*. The basic idea is as shown in Fig. 10.22.

Inheritance is not limited to a single level. For instance, we can see that mopeds and scooters are two-wheelers; whereas cars are four-wheelers. Therefore, we can group (or generalise) scooters and mopeds into another class called *two-wheeler*. The cars can go into another class called *four-wheeler.* If we are sure that we will not add trucks, jeeps or anything else to the family of four-wheelers, we can keep car as a directly subclass of the *vehicle* super class, similar to the one shown earlier. However, if we do add further categories to the sub classes four-wheeler and two-wheeler, our new inheritance relationship would look as shown in Fig. 10.23.

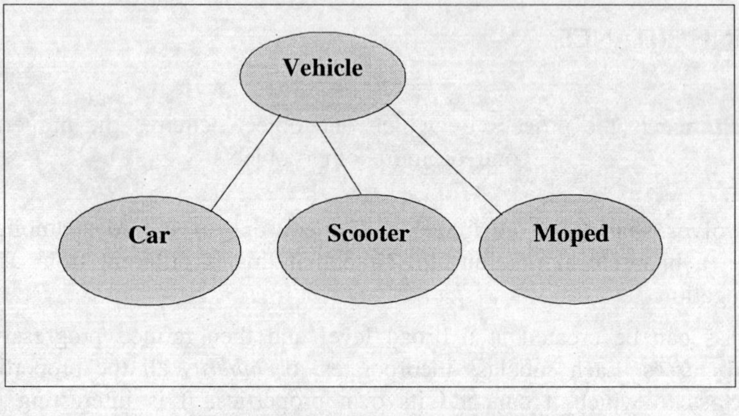

Fig. 10.22 Inheritance concept

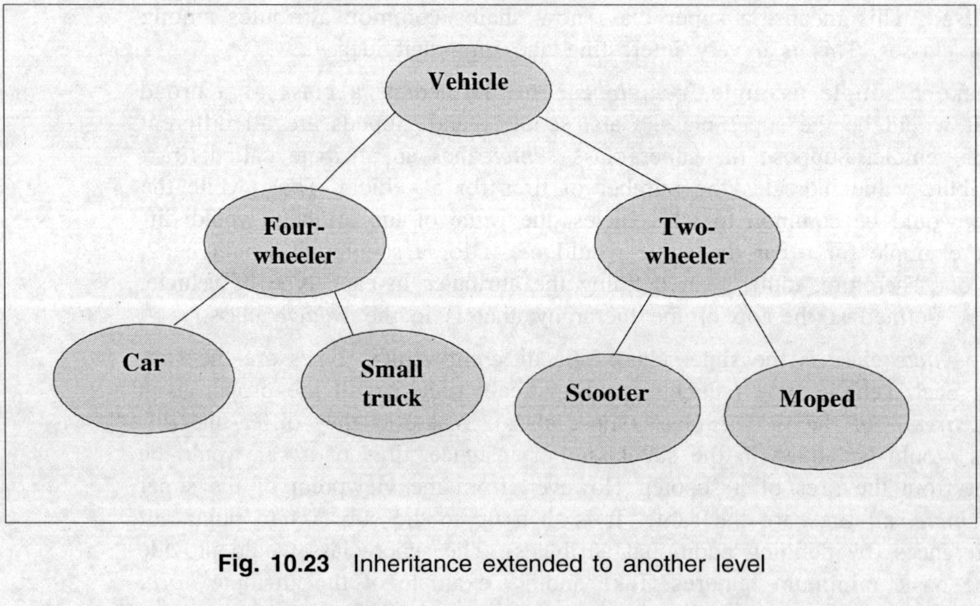

Fig. 10.23 Inheritance extended to another level

As the figure shows, inheritance can be extended to more than one level. Why does one need to extend inheritance to more than one level anyway? The reason for adding another level of inheritance is to combine classes into still finer groups. Thus, classes are not only grouped, but they are also specialised. For example, cars and small trucks are not particular cases of vehicles: they are particular cases of four-wheelers.

This kind of extention gives software designers and developers a better level of control. Thus, only the very basic and common features would be kept in the vehicle class. It would be fine-tuned to have features of only four-wheelers in the four-wheeler class. Similarly the two-wheeler class would contain features of only two wheelers. Obviously, apart from inheriting properties from its super class, a class can have its own additional properties. A class can pass on both the inherited and the new properties to its subclass. Clearly, this is very useful when writing software as it reduced the chances of duplication of efforts. Once the super class is created, the subclasses can inherit all its attributes and methods automatically, so there is no need to write them once again. As discussed, this can be extended any desired level.

Also, any other application that needs to deal with vehicle information can simply use the vehicle class and inherit its own subclasses from this generic class. Therefore, we do not need to write separate programs for this. That is, we can reuse the programs written for *vehicle* super class. This feature is called **code reusability.**

Inheritance is a logical extension of the concept of abstraction. Actually, the concept of inheritance was present even in the days of procedural programming. This was achieved by writing common procedures, which could be reused by other programs/procedures. However, inheritance takes this idea a step ahead. Now, the relationships between classes can be defined, which allows for not only code reuse but also better design, by factoring in commonalities of the various classes. The designer's job here is to start thinking about such commonalities, and look for them in the classes that are being designed. For instance, an application could have student and teacher as two classes. Obviously, they may share some basic attributes, such as name, date of birth, sex, and others. These and other such common attributes can be abstracted to form a super class called person. Student and teacher could become the subclasses of this super class, thus inheriting the properties of the person super class. Since the super class forms the foundation or base of sharing, it is also called **base class**.

Object technology specifies many features that are expected to make software engineering and development better. Examples of these features are abstraction (focus on what needs to be done, not how to do it), inheritance (create hierarchies of objects so as to make data and code sharing effective), polymorphism (allow the same method to perform different tasks, depending on the context), and so on.

Of course, the similarities between a student and a teacher end at some point. That is when the idea of generalisation no longer continues to be true and specialisation begins. Once we are through with all the possible commonalities between a student and a teacher, we should carve out a person class, and include all these common features in this class. At the next stage, we need to think of the differences between the two–that is the specialties of the student, as well as the teacher. For instance, a student would have attributes such as total marks obtained, and ranking among her peers. These are not at all relevant to a teacher who will have some completely unrelated specialties, such as the subject that she teaches. These special attributes of the student and the teacher would go into their respective subclasses. The ideas of generalisation and specialisation are shown in Fig. 10.24. As we can see, generalisation starts from the bottom, and goes to the top. On the other hand, specialisation starts at the top, and moves down to the bottom.

Technically, arrows originating from the subclasses towards the super class show the inheritance relationship. The arrows indicate that the subclass *inherits from* the super class. If class A is the super class and class B is the subclass, this relationship can be shown as depicted in Fig. 10.25.

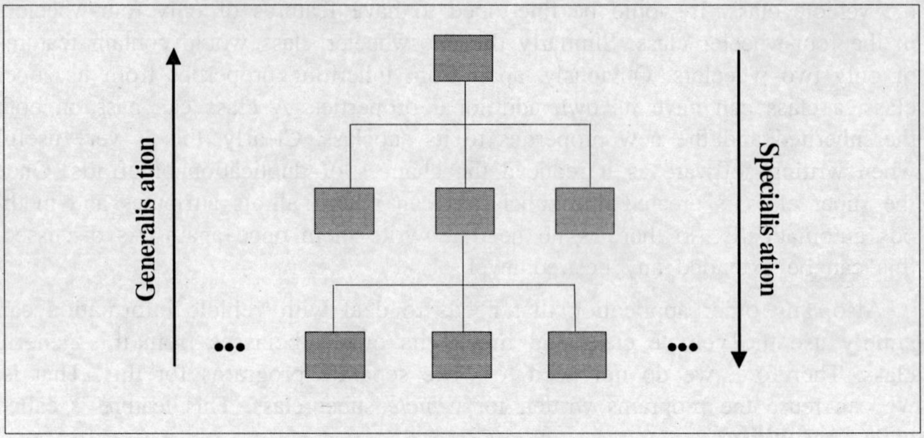

Fig. 10.24 Generalisation and specialisation

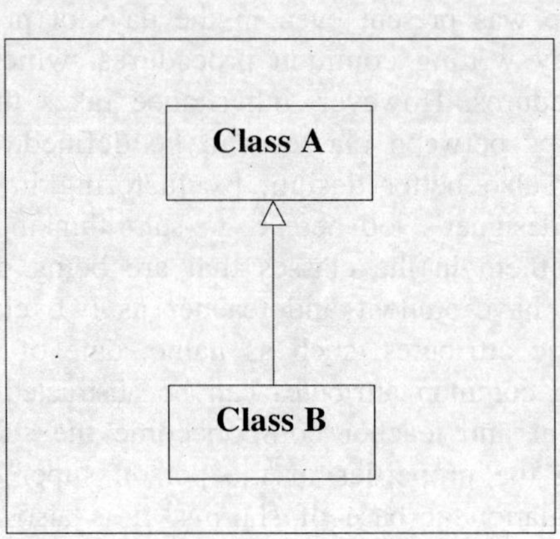

Fig. 10.25 Inheritance relationship

Just as aggregation can be found out by looking for *has a* relationship, inheritance can be found out by looking for *is a* relationship. For instance, when we say that student and person are subclass and super class respectively, we actually mean that student *is a* person. Since a student is a person, it already knows what it means to be a person! Therefore, it needs to highlight only the specialties of a student, which are missing in a person. Thus, in general, a sub class needs to point out only the differences as compared to its super class. A subclass can do all that its super class can, and more!

Other terms for a super class are: *parent class* or *ancestor*. Similarly, other names for a subclass are: *child class* or *descendent*.

10.5 OBJECT TECHNOLOGY AND RDBMS

10.5.1 Identifying a Record Uniquely

We have noted that the basis for identifying a RDBMS record uniquely in a table is the primary key associated with that record. In object technology, an object has an implicit **object ID**, which helps the underlying technology to identify that record. These two concepts gel with each other in the sense that both RDBMS and object technologies believe that records and objects have existence beyond their properties. Of course, the major difference between the two is that while the primary key is explicit (i.e. visible to the entire world), the object ID is implicit (i.e. hidden from the external world). This idea is illustrated in Fig. 10.26.

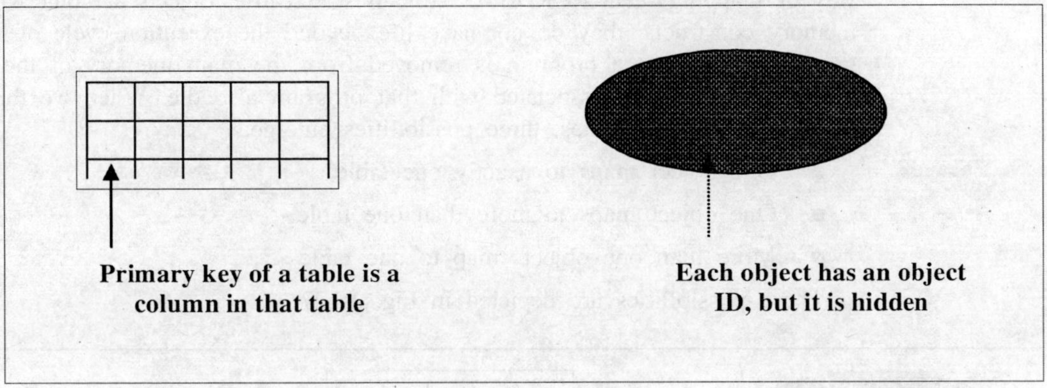

Fig. 10.26 Concept of primary key and object ID

It may seem straightforward to map the concept of primary keys to objects. That is, it may seem that just as a table has a primary key column, a class should have an attribute equivalent to that column. Therefore, a student class would perhaps have student_ID, a salesperson class would have salesperson_ID, and so on. However, there is a lot of debate regarding the usage of such identifiers in objects. Of the many reasons that are quoted, the following are the key ones:

- The main objection to the idea of identifiers comes from the fact that object technology is perceived as an extension of our natural thinking. People consider objects as computer-representation of real-world objects. Therefore, questions are often raised as to why we should have explicit identifiers identifying computer-based objects uniquely, when we do not have any such scheme in the real world!
- Another objection to the idea of special identifiers comes from technologists who believe that the very notion of adding identifiers to objects means that the analyst/designer has already started thinking about how the objects would get stored on the disk (i.e. implementation), rather than what they should do. This could pose the danger of the analyst/designer losing focus.

It may surprise us to read this, given the fact that both RDBMS and object technology actually use identifiers in some way. But as we have noted, RDBMS requires the presence of an identifier in the actual record. On the other hand, object technology associates the identifier with an object internally, and resists having the identifier as an explicit attribute of the object. This should clarify the point that although the basic motive in both the cases is the same, the envisaged usage is quite different.

Regardless of the objections, it is usually seen that we need to add IDs to objects. There is no other way we can easily map them to RDBMS table structures.

10.5.2 Mapping Classes to Tables

If we need to store classes (actually, objects) on a disk, there must be some way of mapping them to RDBMS structures. Because, objects are otherwise in-memory constructs, they do not have life beyond the execution cycle of a program. The moment a program is removed from the main memory of the computer, all the objects associated with that program also die. When we think of mapping objects to tables, three possibilities emerge:

- One object maps to exactly one table
- One object maps to more than one table
- More than one objects map to one table

These possibilities are depicted in Fig. 10.27.

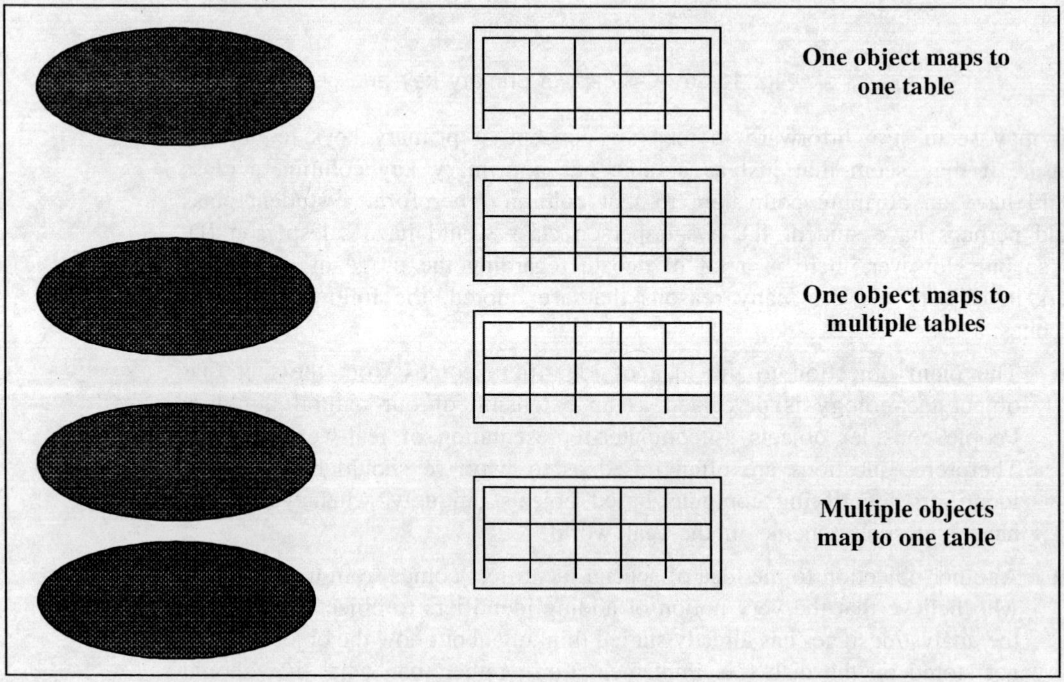

Fig. 10.27 Different possibilities in object-to-table mapping

The objects corresponding to a class can be partitioned horizontally and/or vertically.

n **Horizontal partioning**: If a few instances (i.e. objects) of a class are referenced to more frequently than others, it may be a good idea to place the frequently-accessed instances in one physical table. The ones not frequently accessed can be put in another table. It is imperative that the application using these tables should know which table contains the frequently-accessed data, of it would not benefit from such a partitioning scheme. An example of horizontal partitioning is shown in Table 10.1.

Table 10.1 Horizontal partitioning

Student ID	*Student Name*	*Marks*
01	Atul	62
02	Ana	70
03	Jui	82
04	Harsh	89

(a) Original table

Student ID	*Student Name*	*Marks*
01	Atul	62
02	Ana	70

(b) Horizontal partition number 1

Student ID	*Student Name*	*Marks*
03	Jui	82
04	Harsh	89

(c) Horizontal partition number 2

- **Vertical partioning**: There are after situations when some attributes of a class are more frequently accessed than others. That is, the class may have varying *access patterns*. In such cases, the table corresponding to the class can be partitioned vertically. The frequently accessed attributes can be placed in one table and the other attributes can be placed in another (with appropriate record identifiers). An example is shown in Table 10.2.

Let us now consider an example of mapping a simple class to a table. Let us assume that we have a Student class, containing two attributes: student name, and marks. This is the view of our object model. When we want to map this to an appropriate table, there are two main steps: (a) Outline the corresponding table model for this class, and (b) Write the SQL code corresponding to the table model.

While transforming the object model to the table model, we add a record identifier (student ID). Moreover, we also provide greater details about the table model. For instance, we specify that the student ID must be unique and must not be null, which makes it our ideal primary key. We also mention that the student name must have some value – it cannot be null. However, because two or more students can have the same name, this cannot be a primary key but a secondary one. This would mean that we would create an index on the student name (in addition to the default index on the student ID), thus facilitating a quicker search based on the student name. Marks is a simple attribute without any regards to the key.

Table 10.2 Vertical partition

Student ID	*Student Name*	*Marks*
01	Atul	62
02	Ana	70
03	Jui	82
04	Harsh	89

(a) Original table

Student ID	*Student Name*
01	Atul
02	Ana
03	Jui
04	Harsh

(b) Vertical partition number 2

Student ID	*Marks*
01	62
02	70
03	82
04	89

(c) Vertical partition number 3

The entire process is depicted in Fig. 10.28.

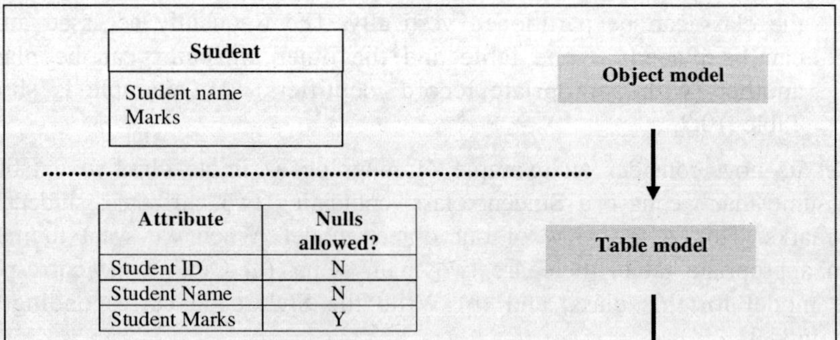

Fig. 10.28 Mapping a class to a table

Mapping classes to tables is usually quite simpleforward. The challenges in mapping begin to surface when we start thinking about mapping associations (i.e. relationships between two or more different classes) to tables. Associations may or may not map to tables, depending on the designer's view, and the problem domain. In general, associations can be binary (which means that values from two classes are derived), ternary (which means that values from three classes are derived), and so on. We will discuss binary associations now.

10.5.3 Mapping Binary Associations to Tables

Binary associations can be largely classified into two types: (a) **Many-to-many associations**, and (b) **One-to-many associations**. Simple examples of these are: many students choosing many subjects for their courses, and thus obtaining some marks in each one (many-to-many); and a school enrolling many students per standard (one-to-many). Depending on the type, we can decide how to map these constructs to tables.

- **Many-to-many associations**

  Many-to-many associations always map to a distinct table. In other words, if we have a class X, another class Y, and their many-to-many association as XY, then we always end up with three tables: one for X, one for Y, and one for XY.

  Let us consider an example. Suppose we have two classes: Student (containing attributes Student name and Address) and Subject (containing Subject name and Details). Many students can choose many subjects. That is, given a student name, we can have multiple subjects chosen by the student; and given a subject name, we can have multiple students choosing that subject. Then we are posed with a problem of not only modelling the student class and the subject class, but also of relating the students with the subjects. Quite clearly, student and subject details would go into their own respective tables. Additionally, we would derive a third table, called Result, which would capture the relationship (i.e. many-to-many association) between the students and the subjects, along with the marks obtained.

Fig. 10.29 illustrates the modelling process for this situation. We will discuss details of this profess after taking a look at the figure.

We have not shown the details of the student and subject classes, which should be easy to understand. In order to depict the association between these two classes, we have created a third table, called Result. This table links the student (based on her ID) with the subject (based on the subject ID), using the marks obtained. As before, we assume that the student ID and subject ID are derived unique identifiers, which are not a part of the basic student and subject classes.

We have mentioned that the primary key of the **Result** table is a combination of the student ID and the subject ID. This is quite logical. After all, the Results table can have multiple records for a student, as well as for a subject. Therefore, the only way to identify a record uniquely is based on a combination of the student ID and the subject ID. This is also the reason why the student ID and subject ID fields cannot have any null values. However, we have allowed the Marks column to allow null values, because it is possible that the examination results are not yet announced.

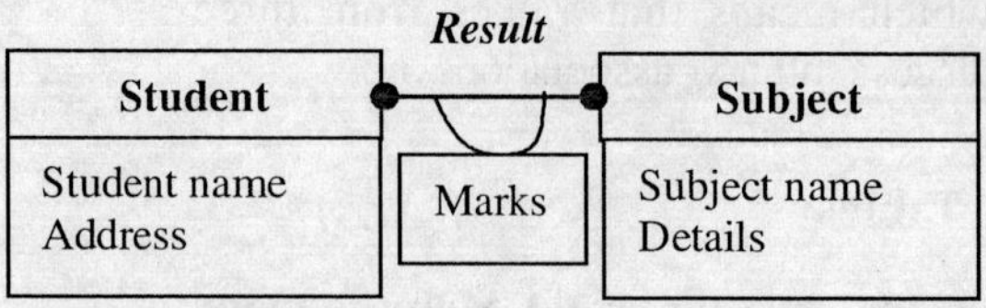

Object model

Meaning: Many students can appear for many subjects. In each case, they would obtain some marks.

Note: We will not show the Student and Subject tables, and assume that they are available. Instead, we will only consider the Result table, which captures the association.

Attribute	Nulls allowed?
Student ID	N
Subject ID	N
Marks	Y

Result table

Table model

```
CREATE TABLE Result
( Student-ID     Integer  Not null,
  Subject-ID     Integer  Not null,
  Marks          Integer,
  PRIMARY KEY (Student-ID, Subject-ID),
  FOREIGN KEY (Student-ID) REFERENCES Student,
  FOREIGN KEY (Subject-ID) REFERENCES Subject));

CREATE SECONDARY INDEX Result-Student-ID-Index
ON Result (Student-ID);

CREATE SECONDARY INDEX Result-Subject-ID-Index
ON Result (Subject-ID);
```

SQL code

Fig. 10.29 Mapping many-to-many association to tables

We have also declared the student ID and the subject ID as foreign keys. This means that they refer to some other tables, where they are primary keys. Of course, these tables are the **Student** table and the **Subject** table, respectively.

For enabling fast searches (e.g. find all subjects chosen by a student, find which students have chosen a particular subject), we have created two secondary indexes: one on the student ID, and another on the subject ID.

- **One-to-many associations**

  To illustrate one-to-many associations, we take the example of a school enrolling many students per standard. A student may or may not actually enroll in any school at all, and yet we may want to maintain information about that student. Also, there can be many schools, in which the students are seeking admission, and we want to store information about all of them. Do not get confused that this causes the relationship to become many-to-many. It is still one-to-many, because for a given school there can be many students, but given a student, there can be only one school. Thus, we know that there must be two tables to start with: Student and School. How do we model their relationship? There are two possibilities:

(a) **Creating a distinct association table**: Similar to the way in which we had earlier modelled the many-to-many association relationship, we can create a third table called as Enrollment. This table will contain the School ID, Student ID, and the standard. We can make the student ID the primary key of this table, since it would always be a unique value. If we examine this carefully, we will note the following advantages:

(i) We are creating a separate table to store the association relationship. Thus, we are not mixing different objects into a single table. This is in line with the encapsulation principle of object technology.

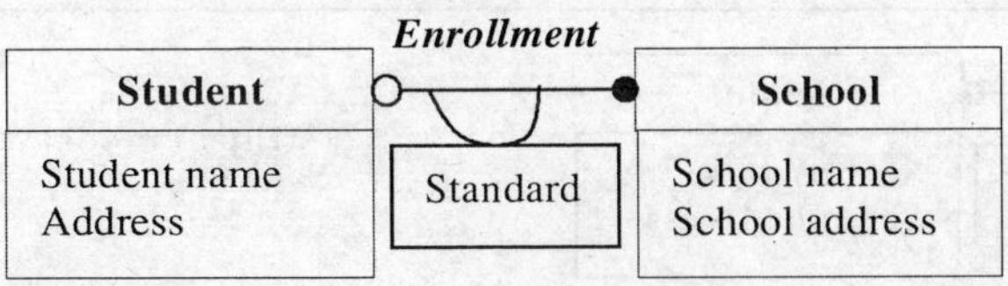

Object model

Meaning: Many students can enroll into the same school. One student can enroll into only one school.

Note: We will not show the Student and School tables, and assume that they are available. Instead, we will only consider the Enrollment table, which captures the association.

Attribute	Nulls allowed?
School ID	N
Student ID	N
Standard	Y

Enrollment table

Table model

```
CREATE TABLE Enrollment
( School-ID      Integer  Not null,
  Student-ID     Integer  Not null,
  Standard       Integer,
  PRIMARY KEY (Student-ID),
  FOREIGN KEY (Student-ID) REFERENCES Student,
  FOREIGN KEY (School-ID) REFERENCES School));
CREATE SECONDARY INDEX Result-School-ID-Index
ON Enrollment (School-ID);
CREATE SECONDARY INDEX Result-Student-ID-Index
ON Enrollment (Student-ID);
```

SQL code

Fig. 10.30 Mapping one-to-many association to tables – Distinct association table

(ii) This design is symmetrical, because we are not complicating any existing objects with additional attributes. Instead, we are creating a third table.

This design also has the following drawbacks:

(i) It leads to one more table than the basic design needs.

(ii) The performance may be slow, since we would need to navigate more tables.

Let us depict this pattern as shown in Fig. 10.30.

Note that we have used a hollow circle at the end of the school class, and a filled circle at the end of the student class. This indicates the one-to-many relationship between a school and its students.

(b) **Hidden foreign key**: In this approach, we do not create a third table to store the association relationship between a school and its students. Instead, we alter the design of the original Student table to include information about which school she studies in. The student table would thus also have School-ID as one of its columns. This column is a foreign key, which refers to the School table. There would be no change in the School table. The design is shown in Fig. 10.31.

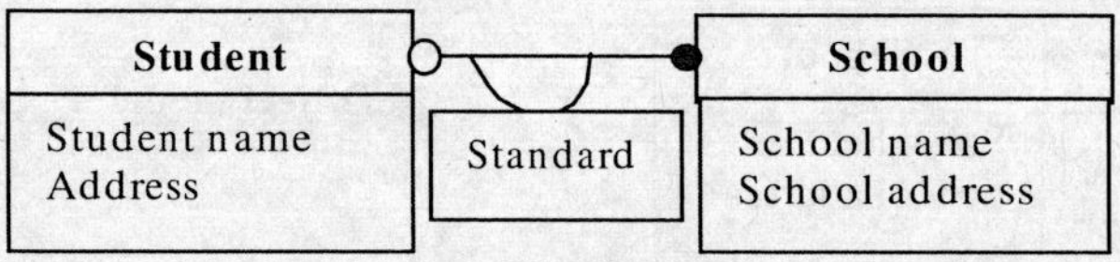

Object model

Meaning: Many students can enroll into the same school. One student can enroll into only one school.

Note: We will not show the School table, and assume that it is available. Instead, we will only consider the Student table, which captures the association.

Attribute	Nulls allowed?
Student ID	N
Student Name	N
Address	Y
School ID	Y
Standard	Y

Student table

Table model

```
CREATE TABLE Student
( Student-ID      Integer          Not null,
  Student-Name    char (30)        Not null,
  Address         char (80),
  School-ID       Integer,
  Standard        Integer,
  PRIMARY KEY (Student-ID),
  FOREIGN KEY (School-ID) REFERENCES School,

CREATE SECONDARY INDEX Result-School-ID-Index
ON Student (School-ID));
```

SQL code

Fig. 10.31 Mapping one-to-many association to tables – Hidden foreign key

The advantages of this approach are apparent. Because of fewer tables, this would work faster. But it also suffers from the drawbacks of being asymmetrical in nature. For instance, even when a student is not enrolled into any school, that student record will still have the column of school ID (although it would be empty). Thus, in this table, we are contaminating the student object with additional information, which can actually be kept in a third, separate table.

As we can see, both the approaches have their own pros and cons. Depending on the needs of the application, the better approach would generally be adopted for each specific use.

10.5.4 Modelling Generalisations to Tables

How do we map generalisation relationships to tables? That is, how do we depict the inheritance relationships between classes in the form of table relationships? To understand this, we will use the generalisation relationship as shown in Fig. 10.32.

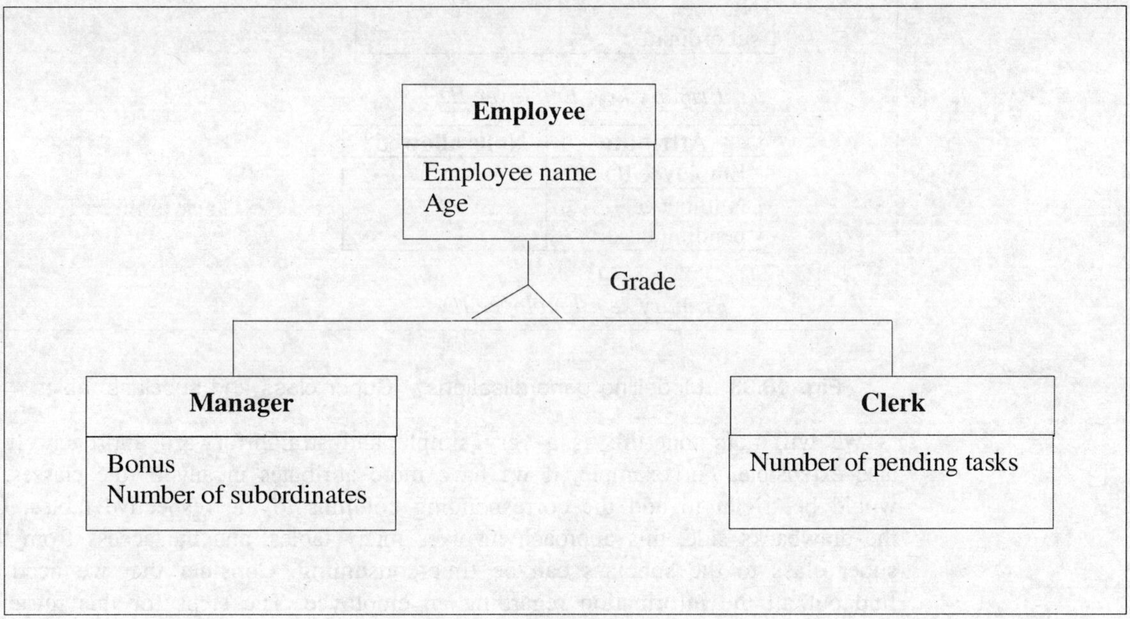

Fig. 10.32 Generalisation example

There are four possible approaches that can be used for this kind of modelling. Let us discuss them one by one.

1. **Super class and subclass tables**

   This is the simplest of all approaches. Here, we map the super class (i.e. Employee) to a table, and the two subclasses (i.e. Manager and Clerk) to two their respective tables. Thus, we have three tables in this design. The identity of an object is maintained throughout the design with the help of a unique employee ID. For instance, an employee, Ana, may occupy a row in the Employee table with 100 as employee ID, and a row in the Manager table, with the same employee ID (i.e. 100). The idea is depicted in Fig. 10.33.

Employee table

Attribute	Nulls allowed?
Employee ID	N
Employee Name	N
Age	Y
Grade	N

Primary key: Employee ID

Manager table

Attribute	Nulls allowed?
Employee ID	N
Bonus	Y
Number of subordinates	Y

Primary key: Employee ID

Clerk table

Attribute	Nulls allowed?
Employee ID	N
Number of pending tasks	Y

Primary key: Employee ID

Fig. 10.33 Modelling generalisations – Super class and subclass tables

We will note that this is a very simple and straightforward approach. It is also extensible. For example, if we have more attributes in any of the classes, it would be trivial to add the corresponding columns to the respective tables. On the drawbacks side, this approach involves many tables, and the access from the super class to the subclass can be time-consuming. Consider that we need to find out all the information regarding an employee. The steps for this retrieval process would be as shown in Fig. 10.34.

Step 1: User provides the *employee name*.
Step 2: Find the row in the Employee table, which corresponds to the *employee name* provided by the user.
Step 3: Retrieve the *employee ID* and *grade* for this employee.
Step 4: Depending on the value of *grade*, go to the appropriate subclass table (i.e. Manager or Clerk).
Step 5: Find the row in the subclass table, which corresponds to the *employee name* provided by the user.

Fig. 10.34 Obtaining a subclass record

For example, suppose the user wants all the information regarding an employee named as *Ana*. The application obtains the employee ID (say *100*) and grade (say *Manager*) of Ana from the Employee table. Since Ana is a manager, the application now looks up the Manager table, and tries to find a match for a row containing the employee ID 100. When it finds one, it retrieves the values of the bonus and the number of subordinates for Ana.

As we can see, this makes the retrieval quite slow. Another problem with this model is actually not noticeable at this juncture. To bring that problem to surface, let us write the SQL code corresponding to our design, as shown in Fig. 10.35.

```
CREATE TABLE Employee
( Employee-ID            Integer        Not null,
  Employee-Name          Char (30)      Not null,
  Age                    Integer,
  Grade                  Char (10)      Not null,

  PRIMARY KEY (Employee-ID));

CREATE SECONDARY INDEX Employee-Name-Index
  ON Employee (Employee-Name);

CREATE TABLE Manager
( Employee-ID            Integer        Not null,
  Bonus                  Integer,
  Number-of-subordinates Integer,

  PRIMARY KEY (Employee-ID),
  FOREIGN KEY (Employee-ID) REFERENCES Employee);

CREATE TABLE Clerk
( Employee-ID                  Integer        Not null,
  Bonus                        Integer,
  Number-of-pending-tasks      Integer,

  PRIMARY KEY (Employee-ID),
  FOREIGN KEY (Employee-ID) REFERENCES Employee);
```

Fig. 10.35 SQL code for super class and subclass tables

The subclass tables include employee ID, and by using the concept of foreign keys, they associate themselves with the super class table. This is perfectly all right. But the problem with this scheme is that there is no direct way for us to prevent the existence of the same employee in both the subclasses. That is, we cannot prevent an employee from becoming a manager as well as a clerk! For instance, we can have an employee, with ID 100, in the Employee table, in the Manager as well as the Clerk tables. We can only stop the application from having more than one employee/manager/clerk within the same table (i.e. as a duplicate entry). Nonetheless, we cannot prevent its occurrence across the subclass tables. We must make appropriate checks for this via additional program code.

2. **Many subclass tables**

   In this approach, we do not have a table corresponding to the super class. Instead, we have one table per subclass. Obviously, in such a design, we must replicate the information that would have been in the super class table into all the subclass tables. The fact that there is no super class table means that we cannot depend on any outside table, when we need to obtain information from a subclass table. All subclass tables must be self-sufficient.

Fig. 10.36 shows the table design for the case where we have no super class table, but only the subclass tables.

Manager table

Attribute	Nulls allowed?
Employee ID	N
Employee name	N
Age	Y
Grade	N
Bonus	Y
Number of subordinates	Y

Primary key: Employee ID

Clerk table

Attribute	Nulls allowed?
Employee ID	N
Employee name	N
Age	Y
Grade	N
Number of pending tasks	Y
Number of subordinates	Y

Primary key: Employee ID

Fig. 10.36 Modelling generalisations – Many subclass tables

Because there is no super class table here, the navigation steps are reduced by one. This also means that a search operation on the subclass table would be faster than it was earlier.

Since we replicate all the super class attributes in the subclass tables, this approach can be used in situations where the super class attributes are small in number, and the subclass attributes are quite high.

Although this approach satisfies the third normal form, the main problem with this approach can be described as follows.

An employee can be a manager as well as a clerk. This is because although the employee ID would be unique within a table (i.e. in the Manager table or in the Clerk table), it may not be unique across both the tables. RDBMS technology does not provide any in-built mechanisms to thwart this problem.

3. **One super class table**

   In this approach, rather than eliminating the super class, we do away with the subclasses. At the same time, we retain the super class. This means that there is only one table in the design now: the super class table. There is no other table.

As we have only the super class, this super class must model all the attributes of the subclasses as well. In other words, we must replicate all the subclass attributes within the super class, and add one column each to the super class table.

Fig. 10.37 illustrates the design of this approach.

Employee table

Attribute	Nulls allowed?
Employee ID	N
Employee name	N
Age	Y
Grade	N
Bonus	Y
Number of subordinates	Y
Number of pending tasks	Y

Primary key: Employee ID

Fig. 10.37 Modelling generalisations – One super class table

What are the characteristics of this model? All the subclasses are tied together. If we have 10 managers and 50 clerks in the organisation, then this model would have 60 records in the employee table. This is because one record will store information about one subclass type (i.e. either manager or clerk). In the case of the manager records, the column *Number of pending tasks* would contain nulls. Similarly, in the case of clerk records, the columns *Bonus* and *Number of subordinates* would contain nulls.

Notably, this table also violates the third normal form. This is because although employee ID is the primary key of the table, the values of the subclass columns such as *bonus*, *number of subordinates* and *number of pending tasks* depend on the value of the *grade* attribute, which is not a primary key of the table.

In spite of its disadvantages, this approach can be considered when the number of subclasses and their attributes are small.

10.6 OBJECT ORIENTED DATABASE MANAGEMENT SYSTEMS (OODBMS)

Object Oriented Database Management Systems (OODBMS) have not become as successful as it was initially thought. Apart from many other reasons, one striking factor behind this is that it is not easy to program for OODBMS systems. Once someone gets used to writing SQL queries, which are almost English-like, it is difficult to comprehend as to why one needs to learn and remember such cryptic syntaxes as used in most OO languages and OODBMS as well. The most practical way ahead seems to be the marriage of object or traditional programs with RDBMS for data storage and retrieval.

10.6.1 Basic Concepts

Although RDBMS is the preferred choice of the computing industry worldwide, a recent development has taken place in the area of the **Object Oriented Database Management Systems** technology. An OODBMS provides a persistent (i.e. permanent) storage for objects. By persistent or permanent storage, we mean storage beyond the life of a program.

OODBMS is generally used in a multi-user client/server environment. It controls the concurrent access to objects, provides locking mechanisms and transactional features, offers security features at the object level and also ensures object backup and restoration.

The biggest difference between a RDBMS and an OODBMS is that whereas the former stores the data related to an object in a table, the latter stores the state of an object. Each object in an OODBMS has a unique Object Identifier (OID), which is used to identify and link it with other objects when needed (e.g. in referential integrity relationships). An OODBMS supports encapsulation and inheritance.

We know that SQL is used in conjunction with RDBMS. OODBMS generally uses class definitions and traditional OOP languages, such as C++ and Java, to define, manipulate and retrieve data. That is, an OODBMS is an extension (on the disk) of the in-memory data structures such as objects. An OODBMS integrates database-handling operations directly into the base OOP language. The idea is shown in Fig. 10.38.

This architecture may raise a doubt. We know that SQL is language-neutral. That is, we can type SQL commands simply on a command prompt, or we can also use SQL inside programming languages such as C++, Java, COBOL, and others with the same basic syntax.

From what we have discussed about OODBMS, it appears that a programmer must be familiar with *OODBMS with C++* or *OODBMS with Java* syntaxes, etc. In other words, are we saying that the syntax for using OODBMS in C++ is different from using OODBMS in Java? Does it mean that we must *relearn* OODBMS syntax the moment we change from one OOP language to another?

This was indeed the case! Thankfully, however, to address this problem, an **Object Database Management Group (ODMG)** was set up. This group has come up with a specification for using OODBMS in a certain way. This specification has three main aspects, as shown in Fig. 10.39.

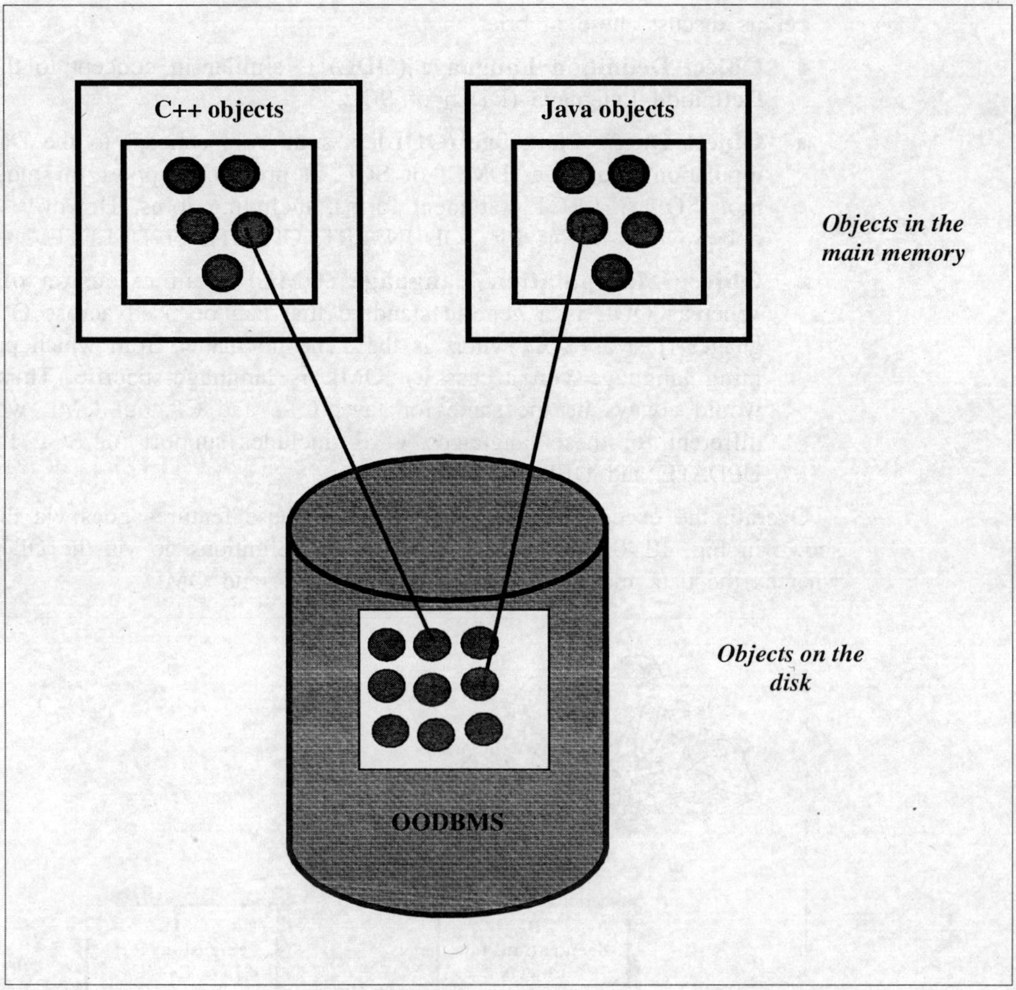

Fig. 10.38 OODBMS concept

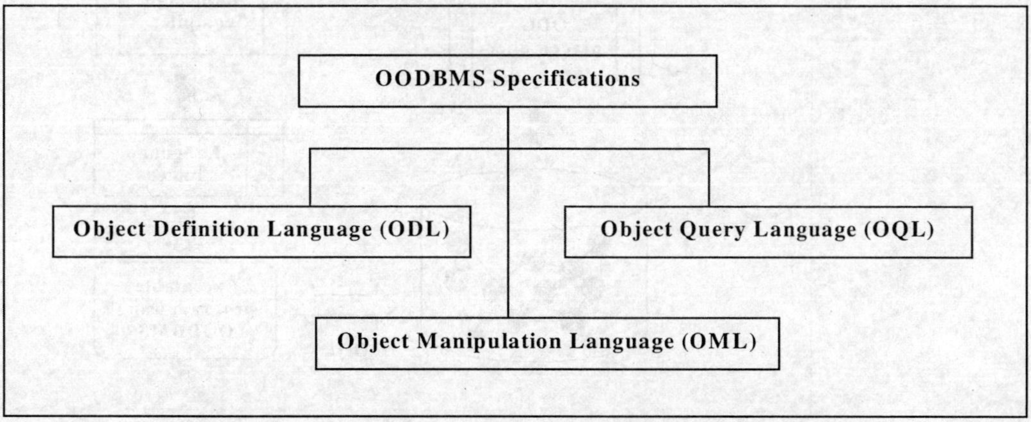

Fig. 10.39 Aspects of OODBMS as per ODMG specifications

Let us discuss these in brief.

- **Object Definition Language (ODL)** is similar in concept to the Data Definition Language (DDL) of SQL.
- **Object Query Language (OQL)** is similar in concept to the Data Manipulation Language (DML) of SQL. It provides support for most common SQL SELECT statement forms, including joins. However, it does not provide support for SQL INSERT, UPDATE or DELETE.
- **Object Manipulation Language (OML)** is an extension of OQL. Whereas OQL is a generic standard that can be used across OOP languages (just as SQL syntax is the same no matter from which programming language you access it), OML is language-specific. Thus, OQL would always be the same for Java, C++ and C#, but OML would be different for these languages. OML includes support for SQL INSERT, UPDATE and DELETE statements.

Overall, the execution of a program using these features goes via the steps shown in Fig. 10.40. As we can see, the data definitions go via the ODL route, whereas the data manipulations go through OQL and OML.

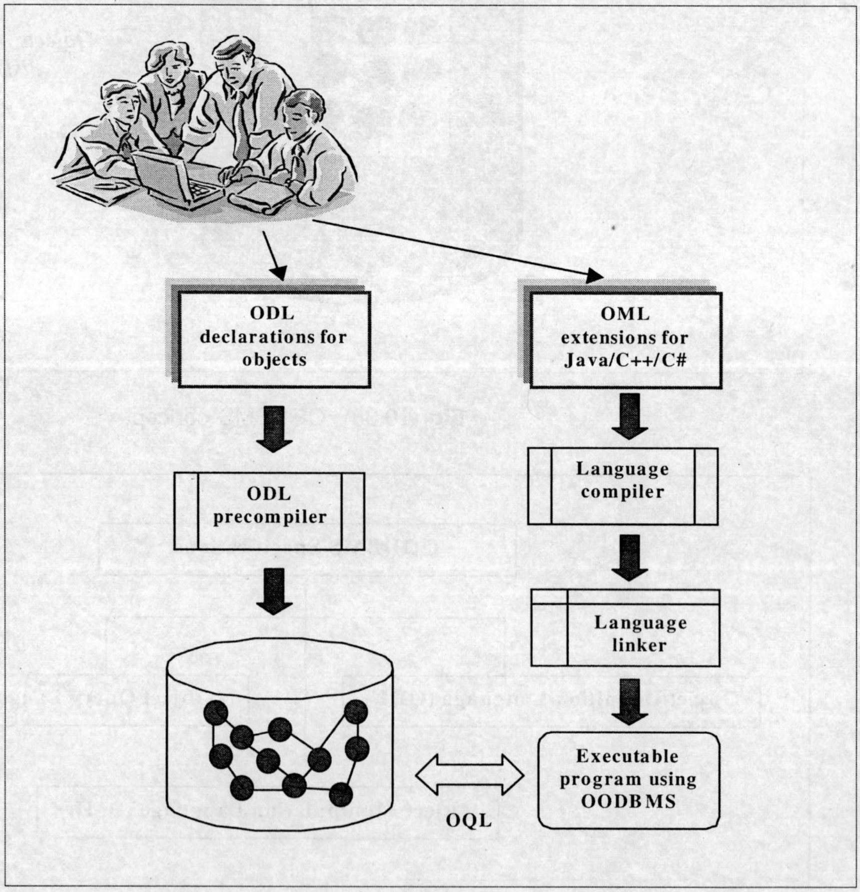

Fig. 10.40 Steps in development of program using OODBMS

We shall later discuss some simple examples of ODL, OQL and OML.

10.6.2 When Should OODBMS be Used?

Traditional business applications require data to be stored in the form of rows and columns. For example, a payroll application would need employee details to be stored in one table, the payment details in another, and so on, all in a tabular form. This makes the conceptual understanding as well as the retrieval of the data quite easy. However, for applications that deal with complicated data types, this style may not be suitable. This is because, in these applications, it is not wise to split the data into rows and columns, and instead, the data must be stored in its original form. In other words, an object should be stored as an object, and not as a group of rows and columns. Fig. 10.41 illustrates the idea.

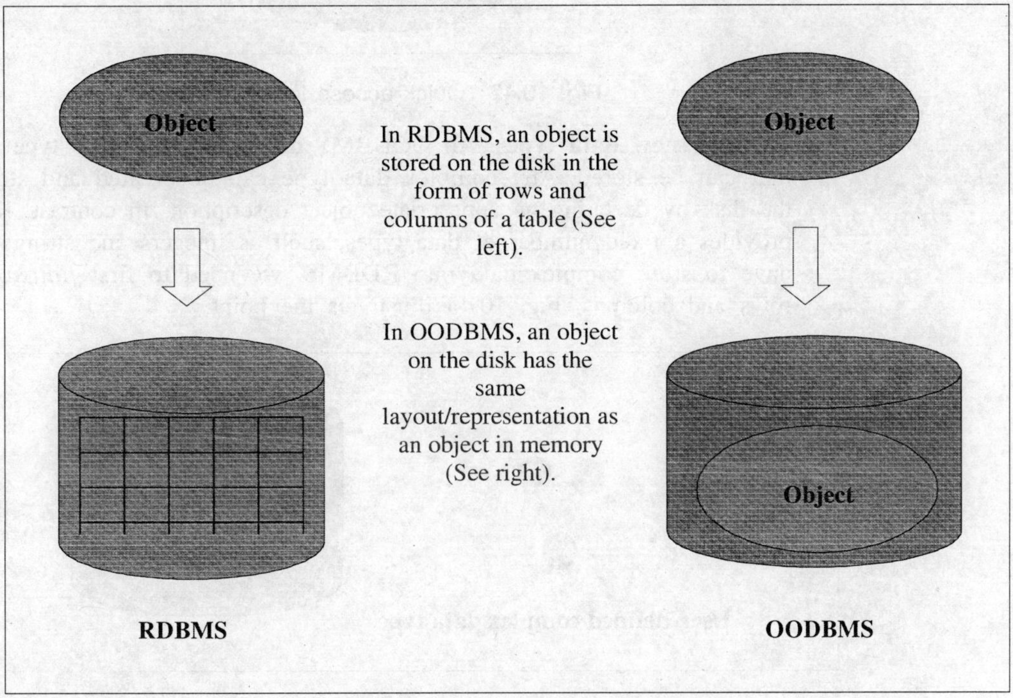

Fig. 10.41 RDBMS versus OODBMS storage concept

What are these applications? Typically, these applications consist of Computer Aided Design (CAD) drawings, Computer Aided Machines (CAM), Computer Aided Software Engineering (CASE) tools, and so on. Therefore, we can say that all engineering, scientific and construction activities, among others, fall within this category.

10.6.3 Advantages of OODBMS

Let us summarise the advantages offered by OODBMS, especially in contrast to the features of RDBMS.

1. **Quicker access to information**: An OODBMS keeps track of objects via their unique object IDs. This means that a search operation moves from one object to another via these IDs, and not through complex foreign key traversals. As a result, the search operations in OODBMS are generally faster than those in RDBMS. Fig. 10.42 shows the idea.

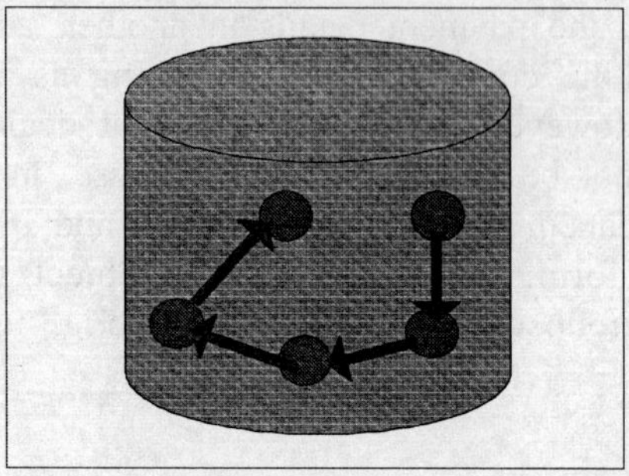

Fig. 10.42 Quick access to information

2. **Creating new data types**: An OODBMS does not restrict the type of data that can be stored. Any complex data type can be created and stored on the disk by declaring an appropriate object description. In contrast, RDBMS provides a fixed number of data types, such as integers and strings. If we have to store complex data into RDBMS, we need to first *flatten* it into rows and columns. Fig. 10.43 illustrates the point.

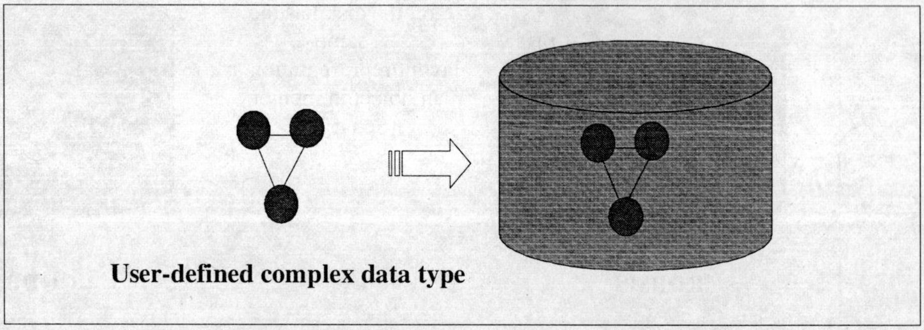

Fig. 10.43 Storing complex data

3. **Integration with OOP languages**: As we have mentioned, OODBMS is actually an extension of OOP languages, such as Java and C++. As such, they represent the in-memory data structures on the disk. This means that there is no impedance mismatch between the language and the DBMS. What do we mean by this? Contrast this approach with the traditional approach of accessing an RDBMS table in a language such as C. In this case, we would typically execute a SELECT query via the C program, which may return multiple rows. The C program stores them in a buffer (i.e. main memory), and processes them one-by-one. Therefore, the view of the C program is one row at a time, whereas that of the RDBMS is multiple rows at one shot. This difference is called imped-

ance mismatch. As opposed to this, an OODBMS deals with one object at a time, just as an OOP language would do. Moreover, OODBMS preserves the original characteristics of an object, because it stores it *as is*. Fig. 10.44 depicts this in a nutshell.

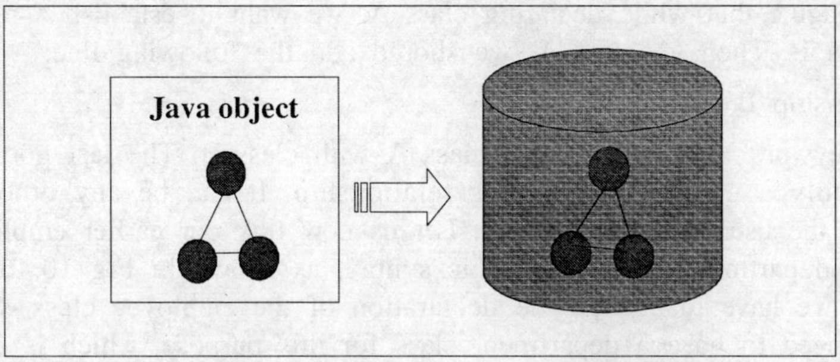

Fig. 10.44 Integration with OOP languages

10.6.4 Examples of ODL, OQL and OML

Having discussed the theory behind OODBMS, let us move on to the syntax of ODL, OQL and OML. Since we do not intend to *teach* these languages here, the focus would be to simply give an overview. More specifically, we shall make an attempt to grasp the broad-level syntaxes, and not worry about the precise rules of these languages.

Declaring classes using ODL

The declaration of a class in ODL involves three main aspects:

- The keyword *interface*
- The name of the class
- A list of attributes of the class

The keyword *interface* in ODL means class. That is, just as we declare a class in Java, C++ or C#, by using the keyword *class*, we need to use the keyword *interface* in the case of OODBMS.

An example of a class declaration in ODL is shown in Fig. 10.45. We can see that this declaration is quite similar to a class declaration in an OOP language.

```
interface employee
{
        attribute integer ID;
        attribute integer name;
        attribute string address;
        attribute string department_ID;
};
```

Fig. 10.45 Declaration of a class in ODL

Declaring class relationships using ODL

We know that SQL uses the concept of foreign key declarations to establish relationships between tables. In a similar fashion, ODL uses the keyword *relationship* for this purpose. Suppose we have two classes–A and B. Furthermore, let us imagine that while declaring class A, we want to establish a relationship with class B. Then, in class A, we should add the following line:

relationship B rel-a-b;

The keyword *relationship* links class A with class B. The last portion 'rel-a-b' is simply a name given to this relationship. It can be any other suitable name, as the user finds appropriate. Let us now link our earlier employee class with the department class using this syntax, as shown in Fig. 10.46. For this purpose, we have to change the declaration of the employee class. Obviously, we will need to have a department class for this purpose, which is not shown here.

```
interface employee
{
        attribute integer ID;
        attribute integer name;
        attribute string address;
        attribute string department_ID;
        relationship department rel-emp-dept;
};
```

Fig. 10.46 Declaration of a relationship in ODL

Declaring keys using ODL

In ODL, an attribute is declared to be a key attribute by using the keyword *key*. The key declaration must be made before the internal description of a class begins. That is, the keyword *key* must follow the class declaration. An example of this is shown in Fig. 10.47.

```
interface employee (key ID)
{
        attribute integer ID;
        attribute integer name;
        attribute string address;
        attribute string department_ID;
};
```

Fig. 10.47 Declaration of a key in ODL

If more than one attribute make up the key, then we should list all these attributes inside a parenthesis after the keyword *key*, as shown in Fig. 10.48.

What we are saying here is that no employee can have the same ID and the same department ID. That is, the combination of the employee ID and the department ID must be unique, although on their own they may be duplicated. If two employees have the same employee ID, their department ID must differ.

Conversely, if their department ID is the same, then their employee ID must be different. Some of the allowed and disallowed values are shown in Fig. 10.49. Note that in part (b) of the figure, we have the employee record A occurring twice within department A, and employee record 300 occurring twice in department D. Both of these cases are disallowed, since within a department, the same employee must not be duplicated. However, in case (a), there is no problem since the combination of employee ID and department ID is always unique.

```
interface employee (key (ID, department_ID))
{
        attribute integer ID;
        attribute integer name;
        attribute string address;
        attribute string department_ID;
};
```

Fig. 10.48 Declaration of a key with multiple attributes in ODL

Employee ID	Department ID
100	A
200	A
200	B
300	C
300	D
400	D
400	E

(a) Allowed set of values

Employee ID	Department ID
100	A
200	A
200	A
300	C
300	D
300	D
400	E

(b) This is not allowed

Fig. 10.49 Examples of keys values: What is allowed, what is not?

Interestingly, the declaration of key in Fig. 10.50 is different from the one shown earlier, and it also has a different meaning.

```
interface employee (key ID, department_ID)
{
        attribute integer ID;
        attribute integer name;
        attribute string address;
        attribute string department_ID;
};
```

Fig. 10.50 Declaration of multiple keys in ODL

Note that we have now removed the bracket surrounding the attributes of the key. This changes the meaning dramatically. The employee ID and the department ID must be independently different. Both attributes are keys by themselves. Now, every employee ID and department ID must be unique on their own. Thus, we no longer need only the combination of the employee ID and the department ID to be unique, but we also need the uniqueness of the two attributes. Thus, now what is allowed and what is not, is shown in Fig. 10.51.

Employee ID	Department ID
100	A
200	B
300	C
400	D
500	E
600	F
700	G

(a) Allowed set of values

Employee ID	Department ID
100	A
200	A
200	B
300	C
300	D
300	D
400	E

(b) This is not allowed

Fig. 10.51 Examples of keys values: What is allowed, what is not

Case (a) is straightforward, as we have unique values in the employee ID and the department ID columns. However, case (b), violates the key declaration in two ways:

- Employee IDs 200 and 300 repeat
- Department IDs A and D repeat

Moreover, as a side-effect, the combination of employee ID and department ID 300-D also repeats.

Reading data using OQL

We have mentioned that the Object Query Language (OQL) provides syntax and features similar to that of the SQL SELECT statement. Let us consider a simple example to understand this, as shown in Fig. 10.52.

```
SELECT e.department_ID
FROM employee e
WHERE e.name = "Ram"
```

Fig. 10.52 OQL query example

All the other major SQL features are also available in OQL, but we shall not discuss them here.

KEY TERMS AND CONCEPTS

Abstraction
Base class
Code reusability
Generalisation
Impedance mismatch
Inheritance
Attribute
Class
Encapsulation
Horizontal partitioning
Information hiding
Many-to-many association

- Message
- Method
- Modelling
- Object
- Object Database Management Group (ODMG)
- Object Definition Language (ODL)
- Object ID
- Object Manipulation Language (OML)
- Object orientation
- Object Oriented Database Management System (OODBMS)
- Object Query Language (OQL)
- Object technology
- One-to-many association
- Relationship
- Semantic gap
- Subclass
- Super class
- Vertical partitioning

CHAPTER SUMMARY

- **Object technology** is based on the concept of **objects**. An object is a self-contained representation of real-life objects.
- An object contains data (**attributes**) as well as the functions that operate on them (**methods**).
- Class is a template for similar kinds of objects. For example, *Person* can be a class, and Atul, Ana, Jui, and Harsh can be the objects of this class.
- Objects interact with each other by passing **messages** in an **Object Oriented** (**OO**) system.
- Object technology has emerged as a very popular method of analysis, design and systems development.
- **Abstraction** is a concept that allows the analyst/designer to focus on key aspects of a system. It frees the user from unnecessary details.
- By using **encapsulation**, attributes of a class can be protected. These are accessible only to the methods of that class. Thus, the outside world cannot access the attributes of the class.
- Encapsulation also ensures that the attributes and methods of a class stay close to each other, in a tight environment.
- The concept of **inheritance** helps create hierarchy of classes. For example, if *Person* is the class at the top (i.e. parent class), then *Man* and *Woman* can be the two classes at one level below (i.e. child classes).
- The parent class in an inheritance relationship is called as the **super class**. The child class is the **subclass**. The inheritance relationship can span many levels.
- There are several challenges in marrying object technology with RDBMS.
- We identify a record in RDBMS uniquely based on its primary key. In the case of an object, the object identifier identifies a unique object.
- There are several ways to model classes so that their data can be stored in RDBMS.
- Objects can be fragmented vertically or horizontally before they are stored in RDBMS tables.
- One object can map to one table, one object can be split into multiple tables, or multiple objects can be combined to form one table. The decision depends on the nature of the application.
- Care needs to be taken while mapping generalisation and binary relationships in objects to RDBMS tables.

- The **Object Oriented Database Management Systems (OODBMS)** allow objects to be stored as objects, and not as RDBMS tables.
- In OODBMS, there are three main aspects, similar to the DDL and DML portions of SQL.
- The **Object Definition Language (ODL)** is similar in concept to Data Definition Language (DDL) of SQL.
- The **Object Query Language (OQL)** is similar in concept to Data Manipulation Language (DML) of SQL.
- The **Object Manipulation Language (OML)** is an extension to OQL. Whereas OQL is a generic standard that can be used across OOP languages (just as SQL syntax is the same no matter from which programming language you access it), OML is language-specific.
- The choice of RDBMS versus OODBMS depends on the nature of the application being developed.

PRACTICE SET

Mark as true or false

1. Object and class mean the same thing.
2. Java is a non-OO language.
3. A method in object technology is similar to a function in traditional technologies.
4. In abstraction, we think about the minute details of an object.
5. Inheritance leads to specialisation relationships.
6. OODBMS uses the concept of tables.
7. A unique object ID identifies every object.
8. OQL is similar to the DML portion of SQL.
9. ODL is similar to the DDL portion of SQL.
10. There is no direct equivalent to DCL in OO technology.

Fill in the blanks

1. Attributes and methods make up _______.

   (a) an object (b) a template

   (c) a program (d) a function

2. The generic template for objects is called a ________.

   (a) method (b) message

   (c) program (d) class

3. The parent class in an inheritance relationship is called as ______.

   (a) subclass (b) super class

   (c) main class (d) father class

4. An example of an OOP language is _____.

(a) C (b) COBOL

(c) C++ (d) Pascal

5. In _____, we protect the attributes of a class.

(a) abstraction (b) polymorphism

(c) encapsulation (d) inheritance

6. To model _______, we need to create tables for super class and subclass.

(a) abstraction (b) polymorphism

(c) classes (d) generalisation

7. In order to store objects in RDBMS, we need to transform them into _______.

(a) classes (b) tables

(c) files (d) segments

8. _____ is similar to DML.

(a) OML (b) OCL

(c) ODL (d) OQL

9. The difference between a programming language and the way it accesses data is called _________.

(a) impedance mismatch (b) hierarchy difference

(c) impedance difference (d) level mismatch

10. In OODBMS, objects are stored as _______.

(a) tables (b) objects

(c) files (d) relations

Provide detailed answers to the following questions

1. Discuss the term *object technology*.
2. What is an object? How is it different from a class?
3. What are attributes and methods?
4. Explain the idea of abstraction.
5. What is inheritance?
6. Describe the meaning of the term encapsulation.
7. What are the various ways in which we can model an object as a table in RDBMS?
8. What is an OODBMS?
9. When should we use OODBMS?
10. Discuss the advantages of OODBMS.

Exercises

1. Learn more about an OOP language, such as Java or C++.
2. Investigate the precise differences between traditional analysis/design techniques and object technology.
3. What are the various ways of accessing RDBMS from an OOP language? (Hint: Learn more about ODBC, JDBC).
4. Given an object that needs to be stored in an RDBMS, which main characteristics would you look for?
5. How would you test a program written in OOP language that accesses RDBMS? (Hint: Look for aspects such as how to map classes to tables, how to represent primary/foreign key relationships, how to take care of referential integrity, etc).
6. Study more about an OODBMS product, such as ObjectStore or Jasmine.
7. Why do you think OODBMS has not caught up as much as it was expected to?
8. Is a hierarchical DBMS same as an OODBMS? Why?
9. What is RUP? (Hint: It stands for *Rational Unified Process*).
10. Find out more about three persons: Booch, Rambaugh and Jacobson and their contributions to object technology. (Hint: They are the pioneers of the Object Oriented Analysis and Design methodologies).

Chapter 11

Advanced Topics in DBMS

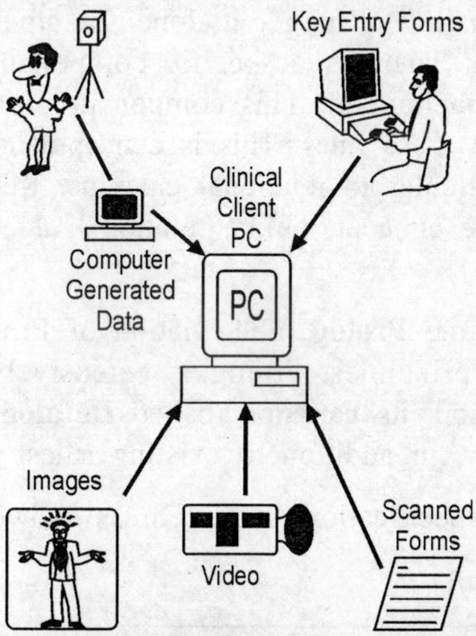

Multimedia in computer applications can show images, graphics, video, animation, and play all kinds of sounds. Multimedia databases takes care of database issues pertaining to multimedia data.

Chapter Highlights

- ◈ Meaning of Deductive Databases
- ◈ Internet Technology and Its Relevance to DBMS
- ◈ Technology of Multimedia Databases
- ◈ Overview of Digital Libraries
- ◈ Mobile Databases

11.1 DEDUCTIVE DATABASES

11.1.1 Features of Deductive Databases

We store information about things in a DBMS.

> A **deductive database system** contains capabilities to define rules. These rules can deduce or infer information to that stored in a database already.

The rules that are used in such databases are based on mathematics. That is why such rules are called **logic databases**.

There are two primary variations of deductive database systems: **expert database systems** and **knowledge-based database systems**. Deductive databases differ from these two types of databases in one major respect: In the case of expert or knowledge-based databases, the data needs to be present in the primary (main) memory of the computer. However, in a deductive database, this restriction is not present. The data can be in primary or secondary memory.

The fundamental concept in declarative databases is the use of a **declarative language**. We specify *what* we want, rather than *how* to get it done. In other words, we specify rules about the information. There is a specific component called as the **inference engine** or **deductive mechanism**. This component of a deductive database finds out new facts based on these rules. This is conceptually similar to the way RDBMS works, and in particular to relational calculus. Recall that relational calculus is also a declarative concept, unlike relational algebra.

There is a programming language by the name **Prolog** (abbreviation of Programming Logic), which is based on similar principles. Prolog is extensively used in deductive database technology. In addition, its variation (called **Datalog**) is also used. Datalog defines rules declaratively, in addition to existing rules.

In deductive databases, two basic types of specifications are used, as shown in Fig. 11.1.

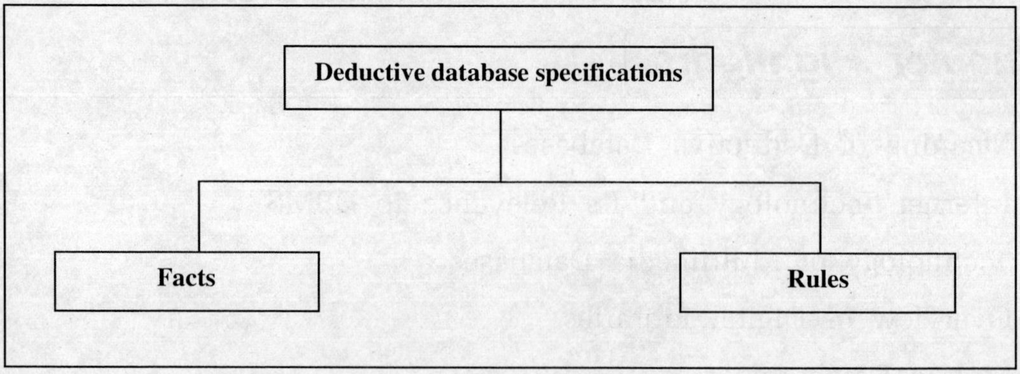

Fig. 11.1 Types of specifications in deductive databases

Let us discuss these types.

- **Facts** are similar to tables in RDBMS. These are described in a manner that is quite close to the describing of relations. However, unlike tables in RDBMS, there is no concept of attributes or columns here. We know that in the case of RDBMS, the value of a column within a row signifies some real-world fact about that row. Here, there is no such concept. Instead, what is important is the *position* of the column in a row.
- **Rules** are similar to the views in RDBMS. Rules specify and describe virtual (non-existing) tables. Often, in RDBMS, we can infer information from database tables by using views. Similarly, we can deduce information from facts by using rules. This shows that facts are similar to tables, whereas rules are similar to views.

We have discussed OODBMS earlier. Where do deductive databases fit with respect to OODBMS? We know that the basic premise in OODBMS is to try and provide a simple mechanism in order to model real-world objects. We try to model the structure and the behaviour of objects in OODBMS. However, this is not the case in deductive databases. Here, the focus is to try and derive more comprehension from existing information by providing additional details in the form of rules. In the near future, the addition of deductive capabilities to existing OODB features is expected to give birth to what would be termed as **Deductive Object Oriented Databases (DOODB).**

We now provide a brief outline of what the Prolog language can do, in order to understand the capabilities of deductive database technology.

11.1.2 An Overview of Logic

What is **mathematical logic?** In our daily lives, when people disagree on certain issues, some say that their arguments are *logical* and that the other party is speaking *illogically*. What does this mean? This simply means that the first group of people is using logical reasoning to arrive at some conclusions. Mathematical logic–also called as **symbolic logic**, deals with the rules of logical reasoning. In early days of computing, mathematical logic was used only at the 1GL machine level – that is the lowest level. However, artificial intelligence is aimed at establishing mathematical logic at higher levels such as 3GL.

The most popular 3GLs, such as COBOL, C, BASIC, C++ are not based on the principle of mathematical logic. These languages were developed to provide data manipulation and computation. However, they cannot be used for simulating an expert's reasoning. They work fine when, say 1000 records are to be read from a file, processed in some way and added into a database. The expert systems developed by using modern languages (such as Prolog) have been specifically designed for **artificial intelligence** attempts to solve problems in various domains. Expert systems can perform intelligent reasoning and explain how they draw their conclusions. Therefore, these programming languages are based on the principles of mathematical logic.

Mathematical logic is based on two factors:

- **Facts** – Facts are pieces of fundamental knowledge. For instance, 'A is son of B' can be a fact, since it is not based on any conditions.

PROLOG is a very concise but effective language. It is very logical in nature, and is usually based on a series of logical/Boolean (Yes/No) answers.

- **Rules** – When facts depend on certain conditions, they become rules. For instance, when we say *'If you get at least 35 marks out of 100, you will be declared a successful candidate'*, it is a rule.

A deductive database system based on artificial intelligence works on a set of facts and rules that describe objects and their relations. Facts are statements that are always unconditionally true while rules declare properties and relations that depend on a given condition.

11.1.3 Knowledge Representation

What is **knowledge representation**? Let us consider a simple example to illustrate the concepts learned so far and see how knowledge can be represented. Suppose we have a relationship, as shown in Fig. 11.2.

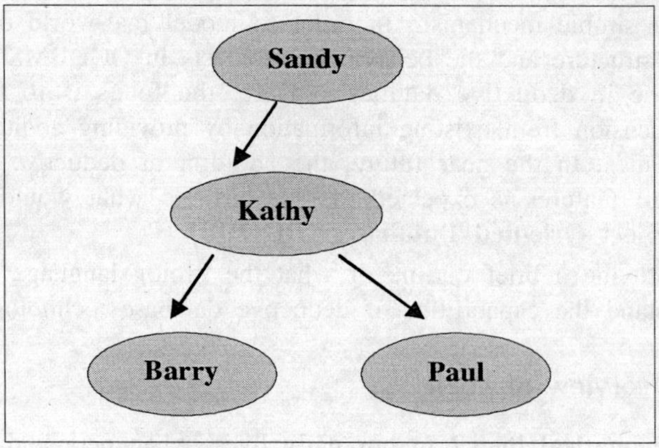

Fig. 11.2 A sample family tree

The figure shows a sample family tree. How would a deductive database system represent this information? Of course, it has to make use of facts and rules for this, as discussed earlier. Let us write this family tree in the Prolog language as shown in Fig. 11.3.

child (Kathy, Sandy) child (Barry, Kathy) child (Paul, Kathy)	Facts
parent (x, y) :- child (y, x)	Rule

Fig. 11.3 A Prolog program (left box) for the family tree

The program (shown in the left box of the figure) consists of four statements: three facts and one rule. The facts represent family relations. They state that Kathy is a child of Sandy and that Barry and Paul are Kathy's children. The fourth clause is a rule that states that 'For all x and y, x is a parent of y if y is a child of x'. This is how knowledge is represented inside a deductive database system. Of course, the exact way in which this is done would differ from language to language. However, the principles of describing facts and rules as knowledge remain the same.

Having established the facts and rules, how do deductive database systems allow us to derive intelligence from them? For this, let us extend the same example. Suppose, someone who does not know much about the family described earlier, wants to know if Kathy is Sandy's child. For this, the following question may be asked to the program:

? child (Kathy, Sandy)

The program would come back with the message:

Yes

The program comes back with a positive message since it finds a fact that states this relation. Similarly, if someone types:

? child (Kathy, Paul)

The program would respond with:

No

Going further, we can query our knowledge established so far to find who is Sandy's child and whose child is Paul.

? child (x, Sandy)

x = Kathy

? child (Paul, x)

x = Kathy

All these answers are based on facts. Remember we had a rule as the fourth statement. How can we use that rule to derive some information? Suppose we ask the program who is Kathy's parent, using this rule.

? parent (x, Kathy)

x = Sandy

Thus, using the basic principles of facts and rules, knowledge can be represented and then used to query that knowledge in a variety of ways. All artificial intelligence systems work on similar principles.

If we study the example carefully, we would realise that to answer a questions such as who is child or parent of whom, we would have also worked in a similar manner. We would have thought about the facts and rules and come up with similar answers. The point is, once we are able to set up all the facts and rules, we can let the artificial intelligence system take care of the answers. As discussed earlier, however, establishing facts and rules itself is not easy, simply because there are so many of them. But for special purpose smaller applications, that should certainly be possible.

A great amount of research is still being carried out on deductive database systems. In the coming years, perhaps artificial intelligence systems based on deductive databases will do things which are unthinkable at the moment.

11.2 INTERNET AND DBMS

11.2.1 What is WWW?

World Wide Web (WWW) is an application that uses the **Internet** for communications, with TCP/IP as the underlying transport mechanism. Many companies set up Internet **Websites**. A Website, like a brochure, is a collection of **Web pages**. These pages on a Website are stored digitally on the **Web server**.

The function of the Web server is to store the Web pages and send them to a client computer as and when it requests for them. The Website address is called as the **Uniform Resource Locator (URL).** It corresponds to the first page (also called as **home page**) of the Website. Internally, a Web page is a computer file stored on the disk of the server. The file contains *tags* written in a codified form. These tags decide how the file would look when displayed on a computer screen.

11.2.2 Web server and Web browser

A Web server is a program running on a server computer. Additionally, it consists of the Website containing a number of Web pages. A Web page constitutes simply a special type of computer file written in a specially designed language called as **Hyper Text Markup Language (HTML)**. Each Web page can contain text, graphics, sound, video and animation that people want to see or hear.

The Web server constantly and passively waits for a request for a Web page from a browser program and when any such request is received, it locates that corresponding page and sends it to the requesting client computer. This request-response model is governed by a protocol called as **Hyper Text Transfer Protocol (HTTP)**. For instance, HTTP software on the client computer prepares the request for a Web page, whereas the HTTP software on the server interprets such a request and prepares a response to be sent back to the client. Thus, both client and server computers need to have HTTP software running on them. We should not confuse HTTP with HTML. HTML is a special language in which the Web pages are written and stored on the server. HTTP is a protocol which governs the dialog between the client and server.

A Web browser acts as the client in the WWW interaction. Using this program, a user requests for a Web page (which is a disk file, as we have noted) stored on a Web server. The Web server locates this Web page and sends it back to the client computer. The Web browser then interprets the Web page written in the HTML language/format and displays it on the screen of the client computer.

Deductive databases are based on principles that are similar to PROLOG and other logic-based languages.

11.2.3 Hyper Text Markup Language (HTML)

A language called *Hyper Text Markup Language (HTML)* is used in order to create Web pages. HTML is used to specify where and how to display headings, where a new paragraph starts, which text to display in what font and color, and so on.

HTML uses *tags* to define the contents of Web pages. Tags are enclosed in angled brackets. For example, a tag <I> indicates the beginning of text in italics. Thus, when a Web page containing a <I> tag is sent by a Web server, the Web browser interprets this tag and starts displaying the contents after this point in italics. Most tags end with a corresponding </> tag. For example, the <I> tag would end with a </I> tag. There are many such tags to create document titles, headings, changing fonts and styles, and so on.

For example, let us consider how the tag pair <U> and </U> can be used to change the text font to underlined. This is shown in Fig. 11.4.

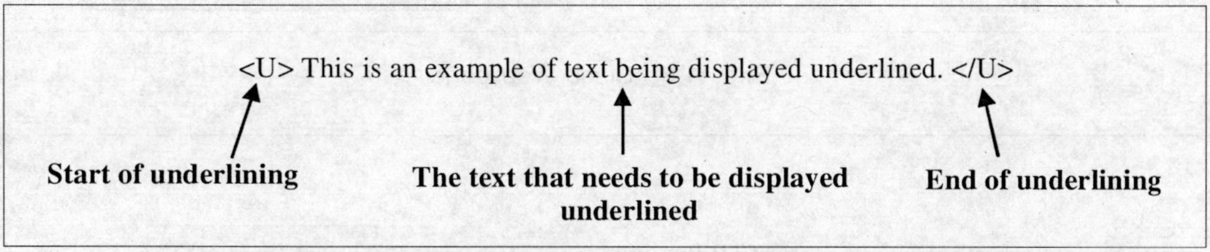

Fig. 11.4 Example of the <U> and </U> HTML tags to make the specified text underlined

When a browser hits the <U> portion of an HTML file, it realises that the following section of the text embedded within the <U> and </U> tags needs to be displayed underlined. Therefore, it displays this text underlined, as shown in Fig. 11.5.

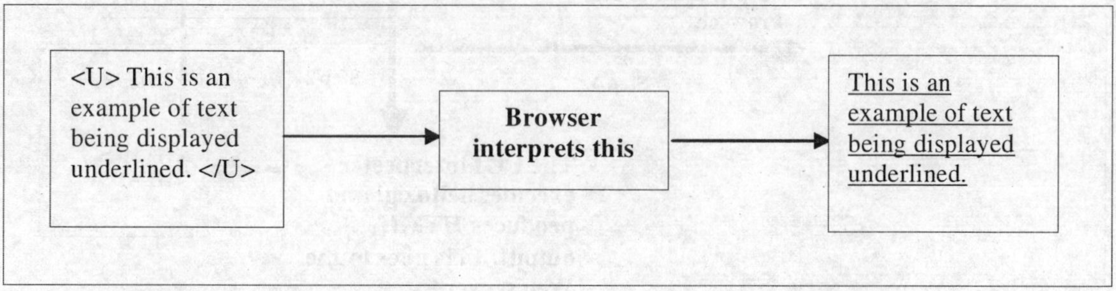

Fig. 11.5 Output resulting from the use of the <U> and </U> HTML tags

11.2.4 Dynamic Web Pages

Many Web pages are **static**. That is, their content does not change on the basis of request made. In other words, when a browser requests the server to send a static Web page, the server does not execute any application program. It simply finds the requested Web page (which is an HTML file on its disk) and sends it back to the browser as it is. Of course, the page should have been created and stored on the server prior to this, and it cannot be created at run time. In contrast, a **dynamic Web page** is a program in response to a Web page request. The output of this program (which is also in HTML) is sent back to the Web browser. For ease of understanding, we can show the differences between static and dynamic Web pages as shown in Fig. 11.6 and Fig. 11.7.

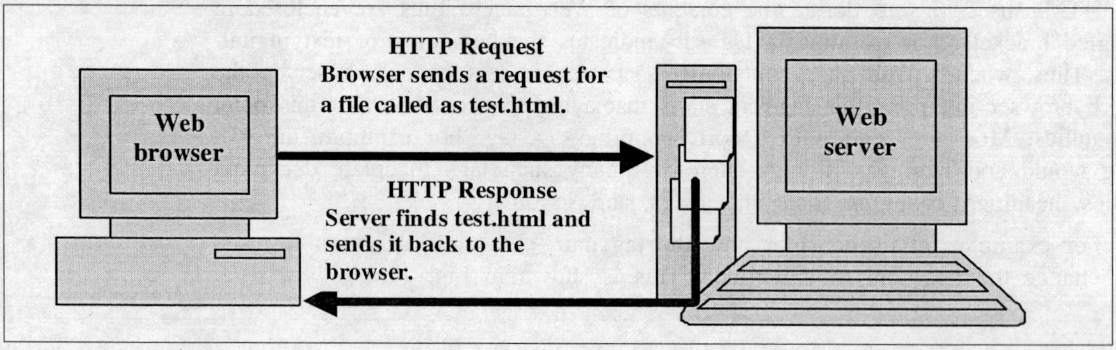

Fig. 11.6 Static Web page

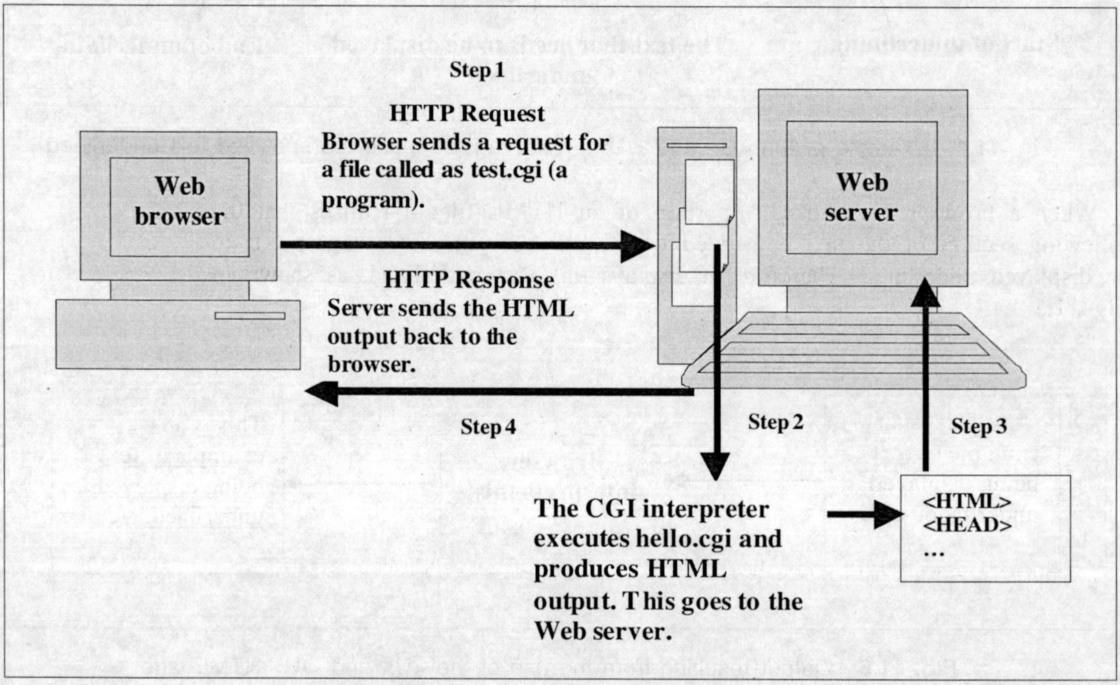

Fig. 11.7 Dynamic Web page

In case of static Web pages, the browser sends the address of the desired Web page in the form of URL to the Web server. After this, the Web server locates the requested file on its disk and sends it back to the browser. In this case, the browser has requested for a file called as test.html. The server locates that file and sends it back to the browser.

Now let us consider what happens in case of a dynamic Web page. Here, the URL does not correspond to the address of a per-created (static) Web page. Instead, it is the address of a program to be executed on the Web server. There are various programming languages/technologies used for this purpose, such as **Active Server Pages (ASP), Java Server Pages (JSP)** or **Common Gateway**

Interface (CGI). These are programs that get executed on the server. Their output is also in plain HTML. This output is sent to the browser for display.

In the following example, the browser sends a request for a program called test.cgi. The Web server locates test.cgi and hands it over to the CGI interpreter program. The CGI interpreter executes the program test.cgi and produces HTML output, which goes back to the Web server. The server sends this HTML output back to the browser. Note how different this is from the retrieval of the static Web page called test.html.

We can now very well understand that dynamic Web pages are extremely important. Imagine that we need to show the Internet users something that is constantly changing: for example, the inventory balance of a product. To do this, we will need to create a program (in ASP, JSP, CGI, etc.). This program would reside on the Web server. This program would will accept a request from the client, and search the product database maintained on the server for the desired product. It would read the inventory record for that product, extract the inventory balance, and send it in HTML format to the browser. The browser will then display the output. It should be noted that inventory transaction such as receipts, issues and returns would be updating the product database records continuously on the server. At any moment, when a user clicks on a particular product to check on the balance, the product code and the URL of the Web page (in which this program for the product database search is stored) are sent from the browser to the server. The server then locates the Web page (knowing that it is a program from the extension such as .asp or .jsp), it loads it in its memory, executes it with the help of the appropriate (ASP, JSP or CGI) compiler/interpreter, and sends the results in HTML format back to the browser. This is how a user gets real time information about various things.

We can now imagine how dynamic Web pages are useful in getting the latest information on weather forecasts, stock prices, and many other subjects. The only point to remember is that some other programs have to do the job of updating the respective databases.

11.2.5 Issues in Web Databases

We shall now examine a few issues related to DBMS that need to be addressed in the context of Web technologies.

1. **Constant availability**: The Internet is always *on*. In other words, at any point of time, someone or the other in the world accesses the Internet. This also means that it needs to be constantly available. Applications running on the Internet must provide for 24×7 support. These applications make heavy use of DBMS technology for storing huge amounts of data. Consequently, it is also very significant that DBMS is able to stand up to such demands. Several approaches are used in order to ensure this. We have already studied most of them, such as data replication, data redundancy and data distribution.
2. **Security**: The Internet is an open platform. The Web can be accessed by anyone armed with a simple Web browser and an Internet connection.

Multimedia is exciting and the way forward. Plain text-based computing will continue to dominate serious business applications for at least a few more decades. However, multimedia applications will become the norm for all entertainment and many business applications as well. It would provide sound, animation, graphics, video, and so on. The faster the hardware and more optimised the compression techniques, the better it will be.

This also means that one need not possess any special privileges to browse the Internet. However, when it comes to accessing specific applications running on the Internet, appropriate security measures to ensure authentication, authorisation, integrity and confidentiality must be in place. The DBMS is closely associated with all these aspects. Many times security breaches on the Internet occur in the form of access to databases directly, bypassing the application. Such attacks must be prevented by creating and practicing an elaborate security policy and by using the appropriate technical tools.

3. **Transaction processing capabilities**: There have been instances when literally millions of users have tried to access the same Website at the same time. Examples of such sites are the ones that host live sports updates, news telecasts, election results, and so on. Such sites must be able to weather the demands of such a high number of users. This also means that the DBMS that these sites use must be able to process transactions at a very rapid pace. It must be able to recover from transactional problems quite quickly. Worse still, if these sites make use of distributed/replicated databases, the transaction processing logic has to take care of these aspects as well.
4. **Concurrency**: We can guess from the above points that Web databases need a high amount of concurrency. The same table, or for that matter, the same row, may be accessed by millions of users at the same time. The DBMS must cater to such requirements by providing a very sophisticated concurrency model. We have discussed all the issues and the possible solutions related to concurrency earlier.
5. **Support for XML**: **Extensible Markup Language (XML)** and its variants have gained a lot of popularity over the last few years. XML is a data description language that allows data to be exchanged between applications quite easily, as opposed to the earlier proprietary standards. These days, most popular DBMS products allow the data to be directly stored or retrieved as XML.

11.3 MULTIMEDIA DATABASES

11.3.1 What is Multimedia?

The modern computer systems can also be used for the following:

- Drawing, storing and viewing pictures
- Storing sounds and playing them back
- Storing videos and playing them back

Computers store textual information in the form of bits and bytes. We can codify various characters of the English language as a series of zeroes and ones. Once this codification is ready, we can continue to use our language of words and sentences, and let the computer treat these as a series of appropriate zeroes and ones, depending on the character.

However, pictures, videos and sounds are not made up of alphabets and numbers. How can a computer recognise and store them? How can we codify information about these so that a computer can store them? Clearly, we cannot have a scheme such as ASCII or EBCDIC here. What is the solution, then?

The concept of **multimedia** came into being to resolve this problem of codification of pictures, videos and sounds. As the name says, multimedia means *multi*ple *media*. Thus, with the use of multimedia, we can not only access the usual textual information, but also information in the form of pictures, videos and sounds, which can be created by using a computer, stored inside a computer and played back.

Multimedia is used in several areas, such as document management, training, marketing, travel, education, entertainment, advertising, control systems, and so on.

11.3.2 Sampling and Quantising

If we want to transform a picture, video or an audio signal such that it can be mapped to the computer-recognisable data of 0 and 1, we must *map* it as digital data. This means that, we must *measure* the signal in the form of numbers; when we do that, the signal becomes equivalent to what it would be when interpreted by a computer!

Two techniques are used together for *measuring* such a signal. They are **sampling** and **quantising**. Put simply, we must determine *how frequently* we should measure the signal and *how much signal range* we should have.

Measuring audio signals at fixed intervals of time is called sampling. Thus, if we decide that an audio signal would be measured 60 times a second, the sampling rate would be 60. So, if we have an audio signal as shown in Fig. 11.8, we can sample it as shown. Obviously, the higher the sampling rate, the better is the representation of the audio signal inside the computer, as we would have more samples.

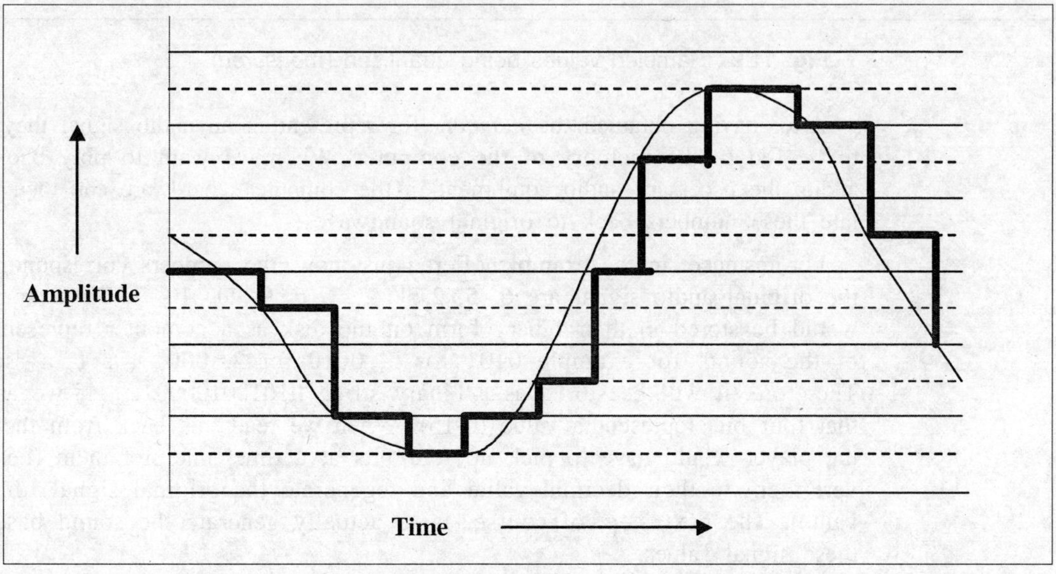

Fig. 11.8 Sampling an audio waveform

Having determined how many times the signal should be *measured*, the next step is to assess the range of amplitudes. If we take 60 samples per second, we would have 60 discrete numbers for the audio signal. In quantising, we assign them numbers depending on their amplitude values. Obviously, a 0 would represent the weakest signal or a lack of signal, whereas a powerful signal would get translated into a high positive value. The question that arises is: how much is the quantising range? The answer is: the higher the range, the better is the audio quality, since finer audio details can be captured on a broader scale. Fig. 11.9 illustrates the idea. The numbers thus obtained are the signal values for the original audio signal, as stored inside a computer.

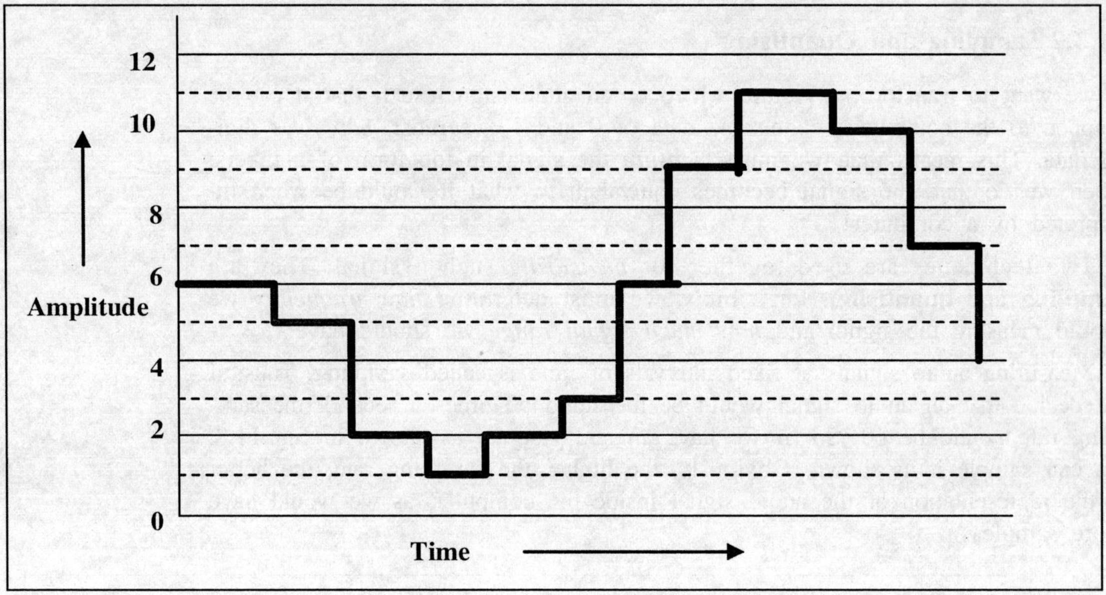

Fig. 11.9 Sampled values being quantised (*measured*)

After having obtained the *numbers* for representing an audio signal they need to be fed to the memory of the computer. When we want to play back this audio, the necessary audio equipment in the computer's hardware can then translate these numbers back to original soundwaves!

For instance, in the example offered just now, the numbers corresponding to the original audio signal are 6, 5, 2, 1, 2, 3, 6, 9, 11, 10, 7. These numbers would be stored in their binary form on the disk as a computer representation of the sound, for example 0101 for 5, 0010 for 2, 0001 for 1, as so on. Therefore, it will be stored as a binary string 010100100001.... if we assume that four bits represent a value (0-15). When we read this back from the disk, the player would have to pick up four bits at a time, interpret them (i.e. convert them to their decimal value and regenerate the original signal for each value). The next step, of course, is to actually generate the sound based on these signal values.

The entire process can be summarised as shown in Fig. 11.10.

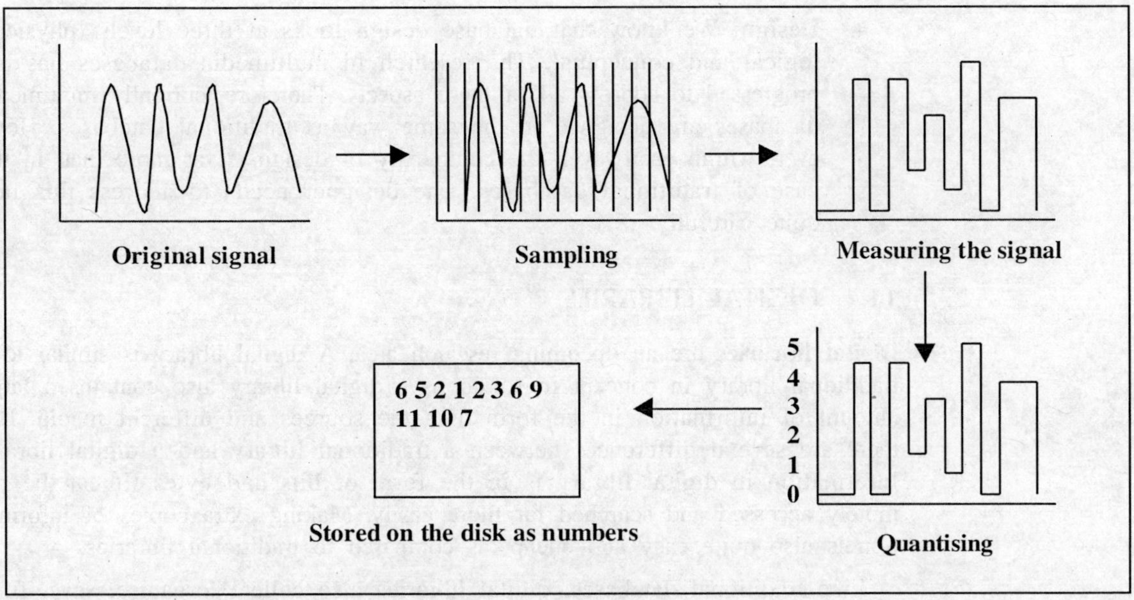

Fig. 11.10 Sampling and quantising

A similar process needs to be employed for graphics/video.

11.3.3 Issues in Multimedia Databases

Multimedia applications can hold thousands of pictures, audio files and videos. They must be stored in the most efficient manner and retrieved as and when necessary in the shortest possible time. To make this possible, the design of multimedia databases must be well thoughtout. Several issues need to be kept in mind while designing multimedia databases. They are:

1. **Performance**: Multimedia applications demand a very high level of performance. For example, video must be delivered at a speed of 60 picture frames per second. If the speed is below this threshold, the video would appear to be shaky and would not appeal to the users. Some of the important techniques used to deal with performance issues are query optimisation and data compression.

2. **Storage**: Storing multimedia files is not easy. One has to think about problems in the form of how to represent, compress, map, archive, buffer and backup such data during any file operation. Several multimedia file standards are available, such as MPEG and JPEG. Vendors who comply with such standards automatically solve some of these problems. DBMS products provide a special data type called as **Binary Large Object (BLOB)**, which allows multimedia data to be stored in the form of bitmaps. The major problem in this category of issues is related to data synchronisation and compression.

3. **Modelling**: Multimedia databases can hold complex objects. Modelling such objects is not easy, since they cannot be easily mapped to the standard data types.

4. **Design**: We know that database design looks at three levels: physical, logical and conceptual. The research in multimedia databases has not progressed to address all of these aspects. Therefore, currently multimedia databases are designed in the same way as traditional databases. However, within each level, the complexity of design is far more than in the case of traditional databases. The designer needs to address this fact quite carefully.

11.4 DIGITAL LIBRARIES

Digital libraries are an upcoming research area. A digital library is similar to a traditional library in concept in so far as a digital library also contains a large amount of information in the form of some sources and different media. But there are several differences between a traditional library and a digital library. Information in digital library is in the form of bits and bytes. It can be remotely accessed and searched far more easily. Making extra copies of information is also quite easy and cheap, as compared to traditional libraries.

Like traditional databases, digital libraries also collect, organise, save, find, process, retrieve and provide data. They can also contain multiple media. Handling of complex data types and different types of data is possible. However, in the case of most digital libraries, there is no central administrator (unlike a Database Administrator or DBA). Also, the quality standards of data in digital libraries is less rigid, because of the lack of centralised control.

11.5 MOBILE DATABASES

11.5.1 What is Mobile Computing?

In the early days all computing was *wired*. In other words, a physical cable needed to exist between computers that communicated with each other and worked together to form a network. This has changed with the advances in the area of **wireless networking**. With wireless networking, computers need not be connected to each other by physical cables. They can communicate with each other via air. This advancement led to the development of **mobile computing**.

Mobile computing allows users to communicate with each other and manage their work while on the move.

Mobile computing is extremely handy for people and organisations who work in geographically diverse areas. Examples of such people are marketing staff, who are constantly on the move making presentations in one city today or negotiating a contact in another city the very next day.

Mobile computing is very interesting and useful. However, it also comes with its own set of problems, as follows:

- *Software problems*: Data management, Transaction management, Data recovery

- *Hardware problems*: Small bandwidth, Limited power supply to the mobile units, Changing locations of required information (e.g. air, ground, vehicles).

11.5.2 Case Study - WAP

To understand how mobile computing works, we shall consider the example of the **Wireless Application Protocol (WAP)**. WAP allows mobile users to access the Internet from their cell phones. We shall quickly summarise how WAP works. The specific ideas related to the working of WAP can be applied to other wireless protocols to a certain extent.

The **WAP gateway** is a device that logically sits between the client (called as **WAP device**) and the server (called as **origin server**). Several new terms have been introduced with the development of WAP. Let us understand them.

- A *WAP device* is any mobile device such as a mobile phone or a PDA that can be used to access mobile computing services. The idea is that the device can be any mobile device as long as it supports WAP.
- An *origin server* is any Web server on the Internet.
- The *WAP gateway* enables a WAP device to communicate with an origin server.

In the wired Internet architecture, both the client (a Web browser) and the server (a Web server) understand and work with the HTTP protocol. Therefore, no such gateway is required between the two. However, in the case of WAP, the client (i.e. a WAP device) runs WAP as the communications protocol, and not HTTP, while the server (the origin server) continues to work with HTTP. Therefore, some translation is required between the two. This is precisely what a WAP gateway is used for; it acts as an interpreter that does two things:

1. It takes WAP requests sent by the client and translates them to HTTP requests for forwarding them on to the origin server.
2. It takes HTTP responses sent by the origin server and translates them to WAP responses for forwarding them on to the client.

This is shown in Fig. 11.11.

We can now describe a simple interaction between a mobile user and the Internet with the help of the following steps:

1. The user presses a button, selects an option (which internally selects the buried URL) or explicitly enters a URL on the mobile device. This is similar to the way in which an Internet user makes a request for a Web page on the browser. This request is received by the **WAP browser** in the mobile device. A WAP browser is a software program running on the WAP device that interprets WAP content, similar to the way a Web browser interprets HTML content. The WAP browser is responsible for sending requests from the WAP device to the WAP gateway and receiving responses from the WAP gateway, and interpreting them (i.e. displaying them on the screen of the mobile device).

Wireless computing is the way forward. People do not like to use wires to connect their computers to the power supply or to the network interface any more. The mobile user is most likely the driver of future computer applications.

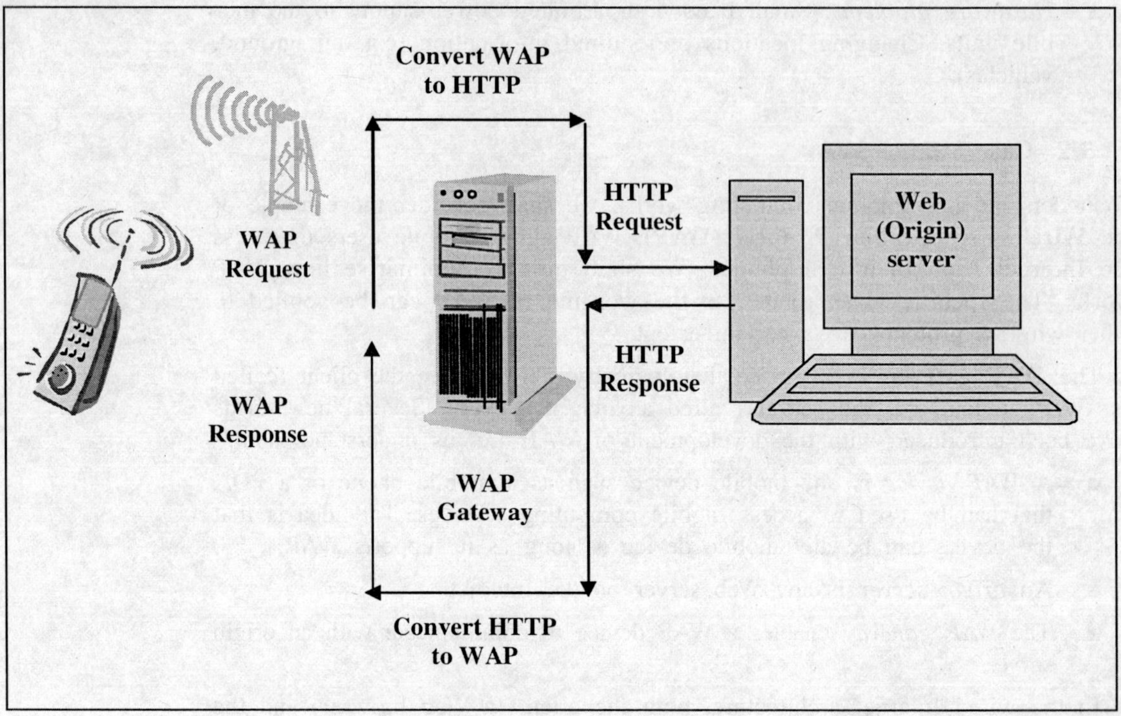

Fig. 11.11 WAP architecture

2. The WAP browser sends the user's request, which travels via the wireless network set up by the network operator to the WAP gateway. This is a **WAP request**, which means that the request is in the form of WAP commands. Note that this is in contrast to the normal interaction between a Web browser and a Web server, which starts with a HTTP request.
3. The WAP gateway receives the WAP request, translates it to the equivalent HTTP request and forwards it to the origin server.
4. The origin server receives the HTTP request from the WAP gateway. This request could be for obtaining a static HTML page, or for executing a dynamic server-side application written in languages such as ASP, JSP, servlets or CGI – just like the normal Internet HTTP requests. In either case, the origin server takes an appropriate action, the final result of which is a HTML page. However, a WAP browser is not created with the intention of interpreting HTML. HTML has now grown into a highly complex language that provides a number of features that are not suited for mobile devices. Therefore, a special program now converts the HTML output to a language called **Wireless Markup Language (WML)**. WML is a highly optimised language that has been invented keeping in mind all the shortcomings of mobile devices and, therefore, suits these devices very well. Of course, rather than first producing HTML output and then translating it into WML, some origin servers now directly produce WML output, bypassing the translation phase. We shall also discuss this possibility and what the WAP gateway does in that case, later. The

point is, the outcome of this process conforms to the WML standards. The origin server then encapsulates these WML contents inside a HTTP response, and sends it back to the WAP gateway.

5. The WAP gateway receives the HTTP response (which has the WML code encapsulated within it) from the origin server. It now translates this HTTP response into **WAP response**, and sends it back to the mobile device. WAP response is a representation of the HTTP response that a mobile device can understand. The WML inside remains as it was.
6. The mobile device now receives the WAP response along with the WML code from the WAP gateway, and hands it over to the WAP browser running on it. The WAP browser takes the WAP response and interprets it. The result of this is the display of the required information on the screen of the mobile device.

This should give us a fair idea about the interaction of a mobile user with the Internet. Of course, it is quite simplistic, and many finer details are not described.

11.5.3 Data in Mobile Applications

Applications running on mobile computers satisfy different needs, such as personal communications, workplace activities and providing updates on certain pieces information. Regardless of their roles, we can classify mobile applications into two categories, as follows.

(a) **Vertical applications**: In **vertical applications**, the users access data within a specified geographical unit (called a **cell**). For example, such applications provide information on emergency services or restaurants within that cell. Any attempts at accessing information outside the boundaries of the cell are not successful.

(b) **Horizontal applications**: Users of mobile computing work together in the **horizontal applications**. Unlike vertical applications, there is no restriction in terms of accessing data within a specific cell. The entire data can be used across the system.

Based on these concepts, mobile data can be classified into three categories, as follows.

(i) **Private data**: The **private data** belongs to a single user. The user is responsible for managing this data. No other user can access this data.

(ii) **Public data**: **Public data** can be accessed by anyone having the authority to browse through it. However, it can be updated by only one user. Examples of such data are scores of a cricket match.

(iii) **Shared data**: The **shared data** can be read and updated by all users.

11.5.4 Mobile Databases: Problem Areas

We can now summarise the problem issues related to mobile databases.

1. **Data distribution and replication**: The distribution of data between the gateway (which is usually called as the **base station**) and the mobile de-

vices is uneven. Since the amount of data that can be passed between the devices and the base station is limited, an attempt is made to provide locally cached data. This can lead to consistency related problems.

2. **Query processing**: The mobile units may be on the move while submitting a query. The exact location of the data should be known before the query is processed completely. Moreover, by the time query processing is over, the device might have moved out. Yet, there is a need to provide complete and correct query results to the mobile device.
3. **Database design**: The problem of name resolution is compounded in mobile databases. This can be attributed to the constant movement and unpredictability about the shutting down of these devices.
4. **Transactions**: The problems of fault tolerance and transaction completeness are compounded in mobile databases. A mobile transaction can serve multiple users working in different base stations. This must be coordinated and managed centrally. It is very difficult to enforce the traditional ACID model of transactions.
5. **Recovery**: Site failures are common because of the limited battery power of mobile devices. When a mobile device moves from one cell to another (in a process called **handoff**), it is common to see a transaction failing because of this movement.

KEY TERMS AND CONCEPTS

Active Server Pages (ASP)
Binary Large Object (BLOB)
Cell
Common Gateway Interface (CGI)
Datalog
Declarative language
Deductive database system
Deductive mechanism
Deductive Object Oriented Databases (DOODB)
Digital libraries
Dynamic Web page
Expert database systems
Facts
Handoff
Home page
Horizontal applications
Hyper Text Markup Language (HTML)
Hyper Text Transfer Protocol (HTTP)
Inference engine
Internet
Java Server Pages (JSP)
Knowledge representation
Knowledge-based database systems
Logic databases
Mathematical logic
Mobile computing
Multimedia
Origin server
Private data
Prolog
Public data
Quantising
Rules
Sampling
Shared data
Static Web page
Symbolic logic
Uniform Resource Locator (URL)

Vertical applications
WAP device
WAP gateway
Web browser
Web page
Web server
Website
Wireless Application Protocol (WAP)
Wireless Markup Language (WML)
Wireless networking
World Wide Web (WWW)

CHAPTER SUMMARY

- **Deductive databases** use **facts** and **rules**.
- Deductive databases are used in Artificial Intelligence (AI).
- Facts are similar to tables. Rules are similar to views.
- A **declarative language** is used in the case of deductive databases.
- The **World Wide Web (WWW)** is an application over the Internet.
- The **Hyper Text Transfer Protocol (HTTP)** is used in the case of the WWW.
- The client in HTTP is a **Web browser**. The **Web server** is the server.
- Web browser sends requests for Web pages, Web server fulfills them.
- A Web page that always shows the same content is called as a **static Web page**.
- A **dynamic Web page** is actually a server-side program.
- Dynamic Web pages provide different results, depending on the context.
- **Hyper Text Markup Language (HTML)** is used to create Web pages.
- Databases are used in dynamic Web pages.
- **Multimedia** means multiple media, such as text, sound, video and graphics.
- Multimedia is transformed into binary values by using **sampling** and **quantising** techniques.
- In sampling, a continuous analog waveform is broken down into slices.
- In quantising, the slices of an analog waveform are measured.
- **Digital libraries** are similar to traditional libraries, but store information in the digital form.
- **Mobile computing** means the ability to use computers while on the move.
- **Wireless networking** has made mobile computing possible.
- Data in mobile computing can be **private, public** or **shared**.

PRACTICE SET

Mark as true or false

1. Deductive databases use procedural language.
2. COBOL is a declarative language.

3. Rules and facts are different things.
4. Static Web pages do not need a program to be executed on the Web server.
5. Dynamic Web pages provide the same output for every request.
6. ASP is an active Web page technology.
7. Sampling and quantising help transform an analog signal into digital form.
8. Digital libraries store data about one fact only.
9. WAP is the name of a wireless protocol.
10. Limited battery life is a problem in mobile computing.

Fill in the blanks

1. Rules in deductive databases are called _________.
   (a) facts (b) definitions
   (c) logical information (d) logical databases
2. _________ is a declarative language.
   (a) C (b) Prolog
   (c) Pascal (d) Java
3. Mathematical logic is also called _____________.
   (a) declarative logic (b) symbolic logic
   (c) simple logic (d) linear logic
4. The _______ protocol is used in WWW application.
   (a) HTTP (b) SMTP
   (c) FTP (d) TELNET
5. _________ is one of the issues in Web databases.
   (a) Database size (b) DBA
   (c) Security (d) Networking
6. Many modern DBMS products provide support for ________,
   (a) HTML (b) SGML
   (c) WML (d) XML
7. When a mobile device moves from one cell to another, it is called as _________.
   (a) handoff (b) move
   (c) transfer (d) passing
8. In _________, an analog signal is broken down into slices.
   (a) slicing (b) sampling
   (c) quantising (d) breaking

9. In _________, an analog signal is measured.
   (a) slicing (b) sampling
   (c) quantising (d) breaking
10. ________ is a tag-based language.
   (a) C (b) HTML
   (c) Prolog (d) Pascal

Provide detailed answers to the following questions

1. What are deductive databases?
2. Explain the concepts of facts and rules.
3. What is Prolog?
4. Describe a static Web page.
5. How is a dynamic Web page different from a static Web page?
6. What are the DBMS issues in Web technologies?
7. What is multimedia?
8. Discuss the DBMS issues in Web technologies.
9. Describe the concept of mobile computing.
10. Explain the DBMS issues in Web technologies.

Exercises

1. Learn more about deductive databases.
2. Study more about the Prolog language.
3. What is Artificial Intelligence (AI)? Find out more about it.
4. Who was Boole? What is his contribution to logic?
5. Find out if digital electronics uses the concept of facts and rules.
6. Study about multimedia databases and multimedia operating systems.
7. Find out how cellular telephony works.
8. What are AMPS, GSM and CDMA in the context of mobile telephony?
9. Study about a few digital library projects.
10. Find out information about the 3G protocol.

Appendix A

Data Structures

We have referred to several **data structures**, such as lists, queues, binary trees, and so on. There is a very interesting theoretical basis behind these data structures. In this appendix, we shall study some of the most common data structures with several examples in the C programming language. Those not familiar with C can skip the programming examples, but are recommended to study the discussions of the various data structures.

A.1 LINKED LISTS

A **linked list** consists of data items that are arranged in a sequential order in such a manner that every data item contains the address of the next item in the list. In other words a data item *points to* the next item in the list. Therefore, an item contains data as well as a pointer to the next item in the list. The basic concept is illustrated in Fig. A.1.

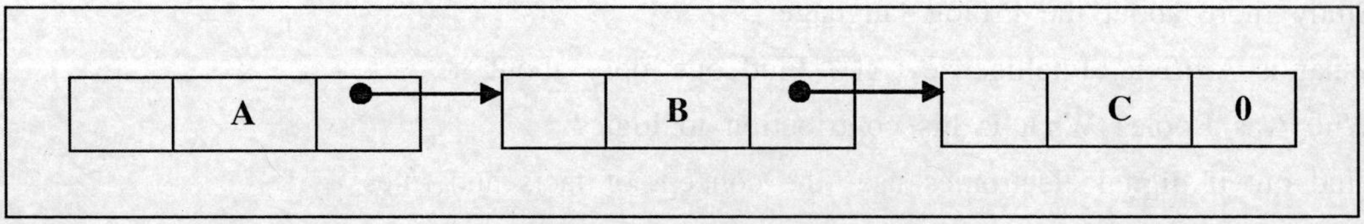

Fig. A.1 Linked list

As we can see, the first item contains data (shown as A), and a pointer to the next item, that is, B. Similarly, the second item contains data as A and a pointer to the next item, that is, C. The third item contains data as C, but its pointer is set to 0 (that is, null). This is because it is the last item in the list, and it has nothing more to point to. The null indicates this fact.

Because of this architecture, where an item points to the next item in the forward direction, all the items are linked together to form a list of items. Because of this property, such a linked list is also called as a **simple linked list** or a **single linked list**.

Linked list provides useful facility for storing data items in such a manner that the list can expand or shrink dynamically. For example, suppose that we need to store the details of employees in a linked list. It is possible that some employees resign, and new ones get added. Also, some employees who had resigned earlier may rejoin. Suppose we need to insert or delete records for these employees in/from the list as and when they join or resign.

What we could do in such a situation is to maintain a linked list of employee records. An employee record would contain the details of the employee, say the Employee ID, Employee name, and Department. Additionally, it would also contain a pointer to the next employee record in the list. Suppose that currently we just have three employees, whose records are shown in Table A.1.

Table A.1 Employee records

Employee ID	*Employee Name*	*Department*
004	Sachin	Statements
007	Mithoo	PROMO
012	Javed	AR

Then a possible linked list implementation of this situation is shown in Fig. A.2.

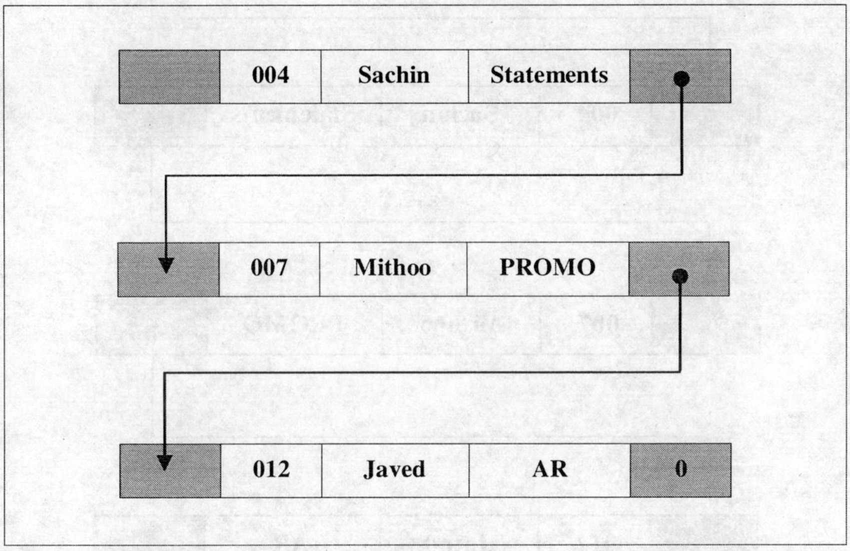

Fig. A.2 Employee records implemented as a linked list

Let us now transform this list into a C language syntax. The result is shown in Fig. A.3. We have not shown the data values to keep things simple. We shall study this in subsequent examples.

```
struct emp
{
     emp_id             int;
     emp_name     char [30];
     department   char [10];
     struct emp   *next;
}:
```

Fig. A.3 Linked list in C

We would realise that several operations on this linked list must be allowed. We should be able to insert an employee at the beginning, in the middle, or at the end of the list. We should be able to modify the values of any employee record. Similarly, we should be able to search for, update, or delete employee records.

We shall not provide the C language code for such a linked list. Instead, we shall wait until we discuss Doubly linked lists.

Figure A.4 shows what happens if we want to insert a new employee record at the first position of the list. See how all records shift one position ahead.

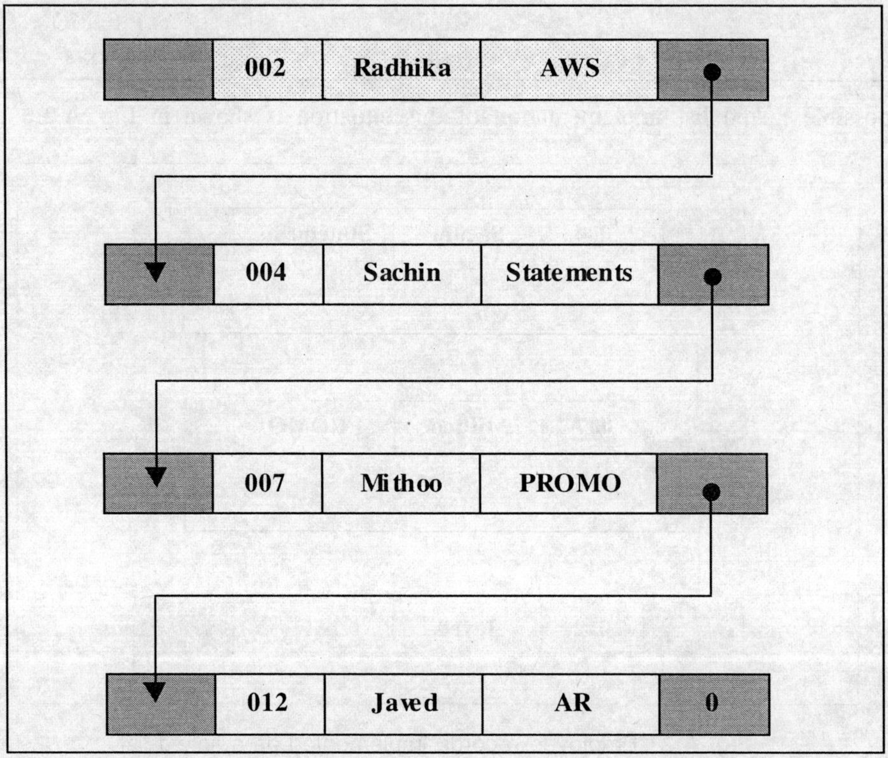

Fig. A.4 Inserting new record at the beginning of the linked list

Figure A.5 shows what happens if we insert a new record in-between the existing linked list records.

Figure A.6 shows the effect of inserting a record at the end of the linked list.

Let us now consider the linked list as consisting of four records as shown in the last diagram. Figure A.7 shows the effect of deleting the last record.

Note that the deletion of items in a list is *logical*, and not *physical*. That is, the record to be deleted (that is, Radhika in this case) is not physically removed, but instead, the mere adjustments of pointer of Javed causes the removal of Radhika automatically from the list.

Now suppose we delete the middle record. The result is shown in Fig. A.8.

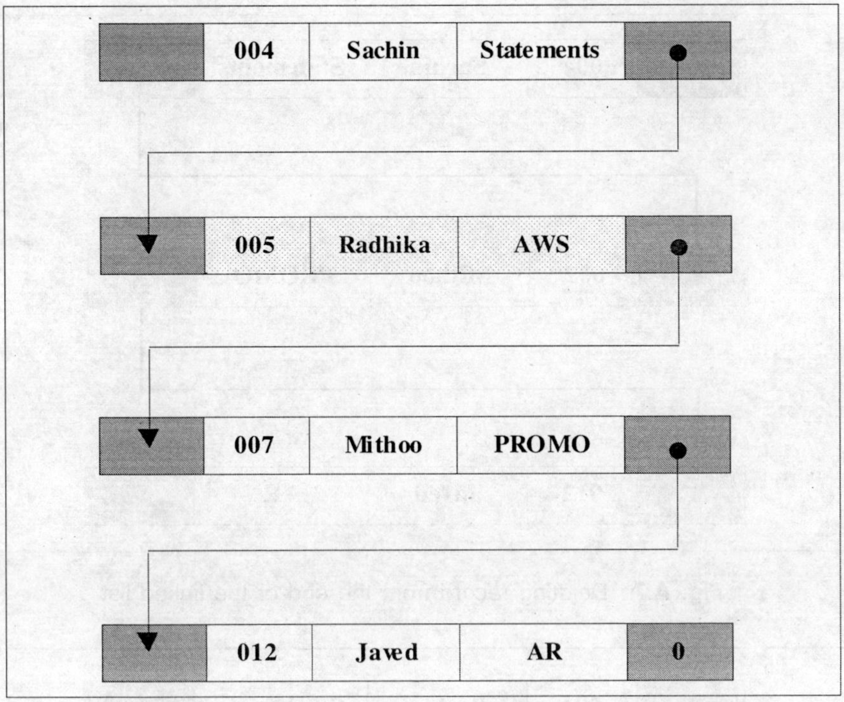

Fig. A.5 Inserting new record in the middle of the linked list

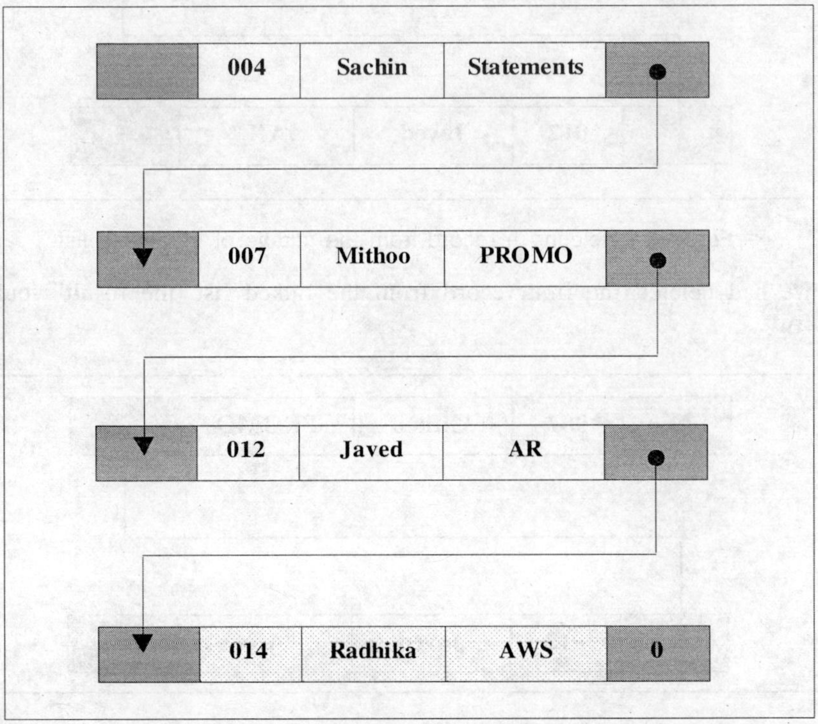

Fig. A.6 Inserting new record at the end of the linked list

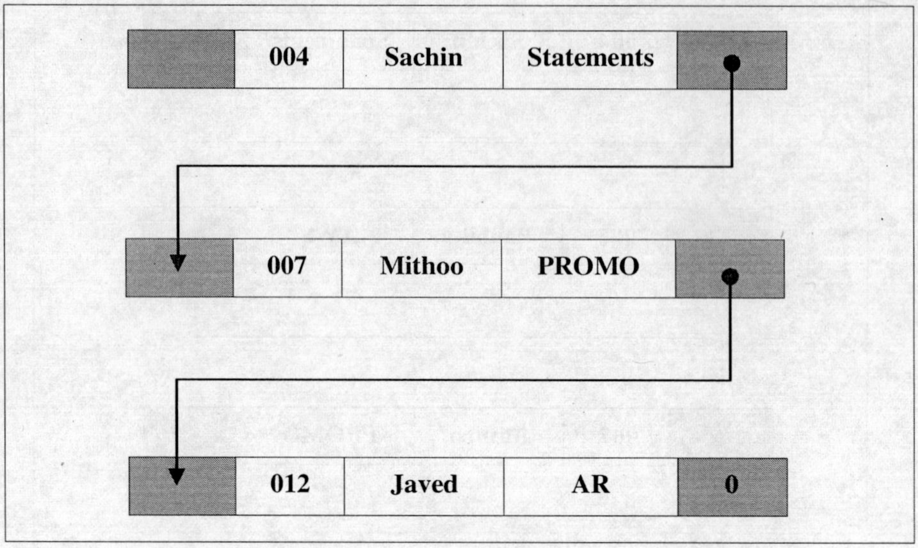

Fig. A.7 Deleting record from the end of the linked list

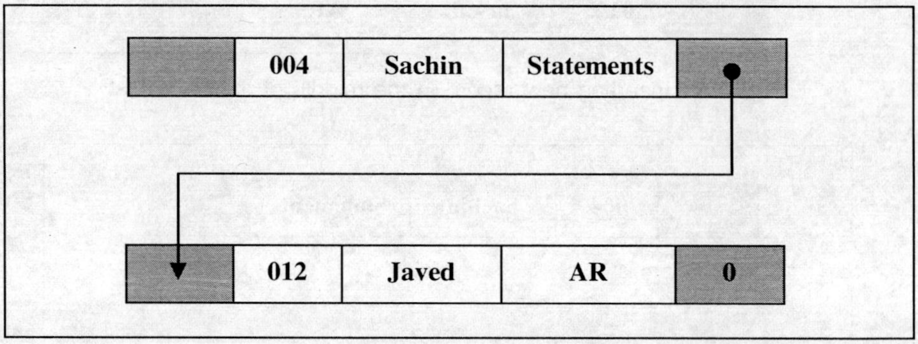

Fig. A.8 Deleting a record from the middle of the linked list

Instead, if we had deleted the first record from the linked list, the result would have been as shown in Fig. A.9.

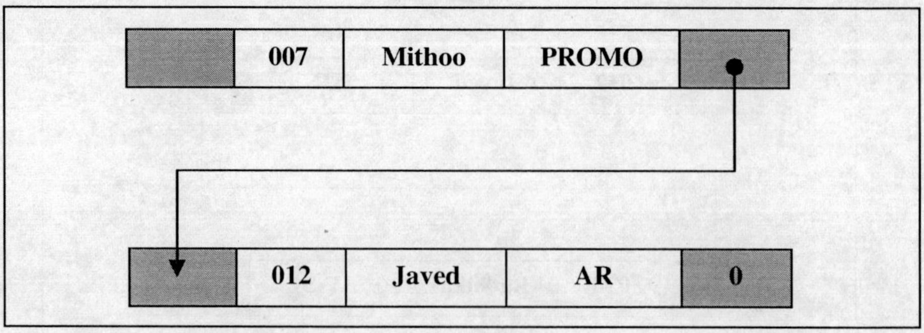

Fig. A.9 Deleting a record from the end of the linked list

In all these operations, we need to adjust the *next* pointer of the structure declared in C, manipulating it so that the items in the list are added or deleted appropriately.

A.2 DOUBLY LINKED LISTS

A **doubly linked list**, also called **two-way linked list**, consists of data as well as pointers to the next item, as well as the previous item. Remember that a single linked list contains just one pointer (usually in the forward direction). Figure A.10 depicts the concept of a doubly linked list.

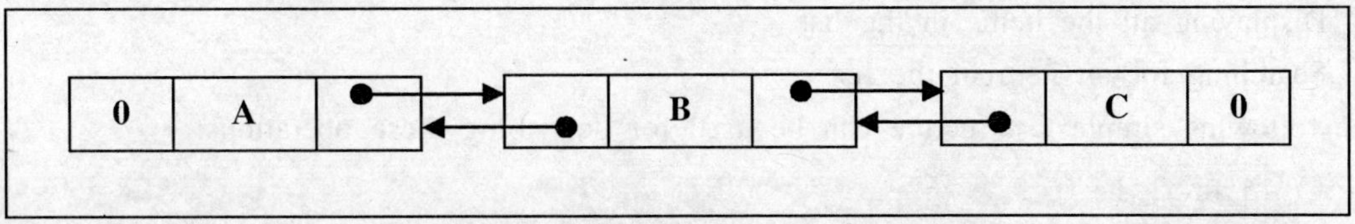

Fig. A.10 Doubly linked list

As shown in the diagram, every item in the list has two links or pointers:

- One link points to the next item in the list in the forward direction.
- The second link points to the previous item in the list in the backward direction.

As before, the first item in the list (shown here as *A*) has nothing to point *back to.* This is because it is the very first item in the list. Because we are using the pointers in both directions, we have shown that the previous pointer of A points to 0, that is, null. We had not done so in the case of a single linked list, because there was no previous pointer at all. Similarly, the last item in the list (shown here as C) has no more items to point to. Therefore, the *next pointer* of the last item in the list contains a dummy value of 0. The other (previous and next) pointers point to the next or the previous item in the list, as appropriate.

Using two links rather than just one provides us with two main advantages:

1. A single linked list has pointers only in one direction (which is usually the forward direction). Therefore, a single linked list cannot be traversed backwards, starting with the last item in the list. In contrast, a doubly linked list can be read in *either* direction, as follows:
   (a) We can start with the first item in the list, and traverse up to the last item in the list in the forward direction. In the example, it means reading the three items in the order A-B-C.
   (b) We can start with the last item in the list, and traverse it back to the first item in the list in the backward direction. In our example, it means reading the three items in the order C-B-A.

   This property of doubly linked lists can be useful in practical situations. It not only simplifies the management of the list, but also can help in reading the records of a file or a database, if they are implemented as a doubly linked list.
2. If there is some problem that causes one of the links (either forward or backward) to fail or to become invalid, that link can be constructed with the help of the other link, which is still intact. Note that this is not possible in the case of a single linked list, because there is only one list, and if it is corrupted, there is no way of re-creating it. Recall our discussion of maintaining pointers in both directions in the Library Management System.

A.2.1 Doubly Linked List Operations

In principle, there is not a major difference between creating a doubly linked list and creating a single linked list. But recall that now we need to maintain two links, in place of just one link. As a result, the basic organisation of a doubly linked list must allow for maintaining two links. We need to focus on the following operations in relation with a doubly linked list:

1. Inserting an item in the list
2. Deleting an item from the list
3. Displaying all the items in the list
4. Searching for an item in the list

The following simple C structure can be used for describing these operations:

```
struct linked_list
{
      int emp_id;
      char emp_name[30];
      char department[10];
      struct linked_list *next;
      struct linked_list *previous;
};
```

A.2.1.1 Inserting an item There are three situations in which a new item can be inserted into a doubly linked list:

1. Insert a new item at the beginning of the list

Figure A.11 shows the insertion of an item to the list at its end. We know that the original list was A-B-C. Because A is the first item in the list, the *previous pointer* of A is 0.

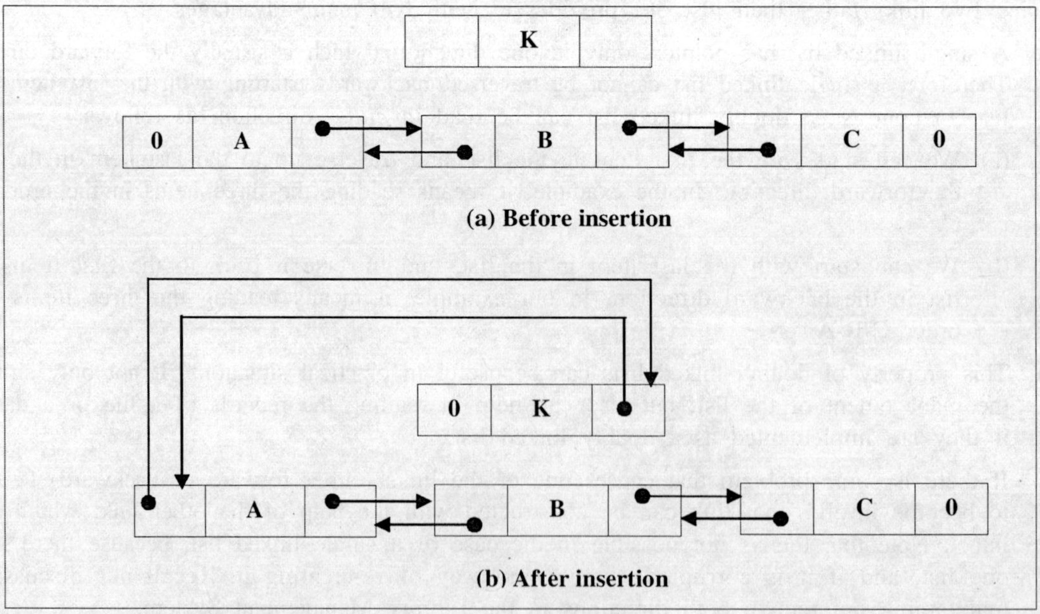

(a) Before insertion

(b) After insertion

Fig. A.11 Insertion of a new item at the beginning of the doubly linked list

The item *K* is being inserted at the first position of the list. Consequently, the previous pointer of the item that was the first item in the list (that is, A) now points to *K*. Also, because this is a doubly linked list, the *next pointer* of *K* points to A. The remaining items of the list are unchanged. In other words, A points to B and B points to C. The *next pointer* of C continues to be 0, which means nothing.

2. Insert a new item in the middle of the list

Let us study the same original linked list, which consisted of three items, A, B and C. Imagine further that the new item K is now to be added in between A and B. We depict the result in Fig. A.12. As we can see, it consists of two mini-operations:

(a) The *next pointer* of A now points to *K*. Additionally, the *previous pointer* of *K* now points to A.

(b) The *next pointer* of *K* points to B. Similarly, the *previous pointer* of B points to *K*.

Note that the pointers between B and C remain unchanged.

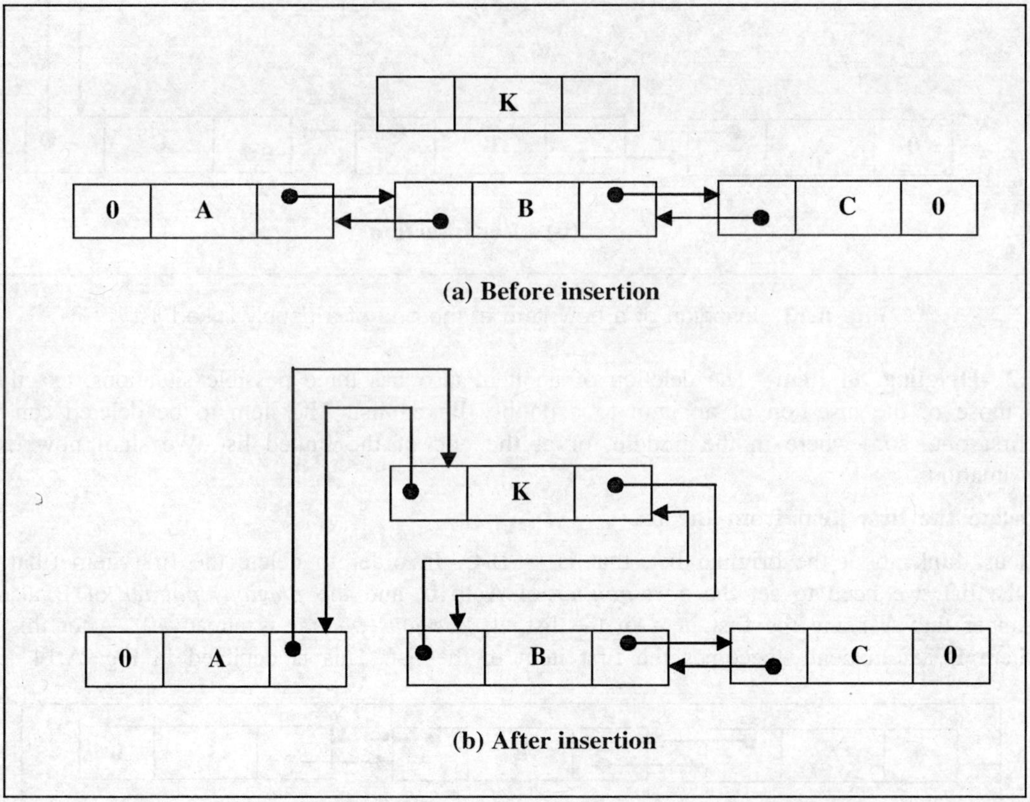

Fig. A.12 Insertion of a new item in the middle of a doubly linked list

3. Insert a new item at the end of the list

This is perhaps the simplest of the three insertion possibilities. Here, the item *K* will be inserted at the end of the list, that is, after C. Thus, the *next pointer* for item C will not be 0 (null) now. Rather, it will point to *K*. By the same logic, the *previous pointer* of *K* will point to C. Last but not the least, the *next pointer* of *K* will now be 0. This is depicted in Fig. A.13.

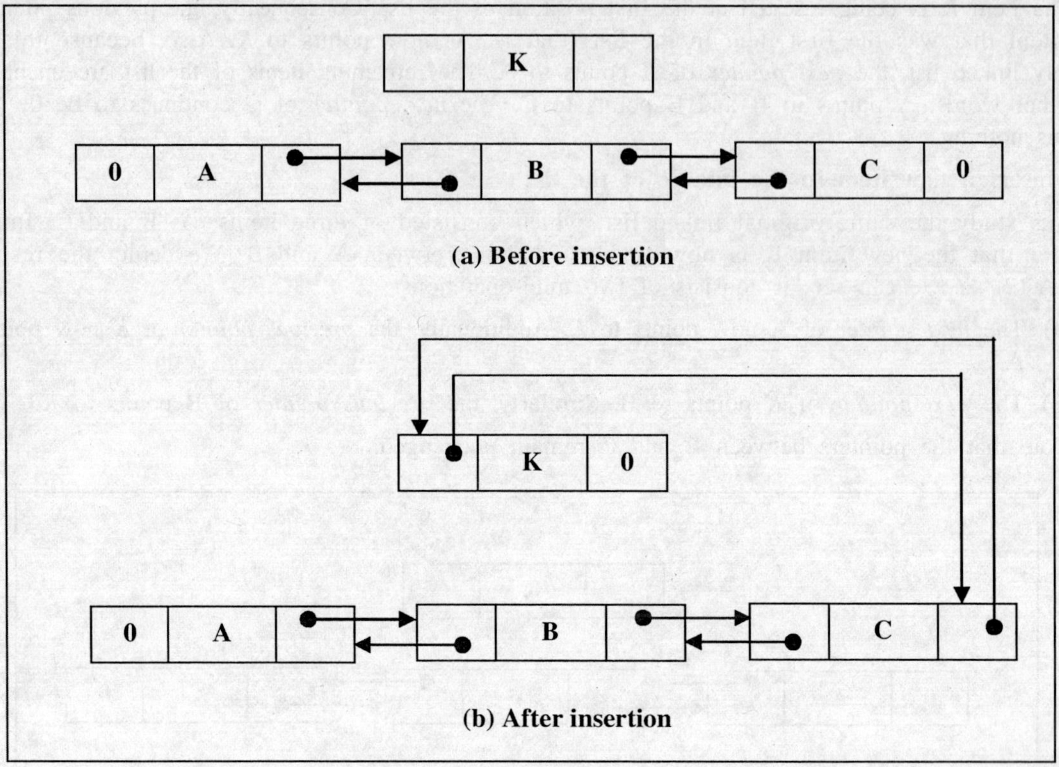

Fig. A.13 Insertion of a new item at the end of a doubly linked list

A.2.1.2 Deleting an item The deletion of an item also has three possible situations, exactly similar to those of the insertion of an item to a doubly linked list. The item to be deleted can be the very first one, somewhere in the middle, or at the end of the linked list. We shall now examine these situations.

1. Delete the first item from the list

Let us think about the original list, that is, A-B-C. In order to delete the first item (that is, A) from the list, we need to set the *next pointer* of A to 0, and the *previous pointer* of B also to 0. (Remember that A being the first item in the list, its *previous pointer* is already 0). After this operation, item B automatically becomes the first item in the list. This is depicted in Fig. A.14.

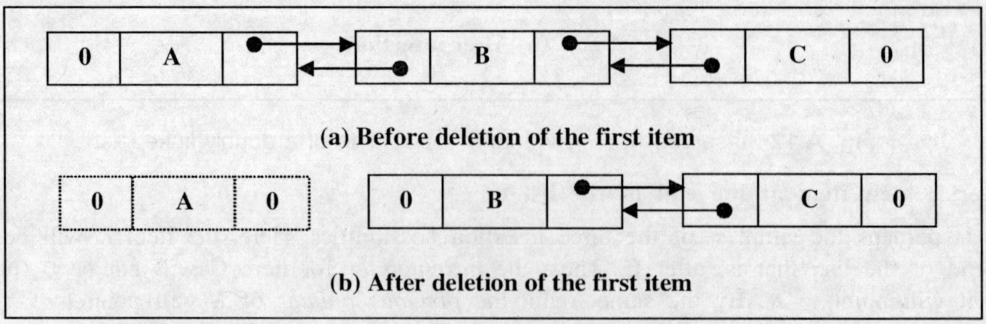

Fig. A.14 Deletion of the first item in a doubly linked list

2. Delete an item in the middle of the list

The deletion of an item somewhere in the middle of a list is more complex than deleting the first or the last item of the list. This is due to the fact that here we need to have the adjustment of the previous and the next pointers of the two items that are adjacent to the item that we want to delete. In this case, from the list A-B-C, we are deleting item B. As a result, the following changes are needed:

(a) The *next pointer* of A, which points to B at the moment, should now point to C.

(b) The *previous pointer* of B is pointing to A. Instead, the *previous pointer* of C should now point to A.

In order to do this, both the *previous pointer* and the *next pointer* of B should be set to 0. This automatically causes the deletion of item B from the list. This is illustrated in Fig. A.15.

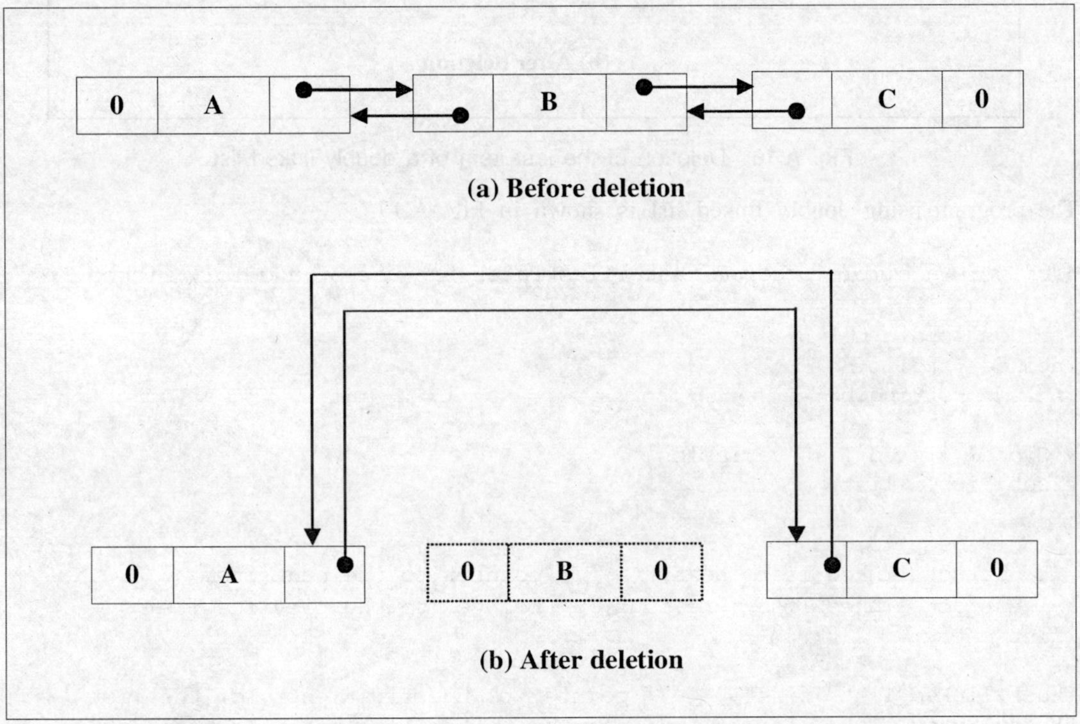

Fig. A.15 Deletion of an item from the middle of a doubly linked list

3. Delete the last item in the list

The deletion of the last item in the list (that is, C in our example) is perhaps the simplest of all deletion operations. To perform this task, we need to reset the *next pointer of* B to 0, which normally points to C. This causes two operations to be performed: B is now the last item in the list; and C is automatically deleted from the list. Similarly, C's *previous pointer* should be reset to 0. This operation is depicted in Fig. A.16.

Because there is nothing to diagrammatically show them, we shall depict the other two operations (that is, displaying all the items in the list and searching for a specific item in the list) with the help of a C program. For simplicity, we shall automatically sort the list while inserting a new item in the list. That is, a new item in the list is automatically added in its right ordered location. For simplicity, we shall consider that the linked list contains just one data item: the employee ID.

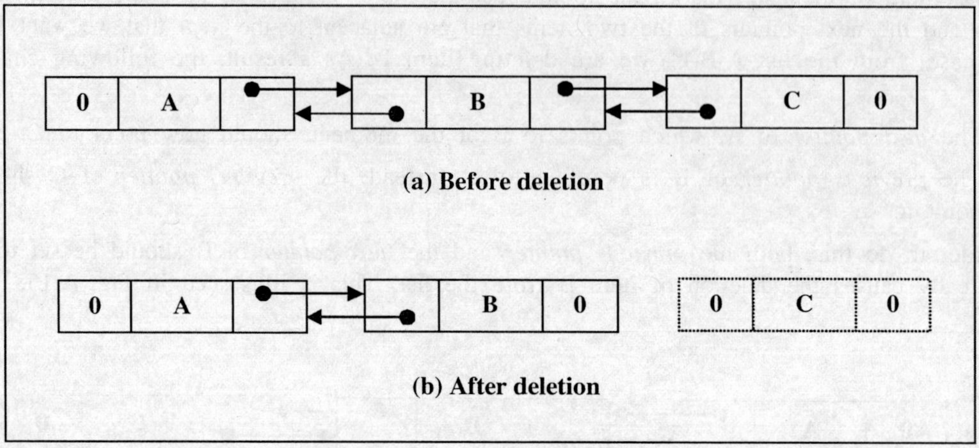

Fig. A.16 Deletion of the last item of a doubly linked list

The program using doubly linked list is shown in Fig. A.17.

```
/* This is a simple program that illustrates the use of a doubly linked list */

#include <stdio.h>
#include <stdlib.h>
#include <string.h>

/* Global linked list variables */
struct linked_list
{
      int emp_id;
      struct linked_list *next;     /* pointer to the next item */
      struct linked_list *previous; /* pointer to the previous item */
} list_entry;

struct linked_list *first;    /* pointer to the first entry of the list */
struct linked_list *last;     /* pointer to the last entry of the list */

/* Function declarations */
char option (void);
void insert (void);
void item_insert (struct linked_list *i, struct linked_list **first, struct
linked_list **last);
void item_delete (struct linked_list **first, struct linked_list **last);
struct linked_list* find (int n);
void list (void);
void search (void);
```

Fig. A.17 Doubly linked list program – Part A

```
/* start of the actual program logic */
void main (void)
{
      first = last = NULL; /* initialize first and last pointers to NULL*/

      for (; ;)
      {
            switch (option ( ))
            {
                  case 1: insert ();
                        break;

                  case 2: item_delete (&first, &last);
                        break;

                  case 3: list ();
                        break;

                  case 4: search ();
                        break;

                  case 5: return;
            }
      }
}

/* User chooses a particular operation to be performed */
char option (void)
{
      char ch;

      /* display the menu of available choices */
      printf ("1. Insert an item\n");
      printf ("2. Delete an item\n");
      printf ("3. Display all items\n");
      printf ("4. Search for an item\n");
      printf ("5. Stop\n");

      do
      {
            printf ("Select your option: ");
            ch = getchar ();
      } while (ch < '1' || ch > '5');

      return ch;
}
```

Fig. A.17 Doubly linked list program – Part B

```
/* Accept and store an item at an appropriate position in the list */
void insert (void)
{
   struct linked_list *rec;
   int k; /* Used to accept user input */

   for (; ;)
   {
      rec = (struct linked_list *) malloc (sizeof (list_entry));

      if (info == NULL)
      {
         printf ("Insufficient memory … Cannot proceed …");
         return;
      }

      /* request user for the next number, 9876 to stop entry */
      printf ("Enter the employee ID to be stored, 9876 to quit: ");
      scanf ("%d", &k);

      if (k == 9876)
         break;
      else
      {
         /* otherwise, add the number to the info structure */
         rec->number = n;
         item_insert (rec, &first, &last);
      }
   }
}
```

Fig. A.17 Doubly linked list program – Part C

```
/* Insert an item into the list */

void item_insert (
   struct linked_list *k, /* new item to be added */
   struct linked_list **first, /* first element in the list */
   struct linked_list **last /* last element in the list */
)
{
   struct linked_list *old, *p;

   /* if this is the very first item to be inserted into the list */
   if (*last == NULL)
   {
      k->next = NULL;
```

```
        k->previous = NULL;
        *last = k;
        *first = k;
        return;
    }

    /* Begin at the start of the list */
    p = *first;
    old = NULL;

    while (p != NULL) /* while there are more items in the list */
    {
        /* if number in the list is less than the one entered by
        the user */
        if (p->emp_id < k->emp_id)
        {
            old = p;
            p = p->next;
        }

        else
        {
            /* if p is not the first item in the list, insert k
            somewhere middle in the list */
            if (p->previous != NULL)
            {
                p->previous->next = k;
                k->next = p;
                k->previous = p->previous;
                p->previous = k;
                return;
            }

            /* k is the new first item */
            k->next = p;
            k->previous = NULL;
            k->previous = k;
            *first = k;
            return;
        }
    }

    /* k should be the last item */
    old->next = k;      k->next = NULL;  k->previous = old;  *last = k;
}
```

Fig. A.17 Doubly linked list program – Part D

```
/* Delete an item from the list */
void item_delete (struct linked_list **first, struct linked_list **last)
{
    struct linked_list *info;
    int k;

    /* accept the employee ID that the user wants to delete */
    printf ("Enter number to be deleted: ");
    scanf ("%d", &k);

    /* find that emp_ID in the list */
    info = find (k);

    /* deletion process only if the item is available in the
    list*/
    if (info != NULL)
    {
        /* if the first item of the list is to be deleted */
        if (*first == info)
        {
            *first = info->next;

            if (*first)
                (*first)->previous = NULL;
            else
                *last = NULL;
        }
        else /* item to be deleted is somewhere in middle */
        {
            info->previous->next = info->next;

            if (info != *last)
                info->next->previous = info->previous;
            else
                *last = info->previous;
        }
        /* free up the allocated space */
        free (info);
    }
}

/* find an item in the list */
struct linked_list* find (int k)
{
    struct linked_list *info = first;

    /* while there are more items in the list */
    while (info != NULL)
    {
```

```
          /* item to be searched is found */
          if (k == info->number) return info;

          /* If not, simply move to the next item in the list */
          info = info->next;
     }

     /* if we are here, it means that the item was not found */
     printf ("The employee ID in the list\n");
     return NULL;
}
```

Fig. A.17 Doubly linked list program – Part E

```
/* Display all the items in the list */
void list (void)
{
     struct linked_list *info = first;

     /* While there are more items in the list */
     while (info != NULL)
     {
          /* display the current item in the list */
          printf ("%d\n", info->emp_id);

          /* move to the next item in the list */
          info = info->next;
     }

     printf ("\n");
}

/* search for a specific item in the list */
void search (void)
{
     int k;
     struct linked_list *info;

     /* accept the number that the user wants to search */
     printf ("Enter the emp ID to be searched: ");
     scanf ("%d", &k);

     /* find that emp ID in the list */
     info = find (k);

     /* display an appropriate result */
     if (info)
          printf ("Item found in the list\n");
     else
          printf ("Item not found in the list\n");
}
```

Fig. A.17 Doubly linked list program – Part F

A.3 QUEUES

Queuing up for anything is generally disliked. A **queue** is very similar to the manner in which we (*are supposed to*) queue up at reservation counters or at bank cashiers' desks. A queue has two important properties:

- A queue is a linear, sequential list of items.
- The items in a queue must be accessed in the order *First In First Out (FIFO).*

In other words, the first item added to a queue must also be the first one to be retrieved. The second item added to a queue is also the second one to be retrieved, and so on. Finally, the last item to be added to the queue is also the last one to be retrieved.

Remember that (*unlike queues of humans*) we can neither store nor retrieve the items in a queue arbitrarily or in any random order.

Imagine that we are creating a queue of items. To do so, let us consider two very simple operations, *write* and *read*. The *write* operation inserts a new item at the end of the queue, whereas the *read* item reads one item from the queue (that is, the first item of the queue). If we go on using these two operations with a few insertions and a few retrievals, the resulting values of the queue would look as shown in Table A.2.

Table A.2 Queue operations

Operation	*Contents of the queue after the operation*
write (p)	p
write (q)	p q
write (r)	p q r
read (*returns p*)	q r
write (s)	q r s
read (*returns q*)	r s
read (*returns r*)	s
write (t)	s t

As we can see, the operations on a queue are always sequential and are FIFO. Moreover, when one item is read from the queue, it is automatically destroyed. In other words, a *read* operation on a queue is **destructive**, unlike what happens with other data structures, such as linked lists. Therefore, if the programmer needs to implement a **non-destructive** reading of a queue, the values, as they are read (and therefore, automatically removed) from the queue, must be stored somewhere else for later access/retrieval.

In order to implement the *write* and *read* operations on a queue, two pointers, *start* and *end* are needed. One pointer (*start*) points at the current beginning of the queue (that is, at the item that is the first in the queue at that point of time). The other pointer (*end*) points at the current end of the queue (that is, at the last storage location available in the queue for a new item). To repeat, insertions into and retrievals from a queue, as discussed earlier, would have the effects on the pointers as shown in Fig. A.18.

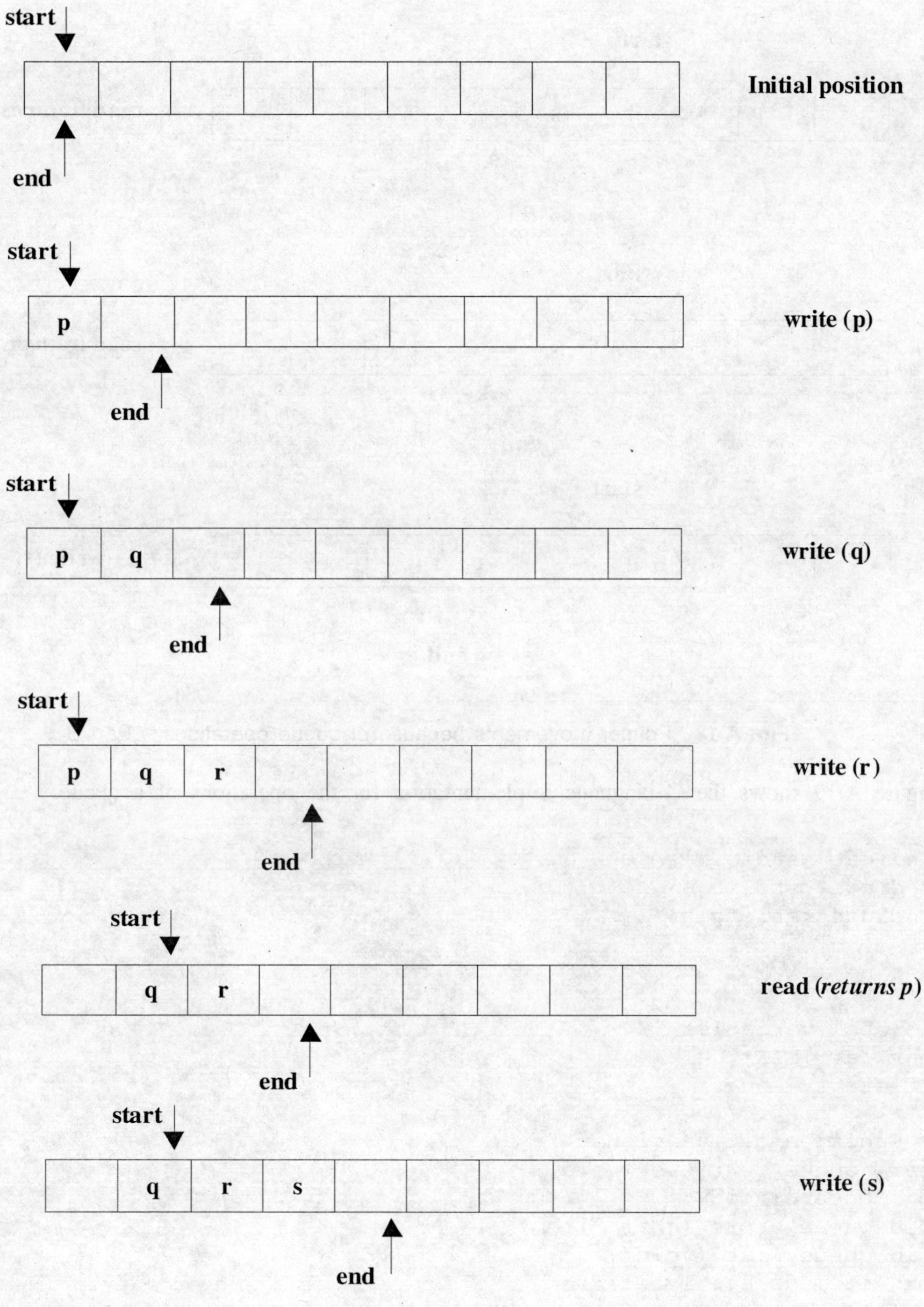

Fig. A.18 Pointer movements because of queue operations – Part A

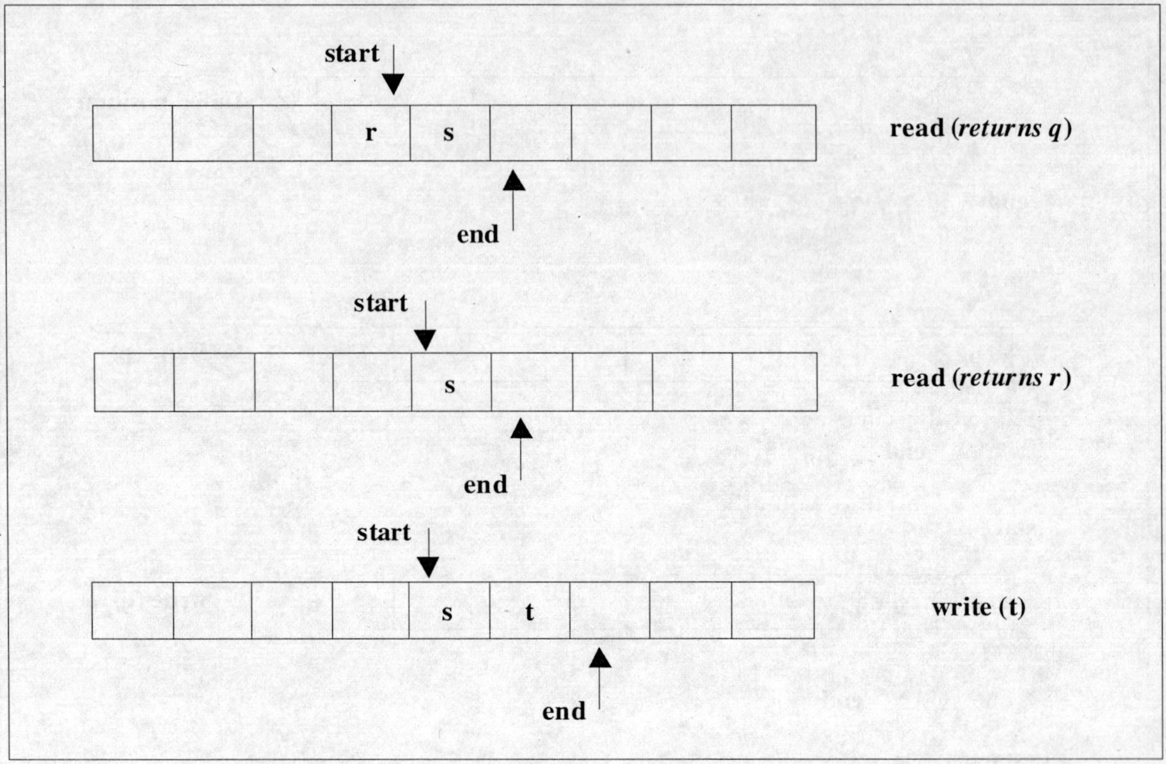

Fig. A.18 Pointer movements because of queue operations – Part B

Figure A.19 shows the C language implementation for the operations of a queue.

```
#include <stdio.h>
#include <stdlib.h>
#include <string.h>

#define     MAX   100

/*Global variables */
char *arr[MAX];
int start, end;

/* Function declarations */
char *queue_retrieve (void);
void enter (void);
void queue_store (char *item);
void queue_list (void);
void item_delete (void);
```

Fig. A.19 Queue program – Part A

```
/* Add an item into the queue */
void enter (void)
{
      char str[50], *ptr;

      do
      {
            printf ("Enter contents of the next item: Number %d: ",
end+1);
            gets (str);

            if(str == NULL)
                  return;
            else
                  ptr = (char *) malloc (strlen (str));

            if (ptr == NULL)
            {
                  printf ("Not enough memory\n");
                  return;
            }

            strcpy (ptr, str);

            if (str [0] != NULL)
                  queue_store (ptr);
      }
      while (*str);
}

/* Display all the queue items on separate lines */
void queue_list (void)
{
      int i;
      printf ("Item number    Contents\n");
      for (i=start; i<end; i++)
            printf ("%d  %s", i+1, arr[i]);
}
/* Delete an item from the queue */
void delete_item (void)
{
      char *ptr;
      ptr = queue_retrieve ( );
      if (ptr == NULL)
            return;

      printf ("%s\n", ptr);
}
```

Fig. A.19 Queue program – Part B

```
/* Add an item to the end of the queue*/
void queue_store (char *ptr)
{
      if (end >= MAX)
      {
            printf ("\nQueue is full. Cannot add new items.");
            return;
      }
      arr[end] = ptr;
      end++;
}
/* Retrieve an item from the queue */
char* queue_retrieve (void)
{
      if (start == end)
      {
            printf ("\nError: Queue is empty.");
            return NULL;
      }
      start++;
      return arr[start-1];
}
```

Fig. A.19 Queue program – Part C

A.3.1 Circular Lists/queues

Interestingly, a list/queue can be circular. In such a case, it is called as a **circular linked list** or a **circular queue**. We may have got an impression that when the items from a queue get deleted, the space for those items is reclaimed. However, it is not true. Those queue slots remain empty. This problem is solved by circular linked lists, which are usually in the form of circular queues.

Put simply, rather than using a linear approach, a circular list takes the circular approach. In other words, items in a circular list are arranged to form a circular shape. This is also the reason why a circular list does not have a beginning or end at all! The representation of a circular queue is as shown in Fig. A.20.

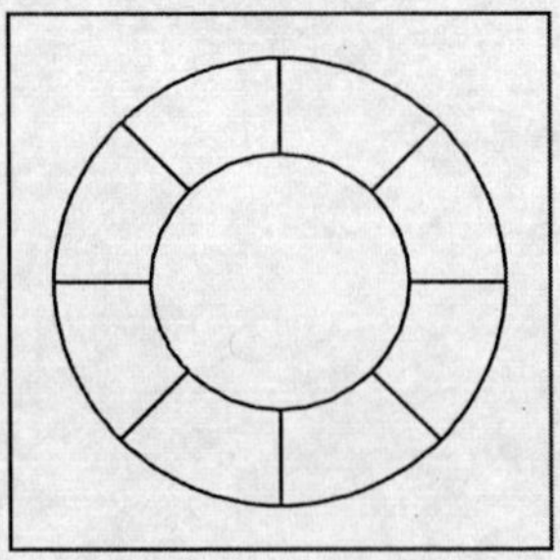

Fig. A.20 Circular queue

What is the effect of making a queue circular, as against keeping it linear?

Well, the functions queue_store and queue_retrieve would have to be altered in the case of a circular queue, as shown in Fig. A.21.

```
void queue_store (char *ptr)
{
      /* The queue is full if (i) end is one less than start, or (ii)
end is at the end of the queue, and start is at the beginning of the
queue */

      if ((end+1 == start) || (end+1 == MAX && start == 0))
      {
            printf ("Queue is full. Cannot add new items.\n");
            return;
      }

      arr[end] = ptr;
      end++;

      /* loop back to the start of the queue to complete the circle
of the queue if end is reached */
      if (end == MAX)
            end = 0;
}

char * queue_retrieve (void)
{
      /* loop back to the beginning of the queue*/
      if (start == MAX)
            start= 0;

      if (start == end)
      {
            printf ("Queue is empty.\n");
            return NULL;
      }

      start++;

      return arr[start-1];
}
```

Fig. A.21 Circular queue implementation

A.4 BINARY TREES

There is another interesting data structure by the name **tree**. Trees come in many forms and shapes (just like real trees!) However, the **binary tree** is a special case, because when it is in a sorted order, it allows us to perform quick search, insertion and deletion operations.

Note that trees in computer science grow from top to bottom, unlike real trees, which grow from bottom to top.

An item in any tree has two pointers or links: one to a left member, and another to a right member. This concept is shown in Fig. A.22.

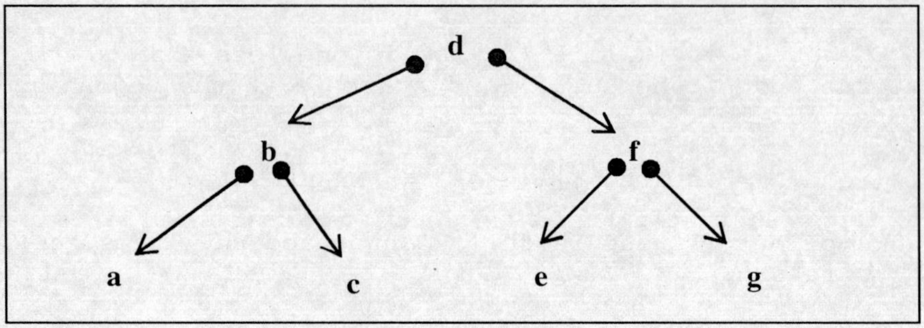

Fig. A.22 Binary tree

In this tree, we say that d is the root of the tree. A data item located on the tree (here a through g) is called as a **node** of the tree. Any portion of a tree (e-f-g) is called as a **sub-tree**. A node that does not have any sub-tree is called as a **terminal node**. For example, a, c, e and g are all examples of terminal nodes, but b, d and f are not. The **height** of the tree is the number of the vertical node positions. In the example, the height is 3. Accessing the items in a tree is called the process of **tree traversal**.

Items of a tree can be retrieved, inserted or deleted in any order. Note that every sub-tree of a tree is itself a tree! Clearly, a tree is a **recursive** (that is, self-repeating) data structure, and therefore, recursive programming techniques are quite commonly used with trees. But it is not mandatory that tree-related programming must always be recursive. Non-recursive tree programming is also possible, but is harder to code and comprehend, as compared to the recursive code version.

A tree can be traversed in three ways:

- **In-order tree traversal**: In this type of traversal, the left sub-tree is traversed first, followed by the root, and finally by the right sub-tree. Thus, the in-order traversal of our tree shown earlier would yield the sequence a-b-c-d-e-f-g.
- **Pre-order tree traversal**: In this traversal, the root is traversed first, followed by the left sub-tree, followed by the right sub-tree. Thus, the pre-order traversal of our sample tree would yield the sequence d-b-a-c-f-e-g.
- **Post-order tree traversal**: In this type, the left sub-tree is accessed first, followed by the right sub-tree, and finally followed by the root. Thus, the post-order traversal of our sample tree shown earlier would yield the sequence a-c-b-e-g-f-d.

Although a tree need not necessarily be in a sorted form, generally, all the practical applications require the use of a sorted tree. We shall also consider sorted trees. Moreover, we shall consider only in-order trees. Note that the other two tree types are simply variations of this type.

The actual view of a tree that has pointers or links between the various items is shown in the form of another tree in Fig. A.23. This view should be kept in mind while working with trees in computer programs. Note how the *next* or *previous* pointers have a value 0 for the nodes that do not point to other nodes in the tree, similar to the empty pointers in linked lists discussed earlier.

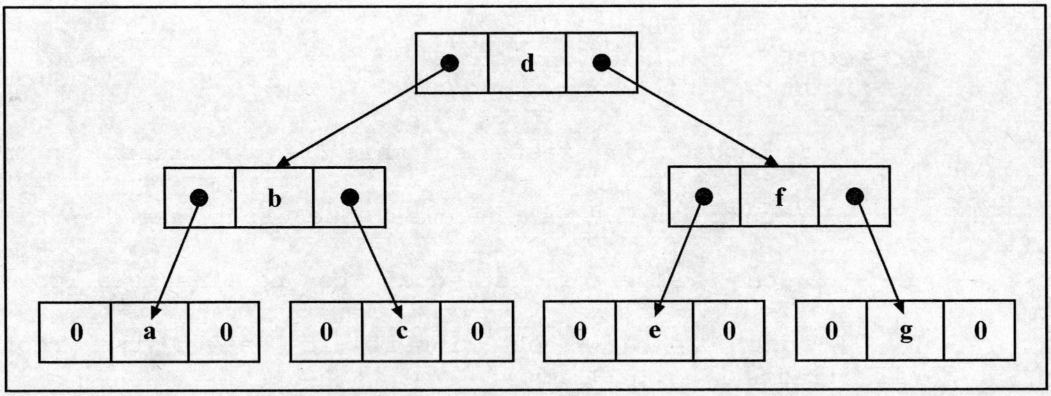

Fig. A.23 Another view of the same tree

We can represent each node in the tree in the form of a C structure, as shown in Fig. A.24.

```
struct tree
{
      int number;          /* data item to be stored */
      struct tree *left;         /* pointer to the left item/node */
      struct tree *right;        /* pointer to the left item/node */
};
```

Fig. A.24 Tree represented as a C structure

We can build a sorted binary tree as shown in Fig. A.25.

```
struct tree *insert_node (struct tree *root,     /* root of the tree */
                        struct tree *r, /* node to be inserted */
int info  /* value of the node that is being inserted */)
{
      /* this is non-recursive portion of the code */

      /* if node to be inserted does not exist, create it */
      if (r == NULL)
      {
            r = (struct tree *) malloc (sizeof (struct tree));

            if (r == NULL)
            {
                  printf ("Error: Insufficient memory\n.");
                  return;
            }

            /* set the left-right pointers of r to null, and set
                 its information to that received from the calling
                 function */
```

```
        r->left  =  NULL;
        r->right  =  NULL;
        r->info  =  info;

        /*  root  does  not  exist,  so  this  is  the  first  entry  */
        if  (root  ==  NULL)
            return  r;  /*  r  becomes  the  root  now  */

        /*  if  the  value  of  the  node  to  be  inserted  is  less
than
            that  of  the  root,  insert  it  before  the  root  */
        if  (info  <  root->info)
            root->left  =  r;
        else
        /*  if  the  value  of  the  node  to  be  inserted  is  greater
            than  that  of  the  root,  insert  it  after  the  root  */
            root->right  =  r;

        return  r;
    }

    /*  these  are  recursive  calls  */

    /* insert the current node in the appropriate position, depending
        on  its  value  */
    if  (info  <  r->info)
        insert_node  (r,  r->left,  info);
    else
        insert_node  (r,  r->right,  info);
}
```

Fig. A.25 Building a sorted binary tree

Once the tree is created, it can be traversed in either of the three ways discussed earlier (in-order, pre-order and post-order). The in-order traversal logic is shown in Fig. A.26.

```
void in_order (struct tree *root)
{
    /* if root does not exist, it means this is an empty tree. So,
    do not display anything */
    if (root == NULL)
        return;

    in_order (root->left);
    print ("%d ", root->number);
    in_order (root->right);
}
```

Fig. A.26 In-order retrieval of binary tree

Note that this logic is also recursive in nature. How would this program work? To understand this, refer to the same sample tree shown in Fig. A.27.

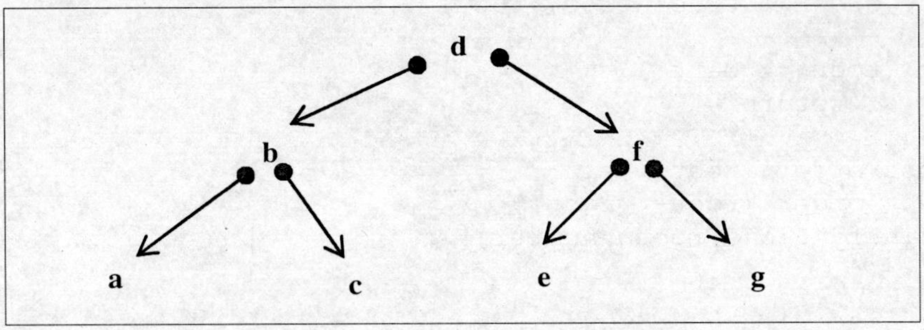

Fig. A.27 Sample binary tree

Let us understand the steps of execution.

1. First, the program checks if the root exists. In this case, the root (d) does exist. So, the program proceeds further.
2. Now, the function calls itself, passing the left node of itself (b). Since this is a recursive call, it would enter the in_order function once more, and call itself once again, passing the new left node of itself (a). This also being a recursive call, it will result into a call to itself passing the new left node of itself (null, this time). This call to itself will now cause the *if* condition (to check if the root is null) to become true. As a result, the recursion ends here. The functions are now executed in the reverse order (with values a and b). This will display a and b.
3. Next, the following function call executes:

   in_order (root->right);
4. This causes a call to itself with the value c now, so it will display c.
5. At this stage, the traversal from d to the left sub-tree is over. So, the function will display d.
6. Now, the right sub-tree of the root (e-f-g) gets displayed similar to the manner in which the left sub-tree was displayed earlier (by using recursive function calls). We will not elaborate on it, as it is exactly similar to the way a-b-c were displayed earlier.

Figure A.28 depicts the pre-order traversal.

```
void pre_order (struct tree *root)
{
      if (root == NULL)
            return;

      printf ("%d", root->number);
      pre_order (root->left);
      printf ("%d", root->right);
}
```

Fig. A.28 Pre-order traversal of the tree

Similarly, the function for a post-order traversal would be as shown in Fig. A.29.

```
void post_order (struct tree *root)
{
      if (root == NULL)
            return;

      post_order (root->left);
      post_order (root->right);
      printf ("%d", root->number);
}
```

Fig. A.29 Post-order traversal of the tree

Appendix B

Sorting Techniques

B.1 SORTING

Sorting of data means arranging it in some order or sequence.

For instance, assume that we have four numbers 78, 16, 18, 70. If we arrange them in an ascending (increasing) order to make the list as 16, 18, 70, 78, then the list is considered as sorted in an ascending order. Similarly, if we arrange these four numbers as 78, 70, 18, 16, then the list is sorted in a descending (decreasing) order.

Sorting need not only be applied to numbers. For example, if there are five alphabets X, I, A, E, T, they can be sorted in either ascending order (A, E, I, T, X) or descending order (X, T, I, E, A).

Sorting techniques have a great importance in computer applications. For instance, consider the following requirements that need the use of sorting techniques.

- Arrange the list of employees in decreasing order of salaries.
- Sort the records in the student file, in order of marks.
- Sort the array of marketing persons in increasing order of their sales figures.

In all such cases, we will have to re-arrange the original information so that it is either in an increasing or a decreasing order of some field (called the **sorting key**). Typical examples of sorting keys are sales figures, student ids and names, marks, grades, totals, summary figures, sales totals, salaries, and so on.

In order to perform sorting efficiently, a number of sorting techniques/algorithms are available. They vary in their complexity, and therefore, efficiency. We shall discuss the following main sorting algorithms.

1. Exchange sort
2. Selection sort
3. Quick sort
4. Tree sort

These four techniques, when applied to computers, are performed quite quickly. But we should know the advantages and drawbacks of each one of them so that we know which ones should be used in which contexts. DBMS makes use of the various sorting techniques quite extensively for retrieving data in the most efficient manner.

B.1.1 Exchange Sort

The basic mechanism in an **exchange sort** technique is to again and again make comparisons, and if required, to swap or exchange the adjacent items. **Bubble sort** is also an example of the exchange sort technique. The name *bubble sort* presents an interesting analogy. Imagine that we are pouring water in a tank. As water is poured, bubbles keep emerging. Every bubble settles down at some location, after a short interval of time. Similarly, imagine that the items to be sorted are *poured* inside the *bubble sorting* algorithm! The output is the items that settle down (arranged) in their correct order, akin to the way the bubbles settle down in the water tank. Hence the name *bubble sort*!

Bubble sort is perhaps the most widely used sorting algorithms for teaching sorting algorithms. However, it is not a recommended method for practical applications. The reason behind this is that although bubble sort is the simplest to understand, and is very poor in terms of performance.

Figure B.1 illustrates a program that performs the bubble sort operation. It first asks the user for a string. It then sorts the string in the ascending order of the alphabet contained in the string.

```
#include <stdio.h>
#include <string.h>
#include <stdlib.h>

/* Function declaration */
void bubble (char *str, int length);

/* driver program, that calls the bubble sort routine */
void main (void)
{
    char str[80];

    /* Accept the input string to be sorted */
    printf ("Enter the original string: ");
    gets (str);

    if (str != NULL)
        bubble (str, strlen (str));
}

/* actual bubble sort functionality */
void bubble (char *str, int length)
{
```

```
    register  int  i,  j;
    register  char  swap;

    /*  outer  loop  executes  length-1  times  */
    for  (i=0;  i<length;  i++)
         for  (j=i+1;  j<length;  j++)
         {
              if  (str[i]  >  str[j])
              {
                   swap  =  str[i];
                   str[i]  =  str[j];
                   str[j]  =  swap;
              }
         }

    printf  ("The  string  sorted  in  the  descending  order  is:%s\n",str);
}
```

Fig. B.1 Bubble sort illustration

Consider that the user has entered a string z y w x. The bubble sort procedure will sort it as w x y z. For this, the following iterations would be performed, for the possible values of the loop counters, i and j. Table B.1 illustrates the step-by-step process for this.

Table B.1 Bubble sort execution

Value of i	*Value of j*	*Current list*
0	0	z y w x
0	1	y z w x
	2	w z y x
	3	w z y x
1	2	w y z x
	3	w x z y
2	3	w x y z

Thus, iteration-wise, there are four logical steps, as follows:

Initial string	z	y	w	x
After round 1	w	z	y	x
After round 2	w	x	z	y
After round 3	w	x	y	z

These steps resemble what happens when the value of i (i.e. the value of the counter of the outer loop) changes.

As we can see from the earlier figure, the total number of steps in the algorithm for sorting 4 items is 6. These steps are:

For i = 0	j = 1, 2, 3	i.e. 3 steps
For i = 1	j = 2, 3	i.e. 2 steps
For i = 2	j = 3	i.e. 1 step
		i.e. total 6 steps

Consider two extreme cases.

- Suppose the initial string entered by the user is w x y z. This string is already in a sorted order. There is no sorting required at all. But how many steps would bubble sort still perform? Unfortunately, it would still perform the same number of steps, that is, 6!
- Now suppose the initial string was z y x w. This string is completely out of order. How many steps would bubble sort still perform? Even in this case, it would perform the same number of steps, that is, 6!

As we can see, the bubble sort technique always needs to perform the same number of steps, regardless of whether the original list is already sorted, somewhat sorted, or is completely out of order! How many steps would this lead to? In our illustration, there were four items to be sorted, and it required 6 steps (which is equal to 4 * 3 / 2).

In general, to sort n values, bubble sort always requires [n * (n – 1) / 2] steps. Thus, to sort 100 values, bubble sort would need to perform (100 * 99 / 2), that is, 4,950 steps!

Obviously, this becomes a mammoth operation as the number of values to be sorted increases! Of course, even though the number of steps in the algorithm is completely independent of the order of the original list, the number of exchanges within those steps (i.e. the satisfaction of the *if* condition in the program listed earlier) is impacted, based on this factor. The more sorted the original list, the lesser is the number of exchange operations required, and the more unsorted the original list, the more is the number of exchange operations required. Note that there are three exchanges for every item that is not in the correct order.

Because the number of steps required in bubble sort is approximately equal to the square of the number of items to be sorted, it is also called as an *n-square algorithm*, where n is the number of items to be sorted.

B.1.2 Selection Sort

The method adopted by the selection sort technique is different from exchange sort. To understand how it works, imagine that we have n items in a list in any sequence and we wish to arrange them in the correct sequence. By employing the selection sort technique, the first item in the list is compared with the remaining (n-1) items of the list. The lowest of all of these is placed in the first position of the output list. Next, the second item from the list is taken out and compared with the remaining (n-2) items of the list. If an item with a value less than that of the second item is found in the (n-2) items, it is swapped with the second item of the list, and so on. This continues for all the remaining items in the list. Thus, the idea is to select the smallest item to fit into the current position or slot of the list.

A C function to perform selection sort is shown in Fig. B.2. Here, we have illustrated the sorting of the alphabets in a string in an ascending order.

```
void selection (char *str, int len)
{
    int i, j, k, swap;
    char temp;

    for (i=0; i<len-1; i++)
    {
        swap = 0;
        k = i;
        temp = str[i];

        for (j=i+1; j<len; j++)
        {
            if (str[j] < temp)
            {
                k = j;
                temp = str[j];
                swap = 1;
            }
        }

        if (swap > 0)
        {
            str[k] = str[i];
            str[i] = temp;
        }
    }
}
```

Fig. B.2 Selection sort logic

Consider that our input string to this logic is b d a c. Let us now track down the progress of the selections ort technique step-by-step on this string. Take a look at Table B.2.

Table B.2 Major steps in selection sort

Value of i	*Current list*
0	b d a c
1	a d b c
2	a b d c
3	a b c d

The internal details of this process are depicted in Table B.3. This should give us a better idea about the precise working of the selection sort technique. We have provided the values of the various variables used in the selection sort process at each step.

Table B.3 Detailed steps in selection sort

i	*j*	*k*	*t*	*swap*	*Current list*
0	1	0	b	0	
	2	0	b	0	
	3	2	a	1	
					a d b c
1	2	1	d	0	
	3	2	b	1	a b d c
2	3	3	c	1	a b c d

We will notice that although the selection sort algorithm differs from exchange sort, it still has the same complexity as exchange sort. This is because it also requires a total of n * (n – 1) / 2 comparisons. The only advantage is that the number of exchanges or swaps required here as compared to the exchange sort is lesser. Therefore, selection sort is somewhat more efficient than exchange sort.

B.1.3 Quick Sort

Quick sort is the most efficient sorting method. It was invented by CAR Hoare. It is built on the idea of creating partitions.

We consider that there are n elements in our list. We need to sort them. The way quick sort works is that it identifies an item (say k) in the list. It then shifts all the items in the list that have a value less than k to the left of k, and all the items that have a value greater than k to the right of k. Thus, we now have two sub-lists, say list-1 and list-2 within the main list, with k standing between list-1 and list-2.

We then identify new k's in the two lists, that is, in list-1 and list-2. Consequently, list-1 and list-2 each will be portioned further into two sub-lists, and so on. This goes on until the entire list is exhausted. Technically, k can be anywhere in the list, but it is generally most efficient to have it in the middle of the list. Thus, if we have a list of items as d a c e b to be sorted, perhaps c is the best candidate for being treated as *k*.

The following example illustrates how quick sort works. Imagine a list of numbers as follows.

43	33	11	55	77	90	40	60	99	22	88	**65**

Step 1: Find out the final position of one of the numbers (that is, k) in the list. As we discussed, it can be any number in the list. We start with the first number, that is, 43. Starting with the last number in the list (that is, 65), search the list from right to left, comparing each number with 43, and stopping at the first number that is less than 43. As we can see, this number is 22. So, we swap 43 with 22. The list now looks as follows.

22	33	11	55	77	90	40	60	99	**43**	88	65

Step 2: Note that the numbers 88 and 65 to the right of 43 are greater than 43. Starting with 22, scan the list into the opposite direction (left to right), comparing each number with 43 and stopping

at the first number, which is greater than 43. This number is 55. So, swap 43 and 55. The new list looks as follows.

22	33	11	**43**	77	90	40	60	99	**55**	88	65

Step 3: Note that the numbers 22, 33 and 11 are all to the left of 43, and are less than 43. Starting with 55, scan the list in the original direction (i.e. right to left), stopping at the first number that is less than 43. It is 40. So, swap 43 and 40. The new list now looks as follows.

22	33	11	**40**	77	90	**43**	60	99	55	88	65

Step 4: Note that numbers to the right of 43 are greater than 43. Starting with 40, scan the list left to right, stopping at the first number, which is greater than 43. It is 77, so swap 77 and 43. The new list looks as follows.

22	33	11	40	**43**	90	77	60	99	55	88	65

Now, note that all the numbers to the left of 43 are less than 43, and all the numbers to the right of 43 are greater than 43. Thus, our original number 43 is at its correct sorted position. Therefore, we now split the list into two halves, one containing the items that are to the left of 43, and the other containing the items that are to the right of 43. This is shown below.

22	33	11	40	90	77	60	99	55	88	65

43

Now, the task is to sort the two sub-lists separately using the same mechanism (identify one item from each of the sub-lists, and go on sorting until that element is in its right position, and then re-split the list into two yet smaller lists, and so on). Continue this process until all the elements are sorted. The actual function for performing such a quick sort operation is shown in Fig. B.3.

```
#include  <stdio.h>
#include  <string.h>

void  quick  (char  *arr,  int  left,  int  right);

/*  driver  function  */

void  main  (void)
{
      char  arr[400];
      int  i  =  0;

      printf  ("Enter  input  string  to  be  sorted:  ");
      gets  (arr);
      i  =  strlen  (arr);

      quick  (arr,  0,  i  -  1);
```

```
    printf("Sorted string is: %s\n", arr);
}

void quick (char *arr, int left, int right)
{
    register int a, b;
    char x,y;

    a = left;
    b = right;

    x = arr[(left+right) / 2];

    do
    {
        while (arr[a] < x && a < right) a++;
        while (x < arr[b] && b > left) b—;

        if (a <= b)
        {
            y = arr[a];
            arr[a] = arr[b];
            arr[b] = y;
            a++; b—;
        }
    }
    while (a <= b);

    if (left < b)
        quick (arr, left, b);           /* recursive call */

    if (a < right)
        quick (arr, a, right);     /* recursive call */
}
```

Fig. B.3 Quick sort example

B.1.4 Tree Sort

The tree sort is based on the algorithm of sorting a binary tree into its correct sequence. Thus, it is similar to the idea of placing a value in its appropriate position of the tree. As we know, a binary tree has a root at the top and roots expanded down the tree. In tree sorting, we organise all these elements in such a fashion that they are arranged from left to right. Fig. B.4 illustrates tree sorting.

```
void tree_sort (int list [ ], int n)
{
     int k, temp, value, j, i, p;
     int step = 1;

     for (k=n; k>=2; k–)
     {
          temp = list [i];
          list [i] = list [k];
          list [k] = temp;

          i = 1;
          value = list [i];
          j = 2;

          if ( (j+1) < k)
               if (list [j+1] > list [j])
                    j++;

          while ((j < (k-1)) && (list [j] > value))
          {
               list [i] = list [j];
               i = j;
               j = 2 * i;

               if ((j+1) < k)
                    if (list[j+1] > list[j])
                         j++;
                    else
                         if (j>n)
                              j = n;

               list [i] = value;
          }

          printf ("\n Step number = %d", step++);

          for (p = 1; p <= n; p++)
               printf (" %d ", list [p]);
     }
}
```

Fig. B.4 Tree sort

The worst case cost of this sort is O (n $\log_2$ n).

Table B.4 summarises the various sorting algorithms in terms of their time and space complexities.

Table B.4 Comparisons of sorting techniques

Sorting technique	*Case*	*Time complexity*	*Space complexity*
Selection sort	Average	O (n^2)	0
	Worst	O (n^2)	0
Bubble sort	Average	O (n^2)	0
	Worst	O (n^2)	0
Insertion sort	Average	O (n^2)	0
	Worst	O (n^2)	0
Merge sort	Average	O (n log n)	O (n)
	Worst	O (n log n)	O (n)
Quick sort	Average	O (n log n)	O (n)
	Worst	O (n^2)	O (n)

B.2 SEARCHING TECHNIQUES

Searching for data is a very common and widely used operation in computer applications. There are many occasions when we need to search for certain information. Examples of such situations are as follows.

- Find out the list of employees who earn more than Rs 20,000 a month.
- Display a list of all the customers who were serviced by a particular sales person in the last month.
- Which tasks in today's schedule are highly critical and of more priority?

As a result, a lot of research has gone into making the searching process more efficient. It should be possible to search for information with the minimum possible efforts, and at the maximum possible speed. The information to be searched can be in the memory (in the form of lists, arrays or trees) or it can be on the disk of the computer (in the form of a disk file or a database). In either case, the success of a searching algorithm depends on how quickly one is able to search for information, regardless of the medium in which it is available. (Of course, information retrieval from a disk would be more time-consuming as compared to the retrieval from the memory. However, the focus here is on the efficiency of the search algorithm, all other things being equal).

At a broad level, searching can take one of the two following forms:

- **Sequential search** (also called as **linear search**)
- **Binary search**

We shall discuss these two mechanisms now.

B.2.1 Sequential Search

Sequential search is the traditional mechanism of searching for information. It is very simple to understand, but can be very poor in performance at times. As the name says, the process of searching for information in a sequential search is sequential (or one after the other). Given a list of items, to find if a particular item exists (or does not exist) in the list, the sequential algorithm shown in Fig. B.5 can be used.

1. Start with a number k = 1.
2. If there are still more items in the list
   Compare the kth element in the list with the item to be searched.
   Else
   Item is not found in the list. Stop.
3. If a match is found
   The item is found in the list. Stop.
   Else
   Add 1 to k, and go back to step 1.

Fig. B.5 Sequential search

The key aspect of this algorithm is that we start with the first item in the list, and go up to the end of the list, or until the item to be searched is found, whichever is earlier.

Table B.5 shows the number of times this algorithm is likely to be executed, depending on the best, average and worst possible cases. Note that we assume that the list contains *N* items.

Table B.5 Sequential search: Likely number of iterations

Case	*Meaning*	*Number of iterations*
Best	The item to be searched is the first item in the list.	1
Average	The item to be searched is found somewhere close to the middle of the list	N/2
Worst	The item to be searched is the last item in the list, or it does not exist at all.	N

Note that the average number of iterations (N/2) is most likely over a period of time. Thus, if we have 10,000 items in a list, on an average, it would require (10,000/2), that is, 5,000 iterations.

Consider an array named *arr*, containing 1000 integers. We can use the function shown in Fig. B.6 to search for a specific number (say *item*) in that array.

```
sequential_search (int item)
{
    int i;

    for (i=0; i<1000; i++)
    {
        if (arr[i] == item)
        {
            printf ("Item found at the position %d in the
            array\n", i+1);
            return;
        }
    }
    printf ("Item not found in the array\n");
}
```

Fig. B.6 Sequential search: Likely number of iterations

The function is quite simple to understand. It basically scans through all the elements of the array one-by-one, starting with the first element of the array. In each case, it compares the current element in the array with the item to be searched for. If a match is found, the processing stops with an appropriate message indicating a successful search. However, if no match is found even after the entire array is exhausted, the function displays a message that the item was not found in the array.

B.3 BINARY SEARCH

Binary search is a vast improvement over the sequential search. However, it cannot always be used, unlike a sequential search. For binary search to work, the items in the list must be in a sorted order [either increasing (ascending) or decreasing (descending)]. This is a pre-requisite for binary search. Note that this is not at all required in the case of a sequential search (although sequential search works equally fine with a sorted/unsorted list). If the list to be searched for a specific item is not sorted, binary search fails.

The approach employed by binary search is called *divide-and-conquer*. Assume that a list contains 1000 elements, which are sorted in an ascending order of their values. An item x is to be searched in that list. Then the approach used by the binary search algorithm is as shown in Fig. B.7.

1. Divide the original list into two equal-sized logical halves. Let us call them Half-1 and Half-2. In this case, the original 1000-element list will be split into two halves, each containing 500 elements.
2. Compare x with the last (500th) element of Half-1. There are three possibilities:
    a. The value of x matches with that of the 500th element of Half-1. If this is the case, the search is successful. Therefore, display an appropriate message and stop processing.
    b. The value of x is greater than that of the 500th element of Half-1. Note that our list was originally sorted in the ascending order. Thus, if the value of x is greater than the last element of Half-1, it means that x is definitely not one of the first 500 elements in the 1,000-element array.
    c. The value of x is less than that of the 500th element of Half-1. Note that our list was originally sorted in the ascending order. Thus, if the value of x is less than the last element of Half-1, it means that if x is in the list, it must definitely be one of the first 500 elements in the 1,000-element array.

Fig. B.7 Binary search algorithm

The result is summarised in Table B.6.

Table B.6 Next action depending on the outcome

Outcome	*Next action*
a. x = Last element of Half-1	Stop processing.
b. x > Last element of Half-1	Search for x within *Half-2*.
c. x < Last element of Half-1	Search for x within *Half-1*.

- Clearly, case a is quite simple, and there is nothing to discuss there. So, we shall now concentrate on case b and c.

- In case b, we need to look for x in *Half-2*. So, we can safely discard *Half-1* altogether, and worry only about *Half-2*. We shall use the same approach as before. We will now divide *Half-2* made up of 500 elements into two halves, each half consisting of 250 elements. Let us call these two halves of *Half-2* as *Half-2-1* and *Half-2-2*. We now compare x with the last element of *Half-2-1*. This will also have three possibilities, a, b or c, as discussed earlier. Depending on that we can stop processing, or divide *Half-2-1* or *Half-2-2* into two halves, and so on. We stop when either a match for x is found, or when we split the list so much that the list cannot be split any further.
- Case c is similar to case b. However, we shall describe it completely, for the sake of completeness. In case b, we need to look for x in *Half-1*. So, we can safely discard *Half-2* altogether, and worry only about *Half-1*. We shall use the same approach as before. We will now divide *Half-1* made up of 500 elements into two halves, each half consisting of 250 elements. Let us call these two halves of *Half-1* as *Half-1-1* and *Half-1-2*. We now compare x with the last element of *Half-1-1*. This will also have three possibilities, a, b or c, as discussed earlier. Depending on that we can stop processing, or divide *Half-1-1* or *Half-1-2* into two halves, and so on. We stop when either a match for x is found, or when we split the list so much that the list cannot be split any further.

An example would help make this discussion clearer. Suppose we have a list of numbers arranged in the ascending order, from 1 to 10, as follows.

1 2 3 4 5 6 7 8 9 10

Assume that we are looking up for a number 8 in the list, which is our x in this example. This would proceed as follows.

1. Divide the original list into two halves, the first half containing numbers 1-5, and the second half containing numbers 6-10.
2. Compare x (8) with the last number of the first half (5). Since 8 > 5, from our earlier logic, case b is true. This means that we should discard the first half (1-5) and look for x in the second half (6-10). Thus, our new list looks as follows.

   6 7 8 9 10
3. Now, we divide the current list (6-10) into two halves, one containing the numbers 6-7 and the other containing the numbers 8-10. We now compare x (8) with the last element of the first half (7). Since x (8) is greater than this, our earlier case b again stands to be proved. This means that we again discard the first half (6-7) and use only the second one. Accordingly, our new list now looks as follows.

   8 9 10
4. We now divide the current list into two halves. The first half would contain 8, and the second half would contain 9 and 10. We now compare x (8) with the last element of the first half (8). Since a match is found, our case a is true. So, we display an appropriate message, indicating that the element to be searched was found, and stop our processing.

Note that the binary search required just two *compare* operations. In contrast, a sequential search would have required 8 *compare* operations. Thus, binary search can be really fast. Of course, the more the number of elements in the list to be searched, the more effective is the binary search, as compared to the sequential search. For smaller lists, the overhead of first sorting the list so as to allow binary search to be possible can be more than performing a sequential search straightaway. So, some judicious decision-making is required in such cases to compare the advantages of sequential search versus binary search.

Fig. B.8 can be used to perform a binary search in a sorted array *arr*, which contains 1000 integer elements. The function expects the item to be searched as the input parameter, and returns the position at which the item is found, or –1 if the item is not found.

```
int binary_search (int arr[ ], int sitem)
{
    int low = 0, high = 999, mid;

    while (low <= high)
    {
        mid = (low + high) / 2;

        if (sitem < arr[mid])
            high = mid - 1;
        else
            if (sitem > arr[mid])
                low = mid + 1;
            else
                return mid; /* item found in the array*/
    }

    return -1;
}
```

Fig. B.8 Binary search

Appendix C

Database Management with Access

C.1 BASIC TABLE DESIGN

When we start the MS-Access software, the screen shown in Fig. C.1 appears. Using this screen, we can create a new database table, or open an existing one.

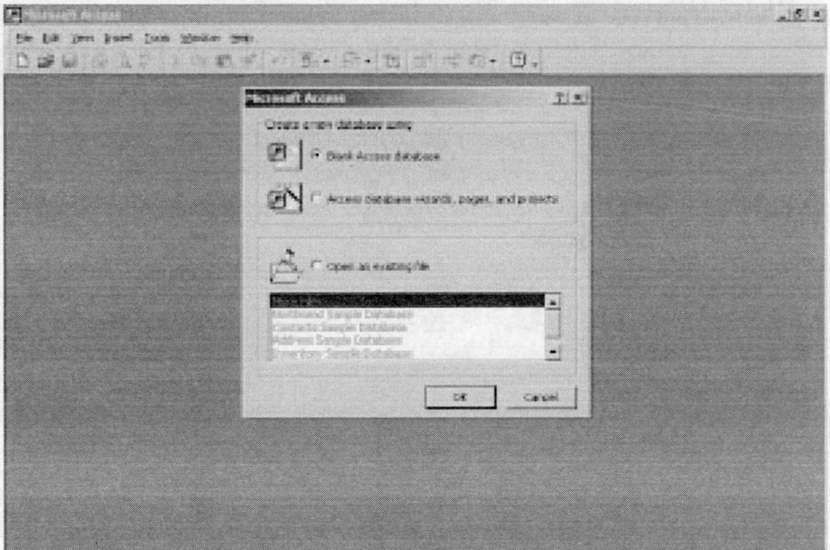

Fig. C.1 MS-Access: The first screen

Let us begin with a blank database, as creating it would teach us many simple concepts. Therefore, we shall select the radio button *Blank Access Database*, and click on OK. MS-Access would prompt us for the desired name and location of the database that we want to create. The result is shown in Fig. C.2.

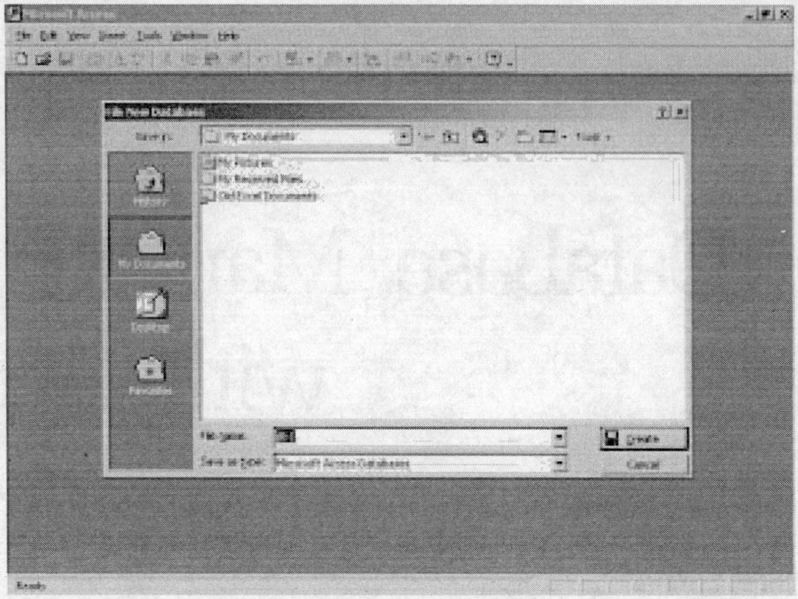

Fig. C.2 Creating a new database

We can change the database name and location (directory/folder), if needed. For now, we shall keep it to the default. That is, we will click on the *Create* button. This presents us with three choices, namely, creating a new database table in the design view, or by using a wizard, or by entering data, as shown in Fig. C.3.

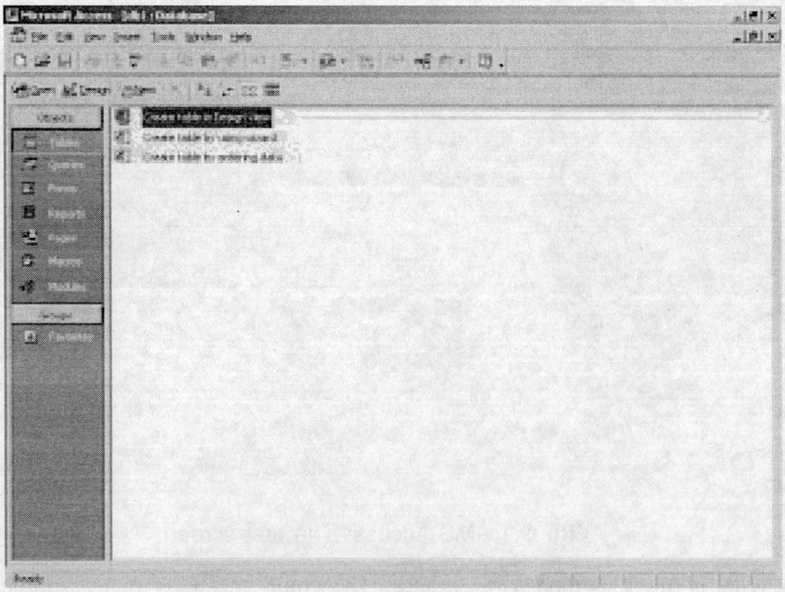

Fig. C.3 Options for creating a new table

Let us begin with the default option of creating a table in the design view. In order to do this, MS-Access shows us the screen shown in Fig. C.4.

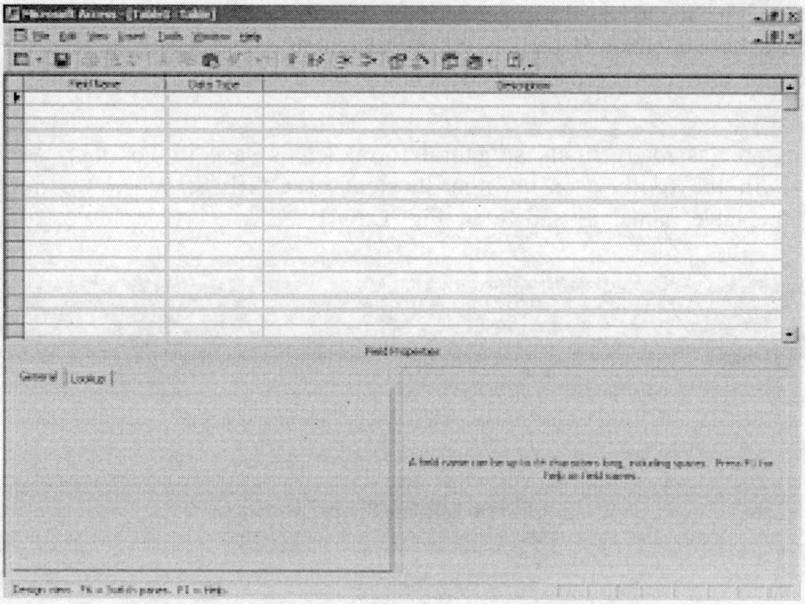

Fig. C.4 Creating a new table in the design view

Now, we can insert column names, data type and optionally, the description for each of the columns. The description is just for our information and has no impact on the database design or contents. We will create a table to store data about people and their credit cards, as shown in Fig. C.5.

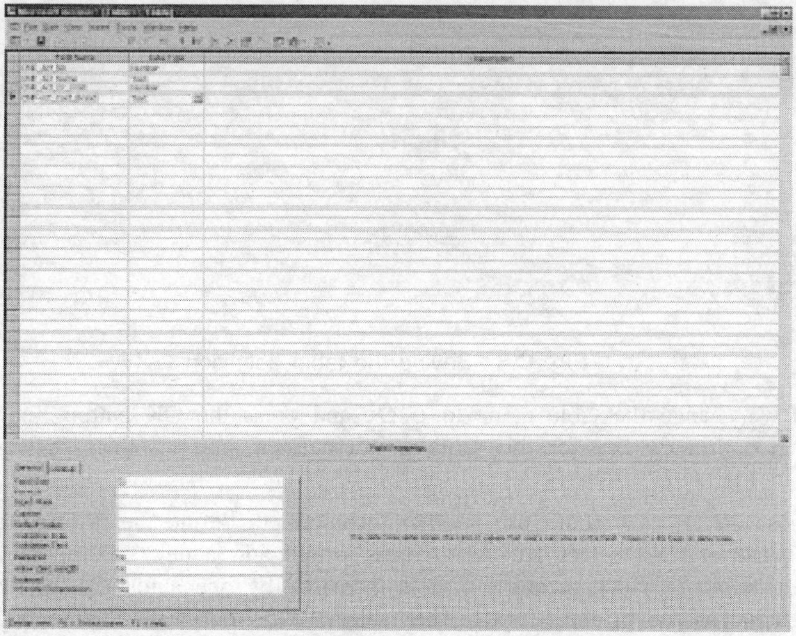

Fig. C.5 Column names and types

There are four columns in the Card Holder Master (CMF) table. They allow us to store the cardholder's account number, name, credit limit, and card type. Associated with each column is a *data type*. A data type identifies the type of data that the column can store (text, numbers, dates, and so on). As we have mentioned earlier, for each column, we can add more description (which we have not done), and also more properties. Depending on the requirements, we can choose an appropriate type.

Now that our table is ready in its structural form, let us save it. For that, we can click on the floppy disk icon in the toolbar, or use the shortcut of CTRL-S. When we do that, MS-Access prompts us for the table name, as shown in Fig. C.6.

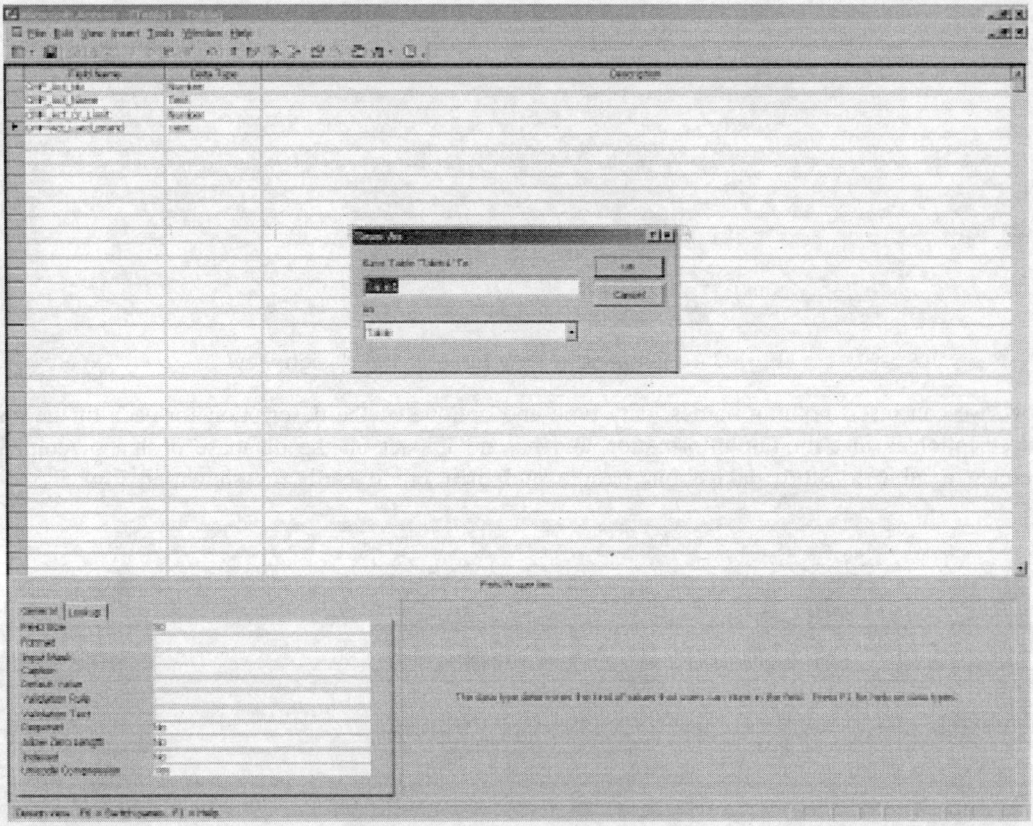

Fig. C.6 Saving the table definition

Imagine that we change the table name to *CMF*, and press the OK button. In response, MS-Access tells us that a primary key for this table is not defined, and whether we want to define one. This is shown in Fig. C.7.

We will choose *No*, as we would use another technique to define the primary key for our table. Why? This is because if we select *Yes*, MS-Access would add a new column on its own, with its data type as AutoNumber (which means that it is increased by one automatically for each row). This would be designated as the primary key of the table. We do not want this to happen. Instead, we want our CMF_Act_No column to be the primary key. How can we do so?

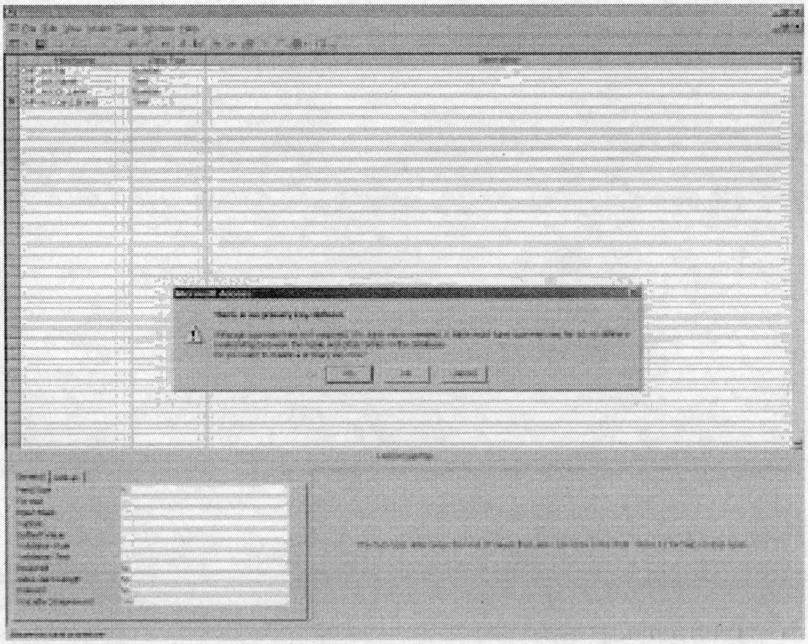

Fig. C.7 Primary key prompt

For designating a column as the primary key of the table, the simplest option is to right click on the column, and choose the *Primary Key* option, as shown in Fig. C.8. The other mechanisms for performing this action are the Edit-Primary Key menu option or the CTRL-K shortcut.

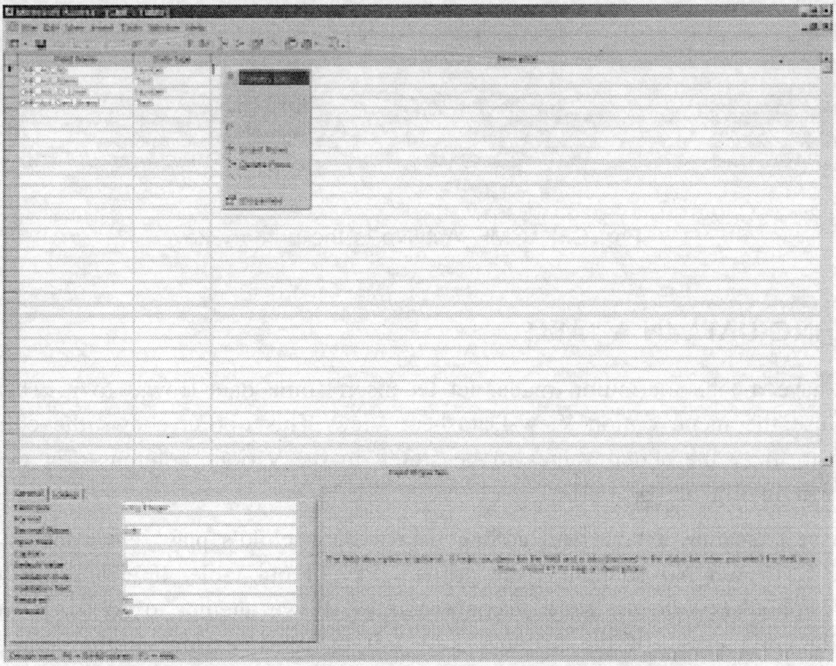

Fig. C.8 Making a column the primary key

Now, the CMF_Act_No column is the primary key of our CMF table. MS-Access shows this fact by adding a small key symbol in the leftmost column of CMF_Act_No, as shown in Fig. C.9.

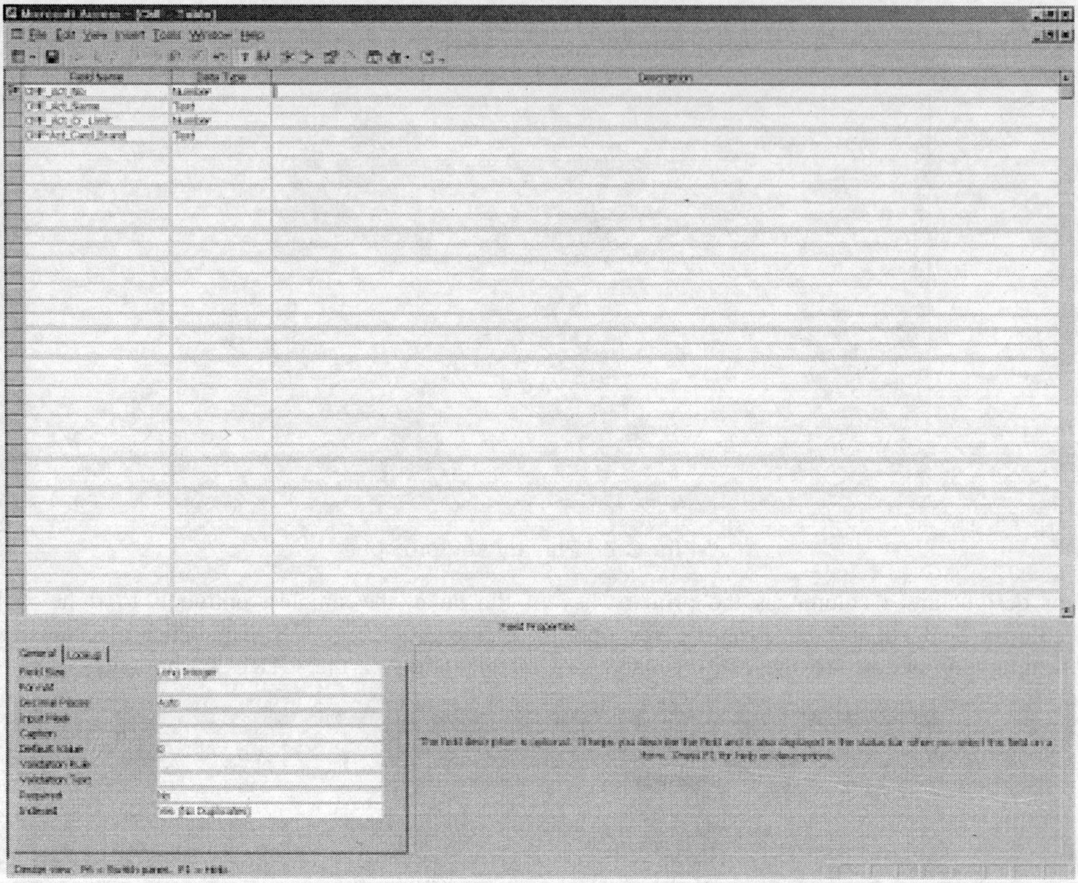

Fig. C.9 CMF_Act_No is the primary key

C.2 INSERTING DATA IN A TABLE

Now that we have a table definition made, let us insert some data (rows) to it. The easiest way to do this is to use the menu option View-Datasheet View. This option shows the columns vertically, and allows us to enter the actual values to be stored in the various columns. Let us add some data values, as shown in Fig. C.10.

As we can see, creating a table and adding data to it is child's play! Now, let us try a trick. We know that the CMF_Act_No column is the primary key of our table. It means that we cannot have two or more cardholders with the same account number. If we attempt to do so, it would violate the principle of the uniqueness of the primary key. Let us try inserting another employee row with CMF_Act_No as a duplicate. The result is shown in Fig. C.11.

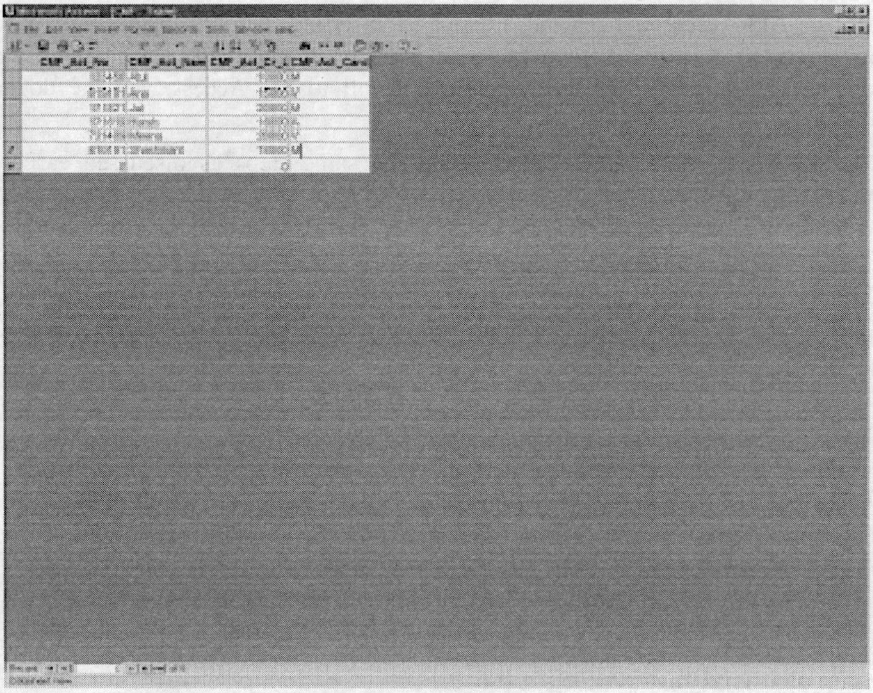

Fig. C.10 Adding rows to the table

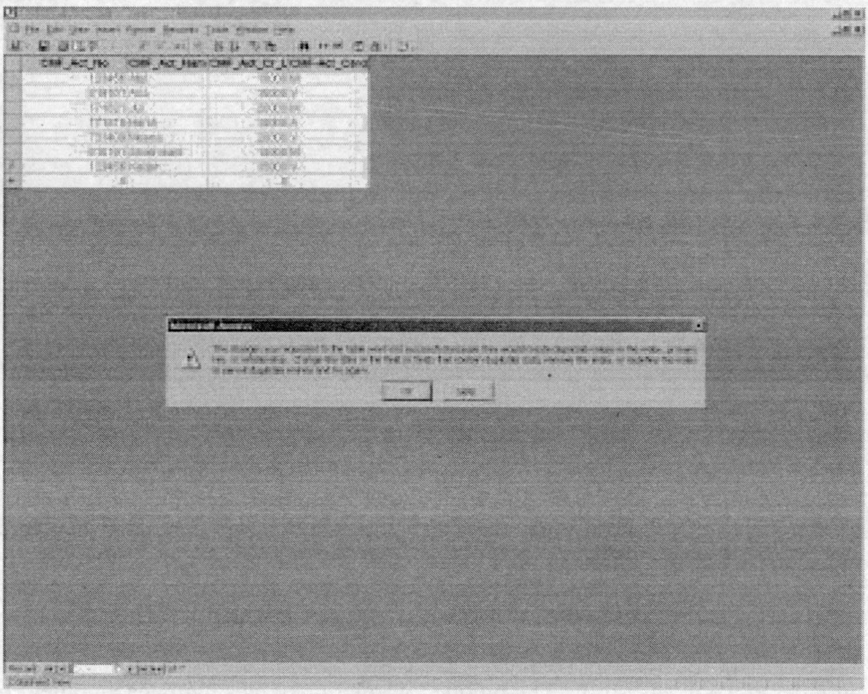

Fig. C.11 Attempt to add a duplicate value to a primary key column

As we can see, MS-Access notices the attempt of inserting a duplicate account number, and prevents us from doing so. Clearly, a good table design should put these verifications while designing the table itself, so that such type of error handling is left to MS-Access, and we do not have to be bothered about it.

Now, let us create one more table, Brand, using the same steps as discussed earlier. The end result is shown in Fig. C.12.

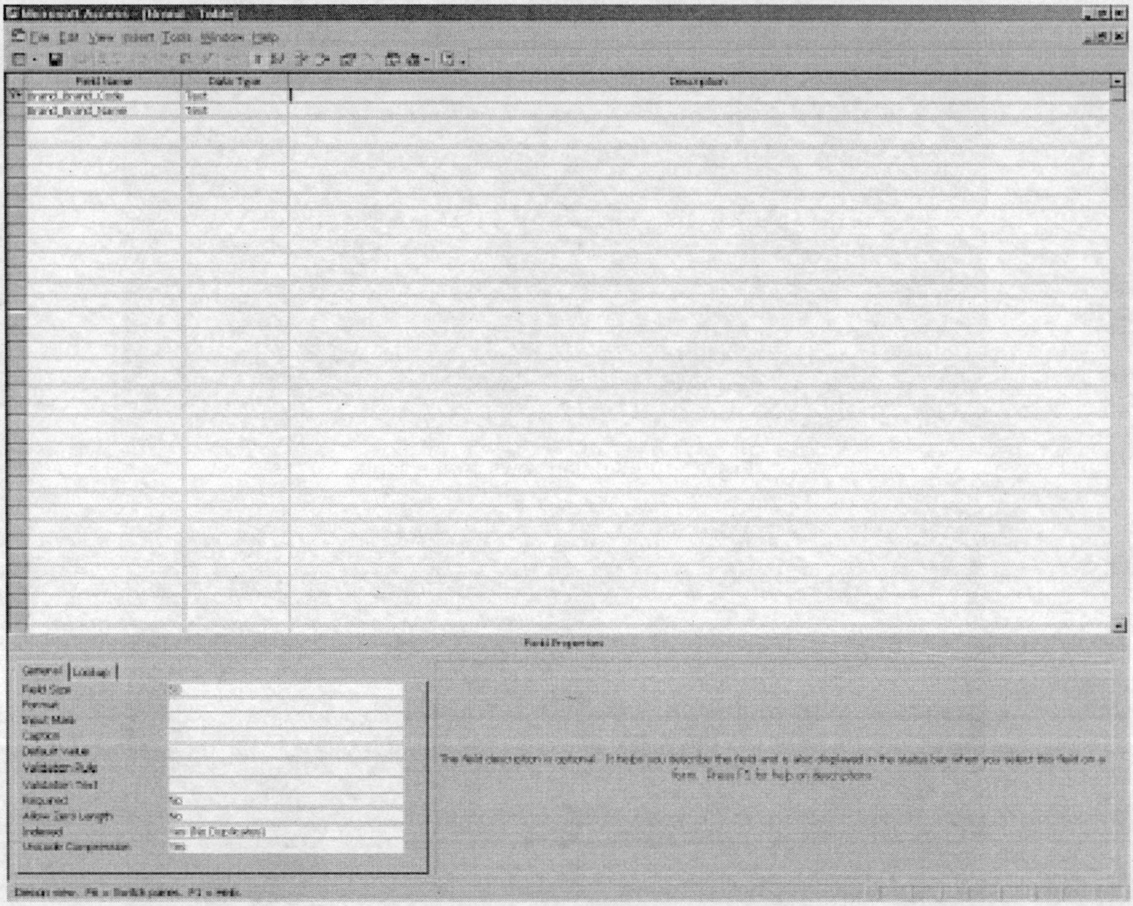

Fig. C.12 Brand table

If we observe carefully, we will realise that the brand identifiers (such as M, V and A) were used in our earlier CMF table. This means that the CMF table and the Brand table are actually related to each other on the basis of the Brand code.

C.3 TABLE RELATIONSHIPS

MS-Access provides a very easy-to-use technique of relating tables with each other. For doing this, we can use the menu option Tools-Relationships. When we do so, MS-Access prompts us to choose the tables we want to be included in the relationship, as shown in Fig. C.13.

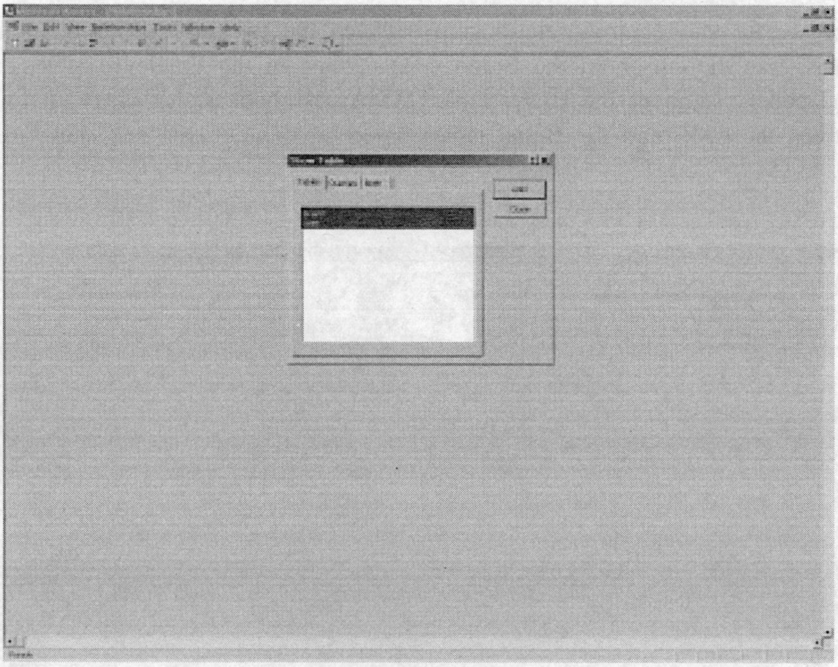

Fig. C.13 Relationships – Part 1

We select both the tables, and press the *Add* button. In response, MS-Access shows both tables, with all their columns, as depicted in Fig. C.14.

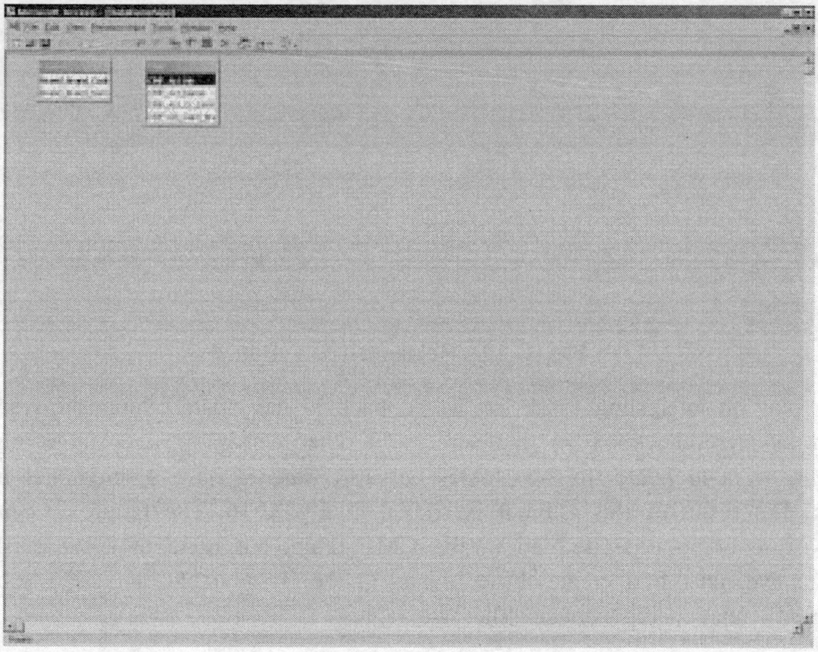

Fig. C.14 Relationships – Part 2

We can now create the required relationship between the two tables, based on the Brand code column. For this, take the cursor on the Brand code column in the Employee table, and then drag it onto the Brand code column of the Brand table. MS-Access notices that we wish to establish a relationship between the CMF and the Brand tables based on this column, and shows us the screen as shown in Fig. C.15.

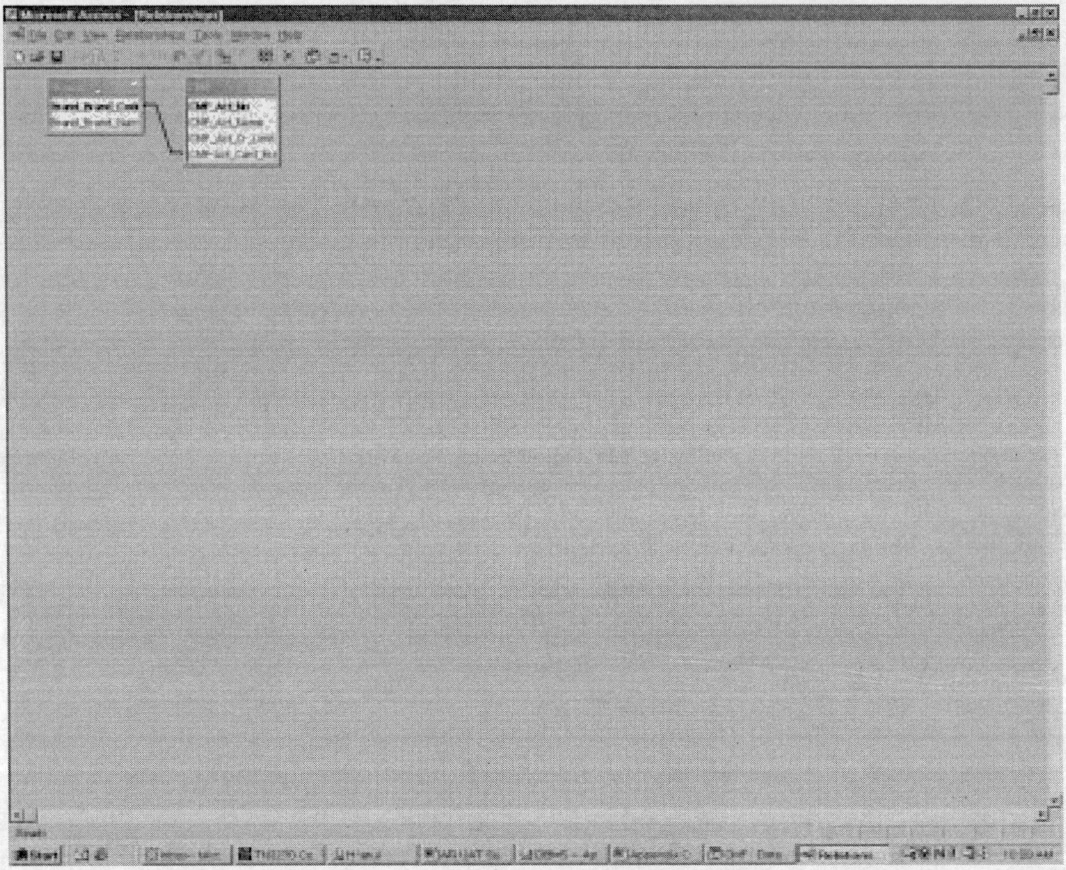

Fig. C.15 Relationships – Part 3

Let us now play an interesting trick. Let us go back to the create relationships screen, and check the *Referential integrity* checkbox on that screen. In other words, we are suggesting to MS-Access that we not only wish to relate the two tables but also want to have a referential integrity between the two tables. The result of this attempt is shown in Fig. C.16. The failure is caused because we have three possible brand type defined in the CMF table, but none of them exists in the Brand table! Therefore, we must first create these brands in the Brand table, and then attempt to create a referential integrity relationship between the two tables.

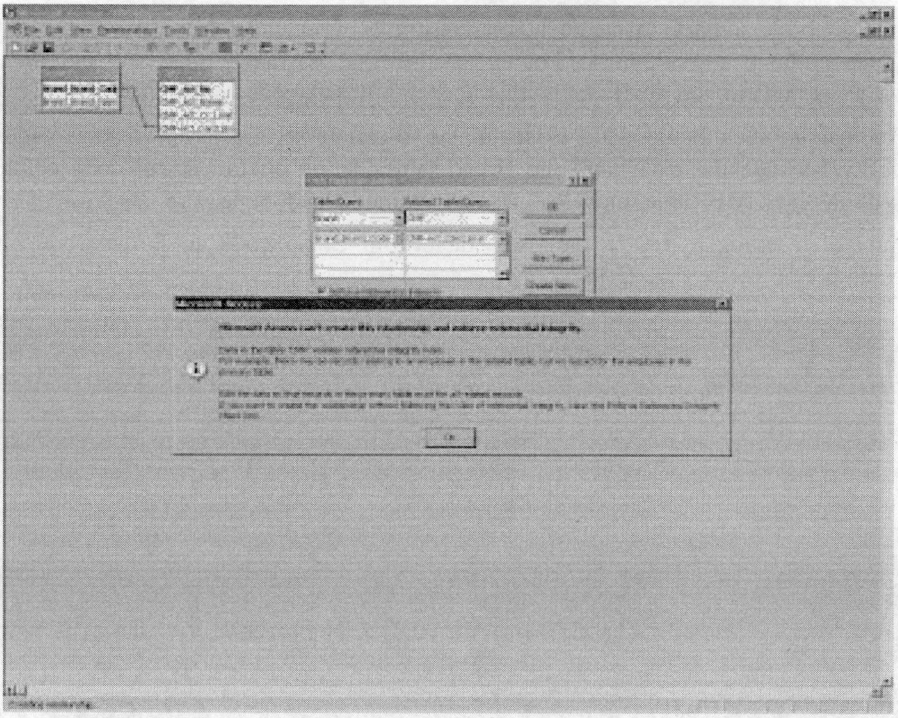

Fig. C.16 Relationships – Part 4

We now create the three brands in the Brand table, as illustrated in Fig. C.17.

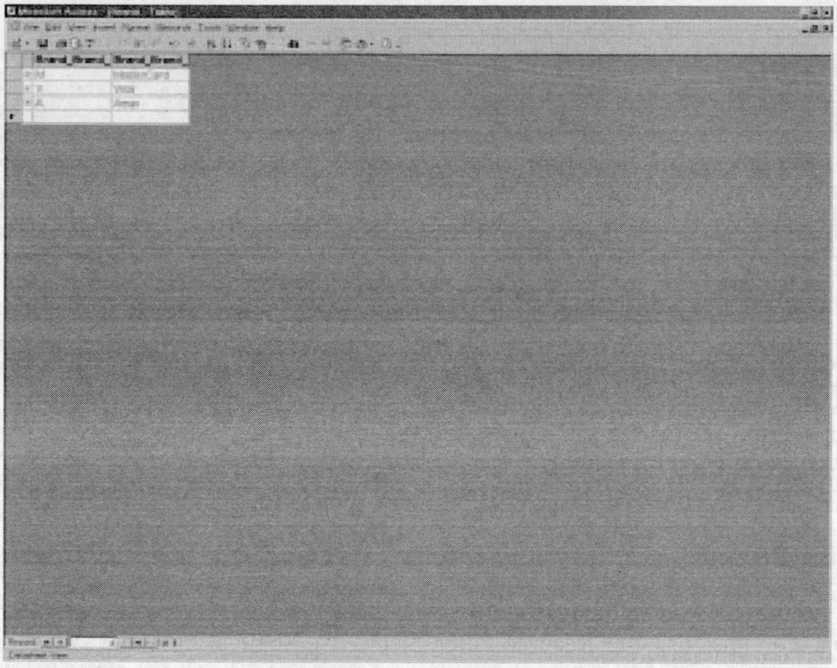

Fig. C.17 Relationships – Part 5

Now if we go back and try to create a relationship between the CMF and Brand tables based on the Brand code column, it will work. Let us assume that we have done so, and then try another trick. Let us try a row in the CMF table that has the Brand code value as T.

Remember that no such brand code exists in the Brand table. Because we have established a referential integrity between the CMF and the Brand tables based on the Brand code column, any code that is present in the CMF table must be present in the Brand table.

Our attempt of inserting a row in the CMF table with Brand code as T, therefore, must and does fail. The result is shown in Fig. C.18.

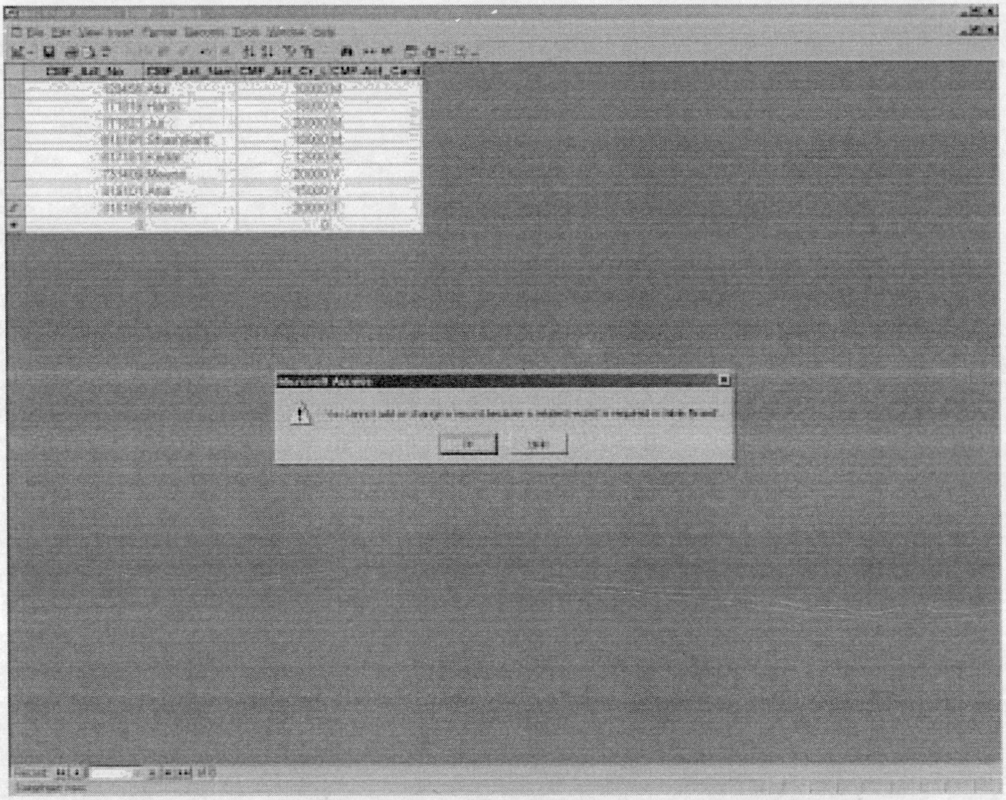

Fig. C.18 Relationships – Part 6

We must add the Brand code to the Brand table and then add a row with this Brand code to the CMF table. That attempt would certainly succeed.

C.4 MISCELLANEOUS FEATURES

C.4.1 Filtering Records

We can filter records based on many conditions, so that we get only those ones that match our selection criteria. For this, use the Records-Filter menu. We shall discuss the Advanced Filter option within this menu. When we select that option, the screen as shown in Fig. C.19 is shown, where we can enter our filter criteria.

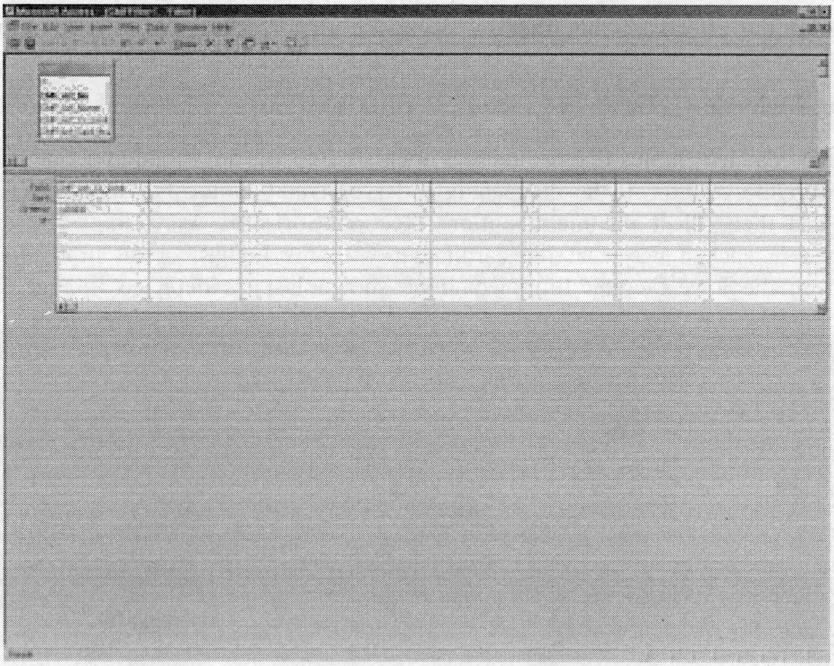

Fig. C.19 Applying filter

The filter that we have applied is to show only the details of cardholders whose credit limit is less than 10,000. When we click the *Apply Filter* button on the screen, we see only the records that satisfy the filtering criterion, as shown in Fig. C.20.

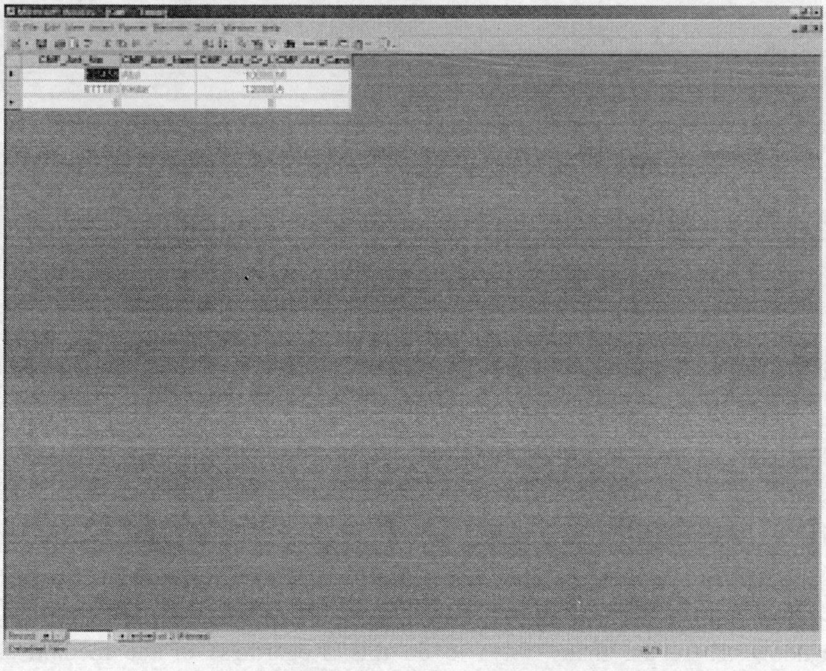

Fig. C.20 Results of the filter

We can cancel the effects of the filter by using the Records-Remove Filter/Sort option.

C.4.2 Sorting Records

We can sort records in a table, that is, reorder them, based on any condition that we want. For instance, let us sort the records in the descending order of credit limits. For this, select the Credit limit column first, and then select the menu options Records-Sort-Sort Ascending. The employee details would be sorted in such a way that the cardholder with the highest credit limit would appear first, and the one with the lowest credit limit would be shown last, as depicted in Fig. C.21.

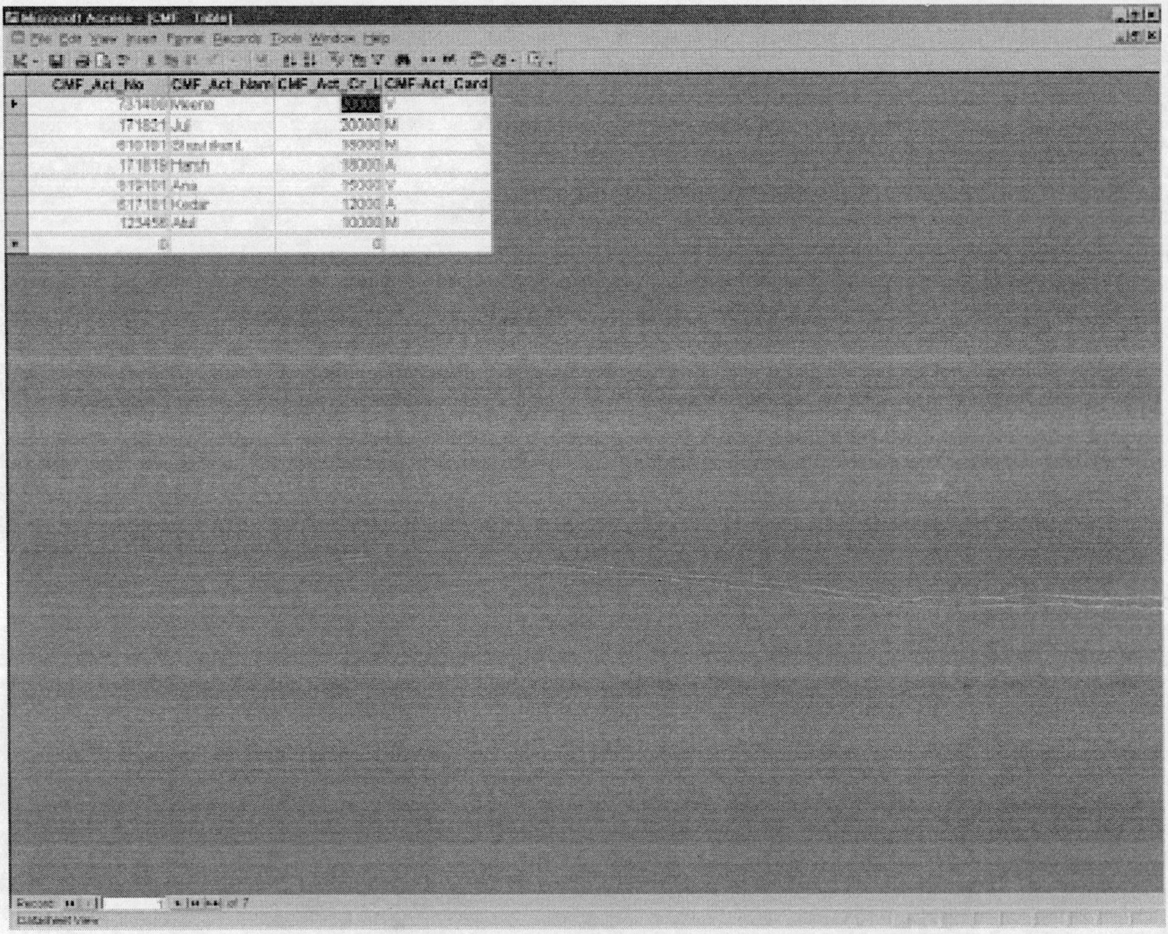

Fig. C.21 Results of the sort

C.5 CREATING REPORTS

We can create reports based on our databases/tables, so that the data can be displayed in a professional manner, and printed, if desired. For this, choose the menu option Insert-Report in the main MS-Access window. There are many ways to do this. Regardless of the method chosen, we get a screen as shown in Fig. C.22.

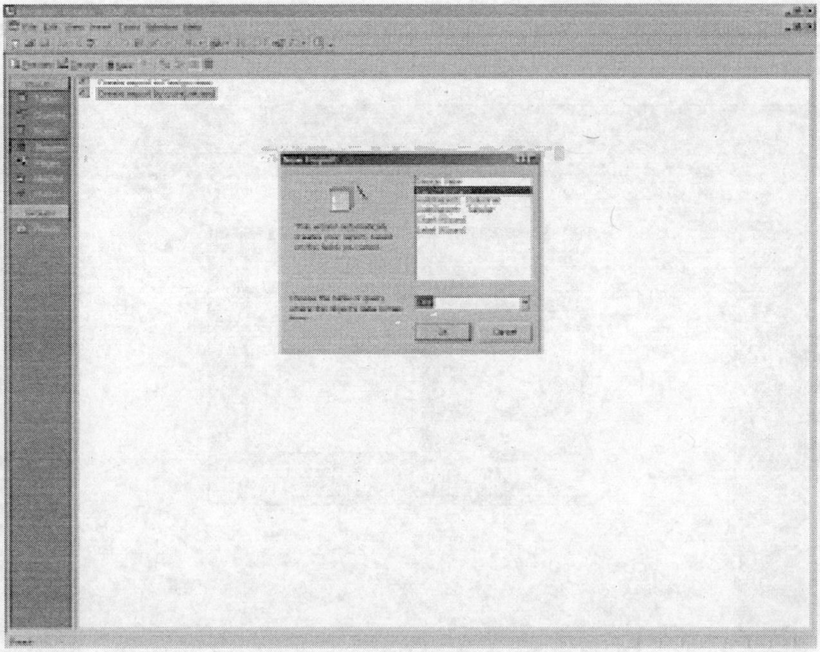

Fig. C.22 Report – Part 1

As shown, we select the *Report Wizard*, and press OK. Ensure that the *Employee* table is selected in the list box shown in the bottom portion of the screen. Now, MS-Access prompts us to select the columns that we would like to see in the report, as shown in Fig. C.23. We will select all and press the *Next* button.

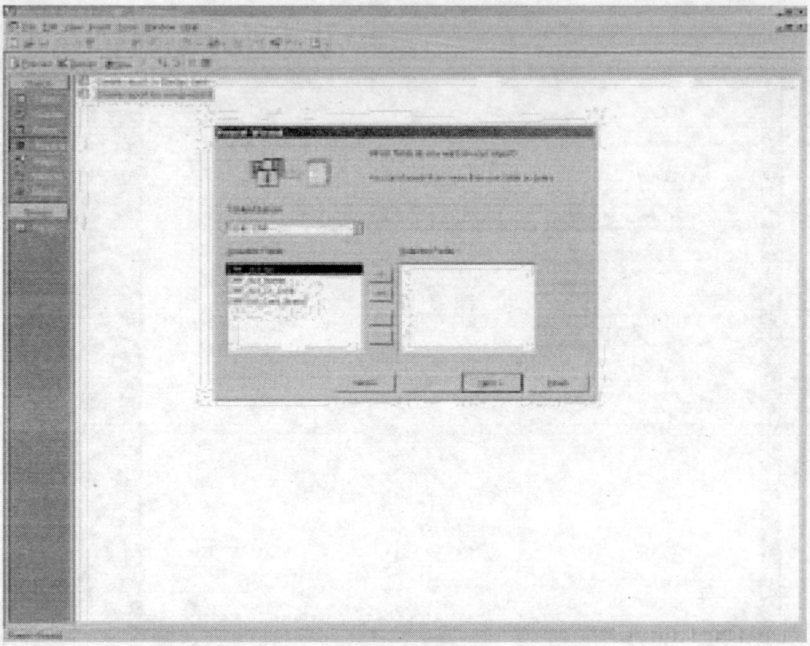

Fig. C.23 Report – Part 2

Now, MS-Access asks us if we want to perform any grouping based on any columns, as shown in Fig. C.24.

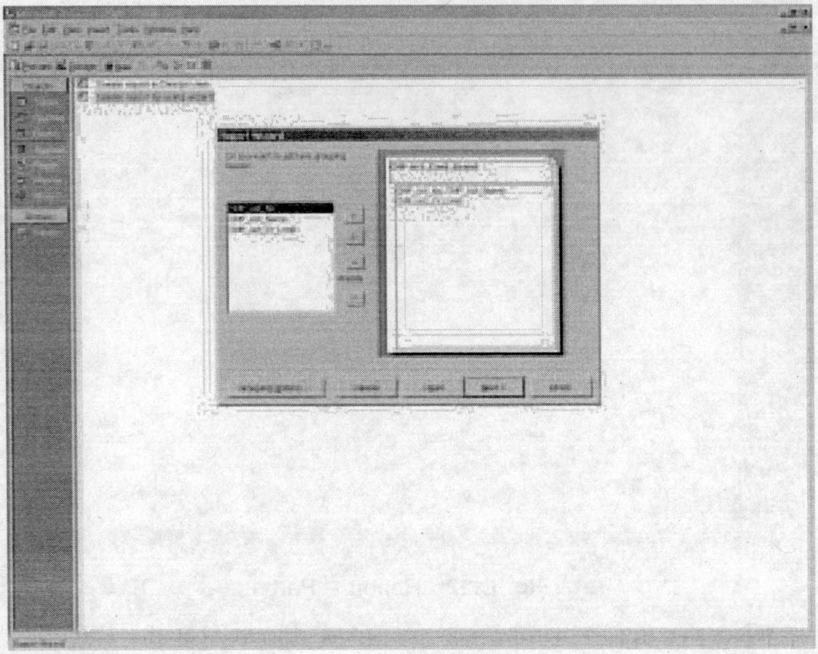

Fig. C.24 Report – Part 3

When we click *Finish*, MS-Access shows us the report as depicted in Fig. C.25.

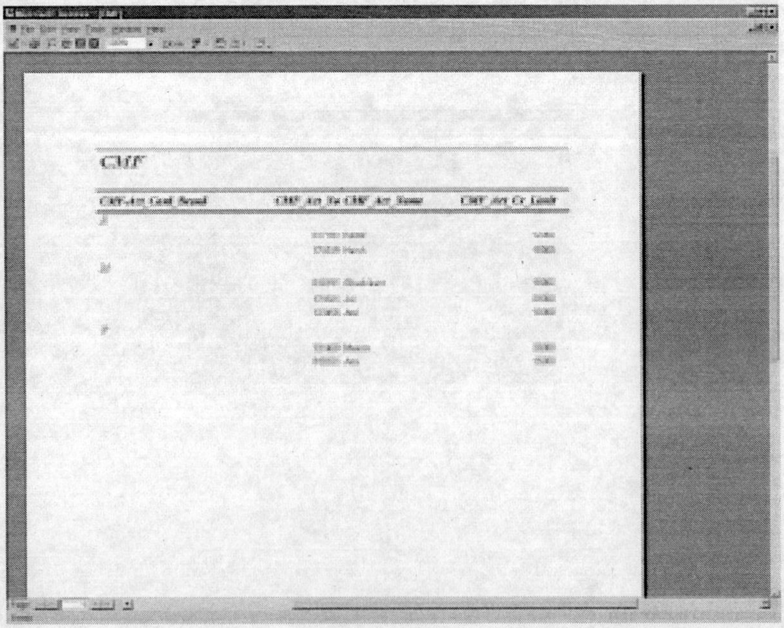

Fig. C.25 Report – Part 4

There are many options and formatting mechanisms in reports. For example, we can easily click a report of all the cardholders per brand, sorted in the descending order of credit limits. This can be achieved with just 5-6 clicks. The resulting report is shown in Fig. C.26.

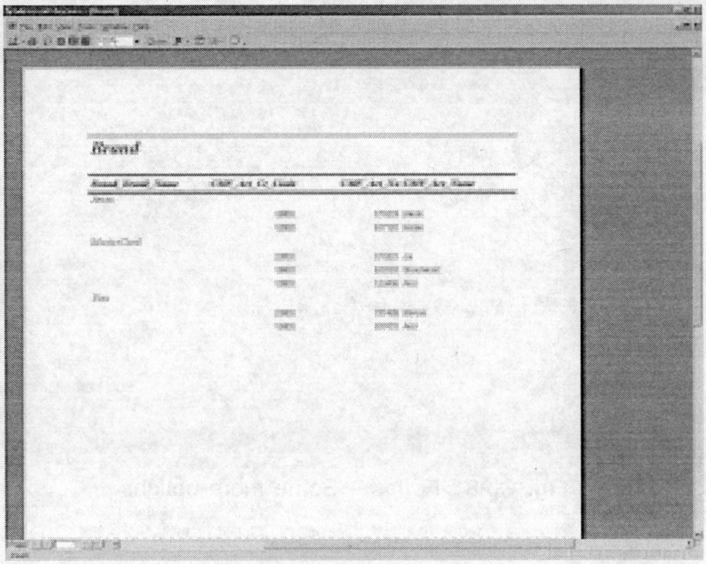

Fig. C.26 Report – Part 5

C.6 FORMS

Forms allow us to enter data in ways other than the default. Figures C.27 and C.28 show a couple of them.

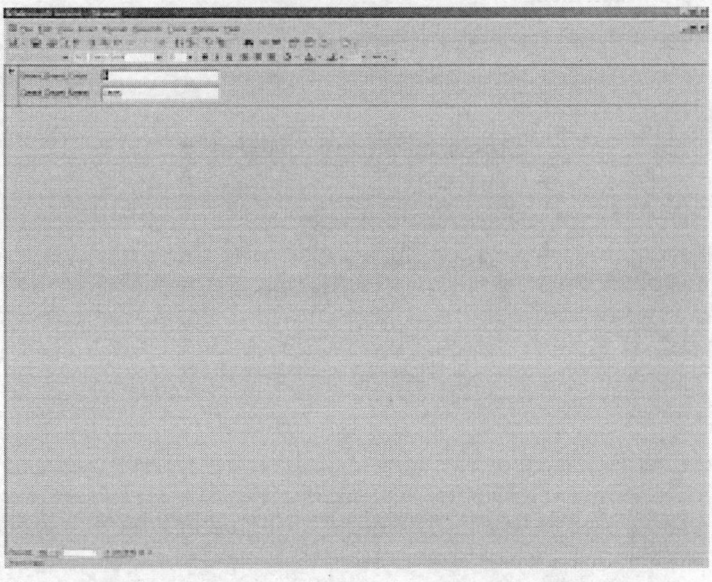

Fig. C.27 Forms – Some options

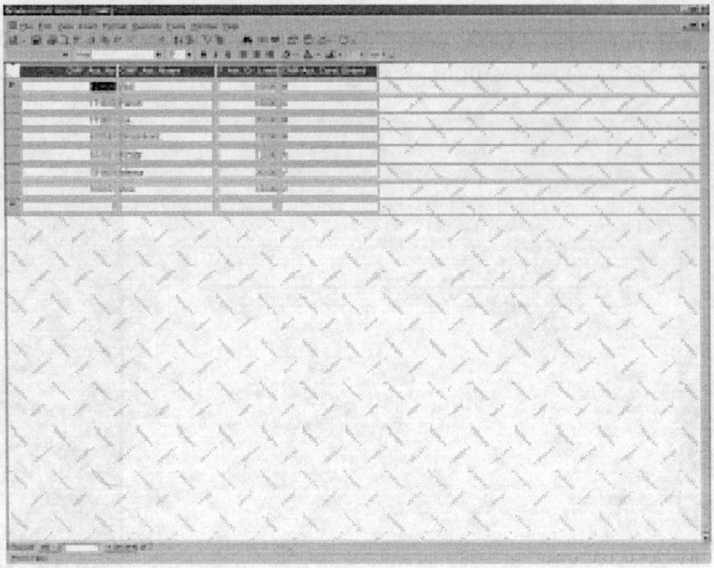

Fig. C.28 Forms – Some more options

C.7 QUERIES

We can write SQL queries to bring data in the manner we want. We also have the option of building the SQL queries in a graphical form, without needing to write them. We can use the drag and drop as well as the other GUI features of MS-Access. Behind the scenes, MS-Access builds the corresponding queries for us.

Figures C.29. C.30, and C.31 show the process of building queries graphically without needing to explicitly code any SQL statements.

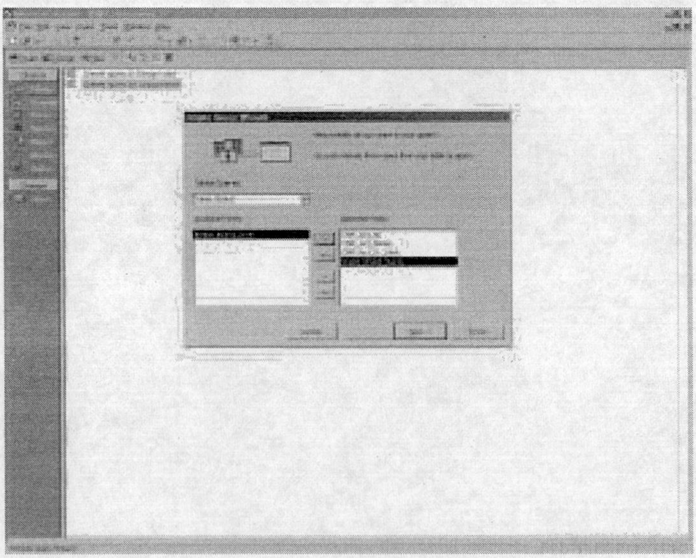

Fig. C.29 Queries – Step 1

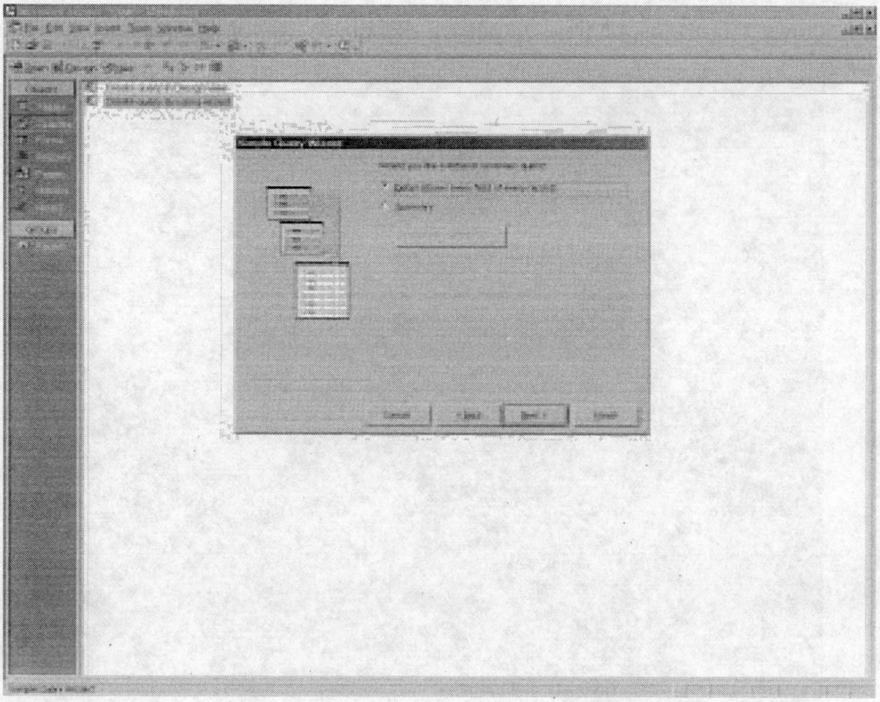

Fig. C.30 Queries – Step 2

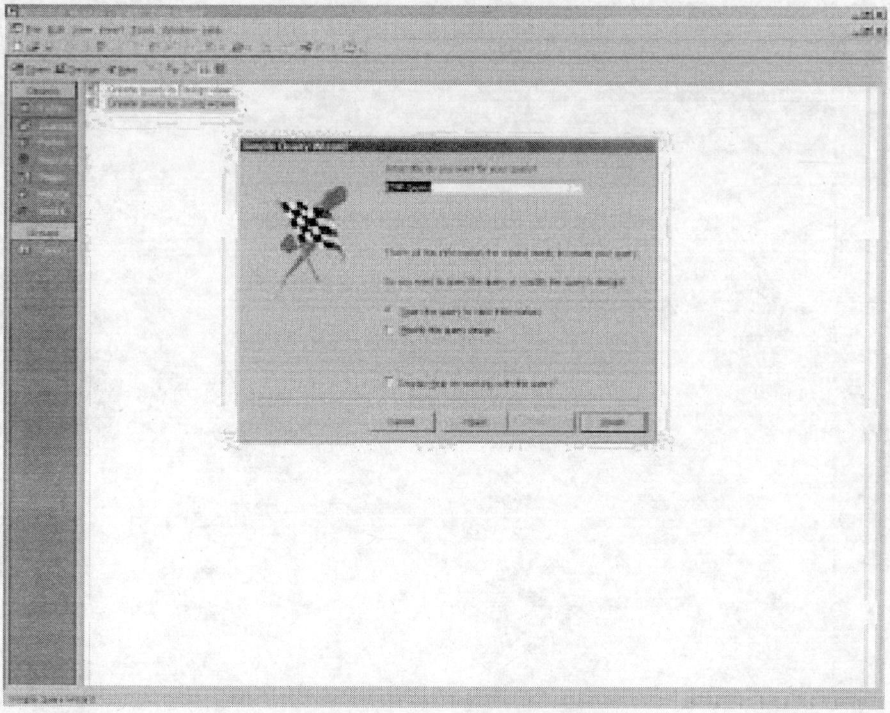

Fig. C.31 Queries – Step 3

Figure C.32 shows the corresponding output of the query we have created.

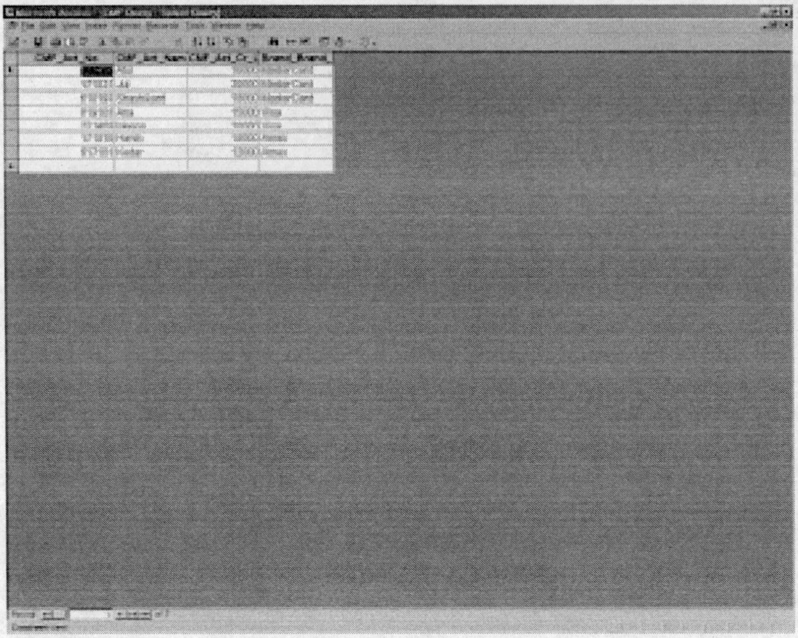

Fig. C.32 Query output

Figure C.33 illustrates the same query in SQL format. Note that MS-Access has created it for us automatically, based on our above operations.

Fig. C.33 Query – SQL view

Appendix D

Case Studies

D.1 INTRODUCTION

In this appendix, we shall examine several case studies to cement our understanding of various DBMS concepts. We shall take up two sets of topics for discussion.

- One is related to the aspects of database design. We have discussed database design in depth, with detailed coverage of the important concept of normalisation. We shall consider some database structures and see whether they fit these discussions, and if not, how we can modify them suitably.
- The other is related to programming examples. We shall consider a few programs that utilise the various concepts in DBMS technology. The primary concept in DBMS programming is the usage of cursors. This is especially used very widely in IBM mainframe applications. This is why we have provided a number of programs that are based on the COBOL programming language. They are actually quite close to real-life programs. For the sake of completeness and for those who are not familiar with COBOL, we have also provided a couple of examples in C.

D.2 DATABASE DESIGN

D.2.1 Credit Card Database

Let us assume that the Cardholders Member (CMF) table contains information about credit card holders and their transactions. For this purpose, we have a table called CMF with the layout shown in Fig. D.1.

What are the possible problems with design? Let us list them down.

1. The CMF table contains information about many facts, such as the cardholders, their credit cards, and also the transactions performed by the cardholders using those cards. This is not desirable, and would lead to many problems as discussed in Fig. D.1.
2. Suppose that a cardholder performs ten transactions using a card on a business day. Then, we will have ten rows for this in the CMF table. Note that information about the cardholder

(such as the name and address) and also the card itself (such as the card name and validity) will also repeat ten times quite unnecessarily.

CM-Act-No
CM-Act-Name
CM-Address
CM-City
CM-Pin
CM-Cr-Limit
CM-Card-Brand-Code
CM-Card-Brand-Name
CM-Validity
CM-Trans-Date
CM-Trans-Time
CM-Trans-Description
CM-Merchant-Code
CM-Amount

Fig. D.1 CMF table layout

3. We cannot enter information about a cardholder until she makes a transaction. This is not acceptable at all.
4. Unless a cardholder holds a particular brand of card (Visa), and worse yet, uses it in a transaction, we cannot store the fact that Visa is an available brand of cards. This is also quite unacceptable.
5. Suppose that a cardholder makes only one transaction with her card, and that transaction for some reason, is invalid. Therefore, we need to delete the row for this transaction from the CMF table. This will mean that there will be no rows for this cardholder in the CMF table anymore. In other words, we have completely lost information about this cardholder!
6. If some details about the cardholder (such as the name or address) change, then we must search for and modify all the rows for this cardholder in the CMF table. The same is true with the brand of a card.

In order to solve these problems, we will break down the tables into the following tables. We will not deliberately state which normal forms are being applied, and how. We would leave it to the reader to think about it and list down its results, and to validate that the following design indeed follows the principles of normal forms.

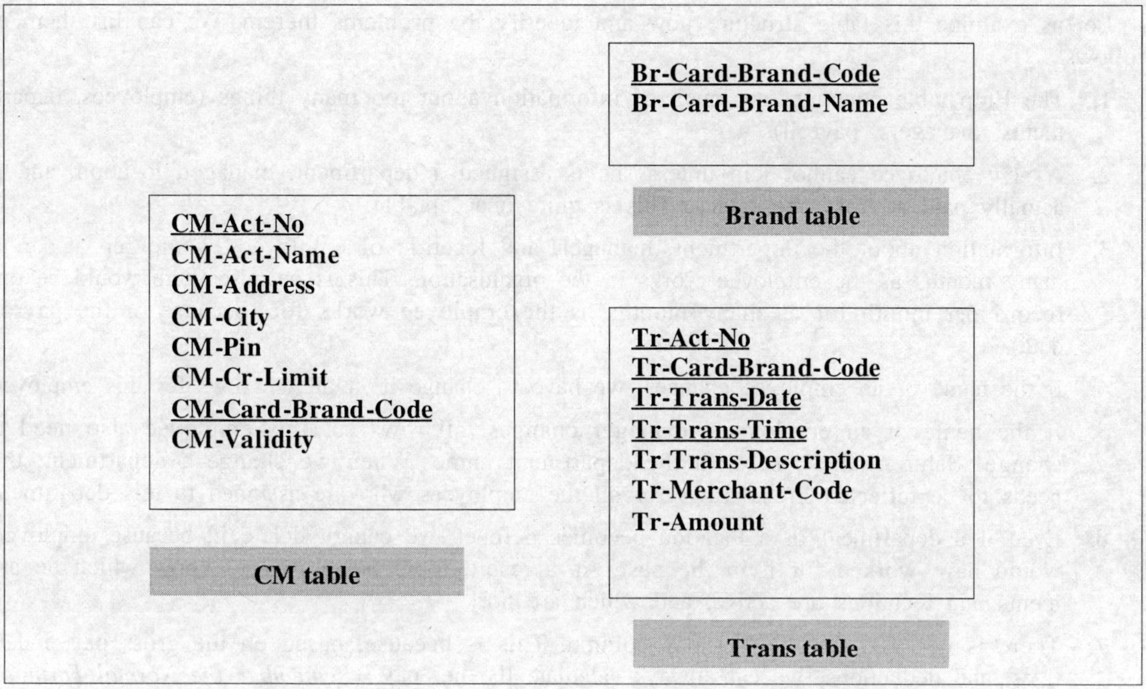

Fig. D.2 Modified table design

Note that the underlined columns form the primary keys of the respective tables.

D.2.2 Employee Database

Let us now think of another example. Assume that we need to store information about the employees in an organisation. Then we can think of a possible database structure as shown in Fig. D.3. We have stored information about the employees, their departments, managers, and payroll.

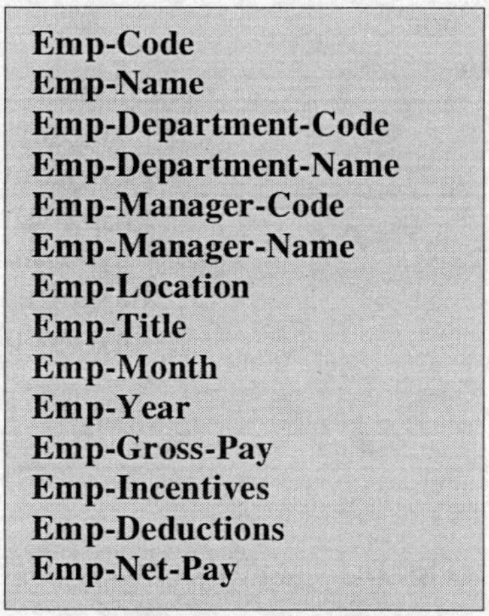

Fig. D.3 Emp table

Let us examine this table structure now and identify the problems therein. We can list them as follows.

1. The Emp table contains too much of information about too many things (employees, departments, managers, payroll).
2. A new employee cannot join unless she is assigned a department, manager, location, and is actually paid at least one salary! This is quite unacceptable.
3. Information about the department, manager, and location of employees would repeat for as many months as the employee works in the organisation. This is because there would be one record per month for as many months as the employee works for (because of the payroll data).
4. If the name of an employee changes, we have to change it in all the rows for this employee.
5. If the name of an employee's manager changes, all rows for this employee also need to change! Same is the case with the department name. When we change a department, this needs to be reflected in the rows for all the employees who are assigned to this department.
6. Even if a department or a location becomes defunct, we cannot delete it, because employees would have worked for it in the past. As a result, there is no way to know which departments and locations are active, and which are not!
7. There is no need for the Net pay column. This is because, based on the gross pay, incentives, and deductions, we can always calculate the net pay. (*Remember the Normal Form associated with this?)*

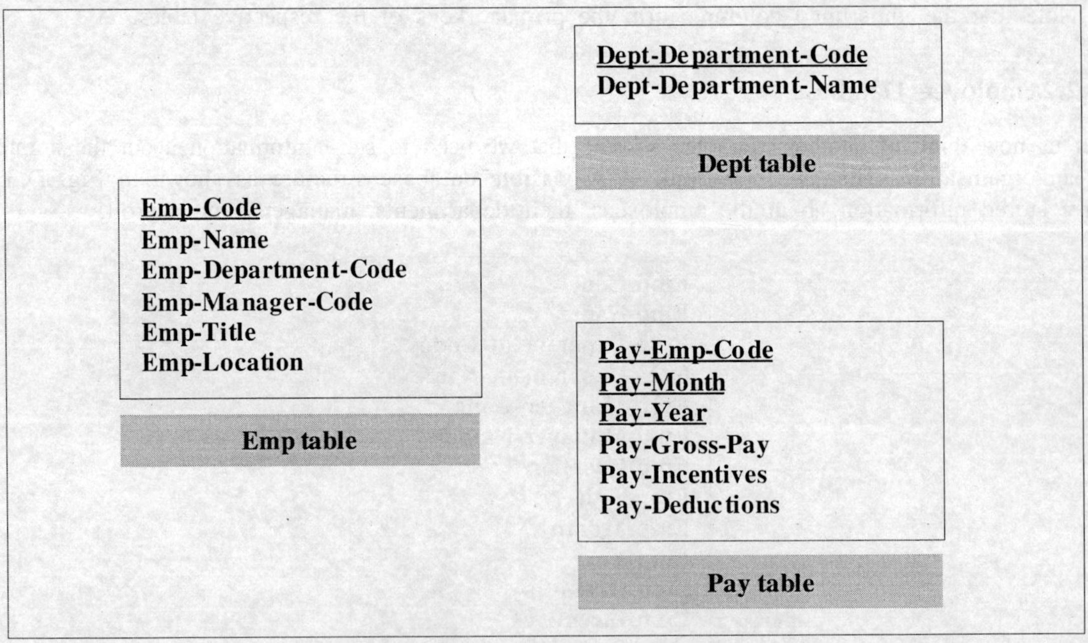

Fig. D.4 Modified table design

As before, we leave it to the reader to verify that the modified table design shown in Fig. D.4 conforms to the principles of Normal Forms.

D.2.3 Weather Database

This example assumes that we want to store the weather information about various cities. What we want to store are details such as the maximum, minimum, and average temperatures on a particular day. We also want to store the temperatures at certain milestones of the day, that is, morning, afternoon, evening, and night. We also want to record whether the day was sunny, cloudy, normal or whether it rained or snowed. Our initial table design is depicted in Fig. D.5.

Wea-Date
Wea-City
Wea-Max-Temp
Wea-Min-Temp
Wea-Avg-Temp
Wea-Mor-Temp
Wea-Aft-Temp
Wea-Eve-Temp
Wea-Nig-Temp
Wea-Rained
Wea-Sunny
Wea-Cloudy
Wea-Snowed
Wea-Normal

Fig. D.5 Weather information table

As before, let us try to find out the possible problems with this table. Does this table contain information about too many things like the previous table designs? Not quite. In fact, the table contains information about just one fact, the weather in a particular city on a particular day. Therefore, most of the problems that could have happened otherwise are clearly eliminated right at the inception. There is just one possible problem, depending on how we define the term *average*.

- If the average temperature means the average of maximum and minimum temperatures, we need not maintain this column, because based on the maximum and minimum values, we can always compute it.
- On the other hand, if the average temperature means the average of the morning, afternoon, evening, and night temperatures, then also we need not store it as a separate column. Because we can always derive it based on the values in these columns.
- However, if the average temperature is calculated based on some other values externally, then we need to maintain this column in our table. This is because we do not have the values from which we can calculate the average temperature.

All other columns in the table seem to be quite perfect. The table does indeed follow the Normal Forms (at least up to 3NF). Therefore, there is no need to change anything in the table design.

Perhaps the only argument can be whether we need so many columns to store information regarding what kind of day it was (rainy, cloudy, ...). Instead, we can use a simple flag to indicate this fact. For instance, if the flag contains R, it means that it was a rainy day. Similarly, C could mean cloudy, and so on.

However, another point is that a day need not be sunny for the whole duration. It may vary many times during the course of the whole day! Therefore, it may snow for a while, then become cloudy, then rainy, and then it may get sunny — all in a single day's course! Therefore, we need these many fields. But then we can also have a single indicator field to hold all these combinations.

For instance, we can have a convention of 1 = Snow, 2 = Cloudy, and so on. The indicator field may contain up to four values. So in the case of an extremely volatile day as described above, it would contain 1 2 3 4. On the other hand, on a day where it snows the whole day, it would contain just 1.

Effectively, this decision is not a DBMS decision per say. It is a decision that will have to be taken in any situation. Hence, we shall not discuss it any further, but we mentioned it in detail so that we are aware of all the possibilities.

D.2.4 Cricket Database

Suppose we want to store the performances of players in international cricket. For this purpose, we create a database that has design as shown in Fig. D.6.

Player-Code
Player-Name
Match-Number
For-Team
Against-Team
Ground
Date
How-Out
Bowler
Overs
Maidens
Runs
Wickets
Catches
Umpire-1
Umpire-2
TV-Umpire
Match-referee
Toss
Result

Fig. D.6 Cricket Table

This interesting table is now without its flaws. Let us examine the pitfalls in this table design.

1. Like some of our other databases, there is too much of information in a single table. We are storing information about player, his performance, match data, result, umpires, and referee in the same table. This leads to many problems, some of which are mentioned below.

2. If the name of a player changes, it has to be changed in several rows of the table.

3. The details of umpires and referee per row are unnecessary.

4. The information about toss and result is also unnecessarily duplicated in all the records.

Let us examine how we can solve this problem with the help of the modified database design as shown in Fig. D.7.

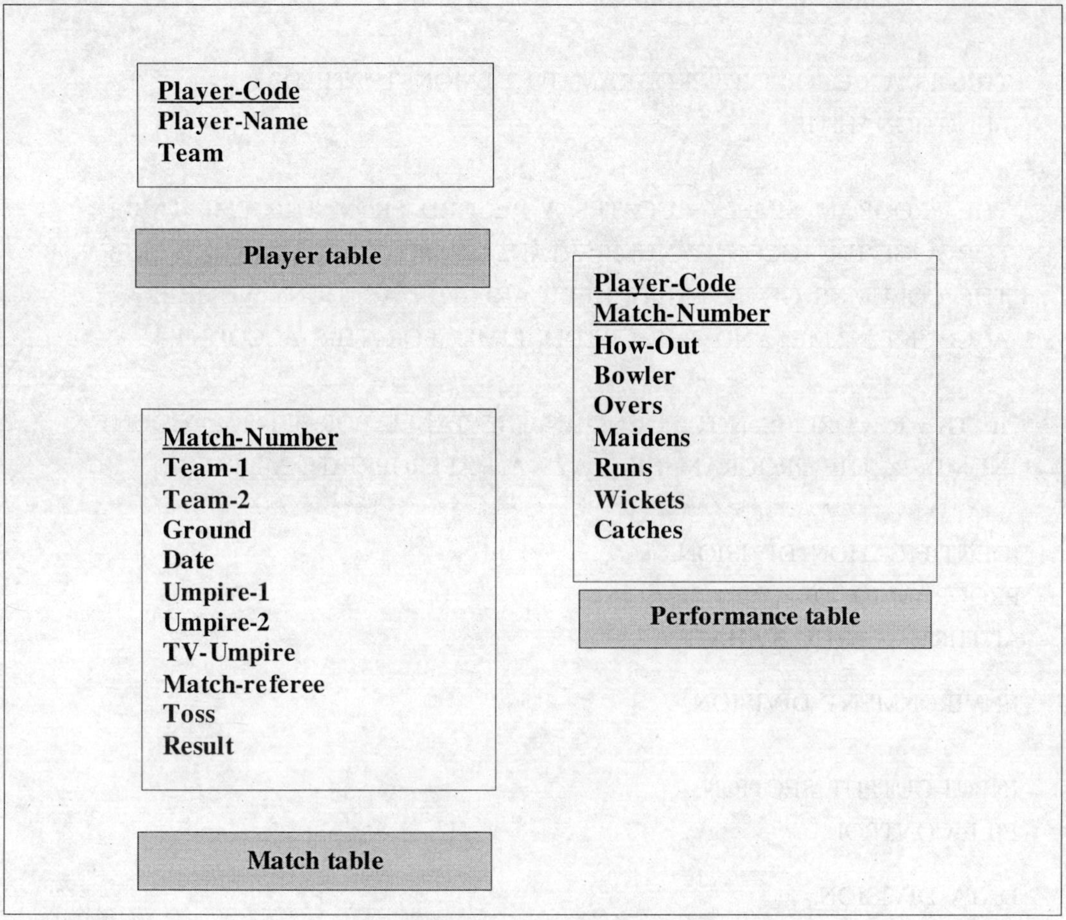

Fig. D.7 Modified table design

Would this database design solve our problems? If you notice, each of the three tables is self-sufficient, and does not contain any unwanted data. They are all linked to each other, too. This linking is on the basis of the match numbers and the player codes.

An interesting exercise would be to try and see if this decomposition of the original table into three tables is lossless or lossy. We would leave this exercise for the reader.

D.3 PROGRAMMING EXAMPLES

In this section, we present a few sample programs to demonstrate DBMS concepts as they are used in application programs. We have used the COBOL programming language to demonstrate this, as it is most widely used with DBMS programming on IBM mainframe computers. The programs are self-explanatory, and contain a lot of comments. So even a reader with little COBOL background should be able to understand them quite easily.

D.3.1 Program for SELECT Operation

```
*****************************************************************
*              PROGRAM DOCUMENTATION
*
* THIS IS A COBOL-DB2 PROGRAM TO DEMONSTRATE DB2
* FUNCTIONALITIES.
*
* THE PROGRAM SIMPLY LOCATES A RECORD FROM THE CMF TABLE
* FOR A GIVEN ACCOUNT NUMBER AND DISPLAYS IT ON THE SCREEN.
* THE COLUMNS OF INTEREST HERE ARE THE ACCOUNT NUMBER,
* ACCOUNT NAME, AND THE CREDIT LIMIT FOR THIS ACCOUNT.
*
* IF THE RECORD IS NOT FOUND IN THE TABLE FOR THAT ACCOUNT
* NUMBER, THE PROGRAM DISPLAYS AN APPROPRIATE MESSAGE.
*****************************************************************
 IDENTIFICATION DIVISION.
 PROGRAM-ID. DB2ONE.
 AUTHOR.    ATUL KAHATE.

 ENVIRONMENT DIVISION.
*
 INPUT-OUTPUT SECTION.
 FILE-CONTROL.

 DATA DIVISION.
 FILE SECTION.

 WORKING-STORAGE SECTION.
*
    EXEC SQL
     INCLUDE SQLCA
    END-EXEC.

    EXEC SQL
     INCLUDE DCLCMF
    END-EXEC.

 PROCEDURE DIVISION.
```

```
*****************************************************************
* 0000-MAINLINE.
* THIS IS A DUMMY PARAGRAPH. IT MERELY CALLS THE MAIN
* PROCESSING LOGIC OF A000-PROCESS PARAGRAPH. IN MORE COMPLEX
* PROGRAMS, IT WOULD CONTAIN MORE COMPLICATED LOGIC.
*****************************************************************
 0000-MAINLINE.

   PERFORM A000-PROCESS          THRU A000-EXIT.
   GOBACK.

 0000-EXIT.
   EXIT.
*****************************************************************
* A000-PROCESS.
* RUN A SELECT QUERY AND DISPLAY THE RESULTS ON THE SCREEN.
*****************************************************************
 A000-PROCESS.

*****************************************************************
* WRITE A SELECT QUERY. NOTE THAT WE ARE USING A
* SELECT-FROM-INTO SYNTAX. AS A RESULT, THE VALUES FROM THE
* TABLE GET POPULATED IN THE VARIABLES MENTIONED IN THE INTO
* CLAUSE. THESE VARIABLES ARE CALLED AS HOST VARIABLES.
*
* IF THE QUERY EXECUTION IS SUCCESSFUL, THEN THE ACCOUNT NUMBER
* AND CREDIT LIMIT VALUES FOR THE GIVEN ACCOUNT NUMBER ARE
* FETCHED IN THE CORRESPONDING HOST VARIABLES SPECIFIED BELOW.
*****************************************************************

   EXEC SQL
    SELECT CMF_ACT_NO, CMF_ACT_NAME, CMF_ACT_CR_LIMIT
      FROM CMF
      INTO :HOST-CMF-ACT-NO, :HOST-CMF-ACT-NAME,
         :HOST-CMF-CR-LIMIT
      WHERE CMF_ACT-NO = 123456789987654
   END-EXEC.
```

```
*****************************************************************
* CHECK SQLCODE. IF IT IS 0, IT MEANS THAT THE ABOVE OPERATION
* WAS SUCCESSFUL. HOWEVER, IF IT IS NOT, THEN THE QUERY HAS
* FAILED FOR SOME REASON. DISPLAY AN ERROR MESSAGE ACCORDINGLY.
*****************************************************************

    IF SQLCODE = 0
     DISPLAY 'ACCOUNT NUMBER: ' HOST-CMF-ACT-NO
     DISPLAY 'ACCOUNT NAME : ' HOST-CMF-ACT-NAME
     DISPLAY 'CREDIT LIMIT : ' HOST-CMF-CR-LIMIT
    ELSE
     DISPLAY '*** ERROR IN SELECT OPERATION ***'
     DISPLAY 'SQLCODE     : ' SQLCODE
    END-IF.
  A000-EXIT.
    EXIT.
```

D.3.2 Program for SELECT with File Operations

```
*****************************************************************
*              PROGRAM DOCUMENTATION
*
* THIS IS A COBOL-DB2 PROGRAM TO DEMONSTRATE DB2
* FUNCTIONALITIES.
*
* THE PROGRAM READS A FILE THAT CONTAINS ACCOUNT NUMBER OF OUR
* INTEREST. THE PROGRAM READS ALL OF THEM ONE-BY-ONE IN A
* SEQUENTIAL FASHION. THIS FILE IS CALLED AS IN-FILE.
*
* FOR EACH ACCOUNT NUMBER READ FROM THE IN-FILE, THE PROGRAM
* SEARCHES IT IN THE CMF TABLE. IF THE ACCOUNT IS FOUND ON THE
* CMF TABLE, THEN THE PROGRAM DISPLAYS IT ON THE SCREEN.
* THE COLUMNS OF INTEREST HERE ARE THE ACCOUNT NUMBER,
* ACCOUNT NAME, AND THE CREDIT LIMIT FOR THIS ACCOUNT.
*
* IF THE RECORD IS NOT FOUND IN THE TABLE FOR THAT ACCOUNT
* NUMBER, THE PROGRAM DISPLAYS AN APPROPRIATE MESSAGE.
*****************************************************************
```

```
IDENTIFICATION DIVISION.
PROGRAM-ID. DB2TWO.
AUTHOR.    ATUL KAHATE.

ENVIRONMENT DIVISION.
*
INPUT-OUTPUT SECTION.
FILE-CONTROL.

*****************************************************************
* THE PROGRAM DECLARES THE IN-FILE AS A SEQUENTIAL FILE THAT
* WOULD BE USED FOR SOME SORT OF PROCESSING.
*****************************************************************

    SELECT IN-FILE ASSIGN TO DISK
    ORGANIZATION IS SEQUENTIAL
    ACCESS MODE IS SEQUENTIAL
    FILE STATUS IS IN-ST.

DATA DIVISION.
FILE SECTION.

*****************************************************************
* THE FOLLOWING STATEMENTS DECLARE THE DESCRIPTION FOR THE CMF
* FILE. IN-FILE CONTAINS JUST ONE FIELD, THE ACCOUNT NUMBER.
*****************************************************************

FD IN-FILE.
01 IN-REC.
   05 IN-ACT-NO            PIC 9(16).

WORKING-STORAGE SECTION.

   EXEC SQL
    INCLUDE SQLCA
   END-EXEC.

   EXEC SQL
    INCLUDE DCLCMF
   END-EXEC.

PROCEDURE DIVISION.
```

```
*****************************************************************
* 0000-MAINLINE.
* THIS PARAGRAPH IS THE MAIN PROCESSING PARAGRAPH. IT CALLS
* THE OTHER PARAGRAPHS THAT PERFORM THE ACTUAL PROCESSING.
*****************************************************************

 0000-MAINLINE.
   PERFORM Z000-INIT                THRU Z000-EXIT.
   PERFORM A000-PROCESS             THRU A000-EXIT
       UNTIL IN-ST = '10'.
   PERFORM C000-CLOSE               THRU C000-EXIT.
   GOBACK.

 0000-EXIT.
   EXIT.
*****************************************************************
* Z000-INIT.
* DO THE INITIALIATIONS, I.E. OPEN THE IN-FILE.
*****************************************************************

 Z000-INIT.

   OPEN INPUT IN-FILE.

   IF IN-ST = '00'
    CONTINUE
   ELSE
    DISPLAY '*** ERROR IN OPENING THE IN FILE ***'
    DISPLAY 'FILE STATUS: ' IN-ST
    PERFORM Z999-STOP-PROGRAM THRU Z999-EXIT
   END-IF.

 0000-EXIT.
   EXIT.

*****************************************************************
* A000-PROCESS.
* READ THE FIRST RECORD FROM THE INPUT FILE. IF THE FILE IS
```

```
* EMPTY, PROCESSING WOULD STOP IMMEDIATELY. OTHERWISE, PERFORM
* THE B000- PARAGRAPH FOR ALL THE RECORDS IN THE INPUT FILE.
*****************************************************************

A000-PROCESS.

   READ IN-FILE.

   EVALUATE IN-ST
    WHEN '00'
      CONTINUE
    WHEN '10'
      DISPLAY '*** INPUT FILE IS EMPTY ***'
      GO TO A000-EXIT
    WHEN OTHER
      DISPLAY '*** ERROR IN READING THE IN FILE ***'
      DISPLAY 'FILE STATUS: ' IN-ST
      PERFORM Z999-STOP-PROGRAM THRU Z999-EXIT
   END-EVALUATE.

   PERFORM B000-PROCESS-IN-FILE THRU B000-EXIT
        UNTIL IN-ST = '10'.

A000-EXIT.
   EXIT.

*****************************************************************
* B000-PROCESS-IN-FILE.
* TRY TO FIND A MATCH IN THE CMF DB2 TABLE FOR THE RECORD READ
* FROM THE INPUT FILE. IF A MATCH IS FOUND, DISPLAY THE FIELDS
* OF INTEREST ON THE SCEREN. IF NO MATCH IS FOUND, DISPLAY THE
* ACCOUNT NUMBER FROM THE INPUT FILE FOR WHICH A MISMATCH HAS
* OCCURRED.
*
* IN THE CASE OF AN ERROR, TERMINATE THE PROGRAM.
*
* OTHERWISE, CONTINUE PROCESSING THE INPUT FILE FOR ALL THE
* RECORDS IN THE FILE.
*****************************************************************
```

```
B000-PROCESS-IN-FILE.

   EXEC SQL
    SELECT CMF_ACT_NO, CMF_ACT_NAME, CMF_ACT_CR_LIMIT
      FROM CMF
      INTO :HOST-CMF-ACT-NO, :HOST-CMF-ACT-NAME,
         :HOST-CMF-CR-LIMIT
      WHERE CMF_ACT_NO = :IN-ACT-NO
   END-EXEC.

*****************************************************************
* CHECK SQLCODE. IF IT IS 0, IT MEANS THAT THE ABOVE OPERATION
* WAS SUCCESSFUL. HOWEVER, IF IT IS NOT, THEN THE QUERY HAS
* FAILED FOR SOME REASON. DISPLAY AN ERROR MESSAGE ACCORDINGLY.
*****************************************************************

   EVALUATE SQLCODE
    WHEN 0
      DISPLAY 'ACCOUNT NUMBER: ' HOST-CMF-ACT-NO
      DISPLAY 'ACCOUNT NAME   : ' HOST-CMF-ACT-NAME
      DISPLAY 'CREDIT LIMIT    : ' HOST-CMF-CR-LIMIT
    WHEN +100
      DISPLAY '*** RECORD NOT FOUND IN CMF TABLE ***'
      DISPLAY 'INPUT ACT NO : ' IN-ACT-NO
    WHEN OTHER
      DISPLAY '*** ERROR IN SELECT OPERATION ***'
      DISPLAY 'SQLCODE     : ' SQLCODE
      PERFORM Z999-STOP-PROGRAM THRU Z999-EXIT
   END-IF.

*****************************************************************
* NOW READ THE NEXT RECORD FROM THE INPUT FILE.
*****************************************************************

   READ IN-FILE.

   EVALUATE IN-ST
    WHEN '00'
      CONTINUE
```

```
     WHEN '10'
        GO TO B000-EXIT
     WHEN OTHER
        DISPLAY '*** ERROR IN READING THE IN FILE ***'
        DISPLAY 'FILE STATUS: ' IN-ST
        PERFORM Z999-STOP-PROGRAM THRU Z999-EXIT
    END-EVALUATE.

 B000-EXIT.
    EXIT.

*****************************************************************
* C000-CLOSE.
* CLOSE THE INPUT FILE.
*****************************************************************

 C000-CLOSE.

    CLOSE IN-FILE.

    IF IN-ST = '00'
     CONTINUE
    ELSE
     DISPLAY '*** ERROR IN CLOSING THE IN FILE ***'
     DISPLAY 'FILE STATUS: ' IN-ST
     PERFORM Z999-STOP-PROGRAM THRU Z999-EXIT
    END-IF.

 C000-EXIT.
    EXIT.

*****************************************************************
* Z999-STOP-PROGRAM.
* THERE IS SOME SORT OF AN ERROR IF CONTROL COMES HERE.
* TERMINATE THE PROGRAM IMMEDIATELY.
*****************************************************************

    DISPLAY '*** THERE IS AN ERROR IN PROGRAM EXECUTION ***'.
    DISPLAY '*** PROGRAM IS BEING TERMINATED ABNORMALLY ***'.
    DISPLAY '*** PLEASE CHECK WHAT HAS HAPPENED ***'.
```

```
Z999-EXIT.
    EXIT.
```

D.3.3 Program for Basic Cursor Operations

```
*****************************************************************
*               PROGRAM DOCUMENTATION
*
* THIS IS A COBOL-DB2 PROGRAM TO DEMONSTRATE DB2
* FUNCTIONALITIES.
*
* THE PROGRAM READS ALL THE RECORDS FROM THE CMF TABLE HAVING
* CREDIT LIMIT BELOW 500. IT WRITES ALL THESE RECORDS TO AN
* OUTPUT FILE. THIS FILE IS CALLED AS OUT-FILE.
*
* THE PROGRAM USES THE CONCEPT OF A CURSOR. USING THE CURSOR,
* THE PROGRAM IS ABLE TO BRING ALL THE RECORDS OF INTEREST
* FROM THE TABLE INTO THE PROGRAM'S MEMORY.
*****************************************************************

IDENTIFICATION DIVISION.
PROGRAM-ID. DB2THREE.
AUTHOR.   ATUL KAHATE.
```


```
*****************************************************************
*               PROGRAM DOCUMENTATION
*
* THIS IS A COBOL-DB2 PROGRAM TO DEMONSTRATE DB2
* FUNCTIONALITIES.
*
* THE PROGRAM READS ALL THE RECORDS FROM THE CMF TABLE HAVING
* CREDIT LIMIT BELOW 500. IT WRITES ALL THESE RECORDS TO AN
* OUTPUT FILE. THIS FILE IS CALLED AS OUT-FILE.
*
* THE PROGRAM USES THE CONCEPT OF A CURSOR. USING THE CURSOR,
* THE PROGRAM IS ABLE TO BRING ALL THE RECORDS OF INTEREST
* FROM THE TABLE INTO THE PROGRAM'S MEMORY.
*****************************************************************
```

```
ENVIRONMENT DIVISION.
*
INPUT-OUTPUT SECTION.
FILE-CONTROL.
*****************************************************************
* THE PROGRAM DECLARES THE OUT-FILE AS A SEQUENTIAL FILE THAT
* WOULD BE USED FOR SOME SORT OF PROCESSING.
*****************************************************************
    SELECT OUT-FILE ASSIGN TO DISK
    ORGANIZATION IS SEQUENTIAL
    ACCESS MODE IS SEQUENTIAL
    FILE STATUS IS OUT-ST.
DATA DIVISION.
FILE SECTION.
*****************************************************************
* THE FOLLOWING STATEMENTS DECLARE THE DESCRIPTION FOR THE OUT
* FILE. WE WRITE THE ACCOUNT NUMBER, NAME, AND CREDIT LIMIT.
*****************************************************************
FD OUT-FILE.
01 OUT-REC.
    05 OUT-ACT-NO           PIC 9(16).
    05 OUT-ACT-NAME         PIC X(30).
    05 OUT-ACT-CR-LIMIT     PIC 9(05).
WORKING-STORAGE SECTION.
01 WS-WRITE-COUNT           PIC 9(10) VALUE 0.
    EXEC SQL
     INCLUDE SQLCA
    END-EXEC.
    EXEC SQL
     INCLUDE DCLCMF
    END-EXEC.
```

```
*****************************************************************
* DECLARE A CURSOR ON THE CMF TABLE TO BRING RECORDS WHERE
* CREDIT LIMIT IS LESS THAN 500.
*****************************************************************

    EXEC SQL
     DECLARE CMFCURSOR AS
       SELECT CMF_ACT_NO, CMF_ACT_NAME, CMF_ACT_CR_LIMIT
       FROM   CMF
       WHERE  CMF_ACT_CR_LIMIT < 500
    END-EXEC.

 PROCEDURE DIVISION.
*****************************************************************
* 0000-MAINLINE.
* THIS PARAGRAPH IS THE MAIN PROCESSING PARAGRAPH. IT CALLS
* THE OTHER PARAGRAPHS THAT PERFORM THE ACTUAL PROCESSING.
*****************************************************************

 0000-MAINLINE.

    PERFORM Z000-INIT          THRU Z000-EXIT.
    PERFORM A000-PROCESS         THRU A000-EXIT
        UNTIL SQLCODE = '100'.
    PERFORM C000-CLOSE          THRU C000-EXIT.
    GOBACK.

 0000-EXIT.
    EXIT.

*****************************************************************
* Z000-INIT.
* DO THE INITIALIATIONS, I.E. OPEN THE OUT-FILE AND THE CURSOR.
*****************************************************************

 Z000-INIT.

    OPEN OUTPUT OUT-FILE.

    IF OUT-ST = '00'
     CONTINUE
```

```
  ELSE
   DISPLAY '*** ERROR IN OPENING THE OUT FILE ***'
   DISPLAY 'FILE STATUS: ' OUT-ST
   PERFORM Z999-STOP-PROGRAM THRU Z999-EXIT
  END-IF.

  EXEC SQL
   OPEN CMFCURSOR
  END-EXEC.

  IF SQLCODE = 0
   CONTINUE
  ELSE
   DISPLAY '*** ERROR IN OPENING CMF CURSOR ***'
   DISPLAY 'SQLCODE : ' SQLCODE
   PERFORM Z999-STOP-PROGRAM THRU Z999-EXIT
  END-IF.

Z000-EXIT.
  EXIT.

*****************************************************************
* A000-PROCESS.
* FETCH THE FIRST ROW FROM THE CURSOR. IF NO SUCH ROW EXISTS,
* PROCESSING WOULD STOP IMMEDIATELY. OTHERWISE, PERFORM
* THE B000- PARAGRAPH FOR ALL THE ROWS IN THE CURSOR.
*****************************************************************

A000-PROCESS.
  EXEC SQL
   FETCH CMFCURSOR
     INTO :HOST-CMF-ACT-NO, :HOST-CMF-ACT-NAME,
       :HOST-CMF-CR-LIMIT
  END-EXEC.

  EVALUATE SQLCODE
   WHEN 0
     CONTINUE
   WHEN 100
```

```
        DISPLAY '*** NO MATCHING ROWS IN CMF TABLE ***'
        GO TO A000-EXIT
      WHEN OTHER
        DISPLAY '*** ERROR IN FETCHING CMF CURSOR ***'
        DISPLAY 'SQLCODE : ' SQLCODE
        PERFORM Z999-STOP-PROGRAM        THRU Z999-EXIT
    END-EVALUATE.

    PERFORM B000-PROCESS-CURSOR         THRU B000-EXIT
         UNTIL SQLCODE = +100.

 A000-EXIT.
    EXIT.

*******************************************************************
* B000-PROCESS-CURSOR.
* FETCH CURSOR AND WRITE RECORD TO THE OUTPUT FILE. REPEAT FOR
* ALL THE MATCHING ROWS IN THE TABLE (I.E. TILL THE CURSOR
* BRINGS IN MORE ROWS FOR PROCESSING).
*******************************************************************

 B000-PROCESS-CURSOR.

*******************************************************************
* CHECK SQLCODE. IF IT IS 0, IT MEANS THAT THE ABOVE OPERATION
* WAS SUCCESSFUL. HOWEVER, IF IT IS NOT, THEN THE QUERY HAS
* FAILED FOR SOME REASON. DISPLAY AN ERROR MESSAGE ACCORDINGLY.
*******************************************************************

    EVALUATE SQLCODE
      WHEN 0
        MOVE HOST-CMF-ACT-NO          TO OUT-ACT-NO
        MOVE HOST-CMF-ACT-NAME        TO OUT-ACT-NAME
        MOVE HOST-CMF-ACT-CR-LIMIT    TO OUT-ACT-CR-LIMIT
      WHEN +100
        GO TO B000-EXIT
      WHEN OTHER
        DISPLAY '*** ERROR IN FETCHING CMF CURSOR ***'
        DISPLAY 'SQLCODE : ' SQLCODE
```

```
        PERFORM Z999-STOP-PROGRAM THRU Z999-EXIT
    END-EVALUATE.

*****************************************************************
* NOW WRITE THE RECORD TO THE OUTPUT FILE.
*****************************************************************

    WRITE OUT-REC.

    EVALUATE OUT-ST
     WHEN '00'
        ADD 1 TO WS-WRITE-COUNT
     WHEN OTHER
        DISPLAY '*** ERROR IN WRITING TO THE OUTPUT FILE ***'
        DISPLAY 'FILE STATUS: ' OUT-ST
        PERFORM Z999-STOP-PROGRAM THRU Z999-EXIT
    END-EVALUATE.

    EXEC SQL
     FETCH CMFCURSOR
        INTO :HOST-CMF-ACT-NO, :HOST-CMF-ACT-NAME,
           :HOST-CMF-CR-LIMIT
    END-EXEC.

  B000-EXIT.
    EXIT.

*****************************************************************
* C000-CLOSE.
* CLOSE THE OUTPUT FILE, CURSOR AND DISPLAY THE RECORD COUNT.
*****************************************************************

  C000-CLOSE.

    CLOSE OUT-FILE.

    IF OUT-ST = '00'
     CONTINUE
    ELSE
     DISPLAY '*** ERROR IN CLOSING THE OUT FILE ***'
     DISPLAY 'FILE STATUS: ' OUT-ST
```

```
     PERFORM Z999-STOP-PROGRAM THRU Z999-EXIT
    END-IF.

    EXEC SQL
     CLOSE CMFCURSOR
    END-EXEC.

    IF SQLCODE = 0
     CONTINUE
    ELSE
     DISPLAY '*** ERROR IN CLOSING CMF CURSOR  ***'
     DISPLAY 'SQLCODE : ' SQLCODE
     PERFORM Z999-STOP-PROGRAM THRU Z999-EXIT
    END-IF.

    DISPLAY '=== NUMBER OF RECORDS WRITTEN TO OUT FILE === '.
    DISPLAY WS-WRITE-COUNT.
    DISPLAY ' ==='.

   C000-EXIT.
    EXIT.

*****************************************************************
* Z999-STOP-PROGRAM.
* THERE IS SOME SORT OF AN ERROR IF CONTROL COMES HERE.
* TERMINATE THE PROGRAM IMMEDIATELY.
*****************************************************************

    DISPLAY '*** THERE IS AN ERROR IN PROGRAM EXECUTION ***'.
    DISPLAY '*** PROGRAM IS BEING TERMINATED ABNORMALLY ***'.
    DISPLAY '*** PLEASE CHECK WHAT HAS HAPPENED      ***'.

   Z999-EXIT.
    EXIT.
```

D.3.4 Program for Advanced Cursor Operations

```
*****************************************************************
*              PROGRAM DOCUMENTATION
*
* THIS IS A COBOL-DB2 PROGRAM TO DEMONSTRATE DB2
```

```
* FUNCTIONALITIES.
*
* WE ASSUME THE FOLLOWING. CMF TABLE CONTAINS THE ACCOUNT
* NUMBERS, NAMES, AND THE TOTAL VALUE OF TRANSACTIONS FOR THE
* ACCOUNT/CARD HOLDER AS OF DATE. THERE IS ANOTHER TABLE
* CALLED AS THE TRANS TABLE. THIS TABLE CONTAINS THE
* TRANSACTIONS PERFORMED BY THE CARDHOLDER. THE SUM OF THE
* AMOUNTS OF ALL THESE TRANSACTIONS MUST MATCH WITH THE TOTAL
* VALUE STORED IN THE CMF TABLE FOR THIS CARDHOLDER. IF IT
* NOT, THEN THERE IS AN ERROR. WE NEED TO WRITE THE NUMBERS,
* NAMES, TOTAL AS IN CMF TABLE AND TOTAL AS IN TRANS TABLE FOR
* ALL MISMATCHES TO A FILE.
*****************************************************************
 IDENTIFICATION DIVISION.
 PROGRAM-ID. DB2FOUR.
 AUTHOR.    ATUL KAHATE.

 ENVIRONMENT DIVISION.
*
 INPUT-OUTPUT SECTION.
 FILE-CONTROL.

*****************************************************************
* THE PROGRAM DECLARES THE OUT-FILE AS A SEQUENTIAL FILE THAT
* WOULD BE USED TO REPORT THE MISMATCHES.
*****************************************************************
    SELECT OUT-FILE ASSIGN TO DISK
    ORGANIZATION IS SEQUENTIAL
    ACCESS MODE IS SEQUENTIAL
    FILE STATUS IS OUT-ST.

 DATA DIVISION.
 FILE SECTION.
*****************************************************************
* THE FOLLOWING STATEMENTS DECLARE THE DESCRIPTION FOR THE OUT
* FILE. WE WRITE THE ACCOUNT NUMBER, NAME, AND CREDIT LIMIT.
*****************************************************************
```

```
FD OUT-FILE.
01 OUT-REC.
   05 OUT-ACT-NO              PIC 9(16).
   05 OUT-ACT-NAME            PIC X(30).
   05 OUT-CMF-TOTAL           PIC 9(10).
   05 OUT-TRANS-TOTAL         PIC 9(10).

WORKING-STORAGE SECTION.
01 WS-WRITE-COUNT             PIC 9(10) VALUE 0.
01 WS-TOTAL                   PIC 9(10) VALUE 0.
01 EOF-CMF                    PIC X(01) VALUE 'N'.

   EXEC SQL
    INCLUDE SQLCA
   END-EXEC.

   EXEC SQL
    INCLUDE DCLCMF
   END-EXEC.

   EXEC SQL
    INCLUDE DCLTRANS
   END-EXEC.

*****************************************************************
* DECLARE A CURSOR ON THE CMF TABLE.
*****************************************************************

   EXEC SQL
    DECLARE CMFCURSOR AS
      SELECT CMF_ACT_NO, CMF_ACT_NAME, CMF_TOTAL
      FROM  CMF
   END-EXEC.

 PROCEDURE DIVISION.
*****************************************************************
* 0000-MAINLINE.
* THIS PARAGRAPH IS THE MAIN PROCESSING PARAGRAPH. IT CALLS
* THE OTHER PARAGRAPHS THAT PERFORM THE ACTUAL PROCESSING.
*****************************************************************
```

```
0000-MAINLINE.
    PERFORM Z000-INIT                     THRU Z000-EXIT.
    PERFORM A000-PROCESS                  THRU A000-EXIT
        UNTIL EOF-CMF = 'Y'.
    PERFORM C000-CLOSE                    THRU C000-EXIT.
    GOBACK.

0000-EXIT.
    EXIT.

**************************************************************
* Z000-INIT.
* DO THE INITIALIATIONS, I.E. OPEN THE OUT-FILE AND THE CURSOR.
**************************************************************
Z000-INIT.

    OPEN OUTPUT OUT-FILE.

    IF OUT-ST = '00'
     CONTINUE
    ELSE
     DISPLAY '*** ERROR IN OPENING THE OUT FILE ***'
     DISPLAY 'FILE STATUS: ' OUT-ST
     PERFORM Z999-STOP-PROGRAM THRU Z999-EXIT
    END-IF.

    EXEC SQL
     OPEN CMFCURSOR
    END-EXEC.

    IF SQLCODE = 0
     CONTINUE
    ELSE
     DISPLAY '*** ERROR IN OPENING CMF CURSOR ***'
     DISPLAY 'SQLCODE : ' SQLCODE
     PERFORM Z999-STOP-PROGRAM THRU Z999-EXIT
    END-IF.

Z000-EXIT.
    EXIT.
```

```
*****************************************************************
* A000-PROCESS.
* FETCH THE FIRST ROW FROM THE CURSOR. IF NO SUCH ROW EXISTS,
* PROCESSING WOULD STOP IMMEDIATELY. OTHERWISE, PERFORM
* THE B000- PARAGRAPH FOR ALL THE ROWS IN THE CURSOR.
*****************************************************************

 A000-PROCESS.
   EXEC SQL
    FETCH CMFCURSOR
      INTO :HOST-CMF-ACT-NO, :HOST-CMF-ACT-NAME,
        :HOST-CMF-TOTAL
   END-EXEC.

   EVALUATE SQLCODE
    WHEN 0
      CONTINUE
    WHEN 100
      DISPLAY '*** NO ROWS IN CMF TABLE ***'
      GO TO A000-EXIT
    WHEN OTHER
      DISPLAY '*** ERROR IN FETCHING CMF CURSOR ***'
      DISPLAY 'SQLCODE : ' SQLCODE
      PERFORM Z999-STOP-PROGRAM THRU Z999-EXIT
   END-EVALUATE.

   PERFORM B000-PROCESS-CURSOR THRU B000-EXIT
       UNTIL EOF-CMF = 'Y'.
 A000-EXIT.
   EXIT.

*****************************************************************
* B000-PROCESS-CURSOR.
* FETCH CURSOR AND DO THE NECESSARY PROCESSING. REPEAT FOR
* ALL THE MATCHING ROWS IN THE TABLE (I.E. TILL THE CURSOR
* BRINGS IN MORE ROWS FOR PROCESSING).
*****************************************************************

 B000-PROCESS-CURSOR.
```

```
*****************************************************************
* CHECK SQLCODE. IF IT IS 0, IT MEANS THAT THE SQL OPERATION
* WAS SUCCESSFUL. HOWEVER, IF IT IS NOT, THEN THE QUERY HAS
* FAILED FOR SOME REASON. DISPLAY AN ERROR MESSAGE ACCORDINGLY.
*****************************************************************

     EVALUATE SQLCODE
      WHEN 0
*****************************************************************
* FIND THE SUM OF TRANSACTIONS FOR THIS ACOCUNT HOLDER FROM THE
* TRANS TABLE. IF IT MATCHES WITH THE TOTAL FETCHED FROM THE
* CMF TABLE, SKIP THIS RECORD. IF IT DOES NOT, WRITE TO OUTPUT
* FILE AS AN ERROR.
*****************************************************************

        PERFORM B100-COMPARE-TOTALS THRU B100-EXIT
      WHEN +100
        MOVE 'Y' TO EOF-CMF
        GO TO B000-EXIT
      WHEN OTHER
        DISPLAY '*** ERROR IN FETCHING CMF CURSOR ***'
        DISPLAY 'SQLCODE : ' SQLCODE
        PERFORM Z999-STOP-PROGRAM THRU Z999-EXIT
     END-EVALUATE.

     EXEC SQL
      FETCH CMFCURSOR
        INTO :HOST-CMF-ACT-NO, :HOST-CMF-ACT-NAME,
           :HOST-CMF-TOTAL
     END-EXEC.

 B000-EXIT.
     EXIT.

*****************************************************************
* B100-COMPARE-TOTALS.
* COMPARE THE TOTAL FROM THE CMF WITH THE TOTALS CALCULATED ON
* THE TRANS TABLE.
*****************************************************************
```

```
B100-COMPARE-TOTALS.

  EXEC SQL
   SELECT SUM (TRANS-AMT)
   INTO :WS-TOTAL
   FROM TRANS
   WHERE TRANS_ACT_NO = :HOST-CMF-ACT-NO
   GROUP BY TRANS_ACT_NO
  END-EXEC.

  EVALUATE SQLCODE
   WHEN 0
     IF WS-SUM = CMF-ACT-TOTAL
      CONTINUE
     ELSE
      PERFORM B110-WRITE THRU B110-EXIT
     END-IF
   WHEN 100
     CONTINUE
   WHEN OTHER
     DISPLAY '*** ERROR IN SELECT ON TRANS TABLE ***'
     DISPLAY 'SQLCODE : ' SQLCODE
     PERFORM Z999-STOP-PROGRAM THRU Z999-EXIT
  END-EVALUATE.

B100-EXIT.
  EXIT.

******************************************************************
* B110-WRITE.
* WRITE MISMATCH RECORD TO THE OUTPUT FILE.
******************************************************************

B110-WRITE.

  MOVE HOST-CMF-ACT-NO          TO OUT-ACT-NO.
  MOVE HOST-CMF-ACT-NAME        TO OUT-ACT-NAME.
  MOVE CMF-ACT-TOTAL            TO OUT-CMF-TOTAL.
  MOVE WS-SUM                   TO OUT-TRANS-TOTAL.
```

```
    WRITE OUT-REC.

    EVALUATE OUT-ST
     WHEN '00'
       ADD 1 TO WS-WRITE-COUNT
     WHEN OTHER
       DISPLAY '*** ERROR IN WRITING TO THE OUTPUT FILE ***'
       DISPLAY 'FILE STATUS: ' OUT-ST
       PERFORM Z999-STOP-PROGRAM THRU Z999-EXIT
    END-EVALUATE.

 B110-EXIT.
    EXIT.

*****************************************************************
* C000-CLOSE.
* CLOSE THE OUTPUT FILE, CURSOR AND DISPLAY THE RECORD COUNT.
*****************************************************************

 C000-CLOSE.

    CLOSE OUT-FILE.

    IF OUT-ST = '00'
     CONTINUE
    ELSE
     DISPLAY '*** ERROR IN CLOSING THE OUT FILE ***'
     DISPLAY 'FILE STATUS: ' OUT-ST
     PERFORM Z999-STOP-PROGRAM THRU Z999-EXIT
    END-IF.

    EXEC SQL
     CLOSE CMFCURSOR
    END-EXEC.

    IF SQLCODE = 0
     CONTINUE
    ELSE
     DISPLAY '*** ERROR IN CLOSING CMF CURSOR ***'
     DISPLAY 'SQLCODE : ' SQLCODE
```

```
    PERFORM Z999-STOP-PROGRAM THRU Z999-EXIT
   END-IF.

   DISPLAY '=== NUMBER OF RECORDS WRITTEN TO OUT FILE === '.
   DISPLAY WS-WRITE-COUNT.
   DISPLAY ' ==='.

 C000-EXIT.
   EXIT.

*****************************************************************
* Z999-STOP-PROGRAM.
* THERE IS SOME SORT OF AN ERROR IF CONTROL COMES HERE.
* TERMINATE THE PROGRAM IMMEDIATELY.
*****************************************************************

   DISPLAY '*** THERE IS AN ERROR IN PROGRAM EXECUTION ***'.
   DISPLAY '*** PROGRAM IS BEING TERMINATED ABNORMALLY ***'.
   DISPLAY '*** PLEASE CHECK WHAT HAS HAPPENED ***'.

 Z999-EXIT.
   EXIT.
```

D.3.5 Program in C for SELECT Operation

```
   /* Program to print the details of an account if it is
found on the CMF table */

 #include <stdio.h>
 #include <file.h>
 #include <string.h>

 #include "dclcmf.h"

 EXEC SQL INCLUDE SQLCA;

 main ( )
 {

     /* Execute the SQL query */
     EXEC SQL
           SELECT CMF_ACT_NO, CMF_ACT_NAME, CMF_ACT_CR_LIMIT
               FROM CMF
```

```
        INTO  :HOST_CMF_ACT_NO,  :HOST_CMF_ACT_NAME,
                        :HOST_CMF_CR_LIMIT
            WHERE  CMF_ACT_NO  =  123456789987654;

    /*  Check  SQLCODE  and  take  an  appropriate  action  */
    if  (SQLCODE  ==  0)
    {
         printf("\nACCOUNT  NUMBER:  %d",  HOST_CMF_ACT_NO);
         printf("\nACCOUNT  NAME   :  %s",  HOST_CMF_ACT_NAME);
         printf("\nCREDIT  LIMIT   :  %d",  HOST_CMF_CR_LIMIT);
    }
else
    {
         printf("\n***  ERROR  IN  SELECT  OPERATION  ***");
         printf("\nSQLCODE         :  %d",  SQLCODE);
    }
}
```

Index

E

F

G

H

N

O

P

Q

R

S

T

U

V

W